UNFETTERED AND ALIVE

Also by Anne Summers

The Misogyny Factor

The Lost Mother. A Story of Art and Love

On Luck

*The End of Equality. Work babies and Women's Choices
in 21st century Australia*

Ducks on the Pond. An autobiography 1945-1976

*Gamble for Power. How Bob Hawke Beat Malcolm Fraser.
The 1983 Election*

Her Story. Australian Women in Print, 1788-1975 (with Margaret Bettison)

*Damned Whores and God's Police. The Colonisation
of Women in Australia.*

ANNE SUMMERS

UNFETTERED AND ALIVE

A Memoir

ALLEN&UNWIN

SYDNEY · MELBOURNE · AUCKLAND · LONDON

First published in 2018

Allen & Unwin
83 Alexander Street
Crows Nest NSW 2065
Australia
Phone: (61 2) 8425 0100
Email: info@allenandunwin.com
Web: www.allenandunwin.com

 A catalogue record for this
book is available from the
National Library of Australia

ISBN 978 1 74331 841 6

Set in 11/15 pt Minion Pro by Midland Typesetters, Australia
Printed and bound in Australia by Griffin Press

10 9 8 7 6 5 4 3 2 1

 The paper in this book is FSC® certified.
FSC® promotes environmentally responsible,
socially beneficial and economically viable
management of the world's forests.

For Chip

One is not born, rather one becomes woman. No biological, psychic or economic destiny defines the figure that the human female takes on in society; it is civilization as a whole that elaborates this inter-mediary product between the male and the eunuch that is called feminine.

Simone de Beauvoir, The Second Sex, 1949

CONTENTS

INTRODUCTION   xi

CHAPTER ONE   'What's the Story, Morning Glory?'   1

CHAPTER TWO   Home of the Brave   38

CHAPTER THREE   The Press Gallery   72

CHAPTER FOUR   Foreign Correspondence   101

CHAPTER FIVE   Mandarins versus Missionaries   139

CHAPTER SIX   'The Times Will Suit Me'   176

CHAPTER SEVEN   'Real Feminists with Real Money'   205

CHAPTER EIGHT   Media Mogulettes in New York City   246

CHAPTER NINE   Paul Keating and the Laminar Flow   286

CHAPTER TEN   The Getting of Anger   332

CHAPTER ELEVEN   Peace and War   368

CHAPTER TWELVE   Unfettered and Alive   410

ACKNOWLEDGEMENTS   445

NOTES   447

INDEX   455

INTRODUCTION

—⇒>●<⇐—

... women are still in their early days. There isn't very much for them to be like without upsetting preconceptions. Some of them are warriors, too, but mostly they're belly dancers or capable little Victorian mothers.

Elizabeth Harrower, *In Certain Circles*, 2014 (written in 1971)

Anne,

You are thirty now.

Already, you have done more with your life than you dreamed was possible. You have published your first book. You are about to start work as a journalist. But what you have already done does not matter so much as what you will do from now. Your life is still ahead of you.

You need to understand that what becomes of you is almost entirely up to you. It is your choice, your decision. You have already shown that you can shape your future. You wanted to be a writer but your much younger and more practical self told you such dreams were not for people like you. Yet you found the grit and the courage to shut your ears to those who had other plans for you, and you learned to put yourself first. That was quite an unusual thing to do back then. You and your close friends talked about lives that would be different from those that had been laid out for you by your parents and teachers but you knew no one who had done it. There were few women you could see to model your selves on. Except in books.

When you were a teenager you wanted something, anything, more engaging than the dreary and stultifying choices that seemed to be the only options for a Catholic girl in the staid city of Adelaide in the late 1950s. It was through books that you learned that there were other lives, different from those of your mother and her three sisters.

At the age of twenty your mother Eileen (but always known by her nickname Tun) married, and over the next fourteen years had six children. You were the first and the only girl. Her oldest sister, Sheila, married at what in those days was considered the very late age of 39 and quickly bore three children. Of the two younger sisters, Gwen entered the convent, becoming a Sister of Mercy, while Nance remained unmarried. She was, as they used to say, a spinster. You were given to understand that the lives of your mother and her sisters represented the only choices available to you. You could marry and have children, you could become a nun or, as the harsh language of the day had it, you could be 'left on the shelf'. As a fourteen-year-old you briefly flirted with the idea of becoming a nun, but you soon outgrew that. You found your spinster aunt to be the most intriguing of your female relatives. You envied Nance her freedom. No 'home duties' for her. That was the term most women in those days used to describe what they did; on the census form, they wrote 'housewife'. Your aunt had a job, in a bank. She was the one who unwittingly first implanted in you the spark of the idea that marriage and kids need not be inevitable. She was just two years older than you are now when she died, of kidney disease. Nance Hogan never got to see what you did with your life, which is a shame because in all likelihood without her example, the path you trod might have been very different.

You left school as soon as it was legal at the age of sixteen and, again perhaps unconsciously following Nance's example, your first job was in a bank. Because you were a girl, you were not allowed to handle the money but you were expected to make cups of tea for the tellers and the manager. It did not occur to you to demur. All you could think about was saving money as fast as you could to buy the typewriter you had convinced yourself was key to your future. You had been writing since you were about seven, fervently contributing to the children's pages of *The Advertiser*, the Catholic newspaper *The Southern Cross* and the ABC's children's radio program, the *Argonauts*. You wrote short stories and plays and even sent off a piece to a national women's magazine. Using a pseudonym of course.

You didn't know women who were doing anything outside the home, let alone making a living with their typewriters, yet you were aware of them from books, many of them written by women. But they were remote creatures, from England or Ireland or even exotic places like France. You had yet to discover how a girl in Adelaide could become one of these women. All you could see was that on the printed page, there were no limits. You could imagine, and you could dream. You could tell yourself, I want to be a writer. I want to write books and be a journalist. You knew there were people, women, who did both. What you needed to figure out was: could you?

You were impatient to discover what life held for you. When you were in your twenties, you realised that life could be an adventure. You did not have to follow a pre-ordained path. In the 1960s all the old rules were starting to dissolve which meant there were opportunities, and choices, that once would not have been there for you. Perhaps the most important lesson of those years was the discovery that you were in charge of yourself. You could choose what to do, and if you realised that marrying young just as the women's liberation movement was turning everyone's life upside down had been the wrong thing for you, you were able to change course. You discovered the French writer Simone de Beauvoir and her revolutionary feminist book *The Second Sex*. It had been published twenty years earlier, in 1949, but its opening words, 'One is not born but, rather, one becomes a woman' had a profound impact on you. These words made you hungry to learn more about this critique of women's traditional roles that presaged new ways of being a woman. You were especially taken with de Beauvoir's later observation, in 1965, 'Women are obliged to play at being what they aren't, to play, for example, at being great courtesans, to fake their personalities. They're on the brink of neurosis,' she said in an interview in *The Paris Review*. 'I feel very sympathetic toward women of that type. They interest me more than the well-balanced housewife and mother. There are, of course, women who interest me even more, those who are both true and independent, who work and create.'[1] She articulated who you wanted to be: a woman who was 'both true and independent', who could 'work and create'. You will spend your entire life trying to do this. Just as, for the rest of your life, you will be trying to come to terms with what it means to be a woman. Because what it means will continue to evolve and change as you become a kind of woman that you did not know existed when you were a teenager.

You will not change who you are; your essential self will remain although it will develop and strengthen, and you will ultimately develop a set of core beliefs and values that will guide you at all times. But you will change what you do, not once or twice but many times, because you will embrace openings that present themselves and each time they will change your life. You will learn that if you reach out, and you are willing to take risks, there is usually no limit to what you can do. You will come to understand that if we defer our dreams they will never be realised. But you will also learn that what matters is not just what you do but your state of being. You ultimately describe yourself as 'unfettered and alive', a fortunate and in many ways privileged state of existence. It's how you are, not who you are.

The road to becoming the woman you are today is long and at times meandering as you did not follow a linear path. You never had a plan beyond your dream of being a writer and a journalist. When people ask, as they used to at so-called 'leadership' conferences, what will you be doing in five years time, you would look at them blankly. Just as you can't answer the question, How do you do what you do? Except by saying, I just do it.

Your life has been a patchwork of the unplanned and unpredictable with all the risks that involved, but also the intense enjoyment of the unexpected. Your haphazard approach, and your willingness to accept the offer of adventures, took you to places and jobs you could never have imagined as well as the ones you'd dreamed about. Like the one you are about to start. Not everything ended well, but you have never been bored. Along the way, you learned that you had to be brave, to absorb the pain of rejection, to not care too much what other people thought of you, to build a self-protective shell unto which you could retreat if you needed to.

The story you are going to tell in this book describes what it was like to become a woman living in an advanced Western economy during the last quarter of the twentieth century and the early decades of the 21st. And what it means to still be evolving as a woman into her eighth decade, something that was unimaginable to you when you were in your twenties. People thought then, as some people no doubt still do, that women had a use-by date. That to be old—even if the definition of 'old' has shifted upwards over the years, and been softened by the term 'older'—meant you were no longer an actor in life. You were meant to retreat to the shadows of family or community, to be content to be a handmaiden to other people's lives. You certainly had no expectation that you would be fit and healthy—and alive—and still reinventing yourself as you passed the 'three score and ten' benchmark that once was seen as our allotted life span.

It is not just you that changed. The very idea of what a woman is—and can be—has changed as well. The possibilities for women in the twentieth century were unparalleled in history, and you were fortunate to be born at the right time to benefit from these changes. Unlike your mother's generation, let alone your grandmothers'. And unlike young women today who are born into a world where they are entitled to take for granted that they can become whoever and whatever they decide and that if their dream is denied, know they have the right to complain. You were born on the cusp of this change. You were part of the generation of women who had the unprecedented benefit of higher education and who were transformed by it. You were swept along by the changes to the world of women, but you also felt the need to help shape them because although many (although certainly not all) of your generation were given these opportunities, they created expectations that were not always delivered.

You also found that being a woman became intrinsic to your story. You were one of those redefining what being a woman was so it was rarely possible to just be a journalist, or a writer or whatever you happened to be doing at the time. Paraphrasing Julia Gillard in her farewell speech on the night she was deposed as Australia's first woman prime minister in 2013, it is simply not possible for women to escape their gender. It is a given. Sometimes it matters. Sometimes it matters a lot. And your life has reflected that. Sometimes it was front and centre to what you were doing, or what was being done to you. Sometimes it barely mattered, but it could never be ignored. Women were, as de Beauvoir noted, 'the other'. And they still are.

So while you did not choose to become a warrior for women you found yourself thrust along on the surge of history, propelled by desire and by anger. You felt keenly the injustice of the unfair ways women were expected to work harder, for less money and for far less recognition. You became angry at the double standards you observed in so many places. And you were incredulous that such injustices could prevail or even be reinstated because you assumed progress and change were linear and irreversible, but the progress of women, especially for women of your generation, turned out to be accompanied by fightback and pushback. In countries like Australia, this has taken the form of conservative governments trying to weaken or reverse gains or entitlements already won, and has given rise to a resurgence of unbelievably ugly forms of sexism and misogyny. In other parts of the world the resistance has been more sinister, even lethal. In 1980 in Pakistan you witnessed the new trend of women being 'encouraged' to cover their heads with the chador. Thirty years later the shooting of the schoolgirl Malala Yousafzai in that country's Swat Valley because she helped girls go to school, showed that resistance to women's equality had become a war. The increasingly anti-women strains of Islam in certain parts of the Middle East and Africa is another example. Yet at the same time, globalisation and communications technology allowed you to know these things were happening and provide ways to fight back.

As you tell your story and reflect on what you have done and what you have learned along the way, you will discover many things. Most of all you will be amazed to discover that the self-doubting and often self-loathing girl you once were is now a confident, shouty, fearless woman who became a journalist and a writer. And who, all these decades later, still is.

Anne

CHAPTER ONE

'WHAT'S THE STORY, MORNING GLORY?'

———◆———

In December 1975, I was in Sydney, aged 30 and feeling pretty pleased with myself because I had achieved my two life's ambitions. A month earlier my book *Damned Whores and God's Police* had been published and now I was starting my new job as a journalist at the *National Times*. I was still almost trembling with pride at having written my first book. I could scarcely believe that my labour of the past four years was now in print; I could hold it in my hand and see my name on its spine. I placed the book on a shelf, inserted between other volumes written by well-known authors, and looked in awe. There I was, in the company of real writers. Although the reviews so far ranged from sceptical to hostile, I did not allow myself to be upset, or deterred. I was a published writer now. I was, I hoped, on my way. And, after brief forays into journalism that mostly involved book reviews or writing for alternative and underground publications, I had just been hired by the mainstream media and was about to become a real journalist. Newspaper jobs were never advertised in the 1970s, and rarely are today, but Max Suich, the wily editor of what was fast becoming a journalistically ground-breaking newspaper, had decided to cast a wider-than-usual net to find new talent. I'd answered an advertisement for 'energetic self-starters' and been put on a three-month trial. Despite having recommendations from a couple of acquaintances who were already on staff, Suich was sceptical about me because I'd been a post-graduate student at the University of Sydney for the past few years. I hastened to assure him that I was not 'a fucking academic'. Apart from my book, which had just a few weeks earlier received front-page treatment by the *National Times*, helping get it—and me—widely known, I was, I told him, an accomplished writer. I exaggerated how much freelance experience I actually had, but was able to point to a couple of articles I'd written for his predecessor, Trevor Kennedy. I'd be valuable from day one, I promised, and proposed he start me as an A grade, three levels from the top of the journalists' salary scale. Suich laughed in my face: 'You'll start as a C', he said. 'You can earn yourself an A.' It took me a year.

Suich wasn't there on my first day but his secretary Maureen Doughty showed me my desk and then left me to it. I must have come in too early, I told myself, because none of the other journalists was there yet. I sat down and picked up the phone, thinking I'd better energetically start and find a story. Around lunchtime David Dale, Susie Anthony and a few other journalists from the *Sydney Morning Herald* stopped by. Was I interested in a spot of lunch? A short time later we were arranging ourselves around a table at the Italo Club, a fairly basic Italian joint upstairs in a building in the heart of Chinatown. By the time I was back at my desk a couple of hours later, I had learned two things about my new job: that lunch was an essential part of our work and there was this thing called the New Journalism.

I ferreted out the article from *New York* magazine in which Tom Wolfe's long essay described the 'new journalism'.[1] It was, I learned, a form of reporting where any topic was fair game, where the reporter could insert herself into the 'story', and draw on techniques of fiction to set scenes and create atmosphere, to evoke people's appearance and explore their emotions rather than just state their age, their sex and, if they were women, their marital and maternal status, as was standard newspaper practice. One of Wolfe's famous and trend-setting early pieces was entitled 'Radical chic',[2] and it described a ritzy fundraising party at conductor Leonard Bernstein's thirteen-room penthouse duplex on Park Avenue. The guests of honour were a bunch of

Black Panthers, the militant African-American group raising hell on the fringes of the civil rights movement by combining black pride and community programs with aggressive, sometimes borderline criminal, political activities. Wolfe's article was an exuberant piece of writing that managed simultaneously to enter the nightmares of the great conductor/composer, and to mock the pretensions (the 'radical chic') of the Park Avenue crowd cosying up to gun-toting, tight-pants-wearing men whose Afros had not 'been shaped and trimmed like a topiary hedge'. Wolfe was rewriting the rules of journalism. The article was merciless in its mockery, but it wasn't satire. The New Journalism depicted the world as it was, with its ugliness and profanities as well as its kindnesses and confusions. It was absorbing and addictive and, where editors allowed it, feverishly imitated by journalists in newspaper offices all around the world, at the least the English-speaking world. I was one of them.

One of my earliest articles, written 'on-spec' since I wasn't sure that Suich would be receptive, described Christmas Day 1975 in Belmore Park near Central Railway in Sydney. A friend and I were driving past on our way to a festive lunch, when we noticed a number of homeless men sprawled on park benches. On the back seat of our car was an array of freshly cooked food, far more than would be needed at our lunch. We each had the same thought. We took one of the turkeys and, in our atheistic version of Christmas cheer, offered it to the men. My article was self-mocking. We had not foreseen how they would claw at the meat with bare hands, stuff it into stomachs so unaccustomed to food of such quantity and richness that they would spew it up immediately. Not only that. We fled, leaving behind our nice plate and our do-gooder naivety, as a couple of the men unzipped their pants and, fumbling for their penises, told us what they'd really like for Christmas.

The next day I left my story on Suich's desk.

'Did you write this?' he demanded some hours later, brandishing my little composition.

I knew it was an unusual piece, I knew the *National Times* was not as adventurous as *Nation Review*, the other weekly newspaper that was enlivening the media scene in the 1970s. The transport magnate Gordon Barton had launched *Nation Review* in 1970 as a newspaper that characterised itself as 'the Ferret: lean and nosy' and in both tone and subject matter, it went where the rest of media seldom trod. Today, it would be seen as utterly misogynist and probably racist as well; it reflected the times, perhaps a little too faithfully.

'It was just an experiment,' I responded somewhat defensively. 'I wanted to try a different way of writing.'

I can't remember his exact words although they were along the lines that it was a great piece of writing, but that I'd better not think that I could spend all my time on this bleeding hearts stuff when there were real stories out there and we—or, to be more precise, I—was going to get them.

That was fine with me. I wanted to broaden my knowledge and I certainly wanted to avoid being typecast as only able to write about women or other subjects that were seen as 'soft'. It annoyed me that there was such a hierarchy of status given to subjects and that I would not be taken seriously as a journalist if I was seen as only interested in 'bleeding hearts' stories. Politics and crime were the big stories of the era and the only way to build a reputation was to write about these. Later, with some of my male colleagues, we would find new ways of writing stories about particularly brutal or squalid examples of sexual abuse, stories the mainstream media in those days never touched outside their crime pages. We learned to bring in the victims' point of view and to explore the murky terrain of he said/she said in ways that had never previously been done in Australian journalism. But for now I was finding my feet, learning as fast as I could and loving every moment of it. I was fortunate that I did not have to serve a cadetship, writing shipping news or covering town hall meetings. I was disadvantaged in that I did not learn shorthand, nor was I ever taught the basics of reporting, but I felt more than compensated by being able to go straight into the big, often very big, stories and to have as much time, and as much space, as I needed.

For the first time since I was a teenager when I'd worked in a bank, I had to go to the office each day. I was unaware until Suich called as I was sitting down with guests to a lunch I was hosting on New Year's Day that journalists worked public holidays: 'Get your arse in here,' he'd commanded. I made my apologies and headed for Jones Street, Broadway. The compensation for working public holidays was an extra two weeks annual leave, I discovered.

That certainly made up for it. I was in a real job, with deadlines, and working alongside a bunch of highly talented, very opinionated and extremely competitive individuals. I had met John Edwards when he worked for Whitlam's Labor minister, Clyde Cameron, in Canberra; later, after writing some memorable political profiles for the *Australian Financial Review*, he was now writing politics for the *National Times*. I knew Yvonne Preston, renowned for her writing on social and political subjects, from around the traps. Both of them had put in a word for me with Suich. I knew a few other journalists who were part of the Sydney Push, that group of free-spirited and argumentative individuals, mostly self-styled libertarians and anarchists, I had gravitated towards soon after arriving in Sydney. Their numbers also included gamblers and labourers as well as academics, students, poets and people who proudly referred to themselves as layabouts. Our Friday night watering-hole was the Criterion in Sussex Street where, I now found, working for the 'capitalist press' was contentious. Our arguments became even more belligerent. I was leaving the safety of the crowd, I realised. I was on my own, I'd have to make my own way.

Eventually I wrote about everything from Defence procurement to children's books, social workers to corrupt cops, rape to armed robberies, from the murder of police sources to the drug habits of the 'gonzo' writer Hunter S. Thompson. But that first week I had started with the familiar, writing a story about what happens to women once they leave a refuge, those safe havens recently established by the women's movement for women and children escaping domestic violence. It was easy, being a subject I already knew, and the women who ran Elsie Women's Refuge in Glebe, which I'd helped start the year before, were only too willing to help. Two women who with their kids had recently been moved into public housing agreed to be interviewed on the record. I found out how to organise a photographer and by Thursday I had the story, complete with pics, on Suich's desk. It was my first published article but it had absolutely zero impact, including with my editor, because the paper came out the weekend of the emotional and rowdy federal election that saw Malcolm Fraser, the Liberal leader who had engineered the 'constitutional coup' that led to the sacking of Labor Prime

Minister Gough Whitlam on 11 November 1975, confirmed in office and the dismissed Whitlam consigned to opposition.

Ironically enough, my very next story, which hit the mark with Suich for being tough, came from knowledge I'd acquired during my radical political activities. For the past several years I had been active in the women's movement, working on a range of issues including publications (I'd helped start *Refractory Girl*, the first women's studies journal) as well as being one of the group that had occupied a vacant house in Glebe and opened Australia's first modern women's refuge, Elsie. I'd also taken part in resident actions aimed at saving low-income housing and some of Sydney's older buildings and in prisoner action groups where I met people on both sides of the law. I was able to use such knowledge several times and it resulted in some of my most successful stories. I would make my name, in that first year, by writing a series of articles about the New South Wales prison system that caused a political ruckus and put pressure on the recently established Royal Commission into NSW prisons. Much of the information that I 'revealed' was common knowledge among lefty lawyers and others who agitated for prison reform, but the rest of the press wasn't interested. Once it was clear that Suich was willing to go down paths other newspapers shied away from, the scope for us to break major stories was almost boundless. The first time it happened was the result of Suich mentioning his suspicion that the police routinely disregarded the law requiring the destruction of fingerprints of people who had been charged but not convicted.

'But everyone knows the cops keep them,' I'd chipped in. 'Where's the story in that?'

'We *suspect* they keep them,' he corrected me. 'We don't know for sure.'

'Yes we do.'

'Can you prove it?'

'Yes.'

It was common knowledge around the courts, with any number of lawyers having first-hand experience of a client's prints being retained. I no longer have the story and I can't remember how I assembled the proof, but I do know that it was not difficult and that the story when it was published caused all sorts of strife. After that, I got put onto a lot more police stories. But I also found myself needing to confront a fundamental question about

what my life had become when Suich asked me to take down a large poster
I had pinned to the wall beside my desk. It showed a stylised photograph of
a NSW police officer with the words 'tomorrow's bacon!' scrawled across
the top. It was a striking piece of work, designed by the renowned graphic
artist Chips Mackinolty for the Earthworks Collective, a group based at the
Tin Sheds at Sydney University that produced powerful political posters.
Now my boss was asking me—or was he telling me?—to take it down. I hesitated. I understood he was in fact asking me to decide whether I was still
an activist, or if I was willing to take my heart off my sleeve and become an
observer and reporter of events. Hadn't I already made that choice by joining
the *National Times*? Or was I trying to have it both ways? It was an argument
that journalists continue to have. We were not expected to have no political views, but we were expected to not put them on display. In the US, this
proscription extended to reporters being discouraged from taking part in
political rallies, lest their presence be seen to compromise their objectivity.
I was astonished to learn that Linda Greenhouse, who covered the Supreme
Court for the *New York Times*, was criticised for joining the massive march
in Washington DC in 1989 in favour of abortion rights. In Australia, the
rules were not as stringent. In 2000 many journalists, including the editor
of the *Sydney Morning Herald*, would join the several hundred thousand
people who walked across the Sydney Harbour Bridge in the March for
Indigenous Reconciliation. But in 1976 I was being told I could not display
an anti-police poster in the newsroom. I had already been attacked by many
of my friends for what they saw as 'selling out'. I'd argued that the *National
Times* was different, that we could expose the kinds of corruption and abuse
of power that our political activism was all about. This was just a different
way of doing it. And, I liked to think, perhaps a more effective way since
we reached a much larger audience and we had the authority of the Fairfax
media company behind us. Not many of my friends bought this argument.
They were purists. Later some like Wendy Bacon, who I knew from the
Sydney Push and who was also active in resident action and women in
prison groups and who had attacked me the most vehemently, themselves
joined the media. She wrote ground-breaking articles about corruption for
the *National Times*. But early in 1976, you were a journalist or you were an
activist. You could not be both, or at least not in the newsroom. For the rest

of my life I would continue to be torn by these conflicting and, it seemed, incompatible desires. It had been a problem for me while I was writing *Damned Whores and God's Police*, although that had been more about how I split my time between writing and activism. As a journalist working for a mainstream newspaper I would never have the latitude enjoyed by Simone de Beauvoir and Jean-Paul Sartre, who were their own publishers, and so could engage politically while they wrote articles and novels (and continued to teach). I had to choose. I took the poster down. For now, at least, I was choosing journalism.

The *National Times* ran articles that were not just long but by the standards of daily newspapers, digressive. We used adjectives and ego-enhancing bylines at a time when the *Sydney Morning Herald*, the flagship publication of the stately Fairfax newspaper empire, regarded these as rare rewards for major pieces or favoured writers. You were more likely to see a piece 'From our Canberra correspondent' than one that disclosed who had actually written the story. The *National Times* was a unique publication. Without the obligation to report on the news of the day, or even the week (although since we went to press at 11 a.m. on Saturday for Sunday morning publication, we could update stories if necessary, to ensure they were current, and sometimes it was legally astute to do so), it became known for its magazine-style journalism. The paper and its reporting staff were free to roam as far as their editor would allow.

The paper had been established in 1971, the idea of Vic Carroll, the man who had turned the *Australian Financial Review* into a commercial and journalistic success during the 1960s. He had presided over the covering of the early days of the oil and minerals exploration booms and supervised political and business coverage that launched the careers of Max Walsh, Robert Gottliebsen, Peter Robinson and Trevor Kennedy. Carroll was a dour man who said little but who, you felt, was always sizing you up under those hooded eyes of his. He was, it turned out. I was amazed, and gratified, to discover later that he thought highly of my work. Carroll had once been a stockbroker and understood the ways of money but he knew that journalism was more than just reporting what was in front of you. The essence of journalism was 'curiosity', he said in 2013 after being awarded an Honorary Doctorate by Macquarie University.[3] Carroll proposed that Fairfax start up a weekend paper that continued, and expanded, the *Financial Review*'s market. He was managing editor of both papers from 1970 to 1975 before, in 1980, being put in charge of transforming the *Sydney Morning Herald* into a modern, quality newspaper.

Max Suich was 33 when he became the paper's second editor in late 1972. He'd been Japan correspondent filing mostly for the *Financial Review*, covering the big trade and economic stories of the relationship between Japan and Australia. He was single-minded and ambitious, and he succeeded in turning the *National Times* into a newspaper legend, attracting and then managing the egos of some extraordinary talent. Suich had reddish, rapidly thinning hair and a wicked grin; he could be decidedly brutal as an editor and brusque as a person, but he was nevertheless kind and even shy in some situations. He became embarrassed when a female reporter asked for the day off to have an abortion.

'Take all the time you need,' he said. 'Just don't talk about it.'

When it came to our work he gave us very free rein. He was adventurous and encouraging and willing to listen to any ideas his staff wanted to run past him.

'What's the story, morning glory?' was Suich's way of greeting every one of his reporters. Whatever the subject, however mundane, or potentially sensational, he was interested in hearing what we had. Everything was 'a story' which I found confusing at first, thinking stories were fiction, but I soon mastered the lingo and relished in the freedom of being able to write about anything that was interesting or, increasingly as I got into stories of crime and corruption, illegal. I began to write more about the police, including the activities of the Special Branch, and about the notorious but previously hard to prove role of some senior police in orchestrating and profiting from criminal activities. And I wrote a great deal about prisons, but also continued to write about subjects that were denigrated as 'bleeding hearts' journalism by Suich and his tough-minded contemporaries. Their Friday lunches, were always at a fancy restaurant, where Suich, Carroll, Walsh, Robinson, Fred Brenchley (covering politics in Canberra, but a frequent visitor to Sydney and later editor of the *Financial Review*) and Paddy McGuinness, the *Financial Review*'s economics editor and, also, later its editor would dissect the problems of the world and, just as importantly, Fairfax their employer.

They were long and extremely liquid affairs. Occasionally, I would be invited to join them. Sometimes Valerie Lawson or Deborah Light from the *Financial Review* might be there, but it was mostly an all-male affair. I was keen to have these men respect me, and I knew there was no better place to be learning, but I did not see any contradiction between being interested in both the tough stuff and stories about the disadvantages or outright suffering of those who were being excluded from the overall benefits of society. They indulged my little one-woman stand, but no one took it seriously. That wasn't where 'the story' was.

People today look back on the *National Times* in the 1970s as some kind of halcyon era of journalism and they are right. Our journalism was different, and so was our sense of ourselves. At first, we thought ourselves lucky to be at the pointy-end of the way journalism was evolving, but before long we took it for granted and I, at least, developed a certain smugness. Not only were we right, we were better.

Our office shared a floor with the *Sun*, the afternoon tabloid that favoured racy headlines and was in frenzied competition with the *Daily Mirror*, produced by the Murdoch stable a few blocks away in Holt Street, Surry Hills. Derryn Hinch, later well-known as a radio host in Melbourne, and in 2016 elected to the Senate as an Independent, was editor of the *Sun*. He was a friendly and approachable guy, with the equally affable Terry Hayes, now an internationally best-selling writer of fiction, as his sidekick. I used to see Hinch at the pub, or drop by his office occasionally, so I knew him well enough to storm in one day in May 1976 to protest the headline, 'Rebel mum suicides in jail'. There were many ways to describe the German radical, Ulrike Meinhof, but 'rebel mum' was a bit too reductionist, even for a Sydney tabloid. Meinhof did have twin daughters but, in teaming up with Andreas Baader to form the Red Army Faction, or the Baader-Meinhof gang as it was colloquially known, she went way further than your average rebel, even in the 1960s. Meinhof advocated, and practised, urban guerilla warfare against the state and individual industrialists and was eventually caught, imprisoned and sentenced. There is still controversy as to whether she suicided—or was murdered—in her cell. The *Sun*, of course, had no room for such ambiguity.

Suich's deputy was Evan Whitton, a tall long-faced man with a deadpan sense of humour that often got lost in translation when his words were interpreted literally, but he had a ferocious dedication to, as he put it, 'naming the guilty men'. He had been a prominent reporter at the Melbourne tabloid *Truth* when it exposed the abortion rackets in the late-1960s—where police protected, and thus perpetuated, abortionists who were not always too particular about the safety or even the lives of the desperate women who sought their services. Later he had worked for News Ltd, first at the *Weekend Australian* and then the *Daily Telegraph* before Vic Carroll brought him over to the *National Times* where he brought the same forensic intensity to organised crime and police corruption in NSW as he had to the Victorian abortion industry. He and I worked closely together on many of my big reporting jobs.

It is difficult to think of any of the reporters engaged by Suich who were not—and, those who survive, mostly still are—stars of journalism. During my three years there I was fortunate enough to work with these writers of extraordinary and distinctive talent—Andrew Clark, John Edwards, David Marr, Paul Kelly, Robert Milliken, Adele Horin, David Hickie, Glennys Bell, Meryl Constance, Yvonne Preston, Bruce Stannard and John Jost—and to count many as lifelong friends. Patrick Cook was the cartoonist and Ward O'Neill drew caricatures. I was thrilled when cartoonist Jenny Coopes, came on board as well. I knew Jenny from the Push but she was also a star in feminist circles for 'The Adventures of Super Fem', a witty regular strip she had drawn in the Whitlam era that parodied Elizabeth Reid, Whitlam's women's adviser, and was published in *Liberaction*, the publication of the iconoclastic Hobart Women's Action Group.

As well as being economics editor for the *Financial Review* P.P. (Paddy) McGuinness contributed an economics column and reviewed films for the *National Times*. His picture byline, showing the dark glasses he always wore because his pale Irish eyes could not tolerate bright light, led to lots of jokes about us being the only newspaper to employ a blind film reviewer. Paddy wore nothing but black long before it became *de rigueur* for the rest of us, and seemed unconcerned about his rapidly expanding girth. He loved his food and drink and was unconvinced of the merits of any form of physical exercise.

Elisabeth Wynhausen was probably my best friend at the office. She was a tough-talking, soft-hearted, eternally optimistic, nervously energetic woman with a thin thatch of soft dark hair, who'd come to the *Natty Times* (as we'd started calling the paper) from the *Bulletin*. We'd known each other through the Balmain Push and the literary world; she aspired to be a 'real' writer and no one I've ever met agonised more over every word. She often pulled all-nighters in the office in order to meet a deadline. We'd come in the next day and she'd be still clacking away, her ashtray piled high, and the floor around her desk littered with ripped, discarded pieces of the three-ply slips of paper we used to type our stories on.

We were a tight and rowdy bunch, banging away on our typewriters, most of us with a cigarette on the go as we typed, pushed the carriage return, ripped out the three-ply, inserted another set and knocked out a few more pars. If we needed space on our desks, to read, or to take notes while we interviewed someone on the phone, we'd simply upend our typewriters onto their backs. There was nothing fancy about the setup; the desks were well-used, the floor was a ghastly pale linoleum which could, and often did, absorb a cigarette butt ground underfoot. If we'd been in a proper newsroom, we could have yelled 'copy' when we'd finished our story and a boy—later there were copygirls as well—would scoop up the story and run it over to the subeditors. But we were a small outfit, about a dozen of us, in a windowless space that had been carved out of the cavernous expanse of the fifth floor of the Herald building in Jones Street, Ultimo, that is now occupied by the University of Technology Sydney. We would separate and collate the three-ply ourselves: one copy for the subs, one for the editor and one to keep. That was seldom the end of the process. Apart from any queries the subs might have, there would be wrangles with Max, decisions about what could be cut so as to fit one of Patrick Cook's acerbic cartoons and, increasingly often with my stories, there would be long hard Friday night negotiations with Frank Hoffey, our defamation lawyer.

Once it was all done, we would stroll across Broadway to The Australian hotel. It was routine for us to have a few rounds after work and on Friday nights to stay on until very late. We mostly drank beer, but the first time I joined my new colleagues I was astonished to see they were drinking Veuve Clicquot. I was embarrassed, too, because I had no money. When it came time for my round, I had to borrow from John Edwards. If you went to the pub any other time, Suich would most likely already be there. The amount of time he, and we, spent at the pub is startling by today's standards. Today if you needed a private chat with a staff member, you would do it over a coffee. In those days, if Suich, or any of the blokes, wanted a really private chat they could go to the front bar where women were still banned. A bunch of Sydney feminists were working on that, staging protests and 'drink-ins' at pubs just a few kilometres further along Parramatta Road. Before long, the 'ladies lounges', those rooms at the back of pubs where, notoriously, women would shell the peas for tea that night while downing a shandy or two, went the way of the girdle and other restricting irritants in the lives of women.

On the fourth floor of the Fairfax building was the photo-compositing room where the pages of the newspapers were laid out and where journalists were mostly forbidden. Sometimes, late on a Friday, I would be allowed to go down to check the final version of my story on 'the stone', as it was still called although the old hot-metal process of making up pages with metal letters had been superseded. Union rules remained the same, however, and there were few unions as protective of their sphere as the Printing and Kindred Industries Union (PKIU). On the fourth floor, photocopying was printers' work, as I discovered when I attempted to make a copy of a page and found myself inadvertently precipitating a potential demarcation dispute. Below us the presses hummed, less noisy than they'd once been but you knew they were there. The only contact we had with the men who ran the presses was at the pub. The father of the chapel, as the head of the PKIU onsite was known, liked to drink with journalists. Especially women journalists.

Women were increasingly being employed in journalism and no longer just on the social pages, which themselves were undergoing a makeover. In 1971 the *Sydney Morning Herald* had replaced its fashion, housewifery, society notes and social pages with 'Look!' a livelier, lifestyle approach that at least nodded to the emerging ideas of women's liberation. Suzanne Baker, a journalist with a background in film, was brought in to do the job although she had moved back to film by the time I started at Fairfax four years later. Gavin Souter's history of Fairfax records that from a ratio of about one woman to every eleven men in the 1950s and 1960s, the numbers of women doubled between 1969 and 1973, from 15 to 31.[4] But although I was part of a distinct minority, it did not feel that way at the *National Times*. Perhaps this was because the ratio of women was greater there than on the other titles, but also because we were not restricted in what we could write. In fact, it was often the other way round, with me wanting to write stories about women and being encouraged, instead, to do the tough pieces about the so-called 'real world'.

The culture of newspapers was undeniably masculine. It wasn't just that the pub was our hangout, or that rough language and swearing were our common parlance; it was that the assumptions about what was important, or what was scandalous, or what was funny all derived from a view of the world that had been built around men's experiences and expectations. Women journalists are as tough and resilient as the men, and certainly none of the women at the *National Times* were shrinking types. Meryl Constance, who Suich had poached from *Choice* to write about consumer issues, and Yvonne Preston, who in the mid-1970s had gone to China as the Fairfax correspondent, were the only women on staff who had children and were less likely to go to the pub after work. But the rest of us—Elisabeth Wynhausen, Adele Horin, Glennys Bell and Jenny Coopes breasted the (back) bar along with the boys. We were assertive and unshockable. That did not mean that I, at least, sometimes wondered what universe I was in. As when Suich told us the story of a renowned American journalist who had broken many international stories during his time in Southeast Asia. On this particular evening, Suich recounted, the journalist was 'rooted' because he'd worked for days on end filing a particularly important scoop.

'Then, instead of going home, he took himself to X.'—Suich named a place that, he had to explain to everyone, was a notorious brothel in that particular city.

His avid listeners roared, whether with admiration, awe or envy, I, the only woman present, could not say. All I knew was that while I wasn't prudish, nor was I able to identify in any way with the story of a journalist who recovered from a hard day at the office by surrounding himself with pliant young Asian hookers.

I was certainly not a pioneer as a woman journalist. Those honours went to women like Margaret Jones, a tall and somewhat stern woman who had been the *Herald's* literary editor (and given me a reviewing assignment when I had first arrived in Sydney). She had been correspondent in Washington where as a woman she was denied admission to the National Press Club and thus prevented from reporting key political stories, and in December 1973 became the paper's first China correspondent. She liked to tell of riding her bike in Peking, as Beijing was still called, and often passing the Chief of the US Liaison Office, as the top American representative was titled before the US formally recognised China in 1979, who was riding his.

'Good morning, Miss Jones,' he would say.

'Good morning, Mr Bush,' she'd reply to the man who in 1989 would become the 41st President of the United States.

Margaret became something of a mentor to me for the few years she was in Sydney before being sent off to Europe in 1980. We regularly went to the theatre together and she gave me advice on how to handle my job. We were dissimilar in temperament (and politics) and there was a significant age difference which meant I often thought her advice a bit off the mark, but I valued her friendship and that she took time to spend with me.

***

The stories that earned me my reputation—and a Walkley Award before the end of my first year in journalism—were a multi-part series on NSW prisons. Like the story on police fingerprinting, they began with my being able to establish as true a number of stories that had been circulating around newsrooms and which were widely known to people who worked in the legal system. Lawyers like Tom Kelly, Rod Madgwick, Jim Staples and Jack Grahame often represented men who were in and out of prison and were outspoken in favour of prison reform, as were academics such as David Brown from the University of New South Wales and a number of newly established prisoner action groups. I was active myself in one of these; I visited prisons and I knew prisoners, some still serving, others who were now out. Much of what I wrote was widely known in these circles. It just hadn't been written about in the press before. And I was able to add a great deal more detail and to get on-the-record corroboration from prison officers and others which added to what was already known. It was information, much of it shocking, that the government, in the form of the Minister for Justice and the Department of Corrective Services, which administered the prison system, had gone to great lengths to keep covered up. For instance, I was able to get a prison officer to confirm that a number of prisoners had been shot during the Bathurst riots of 1974, a couple of them receiving bullet wounds in the back, and that one man had become paraplegic as a result. Prison administrators had always denied this and no one in the media had been able to corroborate it.

NSW prisons were archaic and barbaric, even by the punitive standards of the times. The living conditions of prisoners were appalling and the punishments administered for the most minor infractions were brutal. The prisons became hotbeds of simmering resentment and rage. In 1970, Bathurst jail erupted with a riot that was unable to be kept from the public and which led to calls for an inquiry and reform. Nothing happened. Four years later, the same prison went up again, this time with far more serious consequences. Large sections of the prison were destroyed and the government could not ignore reports of prisoners being savagely beaten and even shot. A Royal Commission was appointed with Justice John Nagle of the Supreme Court heading it. The first day of formal hearings of the Royal Commission was 14 April 1976, two days after my first article appeared. I was encouraged by Suich and Evan Whitton to put together a series of articles reporting on what conditions in NSW prisons were really like. I think we saw ourselves as providing some context to the official inquiry, but also, given the long history of evasion and cover-ups in previous investigations, we wanted to put pressure on the commission to look hard and unflinchingly at a system that, in some places at least, would have given Stalin's gulag a run for its money. I put things on the public record that could not be ignored. My articles have often been credited with forcing the government to establish the Royal Commission. They didn't, but I do like to think they helped ensure that, finally, the veil was lifted. I published material that, in any honest investigation, would have to be thoroughly tested. Under Justice Nagle's leadership, it was.

The first of my six articles, 'The days the screws were turned loose',[5] provided a detailed account of the bashing of four prisoners who had attempted to escape from Sydney's Long Bay prison in October 1973. I followed this with the first-ever published account of the 'reception biff'— the systematic beating of newly arrived intractable prisoners at Grafton Prison by officers with rubber truncheons. I also reported on the new Katingal sensory deprivation unit at Long Bay, designed to replace physical punishment with psychological torture; on the women's prison at Mulawa; on the way the prison officers and their union were dealing with the impending spotlight on their violent and illegal behaviour; and, finally, my detailed eye-witness account of what really happened at Bathurst in 1974. It is true that the public does not really care about prisons, or prisoners (so long as they are safely locked up) and so this was not regular media fare, but it was also true that, by not having these things reported, the public was ignorant of the archaic and inhumane conditions of prisoners in NSW. This was an era of reform in so many other areas of our society. Anti-discrimination legislation was being passed, homosexuality was being decriminalised, institutions such as the public service were being shaken up, first in Canberra by the Whitlam government, and in the states by Labor leaders like Don Dunstan in South Australia and now Neville Wran, who in May 1976 had led the Labor Party to victory in NSW. Few areas of society were not being scrutinised by avid reformers. It was inevitable that prisons would come into focus.

My first article caused a big stir—and not just with the reading public. Fairfax management summoned Suich. The subject matter was unsavoury, he was told: 'Our readers' did not care to know about such things. Suich was told that there should be no further articles about prisons. Then something totally unexpected happened.

For the first time, I took the lift to the 14th floor. It was hard to believe I was still in the same building. No fluorescent lights, or makeshift room dividers. No metal desks with peeling veneers or office chairs lurching drunkenly off their wheels, and certainly no clacking or yelling or raised voices of any kind. The 14th floor was mahogany panelling, Persian carpets, oil portraits of Fairfaxes and whisper quiet. I was shown into an office that I remember as large and elegant and shook the hand of the 75-year-old proprietor of the company, Sir Warwick Fairfax. He was tall and thin with a beaked nose and lots of dark grey hair. He was courteous, but he also seemed to be quite angry about what he'd been confronted with by my story. He was a compassionate and gentle man and he could scarcely believe that such things as I reported were happening in New South Wales.

'Is this true?' he demanded to know.

I handed him two pages on which were pasted a copy of my article together with my annotations. I had treated it like a university essay and documented it with footnotes. I had two and, in most cases, three sources for every single assertion. Sir Warwick looked at me with astonishment. Journalism was definitely changing. It would no longer be enough to tell your editor that your source was a cop you'd had a drink with the night before. These days, as I was soon to find out, the cop was just as likely to be the object of your story, not its source.

After this, I was free to pursue prisons and I did so with zest.

The initial stories, or tips that might become stories, often came from crims or lawyers or academics—but then it was a matter of classic reporting, of following leads, interviewing people and, often, strategising about how to get unwilling people to talk. I liked to just turn up at people's houses, exploit the surprise factor, look them in the eye and—what a phone call, let alone an email can never reveal—assess whether they were telling the truth. It came to be known as 'investigative reporting'—although that was not a term we used then—but since it was the only kind of reporting I had ever done, I did not know it was special or unusual. It was just journalism. It was also similar in all sorts of ways to the kind of research I had done for my book. Looking up facts, interviewing people, scouring old records, making educated guesses. It did not matter whether I was looking at the rioting of convict women at Parramatta jail in the early years of settlement or the conduct of prison officers during uprisings at Bathurst jail in the 1970s; I was trying to find out what happened. The advantage with researching current stories was, of course, that the players were more likely to be around and could often be persuaded to talk.

For the two years since the 1974 Bathurst riots, authorities had always denied that prisoners had been shot and that one man had been left paralysed. Yet it only took a bit of legwork for me to track down 25-year-old Dennis Bugg to a residential care facility in Sydney's eastern suburbs. No one had ever visited Bugg before. No one was supposed to know he even existed. He spent his days watching television in the company of several other equally immobile young men, most of them paralysed as a result of motorcycle accidents. I had not made an appointment, or announced myself, so at first they regarded me curiously when I simply walked in and asked which one of them was Dennis. When they saw that I was an unaccompanied young woman who was interested in one of their number, several of them began making sexually explicit catcalls. I engaged in harmless banter with them. I wasn't offended by what they were saying. Rather, I felt immensely sorry for these men, their lost lives and the fact that no one cared about them.

Bugg was serving a sentence for stealing, which had been supplemented with extra time for trying to escape, when he had been shot in the back during the riot on 3 February 1974. He had been due for parole two days later. After he dropped to the ground three other prisoners helped carry him to safety.

'They fired at us all the way,' Bugg told me.

Bugg finally got his parole on 12 February, but by then he was incapacitated in Sydney's Prince Henry Hospital. The Corrective Services department turned down his parole officer's request for $1500 to pay for a wheelchair and other equipment. Instead, Bugg was charged under the Crimes Act with offences relating to the riots at Bathurst. A few times he rode his hospital-supplied wheelchair into the traffic on busy nearby Anzac Parade, which was interpreted as a suicide attempt, so he was scheduled to Callan Park, a psychiatric institution. After just a month Callan Park demanded he be removed, saying he was a medical patient, not a psych case. Bugg was sent to the home where I found him three years later. During that time, neither Bugg nor his family had ever paid a bill for his care; the home told me 'the government' paid. The charges were never proceeded with. Dennis Bugg was simply hidden away from public view—and public scrutiny.

I also found a prison officer who went on the record and described the floggings 'the screws'—as the prison officers were called—were expected to administer regularly to 'tracs', the so-called intractable prisoners, who were sent 'to the Jacaranda festival' as the notorious Grafton jail was known. The 'reception biff' at Grafton was famous throughout the NSW prison system and crims dreaded being sent there. Better to endure the freezing cold of the windowless and non-heated stone cells at Bathurst, and the occasional biff, than the guaranteed savage beating of your naked body when you arrived in the warm climate of northern New South Wales and which was followed by a regular weekly walloping. I interviewed Max Williams who had spent 27 years of his life in institutions of one kind or another, including a stint at Grafton in the 1950s. For a time he and fellow Grafton inmate Darcy Dugan were Australia's two most notorious criminals. 'We used to get a hiding

regularly about once a week. I used to get flogged on Thursdays,' he told
me. 'Just in normal conversation someone would say "Aren't you due to be
biffed?" And I'd say, Jeez, what's today? It was Thursday. Well it was my biff.
And this was every week.' Grafton had broken Max. He'd lost his hair and
nearly half his body weight. Like many other prisoners, he turned to writing
as a means of expression and escape. After his eventual release he became
a renowned poet. He was a gentle man but his past never left him. He will-
ingly told me about it and Justice Nagle made sure that he gave evidence to
the Royal Commission; his description of Australia's Gulag featured on the
second page of Nagle's final report. Grafton was, Nagle reported, 'a regime
of terror'.[6]

I was also able to obtain corroboration for an atrocity that occurred after
the Royal Commission had ended its inquiry.[7] I learned from his lawyer that
two days after the commission finished taking its evidence, Bernie Matthews
had been beaten unconscious by the screws at Katingal. The whole rationale
for Katingal was that it was supposed to use sensory deprivation instead of
physical brutality to quell prisoners. But Matthews, who had endured the
Grafton 'biff' five years earlier when he'd been sent there for trying to escape
from Parramatta, had been bashed at Katingal as well. I found out the name
of the doctor who had treated Matthews and who confirmed his injuries and
I then called the superintendent of Katingal, whose spluttering obfuscations
were certainly not a denial of what had happened.

Bernie Matthews had been an important witness at the Royal Commission,
giving first-hand accounts of brutality that was so severe it was hard to comprehend it was happening in New South Wales in the 1970s. Now clearly he
was getting paid back. Matthews became a writer while he was in prison,
writing poetry and plays and, since his release, has published *Intractable*,
a book about his prison experiences[8] and he still maintains a blog. I had met
Bernie at Parramatta and I gave him his first job as a journalist, getting him
to write a review for 'BookWorld', the paper's book pages which I edited for
a time. I think he was the first serving crim to write for the paper.

The Nagle Report began with an 1843 quote: 'Society has the right to
punish, but not to corrupt those punished.' It was from a book by Gustave
de Beaumont, a French magistrate and prison reformer, and the man who
accompanied Alexis de Tocqueville on his famous journey to inspect the

emerging democracy of the colonies in America in 1831–32. The report 'laid out the horror of the 33-year Grafton regime, recommended closure of the state's newest prison, Katingal, and made a large number of mainly reformist recommendations for improvement in prison conditions and amenities', wrote David Brown in an assessment of the Royal Commission 25 years later.[9] The NSW prison system had developed into a ruthless regime where deprivation of liberty was no longer seen as sufficient punishment. There is no doubt that many of the prisoners I interviewed or wrote about were dangerous and violent men, but many of them had become so because of what was done to them in prison. Max Williams had been released after serving ten years for stealing an alarm clock and for several escape attempts—and went straight to a gun shop. He planned to kill two of the screws and then shoot the rest of them when they turned up for their mates' funeral. Mad as a cut snake, he remained free for seven days before being sent back to prison. As I noted in my article, you could not describe Grafton as rehabilitative. I knew other crims who were sexually impotent after being released. Many had severe psychological problems. Anyone who'd been to Grafton had trouble looking you in the eye, something that had earned a flogging inside.

In the 1970s as we tried to grapple with notions of crime and punishment, and liberty and incarceration, we absorbed the new literature that was addressing these issues in a profound and unprecedented way. Aleksandr Solzhenitsyn's *The Gulag Archipelago* was published in English in 1974 and the French philosopher Michel Foucault's very influential *Discipline and Punish*, about the evolution of Western prisons, came out in 1975. This was the environment in which my articles were published and that, together with the Royal Commission offering the hope that justice might be at hand, gave them a resonance they might otherwise not have had. It was also a time when many, including me, were campaigning actively for individual prisoners who, we judged, had been treated unfairly by the system. The Free Sandra Willson campaign, instigated by a group of women calling themselves Women Behind Bars, succeeded when Willson was released in 1977 after eighteen years served 'at the Governor's pleasure' for murdering a taxi driver in Sydney. Our case was not that she wasn't guilty of the worst crime imaginable, but that the state had given her an indeterminate sentence. A life sentence for murder was generally around thirteen years then, but and ours, was finally over. Just a few days later came the phone call saying I'd won a Walkley Award for Best Newspaper Feature for my prison articles. It felt like an obscene intrusion and I did not want to tell the family, but they had welcomed the distraction. On 5 November I found myself in Perth's Sheraton Hotel listening to speeches by the premier, Sir Charles Court, and the widow of Sir William Walkley, the founder of Ampol Petroleum who had created the awards in 1956, and who had died just a few months earlier. The Walkleys were a lot smaller than they are today, with just five awards, all of them for print journalism, but I suspect they are still an equally inebriated event. I rampaged around the room giving my views to anyone who would listen, as well as those who seemed reluctant to hear my opinions. As I recall, there were very few women there and certainly no other female winners. But I received many compliments and congratulations from women in the industry, many of whom expressed genuine pride at a rare win by a member of their sex. A few people were pleased because I was a late-starter; it meant that there was hope for other oldies. I was 31 at the time and, I am pretty certain, the youngest winner. I felt an immense pride at winning this prize because of the tough subject matter. In some ways I was more proud than when I'd published *Damned Whores*, one year to the day earlier. My book had been reprinted three times in 1976 but that seemed remote from me; I could not see people buying or reading it. I received almost no feedback. Journalism was more tangible. It was immediate, and the reaction—whatever it was—instantaneous. Gratifying. Or terrifying. Depending on the story.

After a year I felt I was getting the hang of journalism. I liked it and it seemed that I was good at it. I had learned so much in a very short time and I hoped I would be able to continue to develop. Suich and Whitton pushed me. I was now investigating procurement in the Defence department, probing for potential corruption in the multi-million-dollar deals that kept the military supplied. I was hoping I might uncover something similar to the Lockheed aircraft bribery scandals that had been exposed in several European and Asian countries. Australia purchased aircraft from Lockheed. I did not know where I would end up, with the story or with my life. I just knew that, for now, I was where I wanted to be. I felt I could do anything, not just because of what I was doing at the paper but because of another challenge I had set myself. Ever since I had been fished from the

'They have an absolute contempt for women. A hatred,' Ross told Stannard. 'They despise any girl who is prepared to have sex.'

Stannard returned to Sydney and got on the phone. He had been sceptical initially that such a story could be true—in the 1970s surely such behaviour would not be tolerated. But a quick chat with an Ingham detective-sergeant confirmed not only that rape was common—between 30 and 40 local women had been raped, he said—but the police were largely powerless to do anything about it for lack of evidence. They did not even bother to record the complaints any more.

Evan Whitton was in the chair at the time because Suich was on assignment in Tokyo. As a former *Truth* reporter he had a nose for a good crime story and was keen to pursue this one but, partly guided by the young American writer Bruce Hanford who had joined the paper at Whitton's instigation, he agreed to a novel approach. It was unusual for the paper to send any of us much farther afield than a nearby capital city; it was unheard of to send a team of three to a place as distant as Ingham but it turned out to be an inspired decision. The team was Stannard, who had got the original story; Hanford, who would bring an editor's eye and a gonzo sensibility to the exercise; and me, the feminist who had written at length about rape in her book and who could now draw on that background when she interviewed the young women who had been 'trained'. What we did was a first for Australian journalism: a team effort where we split the reporting along gender lines and where we inserted ourselves into the story, New Journalism style, as we tried to get the truth about what was happening to the girls in this town.

We spent just a day in Ingham, driving to and from Townsville in a rented car, and checking into a motel room that would serve as our base and from where we could make telephone calls. We had done enough preliminary work to know who we wanted to talk to, and where to find them, but we still managed to cover an enormous amount of ground in a very short time. I concentrated on tracking down and talking to several of the young girls while Stannard and Hanford talked to the cops, to the local newspaper editor and to several of the perpetrators including, amazingly, the man who was the chief organiser of the 'trains'.

'None of the sheilas get raped or anything like that,' he told the two Bruces. 'It's just the way they are.'

I heard a very different story.

A seventeen-year-old who we called X and who had a baby told me how she had been raped at age thirteen when two girls in a car with some boys had invited her to come into town with them: 'Instead of going to town, they took me out near the mill. There were five men and they all raped me. I reported it to the police. But I didn't have enough evidence. I wasn't bruised enough.' She knew the men but they avoided her for some months afterwards, crossing the street so as not to have to talk to her. That all changed, she told me, after she had the baby that had resulted from the rape and, two days before the birth, the same men raped her little sister. The boys were 'real proud' after that, X told me.

I heard similar stories from a couple of other girls and I could not help but be reminded of similar humiliations that I had endured as a teenager. The difference was that I never was subjected to attacks by multiple men, but there was always immense pressure from the man who had asked you out, paid for dinner or even just given you a ride home from a party. Wanting to be liked, thinking giving in to sex would make me popular, the sheer terror of a pregnancy resulting from forced sex; it all came flooding back as I witnessed the misery of these girls as they recounted what had happened to them. I met with a teacher at Ingham's high school who said: 'It got that way that when I saw a girl crying at my door, I would go cold all over and think to myself, Oh no. Not again.'

The article caused a sensation. The story itself was scandalous but the way it was reported was also unprecedented. It brought together the points of view of so many of the players, including court and law enforcement officials, as well as the on-the-record comments of alleged rapists and their victims. It contained judgements and commentary that was unusual for newspaper reporting at the time, including my observation that what happened in Ingham was just a more blatant example of what happened to women everywhere. What we ran was raw, and it was recent. We published the story just days after we'd returned from Ingham, running it over four pages of the paper, complete with photographs of the hotel where the trains often started and the courthouse where justice was never dispensed. It became a political issue in Queensland and led to a debate about the state's rape laws, led by a Liberal Party MP Rosemary Kyburz who championed the girls of Ingham. Somewhat unfairly, since I had been just one of a three-person team, my name was the one that became associated with this story and this persisted for years afterwards. The story was re-reported by overseas media, it was turned into a film, was the subject of documentaries and an extensive number of debates and other forms of follow-up. For years it was synonymous with ground-breaking journalism, and with bringing a subject like rape from the crime blotter and into the feature pages where it would be read by a huge, largely unprepared and therefore utterly shocked audience. It was not a story that people forgot.

Less than a year later, David Marr and I teamed up to report on another gruesome sexual activity.[11] This one took place much closer to home, at St Paul's College at the University of Sydney. But the paper's introduction to the story compared it to what happened at Ingham, describing it as 'a similarly ugly custom apparently sanctioned among the more sophisticated and highly educated sons of New South Wales society'.

We reported on the annual valedictory dinner held just three weeks earlier on 3 November 1977. After the formal proceedings—including a witty after-dinner speech by Sydney University Law Professor, former Pauline (as the college's alumni were known), and later High Court Justice, Dyson Heydon—staff and many senior students retired for their after-dinner ports. It was then, we wrote, that 'another custom, less formal, but nevertheless traditional, begins.' The Animal Act of the Year, we reported, has traditionally gone to the student who in the eyes of his peers has committed an act 'which contravenes commonly accepted social mores in some extravagant fashion'. There were just two nominees: a fellow who had led a team that sprayed cat's blood on a corridor at nearby Women's College, and another who had sexually humiliated his girlfriend, also from Women's College, in July that year by organising a gangbang on her. The gangbanger won. After accepting his trophy, a nickel-plated sports cup, the winner, whose gross exploits had been described in disgusting detail in the nomination, proceeded to simulate sexual intercourse with a life-sized plastic doll. During these proceedings, 'one of the nominators called out her nickname and she was instantly recognisable as the winner's girlfriend'. The college reacted immediately and by the next morning the winner and three of his mates had been suspended from college. It was a bridge too far, apparently, for a sex aid to be used and for the 'mention of a lady's name in the mess'.

The young woman heard the same night that her name had been called out at the dinner. She was beside herself with shock and outrage. She was from the country and was not a sophisticated person, which was one reason her parents wanted her at Women's College where, they had assumed, she would be safe. The morning after the dinner, accompanied by her mother, she went to see Barbara Ramjan, the president of the Students' Representative Council (SRC). At the time of the sexual acts she had confided in several close friends, seen a gynaecologist and sought the services of a student counsellor. Now, several months later, she was making a formal complaint to the SRC. The young woman had thought that perhaps Ramjan, the first woman in more than twenty years to occupy this position, and the now feminist-dominated SRC, might spray-paint St Paul's College with some derogatory graffiti. Instead, Ramjan contacted me. I went to the City Road offices of the student union, to meet the young woman and to hear her story. At my request, she signed a statutory declaration that set out in gruesome detail what had happened to her that July night when, drunk and stoned, she had sexual intercourse with her boyfriend and three of his mates. She swore that she had consented to the boyfriend but not to his mates. Her mother told me they had consulted a solicitor, a family friend, who had advised them not to press criminal charges; no lawyer in Sydney would touch the case, he said, because of the family connections of one of the students.

Back in the office, we decided that David Marr should interview the young men and the college authorities. The men told David that the woman had consented; they provided details that were meant to support their version. Their interviews were unsworn but David was 'impressed' by what they told him. He was not convinced that what happened that night was rape. We repaired to my place to argue about the story. We spent several days at my flat in Elizabeth Bay, that overlooked the boats bobbing on Rushcutters Bay six floors below, going over the materials. We were unable to agree on how to interpret what we had been told. It boiled down to the simple fact that I believed the girl and David believed the boys. Neither of us would budge so, we decided, we needed to make our differing views part of the story. Doing so reflected the reality of so many alleged rape stories; it all came down to he said/she said. In this case, however, there were also other factors at play: the unequal contest between an inexperienced country family and one of the biggest names in Sydney's legal fraternity, the fact that the university had declined to become involved, leaving St Paul's College to handle things. The college had only one sanction: expulsion. Given that two of the boys were about to complete their studies within weeks, this was not much of a punishment. In any event, the college was reluctant to do anything because they believed, and supported, the men's version of events. None of this gave any satisfaction, let alone justice, to the young woman. One thing David and I did agree on was, we wrote, that 'whatever form of consent may have been given—or assumed—on that night in July, it did not include a willingness to be subjected to public slander'. The young woman's life was wrecked. She left university and went back to the farm. Our story, which had at its heart the sexual abuse and public humiliation of a naive young woman, reverberated around Sydney but not much changed. In 2016, Fairfax reported similar activities at St Paul's.[12] What happened to the young woman in 1976 is now called 'slut-shaming' and social media today provides Paulines and other young men with potent new tools such as a Facebook 'pro-rape page' but the college's attitude remained atavistically protective of such abusive behaviour. St Paul's at first announced it would not cooperate with an inquiry into the culture of college life, instigated by the university, by now willing to take some responsibility for what happens on campus. In June 2017, however, after yet further allegations of sexual abuse were made against students at St. Paul's, the college announced it would join the review being conducted by former Sex Discrimination Commissioner Elizabeth Broderick.[13]

I had been living in Sydney for seven years by 1978, and by now knew the town well. After starting out in Newtown, then Balmain, Annandale and Leichhardt, I had decided the eastern suburbs were where I wanted to be. I liked Kings Cross, which was full of strip clubs and other questionable joints but which also had good food shopping, and for the rest of my time in Sydney I would live a short stroll away in Elizabeth Bay. Partly through living there, I now knew lots of people on both sides of the law and prided myself on being 'in the know' about what a dirty little town Sydney really was. But at times even I was astounded at just how crooked the place was. It was common knowledge that many police were corrupt. I'd been to the Forbes Club and Club 33, illegal casinos in Darlinghurst that were always packed with punters, where the drinks were free and where you could always spot a copper or two enjoying a good old time. I was pretty sure I'd seen the Police Commissioner at the Forbes Club one night. I also knew the rumours that some police actually organised bank robberies, making the crims do the dangerous work of breaking in and blowing the safes, and then taking most of the proceeds for themselves. But while we 'knew' this, there was no proof. And while there was no proof, the Sydney corruption mill ground on, seemingly unstoppable.

But in March 1978 I managed to get hold of a 64-page transcript of a record of interview, conducted between 18 July and 17 August 1971 between a number of NSW senior police officials and Shirley Brifman, a well-known prostitute who had operated a series of brothels around the area where I now lived. Her most famous one was located in a fancy apartment building, The Reef, in Ithaca Road just steps from my front door. In her record of interview Brifman had made sensational allegations against 34 named police officers. She had paid regular protection money of $100 a week to two cops, Michael Phelan and Freddy Krahe, and had had dealings that were illegal with more than 30 others. In return for these payments, Krahe and Phelan were supposed to protect her business and keep away any 'gunnies', as non-police standover men were known. Krahe was especially important; he ensured that each time she changed address, which was often, her phone number 35 3837 which, she claimed was known to 'millions of men', moved with her. He arranged for a complaining neighbour at Ithaca Road to be burgled; he often stored stolen goods at Brifman's place and, perhaps not surprisingly, he regularly availed himself of Brifman's sexual favours. This cosy little arrangement had come to an abrupt end in early 1971 when Brifman was charged with procuring a thirteen-year-old girl for prostitution. It turned out the girl was her daughter. Events soon spiralled out of control. As Michael Duffy and Nick Hordern have pointed out, the appointment of a new head of the CID, to replace the corrupt Don Fergusson who had suicided in February 1970, signalled the end of this blatant corruption.[14] An enraged Shirley Brifman was hell-bent on revenge. It came in the form of a live ABC television interview, where she made explosive allegations against police in NSW and Queensland. Not long afterwards, she was sitting down with senior NSW police, answering 320 questions about the allegations. It was rumoured at the time that Shirley Brifman had named names. Lots of them. Which is no doubt why she ended up dead in her Brisbane apartment in March 1972, a few days before her trial on the underage girl was about to begin. (She was originally from Brisbane and had begun her sex trade career there.) The media said her death was the result of a heart attack, or a drug overdose. There was no autopsy or inquest so no one could be sure but the word around police circles in Sydney was that Freddie Krahe had flown north and, with the help of a Brisbane detective by the name of Tony Murphy, had gone to Brifman's apartment and forced drugs down her throat. Now, six years after her death, I had a copy of her record of interview.

It was every bit as sensational as rumour had had it, but it was also highly defamatory. The 34 police officers named were each accused of specific offences, from accepting bribes, to colluding with wealthy homeowners to rob their houses in return for a share of the insurance, to accepting money from underage girls in return for not informing child protection services, to organising bank robberies, and, of course, accepting free sex at the brothel. How to get these allegations into print was going to be one of the biggest challenges the paper had ever faced. There was really only one way, and that was to get the protection of parliamentary privilege for the documents. If a politician was prepared to read the transcripts into Hansard, they would attract privilege, and the media could report their content. There was no chance of any NSW parliamentarian doing this. Too many of them either had questionable connections themselves or would have been prevented by their parties from such a provocative attempt to upset the existing order. However, in South Australia, Peter Duncan, the young and radical Attorney-General in the Dunstan government, and a friend of mine since our days at the University of Adelaide, was known to be anxious to curtail the activities of Abe Saffron, the well-known Sydney crime figure, who was trying to get a foothold in Adelaide. In March 1978 Duncan tabled in the South Australian Parliament three documents: 1. Abe Saffron's NSW police record, 2. A record of police interview with two Sydney journalists, Tony Reeves and Barry Ward relating to the disappearance and suspected murder

of Juanita Nielsen, a community newspaper publisher who had been campaigning against development in Victoria Street, Kings Cross, and 3. The
Brifman transcript. In our article, published on 13 March, the *National
Times* wrote the tabled documents 'might perhaps best be described as the
Saffron papers'.[15] The connection with Saffron in each of these documents
was the by-now former policeman Freddie Krahe who, Duncan asserted in
the SA Parliament, 'is a well-known business associate of Saffron'. Krahe
was suspected as being instrumental in the disappearance and murder
of Nielsen, and of course the ex-cop had a starring role in the Brifman
tapes. The tabling of these documents helped Duncan to create a climate
of apprehension about Saffron; he was able to use this, together with his
announcement that the government would oppose the issuance or renewal
of all Saffron's liquor licences, to negotiate the crime organisation's exit from
South Australia. He agreed to give them a year to wind up their operations.[16]

With the transcript tabled, we had some cover but would it be enough
to satisfy our lawyer and Fairfax management? Any misjudgement could be
catastrophically expensive for the company if 30 or more cops were able to
sue, but that was not the only danger. Someone from the paper had had to call
Krahe for a comment on his association with Saffron (which he denied), so
he had prior warning that we were intending to publish. We were pretty sure
that Krahe had killed at least two women. It was decided my byline would
not appear on the story. The pages were subbed and laid out, with a larger
than usual bold headline, 'POLICE CORRUPTION ALLEGATIONS', but
the story was back in the paper, on page 8, and was not puffed on the cover.
Frank Hoffey arrived at around 5 p.m. on Friday. He handled defamation
for Stephen Jacques, Fairfax's legal firm, and was a frequent presence in our
office. He was a New Zealander, an affable sandy-haired man of about 40
whose genius was he could always provide the legal reasoning that allowed
our story to be published. Unlike many other defamation lawyers I subsequently worked with, Hoffey was creative rather than cautious. He shared
the journalist's enthusiasm for getting the story into print and his role was
to ensure it was legally defensible. 'The form of words was ours, the law
was his, and the published version the result of our negotiations with him,'
was the way Max Suich later described how we worked. 'What we sought
from Frank was his "form of words", advice that if the complainant sued,

it could be successfully defended in his opinion'. Hoffey had great confidence in his ability to do this and he was rarely wrong. But this night he was worried. The Brifman transcript had been *tabled* as distinct from being incorporated in Hansard, which meant the contents were not part of the official parliamentary record. That, Hoffey judged, reduced the privilege. None of us dared contemplate that there might be *no* privilege attached to the documents. There was also the problem that the *National Times* was a national newspaper, so whatever privilege existed might be confined to South Australia. Would that prevent these NSW-based cops from suing? We went backwards and forwards for hours. Hoffey said it was dicey and, for once, was unwilling to take responsibility. 'Management would have to make the call,' he said.

Graham Wilkinson, the editorial manager, had the head of the International Press Association at his house for dinner when Hoffey rang. He had had a few drinks, which perhaps made him less cautious than usual but nor did he want to appear in front of his international guest to be anything less than enthusiastically promoting freedom of the press when it came to approving a story that alleged extensive police corruption in Sydney. He gave us the all clear. I think I virtually collapsed with elation; it had been a fifteen-hour day. The next day I would turn 33 and on Sunday the *National Times* would hit the streets with one of the most important stories it had ever published.

There was scarcely a ripple. I could not believe that our naming these cops, and the crimes they had committed, was not a major scandal. But of course no other media would follow up as they knew the legal pitfalls. Premier Neville Wran did ask his Police Commissioner Mervyn Wood for a report, which came back with the finding that all the allegations had been investigated. When we asked the Police department what had happened to each of the named cops, we were given 'preserving privacy' as a reason for declining to answer. Frustrated, we decided to push back. Two weeks later we ran an article that described the corrupt activities of each of the 27 cops who were still alive. This time David Hickie and I shared the byline. We did not name the cops, instead using a letter of the alphabet for each one, but there was no doubt some of them were identifiable from the descriptions contained in the earlier article. The first writ arrived on Monday, from a man who was now a chief superintendent in the Commonwealth Police. He delivered it in person to our offices, to Hickie and myself, along with a solicitor's letter seeking to restrain us from publishing any further material about him. Abe Saffron's son also rang the paper, just to let us know we were on the radar. I was concerned about the writs but I was more worried to learn that Freddy Krahe was now also an employee of Fairfax. He'd been hired by the *Sun*, apparently, to help them gather material to defend a defamation case brought by Darcy Dugan but there were rumours that other parts of the organisation had called on him to do strong-arm work. I was uneasy, even a little scared, but told myself that surely Krahe would not harm another employee. But then several senior Fairfax executives told me I should not be living alone (I was). Suich said he would pay for me to move to an apartment somewhere out of the Cross for a month or so. It was then I realised that I did not have the stomach for this particular type of journalism. I was already angry and upset that Whitton had not offered me the deputy editor's job when he was slated to replace Suich who was leaving in a few weeks. I had been led to believe I would get the job but, without warning, it was announced Paul Kelly from our Canberra bureau would be the deputy. I decided that it was time for me to do something else. Andrew Clark told me about a fellowship for journalists in the United States that he had been awarded some years earlier and encouraged me to go for it. If I was successful, it would mean nine months travelling around America. It sounded like a CIA-funded ploy, but I didn't care. I applied.

While I waited to hear, I kept writing although I now steered clear of police corruption. In June I'd written about the disappearance of a young woman, Trudie Adams, from the Northern Beaches in Sydney who had last been seen getting into the back of a panel van, a vehicle I referred to as 'the mobile bedrooms of the young'. Two young women got in touch; they knew all about panel vans, they told me, as they'd been 'surfie chicks' in Cronulla in the early 1970s and had written a novel about their experiences. They enclosed a few pages. I'd gone around to the house they shared in Annandale to check them out. They were hilarious, both excited to have a 'real' journalist take them seriously, but anxious to appear supercool. They gave me drinks, a book of Dorothy Parker poems and their manuscript. I said I'd help them get published. A week later Suich and I had lunch with them and soon these very impressive nineteen-year-olds were writing a column in the *Sun Herald* under the byline of the Salami Sisters. In mid-August, just before I left for America to take up the US fellowship which I was thrilled to learn I had been accepted for, I wrote to Hilary McPhee and Di Gribble. Three years earlier they had formed McPhee Gribble Publishers and were making a name for themselves with literary works by emerging writers such as Helen Garner. I had a novel that might interest them, I wrote. As I was leaving Australia in a few days, it was best if they contacted the girls direct: 'Their names are Gabrielle Carey and Kathy Lette . . .' The book, of course, was *Puberty Blues* and McPhee Gribble published it the next year.

A year earlier Suich had talked me out of it when I had tried to resign from the paper to work full-time on a book. I had intended to write a biography of Adela Pankhurst Walsh, the daughter of British suffragette Emmeline Pankhurst, who had come to Australia in 1914. I'd first encountered her while I was researching *Damned Whores* and had become intrigued by the story of this English radical pacifist, who had joined Vida Goldstein's Women's Peace Army in Melbourne to fight the 1916 conscription referendum but then with her husband Tom Walsh, a communist and an official with the Seamen's Union, had done a startling political about-face and become sympathisers with Japan in the late 1930s. She was briefly interned during the war. I'd tried to work on the book at nights and weekends but I'd made little progress. I knew lots of journalists wrote books, and the two occupations seemed to complement, even feed off each other, but it didn't work that way for me. I spent too much time on my journalism and I was too much of a party girl. I was single and young; I would be at the pub, or having dinner with friends, having fun. Maybe if I'd had a partner and a domestic life I might have managed to go straight from the office to my typewriter at home. The only way I could see myself finishing a book was to leave journalism and write full-time. Suich had sweet-talked me into staying then, but now I felt I needed to test what my vocation was: journalist or writer. And what about my feminism? I felt guilty because my unpredictable hours meant I could no longer commit to being a regular on the roster at Elsie Women's Refuge. I did find time for other less-demanding women-related

activities as an editorial board member of Sisters Inc., a new feminist publishing venture in Melbourne, and I was the Australian member of the
advisory group for Virago, the feminist publishers in London started by
Carmen Callil, the dynamo Australian-born London publisher. Soon I was
receiving regular packages of paperbacks with their trademark dark green
spines and being introduced to writers such as Maya Angelou and Vera
Brittain. I also retained the small editorial consultancy with Penguin Books
that I had had since before *Damned Whores* had been published, and in
June I began to write a fortnightly column on the Australian book trade
for Fred Brenchley, who was now editing the *Financial Review*. There were
constant invitations to talk, at conferences or seminars—even on television.
One such appearance, on a commercial station's morning show, led to an
invitation to do a regular spot. I was establishing a pattern that I have found
myself unable to alter ever since: doing too many things, stretching myself
too thin, never able to refuse an invitation or an opportunity, never satisfied,
always restless. I was startled to learn that some of my colleagues thought
of me as 'ruthlessly ambitious'. I saw myself as driven, as single-minded,
someone with boundless energy who could never see a reason not to take
on another challenge, but 'ruthless'? I could not see that.

I hoped that in America I might be able to make sense of my life. Maybe
distance, and a vastly different culture, would give me perspective. What
kind of writer was I? How did being a woman fit into all of this? Earlier that
year, at Writers' Week in Adelaide, I had asked the novelist Thea Astley what
she thought of the fact that none of the major featured women writers had
presented themselves as women, preferring instead to be identified by their
nationality. Margaret Atwood was a Canadian, Fay Zwicky an Australian.
I commented that I was disappointed the feminist voice was not present
in Adelaide.

'When you pick up your biro to write you shed your sex,' Astley had said
to me.

I didn't argue with her, but I didn't want to agree either. I did not see
how you could 'shed' your sex, unless it was to put on a false skin and play
at being something other than who you were. But nor did I know what it
meant to write as a woman. I was a woman. Who wrote. I was a reporter, an
observer but I was also a catalyst, someone who revelled in action, especially

action that championed women. I had no idea how to reconcile being a realist and an idealist, an observer and an activist. Maybe it simply was not possible.

At a party I met Jill Neville, a dazzlingly smart and interesting woman who was a writer. She was more than a decade older than me and had come of age at an even worse time. She had escaped to England before she was 21 and only came back to Sydney occasionally to see her family. She and I hit it off immediately as we talked about how to cope with the world as a bright, successful woman. 'We are still a minority,' she said. 'And something men don't understand. Nor,' she elaborated, 'do women who are married or not ambitious.' Yes, I thought, she's right. There are not many of us. Not yet.

CHAPTER TWO

HOME OF THE BRAVE

—————⟶•◦•⟵—————

We left JFK Airport in a battered yellow taxi. Not, to my disappointment, a classic Checkers cab. It was winter and late afternoon so the sky was already dark. We bounced along the expressway through Queens on our way to Manhattan, past what seemed like endless cemeteries. The traffic moved fast. Our driver was not about to have anyone pass us so we moved even faster. My usual nervousness in cars faded in the face of my fascination with being in New York for the first time.

I noticed several burning car wrecks on the side of the road. Our driver was uncommunicative, angry even, as if whatever problems he had in life were the fault of these two unwitting passengers. I was just a wide-eyed young Australian but my companion, the man I was starting to feel comfortable calling my boyfriend, was an American. He had been able to return to the US after years in exile in Australia as a draft dodger because of the amnesty offered by the newly inaugurated President Jimmy Carter. He was having a complicated reaction to the country of his birth which in many ways mirrored the complications of our nascent relationship. We'd started in Canada, then gone to Washington State, where his parents lived in a small semi-rural community that was beautiful and peaceful and bland.

Now we were in a very different America.

It was early 1977 and I was the first person I knew to go to the United States. Most of us were anti-American, at least its politics but also what we saw as its vapid consumerist culture, and that in itself was reason enough not to want to visit. We'd been opposed to the Vietnam War, which had ended two years earlier, and angry at America, at what we saw as the gross misuse of its power, using military force, for instance, to invade countries in Central America to protect the interests of US corporations. At the same time, there were many Americans I admired. It was American writers and activists who gave us the arguments against the war and against the capitalist system. We relied on the inflammatory and provocative writings of American women in the early days of women's liberation. As a teenager in Adelaide I had absorbed the poetry of Lawrence Ferlinghetti, founder of the famous City Lights Bookstore in San Francisco, and Allen Ginsberg and other Beats. I had been *On the Road* with Jack Kerouac and now a different American fiction was nudging its way into my consciousness, as books by women exploded into the literary firmament. It had started in 1972 with the Canadian Margaret Atwood's *Surfacing*, an astonishing book that enabled me to see on the page, for the very first time, a woman with whom I could fully identify. A year later *Fear of Flying*, Erica Jong's raucous sexual romp that gave us the memorable phrase 'the zipless fuck' to describe casual encounters, became an international bestseller. Lisa Alther quickly followed in 1975 with *Kinflicks*, another novel that demonstrated women could be as sexually explicit in their writings as men, and in 1977 Marilyn French would blow everyone out of the water with *The Women's Room*, a novel of female empowerment that seemingly every woman I ever met had had her life changed by. And as well as the writing, America offered music. There was jazz and there was folk and there was rock 'n' roll.

We stayed with Phillip Frazer, a supercool lefty entrepreneur who had just arrived in New York intending to continue his work with alternative publishing. In Melbourne, he had published a weekly pop music newspaper *Go Set* and subsequently *The Digger*, a political and cultural newspaper that captured the spirit of the times. Frazer's girlfriend, Paula Longendyke, was an artist who had a large loft downtown on Park Place in what is now known as Tribeca. In New York lingo, 'downtown' was anywhere below 14th Street but we were ten blocks below Canal Street, not far from Wall Street, and that was definitely not a residential area in the 1970s. We were lucky to have a free place to stay; the loft was very large, with huge windows allowing light onto the raw floorboards and unpainted walls. Today, even in its totally unrenovated state, it would sell for millions. At the time it felt to me like living in a cardboard box. We were a good twenty blocks away from what I thought of as the bohemian New York of Greenwich Village, and even a long way south of Soho, whose old industrial buildings and cobblestoned streets had already attracted a colony of artists. I was with pioneers, the artists and writers whose low income required them to find ever cheaper places to live and work. It was eye-opening and, in many ways, exciting. We spent a wintry weekend at minimalist artist Frank Stella's extraordinary house in the Hamptons. Paula had the keys as she was a friend of the artist, although I doubt he knew we were enjoying his hospitality. I wondered at the curved floorboards until someone mentioned they'd come from an ancient ship. It was my first exposure to the grey and blustery waters of the Atlantic Ocean, and to a beach that was open only to those wealthy enough to own houses along its frontage.

I was much too sophisticated to admit that I wanted to see any of the city's fabled landmarks. Only tourists cared about the Empire State Building, Times Square or Central Park, I told myself. Skyscrapers, like the twin towers of the World Trade Centre, located a couple of blocks below Park Place, which had opened just four years earlier, did not interest me. I was there for the ideas, the politics, and the music and with Frazer's journalistic and political connections I was in the right place. Yet I felt some disappointment. I was not sure what I had expected, but it wasn't this.

New York had not yet become the Big Apple, the exciting place that lured millions of tourists each year. The brilliant 'I(heart)NY' logo and marketing campaign were a year away from launch. In the 1970s, the city was unattractive and quite dangerous. Street crime was high, the subway was not safe and there was an air of menace in some areas, even if you stuck to the main streets. The streetlights were orange, casting an eerie yellowish glow on everything. People picked their way through these dim and grimy streets like alien creatures. Shop fronts were barred, or boarded and shuttered. I felt I was in a dystopian world, not unlike the one that would enter film legend a few years later with *Blade Runner*. Spurts of steam erupted constantly from beneath the streets. In some places, tall funnels channelled the steam into the night. One night I got off at the wrong subway stop and had to walk three blocks through what seemed like a war zone. The streets were amuck with garbage, broken glass, dumped wrecks of cars. Overhead was a giant uncompleted overpass, a highway to nowhere. It gave the scene a sense of a future that was not going to arrive.

I would turn 32 in a few weeks, time I made some decisions about my life. I had just completed my first year in journalism. I had won a Walkley Award, the highest honour of our profession, so I should have been revelling in my success but I was still breathless with shock and disbelief from the death of my seventeen-year-old brother Jamie, and I was questioning the relevance of everything around me. I had taken leave from the *National Times*, but I did not see how I could go back—to the job and to my old life. To just resume normality seemed obscene. You can't lose your little brother and stay the same. I'd gone to America in part to see if I could lose myself in love with my new companion, perhaps stay in New York and find work. Shortly after I arrived, I'd published an article about the recent outlawing of rape in marriage in South Australia in the new left-wing monthly magazine, *Seven Days*, thanks to Phillip Frazer who was on the editorial staff. In 1894 my home state had become the first Australian state, and only the fourth place in the world (after Wyoming, Colorado and New Zealand), to give women the vote. Now premier Don Dunstan, who later that year would win his third state election, was adding to his already impressive list of reforms. His government had already decriminalised homosexuality, introduced Aboriginal land rights, got rid of an electoral gerrymander, established the South Australian Film Corporation and the Adelaide Festival of Arts, and in 1975 had become the first state in Australia to legislate against sex discrimination. The conversation about rape in marriage—that there was any such thing—was only just getting started in feminist, legal and political circles and it is fair to say that many people were not yet willing to see it as a crime. South Australia, the staid state where I had grown up, was once again leading the world in pioneering social reform. The people at *Seven Days* were impressed.

One night word went around that Patti Smith was performing somewhere near us. We joined the throng, trudging south, shoulders hunched

against the late-February freeze, then milled around in the street outside
the venue that looked like a neglected garage. New York might be strange,
ugly and alien but it was the place where the world's best writers and singers
and poets lived and worked and were liable to appear at your local. And
Australians could make it here: Frazer was in publishing and underground
artist Tim Burns currently had a show. I took a train way uptown to near
Columbia University to visit Glenda Adams, who had just published *Lies
and Stories*, a collection of short stories.

It was alluring, but was it enough to persuade me to stay?

In the end it wasn't. Patti Smith had not appeared. The crowd peeled
off when they realised it was just her band. New York offered phantasms
aplenty, but how much was graspable? I'd had an article published, but I
had not been paid for it. How could I get enough money to live? I was not
sure about the life in downtown lofts but my glimpse of another New York
was just as strange. I spent a few days in an Upper East Side apartment
where the view was of scrubbed streets and the pair of potted ficus trees in
the living room had already reached the low ceiling and were now doing
a U-turn and starting to grow downwards. If there were no limits at all in
downtown New York, uptown was far too constrained for my liking. I did
not feel I belonged in either place. And, I had to admit to myself, I was
afraid of having no job and no place of my own. I was not a risk-taker,
I realised. In early 1977 I went back to Sydney, and back to the *National
Times*. But I was now a different person. Jamie's death and the end of the
relationship in America had changed me. The romance had been stormy
enough, but it reached a crescendo one night in Scottsdale, Arizona where
we'd gone in pursuit of the Lockheed bribery scandal story that I had been
chasing in Australia and had decided to pursue further while I was in the US.
We'd brazenly presented ourselves at the front door of a former Lockheed
executive. I'd explained I was a reporter from Australia and wanted to talk
to him. He was extremely courteous. He invited us in, offered us drinks,
introduced me to his wife—and then took my companion (who was also a
journalist but he was not the one doing this story) into his study and shut
the door. Our fight that night was so ferocious we were asked to leave the
hotel where we were staying.

'How dare you,' I'd raged at him. 'It was *my* story.'

I was going to stay in mainstream journalism. I wanted the immediacy of writing about the world as it was now. I enjoyed being able to interview people, to get their stories, or at least their sides of the stories I was chasing, and I liked the almost instant gratification of weekly publication. Academia held no allure but I did have one final obligation to Henry Mayer, my professor in the department of government at the University of Sydney. I doubt that I could have written *Damned Whores and God's Police* without Mayer's intellectual encouragement and his practical assistance, and I wanted to show my gratitude. Henry Mayer had been a 'Dunera boy', one of 2542 German Jewish refugees and others who, mostly wrongly, had been classified as 'enemy aliens' and deported from London, under conditions of appalling privation on the *Dunera*, a converted passenger ship. They'd arrived in Sydney in September 1940 and then been interned at a prison camp in Hay for the rest of the war. Like so many of the Dunera boys, Mayer was phenomenally successful in his chosen career. He was nominally professor of political theory, but he also wrote a pioneering book about abortion in Australia, created the field of media studies, and was fascinated by the 'new' movements of the late 1960s and early 1970s: the student movement, the women's movement and the gay liberation movement. He regarded them as serious politically, with solid intellectual foundations and having the capacity to be transformative in ways that the 'old' politics could not. The government department in the early 1970s swirled with unorthodoxy. Dennis Altman, Lex Watson and Sue Wills, early writers about gay liberation, were there and Warren Osmond and Peter King and many other advocates of New Left politics. Henry Mayer had provided me with an academic home that was both convivial and challenging, but he had an academic reputation to tend to, and that was partly measured by how many degrees he could deliver. Mayer had protected me for several years, signing the forms that meant I received the Commonwealth Scholarship living allowance and could survive and keep writing without needing to take more than occasional tutoring or seminar work. Now, in return, I had to deliver him a doctorate. The university had never before accepted an already-published book as fulfilling the requirement, but Mayer set to work to create a precedent. I undertook to do whatever the Dean of Arts required—short of his initial, ridiculous, and later withdrawn, demand that we have the entire book typed so it could be submitted as a conventional thesis. I tendered a hardcover copy of the book, together with some additional research and several supplementary papers that were typed and bound like a normal thesis. That seemed to satisfy everyone. But then the chief examiner, the renowned historian and folklorist Ian Turner, had died before he could write his report, so a replacement had to be found and given time to read the material. It was not until mid-1979 that I finally received the degree.

In September 1978 I was back in the US, but this time in the Midwest and about to experience a very different America. I had been awarded the journalist's scholarship I'd applied for from the World Press Institute, the WPI as it was known, a body funded by US media organisations to give foreign journalists exposure to American society. The WPI was based at Macalester College in St Paul, Minnesota, which lay adjacent to the city of Minneapolis, the two places being known as the Twin Cities. It was a huge adjustment for me. For the first time in my life, I had to live in a dorm, use communal bathrooms and line up in the student cafeteria for stuff that I could not bring myself to call 'food'. Against that, we had pretty free access to rental cars and so were very mobile; along with a few of my more adventurous new colleagues, we wasted no time in getting to know the bars of Minneapolis. The eleven of us on the program that year were a very diverse group that included two men who worked for state-owned newspapers, in Burma and Zambia; the first-ever woman journalist in Nepal; two whose countries were either an authoritarian state or under military rule (South Africa and Uruguay); and several freelancers. I was hugely challenged by the fact that everyone thought of themselves as journalists. To my mind, a journalist worked for a free press and was constrained only by one's editor and one's audience. Could the same term apply if you worked for the state, or were subject to censorship? There were also immense cultural and other differences between us, and several in the group had only minimal English. It was going to be an interesting time.

We spent the first few weeks in Minnesota getting acquainted with its quite extraordinary people, politics and climate before embarking upon several months of countrywide travel. Minnesota had long been a crucible for ultra-radical politics, and leaned towards the Democratic Party in electoral politics, producing such national leaders as Hubert Humphrey and Walter Mondale. Politics was a prominent and, to me, alluring part of the WPI agenda. Our exposure to mainstream American politics included attending a press conference with President Carter; watching the Chinese Vice-premier Deng Xiao Ping arriving in January 1979 at the historic state dinner in Washington that marked the US recognising China and the first visit of such a high-ranking Chinese official; and observing Ronald Reagan in Minneapolis in 1978 during his nation-wide travels trying to secure support for the presidential nomination. We also were given entrée to alternative political organisations, such as Jesse Jackson's Operation PUSH in Chicago and some local Native American groups. Interestingly, no women's groups were included on our itinerary, even though this was 1978 and the second-wave women's movement had been underway in the US for close to a decade. But we did meet with an extremely broad array of people, including the CEO of America's biggest farm-machinery corporation, the entire editorial board of the *Chicago Tribune*, and the man who gave the daily press briefings in Henry Kissinger's State Department.

I ended up leaving the program a few months early, in February 1979, because Max Walsh, managing editor of the *Australian Financial Review*, had made me the irresistible offer to be the paper's political correspondent in Canberra, but my time at WPI turned out to be extremely good training for the Canberra Press Gallery. Although at the time I often chafed about the way we were treated, herded—like sheep, I complained—on and off minibuses and private planes, into boardrooms and briefing sessions, running to schedules that we had no say in drawing up, up early to be at airports, and then hanging around in bars late at night because we had nowhere else to go. Meeting the people who ran America. The only difference from what I would find myself doing subsequently in Canberra was that we did not have to file stories each day, although I did keep a detailed journal of our activities, and to earn extra money since my salary was stopped while I was with WPI, I wrote freelance articles for the papers back home whenever I could.

Leaving the program early meant I missed out on the visit to the head-quarters of the Strategic Air Command and the briefings on Soviet weapons capabilities. Nor did I get to meet David Duke, National Director of the Knights of the Ku Klux Klan. But in those five months, I had the most extraordinary exposure to the very best—as well as some of the worst—of the United States, and I knew that I could never again arrive at those simple broad dismissive judgements I had made during my first visit in 1977. America was a disarmingly complex country, and it was impossible for me not to become totally engaged with the place. But it also frightened me.

Macalester College was situated on Grand Avenue, just a block away from Summit Avenue, one of the Twin Cities' great boulevards that stretched for 10 kilometres from St Paul to the Mississippi River, where St Paul meets Minneapolis. On my first morning I went for a walk under its grand canopy of elm trees admiring the historic houses, many of them grand mansions. Sadly, the trees were under threat from Dutch Elm disease and were circled with red paint, meaning they were soon to be torn down. It would be 80 years before their replacements grew to the same height. St Paul was not a city that was well-known to most Australians, but I knew that both F. Scott Fitzgerald and Kate Millett had been born there. Millett had left the city in 1965 after her graduation, but no doubt her English major at the University of Minnesota helped spark the radical thinking in *Sexual Politics*, her 1970 book that opened my eyes to the misogyny that lay at the core of the writings of Norman Mailer, D.H. Lawrence and Henry Miller, three writers I had previously admired so much. It was extraordinarily disturbing for me to realise how much self-loathing was required for me, a woman, to actually *like*, even venerate, books whose essential premise was denigration, if not pure hatred, of women. Once I came to this realisation I could never again ignore such misogyny, in literature or in life.

Fitzgerald had written his first novel, *This Side of Paradise*, while living at 599 Summit in 1919. After it was accepted for publication he had sup-posedly run down Summit Avenue, grabbing strangers and telling them, 'I'm famous'. Jean-Paul Sartre, Simone de Beauvoir's lifelong companion, had done a similar thing in 1937 when the venerable French publishing house Gallimard finally accepted his first novel, *Nausea*. 'Today I walk the streets like an author,' he said.[1] I had also felt transformed in 1975 when Penguin Books published *Damned Whores and God's Police*. Now I, too, could say I was an author, a member of that special, select and, to me, admirable group of people who turned words into books. That was now three years ago. I wondered whether I would ever feel that way again. Would I still be able to write books now that I seemed to be funnelling myself full-time into journalism? I did not know, but later that week I bought, for $35 from a woman who lived on Summit Avenue, an original Corona portable typewriter with old-fashioned parchment coloured keys edged in silver. It was very light, with a built-in carrying case, the kind that war correspondents would have used. I could picture Martha Gellhorn using it to bash out stories during the Spanish Civil War. The spacing was a bit erratic, but I didn't mind. It made me feel both literary and journalistic; through this machine, I felt connected to writers who had gone before me. This American journey was going to take me somewhere, I was determined, and it would have to be through my writing.

———

It was September when I arrived and fall, as Americans refer to autumn, was in all its glory. I had never seen such colours. In evergreen Australia, deciduous trees are relatively uncommon and except for cold-climate cities such as Canberra, it is rare to see turning leaves. Nowhere in Australia are there trees with the range and depth of colour, from palest blond to brilliant scarlet, that I saw in Minnesota that year. Then as the leaves fell and the weather turned, I found myself experiencing a Northern Hemisphere winter for the first time. The American Midwest is so cold that people dig up their rose bushes and store them, wrapped in hessian, in their basements until the spring. There are days when it is too cold for children to go to school, and there are covered walkways between all buildings downtown so that it is rarely necessary to expose oneself to the elements. You drive from heated garage in heated car to your heated destination, which is invariably an underground carpark that sits below whatever building you are visiting. I quickly learned what cold weather felt like. My face hurt, my ears and nose turned red, and one day when I unwittingly walked with wet hair from the Macalester dorm to the rental car parked just across the street, I was amazed to find my hair had frozen by the time I opened the car door. After a few weeks of this, I began to wear makeup again for the first time in years; it was one layer of protection against the cold. As were the puffer jackets the WPI provided for us all; we looked ridiculous, like Michelin Men of varying heights and colours, but we were warm. We soon learned how to drive in the snow, how to look for treacherous black ice and, above all, how to keep ourselves protected from weather that could kill you. It was gruelling enough for me but for my companions from warm countries such as Jamaica, Zambia and Burma, it was sheer misery.

In October the WPI program took us to South Dakota, to inspect the Pine Ridge Indian reservation. I had never seen a worse place. While the poverty-caused squalor was probably comparable to the extreme deprivation I had seen in some remote Aboriginal settlements, the difference here was the weather. Already the temperatures were heading for sub-zero, and winter had not even begun. I saw that none of the 'houses' had insulated walls, or any form of heating, or even any glass in their windows. One cold-water tap served several dwellings. We met with the chairman of the reservation, Chief Elijah Whirlwind Horse, but there was little he could say to put any kind of spin on this dire situation. It was not surprising to discover there were severe problems with drugs and alcohol on Pine Ridge. I had already had some contact with Native Americans while I was in St Paul. The WPI had arranged for us to go north to an Indian reservation to observe a weekend of ceremonies, including spending time in a sweat lodge, which was a teepee-like structure that had been converted into a sauna. We'd also attended a pow wow in a suburban hall. I had found it sad. It seemed almost demeaning that these tribal elders, wearing full ceremonial regalia, were conducting their ancient dances on the hardwood floors of an assembly hall, where on another night bingo would be played or young girls would meet to rehearse their debutante dances. I had gone outside the WPI program to make contact with American Indian Movement (AIM) leaders in Minnesota; I was keen to learn more than we were being spoon-fed on the official program. We met Curtis Baldeagle and Clyde Bellecourt, two long-time activists, and their lawyer, Ken Tilsen. I soon learned about the political struggle, the 'survival schools' that taught only an American

Indian curriculum, and other strategies for restoring pride and developing political potency. But I decided to investigate further, now that we were on the ground in this place that was so rich in American Indian history. I knew that Russell Means was imprisoned in South Dakota, so I did what I would have done in Sydney: I called the State Penitentiary. As luck would have it, the warden, Herman S. Solem, had 'been in Sydney in '44', and he promptly granted my request to visit the next day to interview his most famous prisoner.

Means was notorious for many things, but his current claim to making history was that he was the only person in the US serving jail time for a crime—'riot to obstruct justice'—that no longer existed on the statute books. (Means had claimed self-defence when he was charged for having fought back against a baton-wielding FBI agent, and within weeks of his conviction, the offence was removed from the statutes.) Not that that was seen as a reason to release him, nor to protect him while he was imprisoned. A few weeks before I met him, another inmate had stabbed him. Means was, I believed at the time, a political prisoner. His recent imprisonment was the result of continuing FBI harassment for his involvement in the siege at Wounded Knee where on 27 February 1973, Means had led the occupation and seizure of hostages at a white-owned store named Sioux Enterprises. Wounded Knee was a small town in South Dakota where in 1890, US cavalry troops massacred 350 members of the Lakota Sioux Nation, including its Chief Big Foot, an atrocity that is said to have ended the official resistance of American Indians to the occupation of their lands. The 1973 siege lasted more than two months and received massive media attention, which led to high-profile supporters and civil rights activists flying supplies into the besieged town. 'The country is still good at ignoring Indians, but for a time Mr Means and the American Indian Movement punctured that invisibility', reported the *New York Times* in an obituary for Means four decades later. 'By raising hell for 71 days in one of the most remote corners of the continent, on behalf of an abused and forgotten people, he and his allies captured the attention of the world.'[2] In January 1974, when Means attended court in St Paul for what would ultimately be an unsuccessful prosecution for his role in the siege, he wore traditional clothes and was accompanied by the actor Marlon Brando. The previous year Brando had refused to attend the Academy Awards to accept his Best Actor Oscar for his performance in *The Godfather*. Instead, Sasheen Littlefeather walked onto the stage. She declined to accept the statue, saying Brando did not want it, then read part of a speech he had written for the occasion: 'I would have been here tonight to speak to you directly, but I felt that perhaps I could be of better use if I went to Wounded Knee . . .'[3] He then went on to attack Hollywood for being 'as responsible as any for degrading the Indian and making a mockery of his character, describing his as savage, hostile and evil . . . When Indian children watch television, and they watch films, and when they see their race depicted as they are in films, their minds become injured in ways we can never know.'[4]

I presented myself at the South Dakota State Penitentiary on a Saturday morning and was admitted, along with another WPI colleague who was going to photograph the event, with tape-recorders and cameras. Unlike when I had visited NSW prisons, we were not searched and we were taken to a private room where we enjoyed a three-hour face-to-face encounter with Means. He was a tall, good-looking man who wore his black hair in long braids; he told us his life story and gave us his political analysis of where AIM was heading. Means had been born on Pine Ridge but had been 'relocated' to Cleveland under President Eisenhower's *Indian Relocation Act of 1956*, a law that ostensibly directed people to move to cities where employment opportunities would be greater. However, when seen in conjunction with the large number of 'termination laws' that were passed during the period from 1940 to the 1960s—which removed Indian sovereignty from lands that previously had been ceded to them—it removed federal government responsibility for American Indians, including health, welfare and education funding, and gave criminal jurisdiction over American Indians lands to the states. It was obvious what was happening. American Indians were to be 'assimilated', according to the official language of the day, but the word 'termination' that was used in many laws told the true story. This was nothing short of attempted genocide.

Means told us that less than 10 per cent of land originally granted to Native Americans by the US government via treaties now remained in American Indian hands. These lands had been discovered to contain oil, uranium and other valuable resources and so a whole industry was now devoted to trying to undo these treaties. People like Means were getting in the way. I wondered how much longer he would survive, especially as he was due to be granted a special work release whereby he would work at Pine Ridge during the day and be held at the local jail each night. I saw it is as a device for the federal government to be able to wash its hands of responsibility for whatever happened to him. (As it turns out, Means lived until 2012, remaining a political activist until at least the late 1980s, and later becoming a screen actor; in 1992, he starred as Chief Chingachgook in *The Last of the Mohicans* with Daniel Day-Lewis.)

Our amazing day was not yet over; after we had finished our visit with Means, Warden Solem asked if we'd like to talk to William Schilling, the man who had stabbed Means and who was now languishing in The Hole. Never in all my investigating of prisons in NSW for the *National Times* had I ever had access even to prisoner cells, let alone to punishment areas. We were escorted deep into the entrails of the penitentiary, through countless locked and electronic doors, until we reached an area that was remote from all human contact—a large concrete area which had ten 'cages' along one wall. Anyone who had seen how Hannibal Lecter was incarcerated in the film *Silence of the Lambs* will be familiar with the setup: the cells are each 12 × 6 feet (3.4 × 1.8 metres), with three concrete walls and bars on the front. There was just a bed and a toilet. The prisoners were allowed out once a week for a shower; they could have books but no newspapers or tobacco. I taped my hour-long conversation with Schilling, who was no doubt pleased to have a distraction from his solitary confinement. He was serving 90 days in The Hole for possession of an illegal weapon; a federal grand jury had dismissed the charge of stabbing Means—on the grounds of self-defence. Schilling told us that he had previously stabbed another Indian a few months earlier, and a black man in another prison. At no time did the guards intervene to stop him. In fact, one might see it all as a bit of a setup. Schilling was also notorious for having pulled off the biggest bank robbery in US history, more than $1 million from a bank in Reno, Nevada. He explained to us in great detail how he had done it. He was an escapee at the time but had managed to do a special locksmithing course, had located and analysed each of the 21 alarm systems for the bank and made keys for each of the doors. Although he got 25 years for this crime, his sentence was being served concurrently with his

a massive Henry Moore sculpture, around which wound a large lake with
white swans, ducks, geese and huge Japanese carp. The lake was kept
heated throughout the winter, we were told, so that the swans would
survive. The water from the lake was then circulated through the three
buildings, which exemplified corporate largesse. There was a 400-seat
concert auditorium in the atrium and luxurious open plan offices opened
straight off a tropical garden. Deere boasted a huge art collection and an
artist-in-residence: a concert pianist, Barbara Nissman, who was kept
on retainer to play for the workers. We sat in the boardroom, hosted by
a dozen top executives including William Hewitt, the chairman of the
company, whose vision it had been to create these headquarters, commission the Finnish-American architect Eero Saarinen to design them and
to fill them with art. We repaired to the corporate dining room, where an
entire wall was covered with a specially-commissioned Aubusson tapestry
and given a sumptuous lunch, including French wines. This was unusual
since most WPI lunches were strictly coffee events. Later, when we were
shown around the building, I found it chilling to walk through these corridors of corporate power. It wasn't that they weren't beautiful, but I baulked
at the artifice. It was like walking through a museum, with paintings on
every wall and glass cases displaying Roman and Mexican antiquities. The
beautiful young girls seated every few hundred metres were like museum
attendants, guarding the precious collection. Hewitt prided himself on his
collection of primitive art. He made sure to collect something from every
country he visited, he told us. I was especially offended to see two very large
bark paintings from Arnhem Land. The beige carpets, beige desk dividers
and white noise created what I considered to be a monochromatic prison.
People strolled through the corridors in twos and threes, promenading,
rather than rushing to meetings. There was no external view. No city
skyline, no car park, nothing at all urban to intrude on the perfect tranquillity of the place. This was another instance of the kind of control that
Otto Silha advocated, but this went even further in some ways because it
was an attempt to control people's entire lives. This was a company town,
of course, with Deere providing almost all the employment. There were
traffic jams of people wanting to apply whenever there were vacancies in
their plants, Hewitt had boasted. The company provided health insurance,

credit and any other welfare services needed by their staff. And, it turned out, they were needed.

After the formal visit to the plant, there was the cruise on the Mississippi, followed by a fine dinner in a converted mansion where the wines flowed and lips were loosened. I sat next to a woman whose husband was in public relations for the company and who was trying to start a women's refuge. The perfection we had been shown, she told me, in reality masked a community that was rife with alcohol and drug addiction and domestic violence. Another of our group discovered that one-third of those working at the foundry were drug-addicted. We visited other corporate headquarters that were almost as lavish and where the company philosophy of taking total control of employees' lives was similar. These companies were more important than government, I realised, in the impact they had on the lives of the people who worked for them. And in the influence they had around the world. We had asked Hewitt whether he would follow the example of other companies and pull out of South Africa. He took the question seriously. Last time he'd been there, he told us, he had asked the opinion of every black person he'd met and the unanimous view was that Deere should stay in South Africa and provide jobs. It was pointless to ask if he had ventured outside the Deere plant to secure these responses.

I had initially wondered why this company was spending so much time and such an extraordinary amount of money on our group. We had each been given expensive gifts including Parker Pens (a lot more special then than they are today) yet we were, let's face it, hardly the world's top-drawer journalists. What could they possibly hope to get out of it? Then I realised: we were mostly from countries where Deere did some but seemingly not enough business. We would be useful contacts once we returned home and were reminded of the largesse we had enjoyed at Deere's headquarters. Once, I thought grimly to myself, American companies like United Fruit needed the US Marines to help them open up new markets. Now it was all smooth talking, greased palms and public relations. And that was where the media came in.

I attended a Macalester Women's Club lunch as a guest of the wife in my academic host family. It was like time-travelling back to the 1950s. The women looked as if they had walked out of the pages of an old copy of *Good Housekeeping*: fringed pageboy haircuts, dresses with pinched-in waists and full skirts, and everyone was introduced by the jobs their husbands did. And these were the wives of *academics*! It was fifteen years since the publication of *The Feminine Mystique*, yet these women seemed to still live in a world that I assumed had been shaken up if not totally subverted by that book and the women's movement it helped spawn. The young students weren't much better. I chatted with a couple of the Resident Assistants, whose job it was to enforce the rules in the dormitory, and they told me that the students were more conservative than ten years ago: 'Most of the women wouldn't call themselves feminists,' one of the young women told me. 'They are more assertive, they know what they want. They intend to have careers, and they don't let men push them around.' I wondered if any of these young students had encountered the Macalester Women's Club. On the other hand, my host had told me that she had changed her mind about voting Republican in the forthcoming mid-term congressional elections because the candidate had said he was opposed to an extension of time for ratification of the Equal Rights Amendment. The ERA was the proposed constitutional amendment that would guarantee equality of the sexes, which Congress had passed in 1972 and which needed to be ratified by 38 states within seven years in order to come into effect. That deadline was almost up, and because they were still three states short of the number needed for ratification, its supporters were seeking more time to get this crucial amendment passed. (Although they ultimately won a three-year extension, to 1982, the measure failed to secure the necessary 38 states' ratification.)

'I'm not usually a single-issue voter,' she told me, 'but there are times when you have to lay everything else aside, when there is something that important.'

She voted Democrat.

The students at Macalester were for the most part not interested in politics. One of the teachers had surveyed the class of 1982 and found that students were, in his view, over-influenced by the 'anti-American neo-modernism of the 1960s'. They read *Rolling Stone* and watched *Animal House*. They were more attracted to political satire than actual politics. Most of the students left blank the answer to 'the man or woman you most admire'. The only students who answered that question were what were then called minority students, who put down Muhammad Ali, Barbara Jordan or Anwar Sadat.

—>❧<—

The idea of the host families was so we foreigners could be exposed to typical American family life and awkward as it was at the time, it certainly did that—although perhaps not always in the way the WPI intended. My St Paul host family lived in a gated community. It was not exclusionary, they explained to me, it was more a security thing—although I noted that the gate was broken when we drove in the first time. They did not mind Jews, my host 'mother' explained, and they were not against blacks, but none would be able to afford to live in such an expensive area. My first Thanksgiving in America was with them. It was a subdued and painful meal; we were so excessively polite it created a lot of tension. I was very conscious that my newly acquired Native American friends were marking Thanksgiving with a hunger fast, so I could only pick at the vast quantities of turkey and other foods that are the hallmark of this American feast. There were other tensions, too. The wife seemed suspicious that I was flirting with her husband; in fact, I was just trying to make conversation to make the evening more relaxing. She yelled at me not to put tampons or pads down the toilet.

'Use newspaper,' she said, but she did not tell me where I could find it.

I assured her that I did not have my period so there was no need to worry. I knew I needed to be friends with her or this relationship was going to be disastrous so I asked her about the volunteer job I knew she had at the Science Museum. It was as if a light had been switched on; she was transformed. She brought out books and maps and explained to me all about Mayan culture. The ice broken, she then told me a lot more. That she had cancer; that her husband who ran six miles every day was a recovering alcoholic, who although he was a high-powered lawyer, did pottery in his spare time. I wondered whether to tell her about Jamie. In the end I did, and I was glad because it meant we were able to have an adult conversation about cancer. She and I became friends for the rest of my time in St Paul.

I could not say quite the same of my farm host family, for whom I might as well have been from Mars. The wife had been a Minnesota Housewife of the Year and she turned out a second Thanksgiving meal for me, which was a splendid demonstration of her culinary expertise. We had every possible kind of American delicacy in enormous quantities that, my guilt about the American Indians set aside for now, I had no trouble scoffing down. The trouble came when I declined their invitation to accompany them to church the next morning. When I awoke, the house was empty but a radio had been left just outside my door; it was playing religious music. An open Bible lay beside my place-setting for breakfast. Later, while the erstwhile Housewife of the Year prepared lunch, her laconic husband attempted conversation with me:

'Is Australia wet or dry?' he asked.

I started to explain to him about the various regions of the country, our deserts and our tropics and everything in-between, when he interrupted me:

'Is it whiskey or is it beer you drink down there?'

'Everything,' I assured him.

I'd noted sourly that the wine glasses on the dinner table the night before had been filled with apple juice. So *that* was why he had kept making frequent trips to the garage!

Nor had I enjoyed the hayride, the entertainment organised for 'the young people' the night I'd arrived. We had had to protect ourselves against the freezing weather with snowmobile suits, ski jackets, hats, gloves and lots of beer with Schnapps chasers. This meant we needed frequent pit stops, boys to one side, girls to the other, while we struggled out of cumbersome clothing so we could pee in the cornfields. And that, of course, was the moment the wag left behind on the hay cart turned the spotlight on the girls, exposing their naked bottoms. Hilarious. I could not get back to the city fast enough.

In addition to whatever entertainment our host families provided, the WPI arranged a busy program of group social outings. We went to a baseball game, an art show opening and countless parties. We met nothing but friendliness and warmth, although often the hospitality was strained and most of the time I felt patronised. One of our group, Sophia, was from Poland and she was the centre of attention, and not only because, for the first time, a Pole had just been elected Pope. Sophia was a very good-looking woman who attracted second looks wherever she went, but there were also a lot of Poles in Minnesota and so many people felt a strong connection with her. It was more difficult for those of the group who were from countries that Americans considered uninteresting. Manjula from Nepal, Carlos from Uruguay, Kyi from Burma and Fred from Zambia had the hardest time, being from places that our hosts had either never heard of or could find nothing they wanted to ask about them. Carlos from Portugal, David from Argentina, Elaine from South Africa, Patrick from Jamaica, and Roberto from Italy at least were from countries people knew about. But everyone had heard of Australia. Almost every single person I met while I was in the Midwest had just read *The Thornbirds* by Colleen McCullough which had been published the previous year (and, when it was made into a TV mini-series in 1983, would become the second most-watched show ever—after *Roots*) and it had instilled in them a desire to go to Australia, they enthusiastically told me. Or, and this from some of the older men I encountered, they'd been in Sydney in '44 and asked if I knew some codger they'd met in a bar back then. A few people asked me where they could buy a cheap opal.

I felt immense frustration about being Australian. I was having my very essence reduced to a trashy novel, reminiscences from a war that had ended 33 years earlier or the desire to purchase what I considered to be an ugly and overrated gemstone. I thought I came from a lively and interesting place. I was well versed in A.A. Phillips's concept of the cultural cringe[5] and rejected the idea that we Australians had anything to apologise for. I thought the stereotyping that was at the heart of *The Thornbirds* was crass and embarrassing—as if we all lived in The Outback!—but when I tried to express this view, I received hostile stares, as if I was criticising them for having liked this book. In a way, of course, I was. I'd read about this feeling in the literature of Martin Boyd and Henry Handel Richardson, the state of mind that you can never communicate to the Other because they have already decided what an Australian is, and their view was a decidedly condescending one. But I'd thought while this kind of patronising was to be expected from the English, or even some Europeans, I did not expect it in America, the land that supposedly embraced everyone. I'd never experienced it before and I found it very dispiriting.

In mid-November the group travelled to Chicago. I knew very little about what was known, for good reason, as 'the windy city'—there actually were chains in the street for people to hold onto so they would not be blown over. I was stunned by its beauty, the river that ran through downtown and the Parisienne style bridges that crossed it every few blocks, and its skyscraper architecture could certainly give New York a run for its money. Soon, in our meetings with newspapers, with community organisations and with the legendary author and radio commentator Studs Terkel, we were learning that this was a town with a strong social conscience. Outside the group, I managed to hook up with Abe Peck and Marshall Rosenthal, two radicals from the 1960s. They had both been editors of *Seed*, Chicago's alternative newspaper which ran from 1967 to 1974, but were now working as best they could within establishment media. Peck was with the *Chicago Sun-Times* and told us about the major abortion scandal exposé the paper had recently run. Among the journalistic techniques they had used was to have women take samples of men's urine to dodgy clinics for pregnancy tests; they invariably came back positive. Abe arranged for the paper to publish my article about how Sydney feminists had started Control, an abortion clinic dedicated to ethical and women-friendly services. It was the second piece I had had published in the US. Maybe I could make it here, I mused. Abe also took Carlos Jones, my fellow WPIer from Uruguay, and me to O'Rourkes, a writers' bar that was adorned with portraits and quotes of great Irish writers. Just the place to lose yourself in the bottom of a glass, but we were too impatient to sample all this great city had to offer and we sought Abe's recommendation for a place to hear blues.

'Theresa's,' he said. 'You have to go to Theresa's.'

'You sure you want to go there?' the cab driver asked when we gave him the address of Theresa's Tavern.

We knew about the South Side. It was rough, it was mostly black and it was not a place to hang out, especially if you were white, in those racially tense days. Although it had been ten years since the riots that raged in America's large cities after the killing of Martin Luther King Jr, the anger still simmered. Black areas were neglected. I had been shocked in Washington DC to see that just a couple of blocks away from the White House, an entire neighbourhood that had been razed by fires started by rioters in 1968 was still in ruins. There was no investment in these areas. In fact, the infamous 'redlining'—denying home loans and other financial services based on the racial composition of a neighbourhood—meant that exactly the opposite happened: the inner-city was increasingly being abandoned by white America to unemployment, rundown housing, poverty and its companions: crime and drugs. We would have this explained to us when we met with Jesse Jackson's Operation PUSH the next day, and it was on the South Side of Chicago that a young Barack Obama would work as a community organiser before he embarked on his political odyssey, the road that would lead him to becoming the first African-American President of the United States in 2009.

But we were just going to a bar, a legendary blues bar that had been recommended by a white guy. Surely we'd be okay. It was snowing heavily as we pulled up outside 4801 S. Indiana Avenue, giving the surrounding slums a benign, even beautiful, appearance. As we picked our way through the crunchy snow towards the basement entrance, murmurs came from the shadows:

'Fuck off, honky.'

The room was a narrow space with a long wooden bar along the right-hand wall and a small stage at the back. It was not crowded but we saw at a glance that there were no other white people there. All the looks we got were hostile. Maybe it wasn't going to be so okay. Carlos wanted to leave.

'How can we?' I muttered. The cab had sped off the second we had got out.

We breasted the bar, positioning ourselves near the corner closest to the stage and, using an exaggerated-Australian accent, I ordered some drinks. Was I imagining it or did the tension ease slightly? We sipped on our Scotches, trying to look relaxed.

'When will the music start?' I asked the woman behind the bar. I think now that she must have been Theresa McLaurin Needham, the woman who had opened this little tavern back in 1949. She did not want to talk.

When they're ready, was her terse response.

Carlos and I murmured to each other that if the music did not start soon, we would just finish our drinks and call for a cab. While we were talking

I became aware that a man was standing nearby, at the end of the bar, and he was looking right at us. He was tall and immaculately dressed, in a tailored grey coat, buttoned up, and a dark-coloured homburg hat. He made eye contact with me as he slid his hand into his coat—and pulled out a huge gun. I recognised it from the movies: it was a Magnum .37, the kind Clint Eastwood sported in the *Dirty Harry* films. The man pushed the weapon along the bar towards me.

'Why don't you mind my gun while I sing?' he said.

There seemed to be a collective intake of breath throughout the tavern as everyone watched to see what we would do. It was a test, of course, and one that we could not fail. I had never seen a gun before and I was scared shitless, but I knew this was not a time for showing one's feelings.

'Sure,' I said. And turned back to Carlos and resumed talking.

Theresa rushed up and grabbed the gun and put it under the bar. She yelled at the man, then made calming noises in our direction. The room relaxed; normal noise began again, but only for a few minutes because soon a deep raw sound began to envelop us. I turned around and there on the stage was the man who'd had the gun. He'd taken off his coat but not his hat, and he was grasping the microphone, looking straight at me—and, backed by a small band, he was singing a song that was deep and mournful, rich and sad.

Afterwards he came over to the bar. He bought us drinks, wanted to know where we were from. He introduced himself: his name was Junior Wells. Later I would learn that he was one of the legendary Chicago bluesmen. In his memoir *Life*, the Rolling Stones' Keith Richards describes almost reverentially how in the early 1960s, he and Mick Jagger had travelled to Manchester to hear Muddy Waters and Junior Wells perform. Wells had got his start in 1952, in Waters' band during a recording session at Chicago's iconic Chess Studios, a place that was on Richards' must-visit list when he first went to Chicago. But that night in Theresa's Tavern I knew none of this. I was just soaking up the best music I had ever heard. The hostility of the room had evaporated and now Carlos and I were laughing and relaxed; we were having a good time. We were no longer the unwelcome intruders; we were now treated with generosity and kindness. How long were we staying? Wells wanted to know. He would take us to places where we would hear the very best music Chicago had to offer. With him, he said, we could go anywhere. Sadly, we were leaving the very next night. Even sadder, it was now 2 a.m. and Theresa's was closing. Although many bars in the US stayed open until 4 a.m., Theresa's was not one of them. Carlos and I said our goodbyes and made for the door. Junior Wells stopped us.

'Call these people a cab,' he instructed Theresa.

'It's not safe,' he said to us. 'There's some bad niggers out there.'

When it arrived, Junior Wells escorted us to the cab and sent us safely on our way.

A few weeks later the WPI group travelled to Atlanta where our itinerary included a meeting with Andrew Young, President Carter's Ambassador to the UN, the first African-American to hold this position. But we had some free time so on Saturday night Carlos and I headed for the Agora Ballroom on Peachtree where, someone had told us, the music was good. There was a cover charge of $5.50 and all the beer you could drink. It was a big barn of a place. We grabbed our plastic cups of beer and settled ourselves up on the balcony, from where you had a good view of the stage, and waited to see how the evening would unfold.

Soon a large man came on and settled in with his guitar and started to sing. It was classic Delta blues.

'This is the real thing!' I said excitedly to Carlos.

The man seemed to be a bit drunk, slurring as he introduced songs and joked with the audience. He sang for an hour and then, before he left the stage, he introduced himself:

'My name is Muddy "Mississippi River" Waters,' he said. 'And it has been my pleasure to sing for you.'

I could not believe that we had just heard one of the greatest blues singers of all time. The sign out the front had simply said 'Blues'. We had no clue that we were to sit in on such a legend. Then he came back. Muddy Waters was going to do a second set. He performed for another hour. He went through four harmonica players, imperiously dismissing each one. He was followed by an albino piano player who was billed as Piano Red, but who called himself Dr Feelgood.

'You'll feel good for three weeks after this,' he said as he played. 'I can cure cancer and heart attacks with my music.'

He and Muddy Waters certainly cured my blues. I was agonising over Max Walsh's job offer. I had to give him an answer soon. I knew it would be life-changing if I accepted. Living in Canberra, working in Parliament House, my whole life diverted into politics—what was I letting myself in for? I was glad to have stumbled on that place on Peachtree that night as I knew that I would most likely never again hear such performers, and certainly not by just walking off the street. But at least I would have a memory to cherish.

In late November I returned to a very different New York. Max Suich, now editor of the *Sun-Herald* and apparently able to issue orders to our US bureau, had generously arranged for a limo to meet me at JFK and the driver had been instructed to take the scenic route. I could scarcely believe I was in the same city where just eighteen months earlier I'd bounced through Queens in a yellow cab. We drove through Central Park at dusk as the tiny white bulbs draped over the trees near the Tavern on the Green were just starting to twinkle and the lights were coming on in the grand old apartment buildings along Central Park West. Peering out the car window I could see formations of woods and stone bridges and curved roads that could have been from an illustrated children's book. The smell of roasting chestnuts wafted through the haze. I saw a woman doing ballet practice; she raised her leg skywards, seemingly oblivious to the car that had crashed the night before into the fence she was using as a barre.

This time, I was staying in the heart of Greenwich Village on Bleecker Street with Elisabeth Wynhausen, my old colleague from the *National Times* and her husband, Don Anderson, a lecturer in English at the University of Sydney. He had come to help her get set up for her planned writing career in New York and would soon be going back to Sydney. In the meantime, the three of us grabbed every experience the neighbourhood had to offer. There were bars, where the red wine was not kept in the refrigerator, as it invariably was in the Midwest, and restaurants where not every dish came with cheese. This New York was bright and crowded and noisy and with lots of—as New Yorkers liked to say—'attitude'. Elisabeth showed me her

in November to fly to San Francisco for a Women Against Pornography Conference. I was becoming intrigued by the way American feminists were preoccupied with—I would have said obsessed by—pornography. It seemed to me that this issue got people far more exercised than, say, equal pay or childcare (which did not seem to be on anyone's radars) or even abortion rights. I hoped the conference might enlighten me. It only left me more confused, especially after we marched through a porn district denouncing the merchants for their exploitation of women, yet no one did any more than raise a fist. If this had been back in Sydney, I think we might have been more aggressive, but this wasn't my march and it wasn't for me to set the tone. But if you wanted to Smash Porn, why not start with smashing a few windows? I could not understand it, but at the same time I was grateful that simply identifying with the women's movement opened every door. I could go to any meeting, introduce myself to anyone and be met with friendliness and a willingness to hear how we tackled issues in Australia. I was also able to meet writers, to share books and addresses, and to feel that I might be welcome in this world I so much sought to be part of. The writer Tillie Olsen, whose powerful 1978 book of essays *Silences* documented the ways women were held back from writing, and Adrienne Rich, the poet, both treated me like a friend, as did Diana Russell who in 1976 had co-edited the proceedings of a five-day international tribunal held in Brussels on crimes against women. This was another subject we were starting to understand: how pervasive violence against women was and how it kept women 'in their place'. I'd got hold of Russell's book with its introduction by Simone de Beauvoir, who although unable to attend herself had sent a stirring message. The time of trying to integrate women into male society was over, she said. 'I salute this Tribunal as being the start of a radical decolonization of women.'[6]

I also met a lot of women on my several visits to New York. Ellen Moers, who had just published *Literary Women*, a pioneering work of feminist literary criticism, held a 'literary lunch' for me at the New York Racquet Club, while someone else held a dinner at her apartment on the Upper West Side where my shock at being served by a black maid was only somewhat mitigated by the terrific company. I met Midge Mackenzie, the London-based filmmaker who loved to wear Navaho jewellery, lots of it, and who had just produced *Shoulder to Shoulder*, a stirring history of the suffragettes for the BBC. She and I got on immediately, as I did with Paula Weideger, a tall interesting-looking woman with arresting grey eyes and a full head of black curly hair. She had just published *Menstruation and Menopause*, which explored the social and psychological history as well as current attitudes to two more subjects that no one yet was talking much about. I met up with Paula and Susan Brownmiller late one afternoon at the Allen Room, a space reserved for writers at the New York Public Library, where both of them were working on their next books. We went for a drink at the Algonquin with all its history of the *New Yorker* circle of writers, and then downtown to the Spring Street Café for dinner. I envied them their writers' lives.

In early January 1979, Paula and I drove upstate to Purchase where there was an exhibition of the Mexican artist Frida Kahlo. This was the first time I had encountered Kahlo and learned that she had injured her spine in a bus accident when she was in her early-twenties and her entire life had been wracked by pain. 'Her paintings are a graphic record of her suffering, much of it specific suffering as a woman,' I wrote in my diary. 'She depicts abortion and childbirth in a direct realistic way.' I was mesmerised. I had never seen such pain—and pain that I could relate to—on a contemporary canvas. The work was raw with rage. It was too much for a group of self-improving house-wives who had started to walk through the show at the same time as Paula and me. They took one long, horrified look and fled. Paula and I talked a lot. She had a studio apartment overlooking Gramercy Park where we would eat and talk. Our conversations covered the universe but kept coming back to the subject that was pretty central to both our lives: sex and the single feminist. How did we find the right men, and how did we conduct ourselves with them? How did we maintain our freedom and our independence while not frightening them away? Neither of us wanted to be—or could imagine being—subservient. We had sexual needs, but we also had emotional pride. We wanted to be able to surrender ourselves to passion and, possibly, love. Just not at any price. This was not a conversation that was being had in the women's movement at that time. Instead, the focus of many feminists now was how to dispense entirely with men. They wanted to be woman-centred or, more radically, 'woman-identified' as the current language had it. Many women who had not previously seen themselves as lesbians were identifying as such, and some were arguing that you could not even be a real feminist if you were 'male-identified'. Paula and I felt we did not belong in that conversation so we were trying to figure it out for ourselves.

I could not disguise the fascination I felt for Jane Alpert who I'd already met several times through my new feminist friends in New York, and now I arranged to have dinner with her. In my student radical days my friends and I had followed the activities of the Weathermen, but we could never bring ourselves to embrace their kind of violence. The organisation became known as the Weather Underground after so many of their members had gone on the run after bombing public buildings. Alpert had been arrested in 1969 for her role in bombing a New York Federal Building, but had jumped bail (costing her parents $20,000) and gone underground for more than four years. She moved around the country with apparent ease, getting money and other support from former colleagues. For a time, she told me, she was working in a small town in New Mexico where, by an amazing coincidence, she ran into Mark Rudd, another Weatherperson also on the run.[7] For the last year or so, she said, she had worked at an orthodox Jewish school in Colorado, using the name Carla Weinstein. They had no idea who she was. With a wry kind of pride Alpert showed me her FBI 'Most Wanted' poster although, she told me, she had now renounced terrorism and dismissed the Weather Underground as a bunch of rich kids living off their parents. She had become a radical feminist and while still on the run, had sent an essay to *Ms.* magazine which was published in the August 1973 issue under the title 'Mother Right'. She had included a copy of her fingerprints with the manuscript so the *Ms.* editors could verify its authenticity. The essay was extraordinarily influential and was reprinted many times in feminist anthologies. Alpert became one of the first feminists to argue that women possessed unique female qualities, based on their biology—their ability to bear children, whether or not they exercised this ability—that made them intrinsically superior to men. Many women found this thesis attractive; it provided a rationale for disengaging with men and leaving behind what was a long and exhausting struggle merely to be listened to. It fed into the emerging radical feminism that was now condemning many of their foremothers as being too 'male-oriented', too associated with the left in politics and not being driven by purely female needs and goals. This theme was taken-up by other writers such as Adrienne Rich and the sociologist Carol Gilligan. It was to become a fiercely contested aspect of feminism in the 1980s and not one that I was attracted to. I felt that however burdensome the struggle to be treated as equals was, and I certainly found it wearing and I was often dispirited at how hard it was all becoming, we could not abandon it. For some women, the answer might be to leave the mainstream world to live and work in all-female communities, but that was not for me. Nor, I was pretty sure, was it for most women.

Alpert had turned herself in in late 1974 and served almost three years in prison. She had not long been released when we met. I was keen to know how she saw American politics now, after her experiences. She astonished me with a passionate defence of the American political system; this woman who had hated her country so much that she had planted bombs in crowded buildings (and was very lucky she had not killed anyone) now argued that Watergate had proved that America could redeem itself. I had never heard anyone contend that. To me, Watergate was evidence of the corruption of American politics, of the criminal lengths that the Republican Party was prepared to go, with presidential acquiescence, to win re-election. It was only in America that I was confronted with this point of view: that the impeachment of Richard Nixon and his resignation proved the system could correct and cleanse itself. It was a fair enough argument, I conceded, but then Alpert got very embarrassed at how her new-found patriotism made her sound so conservative.

I happened to be in New York the Sunday in January 1979 for the press conference held by Bella Abzug after President Carter had fired her the previous Friday as co-chair of the National Advisory Committee for Women. More than half the 30 members of the committee had resigned in protest. I rushed to the offices of *Ms.* magazine on 41st and Lexington where the press conference was being held. *Ms.* magazine had been founded by Gloria Steinem four years earlier and had already acquired iconic status. For me, this was hallowed feminist ground and I was excited to have the chance to see these legendary women at such close quarters. Bella Abzug had been a Democratic congresswoman for New York; the media usually attached the word 'feisty' to any mention of her because she was a fiery and outspoken woman. She always wore a hat with a brim and that, as much as her strong Brooklyn accent and her entertaining turn of phrase, became her signature. President Carter had set up the Advisory Committee by Executive Order to advise him on implementing the recommendations of the Houston Conference, a 20,000 strong gathering of women in November 1977, the first and only national women's conference ever to be funded by the American government, and intended to be the United States' response to International Women's Year in 1975.

Bella Abzug told the press conference that she believed that she and President Carter had had a good meeting. She had told him, she said, she was glad that he had asked for advice since none of his cabinet had taken up the opportunity to learn how the Houston recommendations might impact on their portfolios. She had no idea that they were already intending to get rid of her.

She learned that Hamilton Jordan, the President's key adviser (and later Chief-of-Staff), had described Abzug as 'too confrontationary'. The President had also had a problem, apparently, when she tried to explain to him that economics is a women's question.

'We fear that the anti-inflation policies of the President will impact gravely on women,' Abzug said.

But apparently he was only interested in the progress of the Equal Rights Amendment not in Abzug or the rest of the committee's opinion about what was needed for women.

'They want to even label our issues for us,' Abzug said. 'We're allowed to talk about equal rights or battered women, but not about the economy.'

'Obviously they want us to consent, not to advise.'

This was a clever line, I thought, turning on its head the role of the Senate 'to advise and consent' as stipulated by the US constitution. I was tremendously impressed by Abzug, especially by her insistence that women needed to be included in economic policy. I don't think I had heard this articulated so clearly before. It made sense, but it was a new thought and I needed to consider what the implications were. It was the first time I had heard Gloria Steinem speak and I was less impressed by her chatty, jokey style. She dubbed Bella's sacking 'the Friday afternoon massacre', an allusion to Richard Nixon's notorious Saturday night massacre during Watergate. I would later learn at first-hand how adept a phrasemaker Steinem was, but it seemed to me this day that her turn-of-phrase disguised an absence of content. I was far more attracted to Bella Abzug's gutsy way of putting meat on the bone.

I spent my last week visiting New York literary agents. I was amazed at the ease with which I gained appointments to see Lois Wallace, Elaine Markson and several other big names. They were for the most part friendly, although none of them thought there was a market in New York for *Damned Whores*. I knew I was hampered by not having a strong enough idea to propose but perhaps, I thought, if I went straight to an editor at a big publishing house I could find someone who would have sufficient faith to nurture me the way John Hooker, the publisher at Penguin in Australia, had done. After an introduction from Robert Hughes, the art critic for *Time*, an Australian and a friend, I sat down with Chuck Elliott, Hughes's editor at Knopf and told him I'd like to write a book about Australia. I had what I thought at the time was an interesting take on the country and its place in the world.

'Australia is boring,' he told me. 'No one cares about it.'

He showed me his latest bestseller. It was a book about a super-tanker.

'It does not really matter what the subject is,' he said. 'It's how you tell the story.'

Unless the story was Australia, apparently.

I went to drinks with a businessman I had met in the Midwest who was on the board of one of New York's top publishing houses. He had said he could put me in touch with the right editor. We met at a well-known midtown hotel but as I began to babble about my ideas for the book, I felt his hand creeping up my thigh.

In the end, I did not stay and surrender myself to whatever America might have to offer. I opted for the small pond, the safety and security of a job, a salary, a title, a zone of comfort where I would be tested but where I would not risk everything. I knew I was again experiencing the indecision of my previous visit to New York. If I was going to change my life, follow that big dream of being a writer in America, now was the time to do it. But it did not happen. In the end I was not brave enough.

CHAPTER THREE

THE PRESS GALLERY

'I figure it's a 24-hour-a-day job with sufficient psychological rewards to offset any personal inconvenience,' Maximilian Walsh, the managing editor, had written in his lengthy letter appointing me as Canberra political correspondent for the *Australian Financial Review*.

I needed to be out 'beating the bushes; it is not an in-office end-of-phone job,' he wrote. I was new to Canberra, new to political reporting and new to daily journalism. Walsh was taking a huge risk with me so he took some time in his letter to set out his expectations, to warn me of the pitfalls, and to encourage me to be confident and adventurous. As well as reporting the main political news of the day, I would write the weekly column 'Canberra Observed' that had been essential reading for all political aficionados when he himself had written it before transferring to Sydney to take the editor's chair some years earlier. The column had a long and variable history. Sometimes it broke news, but mostly it was intended to provide a perspective on the week in Canberra. 'I want to see that column become not only required reading for anybody seriously interested in politics but also for it to be qualitatively superior to any alternative,' he told me. This was a big ask given my lack of experience and that I was up against reporters like Laurie Oakes, Paul Kelly, Michelle Grattan, Peter Bowers and others who had been in the Gallery for years, and who had a far more thorough knowledge of politics, and its history, than I did.

I had started the job in a state of high anxiety, which I hoped I was hiding from my new colleagues. If I could not put on a bold front, I would have no hope of succeeding. While I was still in the US, after I'd already agreed to take the position, I had been almost paralysed with doubt and fear about whether I could do it. Was I qualified? I was not across the big political issues of the day. Whenever I could get hold of the *Financial Review* (not easy in the Midwest before the internet) to check out what they were covering, I was horrified to read front-page stories about the law of the sea, about Treasury bond tap and tender issues and other topics that I had never even heard of. I kept asking myself whether my doubts were just feelings of female insecurity. I would not be the first woman political correspondent. Michelle Grattan at the *Age* and Gay Davidson at the *Canberra Times* had already broken that barrier, although I would be the first woman to do the job for the F*inancial Review*. But I did not think my sex was the reason I was scared. I was taking on a very big job, where I would be writing about the Prime Minister and the government, and I was frightened of making a fool of myself for not knowing enough. Any failures on my part would be very public—quite possibly on page one of the country's only financial daily. Yet, I kept telling myself, the man who recruited me seemed totally confident: If he thought I could do it, I should not let my own misgivings hold me back.

Before he had been promoted at the age of 37 to the editorship of the *Financial Review*, Max—or Thanksa (Thanks a million/rhyming slang for Maximilian) as many people in the Gallery called him—Walsh had been a standout member of his generation of journalists, which included such luminaries as the *Age's* Alan Barnes and Peter Smark, Fred Brenchley from the *Financial Review*, and Laurie Oakes from the *Melbourne Sun-Pictorial*. They were hard-living, hard-drinking champions of the long lunch, reporters who were intensely competitive with each other. They lived to break news and would have scorned being dependent on what Paul Keating used to call 'the quality drip'—stories which when he was Treasurer and later Prime Minister he arranged to feed to acquiescent journalists. Which is not to say that Walsh and his generation did not cultivate highly placed sources for information, but they were more likely to test what they were given, sometimes even to use it against the source, rather than merely transcribe what they had been told. Walsh, in particular, remade political writing.

Walsh came from the tabloid *Daily Mirror* to the *Financial Review* at the invitation of Max Newton, the brilliant editor who had transformed the paper from a weekly into a daily, and he accepted Newton's theory that all politics was essentially about economics. When Newton left the *Financial Review* to join Rupert Murdoch and launch the *Australian*, his successor, Vic Carroll, put Walsh onto the major business and finance stories of the day where he rapidly showed his acumen. He built a knowledge of the real world of business and its connections to politics, as well as some of the sometimes shady people involved in business. Combined with an Economics degree he had acquired by going part-time to the University of Sydney while still working police rounds for the *Mirror*, Walsh possessed talents previously rare or non-existent in the Canberra Press Gallery. Carroll recognised this when he sent Walsh to be the paper's political correspondent. With the new, upmarket byline Maximilian Walsh, he combined the toughness he'd learned hanging around cops with the expertise he'd picked up at night school to perfect a new form of political journalism. He forsook objectivity to take stands on issues, especially economic matters such as protectionism, and to use his journalism to educate his readers on the perils for the nation of hiding behind a tariff wall. 'Walsh's daily reports, weekly "Canberra Observed" column in the *AFR* and another weekly column in the Sunday *Sun-Herald*, became mandatory reading for mandarins, politicians, lobbyists and the rest of the parliamentary press gallery,' wrote journalist Andrew Clark in a biography of Walsh on the Australian Media Hall of Fame website.[1] 'He informed, inspired, infuriated, and irritated. Most of all, he set the agenda. Walsh had imitators and followers, but no one supplanted him.'

Walsh was aggressive in his analysis, especially of the performance of politicians who had rarely been subjected to such incisive probing. His forensic dissection of Prime Minister William McMahon, sharing with readers of the *National Times* in September 1971 what anyone acquainted with the man knew, that he was shallow and untalented, further cemented his reputation. Unusually among Canberra journalists, Walsh was stylish. He was a snappy dresser. He acquired a heritage house in the toney dress circle, inner-Canberra suburb of Forrest where he entertained well. (He sold the house to Fairfax when he went to Sydney, and it became a perk for the paper's Canberra bureau chief; I lived there for four years.) His colleagues called him 'word-a-day-Walsh' for his penchant for using a new, and unfamiliar, word almost every day in his stories. Australian journalists who today frequently use 'swingeing' and 'schadenfreude' might not know it, but Max Walsh introduced these words to the vocabulary of political journalism. Walsh was also not afraid of a fight and soon he and I were shoulder-to-shoulder in a battle between the Prime Minister and the paper the likes of which had rarely been seen before in the Canberra Press Gallery.

Walsh may have seen something of himself in me which was why he was bringing me from a totally different type of journalism into his old job. I was also someone from outside the traps, who'd made a name for herself writing pioneering pieces, who might be able to transfer those skills to political writing. I have always been grateful for the guidance he gave me in those early months, yet I still found it very hard. I had, literally, been thrown in the deep end and some days I had no idea what I should be doing. What was the story? What was the angle? I didn't want to be mollycoddled but I did need steering and, while most of my colleagues in the bureau were friendly and helpful, sometimes I found myself floundering.

'I can see the absolute terror in your eyes,' a journalist from another newspaper told me one night over dinner.

He was trying to be sympathetic, and suggesting I bullshit my way through as everyone else did, but I wasn't sure that I yet knew enough to be able to do that. Still, I was reassured to hear that others were faking it too.

Walsh and I had a number of fallings-out but, when it mattered he always backed me, and his advice on how to approach the 'Canberra Observed' column was astute: 'Two points you should constantly remind yourself about in writing the column is that if there is a topic of popular conversation in Canberra,' Walsh wrote, 'it is usually worth writing about even if it is a little unconventional'. The second point has informed my writing ever since. 'No matter what you are writing about you should always try to give the reader some[thing] new in the way of information. Your opinions are not going to be marketable for some time and even when they are you should sell them subliminally not shove them down people's throats'. I have now been writing opinion columns for close to four decades and still follow that advice: in each column I do my best to give my readers new facts or other material relevant to the topic I am writing about.

———◦◦◦———

Despite my trepidation about the actual job, I loved going to work. I literally ran up the steps each morning into what is now old Parliament House. Some days I used the Senate entrance, which was the most direct route to our office, but once or twice a week I would go in the front doors and be sure first of all to pass over the spot where four years earlier the just-sacked Gough Whitlam had referred to Malcolm Fraser as 'Kerr's cur'. Now Fraser was still there, ensconced in the Prime Ministerial suite. I would walk up the short staircase just inside the Parliament House entrance into Kings Hall, the grand pillared space that was the epicentre of the building. Parliament House had opened in 1927 and was often referred to as 'the wedding cake' for its squat, tiered, blindingly-white structure. It is now the Museum of Australian Democracy—the new, much-larger, Parliament House, built on top of Capital Hill, opened in 1988—and the old interiors are perfectly preserved. When I visited in June 2016 to refresh my memory of the layout, I was surprised at how small the spaces were. Kings Hall had certainly shrunk.

The main entrances to both the Senate and the House of Representatives opened from Kings Hall so there were always politicians scurrying towards the chambers, especially if the bells were ringing, green for the Reps or red for the Senate, calling all members or senators to a vote. You would also see the mandarins—the senior public servants, all of them men, grey-suited and circumspect, briefcases held tightly—making their way across Kings Hall, towards the offices of their minister. Later in the day, Kings Hall was the ideal location for a loitering journalist as you could literally run into anyone there. Once I'd learned to recognise all the ministers, the MPs and the key public servants, I, too, would often hang around Kings Hall in the hope of being able to grab a few informative words with someone who knew what was going on.

The Press Gallery ran across the roof of the building. Literally. A wooden walkway joined the two ends. The *Fin Review* office was on the Senate side. We were part of the Fairfax corridor, with the *Age*, the *SMH*, the *Sun-Herald* and Channel 7 all having adjacent offices. The *National Times* was a bit further along, off an even-smaller corridor that housed what were known as 'one-man bureaux'. The offices were all small and cramped. Ours had six metal desks jammed into a space that must have been no more than six by three metres. In Sydney, they were starting to get 'the new technology' that would supposedly make production of the paper more efficient but in Canberra we still bashed out our stories on typewriters then rushed the pages into the telex room across the corridor where two operators, Beryl and Yvonne, typed them out again for transmission. In Sydney, after the subeditors had read them, the stories were sent to the compositors who typed them a third time. There was massive scope for error in having copy retyped so many times, especially as there was little time for proof-reading. Sometimes, mistakes were deliberately introduced. When Paddy McGuinness became editor-in-chief, in 1982, he was enraged when every single time he referred in an editorial to the Treasury Secretary Mr John Stone—and since Stone and Treasury were frequently mentioned in his edi-torials, it happened often—it always ended up in the paper as 'Mr Johnstone'. The outspoken and image-conscious Stone refused to believe that this was not deliberate mischief by the editor, rather than subversion by the printers.

The ABC, AAP, News Limited and the *Canberra Times* were located at the other end, on the roof of the Reps. The Prime Minister's Press Office was at that end, too, presided over by the gruff and domineering David Barnett. Barnett was a tall man who had the slightly stooped appearance of someone who is trying to appear shorter. Perhaps he did not want to compete with his boss who was a tall 195 centimetres and who, physically and psychologically, dominated every room he entered. Barnett always had a worried air about him and although he laughed a lot, it was a bitter sardonic sort of laugh that he seemed to use defensively against both crit-icism and attack. Malcolm Fraser always blamed him for any negative stories and I soon got the impression that Barnett had to scramble as hard as the rest of us to get information. The big difference was, of course, that Barnett's source was the Prime Minister, whereas more often than not, ours was Barnett. Before he took the job, Barnett had been an AAP reporter and was renowned for his fast and impeccable shorthand. He had accompanied Gough Whitlam, then Leader of the Opposition, on his historic visit to

China in 1971 and was present on 5 July when Premier Zhou Enlai finally sat down with Whitlam in the Great Hall of the People and conducted an intensive conversation lasting several hours. In a highly unusual move, the journalists were permitted to stay. Barnett's transcript of the entire conversation, as translated, stands as the record of that extraordinary moment in Australian–Chinese diplomacy.[2] Barnett also used his shorthand to take notes of what Fraser told him, which must have unnerved the man who could never bring himself to trust anyone, even—or perhaps especially—those on his personal staff. Malcolm Fraser was known as a tough bastard who showed no warmth or courtesy towards his staff. Someone I knew who worked for him for several years told me he never once said Good Morning or inquired about his family.

The Press Office was located strategically near the boxes, the hub from which all information and gossip radiated. The boxes were a wall of large wooden pigeonholes where news releases, government and parliamentary reports, answers to Questions on Notice and other material for the media were distributed. Each organisation was allocated a box, its name and number crudely created with a Dymo-label printer; ours was right in the middle, number 29, just under the *Australian* which was 28. If something was urgent, whoever was dropping it pressed a loud buzzer that could be heard throughout the Gallery and the most junior person in each office would be sent off to get it. Over the course of a day, dozens of documents and pieces of paper were dropped in these boxes; not only the politicians—government and opposition—distributed press releases but so did lobbyists, NGOs and any organisation that had a message to get out. There was no security at Parliament House and anyone could walk up to the Press Gallery and drop off a release. We cleared the boxes constantly and did a quick triage to see what would go to a journo or could be tossed straight into the bin. It was rare to find anything but public releases in the boxes, but I had the great fortune to have a series of extremely damaging internal Liberal Party memos dropped into our box over several Sundays, usually a quiet news day, so my stories got front-page treatment. I never found out who my benefactor was but there was no doubt they were genuine. The audible gulp at the other end of the phone when I rang the first time, seeking confirmation from the Liberal Party federal director, Tony Eggleton, was proof enough. By the third time it happened, he was becoming almost resigned to the treachery and had decided the best tactic was simply to ride it out. The Prime Minister, who was the subject of trenchant criticism in these documents, was less forgiving. I was dropped from his media Christmas party invitation list as part of my punishment.

There was tremendous camaraderie in the Gallery. We had no choice but to get along because we were all jam-packed in together. That did not mean there weren't rivalries and jealousies and, of course, everyone wanted to be the one to break a big story. And if someone had a scoop, it was never a secret. The Gallery was village-like in the way gossip travelled. It was said that if someone started a rumour at one end of the Gallery it would take no more than eleven seconds for it to travel to the other end, often receiving some embellishment along the way. When word went around that someone had 'the big one' the rest of us would do whatever we could to try to find out what it was. 'Take X from the [scoop-getter's] bureau down to the non-members' bar,' I'd instruct one of my juniors, 'see what he knows.' But scoops were fiercely guarded, and even office colleagues often did not know what the story was. Like the rest of us, they would have to wait until the next morning when the papers arrived to find out that a minister was to be sacked or whatever the story was. Then our editors would be on the phone: Why didn't you have that? How are you going to follow it up?

Like journalists everywhere, those in the Gallery were a cynical lot. I quickly learned that no person or policy was ever greeted positively, let alone with unadulterated enthusiasm. I had learned scepticism in the Sydney Push and could argue against any proposition that was put to me, but I had trouble with this constant negativity. I had to learn to tread the perilous path between political neutrality—we could not of course favour any political party in what we wrote, regardless of our personal views or how we voted—and my own principles. I did not always manage. Very early on, 10 April 1979, I walked out of a press conference where Bill Hayden, the Leader of the Opposition, was releasing the report of a Special Committee of Inquiry into the ALP because he opened proceedings with a joke about rape. Hayden said that one of his Queensland enemies was putting it around that when he, Hayden, had been a police sergeant he had raped a woman in the back of a police car. He wanted, he told us, to put the record straight:

'I wasn't a sergeant, I was a constable first class; secondly, it wasn't a police car and, third, the woman had promised she wouldn't squeal.' I could not believe my ears. I felt I had two choices: to stand up and remonstrate with him, or to walk out. I thought that leaving was more professional than getting into a slanging match with the country's alternative Prime Minister. Alan Ramsey, one of Hayden's press secretaries, who had himself been a controversial Press Gallery figure in the past and later would be a notable reporter and columnist with the *Sydney Morning Herald*, followed me out and tried to hose me down. I'd been grateful to Hayden just four years earlier when, as Minister for Social Security in the Whitlam government, he had turned up unannounced at Elsie Women's Refuge in Glebe, seen the appalling conditions in which we were operating, and arranged to get us federal funds.[3] But in Canberra, I discovered, Hayden often strayed into embarrassing or even somewhat predatory behaviour when he had had a few drinks. That day after the press conference was not the only time during Hayden's tenure that Ramsey would have to explain away, and apologise to me for, outrageous acts of sexism by his boss.

My reaction to Hayden's joke was one indication that I was still very much an outsider. My colleagues did not seem bothered by such things. Either they had not been sensitised to understand how offensive to women these conversations were, or they were so totally accustomed to such talk and the assumptions that underscored them, that they did not even register. It was probably both. Either way, I was out of step. I intended to be utterly professional in how I approached my job, and I could swear with the best of them, so I wasn't worried about that kind of language, but I did not think it was reasonable that I should have to listen to talk that was insulting or offensive to my very being as a woman. Maybe I would never fit in.

My first test in the new job came after just three weeks. What I could never have expected was that it would be my boss and mentor who precipitated it. Walsh had come from Sydney to visit the bureau, and startled and embarrassed me by sitting down at one of the typewriters to bash out a 'rough draft', as he put it, of my 'Canberra Observed' column. It was a big speculative piece about the possible future federal intentions of NSW Premier Neville Wran, the kind of article that only someone with the credibility resulting from years of political experience could write. I certainly could not, but Max argued that this column would 'make me', put me on the map, announce that I was going to be a significant player in the Gallery. He told me to rewrite the piece in my own language. He had already put my byline on it. The rest of the office watched to see what I would do. Then all of them—Judith Hoare, Greg Hywood, Paul Malone and Mungo MacCallum who had recently been hired to write a weekly sketch column— conspicuously got up and left. Obviously they were going to caucus in the non-members' bar. I inserted a page into the typewriter, looked at Max's draft and realised that all I could do would be to alter a word, here or there. It would still be his piece. His ideas. His characteristic bold style. I was still staring miserably at the page when Mungo returned:

'It's none of my business,' he said, 'but someone has to tell you. If you do this, you are finished in Canberra. You'll be a laughing stock.'

It was what I needed. I flashed him a grateful smile and went to the tele-printer room to retrieve the two pages I had already placed in the basket for transmission. I replaced them with Max's full article and changed my byline for his. I then rang Sydney and told them that this week's column was being filed by Max Walsh and that if my byline appeared anywhere near it, I would resign. It all blew over as quickly as political winds change in Canberra. Strange as it was for my boss to have written my column, Max's byline on the piece signalled to my new colleagues that I would not be a pushover. Max took it in good grace. I don't think he was intentionally testing me, he just was frustrated that he no longer had a column as an outlet for his big ideas. My standing in the Gallery seemed to improve somewhat but I was still new, someone it was too soon to make judgements about.

Another sign that I had not yet been totally accepted by my colleagues was that, unlike almost everyone else in the Gallery, I did not have a nickname. The names were occasionally unkind, often amusing and usually so apt that, even 30 years on, it would not be wise to match some of them to their owners. One of the network cameramen was 'tosser' because, so it was said, he'd had the name 'Throwing Stick' as a boy scout. There was also 'dogsy', a guy who was always desperate for sex; and 'dogsballs' (let's just say that when skinny-dipping at a Gallery barbecue people had glimpsed rather too much of him); and 'dipstick', a well-known womaniser; 'the toad', an especially unhandsome man; and a fellow who was known as 'blacks', because he was prone to rifling through colleagues' carbons to check their stories (a practice akin to stealing, that was regarded with contempt). Mungo MacCallum, although about the same age as most of us, was already enough of a legend to be simply Mungo. Sometimes, the names were affectionate and there was no need to be discreet. Michelle Grattan was known as 'Hondo' after Hondo Grattan, the famous harness-racing horse that had won several championships in the early 1970s. Michelle was renowned for her indefatigable pursuit of stories and her doggedness when it came to details. She triple-checked everything and her stories were guaranteed to be accurate. She would ring ministers or bureaucrats or anyone she thought could help with her story at all hours; it became something of a badge of honour for a minister to boast he'd 'got a call from bloody Michelle at 2 bloody am.' Peter Harvey, the popular Channel 9 reporter, was 'four balls', because of his extremely deep voice. But no one had been able to come up with a name for me. They did not know me well enough to use some of the names given to me by close friends: 'the moth', in reference to my late-night sociability, or 'HL' (hollow legs), for my ability to put away large quantities of red wine. As it turned out, events would ensure that I would get my own nickname before the year was out.

We worked long hours, although by the standards of today our output was small. I rarely wrote more than one story a day. I would usually come in at around ten. I had already thoroughly digested at least the political stories in the five newspapers I had delivered at home, so the mornings were spent chatting with colleagues, picking up any gossip, and starting to figure out what the day's stories might be. Sometimes there were press conferences or other scheduled events and, at 2 o'clock each sitting day, there was Question Time. We had our own two-tiered gallery, behind the Speaker's Chair, from where we could look down on proceedings. (None of us would deign to attend Senate Question Time; we were interested only in the main game, the place where the government was formed.) The key media had seats in the lower gallery so we were close to the action on the floor below. We could sense the mood, pick up tensions, and get a sense of any drama that might be about to unfold. Politicians, especially ministers, would constantly and often anxiously glance up at us, as if to try to register how their performances were being judged. Today, the Press Gallery section of the chamber is high up, destroying that connection, and most journalists, if they watch it at all, follow Question Time on their television monitors. No political correspondent would have dreamed of not being there during the Fraser and Hawke governments. A lot more happened then. Questions were less scripted; even Dorothy Dixers had some content to them, and there was rarely anything predictable about how an issue was going to be dealt with. News stories often came out of Question Time. I usually finished filing my story by 9 p.m. but that was not the end of the working day. That time of night was ideal for prowling corridors, looking for MPs who might have had a few drinks and thus be a bit talkative, or for meeting ministers in their offices. Otherwise, I'd just head for the non-members bar, which was always full of lobbyists and politicians as well as journalistic colleagues. Like the 'Sheltered Workshop', as the parliamentary cafeteria was called, it was a place to catch up with colleagues, to be sure to know if there was a whiff of a story in the air, to just keep up with the events of the day. By the time everyone had already put in a twelve-hour day, the non-members was packed and it stayed that way until closing time which was, I think, midnight.

Journalism was a hard-drinking occupation then. And not just in the evenings. Some, like Mungo, would get an early start in the non-members. Others, like me, would wait until lunchtime when we might head into Civic, Canberra's idea of a central business district, to Charlies, the famous restaurant run by Mez O'Neill, whose ebullient personality was as much a factor in the place's popularity as its bill of fare. Mez was married to Garry O'Neill from the *Herald Sun* and we'd been friends since October 1976, when I'd come to Canberra for the first time as a journalist to cover Hunter S. Thompson's lunchtime address to the National Press Club for the *National Times*. I'd ended up at Charlies that night and been immediately captivated by the patrons. Not just the journos and politicians, but all sorts of other characters. Like Mary Scott who, with her wiry frame and very long blonde hair, looked a lot more like the Mary of Peter, Paul and Mary, the famous singing trio, than the senior health bureaucrat she was. But she also owned a farm and took care of injured wildlife. It was not unusual for Mary to have a wallaby or other small native animal in her shoulder bag; nor was it uncommon for one of these creatures to venture out. The first time I saw a kangaroo taking tentative hops around Charlies I wondered whether I'd had too much to drink. There was nothing like this in Sydney, I thought. Every night at Charlies was an experience; dinner could take many hours because so much table-hopping was involved. It was before my time, of course, but Mez often told me stories of the night of the dismissal of the Whitlam government when it seemed that the entire Press Gallery, along with every member of the sacked government, had ended up at Charlies. The place quickly ran out of food but fortunately Mez had adequate stocks of alcohol. People were still there at 6 a.m. When she went to clean up, she told me, there was more than one cabinet submission among the rubbish.

Charlies was less crowded at lunchtime, which meant we could be sure of getting served quickly. We might have a pre-lunch beer or gin and tonic, a bottle or two of wine with our meal—if there were four of us—and maybe squeeze in a quick cognac afterwards, before driving back across Commonwealth Avenue Bridge and getting ourselves up into the Gallery by Question Time. Within a few years, even the Press Gallery got health conscious and at lunchtime you were more likely to see journalists jogging round Lake Burley Griffin than quaffing cognac at Charlies. But the ritual of Friday nights at the National Press Club was unaffected. This was *de rigueur* for political journos because so many bureaucrats drank there, and it was an opportunity to talk informally, to develop a sufficient rapport that you could ring them when you needed information in their area. The ever loquacious John Stone, surrounded by his Treasury deputies, Chris Higgins and Ted Evans and first assistant secretaries, were always there. At first I found this beer-fuelled banter intimidating. I had difficulty finding the right words and demeanour. Nor did I really like beer, certainly not in the quantities required to survive those Friday nights, but I stuck at it. I knew how to make myself part of groups, even those who did not want me. I'd done it in Sydney because I wanted to be at the exciting heart of the women's liberation movement. Now it was my job to cosy up to people who wanted to talk trade or monetary policy, my new favourite subjects, and I had no choice but to do it.

After a few months of living in a rented house in Turner, on the northern side of Canberra, I decided I should buy a house. It would be my first-ever big financial commitment. I was 34 and I had no shares, no savings, nothing to show for the fact I worked. Time to start being responsible, I thought. That I was thinking this way meant I had now discarded my previously held anarchist view, first expressed by Frenchman Pierre Proudhon in 1840, that 'property is theft'. I found a brick duplex in Hamilton Row, Yarralumla that had a huge side garden that included an aboveground swimming pool. I envisaged Saturday lunches under the pergola. The house itself would need a bit of sprucing up, perhaps a paint job and the carpet could be replaced, but we were a lot less obsessed about renovations and the need for a perfect kitchen than we are today. I thought I could move in right away. I applied to my bank, then known as the Bank of New South Wales, for a mortgage on the $89,000 property. I did not expect any problems. I had a reputable and high-profile job, where I earned $31,000, good money for the time, plus I had a company car and generous expense account. I had no dependents and no debts. There was no doubt I had the capacity to meet the repayments, so I was amazed when the bank rejected the application. The reason was simple: they did not lend to women. No amount of remonstrating, or even a letter from the managing editor of the *Financial Review* would persuade them to review, or make an exception to, the policy. Blanket rule. Women could not borrow. I suppose I was angry but I was more worried about the very practical matter that I had already signed a contract to buy the property. A close friend said he'd speak to his father, who had a senior position at the Commonwealth Bank. I got a positive response. They would lend me the money—just as long as I had a male guarantor. I had no choice but to go along with that humiliating requirement. There was no income check on the person who signed. He just needed to be male.

Most of the time, being a woman was not a disadvantage in the Press Gallery. All of us, male and female, were a hard-working lot, who were judged by the stories we got. Mostly my sex was not a factor with ministers; the key thing was the newspaper I worked for. If they wanted to talk to the business world and the political class, the *Financial Review* was the way to reach them. But there were some who responded to my serious questions with bedroom eyes, much to my annoyance, and others, such as Michael Hodgman, a Liberal backbencher from Tasmania (whose son is currently Premier of Tasmania) and who was known as Mouth from the South because he never stopped talking, who seemingly could not help themselves. When I rang him one day in his capacity as chairman of a committee that was examining proposed amendments to an ASIO Bill, to check on the status of the amendments, he asked whether I'd mind if he made a sexist comment. What could I say? He told me that when he'd looked up at me in the Press Gallery during Question Time that day, I had reminded him of Jane Fonda. He then went on to talk about the recent revelations that the FBI had bugged Fonda's bed during her anti-war days.

'I bet they heard plenty of things apart from her war plans,' he said to me.

I never had the experience, recounted to me by a young radio reporter, of literally being chased around a cabinet minister's desk when she went to interview him one night. But one Sunday evening I agreed to visit a cabinet minister in his apartment, the idea being that we would have time for an extended chat about some of his portfolio issues. When I arrived and saw the lowered lights, the open bottle of wine and his smarmy smile, I got myself out of there as fast as I could. I doubt that Laurie Oakes or Paul Kelly got a similar reception if they dropped into a minister's flat for an informal chat. I was not aware of any sexual harassment of women by their Press Gallery colleagues, although it is highly likely that we simply just did not talk about such behaviour in those days before the Sex Discrimination Act. Or that it was unchallenged because it was the way things were back then. Or that because it was not happening in my own bureau, I simply was not aware of what went on in other offices. And while most of the women reporters were professional in their relations with politicians, annoyingly there was sometimes one or two who thought it was just fine to wear a sexy outfit and bat their eyelashes in order to give themselves a supposed advantage. I was very tough on a woman in my bureau who came to work one day with a dress that was slit practically to her waist. Flirtations were one thing, and there were plenty, and there were full-on affairs that were mostly kept very discreet, especially if they involved a journalist and a politician. But there were a few politicians who felt entitled to grab what they could—and their names were on a 'sleaze list' of politicians to avoid being alone with. On Monday my cabinet minister's name was added to it. The list was informal, just girls looking out for each other, an example of sisterhood in what was in most other ways a totally male-dominated place.

One year, Fraser accepted an invitation from the Queensland Irish Club in Brisbane to address its famous St Patrick's Day breakfast. There was just one problem: the club did not admit women, a rule that was not changed until 1986, and this meant that Michelle Grattan and I, the two women in the travelling press corps, were not allowed to attend. We kicked up a fuss. But those Irish ears were deaf to our arguing that they were preventing us from doing our jobs. Michelle and I stood outside the club during the breakfast, giving radio interviews, and doing our best to take a stand against sexism. We had made a half-hearted attempt to argue to the Prime Minister that he should not give his imprimatur to such a blatantly discriminatory event, but Fraser was unmoved. Women's equality was barely on Fraser's personal radar. Even though it was not, strictly speaking, part of my beat, I did my best to keep across what passed for women's policy in those days. I wrote one or two articles on women's refuge funding and I kept in touch with Senator Susan Ryan, who had been a member of the Women's Electoral Lobby and who in 1975 had been elected as senator for the ACT. She had made reducing the gender gap in Labor's vote a priority on her political agenda, commissioning research that showed that women's votes could put Labor in office. She then set about persuading her party to adopt policies that might attract the votes of women. She made sure I got copies of all the research.

Travelling with Fraser was part of the job and as he travelled a lot, so did I. Sometimes it was just to a capital city, as with the St Patrick's Day breakfast in Brisbane, and that was always a very straightforward trip. We journalists were responsible for getting ourselves to Fairbairn RAAF base, just on the other side of Canberra Airport, where we would board the VIP plane and head for our destination where a mini-bus would usually be waiting for the press party. We'd then follow along behind Fraser who was in his official Commonwealth car. If it was a dinner, the press would usually be offered seats and a meal while we dutifully checked the text of his speech against delivery, but many times we would have to just stand around and kill time while the Prime Minister went about whatever business he had. Afterwards, if we were lucky, Fraser would say a few words to us but more likely we'd get a briefing from Barnett or one of the other press secretaries. Then there'd be a rush for the nearest public phones so we could file our stories. Michelle Grattan invariably got there first and this led to constant grumbling, especially if there was only one phone and she took her time to dictate her story.

'That woman needs a phone in her handbag,' one of my colleagues said once while we waited our turns to dictate our copy.

We of course had no idea how much journalism, and the way we did our jobs, would change once we all had such phones. Not to mention Wi-Fi and 4G, enabling us to file from anywhere in the world. Then, we were totally dependent on our organisations' switchboard. Many times, the kind women who answered 20944, the Fairfax number, were my lifeline. Whether I was somewhere in remote Africa or merely in a small town in Tasmania, 'Switch'—as we called whoever answered—would deal with whatever it was, from getting a copytaker to capture my garbled words in the ten minutes I had before the VIP took off; to finding an inebriated editor in a restaurant somewhere and making him take the call; to simply being a reassuring voice in whatever madness I found myself. Once in Sydney, I visited the switchboard and met the surprisingly small number of women who did this heroic job. We went to the pub so I could thank them. Apparently I was one of the very few journalists who ever did that.

So much of political journalism involved getting on the bus, or off the plane, or into the holding area—and then waiting. And waiting. It was extremely boring. We Press Gallery journalists got to know each other pretty well as we swapped stories during those interminable waits. We had no smart phones or Twitter or Facebook to soak up the time. Sometimes we would have to wait on the plane for Fraser. We waited one night for what seemed like hours at an airport somewhere near the Gold Coast. We were on a smaller-than-usual plane and there were only a few journalists and several Fraser staffers, including his speech writer Alan Jones who would go on to become a famous coach with both rugby codes and, much later, one of the country's more notorious shock jocks. We passed the time by getting stuck into the Grange Hermitage. Every VIP was well-stocked with this premium Australian wine. By the time an equally well-watered Fraser arrived, the pilots were concerned we were going to miss the curfew in Melbourne so it was a very fast wheels-up. Fraser barely had time to buckle up. Not that he noticed. We learned that he had sunk a bottle of Scotch with

Sir Jack Egerton, the legendary Labor fixer (whose acceptance of a knight-hood from Fraser had led to his expulsion from the ALP), while the two of them worked on a plot involving preferences and other sweeteners to try to save the seat of McPherson, where there was to be a by-election following the sudden death of Eric Robinson, Fraser's former Finance Minister. Once we were in the air, an unusually convivial Fraser got out his camera and began photographing everyone. At his insistence, I posed sitting on Jones's knee. It was rare to see Fraser so relaxed and so playful, at least while journalists were around. That was the only time I could recall, but then again it was an exciting trip all round. In order to make the curfew at Essendon, we made the two-and-a-half-hour trip in two hours and seven minutes.

Fraser could be very irritable and impatient and that included while he was travelling. On a trip to the Thiess coalmines in Central Queensland in early 1979, he'd simply refused to wait when, due to a misunderstand-ing about the time of a rendezvous back at the air strip, the bus carrying journalists and his own officials arrived a few minutes late. As we left the bus and ran towards the RAAF Chinook helicopter that had ferried us all there, Fraser simply ordered the pilots to take off. Did I just imagine that was Fraser's face at the window, laughing at us from inside the ascending chopper? Fortunately, Sir Leslie Thiess came to our rescue with his private jet. It held fewer passengers than the Chinook so several trips were needed to get us all to the next destination. On another occasion, 27 April 1979, again when we were flying back from Queensland, Fraser decided he wanted to go straight to Melbourne, rather than drop the press off in Canberra as promised. It must have been a Friday and he was anxious to have a weekend on his property 'Nareen' in the western district of Victoria. It meant a couple of extra hours flying time for us journos, but they turned on the '74 Grange to shut us up and by the time we got back to Canberra, most of us had no idea how long we'd been flying—or even where we had been.

I gradually got to know most of the ministers, trying to call on as many of them as possible as often as they would see me. Often the visits were late at night, after dinner, while Parliament was still sitting and a division could be called at any time so no one could leave the building. I had so much ground to make up if I was to be able to compete with the other political chiefs. Most of them had been in the gallery for years. A few, like Wally Brown from the *Courier Mail*, Neil O'Reilly from the *Sun-Herald* and Alan Reid from *The Bulletin*, had been there for decades. After every cabinet meeting I would gamely call the offices of key ministers such as Treasurer John Howard; Foreign Affairs Minister Andrew Peacock; Philip Lynch the Industry Minister, who was a renowned player, ably assisted by Brian Buckley, his Svengali like press secretary and renowned political fixer; or Transport Minister Peter Nixon and ask if I could have 'a few minutes with the boss'. Increasingly, they agreed and I would find myself sitting on one of the green leather couches in the corridors outside their offices. More often than not, Paul Kelly or Michelle Grattan would be sitting there as well. Once inside, I had to work fast to develop the relationship, encourage the minister to trust me—and try to get a story for the next day's paper.

Some ministers were harder to crack. It took me months to get a meeting with Jim Killen, the Defence Minister. Eventually, I got the summons to come to his office one morning. He had one of the best offices in Parliament House, better, in my opinion, than the box-like set of rooms that went under the name of 'the Prime Ministerial suite'. Killen's office was at the front of the building, too, but he had doors that opened out onto a terrace. The doors were open this day, revealing the Burley Griffin vision for Canberra in all its splendour, and it was magnificent. Our eyes travelled down the hill towards the lake and, across the water, up the broad avenue of Anzac Parade leading to the distant Australian War Memorial. There could be no more fitting vista for a Defence Minister.

Killen was a dapper and courtly man whose upper lip sported a neat moustache. He was old-fashioned courteous, with a bit of rogue thrown in. He was definitely a ladies' man although, unlike some of his younger colleagues, far too aware of our respective roles to entertain flirting with me. After he greeted me, he resumed his seat behind his desk. A cask of white wine was perched on one corner, within easy reach.

'Lent,' he explained, as he refilled his glass.

Otherwise it would have been whisky.

It was our first meeting so it was formal and uninformative, but I did get to experience the very entertaining ways of Australia's Defence Minister.

A blowfly had buzzed-in through the open doors and annoyingly zoomed in on us. The minister made a few ineffectual attempts to shoo it away, but when that did not work he picked up a heavy, serious-looking book. Within seconds, mashed fly embellished the cover of The *Strategic Basis of Australian Defence Policy*, the government's most secret document, the one that prioritised actual and possible threats to the country and assessed whether military might need to be deployed to meet them. Killen placed the book back on his desk. I looked at it longingly; if only I could have got my hands on that, I thought, I could have got more out of this meeting than a few laughs.

I never was able to simply ring a minister, let alone the Prime Minister, and get a rundown on what had happened that day in cabinet, as I was sure some of my colleagues did, but it did get easier. By the end of my first year, I felt I was getting on top of the political scene and was feeling more confident about the job. I was also starting to overcome my doubts that I would never be able to reconcile myself to the manipulation politicians engage in. These efforts seemingly reached new levels under Fraser. While the press was grateful to David Barnett for introducing transcripts of every one of the Prime Minister's utterances, some of his other innovations were less welcome. He initiated the door-stop, today a standard device used by all politicians, but then exclusively a tool for the Prime Minister to create a few minutes of television footage or a radio sound-bite on the subject he wanted to emphasise that day, without the burden of having to answer any questions. In my first three years in Canberra, Fraser did not give a single full-scale press conference where he submitted to questions on subjects of the journalists' choosing. Even worse than the door-stop was the T-fac, the television-only opportunity, where Barnett allowed the cameras in to film the Prime Minister's response to what he determined was the subject of the day. These T-facs were resented by print journalists, who had no comparable way of getting access, but in the end it was the television reporters themselves who killed them. The likes of Laurie Oakes, Peter Harvey, Channel 7's Laurie Wilson and the ABC's Ken Begg were experienced journalists who wanted to report—and give commentary—to air, not just provide narratives to images of the Prime Minister's choosing. The practice ended with the Fraser government.

I was finding the political process increasingly fascinating. I was well-placed to observe the feints and the ethics of politics as well as the behaviour of the players themselves. It was instructive to observe their fear and anxiety. Men who had been barristers or businessmen, at the top of their game, men who had run organisations or been figures of substance in their communities were very different people when they got to Canberra and had to calculate their standing in an entirely different kind of hierarchy. The skills needed to survive, let alone advance, were not the same as those they had used to succeed in the past, and many of them were palpably lost and diminished by their continual angst about their political prospects. Maybe at weekends they were still top dog at home in the paterfamilias role, but in Canberra a surprising number of them became supine, like schoolboys, needing to please, always looking-out for how they were doing. The anxiety became palpable when a ministerial reshuffle was imminent. Then it was ministers calling journalists. 'Have you heard anything?' they'd plead.

I stayed on the perimeter, observing and judging, writing about it as best I could. I never became a player. But that did not mean I escaped the ire of these men (there were very few women politicians then) who had so much skin in the game. Paul Keating once left an angry three-page handwritten letter on my desk. Keating, who was the shadow spokesman on Minerals and Energy, was a frequent visitor to our office as we were the only paper that covered these issues, but he was also a big factional player and he was annoyed at me for a political piece. Whether it was because I got it wrong or—perhaps more damagingly—got it right, I can no longer remember. But you were never left wondering what he thought about your journalism. It was the same with Malcolm Fraser.

The phone had rung at home early one morning. The Prime Minister was on the line.

'Your story is wrong,' he said.

That day the paper had splashed with my exclusive budget leak. I did not have the entire budget document as Laurie Oakes did one year, but it was a respectable-enough scoop. A cabinet minister had given it to me. Even this long after the event, I do not feel I can name the source and thus reveal the motive for the leak and hence my confidence that it was indeed from the budget due to be delivered in a few days' time. Now here was Malcolm Fraser

However when Walsh rang a short time later, Barnett told him that if another person from the *Financial Review* were to apply, the decision might be reconsidered. If the *Financial Review* was able 'to squeeze a story out of the paper, we can squeeze Summers off the plane', Barnett said. I had been outraged a few days earlier to discover that Fraser had given Short an exclusive one-on-one interview. The convention was that such interviews only be given to political correspondents. I persuaded Walsh that in my opinion this was a clear example of Short, with the active collaboration of the government, trying to undermine my position. Walsh did not publish the interview.

I heard later from people in the Sydney office who overheard the phone call, that Walsh called Barnett a 'grey little scumbag' and a 'cringing toady'. Max Walsh was from the Paul Keating school of invective; indeed as two boys who had both grown up Catholic and made it out of working-class suburbs of Sydney to the top of their respective professions, the two had a lot in common. They were now also good friends. In May 2007, Walsh hosted a large gathering of former colleagues and other friends at his home in Sydney's Mosman to celebrate his 70th birthday. It was similar in its range of attendees, its utter informality and copious amounts of alcohol consumed to the annual parties Walsh had hosted each year, starting in the late 1970s and lasting for around seven years, to celebrate his deputy Fred Brenchley's getting the all-clear on cancer. At one of these parties Elisabeth Wynhausen and I had decided we needed to cool down and had discarded all of our clothes and jumped into the pool on the front lawn. I'd been mortified to recall the next day how I had insouciantly handed my watch and earrings to Jennie Suich, the wife of my boss Max, for safekeeping. Fortunately Jennie was as unflappable as she was unshockable. In 2007 we were all a lot older and this party was free of such incidents, but it was memorable for an intervention by Paul Keating who decided the party was a little too informal and that someone needed to say something about the man whose birthday we were celebrating. There is no record of that speech but those of us who were present remember that it was a fervent tribute from Australia's former Treasurer to the man he acknowledged as having taught him more about economics than any other person. Keating not only has a way with words, he always has something to say, and he used both gifts that afternoon to sketch for an avid audience a comprehensive portrait of Walsh and his contribution to journalism, to politics and, ultimately, to the betterment of Australia.

⇒●⇐

On 25 January, the morning after Walsh's call to Barnett, the paper ran a front-page story, 'PM Bans *Financial Review* journalist' under the byline of Maximilian Walsh, managing editor. The paper would not tolerate the government managing news or dictating who were acceptable journalists, Walsh wrote. He announced that I would cover the trip anyway—flying commercial. Walsh then went on the ABC's *AM* radio program that morning and accused the Prime Minister of sex discrimination and news management. Now we really were at war.

My phone rang like crazy all day. Airlines offered me free travel, every media outlet in the country wanted an interview. I was trying to write a 'Canberra Observed', to book my tickets for a trip that had originally been just to Washington and London but had now, Fraser had just announced, been extended to Paris and Bonn. I also had the problem that in his article Walsh had referred to me as Dr Anne Summers. I had been intending to keep secret that a few months earlier, I had been formally awarded a PhD by the University of Sydney. Not only was a post-graduate qualification super-fluous in journalism but I was already seen as enough of a blow-in without the added burden of a title. I knew I'd pay for it—and I did. I finally got a nickname. For the rest of my time in the Press Gallery, I'd be known as 'doc', 'the doctor' or, by a few people, as 'quack'. And the title has stuck to me ever since. Although I rarely use it in everyday transactions, people somehow seem to know to call me 'Dr'. It used to embarrass me; I did not like looking as if, to use that great Australian expression, I had 'tickets on myself', but I am now resigned to it and accept that it is just part of my name, even, my 'brand'.

Before this already eventful day was over, John Short had resigned from the *Financial Review* to take a position as adviser to Michael MacKellar, who was Minister for Immigration and Ethnic Affairs. I was appointed Bureau Chief, effective immediately, so there would be no ambiguity about the fact I was the sole representative of the paper when I followed Fraser round the world. Just before I flew out, on 27 January, on a Pan Am flight whose other passengers included Rupert Murdoch, the US Ambassador to Australia and a Who's Who of the Australian film industry, I decided with Walsh's concurrence that I would also try to visit Moscow. A week earlier, US President Jimmy Carter had announced that his country would boycott the Moscow Olympic Games to be held in July that year unless Russia withdrew its troops from Afghanistan. I was travelling solo so I could determine my itinerary. It would be easy enough to get to Moscow from Bonn. There were just two problems. I had not had time to apply for a visa for the Soviet Union before I'd left, and I had a very strong suspicion that I was pregnant.

The visa I could deal with once I got to London. The other problem was not so simple. I had been using contraceptives but my period was late and I had sore breasts, so I had to take seriously that I might be pregnant. I contacted Control, the feminist abortion referral service, and asked about a menstrual extraction. This procedure, I'd heard, could sort me out without even needing a pregnancy test. They advised against it: an early extraction could often miss a fertilised egg and thus be a waste of time, they'd said. They suggested instead a herbal remedy three times a day, for three days. It sounded like what we once disparagingly referred to as an 'old wives tale', but they assured me that it had 'worked' with other women, which meant that it had brought on either a period or a miscarriage. It did not work with me, but I had to put this possible pregnancy out of my mind while I set out to chase Australia's Prime Minister around the world.

In London, I savoured the luxury of Claridge's Hotel. On my first night there, after I'd been to the Soviet Embassy to apply for a visa and before Fraser and the travelling party arrived, I had rung down to ask about room service. There was no menu in the room so I did not know how to order. I tired of waiting for someone to bring me the menu so I stepped into the bath I'd started to run as soon as I'd got to my room. No sooner had I slid into its deep steaming water than the door opened and a butler appeared. He had not knocked and he appeared not to notice that I was naked; he merely asked what Madam would like to eat. This was the service aristocratic England was accustomed to apparently. As was the fact that when I went to check-out, Claridge's told me they did not accept credit cards. 'Perfectly all right, Madam,' I was assured. 'We will send you the account.' And, a few weeks later, they did. More disconcerting was the fact that while

I was out covering Fraser the next day, someone had clearly been through my things. I doubted an English butler would have any interest in finding where I had hidden my diary and, just to let me know, left it out on the desk.

The trip was dominated by talk of war. An unsourced story had appeared on the ABC and in the Sunday papers stating that President Carter was prepared to use tactical nuclear weapons against the Soviet Union if it invaded Iran. Fraser took advantage of this story to change his travel plans to return to Washington to report personally to Jimmy Carter on the outcome of his talks with Margaret Thatcher, France's Giscard d'Estaing and Helmut Schmidt. The German Chancellor had suggested he do this, Fraser told a believing Australian press party. In fact, Fraser said, Schmidt had even rung President Carter to ensure that the Australian Prime Minister would be able to secure a meeting. You had to give Fraser full marks for knowing how to extract maximum political advantage out of a situation. In Paris, I had gone to the Soviet Embassy in yet another attempt to get a visa for Moscow but now, I informed Max Walsh, I thought I'd better follow them all to Washington. He agreed.

At each stop on the visit, I managed to arrive first and be there on the tarmac—you could do that in those days—to greet the official party. In Paris, the travelling press ignored Fraser and all gathered around me for an update on my status as an outcast. This infuriated Barnett and he realised there was only one way to kill this story: he informed me that a seat had been found for me on the VIP to Washington. I rang Max to tell him.

'That's a shame, doctor,' he said. 'We'd booked you on the Concorde.'

After Washington, I travelled as far as Honolulu with the official party. We went to Pearl Harbor and watched Fraser drop his large frame into the narrow opening of an American submarine. I was going to be travelling on my own again as I'd had to give up my seat on the VIP to an Australian Defence official. But I did not mind. I was anxious to get home as soon as possible and deal with what I was now certain was a pregnancy. I felt I had no choice but to have an abortion and I just wanted to get it over with. As I was leaving earlier than the others, I offered to carry back the canister of film of Fraser at Pearl Harbor shot by a pool TV cameraman and hand it over to the waiting network courier when I landed in Sydney. My plane did not leave until midnight so after packing, I dropped the briefing book into the rubbish bin in my room and went down to the hotel bar for a farewell drink with the other journalists. Media were supplied with these briefing books for every trip; they were usually substantial documents that contained information ranging from weather and clothing recommendations to low-classified political briefs about the countries to be visited, their key people and various other pieces of background that might be useful for fleshing out our stories. As was my practice when I checked out of a hotel, I left the door open.

I was enjoying my goodbye drinks when I realised that a tense and angry David Barnett was standing by our table.

'Can I speak with you,' he said.

'Of course, David,' I said, not moving.

'In private,' he said.

I followed him into the hotel lobby where he turned and confronted me: 'Why did you leave your door open?'

'If you mean my hotel room, I left it open because I had checked out,' I said. 'I always leave my door open to show that I have gone.'

'That wasn't the only reason, was it?'

I stared at him.

'You had left something there, hadn't you?' He was getting edgy. 'Who was it for? Who was coming to get it?'

I realised he must be referring to the briefing book.

'Yes, David,' I said, still thinking this was a joke. 'I left it there for the Russians. They are dying to know what we think about the British . . .'

Then it struck me.

'Hang on! How the hell did you know that I had left anything in my room? What were you doing in my room?'

'It wasn't me,' he said.

I got it out of him: apparently it was standard practice for ASIO to 'sweep' all hotel rooms after delegation members checked out, and this applied to the media as well. The ASIO operative had reported to Barnett that I had left the book behind.

'Didn't you know it was classified?' David said.

'Didn't you know it was heavy?' I countered, 'and that I am carrying footage of your boss back to Australia so his adoring public can see him on television. I didn't have room to carry the stupid briefing book as well.'

'It's not the first time, is it?'

I looked at him blankly.

'It's not the first time you have talked to the Russians. You visited them in London and also in Paris. Why?'

I was stunned. I remembered those efforts to get a visa for Moscow, how uncooperative the consulates in both cities had been and what an infuriating waste of time it had been.

I lost it.

'David, you have caught me red-handed,' I said. 'Yes, I did try to sell them the briefing book and guess what, they weren't interested. So I thought, okay I'll just give it to them, so I left it in a hotel room in Honolulu where I fully expect a surfboard riding Soviet agent has by now collected it and teams of cipher agents are going through it as we speak, trying to understand what the fuck Malcolm Fraser thought he was doing over Afghanistan.'

Barnett was grinning sheepishly. He fluttered his hands in a deprecating gesture.

'I had to check,' he said. 'See it from my point of view.'

I certainly wasn't going to do that. He was the person who had tried to set me up so I would lose my job. He had not calculated on Max Walsh standing up to Fraser, and he had seriously underestimated how much of a fighter I can be. But in a funny way he had done me a favour. I was now Bureau Chief of Australia's financial daily newspaper. From now on, the Prime Minister's office had to deal with me. From now on, I would always have a seat on the Prime Minister's plane, and a place at press briefings. I would get my own regular one-on-ones with Malcolm Fraser; cabinet ministers would see me after meetings and share bits and pieces of information; I would start to get my share of the big leaks (something I felt very ambivalent about but it meant I was accepted into the main game); and, perhaps most important of all, everyone now knew my name. I no longer had to explain who I was when I called a bureaucrat or business leader for the first time. They knew who I was and they took me seriously. I would move into the spacious company house in Forrest and, for the first time in my life, enjoy an ensuite bathroom and a walk-in robe, as well as an inground swimming pool and several rooms for entertaining which, I decided, was something I should start doing. I had been in Canberra a year, and my career as a political reporter and commentator was about to really take off.

In 2011, I obtained my ASIO files. They revealed that Australia's domestic security agency had been keeping an eye on me since I was a student protester in Adelaide in 1966. My file contains extensive notes on my activities as a student protestor, as a woman's movement activist, and they even kept track of some of my journalistic endeavours while I was at the *National Times*.[4] There were notes on my attending press drinks at the Soviet Embassy with a man they—but not I—knew to be the chief KGB agent in Australia. They recorded in some detail how Sir Geoffrey Yeend, the Secretary of the Department of the Prime Minister and Cabinet, expedited my getting a high-level security clearance so I could be appointed to run the Office of the Status of Women in late-1983. But there was absolutely no record of ASIO watching me in Paris, in London or in Honolulu. If it was indeed Australia's domestic intelligence service ASIO—rather than ASIS Australia's overseas intelligence service—working overseas in the way Barnett described, it had evidently not thought any of this worth noting in my file. Or maybe it wasn't a security exercise at all. Perhaps it was just, pure and simple, political revenge.

CHAPTER FOUR

FOREIGN CORRESPONDENCE

———◦◦◦———

While I was in Canberra mostly my journalism was focused on writing about Australian politics, but I was given two tremendously challenging and rewarding overseas assignments, one to southern Africa, the other to Pakistan, as a result of Max Walsh's conviction that his leading journalists should be encouraged to test themselves in different environments. It was an innovative approach shared by few other editors. Walsh was willing to take risks, and to spend money on his reporters. If it paid off, he and his paper had yet another laurel to burnish an already sterling reputation. If not, well better luck next time. I had only been in Canberra a few months when Walsh suggested I travel round southern Africa in the weeks preceding the Commonwealth Heads of Government (CHOGM) meeting to be held in Lusaka, Zambia in early August 1979. I would of course go to CHOGM as a member of the Press Gallery covering the Prime Minister but if I went a few weeks early, he said, I could report on South Africa's brutal apartheid system. I could also visit a few countries in the region, perhaps Namibia and Mozambique, from where the Portuguese had fled just four years before, as well as Rhodesia, which was still holding out against ceding political power to its black majority. Walsh told me to put together a possible itinerary. I could scarcely believe my good fortune: I was going to spend a month in southern

Africa. I sought out anyone I could find with southern African connections. I got myself a second passport, knowing that no African country would accept one that had been stamped by South Africa and, inoculations organised, and excitement and wariness competing inside my fevered brain, I flew into Johannesburg for my first outing as a foreign correspondent.

The future of Rhodesia was going to dominate the CHOGM meeting, which was the first to be held in Africa, and there were threats from most of the black countries to sever diplomatic relations with Britain if she recognised the new puppet regime in Rhodesia (Zimbabwe today), as the country was then being called. This would be tantamount to a breakup of the commonwealth, so there was a lot riding on this meeting and Australia would have a central role. Rhodesia was a former British colony of about 275,000 white people and a black population of just under five million that, along with South Africa and Namibia, was the last standout in southern Africa against majority black rule. In 1965 Rhodesia's Prime Minister Ian Smith had unilaterally declared independence from Britain in order to protect white rule, an action that led to the country being isolated internationally. Rhodesia was getting strong military support from South Africa, and had installed a puppet government headed by a black bishop, Abel Muzorewa, but under a constitution that ensured all political and military power was retained in the hands of the whites. No other country apart from South Africa recognised this regime but the newly elected Prime Minister of Britain, Margaret Thatcher, was making noises she might follow suit. Britain feared that Russia or Cuba might intervene, as they had in Angola. With Thatcher referring to the putative leaders of a majority-rule government in Rhodesia as 'terrorists', negotiations were not going to be easy. Malcolm Fraser, Australia's Prime Minister, was expected to play a key role in getting his ideological soul mate to agree to a solution that would end what all sides knew was an untenable, and increasingly violent, situation.

This was the overall context for my trip. Each of the countries I visited before ending up in Lusaka would embody important elements of the struggle for black majority rule that was now the political imperative in Africa. Most critical of these was, of course, South Africa. I had introductions to a Who's Who of the anti-apartheid movement. Relatives and political supporters in Australia had briefed and backgrounded me so that I understood not just the complexity of the issues, but also the dangers for people on the ground of even talking to me. I was counselled to never write names in diaries or notebooks, nor confide in anyone whose credentials I was not certain of. I had to be very, very careful, I was warned.

It was less than two years since the 30-year-old Black Consciousness leader Steve Biko had been murdered while in police custody, and only three years since the Soweto Uprising when up to 10,000 school children in Soweto, the poverty-stricken black township adjoining Johannesburg, had taken to the streets to protest against the directive that the Afrikaans language be used to teach certain subjects in schools. The police had fired on the children, killing around 23 on the first day and leading to riots that lasted for days and ultimately led to the death of as many as 700 with a further 1000 injured. The world had been shocked by the press images of the murdered children. In response to the international outrage, the South African government had announced a series of reforms. 'Petty apartheid', the laws requiring the colour-segregation of public places, including transport, restaurants and beaches, were to be relaxed. But no one was fooled. The infamous 'pass laws' were retained; these required all non-whites to carry identification at all times or risk being arrested and detained. And people were still being arrested for no reason and held for months on end without trial.

I was going to see first-hand what apartheid was all about. I was very lucky to have as my guide Bruce Haigh, Second Secretary, Politics at the Australian Embassy in Pretoria, the national capital of South Africa. Haigh was an activist diplomat who made it his business to be close to the regime's opponents, and took considerable personal risks in doing so. He had befriended Steve Biko and other activists. Just eighteen months before I met him, Haigh had helped newspaper editor Donald Woods to escape from South Africa. (Richard Attenborough later portrayed this courageous act in his film *Cry Freedom*.) After the Biko murder, Woods had been placed under a five year 'ban', whereby he was stripped of the editorship of the *Daily Dispatch* newspaper and prevented from travelling, writing, speaking in public or even from working. Haigh introduced me to a number of activists. He also took it on himself to show me what South Africa was really like.

We went to Bophuthatswana, one of the *bantustans* or so-called 'home-lands' that had been granted to African people by the South African government in 1977 under their 'separate but equal' policy. It was no coin-cidence, Haigh demonstrated to me, that the lands on which white people were allowed to settle were rich, fertile, contiguous and often coastal areas, whereas the black lands were without exception land-locked and barren pockets that seemed to have been picked for their aridity. This place was home to more than one million people, yet only 10 per cent of its 40,000 square kilometres was arable. It had mineral resources but at the time of my visit, the benefits from these had yet to be shared with the population.

We went to a primary school where hundreds of enthusiastic students crowded into tin sheds that served as class rooms and where the only learning equipment was the kind of rudimentary slate boards and chalk that would have been considered outmoded when I was a child. The kids learned to tell the time from a clock made from cardboard. The Australian government provided aid to this school, and when I was introduced as Australian, the kids crowded around, screaming their gratitude. It was a sickening experi-ence, and the image of those laughing children in their squalid dustbowl of a school was still firmly in my memory when, late one afternoon, I inter-viewed Dr Piet Koornhof, the Minister for Cooperation and Development, at his home. This man was the enforcer of apartheid. He was responsible for the forcible removal of thousands of black people from residential areas that had been declared to be 'white' to places such as Bophuthatswana where they were condemned to lives of inactivity and poverty.

'Think of the homelands as being like the Greek islands,' he said to me. 'But whereas the Greek islands are separated by water, in South Africa, the homelands are separated by land.'

I looked at him in disbelief.

'But how do account for the disparities between white and black lands?' I asked him. 'Why is it that the white lands are good for agriculture and grazing but the black lands are arid?'

Koornhof was angry at the question. He had apparently assumed, given the name of my newspaper, that I would at least be obsequious, even if I did not agree with his country's policies. He had recently got into trouble for telling the National Press Club in Washington that 'apartheid is dead'.

He'd been forced to back down after the outcry and, just the evening before our interview, he had made a statement: 'the caricature of apartheid is dead.' Now, he was saying to me 'off-the-record' that he was 'very sad' about Australia's 'harsher and harsher' attitudes towards South Africa. He reminisced about the days when Australia and South Africa had played sport against one another and was clearly disappointed that I did not share his nostalgia.

Piet Koornhof was, of course, a member of the ruling National Party and prior to entering Parliament he had been national secretary of the Broederbond, the secret, all-male, Calvinist organisation that had essentially created apartheid. From 1948, every single Prime Minister and President of South Africa was a member of the Broederbond. This ended only in 1994, when the first free elections led to the election of Nelson Mandela as South Africa's first black African President.

Koornhof had worked for the notorious Hendrik Veorwoerd, known as the architect of apartheid, who was Prime Minister of South Africa from 1958 until his assassination on the floor of the Parliament in 1966. But Koornhof had also been a Rhodes Scholar, and at Oxford he had written a doctoral dissertation on the 'inevitable urbanization' of black people in South Africa. I learned later that in 1986 he was 'punished' by being appointed South African Ambassador to the United States, after telling the Prime Minister P.W. Botha that peace would never come to South Africa until Nelson Mandela was released. Later still, in 1993, Dr Koornhof scandalised his former colleagues by leaving his wife (and, I presume, the comfortable house where I interviewed him) for a young coloured woman with whom he went on to have five children. The following year, he testified before the Truth and Reconciliation Commission, and was one of the few former ministers of the apartheid regime to acknowledge and take responsibility for the atrocities that had occurred during those years.

That afternoon in July 1979, I was amazed at what this man said and seemed to believe. But I was even more astonished by the fact that his house was on a main road and the two of us, sitting in comfort in well-stuffed armchairs, were clearly visible from the street. There was no security. It would have been so easy to lob a bomb through that window, I thought. That morning, Bruce Haigh had taken me to Soweto, the black township where more than one million people lived in conditions of extraordinary squalor and deprivation. But, as I was to learn, the activists in South Africa were not guerilla fighters as were, for instance, Robert Mugabe's Zimbabwe African National Union (ZANU) Party, who from their base in neighbouring Mozambique were waging a war of liberation to regain Rhodesia. Together with Joshua Nkomo's Zimbabwe African People's Union (ZAPU), based in Zambia, they formed the Patriotic Front and were intent on ending white rule in Zimbabwe. In South Africa, there was no armed struggle and the black people were extraordinarily passive, it seemed to me. The whole system depended on their compliance, the thousands of maids and other domestic staff whose live-in labour made possible the comfortable lives enjoyed by Dr Koornhof and the rest of the white population. The English population also benefited, as did other white non-Afrikaaners, such as South Africa's many Jews (who had themselves mostly fled there from persecution in pre-war Europe). In 1977, the 4.3 million whites amounted to just under 17 per cent of the population, yet even the poorest white person enjoyed luxury, and legal rights, simply not available to the black majority. I found it baffling that there was so little physical resistance but, of course, this was deterred by such measures as requiring blacks to have ten continuous years with one employer before they could obtain the notorious 'pass' that enabled them to live legally in South Africa, outside the *bantustans*. The system was utterly repressive and—so far, at least—it had mostly succeeded. Yet resentment simmered everywhere; hatred glowered in many eyes. South Africa's blacks appeared (to me anyway) abject and cowed, but they were not acquiescent. The Soweto uprising had been unprecedented, but it had happened. And it was children who had led the way. Perhaps it was a sign of things to come.

Most of the houses in Soweto were three-roomed very basic shelters, with no bathrooms, or electricity, which housed up to twenty people each. There were no gardens, hardly any trees, no street names or numbers but, incongruously, each house was fenced, as if it were sitting on a lush suburban plot. Street lighting came from arc lights set on high poles, giving the place the appearance of a prison, or a concentration camp. To my great surprise, there were a few houses that, while not being mansions, were large and obviously occupied by well-off people. Haigh pointed out Winnie Mandela's house, and another that belonged to Dr Nthato Motlana, a doctor and a prominent anti-apartheid activist I was due to meet the next day. Motlana had been charged, alongside Mandela and others, for taking part in the ANC's 1952 Campaign of Defiance, whereby people defied the race laws and sat on benches reserved for another colour, or entered libraries that were for whites only. Motlana had received a suspended sentence. Following the Soweto uprising he became one of the Committee of Ten, local citizens who united to provide leadership to the community in the wake of the massacre. He was detained and held without trial for five months.

Mostly, though, Soweto was a desolate place. There was street after street of these dwellings—it was hard to call them houses—stretching as far as the eye could see. There were no proper shops, just one primitive clinic and at the school we visited, the cement floors were cracked and kids were crammed three to a desk. Wrecked cars littered the streets. This was where people struggled to live and to give a chance to their kids, whose perfectly laundered and starched white shirts were a seeming miracle in this dustbowl, where women garbed in bright-coloured dresses and headgear cooked and cleaned and shopped and gossiped as women do everywhere. It was as if they had no idea that just up the road were oases of plenitude, where houses were large and built of brick, where gardens bloomed with colour and lush greenery. But of course they did. These were the women who were the maids who served the white children, who did all the work while the women of the house played tennis or lunched or lounged about, secure in the knowledge that their affairs were in good black hands.

It was while Haigh was showing me Soweto in all its confronting squalor that the security police stopped us. White people were forbidden to visit the townships. They demanded to know what we were doing there.

'I am an Australian diplomat,' Haigh said, offering them his official passport. 'We allow your diplomats in Australia to travel wherever they wish in our country, so I am entitled to do the same here.'

I was sitting beside him in the front of the four-wheeled drive vehicle. I had been scribbling in my notebook and had not had time to conceal it when we were stopped. It was absolutely, totally forbidden for journalists to visit Soweto. We looked at each other.

'Stay calm,' he said to me.

The police had taken Haigh's passport and were radioing back to base. He'd told them I was a newly arrived member of the embassy staff who did not yet have a passport or ID. There was a lot of conferring and head-shaking and foot-shuffling, but eventually they came back to our vehicle and allowed us to go on our way.

For the next two days, I met with dozens of people, most of them anti-apartheid activists of one kind or another. I met lawyers, doctors, journalists, students; some of them famous like Helen Suzman, the parliamentarian who for many years was the only MP who opposed apartheid and who regularly visited Mandela in prison, or John Kane-Berman, a well-known journalist with the *Financial Mail*; but most of them were anxious for our meetings not to be known to the state. I followed my instructions and made sure that my interview notes and the names of the people I'd spoken to were in separate notebooks. I hoped no one would be able to crack my private code.

I was surprised at the inefficiency of South Africa. For all that Johannesburg looked like a modern city, with its skyscrapers and highways, it functioned liked the cumbersome over-bureaucratised state that it was. Television had only just been introduced that year, and was strictly controlled by the state. There was no chance of images of apartheid being beamed out of the country. Repression, more than mining, was the country's main industry and it dominated everything. It was impossible to get anything done on the phone. Even the Anglo-American Corporation, the mining giant, insisted I made my interview requests in writing. Not easy when I was only there for two days and there was no faxing, let alone email. Everything had to be done by telex, which meant I had to get the operator at the hotel to help me. The Information Department, which was meant to arrange foreign journalists' access to politicians, treated me with utter suspicion. I could not interview Dr Koornhof, I was told, because he was out of the country. I knew that was a lie because he'd been quoted at a local event in that morning's newspaper so I pushed back, and miraculously Koornhof reappeared in the country, ready to meet with me. Everyone seemed nervy and uptight. There were uniforms everywhere, including in the bureaucracy, where most positions appeared to require epaulettes and shiny brass buttons.

Mozambique opened my eyes to the reality of a country recently 'liberated' from colonial rule. The Polana Hotel where I stayed was once grand. It had been, I was told, *the* place for holidaying white South Africans, with its large airy rooms, its gardens flowing down to a beach where the Indian Ocean lapped at the shores. But four years of neglect, partly no doubt as a result of it now being state owned, had changed all that. The water in the taps in my room ran brown and, I'd been warned, under no circumstances was I to drink it. In the dining room, there were few choices on the menu, although what food there was was excellent and the waiters struggled to maintain appearances. They did silver service and they still wore livery, although their sandshoes were acknowledgement that standards were not what they'd once been. A large man wheeled around a trolley with covered dishes containing dessert but each one, when opened, revealed just humble quivering jellies and pieces of swiss roll. None of the cream-laden delicacies that would once have tempted diners. The shelves of the local supermarket were almost entirely empty. There was very little food in the country, I was told by X, the representative from the Revolutionary Front for the Independence of East Timor (Fretilin), which had established an embassy in Maputo and was training young men for its revolution. He took me on a tour of the city and its environs, showing me the chaos that had descended on the country since 1975.

Mozambique had been a Portuguese colony since around 1500, although efforts to develop the country were sporadic and, compared with some of their other colonial endeavours, half-hearted. But in the mid-1960s as part of the continuing worldwide uprising against colonialism, FRELIMO, a Marxist party, had led a guerilla war of independence. The war succeeded, somewhat abruptly, when democracy returned to Portugal and in June 1975, Mozambique acquired its independence. One of the first laws of the new government was to require all Portuguese to leave the country immediately, allowed to take just 20 kilograms of luggage with them. Now a civil war was raging. The national front—funded and largely organised by the South African and Rhodesian governments—was trying to bring down the government of Samora Machel.[1] My most striking memory of Maputo was the number of road accidents. Every few hundred metres we encountered yet another car wreck, some of them very serious with bodies strewn all over the road. The South Africans are sending cars in, said my Fretilin guide, but very few people know how to drive. The Portuguese had kept that skill to themselves apparently.

My reason for going to Mozambique had been to try to interview Robert Mugabe. In 1974, after spending eleven years in a Rhodesian prison, he and compatriot Edgar Tekere had made Maputo their base for the revolutionary war ZANU was waging against the regime of Ian Smith. Before the interview could be scheduled, I had to be 'screened', I was informed by the ZANU press office. This had involved meeting in a bar with several of Mugabe's men, all of whom wore the full Che Guevara guerilla garb: khaki pants, leather vests, berets, sunglasses, guns. Justin Nyoka, who headed the ZANU Public Information department, would decide if I could get to interview Comrade Mugabe. It seemed to me that the meeting was more a flirtation than a screening but I remained professional and explained how my newspaper would be a wonderful vehicle for their leader to get his views on how independence should be won for Zimbabwe to an Australian audience. There was only miniscule diplomatic representation in Mozambique, so the Australian government had no direct contact with Mugabe and his men. Australia's Prime Minister, Malcolm Fraser and his Foreign Minister, Andrew Peacock, would be flying into Lusaka in just a few days, I explained. My interview offered the perfect way to get the ZANU point of view in front of CHOGM. Nyoka was noncommittal. I explained that I would be flying to Tanzania, en route to Lusaka, the day after tomorrow; I needed the interview before then.

A few days later I was at the airport, angry and disappointed. I had not got the interview. I had waited. I had called Justin Nyoka as often as Maputo's failing telephone system would allow, but I could not get a commitment. Instead, he gave me Edgar Tekere, who did not fit my preconceptions of what a guerilla should be like. He was a tall, softly spoken man, the son of an Anglican priest, who laughed a lot during our interview and he began each answer with a rhetorical question. But he was, I reminded myself, committed to armed struggle, he had spent years in prison and he had recently succeeded Mugabe as Secretary-General of ZANU, which organisation he—and not Mugabe—had co-founded. Getting to talk to him was something, I suppose, and the paper had run my lengthy Q&A with him. When I re-read the interview while writing this, I was surprised at how significant it really was. Tekere disclosed details of ZANU's military position in Zimbabwe, its political position on a number of key issues to be addressed in Lusaka and was clearly sending messages to British and other Commonwealth diplomats. Perhaps most important of all, he told me that while ZANU enjoyed 'the support of socialist countries to varying degrees', it would not be allowing Cuban troops to join the fight. It was the fear that Cuba, acting as proxy for the Soviet Union, might send in troops that was one factor driving Malcolm Fraser's efforts to secure a political solution in Zimbabwe.

But no one had heard of Edgar Tekere and I was worried that I had failed in my first assignment as a foreign correspondent. I had not been able to snare the top guy. I had yet to learn that securing an interview with a foreign political leader takes time and patience and that success had very long odds. Now I was heading to Lusaka where I would join my colleagues in the Canberra Press Gallery who were flying in with Fraser. I'd attend the briefings, write about the CHOGM meeting, report on the expected stoush between Fraser and Thatcher; in other words, I'd be just another hack, doing what all the others were doing. I had dashed my chance of breaking out and getting my own special story, the big scoop of an interview with the world-famous Robert Mugabe. Oriana Fallaci had nothing to fear, I told myself bitterly. The bold Italian journalist Fallaci was my idol and, if we'd had such a term then, my role model. I admired her without reservation. Her *Interview with History* had been published just three years earlier. It was a collection of her most famous and audacious interviews, with the likes of Henry Kissinger, the Shah of Iran, Indira Gandhi and Golda Meir. Fallaci was not only able to sit down with such people; she gave them hell when she did. Her trademark was to berate, confront or otherwise embarrass her subjects. In 1972, she famously reported Kissinger describing himself as 'the cowboy who leads the wagon train by riding ahead alone on his horse'. Kissinger later said this was the most 'disastrous' media interview he had ever given. Just a month after I failed to interview Mugabe, in September 1979, Fallaci would again make headlines when during her interview with the Ayatollah Khomeini, she ripped off the chador she had been required to don in order to meet the Iranian leader and challenged him to confront her full face and her hair.

Still angry, I watched miserably from the Maputo departure lounge as a spanking-new plane, with a huge giraffe painted on its tail, took off. Wondering what was happening to my flight, I went over to the counter. It turned out that flights were not called at this tiny excuse for an airport. The plane I'd just seen speed down the runway was heading for Tanzania. Not only that, on board was Robert Mugabe and his team, on their way to Lusaka. Worse, there would not be another plane for days. And worse still, my luggage was on that plane.

The only way I would be able to get to Lusaka would be to return to South Africa and find a flight from there. I made my way to the train station where there was a dirty old local, with just one class of travel, that would stop frequently until it reached the border where I'd transfer to a South African train. Before I boarded I had to be inspected by customs, to ensure I was taking nothing illegally out of the country. That was a bit of joke, I thought to myself, it was not like there'd been anything to buy in Maputo. I had nothing except the clothes I was wearing, a sleeveless knee-length red dress, and my handbag. I did not have a jacket or even a cardigan, although I had had the wit to keep my typewriter and tape-recorder with me. Now the customs men were homing in on my bright yellow, and admittedly snazzy, Olivetti portable and my small tape-recorder. I was taking them out of the country illegally, they declared. Where was my export permit? It was useless to state that items such as these were not procurable anywhere in Mozambique because that, of course, was why they wanted them. Grimly, I handed over my tools of trade, demanded token pieces of paper as receipts in return and carrying only my bag slung over my shoulder, walked down the platform.

As the train chugged away from the station, I realised that I was alone in my compartment. The corridors were teeming with people looking for seats so once I'd beckoned that it was okay to join me, an astonished-looking crowd of school kids poured in. They made sure to keep a respectful distance between the white lady and their dark bodies. We did a lot of reassuring smiling at each other. As the train stopped at each station the crowd in my compartment changed, but what did not alter was the initial look of incomprehension and wariness on their faces when they saw me. 'Are you *sure* it's okay?' everyone seemed to be saying. They all knew that a few hundred kilometres further west, once we reached the South African border, what we were doing would be against the law. And they, not me, were the ones who would be punished. But we weren't there yet so I continued to share the relative luxury of my space.

It soon got dark and adults, almost all of them men, replaced the school kids as my travelling companions. Again, there was a lot of smiling as they sought to calm any nervousness I might have felt. I was still too angry and upset at myself for missing the plane, losing my luggage and my typewriter to have any concerns about anything else. We stopped for a while at a station where everyone seemed to get off, to stretch legs and to buy food. Cautiously, I stepped down onto the platform. I was nervous at being stranded here if the train suddenly took off but I savoured my luck at being able to see this tiny outpost. The place was noisy and dirty and full of laughter and the uncensored sounds of people simply living and dealing with each other. Back on the train, the men in my compartment started opening bags of sandwiches. I realised they must be on their way to work in the diamond mines. These men were the backbone of the South African economy, imported labour, paid a pittance, forced to live for months on end in harsh barracks-style accommodation, sentenced to instant death if they were caught stealing even the smallest stone. One of them noticed my hungry glances. After buying the train ticket, I had no money left. A man shyly offered half his sandwich; he took measures to demonstrate to me that his black skin had not touched the bread, that it was okay for me to accept his offering. I gratefully devoured the food but I felt overcome by shame that there was this hierarchy based on race and that, for no reason at all, my skin colour placed me near its top.

The train stopped. I realised from watching the miners that we had to disembark. With gestures, they made me understand I had to have my passport stamped and then walk a short distance to Komatipoort, the South African border town, where another newer and sleeker train waited. Bright klieg-like lights revealed the platform to be so clean it could have satisfied hospital standards, but I felt as if I was walking onto a World War II movie set. Every few metres stood a uniformed guard, his peaked cap resembling those worn (at least in the movies) by Nazis, and beside each guard a large and savage Alsatian dog. The dogs surged and strained at their leashes and

I cowed as I passed them. But I soon understood that they were not barking at me. It was the men beside me, those generous souls who had shared their sandwiches, who were the target of the dogs' fury. These men, too, shrank back, but other guards emerged behind us and forced the men to march past the dogs and ordered them to form a line in front of a small table where another guard sat, papers spread out in front of him. I needed to go to the toilet and found myself forced to use the one marked 'Blankes Dames'. Then I joined the line, feeling really frightened for the first time since I had arrived in southern Africa.

Suddenly, two guards were at my side. They were pulling me by the arm and dragging me out of the queue. It was quickly apparent that I had made a dreadful mistake in joining the black line. The guards were friendly enough, but insistent. I lowered my eyes in embarrassment as I was escorted past the miners to the very front of the line. I was pushed ahead of an Indian woman and her five children who, until my arrival, had been first in the queue. When I squatted down to rest the papers on my leg while I filled them out, a chair was brought for me. I was treated with courtesy despite the fact that I looked like a ruffian; I had not been able to change my clothes for a couple of days. I remembered that I had a bundle of Fretilin leaflets in my handbag. All communist organisations were proscribed in South Africa; it was a crime to even possess, let alone distribute, their publications. But my skin colour saved me, just as my sex had saved me in Soweto. It simply did not occur to these guards that this white woman would be smuggling subversive literature, just as it did not cross the minds of the police in Soweto that I was anything other than a secretary at the embassy. The man at the little table looked at my passport, checked the visa that had been awarded me by the embassy in Canberra, and waved me through. I was taken to the other train and guided towards a compartment. Three women were already seated there, a mother and two daughters, all Afrikaans, plump and smug. They wrinkled their noses in disgust. I probably did smell by now. As we sped towards Johannesburg I shrank into my corner, unable to overlook the difference between the two train trips. The government might be touting the end of petty apartheid but if it was happening at all, it was only in the big cities, in front of the international gaze. Move to rural South Africa and, as I had just observed, nothing had changed.

Nassau in 1985 appointed him, by then no longer Prime Minister, a member of the Eminent Persons Group that was charged with encouraging political dialogue around the world to end apartheid. The Lusaka meeting had been full of drama. Joseph Nkomo, leader of ZAPU, which with Mugabe's ZANU formed the Patriotic Front alliance fighting for majority rule in Zimbabwe, had very undiplomatically taken a seat inside the conference room and was thrown out. The ZANU guerillas had put down their arms to work the diplomatic route and been far more effective. But the biggest drama of all was how Fraser dealt with Margaret Thatcher. It had taken enormous effort to get Thatcher to agree to set aside her earlier support for the new puppet Zimbabwe government and to sign on for new, supervised free elections, but Fraser was worried that she might get cold feet at the last minute. She was under great pressure from the conservatives in her party who felt that any repudiation of their 'kith and kin' in Rhodesia was unconscionable.

So Fraser leaked the communiqué. He called us Australian journalists in and gave us the not-yet-finalised document. He justified this by pointing to the nine-hour time delay between Australia and Zambia; if the Aussies had had to wait for the official release, the British press who were in a much-closer time zone, would scoop our coverage. Thatcher was angry enough when she learned about this, from a note passed to her by her Foreign Secretary Lord Peter Carrington while she was trapped at a church service and unable to intervene. But she went into orbit when she turned up to a barbecue hosted by Fraser that Sunday afternoon to discover he had invited eight leading British journalists for a background briefing. The draft communiqué now a fait accompli—even before the other heads of government had signed-off on it—and Thatcher was locked in. Fraser had triumphed. And so had the black countries and the Patriotic Front. Fraser would attend the Independence celebrations in Zimbabwe the following April, and Australia was the first country to extend diplomatic recognition to the new democracy. We journalists never figured out how to account for Fraser's strong and enduring abhorrence of racism. It seemed so at odds with his conservative, even reactionary, views on so many other topics, yet it was a consistent theme of his government. There was no greater illustration of the man's complexities. In 1981 he prevented a plane carrying South African football players from re-fuelling in Australia. Having helped bring majority rule in Zimbabwe he set his sights on South Africa, and argued ardently for why apartheid had to end. And his anti-racism views were not confined to Africa. He controversially allowed large numbers of Vietnamese boat people into Australia; championed multiculturalism including establishing the Special Broadcasting Service (SBS) radio and television network; and enacted land rights legislation. When he died in 2015, Malcolm Fraser received heartfelt tributes from many Indigenous Australians.

On the final night of CHOGM, Michelle Grattan and I danced with the guerillas in a series of Lusaka nightspots. We drank cognac with Edgar Tekere, Richard Hove and Simba Makoni. Less than a year later, all three men would be ministers in Mugabe's government. They would all eventually fall out with their despotic leader and in 2008, Makoni, endorsed by Tekere, ran for President against Mugabe. On this night, however, in between dancing, the talk was all of revolution: how to manage the increasingly-fractious Patriotic Front, and what to do about the Voice of Free Africa, the Rhodesian propaganda service that was getting to some of Tekere's troops. Sitting there that night, talking and drinking, it was easy to forget that just a few hundred kilometres away across the border in Zimbabwe the war was still raging. A couple of weeks earlier, I had had my first experience of that war when I had flown from Bulawayo to Salisbury, the capital of what everyone on the crammed DC4 was still calling Rhodesia. As the plane had taken off, it had seemed to rise straight up and then it turned, violently.

'That's what's called a corkscrew takeoff,' said the young man sitting next to me. He was wearing an army uniform. As the plane pushed into the atmosphere, the flight attendant came crawling up the aisle on her stomach. She had a torch clenched between her teeth, a tiny notebook in her hand, taking drink orders. Since it was only a twenty-minute flight, I did not bother ordering anything, but I heard everyone around me ordering two, or even three, double Scotches. A blue light suddenly flashed outside the plane's window.

'It's a SAM,' said my companion, seeing that I was startled. 'The terrs are firing at us.'

I took 'terrs' to mean the terrorists, but I had to ask: 'What's a SAM?'

'Surface to air missile,' he offered. 'They'll fire at us when we land, too. They usually miss.'

So that's why everyone had ordered the stiff drinks, I thought to myself. I regretted I had not followed their example.

The flight attendant had not bothered with glasses but had walked the aisle with a basket full of miniature bottles the moment the plane flattened-out.

In the nightclub, Tekere's bodyguards waited at a discrete distance until the Secretary-General was ready to leave. They then organised for another shiny, new Mercedes-Benz vehicle to drive Michelle and me back to our hotel. I was a little shocked to see Red Cross signs on the car doors. Oh well, I thought, I guess they are all on the same side.

Once CHOGM was over I said goodbye to my press gallery colleagues who were returning to Canberra with the Prime Minister and headed back to Johannesburg. I was going home via New York, where I'd planned a few days holiday and I was on a Pan Am flight later that evening. When I checked-in, I was told that the seat I'd requested was available. Puzzled, I took the boarding pass. I had not requested a seat. Who would I be sitting next to, I wondered? He turned out to be a non-descript middle-aged man in a suit. He ignored me as I stepped over him to get to my window seat and seemed more interested in talking to his two companions, one of whom was seated across the aisle, the other in front of him. Why didn't they sit together? I wondered.

As soon as were airborne I took out my book. It was *The Super-Afrikaners. Inside the Afrikaner Broederbond*, an exposé by investigative journalists Ivor Wilkins and Hans Strydom of the secret Afrikaner all-male fraternity that supposedly ran South Africa. The book had created a big stir when it was published the previous year, not just because it had actually dared to expose the existence of this group that had never been previously publicly acknowledged but, even more sensationally, an Index listed 7500 names, reputed to be a near-complete list of all its members. I was running my finger down the list, to see if any of the government people I had interviewed were included, when my travelling companion said to me:

'I'm in there.'

He reached for the book and indicated a name: 'That's me.' He then reached into his pocket and pulled out a business card. It listed his name and his occupation: Mayor of Stellenbosch. Stellenbosch, I knew, was the spiritual and intellectual heartland of Afrikaner South Africa. It was a small city in the Western Cape province, about 50 kilometres from Cape Town, whose population was totally white and which prided itself on making no concessions to the English minority. It was where the Afrikaner University was located, the place where the next generation was trained to assume leadership of the country's political, military and religious institutions.

Just then the flight attendant arrived with the drinks trolley, and as I sipped my pre-dinner bloody mary, the man began to engage me.

'What were you doing in South Africa? Where did you go? Did you like our country?'

'I could not accept the country's apartheid laws,' I told him. I found the institutional oppression of the country's black majority abhorrent.

'But that is changing,' he assured me.

I disagreed. 'Maybe in Johannesburg the Whites Only signs were coming down,' I said, 'but once you got out into the country it was business as usual.'

By now our dinner had been served and we were both into our glasses of red wine.

'Let me buy you another drink,' said my companion.

He made sure my glass was never empty as he continued to question me: 'Who had I interviewed? What were their names? Did anyone criticise the government?' I smiled to myself. The poor man has obviously not been briefed on the capacity of Australians—especially of journalists—to hold their liquor. Eventually it was his voice that became slurred, and he was the one who first fell asleep.

When I awoke it was light outside, and we were only an hour or so from New York. I noticed that my companion was standing in the aisle, conferring with his friends. When he saw that I was awake, he introduced them, telling me they were diamond dealers going to New York on business. My companion sat down and his friend seated in front of him passed over two glasses of what looked like champagne and orange juice. I protested that it was a bit early in the day but the man insisted:

'It's my birthday,' he said. 'You must help me celebrate.'

As I gamely sipped, the questions resumed. 'Where are you staying in New York? We'd love to take you to dinner.' I was vague and instead turned the questions back on him: 'Where are *you* staying? What are you going to be doing?'

'We've got meetings on 45th Street,' the man across the aisle called over. 'You know, the diamond district.'

I knew enough about New York to know that the diamond district was on 47th Street. These guys aren't diamond dealers, I thought. I was shaken at the thought of how much trouble the South African government appeared to have taken to try to find out who I'd spoken to. Three men! All the way to New York!

We were soon on the ground and, I noticed with relief that once I had cleared customs, the men had disappeared. I headed for Seventh Avenue South in the Village, where I had the use of a friend's apartment. I was intending to complete at least a draft of the three articles I proposed to write on South Africa while everything was still fresh in my mind. They would follow-on from the pieces I had written on Mozambique, Namibia and Rhodesia while I had been on the road, as well as the daily articles I had filed from Lusaka. I got out my notebooks and as I arranged them in order, I remembered a conversation I'd had with the journalist John Kane-Bermann.

'Be careful with your notebooks,' he'd warned me when I'd spoken to him just before I got onto the plane for New York. 'They will have been watching you but they will want to know who you have spoken with.'

Of course, I reassured him. Privately, I thought he was being rather paranoid. Even for South Africa.

I was careful of course. There had been no need to hide the fact that I'd met with well-known anti-apartheid figures such as Helen Suzman, Ken Rashidi, Helen Joseph, Dr Nthato Motlana or the various government officials, but there were others who could get into trouble if it was known they were talking to a foreign journalist. One of these was Zwelakhe Sisulu, the son of Walter Sisulu who was still imprisoned on Robben Island with Nelson Mandela, and several other activists and journalists who had been particularly helpful. I had not used their names in my notebooks and I had not written down anywhere the code I'd used to help me identify them.

Before I could even start writing, I began to feel dizzy and nauseous and I had a splitting headache. I must be getting the flu, I thought. A tremendous weariness enveloped me and I found that I could not work, so I climbed into bed. I woke up three days later.

With just a day or two left of my Manhattan stay, I decided to go out. I went shopping, I went for a walk with Kate Jennings, a writer friend from Sydney who now lived in New York; and had a drink with Frank Hoffey, the brilliant defamation lawyer who had always found a way to help me get into print what I wanted to report when I was at the *National Times*. He had moved from Sydney to New York a few months earlier. Then it was time to leave and I went back to the apartment to pack. I then did something for which I have never forgiven myself. Instead of carrying them with me, I packed my notebooks and the drafts of my articles into one of my suitcases, and checked it through. I felt it was safe to do so as, I had been assured by South African Airways, which had written my ticket although the carrier was Pan Am, that it was a direct flight. In fact, the flight stopped in Los Angeles where we changed planes, and again in Auckland. On the morning of 18 August, I arrived back in Sydney. One of my two bags did not.

Luggage is never really lost, of course. But a week later, Pan Am wrote to tell me they had been unable to find my bag and requested further information so they could have their Central Tracing Office in New York take over the search. Then, just over two weeks after my return, Qantas got in touch to say my bag had been found—in Vienna. Nothing seemed to be missing. I examined the notebooks carefully. They were all there but I realised, heart lurching, that although I had not attached names to the actual interviews, I had compiled a list of people I'd intended to try to contact. The list was in another book but it would be easy enough to match it with my notes of the people I had spoken to. But who would do that, I reasoned? I had already left South Africa. I should not have let the notebooks out of my hands, but they were on a flight to Sydney. No one could possibly have seen them. Then I realised something. In New York, I had slipped some pamphlets about Stellenbosch given to me by the man who said he was the mayor into one of the notebooks. They weren't there. That's when I started asking questions. Qantas? Why would Qantas be able to find luggage from a Pan Am flight? How could luggage tagged for Sydney end up in Vienna? I rang John Kane-Berman who gave me the ghastly news. Three of the people I had interviewed, included Zwelakhe Sisulu, had been arrested. I felt sick.[2] I had put people's lives in danger. Although I had my notebooks back, I did not feel able to write my planned series of articles. Maybe exposing the evils of South Africa would be the best—perhaps the only—way to atone for my incompetence. But I was paralysed by remorse. I found myself totally unable to write anything.

And then on 25 September, three weeks after my bag was returned to me, I received a phone call at work from a young woman. She would not tell me her name, but she had some information for me.

'ASIO took your South African files,' she told me.

I was thunderstruck. Only a few people at Fairfax knew about the missing luggage. I had been far too embarrassed to make my blunder public, yet this stranger knew. She said she worked for ASIO on campus, keeping an eye on left-wing groups. She said that she had been 'disgusted' to hear from two of her ASIO colleagues that my files had been stolen. She did not think I was the sort of person who did not have the best interests of Australia at heart, which was how she rationalised spying on students. I gave her my home phone number and asked if she would ring me again if she could find out what had happened to my files. From the way she spoke, she did not seem to know that they had been returned to me. I did not know what to make of her call. I still don't. In the note for my file I wrote straight afterwards, I noted that Pan Am had told me they were perplexed at their inability to find the luggage and were equally mystified by how it had ultimately turned up. 'Was there any politically sensitive material in the files?' the managing director of Pam Am had asked me. He conceded that was the only explanation for the disappearance of the luggage in the first place, and for the preposterous explanation from Qantas that it had gone astray to Vienna.

On 5 October, I wrote a column for the *Financial Review* about this episode, disguising the gender of my caller, and speculating that if the information was true it meant that, contrary to the instructions of the Whitlam government, ASIO still maintained connections with the notorious South African Bureau of State Security, or BOSS as it was known. ASIO must have intercepted my bag in Sydney, rifled through my belongings and, I could scarcely bear to think about it, read my notebooks, at the request of BOSS. Yet, when I finally got access to my quite extensive ASIO file many years later, although it included a copy of this column, there was no commentary as to its accuracy.

The only possible motivation for stealing my luggage, and reading my notebooks and draft articles, was to accomplish what the men on the plane from Johannesburg had failed to discover: who I had spoken to and what they had told me. Melodramatic as it sounded, I could not escape concluding that a drug in the champagne I'd been given on the plane must have caused me to be so sick in New York. A further motive might have been merely to delay publication of my articles; the files were returned to me, after all. My articles would have less currency the longer it took me to write them. With any luck, they might have concluded, I would just give up and not write anything. In the meantime, they had rounded-up the people I'd talked to. The repressive state rolled on.

My article on South Africa was eventually published on 10 October, three months after I had first arrived in the country. It was a tough-enough piece. I dismissed the changes to apartheid as cosmetic and argued that the regime had not changed its basic purpose. 'The ultimate goal of apartheid,' I wrote, 'and one that is non-negotiable is to assign all blacks to a homeland and to oblige them to give up South African citizenship.' I compared the process with the expulsion of Chinese from Vietnam: 'The homelands residents are the boatpeople of South Africa.' But the piece had no context and thus not much currency. It was no longer part of the build-up to CHOGM, able to be seen in the light of the efforts to dismantle minority rule in Zimbabwe. It was just another isolated article about a country that was doing its best to stay out of the international spotlight while it continued on its evil mission to deny basic rights to its non-white citizens. What was so startling was the lengths the country had gone to in order to prevent my writing about it. The bitter lesson for me was how utterly inept I had been, and the consequences that had had for other people. I'd best stick to the small playpen of Canberra, I concluded bitterly.

———⟶⟵———

Yet, less than a year later, Max Walsh had sent me off again, this time to Pakistan. This assignment was also tied to a Prime Ministerial CHOGM trip. Fraser was travelling to New Delhi for a CHOGM regional meeting, and

Max had suggested I peel off at the end and try to interview President Zia ul–Haq, the general who had seized power two years earlier, deposing Prime Minister Zulfikar Ali Bhutto, who was later executed. Before I left Canberra, I had made a formal request through the Pakistani High Commission and once in New Delhi, while the rest of the press party took the day off to visit the Taj Mahal, I found myself being shunted between bureaucrats in the soulless offices of the Pakistani Embassy, trying to firm up the interview. Go to Islamabad and wait, I was advised, and that was how I came to be in Lahore, on my way to Islamabad, and discovering how very different Pakistan was from the laidback countries of most of southern Africa.

I discovered in less than an hour the truth of the saying of the time, that in Pakistan there are three sexes: men, women and Western women. I was trying to get my bearings in an overcrowded Lahore airport, picking my way through bunches of people who clung together in seeming trepidation, anxious perhaps about the looming adventure of flight. The next day, 11 September, was a major public holiday: 48 years since the death of Muhammad Ali Jinnah, the founder of Pakistan, and millions were on the move, visiting their families. It was almost impossible to move in the airport. I found myself trying to edge around a bunch of women who were squatting on the cold floor, in a circle around their bundles of belongings. They were tiny, these women, almost miniature people, the smallest adult human beings I had ever seen, clad in light-coloured robes. It was a chaotic and contradictory scene: women covered and not moving, animals squawking, a sense of nothing happening, yet the only reason to be there was to travel. It felt more like a bus stop than that most modern of places: an airport. Were these women nuns? Or an example of the creeping Islamisation being instigated by President ul-Huq? Women were being, for now, merely encouraged to cover up. Wear the chador, at least. Compulsion would replace encouragement before long. Or maybe these women were just in traditional tribal garb? No one seemed to take any notice of me, despite my height, my informal clothes, and the fact that I was female, with unruly uncovered hair. At Lahore airport and, later, in Islamabad and travelling to the border, I was able to get at least a superficial glimpse of the craziness and the paradox that was Pakistan in 1980: the ultra-modern and the medieval in lockstep. Or in contest?

The line was very long and moved slowly. When I eventually made it to the front, the young man at the information counter beamed, as if it were the happiest moment in his life to have before him a scruffy and travel-worn woman whose jeans and checked cotton shirt, purchased in a bazaar in New Delhi a few days earlier, clearly branded her as epitomising Western decadence. I asked for directions. I was in transit to Islamabad. His instructions, delivered in highly excitable English, were difficult to understand. The man noticed my hesitation.

'Let me show you,' he said as, abandoning a lengthening line of travellers needing help, he leapt over the counter, grabbed my hand and started pulling me towards the door. As soon as we were outside, in a chaotic and noisy space where decrepit vehicles played dodgem cars, the man's warmly ingratiating manner changed: 'There is a hotel we can go to,' he said, waving his arm towards some buildings on the perimeter of the car park. He was not coercive, rather his dark eyes looked pleadingly at me as if to say, I know all you Western women are whores so why not with me? 'No!' I said firmly as I disentangled my arm and marched back into the terminal, from where, it turned out, my next flight would soon be leaving.

It did not occur to me to be nervous, let alone frightened, during my week in Pakistan. I took risks that today would be inconceivable. The political, and religious landscape of Pakistan is vastly different post 9/11; post the assassination of several of its Prime Ministers; post the movement of the Taliban into sections of the country; post the capture and killing of Osama bin Laden who, it turned out, had been hiding out in Pakistan for some years. Today, Westerners cannot move freely, and even within protected compounds are at risk from suicide bombers. Journalists face particular perils such as befell Daniel Pearl from the *Wall Street Journal*, who was kidnapped and executed in 2002. But in 1980 it was not yet dangerous for a Westerner, even a Western woman, to travel alone to places that today are more-or-less no-go areas. Or, maybe, I was just lucky.

I checked into the Holiday Inn Islamabad and began immediately to organise my work. I would meet with the Foreign Affairs Minister, with whom I had an introduction, as well as making contact with local journalists and foreign diplomats. I also hoped to travel to the Afghan border, of course, through the famous Khyber Pass, but my most pressing task—the reason I had come to Pakistan—was to keep pushing for the interview with the President. I went to the hotel coffee shop for some lunch. I was fascinated to see, for the first time, a number of Arab men in thobes and headdresses. I fell into conversation with one of them. Sheik A was a diplomat, he told me, from one of the Gulf States. He invited me to have dinner with him the following night. Later that afternoon I wandered down to the bar where correspondents from various Western newspapers were hanging out. They were friendly enough, if perhaps a little patronising to someone who was new to the scene and who clearly knew nothing. There was talk of how the Russian occupation of Afghanistan was going; it had been nine months since the invasion and refugees were starting to come across into Pakistan. 'It would be interesting to talk to them,' I ventured. 'No way,' was the consensus from the blokes at the bar. 'You can't get to the border.'

The next morning, the day of the big holiday, everything was closed but I asked the hotel about hiring a local driver. They soon found me M., a young man who seemed affable and who agreed to drive me for the rest of my stay. I said I wanted to go to Peshawar. 'No problem,' he said. We agreed to go Sunday. On our way, my driver took me to Murree, a summer resort in the hills outside Rawalpindi, the old city that lies adjacent to Pakistan's capital of Islamabad, and one of the most beautiful places on earth. He introduced me to his family, which I took as meaning he wanted me to know that I could trust him not to behave the way the guy at the airline counter in Lahore had. I was relieved. I was going to be spending a lot of time with M., and in some very remote and potentially dangerous places.

The drive to the outpost of Peshawar, the last town before the Afghan border, took a couple of hours. We stopped so I could see the Old Town. I walked through a bazaar, conspicuous not only as a Western woman wearing just jeans and a cotton shirt, but as the only woman around. I did not feel any hostility towards me. Bemusement perhaps. In the stalls along the dusty streets, ancient vendors presided over baskets piled high with spices and other substances.

'You want heroin?' a bright-eyed boy called out to me. 'You come with me?'

'No thanks.'

Was that really hashish? I wondered, peering more closely at one of the piled-up baskets in front of an old man.

'Madam, like?' he asked, apparently seeing no difference between the drug, the quantities of which would make several of my friends back in Australia gasp in wonder, and the baskets of turmeric, cumin and other spices he had on offer. No, Madam would not like. She might be foolhardy, travelling by herself to what was fast becoming a war zone, but she was not insane. She was not going to even think about what could happen if she was discovered carrying the tiniest quantity of this drug as she made her way home through Bangkok and Singapore.

I had been given permission to visit the Afghan refugee camps at Jamrud and Aza Khel, outside Peshawar. In these tent cities, people surrounded me, begging for help. 'Tell your government,' they said, eyes fixed on mine, testing my sincerity, 'tell your government we need Kalashnikov.' 'I can write about your situation,' was the best I could offer. And indeed as soon as I was back in Islamabad I went to see the people at UNHCR, to get more material for an article about the displacement of tribal people by the Russians, but I knew that no one back in Canberra was going to care about these people.

We then headed for the border. The road was narrow as it wound tightly around the large mountain range that divides Pakistan from Afghanistan. The landscape was dusty, brown, inhospitable-seeming, with low-slung mountains in the distance giving the terrain its only relief. I saw tank traps, formations of rock blocks, similar to today's ubiquitous bollards outside public buildings, and left by the British after World War II. The Khyber Pass, the only way from Europe to Asia though the mountains to Pakistan and, beyond there, the riches of India, is not known as the 'gateway of conquerors' for nothing. The road was isolated, unpatrolled and, I had been warned, the domain of various gangs, some of whom might demand money. I hoped that was all they would want. At Landi Kotal, a town midway to the border, we saw a sign: 'Visitors are requested not to stop or sleep at remote or lonely places. They must try to reach Peshawar before nightfall.' We were stopped once by some kind of militia who searched the car. They were convinced that the only Westerners who travelled in these parts were drug-smugglers. Another three or four times groups of men, brandishing rifles, demanded money. Each time I handed over the amount advised by M., huge wads of local currency that amounted to just a few Australian dollars. One group, obviously officials, at Jamrud Fort, even gave me the bottom copy of an in-triplicate receipt. There was no paper acknowledgement for the other 'taxes' that I had handed over, although I kept track of the amounts so I could claim them on my expenses. There were men in the Canberra Press Gallery who boasted of claiming for brothels on their expenses, so I didn't see why I could not make a legitimate claim for *baksheesh*.

After being stopped the first few times at no cost except a few dollars, I relaxed enough to start to worry about what for me was the most terrifying part of the trip: the traffic. The road was mostly narrow, with sharp hairpin bends, and as we crawled higher and higher in our tiny car, I steeled myself at each bend for the gaudily decorated and overcrowded bus that would invariably come hurtling towards us. There was scarcely room to pass, especially at speed. Each time we survived what I thought was an inevitable head-on collision, I breathed heavily with relief. M. was highly amused by my fear. 'Allah will look after us,' he reassured me cheerily, though I noticed that he, too, closed his eyes as the buses sped towards us. Fortunately Allah did ensure our safe passage and we made it to the Afghan border. I stood beside the sign that noted Kabul was 225 kilometres away, and looked down on the road between the two countries. The border functioned as a duty-free port and it was quite astonishing to watch the steady procession of men and black burkha-clad women, looking like mobile tents, trudging eastwards, their backs burdened by contraband. They were carrying stoves, refrigerators, car-parts, rugs, furniture, huge cartons containing cigarettes. There were also cases of what looked like Coca-Cola—from Russian-held Afghanistan! It was said that you could buy anything at that border, and that if you wanted something that was not on offer, you'd be told to come back the next day and it would be waiting for you. Watching the human carriers (I saw very few vehicles) walk from Afghanistan with their multifarious goods, I could believe it. I settled for some cigarettes and a bottle of Coke. None of these were intended for consumption, and I was quite annoyed a few months later when a friend who was staying with me in Canberra told me she'd drunk the Coke.

'I'll replace it, of course,' she said.

'That will not be easy,' I told her.

Back in Islamabad, I breasted the bar at the Holiday Inn and, trying to maintain my *sangfroid*, mentioned in passing that I'd just returned from the border.

The other journos looked at me sceptically.

'No way you could have got there,' one of them said disbelievingly. 'The road's closed.'

I continued to press my case for an interview with the President. Be patient, I was told. He will see you. I had been waiting four days now and I was not encouraged. I kept busy, gathering information and perspectives. Whatever the outcome with the President, I would be writing something about my visit to Pakistan. I called on the Thai Embassy and the Japanese, saw the US Political Counsellor and met with local journalists. I was asked to do an interview with a local newspaper, *The Muslim*, about the position of women in Australia. Later, I was surprised to see myself described in the article as 'the young blonde Australian journalist Anne Summers of *Woman's Day* and the first woman Bureau Chief of the *Australian Financial Review*'—I would have put it the other way round, my weekly column for a women's magazine being an add-on to my main job of writing about politics. I was even more surprised to see myself quoted as saying, 'If young smart, brilliant girls begin wearing this garment which has a flare of its own, it will gradually become more popular.' I most assuredly had *not* endorsed 'this garment', the chador, the local version of headscarf, which the Zia ul-Haq government was trying to compel women to wear. The Australian High Commission thought this misquoting of me was hilarious: 'Never knew you were so Islamic,' commented the person who had sent me the article.

The President's people said I might have a better chance of seeing him if I went to Karachi. While I was there I would try to meet the Bhutto women, the widow of the late President, killed by the current President, and his daughter, Benazir. They were apparently under some kind of house arrest. I sent out some feelers. I also heard from the Thai Embassy that I should make contact with their people in Karachi. It was my last night in Islamabad and I was finally going to have the several-times deferred dinner with Sheik A. When I arrived in the hotel lobby I did not, at first, recognise him. Gone were the beguiling robes; in front of me was a man wearing what could only be described as a John Travolta suit: it was clinging, it had flared trousers and it was baby blue. Serves you right Summers, I said to myself as I followed him across the marble floors of the Holiday Inn, you were objectifying him; you don't like it when it's done to you.

'Where are we going?' I asked, trying to rescue the evening.

'To a friend's place,' he said. 'You will see.'

As we climbed into his chauffeur-driven embassy vehicle, I noticed that a group of men who had been lingering near us in the foyer had followed us out, and were clambering into other vehicles that formed themselves into a convoy behind ours. We headed out of town, and as the houses grew fewer I began to feel apprehensive.

'Whose place are we going to?'

'We are nearly there.'

And indeed we were. The cars pulled up outside a nice-looking low-slung desert house, with vines and flowering creepers, and we all piled out. There must have been ten men, most of them wearing robes. And me. Oh shit, I thought to myself, and not a soul in the world knows I am here.

We sat down to dinner. I was placed at the head of the long table. Our host, who was an ambassador from, I think, Tunisia, sat at the other end. We were served on plates of solid gold. My recall of the evening is incomplete. We may have been served by a woman, I am not sure, but I do remember this: these men could not have been nicer, more considerate or more anxious to make me feel welcome and safe. We must have talked politics. However strange it must have seemed to all of us that I was there, and however impossible such a gathering would have been in this country anywhere outside an embassy residence (as I learned this house was), on this occasion being a Western woman was a plus. It was yet another instance of the privileged access journalists have to people, to places and to experiences that lie outside the ambit of their usual lives. As conduits to the wide world of our audiences, we are often used and manipulated and misled for craven motives, but we also get to see and do extraordinary and amazing things and meet the world's best (as well as its worst) people. It is a trade that allows seamless access and interchange and where work relations often gravitate into friendships and more.

While I was having no luck getting to meet with President Zia, I did have my interview with the Aga Shahi, the Minister for Foreign Affairs.

His sister lived in Canberra and had kindly arranged this for me. When I arrived at the Ministry of Foreign Affairs it was raining heavily, and as I made my way to the entrance I lost my balance on the slippery terrazzo and fell flat on my face. Worse, I was unable to stop slithering along the wet surface. Very undignified, I thought, trying to scramble to my feet. It was then that I noticed the group of men squatting on the verandah outside the main entrance. They watched me, impassively. By the time I had managed to stand up, I was soaked through. I sent a grim smile in the direction of the men. No response. Inside, the Foreign Minister's aide looked surprised when I asked for a towel.

Minister Shahi was a courtly, dignified man whose eyes made no comment on my bedraggled state. I began to ask him questions, but it soon became clear that he had an agenda of his own. He started telling me about a four-country peace initiative that was to be launched in a week's time. I felt the rising excitement that always accompanied getting a leak, the knowledge that I was going to be able to scoop my colleagues. In this case, those bastards back at the bar of the Holiday Inn.

It was like those times in Canberra when a cabinet minister would 'drop a story' on me. I'd be sitting across the desk, doing my usual routine: 'What happened in cabinet today? Did you make a decision on the national wage case?' (or the airline strike, or whatever was the big issue of the moment).

'Anne, you know I can't discuss confidential cabinet matters,' he'd usually say. 'I thought you just wanted some background.'

But sometimes there'd be that magic moment when he would answer my question, sometimes obliquely, sometimes without reference to an actual cabinet decision, but he'd be talking, he'd be singing, and I'd be trying to gauge whether it would be safe to take notes, whether the magic would dissolve if I lost my lock on his eyes. Afterwards, I'd rush outside, perch myself on one of the leather couches that were positioned along the corridors in the Old Parliament House, and furiously write down everything I could remember.

(It wasn't always a 'he'. There was one woman cabinet minister, Senator Margaret Guilfoyle, who was initially Minister for Social Security and later, the first woman to be Minister for Finance. She sometimes saw it as a sisterly gesture to drop a story on a women journalist. The men would always complain that she was 'a tight-arsed bitch who never told you anything'. I would smile to myself. That's what you think, buster.)

As I listened to the Pakistani Foreign Minister I felt the same rising excitement, the familiar anticipation of the glory that would cover me. This was no grubby little Canberra story; this was a genuine international scoop. I felt I was in the big league. Okay. This was a small country and a little war. It wasn't as if the US Secretary of Defence was telling me a state secret (although that would happen a few years later) but I allowed myself to feel, just for a moment, as if I were Oriana Fallaci. Then I checked myself. Fallaci would not be sitting here passively receiving the minister's version of events. She'd be interrogating the little man, demanding he accept responsibility for the crimes of the Zia regime. Or probing his hypocrisy: asking if he drank liquor or otherwise breached the Islamic code. Instead I was sitting there meekly, my shirt stiffening as it started to dry, wondering how I could check what he was telling me.

All journalism is risky. Sources can lie. They can betray you, say they never said what they told you, leaving the reporter stranded and obliged by the code of ethics not to disclose, in order to denounce, the source. We used to debate this in the gallery. What if your source lies? What if he misleads you? Do you still protect him? Yes, the consensus seemed to be, because there will always be a next time when you'll need him. You can't 'burn' a source unless you are planning a very short career in journalism. And even then, did you really want to be known as a dobber?

Back at the hotel I phoned the Australian Ambassador.[3] The diplomatic circle in Islamabad, a political capital like Canberra and Brasilia, that had no reason for existence outside government, was as bored and isolated as if they were confined to a compound the way diplomats in some other countries are. They thrived on rumour and speculation, hungry for any tid-bit they could report back home to help their careers along. Subsisting on such a diet, they are unusually alert to changes in nuance or phraseology that signals a new policy direction. Like fashion experts, they sense things before they become evident to the eye.

'Does this sound plausible?' I asked, trying out the story on him.

'He had heard a whisper,' he said.

I decided to go with it. Over a scratchy telephone line I dictated to a copy-taker in Sydney the details of the peace initiative that was to be launched under Pakistan's sponsorship in the coming days. The next morning I got a herogram from Max Walsh.

'Great story,' he cabled. 'Reuters picked it up and it's running worldwide.'

I was ecstatic but there was no one to share the glory with. No admiring or envious peers, no angry Prime Minister on the phone, not even the satisfaction of having the paper and seeing my byline over an international scoop. Instead I called Zia's office, and once again I was assured that everything would be okay. The President was going to Baluchistan next week. I could go with him. There would be plenty of time to talk on the plane. I did not believe them. I decided to go to Karachi where, I'd been told, there was a chance I could meet the Bhutto women. An interview with them would in so many ways be better.

I was woken at around 2 a.m. by someone battering on my door.

'Miss, Miss,' a man was calling. It was the desk clerk from downstairs. 'You have a telephone call from Australia.'

I followed him down the eight flights of stairs as, of course, the lift wasn't working, and picked up the phone.

'Doctor!' It was Max Walsh. 'Fraser's called an election. You've got to come home.'

I left the next morning and, as planned, travelled via Karachi but discovered it could take weeks to arrange to meet the Bhutto women. That was out of the question, but then I got a summons from the Thai Consul-General. Could I get myself to Bangkok? Immediately. Since it was on my way, I figured Why not!

I got there too late. The Thai government had invited a select number of journalists to a very special interview that involved travelling to the Cambodian border. They had left an hour before I arrived. I would never get another opportunity to interview Pol Pot, whose murderous Khmer Rouge regime had been toppled in December the previous year, when Vietnam invaded Cambodia. Pol Pot was now hiding out in the jungle near the border. He had, with the support of the Thai government, resumed guerilla activities against the Vietnamese-imposed regime, and it seemed the Thais wanted to showcase this to the international media. It was important because

Pol Pot's was still the internationally recognised government of Cambodia. Back home Malcolm Fraser was locked in a ferocious battle with his Foreign Minister Andrew Peacock about whether to de-recognise Pol Pot. At the meeting they had just attended in New Delhi, Singapore's Prime Minister Lee Kwan Yew had made clear that Pol Pot's regime was to be preferred over the Vietnamese puppets, and the Americans had a similar view. Peacock said he was willing to resign over the issue. On 12 September Fraser had called a federal election, and thus deferred the showdown with Peacock over Pol Pot until after the poll. I met with Gordon Jockel, Australia's Ambassador to Thailand, that afternoon in Bangkok to try to understand this messy diplomatic situation.

That night at the airport, while I waited to fly back to Sydney, I went over in my mind what a disaster the trip had been. I had not managed to interview General Zia; I had not met Benazir Bhutto; and now, I had missed out on a once-in-a-lifetime interview with one of the great mass murderers of our time. At least, I consoled myself, the wires had picked up my story on the four-way peace plan. Then I learned that, just hours after my little story had whizzed around the world, Iraq had invaded Iran. A much bigger story. A real, headline-grabbing war. My little scoop evaporated into the ether.

The federal election of 19 October 1980 swept away the commanding majority Malcolm Fraser had enjoyed since 1975. Labor obtained 49.6 per cent of the vote and won 51 seats, a gain of thirteen. Among the new Labor members was Bob Hawke, former president of the ACTU and a man who was impatient to be Prime Minister. The only question was how long it would take him to dislodge Bill Hayden and then defeat Fraser. Politics was suddenly getting a lot more interesting than it had been for my first two years. The first ructions came from the Liberal Party, however, on 28 April 1981, when Andrew Peacock resigned from cabinet in protest at Fraser's style of government. He had already declined to be reappointed Minister for Foreign Affairs after the 1980 election and had become Minister for Industrial Relations. At a leadership ballot called by the Prime Minister that April evening in 1981, Peacock was defeated. He retired to the backbench. For a time, he and Hawke had nearby offices and the crowds of journalists, lobbyists, politicians and others who trod the constant path to their doors gave the corridor the appearance of housing a government-in-exile.

I was fortunate to be able to cover two leadership challenges, one change of leader and a change of government during my time in the Press Gallery. There had not been such political upheaval since the days of the Whitlam government. We journalists became accustomed to hanging around in Kings Hall waiting to hear the outcome of leadership challenges, something that had not happened since 1971 when, for the first time in Australian political history, a sitting Prime Minister was deposed. John Gorton had instigated a 'spill' to test the numbers for his leadership—and lost. Today, such challenges are more frequent and journalists often learn the outcome, via text from inside the party room, as soon as the counting is completed but we had to wait, often for a very long time, until the party tellers came and gave us the formal results. Bob Hawke had failed in his first challenge to Hayden on 16 July 1982, but seven months later the party installed him as leader at a shadow cabinet meeting in Brisbane just as, in faraway Canberra, Malcolm Fraser was driving to Government House to seek a double-dissolution. Fraser believed he had outwitted Labor which, he calculated, would not change leaders once an election had been called. But, as the press described it at the time, Fraser was caught with his pants down. Labor had already made the switch and it was too late for the election to be called off. Labor went on to win a 25-seat majority in the House of Representatives on 5 March 1983, in a victory that would see Labor remain in power first under Hawke then, from late-1991, under former Treasurer Paul Keating, until 1996.

Hawke had promised reconciliation and consultation after the divisive Fraser years and one of his earliest initiatives was the National Economic Summit, held in April 1983. It was unprecedented for the leaders of business, the trade unions, and state and federal government to come together to agree on a national economic strategy. Many of the business leaders had never met a trade unionist before, and none of the participants—apart from the state premiers—had ever been in the House of Representatives chamber where the summit was held. Hawke knew how to impress. There was a dinner at The Lodge—most of them had never been there before either—and more hospitality at Government House. At the end of the three days, the summit had agreed to Hawke's economic proposal for a Prices and Incomes Accord, designed to return to centralised wage fixing and to control both unemployment and inflation, using tools such as government-provided services and social policies (including the reintroduction of Medicare) that became known as a social wage, and which alleviated the need for wage increases. It was a new and conciliatory way of working, and it became something of a signature approach of the Hawke government. As did policies to benefit women. One of the earliest acts of the government was to upgrade women's policy by moving the Office of Women's Affairs into the Prime Minister's department, and in September it introduced sweeping sex discrimination legislation. Both had been promised during the election and were seen as important in attracting women's votes which, for the first time, were decisive in delivering victory. Not that the Press Gallery was especially interested in either the politics or the policies affecting women. They preferred to focus on what they saw as the main game.

I had taken six weeks off straight after the election to write *Gamble for Power*[4] and I was pleased at how well it was received, especially as it was one of several books written about the election. Perhaps I could become a chronicler of Australian politics in addition to my daily journalism. Like the rest of the Press Gallery, I was caught up in the palpable excitement of the new government, its energy and reformist spirit, and I was relishing reporting this sea change in Australian politics. I could see myself writing more books on politics. Then a phone call changed everything. Susan Ryan, who had become Labor's first-ever woman cabinet minister and was Minister Assisting the Prime Minister on the Status of Women as well as Minister for Education, rang to say she thought I should apply for the newly advertised job of running the upgraded and renamed Office of the Status of Women.

I had not planned on leaving. I liked the rush of daily journalism, the urgency of getting, and confirming, a story, trying to scoop my colleagues from other news outlets. I liked the travel, even if arriving on a Prime Ministerial RAAF plane, and staying in only the best hotels did not really give you an idea of what a place was like. I liked the easy access to power that went with being a journalist, especially with the nation's only daily financial newspaper. I could get virtually anyone in business or politics on the phone, including senior public servants who, I soon learned, were best called at home on Sunday afternoons when they were relaxed and comparatively unguarded. Public servants were not gagged the way they are now. They actually saw it as a duty to help ensure that newspaper reports were accurate and relevant.

I had also just been elected President of the Parliamentary Press Gallery, the first woman to hold the position. I'd been urged to run by colleagues who felt the long-term incumbent, Peter Costigan, bureau chief for the Melbourne *Herald*, was treating it as a sinecure. He did not like being challenged and while the contest might have seemed light-hearted on the surface, underneath it was deadly serious. Costigan ran with what he thought was the hilarious slogan, 'May the best man win'. I countered with 'Go for the Doctor', thinking I might as well capitalise on my newly conferred title with a racing term that meant to try really hard but which, I was informed by Gary O'Neill, had another far racier meaning that had nothing to do with the track. I'd had to campaign, which included asking Gallery gods like Alan Reid, Wally Brown, Rob Chalmers and Ian Fitchett, who had been there for decades, to vote for me, a neophyte, and a woman. And I'd won—by a large margin. How could I walk away—just a few weeks later?

I asked Max Walsh what he thought. He was now with the Packer organisation, working with the *Bulletin* and Channel 9's *Sunday* program. As he was no longer my boss, I thought he might offer an objective opinion; he would certainly grasp the allure of the offer. The Department of Prime Minister and Cabinet (PM&C), where women's policy was now located, was the epicentre of political and bureaucratic power. It would be fascinating to see how it all worked. But it would be a drastic shift to move from reporting to government, from observing to being a player.

'Would look great on your CV,' was all he said.

There were a lot of things to consider. Even though the job was a public service appointment and I would have to go through all the proper processes, I would be seen as Hawke's person. That was unlikely to be an advantage within PM&C. And I would be turning my back on journalism, which had been my life for eight years now. Would I ever be able to return to it? For my generation of journalists, apart from the intrinsic rewards of covering society with your reporting, the job offered us worlds that would not otherwise have been open to us; already my passport had many more stamps than

I could ever have imagined. Only my job as the international board chair of Greenpeace, in the early 2000s, enabled me to travel to more countries. As a journalist, I was able to not just meet a very wide range of political, business and other leaders but to engage with and, in some cases, befriend them. I was able to move easily into entertainment circles, to become on first-name terms with actors and film directors and those in their worlds. It was easy to forget that there was a bargain entailed in this intimacy. As I would discover several times in my future when I again moved from the media, the terms of your entry into this glamorous world are very stark. You learn quickly once you are no longer in the job that you are no longer of any use. The friends quickly disappear and the invitations stop overnight.

Leaving the Press Gallery had its risks but the opportunity, in the end, was irresistible. I was being offered a chance to help advance women's equality in Australia in a unique and unprecedented way. My previous efforts had been through activism or writing. Now I had the prospect of learning how to use the power of the bureaucracy to actually deliver the policies we activists had long argued and campaigned for. The newly elected government had promised to make these policies a priority and had already started to do so. I would be irresponsible, I told myself, if I did not step up to the challenge.

CHAPTER FIVE

MANDARINS VERSUS MISSIONARIES

―――――●>●<●―――――

Were it not for Canberra's ever-present trees, I would have almost been able
to see Parliament House from my new office in the Edmund Barton Building
on Kings Avenue. But I might as well have been a million miles away from
my old workplace, so different was my new world. It was quiet and spacious,
for one thing, and very low-key. None of the crowding or the rowdiness
of the Press Gallery, or the constant hurried movement of politics. Here,
in the centre of bureaucratic power, the colour was beige, the pace was slow
and relations were extremely formal. My PhD was now an advantage: I was
Dr Summers, First Assistant Secretary, Department of the Prime Minister
and Cabinet, or as the mandatory acronyms had it: FAS PM&C.

It was my very first day in the new job and I was being shown where
I fitted in.

'There you are,' said the man who was guiding me through the organisation chart of the department, Status of Women.

Or, as the acronym on the chart described us, SOW.

I looked sharply at the man. Was he sniggering behind that po-face?

'I don't think so,' I said.

This one I had to win. Every division in PM&C was known by its acronym. They included ESP (Economic and Social Policy), INT (International), CAB (Cabinet Office) and P&G (Parliamentary & Government). We had been the Office for Women's Affairs—OWA—before being given a new name to announce our promotion to divisional status with all the power and prestige that went with that, but we would never be taken seriously if our official name was a female pig. I made my case to Alan Rose, the Deputy-Secretary to whom I reported. Maybe he spoke to Sir Geoffrey Yeend, the Secretary, but it was soon official: the acronym for the Office of the Status of Women was changed to OSW.

My path to PM&C had been neither smooth nor inevitable. I had taken a few discreet soundings and been encouraged to go for the advertised job of running women's policy for the Hawke government but I had to be careful. What if I applied and didn't get it? In the end, I told myself, how could I not go for it? My five years with the *Financial Review* had taught me to appreciate the power of PM&C. Imagine, I fantasised, bringing that bureau-cratic clout to ensuring that women's interests were taken into account in government decision-making. I wrote the application, got myself up-to-date on what I hoped were the relevant policy issues, lined up referees and soon found myself in front of the selection panel headed by Ed Visbord, the charming but tough-minded Deputy Secretary of PM&C responsible for the economic areas, and someone I used to speak to quite often in my job at the *Financial Review*. Now he would decide whether a poacher could become a gamekeeper.

It was understandable that the bureaucracy might be nervous about someone joining its ranks who had so recently worked as a journalist. The upgrading of the Office to a division meant its head would have a Top Secret security clearance. Would she be tempted to share cabinet documents with her old mates in the Press Gallery? That thought had not occurred to me. I was there to fight for women's policy, not to play risky games with former colleagues back in the Gallery. But the public service clearly had a problem with me and whatever its reasoning—I was never told—I did not get the job.

It was not yet public but the panel had decided to give the position to Deborah McCulloch who, on paper at least, was far more qualified than me. In 1976 Deborah had been appointed the first women's adviser to the

South Australian Premier, Don Dunstan. I was surprised to learn she had applied for the Canberra job, because she had retreated to a very radical feminism and not been involved in government for some years now, but it was hard to argue with her selection. Despite Susan Ryan's encouragement, there was absolutely no guarantee that I would get the job. It was a public service appointment after all, and a high-level one. But I had expected that if I were passed over, it would be for a safer candidate, someone with current public service credentials. Who would have thought that this selection committee would opt for a radical feminist with no background in Canberra or the public service?

It was going to be profoundly embarrassing for me because the fact I had applied had been leaked to a newspaper. There was also a rather excruciating personal connection: Deborah had lived, and had a child, with John Summers from whom I had separated in 1970 but to whom I was technically still married. Deborah's appointment would be awkward for me, but she and John were no longer living together so it would have no bearing on the ongoing casual friendship I maintained with him. But there was nothing I could do. Or so I thought. It turned out, however, that Susan Ryan was not happy with the outcome. She had wanted someone with a thorough understanding of how Canberra worked, someone who, in her judgement, was enough of a pragmatist to deal with what was likely to be a complicated relationship between the women's movement and the bureaucracy. She also wanted someone who would have the confidence of the Prime Minister. Before I applied, I had sought a meeting with Bob Hawke and asked him if he saw any impediments to my going for the job. I was trying to find out if he had a preferred candidate. No, it turned out. Peter Barron, one of his political advisers, from the muscular NSW Right of the ALP, had had a robust conversation with me about whether I intended to cause any problems for the government if I got the job. Good practice for what lay ahead if I was successful, I told myself at the time.

Ryan decided to push back. I don't know exactly what she did, but I do know this: someone spoke to Yeend, the all-powerful Secretary of PM&C and the nation's most renowned mandarin, and he spoke to Peter Wilenski, the former Whitlam staffer who went on to have a distinguished public service, academic and diplomatic career and who had been recently installed as the head of the Public Service Board (now the Public Service Commission). In early November I got a call: I had the job.

I was relieved. I was pleased. But I was also nervous. Would I have zero credibility with the department now that my appointment was clearly the result of political interference? I did not feel guilty about Deborah because I sincerely believed that I could do a better job and, to her immense credit, she was very gracious about it all. She did not appear to bear me any grudge and subsequently generously gave me public support a couple of times. Although there was a small item about what happened in *The Bulletin*, the rest of the media did not pick it up. It was a good political story, the kind of item the Press Gallery would usually pounce on: political interference in the appointment of a senior public servant. I soon came to understand, with some anger and a great deal of bitterness, that the press had zero interest in anything to do with women's policy. It was true then and it is still true today. The media exhibits an extraordinary myopia in its failure to recognise, and understand, the key role women play in the economy, and how policy to expand women's opportunities is essentially economic policy and of key relevance to all other arms of policy. But the media do not get that. And they are not the only ones. This was to be my key challenge as I took over running OSW.

———◆———

The media *was* interested in my appointment—not the political story behind it, but the fact that one of its own had defected to such a high level in the bureaucracy. Every newspaper reported it, some of them interviewed me and there were some profiles, including in some unexpected places. Perhaps it was not surprising for *Woman's Day* to be interested in the new public face of women's advice to the Prime Minister, but I was astonished when *Vogue* magazine did a comprehensive and very friendly profile, written by Marion von Adlerstein, and accompanied by several stunningly glamorous photos. I had professional hair and makeup for the first time, and the magazine obtained a series of outfits by Australian designers for me to wear during the photo-shoot. That was probably the moment when I realised that fashion and feminism could be friends. I needed to look good in my job. I was the public face of women and I was representing the government, sometimes the Prime Minister himself. I could not look like a dag. I was also now able to feel more confident in my clothes because I had a brand new body. The year before I had had surgery to reduce the size of my breasts. I had always been embarrassed by how big they were. I could never look elegant: my blouses were always busting open, the tops of outfits strained unfashionably across my chest and, perhaps worst of all, it was uncomfortable. My shoulders were always sore from the permanent groove marks of my bra struggling to hold up its weighty burden. I could not run. Two weeks in Melbourne changed that. The surgery transformed me to a size 36C. It was unbelievably painful and the recovery was longer than I had expected but when I was finally able to remove the bandages and raise my arms above my head, I saw in the mirror breasts that sat up—not quite perkily, I was almost 40 after all—and no longer drooped down towards my waist. They seemed normal in size in relation to the rest of my body, which itself was trimmer too because the surgeon had insisted I lose 10 kilograms before he would undertake the operation. I smiled at the new me. I liked her. I could not wait to chuck out all my sensible old heavy-duty bras and fill my drawers with seriously lacy underwear. For work I mostly wore what would become known as the standard 'femocrat' uniform of beige suit, silk blouse and low-heeled pumps. But my suit was by Robert Burton and I also had an array of—for me—unusually elegant frocks by the likes of Weiss and other leading designers, as a result of the introductions from *Vogue*. I paid for these clothes, of course, but was given discounts, which meant I could afford to buy quite a few outfits. I knew I looked good and this gave me added confidence for the battles that I knew would become part of my daily life, and which I would not have the luxury of losing.

I had had to leave the Fairfax house in Forrest and I'd already given up the company car, so it was urgent that I find a place to live and means of getting around. My house in Yarralumla had tenants, so I looked for something close to work that was low maintenance. The garden at the Fairfax house had been a lot of work. I doubted I'd have time for more than a few pot plants in this new job. I was soon settling into a three-bedroom, two-level apartment in Kingston, overlooking Telopea Park; it had a nice big living area and a small modern kitchen. Perfect. It was just a few blocks from Kings Avenue. I could easily have walked to work, except in Canberra nobody ever walked anywhere. Some people, it was rumoured, even drove their rubbish bins from their back door to the front gate on garbage night. Between living without a car in the US and driving the aged Fairfax Ford Falcon for five years, I had not had to think about cars for a very long time. I am totally uninterested in cars as status symbols; I just wanted something functional and reliable, and I needed it quickly. I'd heard Hondas were good. I asked around, did a bit of research and decided that I wanted a Honda Accord, automatic, four doors, colour silver. I went to the Honda showroom in Braddon and there, on the showroom floor, was exactly what I wanted.

'I'll take that one,' I said to the salesman.

He looked at me with utter disgust.

'I bet you'd take more time choosing a hat.'

———————

Late on the evening of 25 November 1983, I was driving my new car home after a dinner at Charlies restaurant when, just metres from my new home, I was pulled over by the police.

'Blow into this bag,' said the officer.

I had already left the *Financial Review* but had not yet officially started at PM&C although the dinner had been with two women I was thinking of hiring as my deputies. I did not think I had had that much to drink, but I knew the *Canberra Times* each day published the names of people who had been before the courts for DUI, together with their blood alcohol reading. I could not bear the embarrassment. What would that do to my carefully planned strategy for engaging the department? For keeping the government onside? My reputation would be shredded, I would be a joke and my chances of effecting significant change for women would be over. No, I could not let that happen. I refused.

I did not know then that Refuse Breath Test was a far more serious offence than actually being over the limit. I was immediately arrested, placed in the police car and driven to the main police headquarters in Civic, with another officer following in my car. I was taken into a room where there was a serious-looking apparatus. It was, I was told, the real breathalyser. Still I refused. I also told them I did not want to call a lawyer. It was too late. I spent the night in the cells.

The next morning Peter Crowley, a friend, a senior lawyer at Gallens Crowley and a brother of Mez O'Neill's, bailed me and I began trying to limit the damage. 'There but for the grace of God go any of us . . ' was Geoff Yeend's soothing response. In fact, the only nastiness was from the media. The Melbourne *Truth* ran a story under the headline: 'Breath test charge for govt libber' and a journalist rang and said if I didn't want him to write about my arrest and likely conviction, I had better give him a cabinet submission. 'Make it a good one he said, 'preferably Defence'.

I reported this to Yeend. In the end, with the aid of bi-partisan character references from Susan Ryan, my new boss, and John Howard, the former Treasurer, who I had to assure that this was in no way usual behaviour on my part, no conviction was recorded and, thanks to the gracious way Yeend responded, no lasting consequences for me or the Office.

I went into OSW determined to be effective, and that meant being pragmatic. I was going to make them—the government, the department, the rest of the public service—take women's policy seriously. One way to set ourselves up as winners, I instinctively knew, was to unsettle the preconceptions everyone had about us. Surprise them. Do the unexpected.

So my first hire was a man. Michael Roche was on the staff of John Dawkins, the Minister for Finance, and had been economics advisor to Bill Hayden when he was Leader of the Opposition. Michael brought economics heft and, coming from Parliament House, he knew the political game. Getting him was a great coup for me and his appointment was a signal, to the Office and to the department, especially to Ed Visbord, that I intended to build-up our skills in economics, taxation and social policy. The government was working on an Accord with the trade unions to contain wages via a boost to non-wage benefits, which meant that targeted social policy was going to be a key area. My second hire was Mary Ann O'Loughlin from the Social Policy Research Unit at the University of New South Wales. We had known each other for some years and I knew she was an effective player as well as having top-rate policy credentials. Mary Ann was also fun to be around. She bubbled over with energy, had a wicked sense of humour, and was utterly fearless when it came to doing what we agreed was needed to advance the status of women. I hoped to recruit more like her. OSW tended to be a dour place and I wanted to lift the mood, make it an exciting place, a policy hub, a place that attracted talent from inside and beyond the bureaucracy.

OSW was coming in from the welfare policy ghetto where too many people thought we belonged. With these two highly qualified experts in place, the Office was superbly equipped to design a range of social and economic policies. We were going to be part of the main game. It was no secret that PM&C was less than thrilled at being required to house a women's policy unit alongside its central (and, in its view, far more important) policy coordination responsibilities. They did not want to have to take the 'women's view' into account when advising the Prime Minister. But I intended to shake up their—and everyone else's—preconceptions of what the 'women's view' was. And it worked. Within a year we were transferred from the Justice area, presided over by Alan Rose, to Ed Visbord's economic domain.

I signalled to PM&C that I intended to work with, not against, them by asking Yeend to assign me a senior person to guide me through the job. I knew nothing about how the bureaucracy worked, and rather than fake it or rely on advice from OSW staff who themselves were newcomers to the department, I decided to ask for help. Paula Rush, a senior officer and a PM&C native who understood the place better than most, was given the job. She was able and energetic and did not share the general PM&C view that we were intruders. She very quickly showed me the essentials and guided me through all kinds of minefields, including an early intervention that saved me some embarrassment.

After cabinet meetings, the submissions we had had any involvement in drafting would be returned to us. A couple of times in the early days, Bob Hawke had written little notes to me in the margins of these official documents.

Nice, I'd thought. I put them in my filing cabinet, in a folder that I intended to take home to place with my personal papers.

'Do you have any returned Cabsubs?' Paula asked me one day. I told her where they were. She gave me one of her looks.

'Those are not personal papers, Anne. They have to go to the National Archives.'

'Can I make a photocopy of the pages with the PM's notes to me?'

'No,' she said. 'They are highly confidential documents and all copies are numbered and have to be accounted for.'

That was how Paula had known where to look for the missing subs. And, rather than use it against me, as some people might have, she saved me from an innocent but very serious mistake.

The work of OSW was astonishingly broad in scope. We had to be across almost every area of policy in order to evaluate submissions to cabinet from other departments. We felt we need not worry too much about employment policy which was in the capable hands of Jenni Neary, who headed the Women's Bureau, the body established by Prime Minister Sir Robert Menzies in 1963 to monitor trends in women's employment and, especially, equal pay. But we had to keep an eye on virtually everything else. All ministers, which in practice meant their departments, were required to fill in the box on the front of cabinet submissions that asked for the 'Impact on Women' of the policy being proposed. Many departments, either from ignorance, laziness or just sheer recalcitrance, opted to write 'Nil'. Our job at OSW was to get around the bureaucracy and persuade them, in the nicest possible way, that there were very few government policies that did not impact one way or another, negatively or positively, on at least some groups of women. The government wanted this information to take into consideration when making decisions. Women's desks were being established in most departments to help inform senior officers and policy makers to figure these things out for themselves, rather than rely on the OSW 'scolds'—as I worried we were becoming known as—to be always having to state what we thought was the bleeding obvious. But of course, to most people, it wasn't.

We had some successes: getting the Department of Transport to create separate baby change rooms at airports, rather than locate these in the women's toilets. We got the Department of Capital Territory to recognise that the proximity of car parks to shopping centres was an issue for women with prams or heavy shopping. But other departments viewed us as an irritating intrusion into what they regarded as their business. We asked Defence if they planned to have married quarters at their proposed new Air Force base in the remote location of Tindall, near Katherine in the Northern Territory? No, they did not. So are you planning brothels? They were affronted. We pointed out the obvious. The 'impact on women' comment required a feminist framing of the issues, and entailed having both information and perspective. This did not come naturally to most departments and some, like the Department of Defence, saw absolutely no reason why it should even try. I learned this in my role as chair of an IDC—which I quickly learned stood for Interdepartmental Committee—that had the job of reviewing some 17,000 job categories in the military and deciding which were 'combat' or 'combat-related'. The recently enacted Sex Discrimination Act (SDA) exempted Defence from having to employ women in jobs in either category. The Defence officials turned up to meetings in full military uniforms, no doubt designed both to impress and intimidate me, and they fought for every single designation to be exempt from having to employ women. I found myself fighting for the right of women to be cooks in the army but that was disallowed, because such jobs were—or could be— 'combat-related'. By the time we had finished, I was convinced that women would now be eligible for fewer jobs than they had had in the separate women's services that were abolished as a result of the SDA, and women integrated into the mainstream military. I was on other IDCs—on Nurse Education, the Repetitive Strain Injury (RSI) Task Force, and the Child Care Steering Group—and I found them hard going. I was not used to the aggression and the competitiveness that seemed to be the bureaucracy's modus operandi, and too often I felt the burr of hostility from those around the table who made it clear that what we were doing was taking them away from more important work.

Early on we received some very welcome, and quite unexpected, help from Geoff Yeend who soon after I arrived established, and himself chaired, the Permanent Heads (as departmental secretaries used to be called) Task Force on the Status of Women (PHTF). This had been a pre-election promise by the Prime Minister in a policy document entitled *Towards Equality*, but I don't think anyone expected the head of PM&C to embrace it with quite such enthusiasm. Yeend was a courtly and civil man who, whatever he may have thought of my appointment, and the political machinations it took to install me, unfailingly treated me with courtesy. He was the quintessential mandarin with an old-school view of how one conducted oneself, especially with the Prime Minister. He was undoubtedly manipulative—that was how mandarins worked—but it was rare to see his fingerprints.

There was no more powerful bureaucratic mechanism than the IDC, and none with the clout of one that consisted entirely of heads of departments. I attended the first meeting and could not help being impressed. Around the table were the heads of Attorney-General's; Finance; Foreign Affairs; Employment and Industrial Relations; Industry, Technology and Commerce; Education; Treasury; Social Security; Community Services; Immigration and Ethnic Affairs; and the Public Service Board.[1] Some in the women's movement criticised the body because, until January 1985 when Helen Williams was appointed to run the department of Education, it comprised only men. Such attacks, like those on Prime Minister Tony Abbott in 2014 for supposedly making himself the Minister for Women by bringing women's policy back to PM&C after a period in the bureaucratic wilderness similar to that it had endured under the Fraser government, fail to understand how power works in Canberra. Susan Ryan, a Canberra native, and the women who contributed to her policy documents, knew exactly how it worked and they knew that it was essential to marshall this bureaucratic power to the benefit of women. The gender of the people at the table, while patently unrepresentative of the population, was not the point, or at least not the main point. What mattered was their mandate and how they exercised it.

The PHTF introduced two extraordinary reforms. John Stone, the cantankerous Treasury Secretary who would soon resign his position and later become a right-wing senator from Queensland, declined to go along with the first initiative on the grounds that Treasury did not actually administer any programs, but the other heads agreed to set up women's units in their departments to monitor the impact on women of the policies and programs they administered, and to account for these in their annual reports.

I have often been given credit for the second reform, but it was actually Yeend's suggestion that a new budget document, the Women's Budget Program (WBP), be produced. His plan was ingenious, an exemplar of using bureaucratic processes to monitor and progress policy. Only an accomplished bureaucrat could have created such a mechanism, and only someone with his power and prestige could have ensured that it was effective. On budget night 1984, the Prime Minister tabled the first WBP in Parliament. It contained reports from thirteen departments describing how their policies impacted on women. I took this document to a meeting of the OECD Working Party on the Role of Women in the Economy in February 1985, where it received high praise and was quickly copied by other member countries. The document effectively required departments to scrutinise their work through a different perspective: that of women's needs. The 1985 WBP, which we had more time to produce, was a substantial document of 300 pages that was an illuminating snapshot of how government policies impacted on women; it also identified gaps in service and thus pointers to where change was needed. Today, a large number of countries, mostly in the developing world, use similar mechanisms to monitor the gender impact of policies. Sadly, Australia no longer does.

Some bureaucrats continued to resist what they saw as OSW's constant interference. Many thought it was just a passing fancy the government would soon tire of, and so need not be taken seriously. They turned out to be right: the cabinet comment requirement was removed in 1987. Others in the bureaucracy did try. OSW was constantly fielding phone calls or attending meetings with public servants who wanted to know how to assess 'impact on women'. In trying to help them, we were both finding our feet policy-wise, and learning how to smooth the rough edges of the very many ways so much of the world impacted on women. In doing so, Australian feminists were in their pragmatic and unplanned way coming up with a new form of activism. The term 'femocrat'—feminist bureaucrat—would become notorious. We were much mocked in the women's movement for our beige suits, our briefcases and our high salaries. We were seen as having 'sold out', as having become mandarins and forgotten where we came from, and who we were supposed to represent. Often the people who scorned us the most were also our biggest mendicants, pleading with us to save policies, increase funding or initiate much-needed policies. At the same time, the bureaucrats, the actual mandarins, saw us as missionaries. In their eyes, we were determined to meddle with a perfectly good system with fervour akin to that of the early Christians and the zealotry of evangelicals. They, of course, saw themselves as professional in their approach to their jobs and personally aloof from the matters they administered or advised on. We femocrats were, in truth, trapped in a no-man's land somewhere between the two, objects of suspicion by both the women's movement and by our work peers and bosses. There were few people we could talk to, as much of what we did was covered by cabinet confidentiality, so every few weeks we femocrats would all have dinner together—to lend each other support, do deals and let off steam.

As well as our oversight role, we had other responsibilities. There was the Aboriginal Women's Task Force that was charged with developing a policy on Indigenous women. Phyllis Daylight and Mary Johnstone, the two task force members, travelled around Australia consulting with other Indigenous women about their needs and in 1986 published their landmark report, *Women's Business*. Phyllis and I met with Charles Perkins, who had just been appointed the first Aboriginal to head the federal Department of Aboriginal Affairs, about how to work together. There was extensive consultation with women in similar or related jobs: regular Commonwealth–State Women's Advisers meetings, and the various advisory groups in TAFE, multicultural affairs, health and other areas. And of course I needed to be in touch with all the major women's organisations, several of whom had representatives on our National Women's Consultative Council (NWCC), which we had set up as a channel for allowing the views of women in the community to be conveyed to the government.

OSW had a very high profile. Women's policy was obviously a government priority; we were clearly in Bob Hawke's good books, and we were in great demand to give advice—or, to put it cynically, to help other organisations look good. As the head of the Office, I had so many invitations and external obligations and travelled so much that I feared I was not spending enough time in the Office. I delegated as much as I could but I was always under pressure to be the one at whatever event it was. I also met frequently with Bill Kelty, the Secretary of the ACTU, and worked with him on designing some of the social-wage policies that were needed for the Accord, and I attended at least one ACTU executive meeting. Then there were individual unions who wanted to see me, a few businesses and, of course, lots of individuals who had views to put or who wanted to get my input into what they were doing. I was constantly asked to be the now mandatory woman on public selection panels and to join all kinds of government advisory bodies. I helped redraft the Commonwealth Style Manual; was put on a Women and Sport group; consulted by the newly established Bicentennial Authority; and, one Sunday in November 1984, was called to Sydney at short notice to an emergency meeting convened by Health Minister Neal Blewett on how to address the looming AIDS crisis—and found myself a member of the AIDS Advisory Committee.

I was also available for Hazel Hawke, the Prime Minister's wife, if she required assistance. Early on, she asked for my input into a speech she was delivering to the National Press Club on Australia Day 1984. In early January I went to Kirribilli House, the Prime Ministerial Sydney residence, where the Hawkes were staying. I was directed to walk around to the front of the house, where the verandahs face onto the glorious waters of Sydney Harbour, the Opera House in full view. It was a sight to distract the busiest bureaucrat, but I was there to meet Hazel so I turned my eyes back to the house.

'G'day Anne!' the unmistakable voice of Bob Hawke greeted me.

I had not seen him. Rather, I had not recognised that the little guy in front of me, wearing nothing but tiny red Speedos, his nut-brown body daubed with white zinc, was the Prime Minister. I was decked out in full femocrat regalia, so I felt distinctly overdressed as I greeted the sunbather.

How we conducted ourselves day-to-day was critical. I was determined that we would become credible players in the political game. The Fraser government had treated the OWA almost sadistically. Its advice was seldom sought, and when proffered was mostly ignored. Not surprisingly, the staff had developed something of a siege mentality. They were used to being defensive and I wanted to change that. Most of the staff welcomed my appointment as someone who was well known, had good feminist credentials, who appeared to have the Prime Minister's ear and who might lift the profile of the Office and its mission. But the reception was not warm. Many were upset that Kath Taperell, who had run OWA during the hard years, had not been given the job. And there were suspicions about where my ultimate loyalties lay. This was evident early on.

I had been in the job for just a few weeks when we learned there was a vacancy on a big agricultural board. Like so many others at the time, this board had never had a woman member. 'We always nominate for these boards,' the veterans of OSW urged me. 'Not,' they conceded, 'that we usually get anyone up.' (I was surprised that even feminists routinely used the 'getting it up' public service parlance.) Let's find someone, I agreed. The Office maintained a Register of Women (ROW), a list of women suitable for board appointments. Disappointingly, it yielded no names I thought were of sufficient calibre for the Prime Minister to take to cabinet, so I decided we would not propose anyone. I detected the first inkling of distrust. I was just there as window-dressing, I could tell some of the veterans were thinking, I was not willing to fight. In fact, I could not wait but I was not going to take on a hopeless cause. Why lose all our credibility on an unqualified nominee? I suggested we boost the Register so that next time we would be better armed. The Office succeeded in expanding the range and depth of ROW and it subsequently yielded names of women whose qualifications made them eminently suitable for appointment to government boards. Indeed some of those early appointees went on to forge impressive board careers in the corporate world.

In addition to the day-to-day work, we had two big assignments. Our biggest initially was to work for society-wide acceptance of the SDA, the wide-ranging anti-discrimination laws that had been introduced to Parliament in 1983, and which would be formally enacted on 1 August 1984. But we also had to develop a complementary policy of affirmative action. Susan Ryan's initial SDA bill had included such provisions but cabinet, wary of alienating business, had stripped them from the legislation and asked they be developed as a separate program. It was to be a priority undertaking when I started at the Office.

Resistance to the SDA had not ended with its enactment. It had been fiercely contested in Parliament, and opposition still raged. It was said the legislation would mean the end of the family, that it would de-sex women, and that it would force women to do jobs they did not want to do. Opponents included conservative state premiers, and none more so than Joh Bjelke-Petersen, the cunning National Party politician who had run Queensland since 1968. He would have no truck with anti-discrimination legislation—and Queensland did not get such laws until 1991, two years after Wayne Goss's Labor government came to office. Susan Ryan decided that OSW should open Women's Information Services (WIS) in those places that had no anti-discrimination laws: Queensland, Tasmania and the ACT. These shop-front offices were intended to provide information to the public about their entitlements under federal laws. They provided useful services, but they were also a political provocation and needed to be carefully managed.

In Brisbane, I found the perfect person to run Queensland Women's Information Service: Quentin Bryce, a lawyer, who lectured at the University of Queensland. She was a locally well-known and respected feminist and human rights activist, and she had served on the National Women's Advisory Council, the body chaired by Dame Beryl Beaurepaire that included other fine advocates such as Wendy McCarthy, Jan Marsh and Evelyn Scott during the Fraser government. NWAC had decision-making powers which it used judiciously to, among other things, commission important research on abortion and on economic issues; work on childcare policies and practices; and ensure the government sent serious representation to the 1980 UN Conference on Women in Copenhagen.

Bryce was tall with striking blonde hair worn twirled on top of her head, she dressed elegantly, usually wore stilettos (at a time when the rest of us were clumping around in lower, more 'sensible' heels). She was always so crisply turned out that it was rumoured she travelled with an iron. She was also married, to the designer Michael Bryce, with whom she had five children. *And* she'd been born in Ilfracombe, a tiny town in central west Queensland. You could not have asked for a more perfect person to counter Bjelke-Petersen's conservative bulwark.

Bryce went on to become federal Sex Discrimination Commissioner in 1988, and to run the fractious national childcare accreditation process for the Keating government, before she moved to the University of Sydney and became principal of Women's College. That job preceded her appointment as Governor of Queensland in 2003 and, in 2008, as Australia's first female Governor-General, when she became a national figure widely regarded with affection and admiration for the grace, creativity and courage with which she tackled the position. But all that was ahead of her in 1984 when she took up the position at QWIS and began a gruelling public education program, that saw her travelling all around the huge state talking to people about why they should welcome the SDA. She endured a lot of resistance and hostility, which she absorbed with charm and humour, but which was a telling indicator that there was not a consensus in Australia, and certainly not in Queensland, that women were entitled to independence and self-reliance. Bryce was invariably gracious and cheerful, even in the face of some pretty awful personal attacks. She seemed to manage the job, with all its travel, and her young family with ease, never showing—to me anyway—any signs of stress. It was only much later, when her children were grown, with families of their own, that she talked publicly about how hard it had been to hold it all together in those difficult days.

Developing the affirmative action policy was even more tricky. We had to come up with a way to deal with the competing pressure from trade unions and women's groups who wanted employers to be made to account publicly for the numbers and remuneration of their female employees, and the resistance from business and its political allies. Chris Ronalds, a barrister and a good friend of mine and Ryan's, was already a consultant to OSW. She was an exuberant character with short blonde hair and an extensive wardrobe of colourful silk shirts who, in additional to her unparalleled legal expertise in what was then still the new field of discrimination law, was known for her extraordinarily generous hospitality. She liked to host big lunches at her Rozelle house where she chopped and cooked and assembled a dazzling array of dishes, usually a mixture of Asian and Italian, for a guest list that usually comprised feminists, politicos, legal types and their hangers on. Ryan had employed Ronalds to draft the SDA, an unusual move since legislation is normally drawn up by the Office of the Parliamentary Counsel. Now, over quite a few dinners and drinks, she and I plotted a legal and political strategy to win acceptance for complementary Affirmative Action legislation. We decided we had to make an economic case for AA, as we called it, and to demonstrate that it would actually be good for business. Ronalds prepared a discussion 'Green' Paper that set out the issues and made the case for AA legislation. The paper had immediate political clout for having an introduction written by the Prime Minister: 'To date, women's skills and talents have not been utilised in our workforce to the fullest extent possible.

The country is the poorer for it.'[2] We tried to make the idea of affirmative action less scary by explaining that it was merely 'the means to achieve equal employment opportunity' and, we assured business, we had no intention of introducing 'American-style quotas'. But we took it further. Rather than just setting out a policy for discussion, we proposed to demonstrate how the law would actually work in practice. Hawke was receptive to my idea of creating a pilot program to test the legislation. He wrote to 28 ASX 200 companies and three universities, inviting them to start complying with the proposed laws on a voluntary basis. Every CEO readily complied with the PM's request—with the exception of Sir Peter Abeles who, despite being a close personal friend of Hawke's, needed personal persuasion. I met with him and after he put me through my paces, he agreed to commit his Ansett Airlines to trial the laws.

OSW was a policy office and we had no experience in running programs so we had to hire a whole new team to conduct the pilot. Soon the normally quiet OSW was punctuated by the rowdy interactions of the six women staffers of the Affirmative Action Research Unit, as they zoomed in and out of the office reporting on their progress. Each of them had to know the corporate world or, in one case, higher education, and they travelled constantly visiting the companies or universities each had been assigned to guide them through the novel task of complying with laws that had yet to be approved by Parliament. The participants ranged from banks located in a major city CBD to the Argyle Mines in remote Western Australia. We were making it up as we went along, but it was surprisingly successful. We worked closely with the Business Council of Australia and its policy head, Geoff Allen, as well as with the ACTU and the university sector. The government established an Advisory Group comprising women, unionists, business and MPs to review progress of the pilot and agree to the draft legislation. The Affirmative Action (Equal Employment Opportunity for Women) legislation was enacted in 1986. Although the Opposition decided at the time not to vote against the bill, it declared its opposition to its principles and wasted no time when it was returned to government a decade later in taking the axe to the law and to the agency that administered it.

I had travelled the country explaining the proposed affirmative action laws to as many audiences as possible, including addressing a packed business luncheon at one of Perth's fanciest hotels. The Premier, Brian Burke, chaired the event and I was seated next to him at the top table. I had not met him before and he certainly made no effort to be either welcoming or charming. He was on a diet and while the rest of us hopped into our chicken, he downed several cups of tea. Maybe that was why he was so grumpy. As I got up to speak, he said in a loud aside to me: 'You better not fucking embarrass me.' I would have liked nothing more, but I knew it was more important to sell the policy to business, and try to get a win for women's employment. You will keep, you bastard, I muttered to myself in a promise that I was never able to keep. I shed no tears, however, when during the 1990s he was twice imprisoned on dishonesty charges and was stripped of his Companion of the Order of Australia, the highest honour our country can bestow on a citizen.

For the most part, the years I spent at OSW were good optimistic times, when progress was palpable and, I was confident, we were really within reach of true equality. Not that we used that term: our talk was of 'improving the status of women'. But we seemed to be getting there. I used to point out in my many speeches that women's pay, while still not at parity, was now at 86 per cent of men's earnings. Just eleven years earlier, in 1970, it had been 65.2 per cent, I'd say, quoting figures from the OECD.[3] The upward trajectory was there—what could possibly stop it? We will soon have equal pay, I would say with utter confidence, just as Gough Whitlam had intended when, in one of the very first acts of his government in 1972, he had authorised intervention in an equal pay case and, reversing the previous government's opposition, had firmly asserted that his government wanted equal pay to be the law of the land. I would not have believed it possible that 30 years later what we now call the gender pay gap would actually have slipped backwards, and in 2016 be at 77 per cent of male earnings.[4] In 1986, I was enthusiastic as I watched women being appointed to jobs they had never previously held, and saw once insuperable barriers break. Just in the time that I was at OSW Dame Roma Mitchell became the first woman chancellor at the University of Adelaide; Helen Williams the first woman to head a federal government department when she was appointed Secretary of the Department of Education, another Susan Ryan appointment; Joan Child, a Victorian Labor MP, became the first woman speaker of the House of Representatives; and Janine Haines became first woman to lead a political party when she was elected leader of the Australian Democrats in 1986. Mary Gaudron became the first woman appointed to the High Court. And these were just the very high-profile appointments to public office; elsewhere women were stepping up, making history and carving new trails of opportunities for others to follow. I felt a sense of achievement and of progress that I did not for one moment think would not be permanent.

The government, apart from a couple of notable exceptions, was firmly onside. Bob Hawke was fully supportive. I was often asked how a man who had had such a reputation as a womaniser before he entered Parliament could possibly understand or empathise with women's issues. I am not in a position to speculate about any contradiction between his past and how he conducted himself in government. All I can say is that in office, he was exemplary. He supported every major proposal we put to him, he was willing to speak on women's issues when it was deemed appropriate and he broke all precedent by moving the second reading of the Affirmative Action legislation when it finally came into Parliament in 1986. Usually Prime Ministers do not introduce legislation.[5] Hawke also liked to point out that he had actually read Simone de Beauvoir's *The Second Sex*, and that this book had introduced him to the feminist principles that he was now willing to have inform much of his government.

Australia now had strong sex discrimination legislation and soon the affirmative action law would require employers to report annually on the numbers of women they employed. This would be a major step in knowing and understanding women's employment patterns. It was less than twenty years since 1966 and the abolition of the 'marriage bar', that required women to resign from the public service, from banks, teaching and a host of other jobs when they married. It was astonishing to realise how recently Australia—and most other Western countries—had employed such blatant discrimination against the majority of women. It would take more than a generation for the economy to make up for this, for women to begin to file into responsible jobs and begin the slow work of advancing up the ladders of opportunity so they might be well-placed, and suitably qualified, to take on senior jobs and leadership roles. Even now, there was still hostility to married women—which was actually mostly code for 'mothers'—being in employment. I could scarcely get my head around this resistance. It was irrational. Married women themselves wanted to work; increasingly, they were sufficiently educated that it would be derelict for a society not to employ them. (Indeed, since 1987, women have constituted a majority of university graduates in Australia.) But the opposition was there and it was loud. The argument now being put forward was that married women were taking jobs from young people (read: young men). It was rubbish, of course, since older women and young people were in different job markets, but it had superficial appeal to those who still firmly believed, in the middle 1980s, that a woman's place was in the home.

So it was not all smooth sailing. There were also, of course, legitimate disagreements about policy issues and about tactics. The women's movement was seldom united and not everything the Office, or I, did met with unqualified approval. No matter how hard I worked, or how genuinely I tried to reach out, I often met unfriendliness. A meeting in Sydney with a group of what were then called 'Multicultural' women became fiercely argumentative about whether I, as an 'Anglo', could understand their issues. I pointed out that I was there, listening, trying to do just that. And there were outright attacks. I attended a show by comedian Sue Ingleton at Canberra Theatre only to hear her say: 'And Anne Summers, she's so far up Bob Hawke's arse . . .' I forget the rest of the sentence. Other attacks were raw and ugly.

One morning I found flung across the windscreen of my car a life-size plastic sex doll. It was deflated, its arms and legs flattened, but the head had been carefully placed so that it faced my steering wheel. I had never seen one of these dolls before and was surprised at how repellent a piece of pink plastic could be. I especially recoiled at the head, with its black painted-on hair, its grotesque makeup and the red-rimmed mouth whose fixed round opening was so patently designed to take a penis. And here it was, on my car. I felt nervous, even a little frightened. Not because this tawdry piece of plastic could hurt me but because whoever put it there could. It was a reminder that there were people—possibly a lot of people—in Canberra and beyond who did not like the way women's policy was getting political priority. And, it was chilling to have to confront that some of them actually hated women. Maybe it wasn't meant for me, friends tried to reassure me. Maybe it was left on your car by accident. Maybe. But if it was intended for me, it was a clear act of hostility.

I had had many surprises when I made the leap from the Canberra Press Gallery to the federal bureaucracy, and by far the biggest was to discover the extent and vehemence of the opposition to any expansion of childcare services. This came not just from sections of the public service, but from within Hawke's own cabinet. I had naively assumed that all ministers would support government policy, so I was quite stunned by the vociferous resistance, particularly from Senator Peter Walsh. Labor Party policy on childcare in the 1980s, Walsh wrote in his *Confessions of a Failed Finance Minister*, had been determined by 'a self-serving, symbiotic coalition of feminist "networkers" on-market sector service providers and early childhood "educators".'[6] He and I were locked in battle over childcare funding and being the Finance Minister, he was probably going to win. It was also awkward that Walsh lived in the same apartment building as me. Our front doors were adjacent. He'd banged on mine more than once, usually after midnight, because he could not find his keys, but usually we passed each other on the stairs with the barest of courtesies.

I became convinced that this was not a financial fight. It was an ideological battle about the place of women in our society and women's right to economic self-reliance. It became obvious that, if we were to make any headway, we needed a circuit-breaker. It came in late 1984, when the Prime Minister called a surprise election. I had been in the job less than a year, but I figured that when faced with bureaucratic obduracy and political hostility, the best—often the only—way to break through was to have the Prime Minister take control of the matter. I knew that what I had in mind was risky, because public servants were supposed to observe proper procedures when dealing with the Prime Minister's office. They were certainly not supposed to use back channels to try to achieve policy outcomes they had failed to win through the 'normal' political process. But what if the 'normal' channels were hell-bent on blocking the very things I had been appointed to deliver? I was in no doubt that circumventing those bureaucrats and cabinet members who were blocking childcare was the right thing to do. But I knew there would probably be consequences.

I could work on this only with a few trusted and courageous people. Both Michael Roche and Mary Ann O'Loughlin were willing to take it on and, together, they had the necessary economic and policy skills. We spent long hours deciding what to propose, but in the end Michael urged simplicity.

'Let's just try to double the number of places,' he said.

He wrote up the policy, and together with the figures to back it up, I presented it on two sheets of plain paper to Bob Hogg, one of Hawke's political advisers, who I met early one morning at the motel where he stayed when he was in Canberra.

When Hawke delivered his election campaign launch speech, his largest single budgetary commitment was the promise of 20,000 new childcare places. Today, when more than a million Australian children use various forms of childcare[7], that does not sound like much, but in 1983 there were just 46,000 government-subsidised childcare places in the entire country. It was a complicated formula, but the new policy was designed to rapidly expand the base number so that future increases in government subsidies would result in an exponential increase in the number of places. We had projected an expansion to 110,000 places by December 1988. The firm commitment from the Prime Minister in his campaign speech meant that once he won the election against Andrew Peacock—which he did, albeit with a somewhat-reduced majority—there would be a mandate to vastly expand childcare services. 'This was a great victory for OSW,' wrote Marian Sawer, who has chronicled the women's advisory functions over several governments, 'and in particular Anne Summers'.[8]

It was indeed a tremendous coup for us, and even more so for the women across Australia for whom access to childcare would open up increased opportunities for education and employment, but we had won this victory through unorthodox means and the question was: were we going to get away with it? And of course, we didn't. Just five months after the election, the government delivered a minibudget that cut $30 million from what was expected to be total expenditure on childcare of $143 million 1985/86.[9] There was massive community protest against this; Marian Sawer reported that the Prime Minister was receiving 600 letters a week.[10] The cut was reduced to $10 million, but in order to keep increasing places with reduced funds, the government cut back on quality. The Childcare Act was amended to repeal the nexus between subsidies and the requirement that childcare workers had stipulated training. The overall result was an increase in the fees parents had to pay and fewer trained workers employed in centres. Our victory came at a high cost but we did achieve a very significant increase in places and spending. Even today, more than 30 years later, there is still a distinct unwillingness on the part of politicians of all parties to address childcare. Although spending on services has risen to a massive $7 billion a year, the policy is irrational and chaotic, and fails to meet what I have always thought should be its primary focus of freeing up women to be able to study or work.

I celebrated my 40th birthday on 12 March 1985 by attending a diplomatic meeting in the morning then flying to Melbourne to attend a NWCC dinner. When I checked into the Southern Cross Hotel just after lunch, I found my room was full of helium-filled balloons, silver, green and purple in colour, a wonderfully frivolous gesture from the staff at OSW. It made me feel a little bit better about being by myself, and working, on this milestone. I could not take them with me, of course, so the next morning I opened the window and let them drift out over the city skyline. I thought of them as representing our feminist dreams, able to soar to our full potential with no force able to stop us.

I had a more formal celebration at the weekend. My parents drove over from Adelaide to attend the party at my apartment in Kingston. It was a relatively low-key evening, with mostly colleagues from my new world. All my rowdy friends in Sydney I would see some other time. My father was mightily impressed that the Prime Minister and his wife were at his daughter's birthday party, although he who insisted on the best of everything, especially when it came to apparel, thought that Dr Scholls sandals was hardly appropriate prime ministerial footwear for a birthday party. Susan Ryan presented me with a Malvern Star Ladies bike. Pink, of course. It was just the thing for a femocrat to be seen riding around the lake in Canberra on Sunday mornings.

My parents stayed on for a few days, which I was not happy about as the visit was extraordinarily stressful. My father was drinking heavily again, and they were fighting. My mother told me she had considered driving the car into a tree on the way over. She had not found it in herself to do that but, she said, they were going to separate. She could not keep living with him the way he was. I was aghast. She'd put up with it for all these years. Why leave now? I was astonished at how upset I was—and at how I was instinctively taking his side. I was the one who was supposed to encourage women to leave distressing relationships. Why didn't I see it that way when it was my own mother? The tension between my parents descended like a cloud on the apartment although my father was subdued most of the time, withdrawn into whatever morbid guilty place where he locked his spirit away. I did not want to have to deal with it—or them. That night I slipped and fell on the stairs and sprained my ankle. I could hardly walk so I retreated to the couch. I became the child again, dependent, forcing my mother into the once familiar domestic role of having to care for me. That way, I could avoid having to deal with the horrible mess that was my parents' lives. I was being a coward and I knew it but I did not know what else to do.

The next morning my mother and I were confronted with the calamity of my father drunk and covered in blood. He had been consigned to the small downstairs bedroom while my mother had taken the spare room upstairs next to my bedroom, and he had evidently spent the night working his way through my liquor cabinet. He was in a terrible state, incoherent and raving, and the walls of his room were splattered with blood. It looked like a murder scene. I was paralysed with horror. My mother looked at me as if to say, See what I have had to deal with? I immediately rang the O'Neills. Great friends that they were, they drove over immediately. Gary brought a couple of boxes and took it upon himself to remove all the alcohol from the apartment, while Mez got on the phone and started ringing rehab places. No one would take him. All we could do, we were advised, was to take him to the emergency department of one of the hospitals. Mez took charge. She cleaned my father up. His wound was not as serious as the amount of blood suggested, but he must have had one hell of a hangover. He was clearly very sick. I could not drive because of my ankle, so Mez took us in my car to Woden Valley Hospital where, we were told, we would just have to wait.

We were there for several hours and it seemed unlikely that a doctor would see him. They clearly took the view it was not their job to deal with drunks. My mother had withdrawn into herself. I found myself starting to feel sympathy for her, but I did not know what on earth we were going to do with my father. It was then that Mez said to him,

'Austin, come with me, we need to have a talk.'

She took him to the end of the corridor, sat him down on one of those cheap plastic hospital chairs, and began an earnest conversation. I could see that he was listening to her. After some time, the two of them rejoined my mother and me, and Mez told us we were all going home. When we got back to Kingston, Mez cleaned up the little room where my father had disgraced himself and put him to bed, and then she left.

The next morning my father apologised for his behaviour and told my mother that he would never drink again. She had heard that so many times before that she was unconvinced but, it turned out, this time it was true. Whatever it was that Mez had said had reached my father in a way that none of his many stints in rehab or his years working with AA had succeeded in doing. Mez told me later that all she had done was to talk frankly to him about what he was doing to himself and his family, and to tell him that he had to stop. And, amazingly, she had got through whatever firewalls he had put between himself and his demons. He never touched alcohol again, and the next few years would be the happiest he and my mother had experienced since they were a bright young couple all those decades ago in Deniliquin during World War II. Every year, on 21 April, their wedding anniversary, he would write her a passionate note on a small card. My mother kept many of these, including the first, dated 21 April 1945, which read 'To dearest little Stinker the best wife in the world. For Our First Anniversary with All my love and wishes that it is the first of many'. I have no idea why my father called his new wife Stinker, but in future years he simply addressed her as Tun, her nickname. The last one, written in April 1988, just five months before he died, and after he had not had a drink in more than three years, read: 'Tun After 43 years I love you more than I did on April 21 1944'.

When I joined OSW I had been adamant that I was not going to have my attention diverted to the international work which, in the past, had occupied a great deal of OWA's attention. I could see how this work had been an attractive substitute for being unable to be effective domestically under the Fraser government; it meant the Office could chalk up some achievements, but I considered domestic policy to be the absolute priority. I could not see the relevance of the UN for what we were doing. When I discovered that Australia was a member of the OECD Working Party on the Role of Women in the Economy, I could see the relevance of attending those meetings, but I still argued that we did not have time for this stuff when there was so much to be done at home. But I allowed myself to be persuaded that Australia had obligations and responsibilities that we needed to treat seriously. In July 1983, the government had ratified the UN Convention on the Elimination of All Forms of Discrimination Against Women (CEDAW). This Convention gave the government the constitutional power it needed for its sex discrimination legislation. The government had successfully nominated Justice Elizabeth Evatt as a member of the committee that monitored the implementation of CEDAW, and which we were obliged to report progress on. Besides, I was told, the UN Conference on Women—the third since International Women's Year in 1975—was coming up in Nairobi later in the year, and as it would conclude the official UN Decade of Women it was a very big deal. I was still not convinced, but the fact that the Preparatory Conference—PrepCom—was being held in New York made it suddenly seem more alluring. In April 1985, along with Senator Pat Giles, who would lead the government's delegation to Nairobi, and Helen Ware who was the OSW international expert, I headed for the US.

I quickly learned that important as the UN work was, and I could see the value in trying to build international consensus around improving the lives of women, I was not the person to be doing it. I did not have the temperament for the politics, the games or the grindingly slow pace of working through the conference document, the *Forward Looking Strategies for the Advancement of Women* (the *FLS*). The purpose of the PrepCom was to try to reach as much consensus as possible on this document before the Nairobi meeting. Ahead of the plenary meetings where this work took place, there were caucuses of the three groups into which the world was then divided:

the Eastern Bloc, the Group of 77—the developing countries or 'Third World' as they were still called then—and the Western bloc, to which Australia belonged. Our meetings were unexpectedly tense. Although chaired with great equanimity by Maureen O'Neill, who headed the Canadian OSW, the meetings were disrupted by the extraordinary aggression and profanity of Alan Keyes, the number two of the US delegation. As someone who'd been around the Labor Party and journalism, I was unshockable when it came to language (and a pretty good swearer myself), but I was surprised by such conduct at the UN and directed against people who were meant to be on the same side. How did he treat his enemies, I wondered? Keyes was African-American, a former diplomat who was a political appointee of the Reagan administration, and he was a master at the use of shock-tactics to try to intimidate us 'allies' into agreement with US positions. Later that day in the plenary session, I introduced myself to Maureen Reagan, the daughter of the President and the leader of the US delegation. We quickly found we had very little in common:

'Honey, you're treading on my toes,' she said when I ventured to express a view on one of the issues we were meant to find common cause on.

I could not wait for the PrepCom to be over. I appreciated the work done by Helen Ware and by Cavan Hogue and John Quinn, the diplomats from the Australian Mission who sat beside me and guided me through, but at the end of the first day, the plenary had discussed just 38 of the several hundred paragraphs in the *FLS*, and reached agreement on only six of them. The rest were put in square brackets, to be dealt with 'later'. I preferred to work at a faster pace—and to be able to judge whether or not I was getting anywhere.

So I was quietly relieved when, in late June, I told the Office that I was withdrawing from the government delegation to Nairobi. I had decided, with encouragement from the PMO, that the interests of Australian women would be better served by my immersing myself in the preparations for the Tax Summit that was to take place in early July and which was likely to agree to major changes to the tax system. It was imperative that women's interests be protected in such a major policy shift. At the request of the Prime Minister, PM&C was developing some major policy proposals around family tax benefits and OSW was at the table: both Michael Roche and Mary Ann O'Loughlin had been seconded to work on them.

I felt guilty about pulling out. On 12 June a TWA plane bound for the US had been hijacked by terrorists from Hezbollah and Islamic Jihad, shortly after taking off from Athens. The hijackers were demanding the release of 700 Shi'ite Muslims from Israeli custody. There were dramatic scenes of the plane at Beirut airport with the pilot seen with a gun to his head. One passenger was killed and his body dumped on the tarmac, others were beaten. The ordeal lasted for two weeks. Shortly after it ended, and just days before our delegation was due to leave for Africa, the Israelis released 700 prisoners. Although they claimed this action was unrelated to the hijacking, our delegation was understandably nervous about the trip and I knew, from attending security briefings, that the threat assessment was grim. Australia was being housed in the same building as the Israelis. This meant we would have the best security possible. But it also made us a target.

In the end, there was no terrorism at Nairobi but we still had to contend with the political fallout from the Middle East. Bill Hayden, the Minister for Foreign Affairs, directed that our delegation abstain on the vote on the entire *FLS* document unless the paragraph equating Zionism with racism was removed. Australia had voted against the conference document in Copenhagen in 1980 on similar grounds. Hayden's decision was a slight improvement—although we were told it had taken a lot of pressure to get him to settle for an abstention—but we in OSW were still angry that, even at an international women's conference, women's policy was deemed to be subservient to Middle East policy. It was a bitter moment. All that work, getting bureaucratic consensus on other controversial clauses in the *FLS*, and getting community groups to sign on, was to be negated by a ritualistic move in the never-ending Middle East death dance. Then a miracle occurred and the women in Nairobi successfully lobbied to have the Zionism clause removed. The *Forward Looking Strategies* was adopted by consensus. When I spoke to Helen Ware, who had taken my place as second-in-charge of the delegation, she was delirious with relief.

'I can't tell you how hideous it would have been for us,' she told me later.

The votes were taken in alphabetical order and Australia would be called early. It would have been a lengthy poll, and the Australians would have sat in isolated ignominy for many minutes till they got to the I's and the next country not to support the *FLS* was called. As it was, being able to support *FLS* made it easier to obey Hayden's other directive: that we join Israel and the United States as the only countries to vote against the paragraph on Palestine.

I was never going to be part of this game. I could see that the combat the bureaucrats so loved might be energising. I could recognise that the crushing of weaker players might satisfy a bloodlust that had few other outlets in a bland city like Canberra (my theory as why Canberra public servants drove like maniacs on the Federal Highway on their way to Sydney was that it was a rare opportunity for risk and excitement). I could see that the financial rewards—in those days, appointments were permanent and superannuation surged into golden nest eggs—might compensate for a lot of things, but I could not see myself staying in that world. I despised the deference to ministers that concealed contempt and sabotage. I hated the continual one-upmanship that passed for normal human discourse. But most of all, I was dismayed by the thought of my working life becoming nothing more than constant trench warfare.

I was no match for seasoned bureaucratic warriors. They had all the time in the world to see off someone they saw as missionary, an advocate for a cause, not mandarins like them, lifelong public servants championing good government (as if the two had to be in conflict). I was weary of the games and, more so, the confected aggression on so many on the committees I was forced to sit on. There was no sense of common good around these tables; it was all about turf and personal advancement and settling ancient scores. I found it both tedious and upsetting. How many hours did I have to spend engaged in these ritualistic battles? The Prime Minister has said he wanted it. Wasn't that good enough? No it wasn't. Most bureaucrats were of the Sir Humphrey Appleby school when it came to government decisions. 'A government decision is something we agree with,' Appleby famously said on the excruciatingly accurate television series *Yes Minister*, 'anything else is just a temporary setback.' It was not surprising that Canberra pretty much came to a standstill when that program aired each week, although ministers and bureaucrats rarely agreed on which bits of the night before's episode were so hilarious.

I was not a bureaucrat, let alone a mandarin. I knew that much. But what was I? Most of my adult life I had been torn between activism and 'advocacy'—wanting to change things—and the cool and often cynical stance of being a mere observer, someone who reported and judged without ever having to take a stand. The journalist in me was constantly at war with the activist and I could not find a way of reconciling the two. They were probably irreconcilable. I had to choose. But at that moment, I was neither. The bureaucrat, even a high-profile one like I was, in the end works mostly behind the scenes, unable to tell people what she has done or, in some instances, what planned atrocities she was able to prevent. Working 'inside' is the way to change things I had reasoned when I applied for the job. The women's movement had accepted the 'femocrat strategy', although with a degree of scepticism. We femocrats were constantly on trial: were we 'selling out'? were we becoming careerists? I suppose I had seen the job as a form of activism. I was proud of what we had been able to do: the biggies like affirmative action, childcare, the Women's Budget Program and the many smaller changes that would remove injustices and make women's lives better, but I did not see it as a lifelong career.

In late November 1985, I went to Europe as a guest of the EEC Visitors Program, travelling to Ireland, Germany and Greece, as well as a mandatory visit to Brussels. I'd initially seen the trip as a chance to meet the women doing comparable jobs to mine, and to check out their thinking, and the progress, around status of women issues generally and, in particular, what we used to call 'positive action'—steps to increase women's employment. But travelling, and meeting some extraordinary people, also allowed me to reflect on what I was doing with my life.

In Dublin I'd met Nell McCafferty, the highly celebrated radical journalist and author. She was, according to a profile in the *Guardian* in 2004, 'a foul-mouthed and fearless social commentator, [who] is one of the great feminist heroes of the liberalisation of Ireland. Part Germaine Greer and part Mae West . . .'[11] She was a pint-sized firebrand, exuding infectious energy, and I felt alive just talking with her. She gave me some of her books and I read them while I was travelling. In quite important ways, reading them changed me. I had to keep putting down *The Armagh Women*, Nell's account of the 'dirty strike' by around 30 IRA women prisoners at Armagh prison to protest ill treatment by brutal guards. These women refused to wash, use the toilet, empty chamber pots or clean their cells. They were emulating a similar strike by IRA men in 1978 at Long Kesh prison but the key difference was that women menstruated and this was puritan and repressed Ireland where, even in 1980, such things were not discussed in front of men. The women were denied sanitary goods, so they started smearing their blood on their cell walls, along with their excrement. The public was scandalised, torn between repulsion and sympathy for these women. Reading about what they endured was almost unbearable but even more confronting was Nell's just-published book, *A Woman to Blame*, about the so-called Kerry babies scandal and the persecution by the legal system and the Catholic Church of a young single woman whose 'illegitimate' baby's body was found washed-up on a beach. This was Ireland in the mid-1980s where abortion was forbidden and even contraceptives only available to married women, and then at the whim of individual pharmacists. Reading about those girls in Ireland with their shameful secret pregnancies and the desperation that led them to allow the babies to die and be hidden in sad little unmarked graves in the countryside, brought back my own Catholic upbringing. We were similarly repressed, unable to even talk about sex let alone protect ourselves when, inevitably, it happened and we got pregnant. I have described elsewhere what happened to me: the terror of parents finding out, being willing to risk my life with a costly and dangerous illegal abortion in order to keep my shameful secret.[12] But that had been 1965. This was a full twenty years later, when women were getting education and jobs, earning good money, having laws protect them from discrimination and inequality, and able to control their fertility with the pill or, if contraceptives failed, abortion. But that was Australia.

Not all places were as progressive. Nor were all people, even Australians whose job it was to represent the policies and values of the federal government. I was guest of honour at a dinner hosted by one of our diplomats in Bonn. Among the invitees were several leading women bureaucrats, doing similar work to me, and Petra Kelly, who was internationally-renowned for having founded the German Greens Party in 1979 and who, in 1983, had been elected to the Bundestag. I had met her in Canberra the year before and was looking forward to resuming our conversation but I found myself seated, not next to the host, which would be usual, but at the far end of the table. I don't know if the host intended this as a hostile act, or whether it was his feeble effort at accommodating what he thought would be a feminist's preference to sit with the spouses. I found myself talking to the diplomat's 'wife'—I was not introduced to her by name—and, on my other side, former General Gert Bastion, Petra's much older partner who, seven years later, would murder Kelly, shooting her through the head while she slept, before turning the gun on himself.

———

A few days later I was on Chios, the small and mostly rugged Greek island close to Turkey, said to be the birthplace of Homer. Here I met up with Margaret Papandreou, the American wife of Andreas Papandreou, the popular and long-serving Prime Minister of Greece; he had come to power at the end of the rule of the colonels and had set about modernising Greek society, especially its education system. Margaret was renowned for championing both women's and peace issues, and she was meeting up with a delegation of Soviet women, one of whom was Valentina Tereshkova, a cosmonaut and the first woman ever to pilot a space vehicle. (In June 1963, she had flown Vostock 6 into space, and remained there for three days, orbiting the earth 48 times.)

We had been driven to a small village high in the mountains by a team of women who were part of a local effort to promote women-owned local tourism. There was a ceremony with speeches. Tereshkova told us how peaceful it had been up there in space, how she had looked down on earth, knowing there were wars and other conflicts taking place far below her, but they seemed to be abstract and meaningless so far from the earth. She called for the end of war, and especially to Star Wars, President Reagan's plan to build a missile-proof shield in space. (This reminded me of Otto Silha's plan for a shield to protect Minnesota from its brutal climate.) Margaret Papandreou beamed. This, it seemed, was the principal reason we were here. It was a declaration of peace, made in the place where the *Iliad*, an epic poem about the Trojan Wars, had quite possibly been recited by Homer. A new legend was to be born from this place: an idea of peace, propagated by women, spread to men of good will everywhere. I was still deeply sceptical of this kind of politics. It was favoured by many Labor women and had led to arguments about whether or not OSW should advocate for women to join the armed forces. I felt we—mostly educated, employed women—had no right to deny girls the technical education that Defence offered and which was the primary reason most people signed up for the military. Besides, if a girl wanted to fly a fighter jet, why shouldn't she? It was still government policy to deny her the opportunity because that was deemed a 'combat' role and was still, despite the SDA, not open to women. It was a fundamental divide in feminism and one that, I suspected, was not going to be easily reconciled.

While Tereshkova was still speaking, a wizened and weatherworn old woman appeared. Her face was deeply lined and tanned and she was leading a donkey that carried on its back a large bundle of what looked like wild thyme. She could have stepped from any of Chios's renowned medieval villages. We would visit one, Mesta, for a traditional feast in the village square later that evening. This woman stood there, uncomprehending, taking in the strange sight of Western women in their smart modern clothes, outlining a dream that was, I realised, almost as remote to me as it was to this peasant woman. My politics were more practical. I liked real and measurable change, but then my life's expectations were limited by where I had been born.

I flew back to Athens with Papandreou. We talked about the spread of feminist ideas, especially to the Third World. She described how during the years 1967–74, when the Western women's movement was developing, Greek women were fighting the junta. Papandreou seemed very popular wherever we went, especially with women who were receptive to her efforts to promote women's issues. The previous year her husband had legislated equal pay for women but, I was told, there was muttering about his wife 'interfering' in politics. Andreas dumped Margaret four years later for a younger woman, but he died in 1996 and did not live to see George, the first of his four children with Margaret, become Prime Minister of Greece in 2009.

We knew none of this of course as we talked in November 1985. I looked past her through the plane's window to the Aegean Sea beneath. That evening in Athens I had dinner with the young journalist from *Ethos*, the communist party newspaper who'd been on the Chios trip. She and her fiancé took me to a private yacht club down the coast. We spent the evening talking about money. I had never met such bourgeois communists. I was going to Paris next, for an OECD meeting. Somehow I knew that my life was about to change radically. Even more than my time in the US in 1978, this trip had opened my eyes to ideas, experiences and people I rarely encountered in my safe little world back in Australia. I was feeling impatient for something new, and more challenging.

While in Paris I made contact with Jacqueline Nonon. She had established the first Women's Bureau in the European Commission in the late 1960s. After working there for a decade she was approached by President Giscard d'Estaing to establish a women's office for France. After just a few months, she resigned in a very public protest against the President's failure to give the office adequate political and financial support. Now she was working at the Commission's Information Office in Paris. She took me to a very special dinner held at the Hotel Royal Monceau on Avenue Hoche of Club 'L', an exclusive women's network set up to rival the men's Club de Siecle. It was a high-powered and ultra-glamorous affair. I met the president of a French bank, France's Ambassador to UNESCO, the world's only female 747 pilot who flew for Air France, and a number of journalists. I was disconcerted to discover midway through the sumptuous meal that I was the guest of honour and expected to speak. I was unprepared and in introducing me, Nonon told the audience all about my job at OSW, leaving me with nothing to talk about. After weeks on the road I was travel-worn, with no decent clothes and looked decidedly frumpish in the midst of this mink-coat wearing group. Worse, I spoke no French. After I sat down there was a polite smattering of applause, but I could tell that I had not made much of an impression. Then another international guest was invited to speak. She was from Texas and was definitely better turned out than I was. I consoled myself by thinking that at least she too would have the same language difficulty, but then shrank back embarrassed as she addressed the group in perfect French.

Some of these women were avowed feminists. Others were there because they were working women who needed a counter to the male networks. Puck Simonet, who ran Club 'L', discussed with me the possibility of setting up a branch in Australia, but I could not imagine such a group. There was no comparison with the Girls' Dinners of femocrats in Canberra. These were usually rowdy, inebriated, letting-off-steam affairs and no one could accuse the attendees of being stylish. If there was to be a Club 'L' in Australia, it would have to be in Sydney or Melbourne, for women in business. In fact such a group was setting itself up in Sydney at about this time. Led by publisher Barbara Cail and involving entrepreneurs Imelda Roche, Carla Zampatti, businesswoman Wendy McCarthy and others, Chief Executive Women was started in 1985 as an offshoot of another French group, Women Chiefs of Enterprise. It is now taken for granted there needs to be networking groups at all levels for women, and the work that in the 1980s was done only at the United Nations or the OECD is now also taken up by the World Economic Forum and other high-level business bodies. Not before time.

During this trip, I received a very tempting job offer.

If I'd thought journalism would be forever closed to me after working for the government, I was relieved to discover that I was wrong. Max Suich, now the chief editorial executive of Fairfax, who had been my first-ever editor at the *National Times*, had kept trying to entice me back almost from the day I left the *Financial Review*. Various jobs, mostly in Sydney, all of them in newspapers, were dangled in front of me. I knew the industry, the company and the people who ran it well enough to know that lures are not firm offers. Nor was I at all certain that I wanted to trade the influence, the high profile and engagement with such a range of issues that my current job gave me for a desk job in Sydney. For all the frustrations of being a femocrat, we could—and we did—actually change things. However hard-fought and compromised the final policy was, we could point to tangible improvement to childcare. OSW *had* become an economic policy force to be reckoned with in PM&C. We *had* pioneered the Women's Budget Program, a policy tool that would be adopted internationally and is still used around the world today. We *had* entrenched anti-discrimination laws. We *were* about to legislate to require all large employers to report on the gender breakdown of their workforce. We *had* got the bureaucracy taking status of women into account when developing policy.

Promotion in the newspaper game meant becoming an editor. That was a powerful and prestigious job within the industry, and of course top editors wielded considerable political power through their publications. But I could not get excited about a job with 'journalists hours', that would see me at the office till at least 10 o'clock every night. I was single. I was 41. I wanted a life. I did not see myself meeting my soul mate in the Fairfax offices in Sydney. Most of the men there about my age were already married. I was tired of affairs and of one-night stands.

'I never hear any gossip about you,' Peter Wilenski once said to me.

I was relieved that I'd managed to fly under the radar with the very few flings I'd enjoyed in Canberra. Most of the time, though, I was sexually lonely and after seven years of living in the national capital, I knew I was unlikely to find what I wanted in that town. I hankered to move into different worlds, mix with people who weren't in politics, who did not know—or care—what an IDC was.

Max Suich was canny. He offered me the one job he knew I would not be able to resist: New York. I agonised about it nevertheless. I drew up lists of Pros and Cons: the lure of an exciting new opportunity versus having been at OSW for just three years, with some important business still unfinished. Someone gave me a poster of the great aviator Amelia Earhart with her famous words: *If you are offered a great adventure, you don't refuse it.* It hadn't ended well for her, but at least she had not died wondering and I was tired of the small and, ultimately, boring pond that was Canberra. The affirmative action laws were not yet through Parliament. Senator Walsh had defied the Prime Minister and denied funding to establish the agency that would administer the laws, and there was a risk the whole package might collapse. I should not leave while this was unresolved. But, I told myself, there is never a good time to leave. There is always unfinished business. And, a pragmatic little voice inside me said: quit while you are ahead. Before people turn on you.

When I announced that I was leaving, to go to New York to become North American manager for my old newspaper employer Fairfax, many of my public service colleagues were astonished.

'You'd give up a permanent job, with super, to go to a dangerous place like New York?'

'I can't wait,' I'd said.

CHAPTER SIX

'THE TIMES WILL SUIT ME'

———⊰⊱———

Finally, I was back in New York. This time I had a job and my own apartment, in a doorman building on the Upper West Side. I took the subway to work, joining the tightly packed throng on the narrow platform at the 72nd Street station. I rode the express 2 or 3 train the one stop to Times Square and spilling out of the carriage at 42nd Street, strode purposefully towards the filthy narrow steps that led up to the chaos of people and traffic just above us in Times Square. Just like a real New Yorker, I told myself. Until I tried to order a black coffee at the deli near the office and was greeted with such hostility that I backed out of the place in bafflement. Later, someone explained that there was 'coffee', which was black, and there was 'regular coffee', which had milk. There would be many other such blunders before I could navigate the town with some ease, but I would always be a foreigner. My accent was a dead giveaway, so even after I'd learned most of the more obvious social cues, and although I began to feel more and more at home as the years rolled on, I realised I would never be able to find my way into the American imagination. That would remain as remote to me as any foreign nation's. It was easy for we visitors to think we knew America because of our familiarity with its movies and television, its music and other cultural creations, but just because we thought we spoke the same language did not mean that we even began to comprehend this curious and infuriating country. The United States was a melting pot, no doubt about that, and New York was the most multicultural of cities where no one questioned your right to be there. If you had money or connections or a claim to fame you would be embraced, as I would discover, but you would never have the grace or certainty of a native. That did not mean you could not have a helluva time and from the moment I arrived at JFK Airport in March 1986, that is what I set out to do.

I was now in the New York I'd always craved. Not the edgy downtown of my first visit, or the elegant Greenwich Village of my most recent trip. I was now in Gotham City, with its canyons and cacophony and in-your-face capitalism. This was the real New York and I was enchanted. I could not wait to devour it. I had been appointed North American manager of John Fairfax & Sons, responsible for supervising the small local staff and overseeing what was then quite a sizeable syndication business. The Fairfax office was on the 24th floor of 1500 Broadway, a 1970s glass sky-scraper overlooking Times Square. It was right across from a New York architectural masterpiece, the 1927 Paramount Building, with its distinctive dome and clock face, and a lobby modelled on the Paris Opera House, where a lot of entertainment companies were located. We were right in the middle of the Broadway theatre district, known as the Great White Way. The distinctive neon lights that lit up the fronts of many buildings were neither as ubiquitous nor as garish as they became after the transformation of Times Square following Mayor Rudolph Guiliani's famous 'cleanup' of the area in the mid-1990s but even then they were the brightest lights of the biggest city. From my window I could look down on the famous news ticker running round the triangular-shaped white tile-clad building that was like a miniature version of the famous Flatiron Building, almost twenty blocks further south. Four blocks away to the north on West 47th street was the famous diamond district where I saw Hasidic Jews for the first time: men dressed all in black—hats, coats, gloves, with long, usually grey, beards—carrying attaché cases and seemingly bent slightly, as if against the wind. Four blocks south was the garment district where racks of clothes were in constant movement from factory to delivery, and where a sharp-eyed observer might spot a celebrity designer, a famous model or, best of all, one of the most powerful figures in New York: a fashion magazine editor.

Each of the Fairfax newspapers had their own correspondent who reported directly to their editors, so my responsibilities towards them were practically non-existent, but I was also North American editor for the *Financial Review*, writing news stories and a regular column as well as a weekly piece for the Natty Times, which had been renamed *Times on Sunday*. After a gap of three years, I hoped I could easily move back into writing. Not that I had any choice as I seemed to have burned my bridges. I had gone to Washington in April for Bob Hawke's visit, and found that the bureaucrats who had been my colleagues just a few months earlier would not talk to me. But nor could I find much common ground with the Press Gallery; I could no longer fall in with their perpetual cynicism. I had views, and values, and no longer wanted to conceal these. I realised, yet again, that I was on my own, no longer part of any herd, but I did not care. I was all fired up. The *New York Times* was just half a block away, on West 43rd Street, and although I did not yet know anyone there, I felt inspired by its mere propinquity.

I already knew that there were many Americas. I would never experience 'the awful realization' of F. Scott Fitzgerald in 1932, when he climbed to the top of the recently completed Empire State Building and took in the view and saw that New York 'was a city after all and not a universe'.[1] He saw beyond the canyons of skyscrapers to the towns and the fields and rivers beyond 'the whole shining edifice that he had reared in his imagination'. The Jazz Age was over, the Wall Street crash had shattered the lives of millions, and the country was settling into a long Depression. But the man who had said there were no second acts in Americans' lives, now saw that also was untrue. Instead, 'from the ruins, lonely and inexplicable as the sphinx, rose the Empire State Building', the place of his epiphany, and evidence that America would never stop inventing itself, would never cease to amaze.

I had seen so much of this perplexing country during my previous visits, and met such a bewildering array of Americans, that I could never be tempted to easy generalisations about this place or its people. I wanted to find a way to write about America that would be engaging and informative and, above all, would not rely on the Yank-bashing stereotypes that Australians responded to so well. It was easy to make fun of America. I decided I would try to do something different. I was in the right place and, it seemed to me, the right time as the Reagan era wound down. I would be an eager observer as America repudiated the harshness of those free-wheeling, free-market years of monetarism and deregulation and moved back, politically, to what I hoped was a replica of its truer self, the country that had been able, through the sixteen years of the leadership of Franklin Delano Roosevelt, to keep its people's spirits alive during the hard years of Depression and war. Australia had turned its back on Malcolm Fraser after eight years of punitive conservative politics and embraced the fairer, more inclusive policies of Labor led by Bob Hawke. I hoped America was ready to do the same and here I was, on the ground, ready to tell the story. If that indeed was the story; the powers-that-be back in Sydney seemed to have other ideas.

'The story,' Max Suich had told me excitedly as he pursued me to leave government and come back to Fairfax, this time in New York, 'the story in America is the capital markets.' Suich was now Fairfax's editorial director but he'd been a reporter before he'd become editor of the *National Times* and for him, 'the story' was the political or, to his mind more likely, the economic circumstances that defined that particular moment in the history of the place you were writing about. When he had represented the *Financial Review* in Tokyo in the late 1960s, 'the story' had been the iron ore negotiations between Japan and Australia. He'd covered the ongoing setting of prices and the determining of supplies that would define the trade relations between the two nations for decades to come, and which would cement Australia's national wealth as being dependent on resources. Suich also covered the men who made this story, the miners such as Russell Madigan and Lang Hancock who had had the foresight to develop the ore and to seek out Japan, so recently our mortal wartime enemy, as a natural trading partner. Now, in New York, 'the story' was how the wide-scale deregulation, including of the financial markets, and the infatuation with monetary policy, was changing not just the broader US economy but the very way Wall Street operated. Bonds were now sexier than stocks and a new product—the junk bond— would soon emerge as one of the definitive errors of the era. Debt was king and leverage was the new way to easy wealth. Leveraged buyouts, or LBOs, as they were known, were the new way to buy and sell companies; debt was deployed against a company's cash flow and assets, which were then broken up and sold to repay the debt. The average return on LBOs in 1986 was 40 per cent, according to *Euromoney* magazine. A 31-year-old computer nerd by the name of Bill Gates had just floated his software company, Microsoft Corp, on the stock exchange, earning himself an instant $350 million and then, sitting back, had watched the stock soar. The stock market was on a dizzying upward spiral. Money was the new god. Greed was good. The savings and loans crisis was starting to reveal itself. Where would it all end?

It was, as journalists say, quite a story. I could see that. I just wasn't sure that it was the story that I wanted to be my main focus. I felt desperately unequipped, for one thing. Suich had arranged for me to be briefed by money market experts and foreign exchange dealers before I'd left Australia, but I had no natural feel for finance and economics. Although I had written for the *Financial Review* for five years before joining OSW, my subject had been politics, which I understood and enjoyed. A few years later, in 1989, when I read *Liar's Poker* by Michael Lewis, an eye-poppingly revealing insider account of the operations of a Wall Street investment banking firm in the late 1980s, I understood how compelling a story it was. By then, of course, the stock market had crashed, the junk bonds and savings and loan scandals had bankrupted thousands of small institutions and provided a grim foretaste of what was to come with the housing collapse that led to the global financial crisis in 2008. But Lewis's books (he wrote several, all of them gripping) and others such as *The Barbarians at the Gate* had the benefit of being retrospective accounts. Although I could see the bigger picture of the dangers in what was happening, I had trouble understanding the story as it was unfolding. When I wrote about the economy or the financial system, I was more likely to approach these subjects the way I would a political story: look for the major issues and trends, identify the key players, and try to tell the story of what they were doing. I had no technical grasp, as was very clear when during an interview with Paul Volcker in late June 1986 I'd asked him a question about monetary policy.

'I thought you were supposed to be a political writer,' he'd said, indicating that I had no idea what I was talking about.

He was right. The Chairman of the Federal Reserve had agreed to this interview as a favour to Bob Hawke. As a parting gift to me the Australian

Prime Minister had written letters of introduction to Defence Secretary Caspar Weinberger, Secretary of State George Schultz and White House Chief of Staff Donald Regan, as well as Volcker. All but Regan had agreed to be interviewed, and although I was never able to pin down a time with Schultz, both Weinberger and Volcker made time to talk to me. Both interviews enhanced my journalistic reputation because Australian reporters usually did not have access to these top-ranking officials. I was extraordinarily lucky to have this kind of leg-up in my very early days as a correspondent in the US. The interview with Volcker was off-the-record. I could not quote him directly, although I could write with authority what he thought about the deregulation of the economy, mounting third world debt and other current economic issues. I was grateful to Volcker for his kindly tolerance, but embarrassed by my ignorance. By then I was able to write my way out of anything, so I produced a three-part series that passed muster, but while I did try to improve my understanding of 'the story', my heart was not in it. I made an effort to cultivate the bankers who made money out of Australia, but I could never think of what to ask them. I went to a briefing at Bain & Co on Australian capital markets. I learned that if I had some money, I could probably make some more. But I found the subject dull and I could not think of interesting or creative ways to write about it. Towards the end of my first year I'd attended the New York Financial Writers' dinner, and soon afterwards a two-day seminar on debt at the Waldorf Astoria. It was another of those occasions where most people's eyes glazed over when they heard my opening line, 'Hi, I'm from the *Australian Financial Review*, it's like the *Wall Street Journal . . .*' No one cared. It wasn't simply that I was female, although the finance world was astonishingly masculine in makeup and ethos. Janine Perrett, who was in New York for the *Australian* news-paper, was totally at ease with business and finance stories. We'd often go for drinks together but we would mostly talk about politics, a subject I felt far more at home with, or gossip about other expatriates. When it came to the capital markets, I simply felt out of place.

I was much more comfortable doing political stories, even an assignment as daunting as my interview with the US Secretary of Defence in early June 1986, a few weeks before I sat down with Volcker. Caspar Weinberger had got the nickname 'Cap the Knife' while serving in the Office of Management and Budget in Washington during the Nixon years, where he engaged in savage cost-cutting, including slashing the Defence budget. He had actually killed the B–1 bomber project, a move that enraged the Pentagon and which Nixon eventually reversed. Now, as Reagan's Defence Secretary, he had presided over the largest military buildup in peacetime. He achieved a 51 per cent increase in real terms of the Defence budget to an astronomical $US293 billion, earning him the accusation that he was 'a draft dodger in the war against the deficit'. He justified this about-face by saying he had been horrified to learn the extent of the Soviet Union's arms buildup. He was not to know, of course, that within a mere three years of our interview the Soviet Union would cease to exist.

Weinberger was an interesting and cultured man, seemingly at odds with the 'cowboy' image of the rest of the Reagan administration. He was a renowned Anglophile, and he was devoted to art and literature; he went to concerts. He brought art into his office, including a bronze bust of General MacArthur and another of an infantryman, a daily reminder of the human cost of what he was undertaking. One of his first acts had been to remove the formal portrait of James V. Forrestal, the first Secretary of Defence, which hung behind his desk. Forrestal had committed suicide in 1949 while on the job, by jumping from a tower of the Bethesda Naval Hospital where he had been admitted for depression. Weinberger replaced the portrait with a 400-year-old Titian he borrowed from Washington's National Gallery of Art. It was a large rectangular picture, using rich red, brown and cream colours, showing Cardinal Marco investing the Abbot of Carrara, with his benefice standing by. 'I found him much more agreeable and soothing to the soul,' Weinberger wrote later in his memoir, *In the Arena: A memoir of the 20th Century*. The Titian 'resided' in his office for the whole seven years he was Defence Secretary.

Weinberger's term had not been without controversy. He was accused of being bewitched by the Pentagon and presiding over excessive waste in procurement. At the time of our interview, he had recently been publicly humiliated by President Reagan, who'd excluded him from a high-level meeting with Secretary-General Gorbachev, and then leaked Weinberger's letter of complaint. And Congress had just passed the Gramm-Rudman amendment, requiring a zero deficit within five years. To achieve this would require brutal budget cuts with at least half of these coming from Defence; his big spending days seemed about to end. But on the day we met, nothing in his demeanour indicated that Caspar Weinberger had anything better to do than spend an hour giving his first-ever interview to an Australian newspaper. I'd been led along what seemed like miles of Pentagon corridors to his office where the Secretary was waiting for me. We sat at a small round conference table, just the two of us, and he gave me his undivided attention. He was remarkably across all details of the Australian alliance, scarcely referring to the thin briefing folder that lay in front of him, and he carefully ensured that he gave me a few items, about Star Wars, about Japan and about the US bases in Australia, that at the time were newsworthy. It was quite a coup for me, and the paper gave it massive coverage, including running a full transcript of the interview. And this time, I did not have to cover-up any gaffes.

After the formal interview was over, I found the nerve to ask him if I could look at the Titian. Weinberger led me over to his desk. Behind it was a huge desktop panel of lights and switches. It resembled the flight deck of a modern jetliner, except that it was two or three times as large.

'That's Western Europe,' he told me.

He was pointing to an area of the panel where several green and orange lights were illuminated. He did not elaborate, but I later learned that this was a massive secure telephone system that enabled him to speak to those under his command anywhere in the world as well as to his political colleagues in Washington. Beside it was the red phone that only the President used. On the wall above the panel was the painting. How appropriate to the politics of the Potomac. The Cardinal, epitomising the power of his era, at that time exercised by the Catholic Church, keeping watch over the man in charge of the most powerful military force in the world.

I lived at 253 West 73rd Street in The Level Club, built in 1927 as a Masonic hotel. The lavish façade of the building was designed to replicate King Solomon's Temple, and the huge foyer was decorated with Masonic symbols.[2] It had been converted to condominium apartments just two years earlier, so I was lucky to be in a marvellous neo-Romanesque building that nevertheless had modern bathrooms and kitchens. I'd rejected the Fairfax apartment as being too small and dingy, overlooking a light well. I wanted to be able to look out my window and see New York, I'd told Such. I'd scanned newspaper advertisements and, luckily for me, not having done any kind of research on the area, I had stumbled on the perfect place. It was just two blocks to Riverside Park and the Hudson River, and three blocks in the other direction to Central Park. Scarcely a Sunday passed when I did not join the multitudes who descended on the park to walk, sunbake, roller-skate, bike, jog, picnic, read or otherwise chill-out in the designated quiet zones or, in the rest of the sprawling park where noise was as natural as the greenery, engaged in the endless forms of exhibitionism that New Yorkers called relaxation.

Food shopping was something else. I had never experienced such choice when it came to food, nor the theatre that was part of the service. At Zabar's, the legendary Jewish delicatessen on Broadway at 80th street, you joined the crush of shoppers for cured meats and fish and whether you ordered one ounce or five pounds, you were shouted at just the same by the men skillfully running their knives across sides of salmon or ladling out dollops of Sevruga. I once stood next to a woman wearing a sable coat who asked for a pound of Beluga as casually as I'd ordered my small container of whitefish salad. She was jostled just like the rest of us as she gave over her hundreds of dollars before the precious purchase was handed to her over the high glass counter. 'Next!' yelled the man who had served her.

Just around the corner from my apartment, on Broadway at 74th Street, was Fairway, with its distinctive blue and black striped awning, one of the best food markets in the city. You could get day-old Israeli tomatoes or corn torn from the earth on Long Island that very morning; if you waited long enough on the Bread Line you had dozens of types of what today is called artisan bread to choose from. And there were cheese and meats and anything else you might feel like. Out the front were the big boxes of slightly less fancy fruit and vegetables. As you paid, you had to tell the young Hispanic women who ran the registers, Inside or Outside. Even inside, the prices were bargain basement compared with what I had paid in Canberra for a far inferior range and quality. There were some things, such as fresh salmon, you simply could not get in Australia. Nor the way New Yorkers were constantly demonstrating their brashness, their humour and their sheer *chutzpah*. Every encounter became a drama. No issue was too tiny to attract belligerence and over-the-top aggression. At times it was confronting and exhausting. No one gave an inch and nobody gave a damn and people would fight over the smallest thing. I was in the line at Fairway one day when the register clerk asked a woman with a large shopping basket of goods where she had got the apple she was munching.

'Inside, or outside?'

'I didn't get this apple here,' the woman replied. 'I brought it in with me.'

The clerk did not believe her, people in the line did not believe her. The murmurs began.

'Give it a rest, lady.'

'Just pay for the fucking apple.'

But, no, she was not going to give it up.

'I've got the receipt,' she said. 'It's in my car.'

And off she went, leaving the ever-lengthening line yelling in protest.

She returned triumphantly a few minutes later with a tiny piece of paper she claimed was the receipt. She did not pay for the apple. That's *chutzpah*.

The Ansonia, one of the most remarkable buildings in New York, was right next door to The Level Club. Built at the turn of the twentieth century, it opened as a hotel in 1904. Eighteen stories high, built of pale-grey stone, the Ansonia is arguably the most extravagant beaux-arts building in New York. Unlike the usual early twentieth century New York grand buildings with their straight lines, and stepped levels, the Ansonia was all curves and carvings, gargoyles and cast-iron filigree. It was, without doubt, one of the most amazing buildings in a city that was not shy about its architectural largesse. Its lavish exterior was part of the architectural tour of New York buildings given by the Sam Waterston character in Woody Allen's 1986 film *Hannah and her Sisters* and in 1992, while I was still living next-door, *Single White Female* starring Jennifer Jason Leigh and Bridget Fonda was filmed inside. The building became very run-down in the mid-twentieth century, but rents were cheap because they were controlled or stabilised so artists and musicians, who liked that Lincoln Centre was just a few blocks to the south, took apartments there. The great soprano Teresa Stratas lived there.

I'd heard her sing Liu in *Turandot* at the Met and I'd seen her in the street. Igor Stravinsky and the tenor Enrico Caruso are supposed to have lived there, as well as other luminaries such as Babe Ruth, Theodore Dreiser, Jack Dempsey and, more recently but before she became a mega-celebrity, Angelina Jolie.

Soon after I moved into The Level Club, I went into the Ansonia and approached the rather large man who was presiding over the lobby. The place was well past its glory days by the mid-1980s, but the grandeur of the building could never be diminished. I looked up in awe at the vaulted ceilings and the elaborate pillars. I said to the concierge that I had seen the sign outside for the baths.

'Were they open to non-residents,' I asked? I'd been hoping I could keep up my swimming in New York.

The man gave me a long look, as if to say, 'You serious, lady?' He took in my straight face and then, rolling his head back, he laughed and laughed. His face was a moist roll of merriment; he dabbed at himself with a handkerchief and heaved his shoulders as another round of laughter overtook him. I stood there politely, waiting for him to tell me what inexcusable crime of etiquette I had committed.

'Those baths, lady,' he told me, still gasping with laughter, 'Those baths. They ain't here anymore, but if they were, you sure wouldn't want to be going to them.'

And off he went again, into another private paroxysm of mirth.

I soon discovered my mistake.

The Ansonia had been home to the now-fabled Continental Baths, the most famous gay bathhouse in New York, which had opened in the basement in 1968. For seven years the Continental Baths was the place to go for hip New Yorkers. And not just for gay men, although it was the first place in New York where they could congregate openly, white towels around their waists, to seek out sex. But the likes of Mick Jagger and Liza Minnelli went as well. It was, apparently, quite a place. As well as the actual baths, there was a health clinic (where patrons could be tested for STDs), a library, a juice bar, a barber shop, a souvenir shop, a café and a gym. But the biggest drawcard, apart from the sex, was the live entertainment. The Continental Baths attracted the biggest names in town: Cab Calloway, Sarah Vaughan, the Andrews Sisters, Lesley Gore and, perhaps not surprisingly, Peter Allen. It was a place that made careers, too. Bette Midler got her start here, with Barry Manilow tickling the ivories as she sang, as did Patti LaBelle. In 1977, two years after the Continental Baths closed, Studio 54 would become the new haven of the fashionable. And, as the disco era took hold, the music definitely took a turn for the worse.

Almost every block in New York had a good story and as I embraced my new city with fervour I wanted to learn as much as I could, to learn its history as well as savour the present. I had never lived anywhere like it. For instance, St Marks Place, the three blocks of East 8th street that run from Astor Place to Tompkins Square, was still a relatively poor block with cold-water tenements and shops that, apart from the very cool St Mark's bookshop that had been a fixture since 1977, ranged from bodegas to head shops to tatty tourist kiosks but it had, even by New York standards, a pretty amazing pedigree. James Fenimore Cooper had lived there in the 1840s; in 1917 Leon Trotsky had moved into No. 77 and written for the *Novy Mir*, a Russian-language communist newspaper which was edited by Russian anarchist Nikolai Bukharin who lived across the street in No. 80. A few years earlier, Russian anarchists Emma Goldman and Alexander Berkman started the progressive Modern School at No. 6. When that closed, it was replaced by a Russian public bath and in 1979 became the world's largest gay bathhouse. In the 1950s, when the area started to become known as the East Village, it was a renowned hangout of the Beats, with Jack Kerouac, William Burroughs and Allen Ginsberg regulars at Gem Spa, a little bar on the corner of Second Avenue that sold newspapers and is renowned for its egg-cream, a peculiarly New York drink of milk, seltzer water and chocolate syrup. In *Just Kids*, Patti Smith recounts Robert Mapplethorpe buying her an egg-cream at the Gem Spa. Five Spot, at No. 2, was a jazz haunt in the early 1960s where musicians like Thelonius Monk, Charlie Mingus and Charlie Parker all played, and early feminist writer Shulamith Firestone, author of *The Dialectic of Sex*, lived at No. 11. And while St Marks Place has been home to an eclectic range of musicians, political types and social rebels—from Andy Warhol who opened his Electric Circus there in 1967 to Abbie Hoffman and Jerry Rubin of the Yippies movement and Lenny Bruce the comedian—by far the most famous resident was the English poet W.H. Auden who lived at

No. 77, for twenty years from 1952 to 1973. It was far from salubrious; for instance, it had no toilet, forcing Auden to use the facilities at the Holiday Cocktail Lounge at No. 75. It was a place that he frequented in any case, as he did like a martini. David Hay, one of my oldest friends, who had made documentary films in Australia and studied at the UCLA Film School in the early 1970s, moved to New York in 1979 and while he contemplated how to jump-start his screenwriting career, took up freelance journalism. He moved into No. 77 in 1983, and for three years lived in Trotsky's old apartment. He was there the day the commemorative plaque for Auden was attached to the front wall of the Holiday. Stephen Spender and Christopher Isherwood were there, David told me, 'I remember looking out my window and seeing them down on the sidewalk.'

My reverie with New York lasted for less than two months. To my horror I discovered that, once again, I was pregnant. It was, I realised, the result of a one-night stand with a visiting Australian with whom I would never dally again, and whom I could never tell. I knew I had no choice about what to do, although it was going to be a challenge to get myself an abortion in New York City—and probably very expensive—but the hormones had already started to kick-in, and I found myself emotionally connecting to what was happening inside me. But, I told myself, there was no way I could have a baby. It might just have been possible the last time I'd been pregnant, in 1979 when I was working in the Press Gallery. Life in Canberra was a lot simpler and support services were on hand, but I'd rejected that choice. I had put myself and my new job first. Had I chosen differently then, today I'd be the single mother of a six-year-old, and no way would I have this job in New York. Now I was 41 and this was probably my last chance, so I had to think very hard about whether I wanted this child. I've never been very clucky or defined myself solely, or even at all, by my ability to bear a child, so I could be a lot more dispassionate than would have been possible for some women. Looking back through my diary I realised that I had probably got pregnant around the time of Simone de Beauvoir's death on 14 April 1986: 'A very sad day for women,' I'd written. 'Her contribution to the explosion of our consciousness was extensive and profound.' De Beauvoir herself never had an abortion, although she famously signed a petition of French women 'confessing' to having broken this law, but she did not hesitate to do whatever it took to put her work first and I would do the same. I wanted to stay in New York and to further hone my craft. I had the biggest assignment of my life in just a few weeks. I could not begin to imagine dealing with morning sickness while I interviewed the US Defence Secretary. I was a writer, I told myself, not a mother. Some women could be both, but not me. I found a gynaecologist on Park Avenue, a wonderfully sympathetic man, a recent immigrant from South Africa, who told me that in my situation— single, newly arrived in America, with a big job—I would be crazy to even consider having the child. I found his words consolingly reinforcing. I had not confided my situation to anyone, preferring to guide myself unaided through this decision. I knew I was doing what was right for me, but that did not mean that I was not sad—and angry. A week later, after the termination, I walked out through the waiting room, which was full of expectant couples. I wondered if they realised that the doctor who was to deliver their babies also did abortions—and would they care? It was behind me now, but I could not overcome my feelings of bitterness and resentment. Men never had to make these decisions. They simply walked away from the bed, usually oblivious to the chaos they had left behind. The man I refused to call 'the father' (I did not think that merely depositing sperm entitled someone to a title that implies effort and commitment) probably occasionally looked back on our night together with a secret little smile. As for me, I treated myself, maxing out my credit card buying three pairs of Bruno Magli stilettos. I had made my choice; it was done. For a time at least, I would be fabulously frivolous. That was my way of asserting that I was back in control of my life. I felt, in the words of the Joni Mitchell song, unfettered and alive.

In July 1986, just a month after the Weinberger interview, I was scheduled to talk with Opposition Leader John Howard. I had booked a fancy restaurant in Washington DC for my dinner with him, hoping it would not be too noisy because he had indicated that he was going to have some things to say. I'd seen him the previous night at a private dinner in New York hosted by Australia's Consul-General, John Taylor, at the plush Beekman Place apartment that went with the job, and attended by a small number of investment bankers and their wives. I was the only journalist present. I'd been startled to see the way that these bankers, especially the Managing Director of Morgan Stanley, put Howard through his paces. He had looked uncomfortable and had not performed well.

'That man has no faith in himself,' remarked the wife of one of those who attended as they drove me home.

I disagreed with that assessment. John Howard was not impressive, but he was ambitious and he was game. He was clearly surprised at the tough time he was being given by these men who would, to a large degree, determine Australia's financial standing in the world markets, but he did not shirk the questions or dissemble. I actually found it horrifying to see these men—these *bankers*—treat a putative Australian Prime Minister as if he were a schoolboy taking a test. He had, after all, been the Treasurer of Australia for six years until the change of government in 1983. The men at this table had already decided to back Vice-President George Bush as the next President. They were utterly confident their wishes would prevail. Wall Street was coming back into the political game in ways that had not been seen since President Roosevelt curbed its influence following the excesses that led to the 1929 crash. Perhaps I did need to pay more attention to what was happening there.

During our dinner in Washington John Howard acknowledged that he was not popular but he felt that might actually be an advantage. People would turn to him because, like his political heroes Ronald Reagan and Margaret Thatcher, he would not be afraid to take tough action which, he argued, people were starting to realise was needed. He was earnest and spoke with conviction as he told me he thought there was an enormous sense of disappointment in Bob Hawke developing in Middle Australia. 'If there's a realisation that things are crook and that changes are needed,' he said, 'there can be quite a significant change in public opinion.'

'The times will suit me,' he said.[3]

I hoped fervently that my tape-recorder, sitting in the breadbasket between us, had picked up this phrase. The restaurant was far noisier than I had anticipated. Howard had confirmed that we were having an on-the-record interview and he had given careful thought to what he was saying.

The phrase 'the times will suit me' became forever associated with him. It would continue to be quoted the whole time he was in public life, although not always in the way he had meant. It was used to mock him when Andrew Peacock deposed him as Liberal Party leader in 1989. It would be ten years before John Howard became Prime Minister of Australia and by then the times were indeed very different, but he was nothing if not adaptable, and he recalibrated himself to accommodate them and went on to win three elections, becoming one of Australia's longest-serving Prime Ministers. His 'the times will suit me' interview with me remained an early defining moment in Howard's dogged journey to the top.

In August 1986 I went to San Francisco, to cover a meeting of what had been known as ANZUS (the Australian, New Zealand and United States alliance). At this meeting the US formally suspended its security obligations to New Zealand, following that country's refusal to allow nuclear-powered US ships into NZ waters. Since the US had a policy of declining to declare which ships were under such power, the refusal amounted to a banning of American ships from NZ. The US reacted swiftly and strongly: New Zealand is 'a friend, but not an ally', declared President Reagan. So it was just Australia and the US at this meeting, and it was a very big story.

I loved the elegant architecture of San Francisco; the rollercoaster-like dips in the streets and the harbour with its Golden Gate Bridge forming a backdrop to the city views, just like in Sydney. American cities each had their distinctive styles. You would never confuse, say, Chicago with New Orleans or Boston with Los Angeles. In Australia, once you left the inner-city, the suburbs tended to meld into an homogenous sameness. San Francisco was divided into distinct districts: Chinatown, the Tenderloin, the Castro, Haight-Ashbury. I especially liked the Italian district, where in 1906 the local merchants had helped put out the Great Fire with casks of wine. Or so it was said. I went to Tosca's, a coffee bar where the jukebox played only operatic arias—and Patti Page. I felt absurdly patriotic to find Joan Sutherland among the opera singers.

I met up with Kim Beazley who, like me, had arrived a day early. I'd known Beazley reasonably well in Canberra, and liked him for his openness and his intellectual curiosity. I had thought that we would probably just stroll around the tourist areas but while in the United States Beazley, who was now the Australian Defence Minister, came with a black stretch limo and a Secret Service detail, so we saw the sights in style. I was amazed that the long vehicle was able to negotiate the notorious serpentine-like turns of Lombard Street. Each time we got out of the car to inspect something, or to duck into a café, the Secret Service men followed at a discreet distance. That did not matter until Beazley got the idea that he wanted to visit the famous City Lights Bookstore, opened in 1953 by the poet Lawrence Ferlinghetti and the renowned hangout of the Beat poets like Allen Ginsberg and writers such as Jack Kerouac. It did not look good arriving at such a place in such a car. It looked even worse when the Secret Service guys, with their buzz cuts and their walkie-talkies and earpieces, came into the bookshop with us. Beazley was fascinated by the place and spent a good hour browsing, including a fair bit of time in the Marxist section. The other patrons were astonished but managed to contain whatever outrage they felt at this intrusion by the enemy. Beazley made a few purchases, including a book on the justification for war. I could not help but compare Beazley and Weinberger, two men running Defence departments, at a time when global military tensions were high, who both had interests and curiosities beyond the responsibilities of their jobs. Perhaps this accounted for Beazley's unusual approach to his. I don't think any other Defence Minister had asked his department for a paper on the moral justification for war.

Although I loved the Level Club, I was worried about how much it was costing me. I had underestimated the cost of living when I'd negotiated my salary. I was paying 60 per cent of my income in rent and I had to pay city, state *and* federal income taxes as well as social security and other deductions. I had to buy furniture for the apartment and I was finding it impossible to get by. I had not been this poor since I was seventeen living in Melbourne, and having to choose between having lunch or taking the tram to work. I had savings in Australia but I was reluctant to use them to subsidise my life in New York, especially as the exchange rate was terrible. Nor, I told myself, should I have to. I was earning what should be good money. It was having the security of a salary that had prompted me to come to New York, but in January 1987, although my pay was increased 3 per cent, all of it was taken up by Reagan's tax 'reforms', and I was notified my rent would increase by $50 a month. I would have to find somewhere cheaper.

I looked at an apartment at 14 West 10th Street, an elegant tree-lined street that was supposedly one of the best blocks in the entire city, in the heart of Greenwich Village. Mark Twain had lived in this house for a year in 1900. The apartment was elegant and light-filled, occupying the entire ground floor of the brownstone. It was the kind of place that New Yorkers lusted after. I was told I was extraordinarily lucky to even have a chance to bid for it. Yes, I would have to dip into my savings to pay the unrefundable 'key money' if my application to rent the place was successful, but at $1500 a month it was considerably less than the $2000 I was currently paying. Even so, I hesitated. I liked the security of a doorman building, and it meant my mail and dry-cleaning would be looked after when I was travelling, even if the doormen were sometimes a little too inquisitive and, on one occasion when I brought an African-American man home, judging by the way he looked at me, censorious. Back in the Village, trying to picture myself living at ground-floor level, I found myself knowing I'd never feel safe. I decided I'd stay on the Upper West Side, look for ways to economise, and ask Suich if he would increase my rent allowance. It was in so many ways the right decision. My financial circumstances would change dramatically before the end of the year, enabling me to buy an apartment in the Level Club; it would be the only address I ever had in New York. But, more saliently, I was spared living in the building where an act of unspeakable violence took place later that year.

The numbers of homeless people in New York horrified me. Many of them slept on the streets, even in the coldest weather. There were as many as ten people, bundled-up against the weather, most of them men, and African-American, just on the one block between my apartment and the subway station. They would rattle cups in the hope of attracting some change. At night, human bundles seeking shelter and rest were in every doorway. It was confronting but I felt impotent. How were you supposed to respond? Choose one person and become his regular donor? Spread around whatever you felt able to share? As an Australian, I strongly believed it was the government's responsibility to provide shelter and other services, but I was in the US now. Things were different here. There was also a lot of street crime and I learned to be alert and defensive. I once found a man's fingers inside my bag as I joined the crush of people threading their way into the 72nd Street subway. When I removed his hand, he just kept moving, avoiding eye contact or any acknowledgement that he'd been trying to pickpocket me. It was a little more dramatic the time I was mugged. I had broken my own rule of being constantly alert, and was strolling along my own street, just a few metres from my front door, my head in the clouds when I heard a terrible scream. I soon realised the noise was coming from my own mouth and that I was reacting instinctually to a man who, standing close behind me, had a knife near my throat as he slashed the strap and made off with my shoulder-bag. It was over in seconds. He'd ran back to his car which—incredibly—was idling right there in the street, holding up the traffic, and sped off. People came from everywhere to help and I quickly recovered my composure. I was upset, of course, because almost everything of value I possessed was in that bag, along with a lot of cash because I was taking a trip the next morning. I was surprised how seriously the police treated what I assumed was a run-of-the-mill mugging. I went to the precinct and was shown mug shots; I was given a crime number: it was 60 something.

'Is that how many crimes have been committed in the city so far this year?' I asked. It was New Year's Day.

The officer looked at me as if to say, 'Get real, lady.'

'That's the number of crimes so far today in this precinct,' he said.

But not even this crime could daunt my enthusiasm for the city. Apart from the everyday theatre of the street, the best thing about living in New York was the ease with which you could see, hear and even meet some of the most powerful, creative or just plain interesting people of the era. I'd attended the wedding of Hester Eisenstein, an American who'd lived in Sydney for some years and become involved in the women's movement. She had written a book on the phenomenon of femocrats. Hester's was the first wedding of a contemporary (rather than, say, a brother) that I'd attended since the 1960s. No one I knew got married anymore. It was also my first Jewish wedding, and I was fascinated by the rituals including the stamping on the glass, but I was even more impressed to learn that Paul Baran and Paul Sweezy were among the guests. I'd written an undergraduate essay on their 1966 classic *Monopoly Capital*, whose extensive documentation of the

Yankee invasions, takeovers and coups against elected governments in Latin America in the service of American capitalism had made it a bible of the student left. And now I would have a chance to meet these two god-like figures. Someone pointed them out. I suppose I did not exactly expect them to be wearing black berets and smoking cheroots, but I certainly could not reconcile the two balding fat men in suits sitting on the other side of the room with the romantic figments of my youthful imagination.

New York is never boring, but sometimes it outdoes itself. In one magic week, in early November 1986, I went, in a state of giddy enthralment, from one amazing event to another. First, on Saturday afternoon, I had gone to an intimate benefit at the Juilliard School and heard both Isaac Stern and Yo-Yo Ma play. At drinks afterwards, I met the Australian architect Harry Seidler, who was in town to work with Donald Trump on the New York property tycoon's bid for the Sydney casino. Then I was introduced to James Wolfensohn, the Australian expatriate of many years, a real Renaissance man who as well as being a leading investment banker, played the cello, would preside over the restoration of Carnegie Hall and, later in 1995, become President of the World Bank. On Tuesday I'd gone to a foreign correspondents' event and heard the great economist J.K. Galbraith talk about the military power of the Superpowers. I was astonished to find that he was 78 (which I thought then was very old) and that not only was he amazingly lucid but he had a liberal outlook that was becoming so rare as to be almost extinct in America in the mid-1980s. Then on Friday I had interviewed the French film director Jean-Jacques Beineix, whose new film *Betty Blue* I'd watched at a private screening a few days earlier. *Betty Blue* went on to get on Oscar nomination and win various awards, but my real interest in Beineix was that he had directed the cult classic *Diva*. I felt quite the fan girl sitting down with him at the Parker Meridian Hotel. And then there was the morning when working my way through the Sunday *New York Times* I'd spotted a small notice about a workshop performance of a new Terrence McNally play that afternoon. An hour later, having paid my $12, I was sitting in the first row at the Manhattan Theatre Club. Right in front of me were F. Murray Abraham and Kathy Bates, in bed together, and about to begin their performance of *Frankie and Johnny in the Clair de Lune*. I knew Abraham from his sullen Salieri in the 1984 Milos Forman movie *Amadeus*, always bitter at being outshone by the mercurial Mozart, but I had not then heard of Kathy Bates. In 1990 she would win an Academy Award, playing a deranged fan in the adaption of Stephen King's book *Misery*, the first of many notable movie performances. Back on stage, the actors suddenly flung back the covers and Abraham leapt out of bed and, stark naked, began to pace around the stage. John Malkovich was doing the same in *Burn This*, another off-Broadway play that was running in New York at the time, and which also would go on to become a smash hit on Broadway, but I was startled to see stage nudity for the first time. You're not in Canberra anymore, I told myself.

I was grateful to be able to have these uplifting experiences after a gruelling visit from my parents a week earlier. I'd flown to London to meet them, together we'd gone on a driving tour of Ireland and then to New York, where I had planned to show them all the sights. They had never visited before. But my father was not well. In April 1986—just three weeks after I'd arrived in New York—he learned that he had prostate cancer. The recommended treatment was for his testicles to be removed, I learned from a panicked phone call from my mother very early one morning. He became immensely depressed about this.

'I've been knackered,' he used to say.

Whether it was the cancer, or losing his manhood, but the fight went out of him. He suddenly became old and I was shocked to see how frail he was. He was just a couple of years older than I am today, yet he seemed elderly. It was awful to watch the power ebbing out of him. It was something that I had observed with almost ghoulish pleasure in once-powerful politicians or businessmen: men who had once used their power in brutish fashion and who were now old and weak and vulnerable and who embodied the fact that power accrues to the position—not the person. Once they were no longer Prime Minister, or Secretary of Defence, or chairman of BHP or whatever powerful position they had once held, these men changed. Sometimes they became bitter and angry about their diminished authority, but often they were transformed into kindly and likeable people who were unrecognisable from their previous selves. Why wasn't it possible for them to be this way when they still had power? Why is our notion of power associated with meanness, even cruelty? Why is so much masculine ego invested in the idea of palpable power? You see it in so many ways: the father who must hold sway over his children, the husband who must dominate his wife, sometimes using violence to assert his control. It is a model of authority that damages us all, men themselves as well as the women who suffer the effects, that is the basis of war and other forms of violence, and it was something, we were to discover, that lurked powerfully in our family. A man who is a kind and considerate leader is often denigrated as weak or ineffectual. A women leader who tries to subvert the model, well we know what happens to her. Even though I felt this way, about the system and many of the individual men who epitomised it, I was nevertheless overcome with sadness to watch my father's diminishment.

The trip was difficult. My father could not walk easily, nor could he hear well, so conversation was hard. He needed to urinate frequently and it was not easy finding public restrooms in New York. 'Freud made the same complaint,' I assured him. We frequently had to stop at a bar and order three Cokes just so that my father could relieve himself. But he and my mother had managed to enjoy their first visit to the Big Apple. They surprised even themselves by catching the subway and meeting me at our appointed destination. We'd done the touristy things like the over-sized sandwiches at the Stage Deli, and visited the top of the World Trade Center, but my father's favourite moment had been a performance of *Madame Butterfly* at the Metropolitan Opera. He'd become quite emotional at being in such a famous place, hearing one of the operas he loved most. We had cheap seats but it was still a magical experience, watching the crystal chandeliers being drawn-up before the curtain rose.

On 17 October my parents attended Mass at St Patrick's Cathedral on Fifth Avenue, to mark the tenth anniversary of Jamie's death. When they returned to my apartment, my mother kept making references to Jamie but I found that I was unable to respond. I was scared of where the conversation might lead. If we talked about Jamie and his death, we would need to acknowledge what was happening to my father, and if we did that, I knew I would have to confront the resentment and anger that I still harboured towards him. Although on the surface things between us might have seemed normal, in reality they were not. I was unable to forget, or forgive, the brutal hostility he'd shown towards me year after year when I was a teenager, nor the torrid scene on my wedding day in 1967, when he'd called me a 'whore' in front of my friends. Although, I told myself, it was all a long time ago, it still hurt. So we did not talk about his illness or his prognosis. We did not talk about what would happen if he became very ill or started to die. As I watched him struggle to stand and to walk, and saw his face reveal how sick he was, I realised that he did not have long to live. Yet we found ourselves incapable of expressing our fears, we were unable to offer him any consolation, and we certainly were unable to put into words how we felt about each other. We had always been this way and we had not changed. All I could do was hug him and offer platitudes that I was not sure that I really meant. I realised that my resentments ran deep, and while I now felt sorry for him and was scared about what lay ahead, I had not been able to find it in myself to start the conversation we needed to have. But then at JFK Airport as I said goodbye, my mother began to weep and then my father totally collapsed into terrible tears, and it became clear that he thought that he would never see me again. Four months later, I got the call I was dreading. The cancer had spread throughout his body, my mother told me over the crackling phone-line. It was now just a matter of time.

———— ⸱⸱⸱ ————

Being a foreign correspondent in New York was a much harder job than I had supposed it would be. I got very little direction from my editors—when I could speak to them. Communications were still amazingly primitive—it could sometimes take up to six hours to get a phone circuit via the international operator—and the top editors were either not there or too busy to talk. We correspondents were pretty much on our own. Malcolm Maiden had come to New York to cover business—including Wall Street—for the *Financial Review*, which was a big relief for me as he was far better qualified to cover the story and I was back in my comfort zone, writing about politics which meant I travelled frequently to Washington DC. I had a White House press pass and could attend press briefings. The Secret Service had evidently not checked the address I'd given on my application, which was just as well because I did not live there, but security was not much of an issue in those days. Without further introductions from an Australian Prime

Minister, I was never again able to secure interviews with people of the calibre of Volcker and Weinberger. In fact, it was almost impossible to talk to anyone from the administration in Washington. Coming from a small and reliable ally certainly had its disadvantages when it came to getting stories. Sometimes I even had difficulty getting the State Department desk officer on the phone. When I looked back over my first year in the US, I had managed a few decent interviews and had broken a few small stories, but I had not been able to develop my writing as I'd hoped this foreign posting would allow. I had been unable to find a way to write about America and Americans in the way that I had planned when I'd first arrived. More and more, I had to settle for covering Australians. Which is not to say it wasn't fun to be writing about Midnight Oil, the Sydney Symphony Orchestra or Circus Oz, or to be keeping an eye on what Australian businessmen were up to. Rupert Murdoch, who was expanding his US businesses, was usually good for a story but it was not what I had set out to do. I was always on the lookout for ways to write what I'd seen as my prime objective: understanding America. But it was not easy. To most Americans, Australia was either exotic or inconsequential. Everyone wanted to go there, they said, although their first preference usually was New Zealand, which had done a much better job marketing itself to Americans than we had. In the 1970s when I'd been in the Midwest, people politely told me they'd read or seen the movie *The Thornbirds*. In 1987 the point of reference was another movie, one that in the US was marketed as *'Crocodile' Dundee*, the quote marks to indicate it wasn't a swamp movie. It wasn't much of a connection, and it certainly was not much of a lure when I put in interview requests. This meant I could not even just report, as there was simply no way to be able to meet a wide-enough range of Americans. Perhaps being located in New York made it even more difficult. I was nothing but a fringe-dweller. Observing only from the periphery, neither a native nor an immigrant. Not knowing the place the way people who were born there; and not striving for a stake, and being willing to set aside criticisms, as immigrants had to do. I simply did not belong.

After two years in New York I could no longer hide my frustrations. I loved the city but not my job, and my personal life was miserable. My several longstanding American friends tended to travel a lot. Paula Weideger had fallen in love with Henri Lessore, an Englishman, and she now spent a lot of time in London. Margot Fox, who I'd met through my ex-husband John Summers, was also on the road constantly in her job as French interpreter for the State Department. When she was in town she was always a lot of fun and, more than once, treated us to the fringe benefits of the job. One remarkable night she took me and a couple of friends to the Blue Note, where Dizzie Gillespie was playing. She had just escorted him on a tour of francophone Africa and he showed his appreciation by getting us good seats and sitting with us after his performance. He asked me for a cigarette. Smoking was forbidden, of course. He did not care and no one was going to stop him, but I did not dare light up. Mostly I hung out with other Australians, those like me who were working temporarily in New York, and my old friends David Hay, Phillip Frazer and Elisabeth Wynhausen, who had moved to the US, perhaps permanently. Elisabeth and I spent a lot of time together, including the day in early November when we'd used our press passes to get to the finishing line of the New York Marathon in Central Park. We'd given Robert de Castella a big, raucous Aussie cheer. He'd been injured and was struggling but he gave us a grateful grin and, we told ourselves, we'd helped him get over the line—in second place. And there was the never-ending stream of Aussie visitors, some of them family or friends who I was pleased to see, others I scarcely knew but who thought they could avail themselves of my services as a tour guide of the Big Apple. I soon learned to rebuff such people. I'd had a few flings and one-night stands with people passing through but nothing serious, and I'd had no luck in hooking-up with any locals. I'd even placed an advertisement in the *New York Review of Books*, the literary publication where people placed personal classified ads searching for soul mates: 'SWF seeks 40-something SWM to share movies, wine, conversations and long walks in the park'—that kind of thing. I can't remember what I said in my ad, but I'd been quite excited when an English professor from Boston responded. We agreed to meet outside a kiosk in the Village. I wore one of my new Bruno Magli high heels, which was a mistake. He barely came up to my waist *and* he was wearing a brown suit. My ad should have said: 'SWF seeks SWM with some fashion sense.' We could find nothing to talk about. My one-and-only date with an American man lasted less than an hour.

———>•<———

In April 1987 Rupert Murdoch established a fourth television network in the US. He had ignored the conventional wisdom that it could not be done, and on 6 April launched the Fox Network with a prime-time debut of *Married—with Children*, a program I described in my piece as 'a smutty sitcom'.[4] It was an instant hit. With its down-market program formula and its aggressively right-wing political agenda promulgated on its Fox News channel that was established a decade later in 1996, Fox grew to become an influential and profitable network, while in the second decade of the 21st century the legacy networks struggled to survive. Just a week before the Fox launch, Murdoch had spent $US300 million to acquire Harper & Row, the third-largest book publisher in the United States, a move which, I wrote, 'further consolidates his worldwide dominance over newspaper, magazine and book publishing'.[5] I had also had some fun in August 1986 with a little scoop about Murdoch gazumping Ronald Reagan by spending $7 million on a fourteen-room, two-storey Spanish style mansion in Bel Air once rented by Katharine Hepburn. President Reagan thought he had finalised the purchase of his dream retirement home with its spectacular views and its Hollywood history, I wrote, but that was before the media mogul came along and, doing what happens all the time in Sydney, made a better offer.[6] I'd got the tip for this story from David Hay, who was now living in LA trying to break into screen-writing, and he had seen a small item in the *Hollywood Reporter*. I stayed with David in his apartment in West Hollywood and had been a witness to a tragedy unfolding right next door, where a friend of his was succumbing to AIDS. A stream of friends came and went, knowing there was nothing they could yet do to stop this calamitous and fatal plague that had assailed the gay community just a few years earlier. I had been visiting New York in 1981 when David told me about the meeting he'd attended, convened by a doctor in the East Village, of men worried about this as-yet unnamed new disease that was striking gay men. Now, just five years later, AIDS had become an epidemic that had already killed almost 49,000 gay men, haemophiliacs and intravenous drug users in the United States. There was widespread panic, but also political revulsion. The Reagan White House refused to acknowledge what was happening. As the medical profession struggled to understand the disease and its origins, the gay community became radicalised

olive green Ford Falcons the military had used to abduct activists were still on the streets. It had been a hard subject to write about, and I felt my series had not done it justice. Fly-in fly-out journalism was not the way to understand a country, I realised, especially one that had endured the kind of trauma that had taken place in Argentina. What I had done was work-manlike, but it was not the kind of journalism I aspired to. It was not the penetrating or elegant writing that I aspired to. I started to doubt myself, to think that perhaps I didn't have it in me. Or perhaps newspapers were not the place for that sort of writing. I was becoming attracted to American magazines and the license they seemed to give writers to explore important topics. Maybe I should be looking for another kind of job.

I'd visited Australia in May and gone to Canberra to catch up with people, and was astonished when Mike Codd, now head of Prime Minister and Cabinet, asked if I'd be interested in coming back to the bureaucracy. I thought I'd burnt that bridge but he told me I'd have no trouble getting a Deputy Secretary's job. I'd also had a very strong overture from Hawke's office that there could be a job there, if I wanted it. I could not see myself going back to Canberra, but it was nice to know that I was seen as having the ability to do such jobs. I'd made the leap back to journalism and that was where I was going to stay, but maybe not where I was at the moment. I met with Suich who asked me what I wanted to do.

'Edit the *Sydney Morning Herald*,' I said without hesitation. The *National Times* would have been the place for me to learn and I would have left New York in a heartbeat if that job had been offered to me.

It was too late, of course. Valerie Lawson had been made editor of the *Times on Sunday*, as it was now called, a month earlier. She asked me to be her deputy. I was insulted enough that I had not been considered for the top job, and I knew she'd shopped the deputy's role to at least one other person, so I said a resounding No. I'd had a senior man in Fairfax beg me to take it. I'd be much better with staff, he said, and with ideas. But I was hurt and angry that yet again I had been passed over for the editor's job. There had been six editors in the nine years since Evan Whitton had succeeded Suich in 1978. I'd looked on with disbelief and some bitterness as David Marr, Brian Toohey, Jeff Penberthy, Robert Haupt and, now, Valerie Lawson had each been given the job. Why not me? I was as qualified as any of them. I did not have editing experience, Suich said when I complained. Neither had any of the other appointees. I was assured that I was being tracked towards something big. If I could just put in the hard slog in a number three or four slot at the *Herald* for the next five to seven years, it would all fall into place. It was hardly enticing. I went back to New York restless and uncertain about what I was going to do with my life.

In mid-1987, Sandra Yates arrived in New York from Sydney with a brief to start a new magazine for teenage girls. Sandra had been deputy managing director of Sungravure, the magazine publishing group owned by Fairfax, and publisher of, among many titles, *Dolly*, the very successful magazine for teenage girls. She had proposed that *Dolly* could be migrated to the US where, she argued, the existing teenage titles were staid and boring. The market could do with a big shake-up. It was a brave idea but Fairfax bought it, and now Sandra was in town looking for premises, getting herself known in the magazine publishing world, lining-up an advertising agency, and recruiting the staff she needed to launch this venture. I was enlisted to help look for office space, so for a couple of months I found myself working closely with her. Sandra was a very down-to-earth person who spoke bluntly and did not waste time with ceremony. She knew what she wanted and she went after it with a focus and determination that I watched with both admiration and amazement. She was creating a totally new product that, after some research, she decided was going to be called *Sassy*. The launch was planned for March the following year. Sandra's enthusiasm was infectious, and what she was doing looked far more exciting and interesting than where I found myself. I wished I could somehow be part of it. So on 4 August 1987, when Sandra took me to lunch at Café Un Deux Trois, a bistro located at 123 West 44th Street, just around the corner from the Fairfax office, and told me that *Ms.* magazine was for sale and she thought that we should get Fairfax to buy it, she would run it in a stable with *Sassy*, and that I should become its editor-in-chief, I did not hesitate.

CHAPTER SEVEN

'REAL FEMINISTS
WITH REAL MONEY'

———◦———

'We've never met but I feel I already know you,' Gloria Steinem flashed her celebrated mega-wattage smile and warmly locked eyes with me. 'After all, we are both members of the revolutionary women's government-in-exile.'

It was mid-August 1987 and we were in the Park Avenue offices of Henry Ansbacher Inc., an investment-banking firm that specialised in media deals. They had been looking for a buyer for *Ms.* magazine and Sandra Yates and I were there to meet Gloria and her long-time friend and business partner, Pat Carbine, to see if they would consider selling to John Fairfax & Sons, the Australian corporation that employed us. I found Gloria charming. She was extraordinarily attractive and looked amazingly youthful. I knew she was 53, eleven years older than me, but with her slim figure, long slender legs and shoulder-length blonde-streaked hair, she barely looked 40. But I thought her words were a strange way to greet someone who wanted to buy the magazine she had founded fifteen years earlier and had toiled through financial salt-mines to try to keep alive. Even meeting with us would seem to be an admission of defeat but, as we were soon to discover, she had no choice but to sell. *Ms.* magazine was on the verge of financial collapse.

Just a few months earlier, 1 had written a front-page story for the *Financial Review* of Kerry Packer's brief involvement with this famous icon of American feminism. I had reported the unusual fact that the Australian media mogul had been personally involved in negotiations over a small-beer deal for *Cleo* magazine, part of his magazine stable, to have rights to use material from *Ms*. It was a surprising marriage, the ultra-glossy and sexually frank commercial magazine pitched at young women (and which ran nude male centrefolds) and the iconic feminist magazine, with its rather stern tone and its embarrassingly low production values. What on earth would *Cleo* find reprintable from *Ms*.? Even more surprising was the fact that Kerry Packer, the proprietor, had joined Trevor Kennedy, the managing director of his company Australian Consolidated Press and *Cleo* editor Lisa Wilkinson at the table in New York for this deal. 'Perhaps the cash-rich Mr Packer is seeking the social and business links the well-connected Ms. Steinem and Ms. Carbine can provide,' I had speculated.[1] At the time, I had been quite angry about this deal because Fairfax had made *Ms*. a similar rights offer, to share copy with *Portfolio*, its working women's magazine. This would have seemed a far more natural 'fit' for *Ms*. material than *Cleo*, although we could not have offered anything like the money Packer paid. I found it strange that the *Ms*. people had not even responded to our offer, and I had called Pat Carbine to tell her how disappointed I was by this.

At a dinner with Clyde Packer, Kerry's brother who lived in Santa Barbara, a few months later, I learned what the talks were really about. He told Sandra and I that James Wolfensohn, the very successful Australian New York-based investment banker who was an adviser to Packer and a friend of Carbine's, had brokered the deal. As Clyde told it, Wolfensohn had undertaken to look for a new investor for *Ms*. because Mort Zuckerman was tired of putting money into the magazine. Zuckerman was a wealthy property developer and media proprietor (he owned the weekly news magazine *US News & World Report* and would later acquire the *Atlantic Monthly* and New York's *Daily News* newspaper) and he was also Gloria Steinem's boyfriend. Kerry had been prepared to buy 60 per cent of *Ms*., Clyde said, but only if he could have editorial control. Steinem and Carbine would never agree to that so the deal had foundered. Nevertheless Kerry had paid them $500,000, which Clyde described as a 'rights' deal that allowed *Cleo* to use any material from *Ms.* This was a hefty injection for an indebted magazine, but it had not been enough to save them.

Steinem showed no signs of resenting the two women she referred to as 'real feminists with real money' who were making an offer for her magazine. Instead we quickly got down to details. First we examined the books of the Ms. Foundation, the not-for-profit body which owned the magazine. We found liabilities of $4.8 million, in addition to $2.2 million worth of subscription liabilities plus $800,000 was needed to publish the final two issues for 1987. All up, around $8 million. The liabilities included deferred salaries for Steinem and Carbine and a loan of $400,000 from Zuckerman. Steinem told me with some bitterness a few months later that Zuckerman had just spent $6 million refurbishing his apartment.

'Half that amount would have saved us,' she said. In reality, it would have taken a lot more than that.

Although the dollar amounts were relatively small for a large publisher like Fairfax, doing the *Ms.* deal was quite complicated. It was not just that we had quickly to get on top of an unfamiliar set of accounts but much of the language, and the way of doing business, was very different from Australia. We discovered, for instance, that the subscriber list which I had thought would be regarded as an asset was regarded by the US tax and accounting regimes as a liability: the income from the subscriptions had been received but the publishers now had an obligation to fulfil those sub-scriptions, and that obligation cost far more than the subscription income. I had not properly understood that in the US, subscribers generally paid only a fraction of the actual cost of producing and mailing a magazine. I should have realised this because when I first arrived in New York, I had been astounded at how inexpensive it was to subscribe to magazines. For instance, an annual subscription to *Vanity Fair* cost $12, just $1 an issue, and a big premium on its newsstand price. Now I was discovering why: the production costs and any profit came from advertising revenue. *Ms.*'s big problem was and—we soon learned—always had been a lack of advertis-ing. And, as we would discover, it was an intractable problem. The major categories of advertisers to women were fashion, cosmetics and food. All of these advertisers demanded supporting, and sympathetic, editorial adjacent to their ads. Most women's magazines were more than happy to surround these ads with recipes, fashion spreads and makeup tips but *Ms.* was meant to be different. Its whole premise was that it did not pander to a traditional stereotype of women, instead inviting advertisers to recognise that the *Ms.* woman was free and independent. She tended to be better-educated and have a higher income than readers of other magazines so she was worth targeting, but while she might cook and wear makeup, and she certainly wore clothes, these were not subjects she wanted to read about in the magazine. It had been a struggle. For all its surface slickness, Madison Avenue was conservative and misogynist, unwilling to buck conventional wisdom about how to reach women. In its early years *Ms.* had had some success, but as the lustre of feminism faded in the early 1980s, with younger women rejecting the label, and the magazine became more defensive and doctrinaire, the ads fell away. *Ms.* became reliant on a controversial diet of automobiles, liquor and cigarette advertising, complemented by some distinctly unattractive spreads for feminine hygiene items, and whatever other products they could pick-up, issue to issue. By mid-1987 revenue was collapsing, *Ms.* was unable to pay its bills and its future looked grim. They were able to produce a nice fat double issue to mark the magazine's fifteenth anniversary in July/August, but then they immediately did a relaunch that was clearly intended to appeal to advertisers. The final four issues for 1987 showed off the slick new design which, except for the poor quality paper stock and pedestrian art direction, no doubt the result of a tight budget, made *Ms.* indistinguishable from most other women's magazines. Gone were the issue-themed covers, instead the smiling faces of well-known or advertiser-alluring women made eye contact with potential readers. One of these women was Cam Starrett, the most senior woman at Avon Products, the cosmetics company (she was Senior VP for Human Resources). Another was Tracey Ullman, the comedian. *Ms.* was changing its approach and was now courting advertisers, it seemed, but it was too late.

The first issue of *Ms.* had appeared as an insert in *New York* magazine in late 1971, and was followed a few months later by the first stand-alone issue with its iconic cover of a multi-armed Indian goddess, representing the many roles and responsibilities of the modern woman. The print run of 300,000 sold-out within a few days, proving there was an audience, generating 30,000 subscribers and enabling Steinem to raise $1 million from Warner Communications in order to begin monthly publication. *Ms.* was an immediate hit. The moment was right, and the magazine quickly developed both influence and a devoted following—and not just in the United States. It became something of a status symbol among many Australian women to brandish the latest issue of *Ms.* But a loyal audience did not necessarily mean the magazine was financially viable, especially when economic downturns led advertisers to cut back on their spends. For Gloria and Pat Carbine, who came on early as the magazine's publisher, responsible for the business side, it had been a long hard struggle to keep the magazine afloat. Over the next fifteen years they had borrowed and begged, sought investor funds, donations from well-heeled women and held countless fundraisers. A special and glamorous $250-a-head benefit was held at the Waldorf Astoria in 1984 to mark Steinem's 50th birthday—and raise money for the Ms. Foundation. 'This is what 50 looks like', had been the theme, echoing a comment Steinem had made ten years earlier when someone had said to her: 'You don't look 40.' But despite all the fundraising, the well was now dry. Steinem was desperately looking for a solution, and that was why we were there.

Although this was the first time I had met Steinem, I knew Pat Carbine from a lunch in Sydney some years earlier hosted by Wendy McCarthy, the feminist and reproductive rights activist, and when I moved to New York in 1986 I had rung her to see if she could recommend a friendly gynaecologist. I was impressed by the warm efficiency of the woman from *Ms.* who'd got back to me with the information—and an invitation to dinner. Her name was Joanne Edgar, a senior editor who had been there since the beginning. I like these women, I thought to myself at the time, so when that extraordinarily serendipitous chain of events a year later saw me become editor-in-chief of *Ms.*, I had every confidence that I was going to enjoy working with them.

In late August, just ten days after our first meeting with Steinem and Carbine and as our negotiations were just starting, Warwick Fairfax launched an audacious $2.3 billion bid to take John Fairfax & Sons private. Warwick, aged 26, was the Harvard-educated son of Sir Warwick Fairfax and his third wife, Mary, and was said to be motivated by his view that his older half-brother James was mismanaging the (highly successful, debt-free) company. Young Warwick, as he was always known to distinguish him from his father, was undoubtedly also infected by that 1980s disease: the desire to leverage wealth from assets that were perceived to be under-utilised. We did not know how this turn of events might affect the *Ms.* acquisition but it seemed prudent that we move as quickly as possible. Three weeks later, on 3 September, we made an offer that comprised cash plus assuming all *Ms.*'s liabilities—so long as we could take possession of the magazine by the end of September, and subject to approval from the Fairfax Board. A couple of days later I flew to Sydney, to help persuade the board to agree to the purchase—and to undertake a crash course in magazine production.

It was the first time I had been back to the fourteenth floor of the Fairfax Building in Jones Street since 1976 when Sir Warwick Fairfax—Young Warwick's father—had summonsed me to his office to discuss my contentious prisons article for the *National Times*. Now, eleven years later, on 14 September, I was in the boardroom trying not to giggle at the unforgettable sight of the five directors, all men, two of them knights and several of whom would fit the description 'crusty', sitting round the imposing board table, solemn oil portraits of Fairfax ancestors looking down on them, flicking through the latest issue of *Ms.* magazine. I doubt if any of them had even seen a feminist publication before. I walked them through my written proposal, arguing that an outlay of around $12.5 million ($8.5 million acquisition price and $4 million ongoing investment) would give Fairfax a prestigious property that would give the company an immediate profile in the American publishing world, as its buying of the *Spectator* magazine a few years earlier had done in the UK. I proposed to make *Ms.* 'a well-written, argumentative and, at times, controversial news magazine which applies a tough-minded feminist perspective to national events, which provides service information to women, and which through its editorial consolidates and improves upon its already impressive demographics.'

The timing was terrible—or great, depending on how you read the tea leaves. Could the board approve an acquisition that was not large in dollar terms, but which represented a significant expansion of the company's US presence, while a takeover offer was on the table? The board was opposed to the takeover and had recommended that shareholders not accept the offer. If Young Warwick succeeded, we faced the hideous prospect that his asset-stripping plans would see the Fairfax magazine group sold on to Kerry Packer and that I would find myself, having left the Fairfax newspaper group, working for Packer. Even worse, the *Ms.* women, having successfully staved off Packer earlier in the year, and agreed to do business with us in part because we were 'not Packer', might find him owning their magazine after all. We hoped we were protected from such a fate by *Ms.* being acquired by Fairfax Publications (US) Ltd, which was a wholly-owned subsidiary of John Fairfax (US) Ltd, the newspaper company, and not therefore owned by Fairfax Magazines.

The board signed off on the purchase and Sandra sent a letter of intent to Henry Ansbacher. It was just six weeks since our lunch at Café Un Deux Trois. We'd done it! But it was too soon to celebrate as we quickly found out. The next day New York *Newsday* broke the story that Australians had bought *Ms.* but, Gloria told me on the phone from New York, her board was still not convinced. They were now chasing another deal, a venture capital injection that would enable them to retain editorial control of the magazine. There was, on Gloria's assessment, only an 80 per cent chance the Ms. Foundation Board would accept the Fairfax offer. This was an astonishing turn of events. We thought we had a deal. Instead, here was the first warning sign that Gloria Steinem was not really willing to let go of *Ms.* magazine.

It was a very tense time. I spent my days with Gill Chalmers, the experienced and down-to-earth editor of *Woman's Day* learning the, to me anyway, mysteries of magazine production and timelines. Every night I was on the phone to New York, lobbying for a favourable decision. Back in New York Sandra was getting on with the business of establishing *Sassy*. She hired 24-year-old Jane Pratt to be editor-in-chief, brought Cheryl Collins, *Dolly's* art director, over from Sydney to start designing a groovy new magazine and hired an advertising agency to start generating buzz. The debut issue of this exciting new publication was slated for March 1988.

On 23 September, the *Ms.* board accepted our offer 'with pleasure' and with no strings attached. We never learned what happened to the white knight or why the Ms. Foundation ultimately agreed to sell to us, but it was highly likely that *Ms.* would have been forced to close had they not accepted the Fairfax offer. I flew out of Sydney that same day. In lieu of notice, I gave the *Financial Review*'s Jenni Hewett the exclusive that Fairfax was now the proud owner of this American feminist icon. On the plane I wrote in my diary how thrilled I was to be embarking on yet another great adventure. And how terrified. This was an astonishing turnaround in my fortunes, and bigger than anything I had ever done before. I hoped that I might be able to bring to *Ms.* my experience in journalism, my feminist sensibility, and the thorough knowledge of women's issues I had accumulated while working at OSW. I had the opportunity to remake *Ms.* so that it was relevant for the 1990s, reflecting where American women were on the still rocky road to true equality and independence, and offering a unique feminist perspective on the issues and obstacles that still stood in their way. I was amazingly confident I could do it. This was the opportunity of a lifetime and I was going to give it everything I had.

Just a week after the Ms. Foundation accepted our offer, the gloomy scenarios of the previous six weeks suddenly became nightmarishly real. Young Warwick agreed to sell the *Financial Review*, the *Times on Sunday* and the Macquarie Network to corporate raider Robert Holmes à Court, and the magazine group and the *Canberra Times* to Kerry Packer. The two newspapers I had worked for until the previous week were both being disposed of. Had it not been for the *Ms.* deal and my exciting new job, I would have been part of the editorial fodder whose future was now so uncertain. Even worse, and what made me feel both guilty and sad, was that so many of the men who had helped me get this extraordinary new opportunity were now casualties. Max Suich, my long time mentor, Greg Gardiner, Fairfax's general manager and Fred Brenchley, another long-time friend and a former editor of the *Financial Review* who had been running the magazine group, would all lose their jobs. No one was able to tell us what the fate of *Ms.* would be under the proposed new arrangements. Sandra and I went to a celebratory dinner with Gloria and Pat but we did not dare tell them anything until we had concrete information about who was to own *Ms.* During the dinner Greg Gardiner rang Sandra to say we were 'Okay'.

On 9 October we signed the deal with the Ms. Foundation. Pat Carbine burst into tears while she and Sandra were signing all the various documents. Gloria and I were in the adjoining room, disguising the tension we each felt by looking at magazines, making small-talk, not referring to the historic event that was taking place a few steps away. We had not thought to bring a photographer so we resolved to do so when we actually handed over the money, once the New York Attorney-General had approved the sale. Exactly one month later on 9 November, Sandra, Jeanne Shelley, the accountant from the Fairfax's New York office, and I handed over the cheques. It was such an extraordinary moment that my body felt utterly unconnected with my emotions. I was physically present in the room but I felt as if I were somewhere else. It was a sign, I suppose, that I was still coming to terms with the tumultuous changes taking place in my life. There was less tension in the room than when we had signed the papers. Whatever emotion Steinem and Carbine felt, neither of them showed it. For Steinem in particular, this moment represented the end of her fight to keep the magazine alive. *Ms.* was now someone else's problem. She probably felt relieved, I surmised, although something told me that she would never really be able to let go. It was too much a part of who she was. Steinem's biographer, the late Carolyn Heilbrun, had addressed this in her 1995 book and concluded that 'the magazine had become like her invalid mother.' As a very young teenager, Gloria had had to assume responsibility for caring for her mentally-ill mother. Her parents had divorced and her older sister was in college so for seven years, living in a rat-infested basement apartment in a poor neighbourhood in Toledo, Ohio, Gloria became, in Heilbrun's words, 'her mother's mother'.[2] It was a very tough time for her, and she only confronted its lasting impact after the sale of *Ms.* In her 1992 book *Revolution from Within*, she revealed her own lack of confidence and 'self-esteem' and argued the need to recognise and nurture the 'child within' each of us. Steinem concluded that her relationship of co-dependency with her mother had dictated how she related to the world. When it came to keeping *Ms.* alive, Heilbrun writes, 'There was no choice, just as there had been none in Toledo'.[3] Steinem remained an adolescent until she was well over 50, contends Heilbrun; she had never been allowed to grow up. Or to complain, or to show emotion. I suspected her lack of emotion the day we signed the

had learned of the impending sale only a day or two earlier. A space had been reserved for me at the top of the table with every other seat taken and the remaining staff standing around the walls staring glumly at me. I was taken aback that Steinem was not there. I had assumed she would steer the meeting. This was terrible for me: no introduction to ease my way in, no assurances to the staff that I was a 'real feminist' they could trust. Steinem's absence that day spoke volumes about how she really felt about the sale and, presumably, about me. She might have sold us the magazine but she was not going to make it easy. In her absence I had no choice but to plunge in alone. I took a deep breath and, after introducing myself, began telling the group what I had done in the past and how proud I was to be joining this legendary magazine. I knew this would be difficult for them, I acknowledged, but said I was looking forward to working with them. I invited questions and I realised that Steinem had at last arrived and was standing behind me when, in responding to a comment someone else had made, she mentioned in that low chuckly voice of hers that she had just come from lunching with Jacqueline Onassis at the Russian Tea Room.

My first day at *Ms.* was 6 November. I had already recruited a secretary, Eileen Moriarty, but when the two of us arrived at the magazine's shambolic offices at 119 West 40th Street, we found no office had been provided for me. The hostility was not overt; it was more passive-aggressive. I asked for a desk. There wasn't one, I was told. 'Okay,' I said, 'I will take over the conference room.' This was hardly an auspicious start. How would I get on with the staff, I wondered, and how difficult would it be for me to start introducing my editorial ideas? Eileen Moriarty had taken a huge leap of faith in agreeing to work for me. She had been earning a high salary with a prominent investment banking firm but she hated the job, she said, and was willing to drop pay to go somewhere she felt would be more humane. She was a cheerful woman with blonde curls and a strong New York accent who was totally unfazed by her new environment; she quickly organised rental furniture and soon the two of us were ensconced in the room whose only window faced a so-called light-shaft, which admitted a few faint rays of sunlight in the morning but was pitch dark by late-afternoon. There was another problem, too. The conference room was at the other end of the floor from the large open space that served as the editorial offices, and could only be reached by negotiating one's way through the advertising and circulation departments. This meant that Eileen and I were constantly tramping backwards and forwards as I tried to assume editorial control of the magazine. Not one editorial staff member ever ventured back to see me. We might have bought the magazine, but it was becoming apparent, we had not bought any kind of cooperation from the staff.

Sandra and I had arranged for the staff to be presented with a small token when they came to work on the first day of our formal ownership. We left on each person's desk a white rosebud tied with a rose ribbon and attached to a card that said 'In friendship' inside and, somewhat gauchely I now see, 'GDay' on the card's envelope. I could hear the exclamations of surprise begin shortly after 10 o'clock as the editorial staffers, cardboard beakers of steaming coffee in hand, began drifting in. The gesture seemed to be appreciated.

Later that day I called an editorial meeting to present the refreshed logo and redesign for the magazine. I knew that we needed a strong visual statement that signified the new direction I intended to take with *Ms*. We had to be well-designed and classy so I had hired Nancy Butkus, the hottest magazine art director in town, to do a redesign and I'd decided to accept her suggestion that we refresh the logo. That would be a strong signal that we were changing. Nancy's cover roughs were sensational: a clean and strong design that made exactly the kind of statement that I knew was necessary. One cover showed a baby dressed in a pinstriped business suit; a perfect metaphor for the 'having it all' anguish of the 1980s. Nancy's new logo removed the full-stop after the 's' in '*Ms*', turned it into a diamond shape and repositioned it underneath the s. At first I was dubious. Was a diamond too frivolous? Nancy persuaded me, however, that it maintained the old logo's simplicity while giving it an eighties lift. I worried that the staff might see it as subverting *Ms*.'s legacy, but I was ready to discuss and defend what I'd done. But when I laid the boards out on the floor, there being nowhere else to present them, not a single person said a word. They simply stared at them and returned to their desks. I had found it remarkable that Steinem and Carbine had not told them of the magazine's insurmountable financial problems and the possibility of a sale. I understood that their hostility masked sadness, and that most of them were having difficulty coping with this suddenly altered reality. Someone must have said something to Steinem because a week or so after we took over, she arranged a day-long counselling session for the staff.

But whatever benefits that session had for individual morale, it did little to persuade them I was not a hostile interloper. I went into the ladies' room and found taped to the main door a cartoon from a magazine that derided Australian women as the Valley Girls of the 1980s, a disparaging and stereotyped reference to the air-headed young women from the San Fernando Valley in Los Angeles. A few weeks earlier, New York *Newsday* had run a headline 'Crocodile Dundee to edit *Ms.*' Great. I was being introduced to New York as a rough and ready Australian, from the same mould as controversial newspaper magnate Rupert Murdoch or Paul Hogan, who played the knockabout Crocodile Dundee in the hit movie of the same name. How could I convince this city that I was a different kind of Australian? A woman, for one thing, and someone who loathed the brash ocker stereotype. But also an Australian who wanted to *lift* the quality of *Ms.* magazine, not turn it into tabloid trash as was Murdoch's style back then.

———◆———

I soon discovered that *Ms.* was chaotic. There was no structure to the editorial staff, no hierarchy or at least not one that was acknowledged. On the masthead everyone appeared to be equal; no one had a title. Was anyone actually in charge? I was surprised to learn that Steinem was not in fact the magazine's editor. That job had been Suzanne Braun Levine's, although you would never know that from the masthead. Just as you would never know that there were in fact editors, a copy editor, a fact-checker and a production manager. Nor were there any secretaries or assistants. Everyone was supposed to do their own 'shit work', answer their own phones, open their own mail, sift through the piles of unsolicited submissions—in addition to doing the essential daily work of commissioning articles and seeing them through the production process. This approach to organisation might have been okay for the women's movement in the 1970s, but it was no way to run a magazine. Nor was it an honest reflection of how power was actually exercised—and remunerated. While most *Ms.* staffers' salaries were very low, those at the (unacknowledged) top paid themselves well, in a couple of cases extremely well.

Suzanne Braun Levine was expected to stand aside for me and she was not happy about it. There was no negotiating this as there was no room for two editors-in-chief. Nor was I prepared to include her name on the masthead as Editor Emerita, as Steinem wanted. The masthead had to reflect the new direction of the magazine, not be a tombstone to the past. *Ms.* was overstaffed given its income so some people would have to go, and I would not retain the various advisory bodies the magazine had been using. There would be fewer names on the masthead than in the past and we would list their job titles. As soon as the deal had been agreed, all staffers had been put on sixty days probation. The new masthead would reflect the new staffing, those *Ms.* staffers I retained as well as new hires such as the art director who had been recommended by Nancy Butkus, but it would also include Steinem and Carbine, who were being retained as consultants. It would not be a totally clean break.

I spent two days interviewing editorial staffers individually while Sandra reviewed the advertising, circulation and marketing people. I wanted to talk to people away from the depressing and enervating environment of the *Ms.* offices, and the hostile bravura of the group, so I'd hired a room in the Grand Hyatt Hotel, which was convenient to the office and to transport. I asked each person to tell me their strengths and weaknesses, to let me know if they wished to continue in their current job or, if there was a choice, was there a job they would prefer to do? Steinem had been anxious to protect the jobs of all *Ms.'s* employees but we were not prepared to give such an under-taking. I needed to make my mark and that meant hiring some new people. Some of the existing staff would have to be cut but I also needed to put the magazine out. I would use my first issue to assess who was indispensable. There was at least one person who had to go right away; she had a serious drinking problem and would return each day after lunch, lie down under her desk and pass out. We insisted that she be dismissed before we got there. They agreed, saying they had been about to sack her anyway, but then failed to honour their undertaking. It was left to Sandra to do. I had found the meetings with the editorial people both depressing and terrifying. Their levels of passivity were astonishing, especially for such a high-energy place as New York. Everyone was completely happy with what they were doing; no one had any ambitions to move to other jobs, let alone other publications. The only requests I received were for pay increases. It was true the editorial staff salaries were extraordinarily low and Sandra and I had already budgeted to pay market rates. But we had also determined that if we were going to pay higher salaries we wanted competent, committed people in every single one of those jobs.

———⟫●⟪———

At first, Gloria Steinem and I seemed to get on well. She was warm and welcoming on my first day, presenting me with a large wooden planter box of Narcissus with a card that said 'for the temporary office of a permanent gardener (of flowers and talent and a better world)'. This was an especially generous gesture since she disapproved, she told me, of my plan to introduce into *Ms.* a page where women wrote about their gardens. I had been struck by how many feminists loved to cultivate plants, even in window boxes or on small terraces, and my idea was to ask well-known women to write about their love of growing things. I had intended to call the page 'The Joy of Growing'. Steinem had no interest in plants and grew nothing in her own apartment but her close friend Robin Morgan, the poet and editor of the feminist anthology *Sisterhood is Powerful* grew roses on her rooftop and would write for the page—as did Kate Millett, Susan Brownmiller, the novelist Marge Piercy and former First Lady, Lady Bird Johnson. Most people to whom I described the idea loved it and eventually Steinem came around; she even came up with 'Earthly Delights' a far better name for the page which l accepted gratefully.

The day after the initial papers were signed I had gone to Steinem's apartment on East 73rd Street. She had invited me to discuss with her how she could help me with the transition. She understood the 'tyranny of expectations', she said, and did not want to burden me with excess information but she wanted to give me as much, and as many introductions, as I thought would be useful. I was impressed by the breadth of her ideas, and her amazingly wide array of contacts, as well as by her generosity in being willing to share these with me. I was already grateful that she had taken me under her wing socially as well, showing me a New York I had never experienced before. Just walking down the street with her, heads turned, people gawked and there was absolutely no problem getting a seat or a table wherever we might want to go. She introduced me to everyone—movie stars, editors and other luminaries and to her 'gang', Robin Morgan and the wonderful Bella Abzug who from 1971 to 1977 had been a member of the US House of Representatives. Both received me warmly and I felt absurdly excited knowing that I could now call upon these trailblazing feminists, perhaps even become friends with them. One night in early November, Gloria took me to Nell's, the smart new nightclub on West 14th Street that was part-owned by the Australian Nell Campbell. It was one of the hottest places in town and almost impossible to get into—unless you were with Gloria Steinem. There was no waiting in the street in the freezing cold behind a velvet rope when you were with Gloria. And of course once we were inside, she knew everyone. As we sat down on one of the club's signature grungy old couches Iman, the gorgeous Somalian supermodel, who later married David Bowie, joined us. 'And who do you most admire?' she said to me. 'Who are your heroes?' I stumbled to come up with a smart answer.

The gap between Steinem's rhetoric and the way she conducted herself would always puzzle me. Her feminist sentiments were impeccable and often expressed in eloquent and colourful language. She was especially adept at popularising the words of others, one example being the slogan 'a woman needs a man like a fish needs a bicycle' which was coined by Irina Dunn, an Australian. But some aspects of her seemed to be at odds with her rhetoric, as I found when I visited her apartment. I found it somewhat disturbing, like being confronted with intimate secrets. Gloria's bed, a loft bed in the front room of her brownstone apartment, was reached by wooden stairs that, like the bed itself, were draped with flimsy white fabric. In Carolyn Heilbrun's view, it resembled a baby's bassinet. She writes that the novelist Alice Walker, at the time a close friend of Gloria's, thought that 'it represents the much-cared-for-baby Steinem believes she never was'.[4] I was astonished to discover that Gloria had once been rather plump and that she had a sister who was grossly overweight. When we dined together she ate very little, whereas I greedily consumed all the offerings of New York's finest restaurants. Once when we had breakfast at the Plaza Hotel, I tucked into Eggs Benedict while she made do with a toasted bran muffin. No butter. Maybe this was why she had a set of physicians' weighing scales wedged in front of the small refrigerator in her kitchen. To open the fridge door, it was necessary to manoeuvre the scales out of the way. Strange stuff for a feminist. Especially one whose magazine regularly urged women to reject the body images foisted on them by the cosmetics and fashion industries. But then Steinem, like many feminists, had a complicated relationship with fashion. She was the beneficiary of designers who wanted to be able to boast that Gloria Steinem wore their label. Early on, I'd asked about a rack of garments being wheeled into the West 40th Street offices. 'They're for Gloria,' I was told. 'She's always being offered clothes.'

Gloria arranged for me to spend time with Betsy Carter, an experienced magazine editor who was currently running a new title called *New York Woman*. She also introduced me to the legendary Clay Felker, the founding editor of *New York* magazine, who had launched the first issue of *Ms.* as a supplement in the magazine in 1971. Felker was a genius of an editor who had changed the way New York was written about. *New York* under Felker was 'all about how the power game is played and who are the winners'[5] in the seven glamour industries that make New York such an alluring place. (Those industries were news media, fashion, finance, theatre, high art, advertising and book publishing.) He had been forced out of *New York* when Rupert Murdoch bought it in 1976 and was now editor of an interesting business magazine called *Manhattan Inc.*

I sat in with Felker while he commissioned a fashion business story, and was relieved to see there were still some hands-on editors left. He liked some of my ideas for *Ms.*, especially my 'Joy of Growing' column, but he disagreed with my plan to run news. 'People don't want news from magazines,' he said. I chose to ignore this and was glad when the popularity of the *Ms. Reporter* vindicated my decision. His suggestions for attracting attention were basically to combine big names with big ideas. I had been thinking along these lines and was pleased to get this reinforcement. I had no shortage of ideas, for stories and for writers, and soon I was hitting the phones to commission people I hoped could deliver a feminist spin on these big ideas. I had begun preparing for my first issue—which would be February 1988 and which would hit the newsstands in late January—in mid-October, even before I had moved into the *Ms.* offices. I was heartened by the warm and positive response I received from virtually everyone I contacted. I was worried there might be suspicion, or condescension—would the 'Crocodile Dundee' headline have stuck?—and I would not have been at all surprised if writers were wary. Instead, my calls were picked up, or quickly returned, and my proposals met with enthusiasm. Soon, writers were calling me, including many who had written in the past for *Ms.* but who told me they had become disenchanted with the direction of the magazine. I was surprised by the deference so many showed towards me. I was learning fast just how much power New York editors have, even on a magazine as egalitarian as *Ms.* supposedly was. Ships' captains and magazine editors, someone had said to me, the two remaining positions of absolute and unqualified power. I was going to need all the power I could muster, I quickly realised, as I was discovering the dismal reputation of the magazine in the industry and with readers. Things were far worse than Sandra or I had understood.

For most of its history, *Ms.* had managed to maintain a circulation of around 500,000. This was barely sustainable in a country where successful women's magazines sold at least 3 or 4 million copies a month but when we took over, the circulation had fallen to a fifteen-year low of 450,000 and advertising revenue was sliding precipitously. If Fairfax had not come along, it is doubtful *Ms.* would have survived the year. The printer was owed hundreds of thousands of dollars and was unlikely to print another issue without receiving a payment. In 1987, the magazine had carried 503 pages of advertising. This was respectable, very respectable in fact when compared with the just 343 pages for the whole of 1986—until you took into account the special fifteen-year anniversary issue of July/August that year, with a nice fat 232-page book-size that was crammed full of ads. It was this issue which had helped Sandra and I persuade the Fairfax Board to buy *Ms.* It proved, we argued, that the advertising support *was* there. All it needed was the professional approach to selling ads that Sandra's extensive sales experience would bring, supported by a marketing campaign which Fairfax could finance—something *Ms.* had never been able to afford in the past. We only found out later that the do-or-die effort to make this anniversary issue a success had involved advertisers being offered deals that did not require them to pay any actual money. We discovered, to our consternation, that many of the contracts had no revenue attached to them. We also found that advertiser resistance to *Ms.* was entrenched and seemingly intractable. In late January 1988 we put on a very expensive dinner at the ritzy Pierre Hotel to signal that things were going to be different from now on. We invited 200 advertisers, but got very few acceptances. Instead our friends and staff members got to enjoy a lavish dinner because, we discovered, it was too late to cancel the event.

Our advertising agency, Della Femina McNamee, had done a couple of quick focus groups on *Ms.* editorial using their own female staff. The response had been overwhelmingly negative. Not one of them read *Ms.* and none of them liked any of the issues they were shown. You would not expect hip women from Madison Avenue to like an issues-based magazine like *Ms.*, I told myself. Except it wasn't just these women. *Ms.*'s own research, done in 1983 and made available to us as part of the sale, showed the magazine had a massive problem in trying to reconcile the needs of the long-term readers— dubbed the 'true faith' readers by the research company—and those they needed to recruit if the magazine was to survive, let alone thrive. The research identified women who, having tried the magazine, did not renew their subscriptions because they found *Ms.* 'too depressing' or because it made them feel guilty. This research revealed what would be an intractable problem for me in trying to achieve the right editorial balance for *Ms.* It was impossible to please, let alone satisfy, both groups. The true faith readers, those who had been loyal to *Ms.* since 1972, wanted to have their fiercely held feminist convictions reinforced and reaffirmed, with a diet of articles that hammered home the basic injustices the world continued to inflict on women. Yet this group was small, around 15,000 of more than 400,000 total subscriptions, and ageing. Younger women said they wanted hope and affirmation that their lives were not all terrible, and they hated being depicted as victims. They did, however, want help with their lives and they wanted to read about women like themselves, ordinary people struggling to fulfil their goals, rather than the corporate high-flyers or celebrities who featured so prominently on the covers of most other women's magazines.

It was obvious we needed to do our own research, to test the magazine afresh and to get some feedback on my editorial ideas. Sandra asked Barbara Riley, an expert market researcher, to come over from Sydney and in late October we went on the road, to Washington DC, St Louis, Chicago and Los Angeles. Sandra had told me that Barbara's expertise was in conducting focus groups, small gatherings of people from a target audience who did not know each other and who would sit around a table and, under Barbara's guidance, talk about the subject under discussion. The client, in this case Sandra and I, observed the proceedings from an adjacent room through a two-way mirror. The groups provided me with valuable insights into the way average American women were feeling about their lives, how they resented what they saw as the burden to 'have it all', for instance. None of them wanted to turn back the clock; if pressed to choose between home and work, they would prefer to work and they definitely wanted their daughters to be able to work and support themselves, but they were affronted at how hard it was to juggle the various components of their lives. Every single woman had heard of *Ms.* and although the groups included a few former subscribers, not a single one of them had a positive view of the magazine. It was disconcerting to hear what a negative view most of them had of feminism and downright alarming to hear their extraordinarily vehement anti-lesbian views. Invariably a member of each group spotted in our classified ads page the very small number of lesbian book ads. In early November, Barbara presented Sandra and me with her verbal report: 'If you want *Ms.* to have any chance of success,' she told us, 'there are three words that should never appear in its pages: feminism, lesbianism and Gloria Steinem.'

I was dreadfully upset by Barbara's report. We had drawn the women in the focus groups from populations we assumed were potential *Ms.* readers but what Barbara was telling us was that even within this group, there was scarcely any tolerance for feminism; no admiration or respect for Gloria Steinem; and a down-right loathing of lesbians. I was under no illusion that *Ms.* could ever become a mass circulation women's magazine, but I had hoped we could get to a circulation of one million. Surely in a country of 230 million people, we could appeal to less than a quarter of one per cent of the population? And surely that group was more tolerant than the population at large? If that was not the case, this presented us with a terrible dilemma. We could not, and would not, ditch the feminist premise of the magazine and nor would we disenfranchise the lesbian women who had stuck loyally with *Ms.* since the beginning, but how were we going to be able to attract new readers? The question of Gloria Steinem was trickier. It seemed to me essential that we start to wean the long-term readers from their reliance on her. For almost fifteen years *Ms.* had become almost neurotically dependent on Steinem, not just to sell ads, but to boost news-stand sales with a quickly turned-out cover story that more often than not was illustrated with her image on the cover but this dependency, we were learning, was self-defeating if the magazine was to grow.

We had to position *Ms.* to advertisers as 'evolving'. We tried to signal this with an ad campaign we ran in the trade press that showed *Ms.* as a woman transitioning, through four separate headshots, from a hippie-looking, headband-wearing 1970s type to a more glamorous 1980s look. It was titled 'We're not the *Ms.* we used to be.' The *Ms.* people were outraged by this ad. Suzanne Braun Levine wrote an angry letter to Sandra and we had numerous complaints from the editors. They saw it as a repudiation of Steinem. We were mystified by this response: Steinem could never be accused of having been a hippie and she was already one of the most glamorous people in the women's movement so it was a stretch to claim that the images were meant to represent her. And they looked nothing like her. But it seemed it was going to be tough to get people to think about *Ms.* as no longer being associated with Gloria Steinem if even this mild effort evoked such a reaction. I did not want to confront the possibility that maybe *Ms.* was so integrally associated with Steinem that without her, the magazine simply did not exist. Our task was not helped by the fact that she remained on our masthead as a consultant, and that I met with her frequently, usually over breakfast, to seek her counsel on various matters. Maybe we should have just cut all ties, but we decided it was better to have Steinem and Carbine in the tent, able to be called-upon when needed and, we required, to refrain from public comments if they did not agree with what we were doing. And Steinem had a contract to write a book. Maybe she would be so relieved to find her freedom that she would be happy to start to disentangle herself.

As I threw myself into producing my first issue, I had to get used to a very different way of working. Starting with the time-lines. With newspapers you could have a good idea one day, and see it on the front page the next. Now I needed to plan two or three months in advance for my next issue, and to learn to be mapping out the next one and the one after that. You needed a long view. And I was amazed at how the editors, as they were called, and who reported to the editor-in-chief (me!), were responsible for shaping stories in ways that Australian journalists and writers would have found shockingly intrusive. It was the same with fact-checkers. I could not believe the potential power they had to rewrite stories that had already been altered, often beyond recognition, by the editors. I knew about the legendary fact-checking department of the *New Yorker*, but had not realised how integral fact-checking was to all American magazines. It was not just 'facts'—such as dates and spellings—that were confirmed. Quotes were read back to people, who of course could deny having ever made the comment. It seemed to me that editing and fact-checking lessened the responsibility of the writer to deliver a well-crafted and complete story. Knowing that facts would be checked anyway encouraged writers to simply leave blanks or, more often, use the ubiquitous TK (which, bizarrely, meant 'to come'), indicating the fact-checker should insert the relevant information. I was astonished to see stories come in that were peppered with TKs, meaning the writer had not bothered to insert the most basic information. This system certainly encouraged laziness on the part of the writer, I thought, but even worse in some ways was the safety net provided by the editors. If a story was badly constructed, poorly written, or otherwise in trouble, it was the job of the editor—not the writer—to fix it. It was not hard to see that writers could succumb to the temptation to allow the editor to do all the hard work. And who got the credit? The writer's name was on the story, not the editor's. What an unfair system, I thought.

Late in 1987 we had moved *Ms.* out of its squalid offices in the garment district to join *Sassy* on the two floors we'd leased in the famous triangular building called One Times Square; it had once been the home of the *New York Times*, and the reason the area once known as Longacre Square had been renamed Times Square in 1904. Now the building was famous for its non-stop news ticker and for the ball which dropped every New Year's Eve. *Ms.* and *Sassy* each had a floor of the building that admittedly had a very small footprint. Everything was new and nice, a far cry from the squalor of the old *Ms.* offices. I think the staff appreciated their new surroundings, despite a few mutterings about it being 'too corporate', and that everyone had cubicles rather than open desks. We were starting to see something of a team spirit, I thought. In the end I had fired only three of the *Ms.* staffers, all of them very junior. I knew I should have been tougher, perhaps cleared out the whole place, but I'd feared I would not be able to produce the first issue without the senior team. I found myself becoming very impressed by several of them, at how hard they worked and how committed they were. Early on, I decided that Marcia Ann Gillespie brought editorial insights and experience that complemented my own and within five months I had appointed her executive editor, effectively my deputy; she became the first African-American woman to hold a senior position at *Ms.*. Marcia had been editor-in-chief of *Essence*, the mass circulation magazine for African-American women and had been hired by *Ms.* as a consultant in the final desperate pre-sale days when the magazine was trying to save itself from oblivion by launching its ill-conceived makeover. Marcia was savvy and smart and a lot of fun, and there was nothing she did not know about women's magazines. She gave me advice on how to achieve what I wanted. I was used to controlling words, editing pieces and ensuring they said what I wanted them to say, but I had never before worked with an Art Director and quickly found I did not have the language to communicate what I wanted. Nor could I always get my ideas across to the editorial team. Sometimes it was cultural, the weird misunderstandings that occur when people think they are speaking the same language, but there were also disagreements and pushback. I was okay with that. I did not want compliant ciphers but I wondered if we would ever achieve a state of mutual trust. I would promise readers in my first Editor's Essay that there would be continuity and change. I wanted to retain the best of the old *Ms.* at the same time as I reshaped the editorial so I asked Letty Cottin Pogrebin if she would write a regular column that had a personal focus. Letty was a bubbly and enthusiastic person, a writer, lecturer and activist around feminist and Jewish issues,

at *Manhattan Inc.*—change the conversation, get people talking about us, looking at us differently.

I knew this was my never-to-be-repeated opportunity to demonstrate my editorial credentials to the New York media which was watching to see what I would do with *Ms.* The Pat Schroeder piece would provide the perfect vehicle to announce to the world that *Ms.* was now a journalistic force to be reckoned with. Just two women had previously run for the Presidential nomination, Senator Margaret Chase Smith for the Republican Party in 1964 and Congresswoman Shirley Chisholm for the Democratic Party in 1972. At this rate, of one woman a decade vying for the Presidency, it was hard to see when the US would ever elect a woman to the White House. The pool of politically qualified women was small and it was shallow. There were only 25 women in the 99th Congress of 1985–87, two of them senators, and just three states had female governors. It seemed the influence of feminism had not yet been felt in electoral politics. This would be the context for my cover story (just as it informed my wanting to introduce regular political coverage into *Ms.*). I was looking for a serious journalistic appraisal of what had happened, the kind of big read one might find in *Esquire* or *Rolling Stone*, but with feminist assumptions. I did not want a soft, predictable piece, an apologia for Schroeder's failure, or a shying away from examining why women were not stepping up in the numbers needed to be a force in US politics. I told the editors of my plan. There was a problem, I was told. What kind of problem, I asked impatiently. I want to do this story, I warned, and I will. The problem was that prior to my arrival someone else had been assigned to write an essay on what the Pat Schroeder decision meant. 'That doesn't matter,' I said. 'We'll kill that assignment. I want my own person.' Looks of horror greeted me. 'We can't kill the piece,' someone said. 'It's Jane O'Reilly.'

I had to be told that Jane O'Reilly was a founding member of what the editors liked to refer to as 'the *Ms.* family'. She had written the famous 'click' article in the first-ever issue of *Ms.*, the one that documented those recognitions that today might be described as 'light-bulb moments', where you see sexism (or, as it used to be called, 'male chauvinism') in action. I was assured that Jane could easily turn her essay into the kind of piece I was looking for. I was unconvinced. I wanted my first cover story to bear *my* stamp, not to be a compromise negotiated with the old guard. I started making calls, working my way through my list of preferred, well-known writers. Every single one of them turned me down. Or, rather, their agents did. In the nicest possible way, of course, but letting me know nevertheless that it was simply unheard of to expect writers of this calibre to drop whatever they were doing to take on an assignment of this kind, especially one that had to be turned around in a matter of weeks. Didn't I know that in the US magazine stories were assigned *months* in advance? No, I did not, but I was fast learning that my own assignment was going to be considerably tougher than I had imagined. I wondered if Tina Brown, the editor-in-chief of *Vanity Fair*, then one of New York's hottest magazines, got the same reaction when she wanted a timely piece.

I had to go back to the editors. 'Okay,' I told them, 'let's get Jane to change her focus and make it a major piece, a cover story. I'll go and see her.' It was quickly made clear to me that would not be a good idea. 'Jane is temperamental,' I was told, 'she does not like to deal with people she doesn't know. Best to let Gloria handle it.' Gloria, in this case, was Gloria Jacobs, one of the senior editors, and someone Jane trusted. I liked Gloria. In the short time we had worked together, I had found her ideas interesting. She might be someone who would survive the transition, I had ruminated. She and I discussed what I had in mind for the article and I crossed my fingers, while she trooped off to the Upper West Side where Jane lived in a shabby but sprawling multi-roomed apartment overlooking Central Park.

The piece was due in early December. Even then it would need a very quick turnaround to get it ready for the February issue that 'closed'—the term used to describe that frantic final week when a magazine is put to bed—in the second week of December. By the end of the first week it had not been delivered and I started to panic. Gloria Jacobs tried to reassure me, but I could tell she was worried. Repeated phone calls to Jane went unanswered. Eventually Jacobs went to her apartment, insisted she be let in, sat down at Jane's word-processor, printed out the piece and brought it back to the office. It was 40 rambling, incoherent and inconsistent pages. It was not an article; it was not even close to being an article. I decided it was unusable. What on earth was I going to do! I had commissioned George Lange, one of New York's top magazine photographers, to do the cover shot. He had produced a sensational image of Pat Schroeder wrapped in the American flag which, I was confident, was going to cause a protest from the American Legion. That would be great publicity for our initial issue. I had a cover shot, but no cover story. Jacobs said she could rescue the piece. I looked at her dubiously, but I had no choice. For almost four days she laboured over the manuscript and when she brought it to me, I could hardly believe the miracle she had wrought. I no longer needed persuading about the value of what American magazine editors do. She had salvaged what I had judged to be an unpublishable piece and turned it into a creditable article that still retained something of Jane's voice. I thanked her profusely and approved it to go into production. The dramas weren't over. Jane O'Reilly sued to have her name removed from the story. The issue had already gone to film, and it would have cost a lot of money to halt production. Lawyers had to be brought in; eventually it was resolved. Welcome to magazine publishing, Anne, I thought to myself.

I pushed on with my plan to open a Washington Bureau and advertised the position of bureau chief. I had wanted a top Washington journalist for the job—another signal that I was shaking things up—but although I received more than 200 applications, none was a big name, or someone from a major news organisation. I was forced to acknowledge that no one was going to leave a prestigious media job to leap into the risky world that I was offering. I interviewed 25 women and selected Peggy Simpson, who had wide Washington experience, knew absolutely everyone, was indefatigable and was able to turn around a story quickly. This was important because I was about to introduce a regular section called the *Ms. Reporter*. It would be printed on salmon-coloured paper (very similar to the *Financial Times*, only glossy) to distinguish it from the rest of the magazine, and would feature short, newsy items on political issues and people. We were, in effect, introducing newspaper-type deadlines to this section of the magazine and Simpson's newspaper background meant she was well-equipped to ensure we always had sufficient, and good, material. Peggy was also consistent and reliable and she never got anything wrong. Indispensable in a journalist. She was a great hire.

The *Ms. Reporter* was to be very popular with readers. They appreciated getting news that no one else published and our focus on political leaders, especially women, and the forthcoming 1988 presidential election made us unique among women's magazines. In 1979, buckling under sky-rocketing cost increases for paper and postage, Steinem and Carbine converted the magazine to not-for-profit status by transferring the ownership to a foundation they also named Ms.. They saved hundreds of thousands of dollars a year in postage costs[6] but they paid a high price, in that they could no longer take political positions and rate candidates. Now we were freed from that constraint and I wanted political coverage to be a *Ms.* hallmark. It would distinguish us from other women's magazines and, if we did it properly, would generate news that would be covered by other media, giving us free publicity. One of my ideas was for a regular *Ms.* poll, but when I told Steinem about this she had argued, persuasively it had seemed at the time, that polls were not reliable in a country where voting was not compulsory. I don't know why I listened to her. Political polls and their findings generate regular news stories. We could have polled voting intentions and all kinds of social issues. It could have been a major part of our rebranding, and I still regret that I did not do it.

Our Washington launch party was held on Capitol Hill on a frigid January night in an elaborate large room, just off the Senate chamber, which meant that a good few senators dropped in during the evening. Peggy Simpson and Ann Lewis, another well-known Washington insider who had also interviewed well and who I had hired to write political commentary, had together ensured that all the major women's organisations and lobbyists were there. Gloria Steinem had delivered the co-chair of the event, the very well-connected Pamela Harriman, who later would be appointed Ambassador to France by President Bill Clinton. Her presence was enough to put us on the Washington map. The room was packed with guests and gate-crashers—the sign of a hot party. Our VIP list included all of the very few women members of Congress, including the diminutive Senator Barbara Mikulski, newly elected from Maryland. She was one of just two women senators then; when she retired in 2017, she had served longer than any other woman in the history of Congress. Pamela, Gloria and I all spoke. I outlined my plans for *Ms.*'s political coverage. It was a presidential election year and *Ms.* would cover the candidates and the issues. We planned to produce a guide to the best candidates for women, I told them.

Senator Edward Kennedy dropped by and headed straight towards Gloria. She introduced us. His face was a deep unhealthy red, his skin was puffy. 'Let's have lunch,' he said, locking eyes with me. Teddy Kennedy's drunken carousing was the talk of the town and the subject of avid media reporting. He and fellow Senator Christopher Dodd from Connecticut frequently cavorted together, often reportedly engaging in sexual activities in public view in restaurants, including a notable incident in 1985 at La Brasserie, one of Kennedy's favourite Washington haunts, that became known as the 'waitress sandwich'.[7] There was plenty of public speculation about the possible reasons for why the 'the last brother', as one biographer dubbed him, was seemingly embarked on some kind of existential suicide mission. Some argued that Teddy had become a reckless drunk after the assassination of his brother Bobby in 1968; others pointed out that the public degradation of women was in the Kennedy DNA and that his brother John, while President, had shamelessly seduced women in semi-public situations, often while his wife was in a nearby room. He did not follow through on the lunch invitation, but a few months later I got to hear Kennedy deliver an address at a Women's Legal Defense Fund conference in Washington. Listening to him espouse women's issues I was struck by the incongruity, given his notorious womanising, of the adoring response of the audience, all them women, presumably feminists. and all aged 40 or more. I'd always been puzzled, and a little repulsed, by the way so many feminists fawned over Kennedy, looking the other way at his treatment of women in return for his votes on issues that mattered. Now I was observing this in action. His Kennedy charm, his glamour, his wealth and his 'feminism' seemed to be an irresistible combination for these women. It occurred to me then that perhaps his feminism was acquired, an act of atonement for the death of Mary Jo Kopechne who had been drowned in Teddy's car off Chappaquiddick Island in 1969, in circumstances that have never been satisfactorily explained. It had been almost twenty years ago, but the stain of that evening had never been erased. In the early 1990s, married again and seemingly calmed and rehabilitated, Kennedy became a very different man, one who ultimately earned respect for his championing of health insurance, civil rights and women's equality. It was hard to see that man the night I met him in Washington.

A few weeks later, when I got an early copy of my first issue of the magazine, I turned the pages with mixed feelings. I was both proud and amazed to have in my hand a copy of *Ms.—Ms.* magazine!—that I had edited. Here was the concrete manifestation of the dramatic change in my life. I loved the cover photo of Pat Schroeder wrapped cheekily in the flag but when I examined the issue I was hypercritical, seeing mostly its faults. I hated this colour, that headline wasn't sharp enough, the cover lines—the words that are meant to 'sell' the inside content—were banal. It was okay, but it didn't knock my socks off. Sandra tried to reassure me, but I knew I had fallen short of what I had wanted to do. I had been so relieved that Jane O'Reilly's piece had been salvaged that I did not allow myself to mourn what could have been. I resolved I was never again going to let myself get caught like this. I wanted to make my mark with big political stories so, I would plan ahead. I called Joan Didion's agent to commission her to cover either the Democratic or Republican Conventions—or both—for *Ms.* They would be held in mid-1988, and it was now early January. Surely that was plenty of notice.

'Sorry, but Miss Didion is not writing about politics anymore,' I was told.

I felt totally deflated. She was the first big name to turn me down. Even Jeane Kirkpatrick, Reagan's former ambassador to the United Nations, and the first woman to hold that position, had left the door open to a future approach when she'd said no to my request to take part in my Conversation series. This was where I paired well-known women from similar fields to talk about their lives and work. The tennis legends Billie Jean King and Martina Navratilova had been the conversants in my first issue. Later, I would pair writers Andrea Dworkin and Erica Jong. I had thought Kirkpatrick would be well-matched with Bella Abzug who had agreed. At least it wasn't an outright No from Kirkpatrick. Most people were at least curious about the new *Ms.* and I found that heartening. Maybe I was going to be able to make this work.

Sandra and I learned, by accident, late one Sunday night in March 1988 that we were to be sold. Young Warwick was disposing of all Fairfax's overseas assets, the New Zealand newspapers, the *Spectator* magazine in the UK—and

Ms. and *Sassy* in the US. I had called Sydney that evening and picked up that something was happening. Sandra's phone was not working so I walked the seven blocks down Broadway to her apartment to tell her the news. She came back to my place and we hit the phones. She was able to wangle a confirmation out of someone in Sydney but, rather than being distraught, it seemed only to spur her to action. I knew she had thought about what to do if this happened, but I did not know that she had a very big and bold plan. 'We,' she told me—she and I—'would buy the magazines ourselves.' I was amazed and admiring. I would never have had the business imagination, or courage, to come up with such an idea myself, but I was certainly up for it. The debut issue of *Sassy* had hit the newsstands a couple of weeks earlier and it was already apparent that Sandra had achieved the most successful new magazine launch since *Elle* in 1985. *Sassy* was the talk of the town. It was cool and it was groovy. Its editorial staff was young and hip so they could talk peer-to-peer, with articles written in teenagers' lingo, rather than the 'talking-down' editorial by adults of the other teen magazines. It had funky art direction and fashion spreads that made the competition look staid. It seemed this new kid on the block was going to shake up the teen magazine category as it was an immediate, huge hit with the teenage girls who were its target audience and was also attracting a tidal wave of advertising. Everyone wanted to be part of *Sassy*. We had a hot property on our hands and Sandra knew exactly what she wanted to do with it. At around 1 a.m. she rang Wilma Jordan, a media broker and investment adviser, who had become famous when as a co-owner of *Esquire* she had negotiated the sale of this iconic magazine to the Hearst Corporation. Sandra briefly outlined the situation. We agreed to meet in Wilma's office at 8 that morning. 'Well, doctor,' Sandra said to me, 'We've got ourselves an investment banker. We are going to buy those magazines'. Within 24 hours she had secured an exclusive option to purchase *Ms.* and *Sassy* for $US14 million, an amount that made good what Fairfax had already outlayed. We issued a press release announcing that Sandra and I intended to do a management buyout—an MBO in the lingo of the day—of John Fairfax (US) Limited. We had five weeks to raise the money and, if we succeeded, it would be only the second-ever women-led management buyout in US corporate history.[8]

'People don't lend money to people who look as if they need it,' Sandra said to me. 'We've got to look like a million dollars'. In reality we had to look like $20 million, as that was the amount we needed: $14 million to repay Fairfax and $6 million to fund our forward operating costs. Sandra had already chopped $3 million off the operating requirements, because of the phenomenal forward ad bookings for *Sassy*. She thought we might not even need the $6 million but, she figured, it would not hurt to have some extra cash up our sleeves. Just in case. Wilma Jordan was lining up meetings with potential investors or partners. We already had one scheduled with Lord Rothermere, owner of the British media empire Associated Newspapers. We had to be ready with our numbers—and we had to look good.

Sandra got herself a Valentino suit, a stunning red number with deceptively simple lines that looked both businesslike and classy. I was inexperienced at such purchases, but after someone steered me towards a personal shopper at Macy's, of all places, I emerged with a classic Anne Klein two-piece suit, with padded shoulders, a hallmark of the time, a long collarless jacket that fitted snuggly over the short skirt. It was also red, a warm invigorating hue that I called Ronald Reagan red; it was the colour women White House correspondents wore for his Press Conferences, knowing he liked it, hoping he'd favour them with a question. I hoped it might favour me in the tumultuous venture we were about to embark on. I chose a soft white silk Georgio Armani crew necked, short-sleeved blouse to go under my suit. It was an astounding $600. I had no idea you could spend that much money on a mere blouse. We each paid $1000 for our suits. I confided to Sandra that while I loved my new outfit, felt it looked fantastic and made me feel totally in control, I was still in shock at how much it had cost.

'Don't worry,' she said, 'we are going to pull this off'. 'Or,' she added, 'we'll be the best-dressed bag ladies in New York.'

However crazy brave the past six months had been, from getting Fairfax to buy *Ms.* to now being tossed overboard as casualties in a corporate war game, this next step was way bigger than anything we had ever done or I could even have imagined. It was just five months since Sandra had handed over the Fairfax cheque to the Ms. Foundation. They had reluctantly sold us their precious property because they had been assured we were a wealthy and established corporation that could ensure *Ms.*'s future, with management and editorial control in the hands of feminist women. We had worked hard to get Fairfax's credentials established in the New York media world. Our energetic and super-stylish marketing manager Pat Cantor, who Sandra had recruited from Hearst, had used the Fairfax heraldic crest on all our stationery and other livery—'that sort of thing impresses Americans,' she'd assured us. Our media agent had planted stories in the business press that boosted the reputation of this old and established Australian publishing house. Now, suddenly, Fairfax was disintegrating and ditching all its overseas properties. On 17 March 1988 the *New York Post* reported that, once again, *Ms.* was for sale.

The offers poured in. Wilma Jordan reported that she had had 'an extraordinary number' of approaches from media groups, financial institutions and even individuals. The big magazine players—Condé Nast, Hearst, and Time Inc. and Associated Newspapers—all put in bids. As did Rupert Murdoch, who not long before had acquired *Seventeen*, which was still the leading magazine in the teenage girl category. Sandra and I had been introduced to him at a function celebrating the visit to New York of the Sydney Symphony Orchestra.

'Interesting that Australians now control the major magazines consumed by teenage girls in America,' Sandra said to Murdoch.

That night he wasn't interested in talking to us—about *Seventeen* or anything else. Maybe he had heard the slogan Sandra had put out on the street: '*Seventeen* is the magazine your grandmother buys for you, *YM*— Young Miss—is the magazine your mother buys you, *Sassy* is the magazine you buy for yourself'. But it was different now. *Sassy* was on the market and Murdoch, like every media company in town, wanted it. We could have sold *Sassy* in a heartbeat, taken the millions and set ourselves up for life. Except for one very big problem: no one at all wanted *Ms.* The market saw *Ms.* as the ugly sister of magazines, we insisted she was an integral part of the deal. We wanted to save *Ms.*, to show the marketplace that a feminist mass-circulation magazine could work.

'We expect when *Sassy* readers grow up they will want to read *Ms.*,' Sandra used to say.

Our numbers actually showed that *Ms.* could become profitable, long before *Sassy*. It was expensive to replace teenage readers (who quickly outgrew the product) whereas *Ms.* readers, if they liked the magazine, had the potential to remain loyal for years, decades even. We were optimistic because the response to my first issue had been so positive. The editorial was being widely praised and this was translating into good numbers. We posted a 100 per cent increase in newsstand sales; our first direct-mail drop had yielded 32,000 responses against our budget of 22,000, and we'd had 1900 early subscription orders when we had expected only 800. Even more importantly, we had done a deal with the National Organisation for Women (NOW), the activist body founded by Betty Friedan, which would enable us to take our rate base (the number of subscriptions we guaranteed to advertisers) from its current 450,000 to 500,000 in July, and to 600,000 the following January. Our projections showed *Ms.* making a big profit within five years. The trouble was, given *Ms.'s* reputation around town, no one wanted to believe this.

In late March, Young Warwick Fairfax had given us a day's warning that he was coming to New York, asking Sandra to book him a 'moderate priced hotel' and to send a car to pick him up from the airport. He arrived at our offices accompanied by Peter King, the South-African born executive who had replaced Greg Gardiner as CEO of Fairfax and an advisor whose function was never made clear. The weedy, bespectacled young man who had orchestrated the takeover that had shredded a great company, wrecked the careers of so many of my friends and had sent his tiny New York outpost reeling into an uncertain future seemed to me to be very ill-at-ease and immature. He was either ignorant or insensitive about the devastation he had wreaked. In Sandra's office, as he and King flicked through copies of *Ms.* and *Sassy*, Warwick told us that we were being sold not because our efforts were not appreciated but because 'it made no sense' to keep us now the magazine division was being sold and there would be no one to manage us. He tried to tell us what a great opportunity he had given us: 'Executives usually only ever get a salary,' he said, 'but we now had a chance to do something more.' 'Found our own dynasty?' Sandra shot back at him.

We had an awkward lunch at Café Un Deux Trois, the place where Sandra had first hatched the plan to get Fairfax to buy *Ms.* Young Warwick sipped his SevenUp, as Sandra tried hard to get him talking while we waited what seemed like forever for the food. Afterwards we guided them back to the Times Square subway station so they could return to Wall Street where, presumably, they were trying to raise more money to keep their deal in place. So, of course, were we.

We hoped we might be able to turn around the market's view of *Ms.* with the very encouraging feedback I was getting for my overall editorial direction. I had made a couple of bad mistakes, such as my anti-fashion photo feature I'd called 'Personal Appearances' of women wearing their own clothes. It was a disaster. I knew *Ms.* readers did not want fashion, but I thought they might appreciate help in how to put their own wardrobes together via seeing what other women like them wore. Our first issue featured Professor Catharine Stimpson, a well-respected professor of English Literature, who had led *Ms.*'s advisory Board of Scholars. It did not work. It wasn't stylish enough for fashionistas and was loathed by those who thought clothes had no place at all in *Ms.* After a few issues, I killed it. But other innovations of mine were better received by both readers and the industry. I'd had editorial appraisals done by industry gurus to include in our sale documents. I'd asked for assessments from *Redbook*'s Sey Chassler, the only male editor-in-chief of a large women's magazine, who'd expanded the editorial formula from recipes to articles about women's rights, and Lenore Hershey, whose eighteen-year tenure running *Ladies' Home Journal*, America's top-selling women's book, made her the unofficial queen of the industry. Both said, independently, that I had accomplished a great deal in a very short time and that I was taking *Ms.* in a direction that was totally new and fresh in the American market. Chassler went so far as to say that I might even be establishing a new genre of women's magazine. This verdict was reinforced a short time later when John Veronis, a merchant banker who specialised in media deals and who had been deputed by Si Newhouse, the owner of Condé Nast, to check-out the *Sassy/Ms.* deal, interviewed Sandra and me. Veronis told me that if I succeeded in what I was trying to do with *Ms.* I would have created a new kind of magazine for women. Heady stuff but although it led to a job offer from Condé Nast's Creative Director Rochelle Udall for me to edit one of their titles, the company decided to pass on our deal.

Sandra and I set up a corporation which we named Matilda Publications Inc. as a nod to our Australian origins. It would be the vehicle for the new ownership. It was fast becoming clear that no media partner wanted to be involved with *Ms.* so we decided we should go to Wall Street and try to raise the money ourselves. We hoped bankers might take a different view of *Ms.*'s prospects. We were running out of options—and time. If we were unable to do a deal by 30 April Fairfax would put the magazines up for auction, *Sassy* would be sold, *Ms.* would fold, and Sandra and I would most likely be out on the street.

Those next few weeks were a hectic and emotionally heart-stopping rollercoaster ride. We learned to measure success by the day, even by the hour, as our deadline loomed and one offer after another either evaporated or did not meet our criteria. We often let off steam during that exciting but extremely stressful time by going to a bar on Broadway in the 70s, which was close to where both Sandra and I lived. Sometimes there would be a group of us, Sandra's exuberant husband Michael Skinner or some of the Australian gang from the office, but often it was just Sandra and me needing to navigate the trickiest situation either of us had ever found ourselves in. The bar was the usual sort of neighbourhood place, with its share of locals huddled over drinks watching one of several television sets that were of course stuck on sports channels, while groups of various descriptions congregated in wooden booths along the outer wall. Max, a stately African-American man of about 70 who always wore an immaculate three-piece dark suit, presided over the bar, so we always referred to the place as Max's. Max took a shine to the Australians, especially to this one, and whenever we appeared he would immediately clear a booth for us. Those evicted had to find other seats, or else leave. We would settle down with our drinks and, more often than we should have, stay until closing time at 2 a.m. We lived off our nerves, so the lack of sleep did not seem to matter. Nor the hangover, although I usually stuck to wine so the damage was not as great as it might have been. Around midnight, the mood in the bar would change, the music would be turned up, and Max would come from behind the bar and invite

In 1975 I realised one of my life's ambitions when I was hired as a journalist at the *National Times*.

'What's the story, morning glory' was how *National Times* editor Max Suich greeted his journalists. Here he is with me in New York in 1977.

I immediately hit it off with writer and feminist Paula Weideger when we met during my first visit to New York in 1976 and we have remained friends ever since.

In 1978 I stayed with Elisabeth Wynhausen in her apartment in Bleecker Street in the Village after she left the *National Times* to move to New York.

At a National Press Club appearance during the 1980 CHOGM meeting in Australia directing a question at British Prime Minister Margaret Thatcher.

While on assignment in Pakistan for the *Financial Review* in 1980 I travelled through the Khyber Pass to reach the Afghan border where refugees were already crossing to escape the Russian invasion.

After I was appointed to run the Office of the Status of Women for the Hawke government, *Vogue* did a profile of me accompanied by a glamorous photo shoot.

Senator Susan Ryan, the Minister Assisting the Prime Minister on the Status of Women, and the first Labor woman Cabinet Minister, visits the office c.1985.

I was the first Australian journalist to interview a US Secretary of Defense when I sat down with Caspar Weinberger in his office at the Pentagon in June 1986.

In an emotional ceremony Pat Carbine and Gloria Steinem signed documents agreeing to sell *Ms.* magazine to John Fairfax & Sons, represented by Sandra Yates and me.

The American Legion protested my use of the American flag on the cover of the first issue of *Ms.* under my editorship, in February 1988, giving us lots of useful publicity.

Senator Edward Kennedy dropped into the party we held in the Capitol Building in January 1988 to launch the new Washington bureau of *Ms.* magazine.

On 30 June 1988, Sandra Yates and I became only the second women in US corporate history to do a management buyout when we raised $20 million on Wall Street to buy *Ms.* and *Sassy.*

Movie star Anne Archer and TV mogul Oprah Winfrey were among the women honoured as *Ms.* Women of the Year 1988 at a special breakfast at the Waldorf-Astoria Hotel in January 1989.

I wore my 'lucky' Anne Klein suit when I stood outside the World Trade Centre in 1989 to pose for this trade ad to try to attract financial advertising for *Ms.*

I was astonished to find that Betty Friedan's name had never appeared in *Ms.* magazine so I remedied that with an interview to mark the 25th anniversary of the publication of *The Feminine Mystique*.

As Editor-in-Chief of *Ms.* I received many invitations to speak, including from women's organisations such as the League of Women Voters' convention in Springfield, Illinois.

In New York in 1990 with designer Daniel Sachs, arts philathropist Howard Gilman, Chip Rolley and my old friend David Hay.

I was thrilled when Paul Keating asked me to be note-taker at his formal meeting with the President of Ireland Mary Robinson during her visit to Canberra in 1992.

In early 1994 when Prime Minister Paul Keating launched a new edition of *Damned Whores and God's Police* I was stunned when he called for reconciliation between Australian women and men.

Almost everyone who ever worked for PJK attended the lunch at Sydney's Bellevue Hotel in December 2012 to celebrate the twentieth anniversary of him becoming Prime Minister, including 'the PMO Annes': Anne de Salis, me and Mary Ann O'Loughlin.

After we moved to Sydney from New York, Chip and I settled in a terrace house in Victoria Street, Kings Cross which is where photographer Peter Brew-Bevan made this beautiful picture.

I visited my parents in Adelaide as often as I could after my father's cancer diagnosis in 1986 and before his death in 1988, including this trip in May 1987.

On my mother's 80th birthday in May 2003, with her five surviving children. My brothers (from left to right) are Greg Cooper, Tony Cooper, David Cooper and Paul Cooper.

GOOD WEEKEND
July 31, 1993
THE AGE MAGAZINE

UNREAL, JEFF

With one of my early *Good Weekend* covers in July 1993 I wanted to illustrate how new, and potentially mischievous, technology could manipulate photographs in believable ways, but Victorian Premier Jeff Kennett was not amused.

With Jeff Allan I was fortunate to have an endlessly energetic and creative Art Director at *Good Weekend* and together we created some memorable work.

I was honoured that Hazel Hawke agreed to launch my autobiography *Ducks on the Pond* in 1999—and surprised at how frank and personal her speech was.

As chair of the board of Greenpeace International I attended Forum 2000 in October 2001 at the invitation of Czech Republic President Vaclev Havel and was tongue-tied to find myself sharing a platform with F.W. de Klerk, the man who released Nelson Mandela and ended apartheid in South Africa.

With Greenpeace campaigner David Logie and Amazon Campaign Coordinator Anne Dingwall on a remote tributary of the Amazon near Porto do Moz. (Photo by Flavio Cannalongu)

I co-curated and emceed the Serious Women's Business conference for nine years including when newly-minted Governor General Quentin Bryce attended, pictured here with SWB founder Taren Hocking and her new-born son Hudson and committee member Megan Dalla-Camina.

In 2011 I was honoured, along with three other feminists, as an Australian Legend by having my image on a postage stamp. My aunty Gwen, S.M. Mercedes, attended the Melbourne launch with me.

I visited Chip several times during the two years he lived in China working on his language proficiency, first in Beijing and, here in 2005, in Shanghai.

My interview with Julia Gillard at the Sydney Opera House on 30 September 2013 was her first public appearance after she was dumped as Prime Minister and was a highly emotional and engaging event.

Julia Gillard and I shared the honours on the *Financial Review*'s 2013 cultural power list. The citation read: 'Gillard made the speech. Summers prosecuted the case. And their live talk shows sold out within hours'.

In 2014 actor Cate Blanchett did me the tremendous honour of agreeing to do a conversation event with me, as well as an extended interview and a rare Australian photoshoot for the cover of *Anne Summers Reports*. Peter Brew-Bevan's image was perfect.

I was unaccountably nervous before my talk with footballer Adam Goodes in April 2015, but he calmed me and we went on to have an inspiring and memorable conversation.

Chip and I at the launch in 2009 of *The Lost Mother*, my book that tells the complex story about the artist who painted my mother as a child, the Russian émigré who bought the portraits and the mother I never really knew.

me to dance. Up and down the room he trotted and swung me, around and around, until I was giddy and giggly and all thoughts of bankers, media tycoons and the jargon of the deal driven from my brain. Max was courteous and considerate, totally the old-fashioned gentleman who swatted away predatory barflies, and waited months before he put the hard word on me. I was single and a fling would probably have been good for me, but I did not want to complicate things at Max's. It was a haven like no other in the city, and that mattered more to me as we hurtled towards whatever our future was going to be.

The breakthrough came when the State Bank of NSW told us they thought the $14 million purchase price represented true value of the assets and was therefore 'bankable'. Their New York manager, the affable Kevin O'Neill (not to be confused with John O'Neill, his boss back in Sydney, the bank's CEO) would lend us $10 million. We just needed to find a source of capital to fund the operating costs. The deal fell into place in late April, when Citicorp's Venture Capital Fund said it was ready to put in $20 million, half of it as mezzanine debt—a term I had not encountered before, and which I learned referred to a high-quality form of debt that is able to be converted to equity—and half as a line of credit. And they were prepared to give Sandra and me equity. The CVC team was led by Steve Sherrill a 33-year-old preppy-looking young man, whose 24-year-old sidekick was Melissa Woolford, a rare woman in the financial world in those days. The two were very keen to do a deal involving *Sassy* and, providing there were tough performance hurdles, agreed to include *Ms.* This was not just good news. It might be a lifeline, because I had just received the alarming news that the newsstand sales for the March issue of *Ms.*—my second—had collapsed; they were one of the lowest sales in *Ms.*'s history. I had defied convention by using the image of a young nuclear family for a cover story on the progress of the American Dream. It was part of my plan to rely less on the standard magazine cover formula of a portrait of an attractive person, often a celebrity, making eye contact with the reader. Instead, I would be more journalistic, using images that illustrated the cover story which, I'd planned, would be less likely to be a profile or an interview than an exploration, from a feminist point of view of course, of a pressing issue or topic. I followed the family cover with a photo of a sad-looking girl in school uniform for a report on the teen pregnancy epidemic, and illustrated a story on women in Arizona politics with a feisty woman in her eighties who'd been prominent in the story we were reporting. All of these issues crashed on the newsstand. Even when they received reader approval, as the Arizona cover did from several key audiences, the failure to sell on the newsstand with the consequent collapse in new subscriptions was disastrous for us. I was forced to concede that the convention was adhered to because it worked. I learned of the famous 'Stolley's law'[9] of covers compiled by Richard Stolley, the founding editor of *People* and based on the magazine's newsstand performance over a decade or more. It wasn't just that covers needed people, it was the kind of people that the rules stipulated. Young is better than old, was the first of the eight laws. Pretty is better, rich is better, movies are better than TV, everything is better than politics and, the final rule, nothing beats a dead celebrity. *People's* cover following John Lennon's murder in 1980 was its biggest-ever seller until 1997, when Princess Diana died. I had had some success with my May cover story about the threats to motherhood of reproductive technologies, which I'd illustrated with a woman and her baby. She was not famous but she was an archetype, a Madonna, beautiful and young, staring straight at you. This was the cover that had caught Condé Nast's attention. Our bankers had loved it, too. Just as well that it distracted from my other failures. But I could not continue to defy reality. For the July issue, I'd brought in Lenore Hershey as a cover consultant and, on her advice, run an arresting stock photo of Cher. It sold its socks off.

For Sherrill and Woolford, the Fairfax buyout was a tiny exercise. Their previous deal had been for more than a billion dollars, but despite the small sums they approached the deal with a similar forensic ferocity and found plenty to quibble with. Every day a new issue arose that usually developed into a crisis that threatened to jeopardise the whole deal. All too often I found myself having to set aside my editorial work to respond to yet another set of bankers' questions. It was time-consuming, and utterly at odds with the mindset needed to tackle the myriad problems at *Ms*. Finally, in mid-June, our lawyers said we were ready to do the deal. It was four months since we had learned of Young Warwick's intention to sell us. We had gained an extension of the five-week deadline once we had an in-principle agreement that we'd raised funds to buy out Fairfax. Each of the parties had completed its due diligence, scrutinising our books with the kind of passionate intensity I soon learned was the particular province of the accountants who worked on these sorts of deals. I had been astounded at the arguments that could be confected and disputes generated where there were no apparent discrepancies. Sandra and I had begun to suspect that some of these professionals were taking advantage of what they presumed was our naivety and, with the meter ticking, inventing issues that would prolong the process. When we protested, we were assured that it was far preferable to resolve any problems in advance of the settlement, when there would be no one else's door to lay them at but ours.

The settlement was delayed several times. The same thing had happened when I had bought my apartment at the Level Club a few months earlier. The mortgage closing was on a much smaller scale, but it still involved all the essential elements of a big corporate deal: lawyers for all parties, brokers, and a mysterious cast of extras whose functions were unclear but who all required fees or 'tips'. Our closing had been deferred three or more times for reasons that made no sense to me. Now, we were finally ready to formally acquire the magazines from Fairfax. The date was set for 30 June.

———————

Sandra and I arrived early at our lawyers' offices, high up in the Pan Am building that straddled Grand Central Station. I had decided to wear the Anne Klein, which I was now calling my lucky suit. Sandra wore a black dress. Both of us sported huge red and white buttons stating our first names. I had found them in a novelty shop. They seemed to me, and Sandra agreed, to add the irreverent touch we both felt was needed to dent the inflated pomposity of the proceedings. I had another button, 'I'd rather be ironing', but in the end decided that one might place too much of a strain on the underdeveloped sense of humour of our American advisers. As it was, our name badges were eyed with bafflement as we all lined up in the conference room for photographs to commemorate the deal. We had dozens of pictures taken: Sandra and me with all the bankers and lawyers and accountants—a long snaky line of ill-matched people brought together by yet another of the exigencies of the 1980s; Sandra and me with the women bankers and lawyers and, finally, just Sandra and me. Behind us was the silver spire of the Chrysler Building. In the photo, it seems to be touching our shoulders, the sun sparkling off its recessed parabolic arches. This iconic New York building was fortuitously providing the backdrop for the beginning of our very great adventure.

Each of the parties had separate conference rooms on the same floor. It scarcely seemed possible that so many parties, each requiring a team of lawyers and accountants, could be involved in what was by New York standards a pretty small deal. Nor could I believe that here we were, Sandra and I, doing an MBO, epitomising 'the story' I had found so difficult to write about just a year before. The Fairfax legal team was in one room, Citibank in another and the State Bank of NSW in a third and, of course, Wilma Jordan and her people. In each room a huddle pored over the tower of documents that constituted the final deal that Citibank had hammered out with the State Bank of NSW and Fairfax. Steve Sherrill had got Fairfax to accept only $12 million plus an earn-out arrangement, instead of the straight $14 million deal covered by our option agreement. Fairfax was not happy but they had much bigger problems, and amounts of money, to worry about as they haggled with both Kerry Packer and Robert Holmes à Court over the spoils of the former Fairfax empire.

Sandra and I had expected that, having got to this point of agreement, the papers would be signed right away, but once again we were disappointed. After a quick lunch in the largest conference room, all parties returned to their separate hideaways. 'What's holding it up?' Sandra asked our principal lawyer. 'It's just a technicality,' he replied. 'Shouldn't be long now'. But it was several more hours; Chinese food was brought in. I marvelled at the efficiency of it all. New teams of support staff, fresh and ready for work, appeared every few hours to do the photocopying, assembling and delivery of documents as they were amended. Fresh coffee was always on hand and the trays of sandwiches constantly replenished. I presumed it was all part of the service. It was and, like all other services rendered, it was billable. Later, we would receive an account for around $17,000 for these staff, the operating costs of the machines, the coffee, the food and the cost of keeping the air-conditioning running after 6 p.m.

Around 10 o'clock Sandra lay down on the floor under the table in the main conference room and had a sleep. I prowled the corridors, listening to the shouts and curses as, right up to the final moment, deal points were disputed and, in some cases, renegotiated. They'd been at it for around twelve hours. What could possibly be left to argue about? In fact there was very little. These were professional dealmakers and they were sharpening their skills, getting the measure of the other guys against whom they might face-off again, across another table, tomorrow or next week. These were not exactly Tom Wolfe's Masters of the Universe—although Steve Sherrill undoubtedly saw himself as part of that world—but they had made themselves indispensable to the frenzied money-churning that had become the hallmark of the 1980s. Although this deal was about money—who was lending how much to whom in return for what kinds of considerations—the closing was not taking place downtown in Citibank's offices on Wall Street, where the money came from. We were in midtown, in the heart of the legal district. The lawyers, as always, had turned the game their way. The longer it went on, the more money they made. The rest of us could not start to make money, or even to function, until they were done.

Finally at 4 a.m. we all gathered again and, blurry-eyed, the principals each signed the many copies of the documents. The bound volume of the deal documents, presented to each of us some weeks later, was almost 20 centimetres thick. As light broke on the first day of July 1988 our new company, Matilda Publications Inc., came into being. We had done it. If it had been exciting enough to buy *Ms.* on behalf of Fairfax, we could scarcely contain our exhilaration that now it was just the two of us who had bought *Ms.* and *Sassy*. If it hadn't been dawn we might have gone for a drink. Instead, Sandra and I collapsed into the town car that was to take us each home. 'I never thought we'd celebrate this deal by falling into a coma,' she said, as we sped off across town into the pink light of the early morning.

CHAPTER EIGHT

MEDIA MOGULETTES
IN NEW YORK CITY

———◆———

Our media empire was just three-weeks-old when catastrophe struck. We were totally blindsided when we learned that *Sassy*, the star of our little stable, the title that was going to be the financial engine of our company, was about to be brought to her knees by a terrifyingly effective boycott organised by right-wing religious groups. When we did the buyout, Sandra and I had taken on tremendous responsibilities, we knew that, and we were both totally ready to do whatever it took to make it work. We now had 75 staff dependent on us; we had a series of tough bank-imposed financial performance hurdles to meet each month; and a large debt to service. We had to maintain *Sassy's* momentum and to continue to build *Ms.* The frenzy of interest in buying *Sassy* by America's largest media companies had convinced us we had a winner. We merely had to keep *Sassy* on course, and although we knew it would be a hard slog with *Ms.*, we did not doubt for a moment our ability to make this venerated but ailing magazine a commercial success.

For those first few weeks in July, we had basked in our success. If before we had been celebrated, now we were the talk of the town. We discovered that, contrary to its reputation for being cool and blasé about accomplishment, New York loves a success story. The media could not get enough of us. Everyone was keen to get a look at the two Aussie women who in raising all that money on Wall Street to buy the two magazines had achieved what no American woman had done. Even more compelling was the sub-text: we, the unknown outsiders, had been able to do what Gloria Steinem, the feted local celebrity, had never been able to do. We had bought *Ms.* magazine. We were on top of the biggest town in the world and we were revelling in it.

The invitations poured in. Both of us were now on everyone's A-list for parties, openings and fundraisers. If I'd wanted to, I could have gone to three or four events every night. I was thrilled to be invited to a party at Leonard Bernstein's apartment. He now lived in the famous Dakota building on West 72nd Street where, I knew, Yoko Ono still lived; so did Lauren Bacall. But when I looked more closely, I saw that the invitation had a price tag. Like almost everything else in New York, this was a fundraiser and it would cost $5000 to attend. I had had a big pay rise as part of the deal but it wasn't that big. I still took the subway to work, I still worked in Times Square and I still shopped at Loehman's, the renowned discount outlet in the Bronx, although now I could afford to venture into stores where the labels were not cut out. I had a generous expense account and I could call anyone in New York or Washington and be confident they would accept an invitation to lunch. Sandra was invited to deliver a prized keynote to the Magazine Publishers Association annual conference, the leading industry event that this year was being held in the Bahamas. It was a gratifying acknowledgement from her peers. I, too, received scores of invitations to speak—women's groups, editors' seminars, political events and even the Harvard Business School. In that talk, which I called 'Media Mogulettes: Organizing a Media MBO in New York City,' I described to a class of some 50 handpicked, already-successful business leaders from around the world in the Executive MBA program, how we had done the buyout, concentrating on the deal-making and money-raising aspects. I used the word 'mogulettes', I explained, not because we were women but because, compared with other media empires, we were small. With just two publications, we scarcely deserved to be called moguls. Not yet at least.

Wilma had estimated that within five years Matilda Publications would be worth $100 million. With our 40 per cent equity, Sandra and I would be rich—at least on paper. By then, we fantasised, we would have started, or acquired, other titles and would be on our way towards building a media empire. Or empire-ette. It was mind-boggling. Just a year earlier I had been miserable, lonely and broke and was seriously thinking of abandoning New York for the safe haven of Sydney. Look at me now, I thought, scarcely able to believe it myself.

On 17 July I flew to Atlanta for the Democratic Party Convention, and enjoying my new status as someone able to hang out with the crème de la crème of the party, I spent the four days going from gathering to meeting to cocktail party to dinner. I even looked in on a couple of sessions at the actual convention. Peggy Simpson, our Washington correspondent, escorted me around and she knew everyone. I was thrilled to be introduced to Ann Richards, just before she went on stage to deliver her famous keynote speech mocking Vice-President George H.W. Bush: 'Poor George, he can't help it, he was born with a silver foot in his mouth.' Richards was the state treasurer of Texas and two years later would be elected Governor. She was a tall, slim woman whose piled-up silver hair made her look very striking. 'Neither snow nor rain can move my hair,' she liked to say. Her clear blue eyes would engage you immediately and deflect from a face that probably had more lines than it should have at her age. Maybe it was the Texas sun or perhaps it was her former habit of filling her water glass with vodka ahead of dreary meetings. She had already given up the drink by the time I met her. Sadly, she lost her battle for a second term as governor of Texas to George W. Bush, the son of the man she had mocked in Atlanta in 1988.

The 1988 convention nominated Michael Dukakis, the former governor of Massachusetts, to be the party's presidential candidate. He would turn out to be a poor choice, easily demolished by the Republican nominee George H.W. Bush, and his hard-nosed team. For some people, the 1988 convention was memorable for the terrible speech by Bill Clinton, a little-known governor from Arkansas, who had been chosen to nominate Dukakis. New York Governor, Mario Cuomo, had instantly gained a national profile in 1984 when he delivered the keynote that attacked Ronald Reagan, as did the relatively unknown state senator from Illinois, Barack Obama, with his speech at the 2004 convention in Boston. But Clinton spoke for too long, had nothing memorable to say and was jeered off the stage. Four years later, when he accepted his party's nomination to be its presidential candidate, at the convention at Madison Square Garden in New York, Clinton drew laughs when he said he was there to finish the speech he had started four years earlier.

I met a dazzling array of political and other luminaries. At one party I was introduced to Joan Didion. She told me she was covering the convention.

'I thought you weren't writing about politics anymore,' I said spitefully.

'Whatever gave you that idea,' she asked?

I realised her agent had not even bothered to tell her about the *Ms.* assignment. Too paltry? Too demeaning? How would I ever overcome the poor opinion so many people had of *Ms.*? I would have a similar experience later that year when I met Susan Sontag at a political fundraiser. She was not interested in *Ms.* magazine, she said to me, and certainly would not dream of writing for it. As soon as someone more interesting appeared—in this case Joe Papp, from the Public Theatre—she turned away from me in mid-sentence and began an animated conversation with him. In October I picked up the *New York Review of Books* and there was 'Insider Baseball', Didion's essay on the Democratic convention. It would become one of her most famous political pieces, quoted and reprinted for many years afterwards. It was exactly what I had wanted for *Ms.* I was starting to realise that I would perhaps never be able to attract writers of this calibre.

I returned to my hotel to find a message from Sandra. 'Call me urgently,' it said. 'No matter how late.' It was after midnight when I reached her.

'What's wrong?' I asked, thinking nothing could be *that* urgent.

'We've had our top six advertisers cancel today.' Sandra spoke with a calmness that merely underscored the calamity she was outlining. 'That's $25 million in revenue, doctor, in case you were wondering.'

I listened, stunned, as she explained that the women who had written to complain about *Sassy* had turned their objections into a fully-fledged consumer boycott, targeting any company that advertised in *Sassy*. Some weeks earlier we'd received a letter from three women in Wabash, Indiana, who called themselves Women Aglow. Lit by the fire of Jesus, apparently. One of them had a teenage daughter who had got one of our direct mailers seeking subscriptions for *Sassy*. This mailing had been extraordinarily successful, so it had clearly hit the spot with large numbers of its target market. In just seven months, *Sassy's* circulation would reach 450,000. It had taken *Elle*, previously the hottest new magazine launch in New York, a year to reach that number from its identical launch circulation of 250,000. The material in the mailer that the Wabash women objected to had never actually appeared in *Sassy*; it had been taken from *Dolly*, the Australian teenage girls' magazine that had been Sandra's model for *Sassy*, but that was immaterial to the storm that was about to descend on us. Sandra and I had not treated the letter seriously. These women were obviously members of the lunatic fringe, we decided. We did not need to worry about them, especially as the magazine was so clearly such a success with teenage girls—its target market. We could not have been more wrong.

When they failed to get a response from us, Women Aglow took their case to Jerry Falwell of the Moral Majority; to Focus on the Family; and to the American Family Association, all of them conservative—I would say right-wing—organisations. *They* took the women from Wabash very seriously and deployed their considerable resources into a letter-writing campaign. Soon we were getting hundreds of letters daily from around the country. We were definitely concerned about this, but we still thought it was a nuisance, nothing more. We did not for a moment consider that the commercial success of *Sassy* could be undermined by an organised letter-writing campaign. But these organisations then provided their members with the names and addresses of the men who ran the parent companies of products advertised in *Sassy* and organised letters to *them*. No company received more than 500 letters. Most received about 100 but, we were astonished to discover, a small number of what were clearly form letters could influence the advertising decisions of a major American corporation. It made no commercial sense. Why on earth would Tambrands, the makers of Tampax tampons, on the basis of a hundred letters from post-menopausal women, withdraw advertising that was reaching hundreds of thousands of girls who were about to make lifelong choices about which brand of feminine protection they would use? It was the same with the cosmetics giant Revlon. These companies were more sensitive to the complaints of the few than the consumer potential of the very many. Revlon, Tambrands, Noxelle, Schering-Plough, Gillette and even the supposedly progressive Reebok were among the advertisers that cancelled their scheduled advertising and threw our little company into financial turmoil. Then, having tasted victory by hitting our advertising revenues, Falwell and his followers went after our newsstand. Walmart, the largest supermarket chain in the United States, agreed not to stock *Sassy*, now purported to be an evil magazine. That was bad enough, but small groups of religious women then began visiting drug stores, supermarkets and convenience stores around the country, urging their managers to drop us. Ultimately, 53 chains delisted *Sassy*, reducing the number of copies in circulation by one-third. We had lost almost all of two of Sassy's three sources of revenue and the third, subscription revenue, would only hold up so long as we could continue to produce a magazine that sizzled with irreverent content and glossy advertising.

While Sandra and the *Sassy* advertising team worked the business side trying to lure back the advertisers, prevent further defections and bring in new ones, it was agreed that I would pursue political remedies. We both assumed that once it became known that our right to publish, and even our very livelihood, was being threatened by this boycott there would be public support. Maybe we'd even become a *cause celebre*. In August I made contact with the American Civil Liberties Union (ACLU) and spoke with Melanne Verveer who ran People for the American Way, a liberal advocacy group that had been founded in 1981 by television producer Norman Lear and Congresswoman Barbara Jordan to fight ring-wing extremism, especially by television evangelists. Verveer, who President Obama would appoint as America's first Ambassador for Global Women's Issues in 2009, was sympathetic and had some practical advice. She compared our situation with the Christian attacks on the recently released Martin Scorsese film, *The Last Temptation of Christ*. 'The movie's producers had got religious leaders to view the film and give frank assessments,' she said. We needed to follow that example and get credible people—parents, adolescent development experts, even kids—to speak out for us. It was good advice and Sandra and I were grateful for her support. But, to my astonishment, the ACLU was dismissive. The right to free speech was paramount in their eyes, which gave the boycotters equal rights with us publishers; they declined to help us. I soon formed the view that the ACLU's purist stance made them useless, both politically and morally. They have a long track record of defending Nazis and other extreme right-wing groups' right to speak and to march, even when such gatherings have led to violence, such as occurred in Charlottesville, Virginia in 2017. Then, a young woman was killed when a white supremacist drove his car into a crowd.

It soon became depressingly obvious that no person or organisation was spontaneously going to speak out in our defence, and we did not have the resources to organise such support. We learned that other media organisations experienced similar boycotts but they kept very quiet about them, taking the view that publicity might encourage other boycotts. Besides, these larger companies could absorb the lost revenue in a way that was impossible for a tiny, indebted outfit like ours. The other way, of course, would have been to fight back, to deny this punishing minority the right to impose its anachronistic views on the majority but there was not much of that in the Reagan years in America. Sandra and I were astounded at the passivity, and the lack of courage, of those we had hoped might stand shoulder-to-shoulder beside us. We even detected a certain amount of glee at our predicament from an industry that was jealous that Sandra had turned the teenage category upside down. Despite what was happening right now, teenage magazines would never again be the same. *Sassy* attracted envy, criticism and—that most reliable arbiter of success—imitation, although it would be fifteen years before the launch of *Teen Vogue*, the magazine that most faithfully followed in the footsteps of *Sassy*. To many in the industry, we were Aussie upstarts, politically naïve, and lacking savvy about the American right-wing.

In September 1988, just weeks into the boycott, we had been unable to meet our first-quarter interest payments. Just three months after we had launched our company, we were technically in default. We had a shortfall in income of between $800,000 and $1 million a month, as a result of the collapse in *Sassy*'s revenue and slower-than-expected ad sales for *Ms*. The precipitous decline in the company's revenues meant that our ambitious plans for *Sassy* and *Ms*. first had to be cut back then, very rapidly, abandoned. Hiring was frozen, and we cancelled our trade advertising plans and direct mail campaigns. We were now having almost daily meetings with the panicked bankers, who did not want to have to report back to their bosses that this high-profile deal was already in trouble. But our performance hurdles were so high, based on the assumption that *Sassy's* income would continue to rise, that while we did our best to maintain business as usual, it was not long before we were looking at disaster. In late January 1989, the State Bank of NSW advised us that we could not draw down the $200,000 revolving line of credit that we needed to meet our payroll, and by mid-February we had completely run out of money. Citibank said they were no longer prepared to put more money in; they proposed that half the company be sold.

The next ten months, until I was fired as *Ms.* editor in December 1989, would be the most stressful time I have ever lived through. My father's description, in a letter he'd written to me the previous year, that trying to please bankers was 'like walking through fire in shoes filled with kerosene', turned out to be apt for the situation in which Sandra and I now found ourselves. We had no option but to look for new money, so once again we called in Wilma Jordan who had advised us on the buyout from Fairfax. She began quietly sounding out an A list of potential partners about taking a 50 per cent share in the company, in return for a $10 million injection of capital as well as assuming our $20 million of debt. The New York Times Company and Time Inc. both expressed interest, as did the Hearst Corporation, although they wanted Citibank to retire some of its debt because they did not agree that the company was worth $30 million. I had already made unsuccessful approaches back in Australia, to Trevor Kennedy at Kerry Packer's Australian Consolidated Press and to Frank Lowy who had recently moved into the media business by buying the Ten Network from Rupert Murdoch. Sandra talked to Si Newhouse and Bernie Leser at Condé Nast but their position had not changed from a year ago; they were interested in *Sassy* but would not even consider *Ms.*

To our surprise, the strongest expression of interest came from Robert Holmes à Court, the Australian businessman who had made his name as a corporate raider who bid for very large companies and, often and surprisingly, managed to win them. He had outwitted the legendary British entertainment mogul Sir Lew Grade to acquire his Associated Communications group, whose assets had included a string of London theatres, a number of film and other entertainment properties, and the rights to 112 Beatles songs. More recently he had made a bid for BHP, Australia's largest company, in what was initially dismissed by the Melbourne establishment as a reckless move by a rank amateur. They quickly changed their tune when Holmes à Court secured a key stake in the company's share register. Now he was looking at us, a tiny indebted company that could not have been less like any of his previous plays. But on 22 February, when Sandra, Wilma and I arrived for our meeting with him at Heytsbury's (the Holmes à Court company) as yet only partially furnished offices on the 24th floor of a swank building on the corner of Fifth Avenue and 56th Street, we were told that Holmes à Court was in London. He wanted me to ring him to discuss the deal. This was most unusual as such conversations would normally be with the bankers, but then Robert Holmes à Court was a most unusual man. I was worried, though, because of a phone call I'd made to him when I'd been with the *Financial Review*—to talk about some $20 million in taxes he'd neglected to pay. He'd sought to deflect me with charm and flattery, but I had written the story anyway. So what was he up to now? Was this trophy hunting or were our financial woes an opportunity for revenge for my article?

When I finally reached him, in Perth, not London, he answered the phone himself, and immediately launched another charm offensive. He told me he'd enjoyed my book on the 1983 Australian federal elections, and mentioned a couple of things from the book that indicated he had indeed read it. He then steered the conversation onto Canberra politics; he especially wanted to talk about Paul Keating, who he referred to as a friend. When I managed to get us onto our deal, he told me he wanted to enter the US media market because it was 'an intellectual activity' populated by 'interesting people', and he was looking for a cheap, opportunity. At $10 million we were certainly cheap, although he said he thought we were too thinly capitalised. He also told me that he liked to invest in immature companies that had a capacity for growth, or companies that had problems that needed solving. He cited as an example of the latter BHP, and its reliance on government steel subsidies.

He did not stipulate which category he thought we fell into. I would have ventured that we actually fit both: we definitely had capacity for growth, and we undoubtedly had a problem with our reliance for revenue on advertising, which reduced our editorial independence and made us vulnerable to boycott, although that was an industry-wide structural weakness that would not change for several decades.

After our conversation I felt absurdly optimistic. Here we were dealing with a principal, someone who called the shots, not one of the corporate eunuchs who needed to refer everything upwards. He said he'd study our document over the weekend and probably come to New York next week to meet us.

While we waited to see if Holmes à Court would come to our rescue, Jane Pratt, the editor of *Sassy*, and I needed to be especially vigilant to not publish anything that might further antagonise advertisers. Our cash flow was so tight we were already stretching payables. This was causing great anxiety with our editors, who had to manage distressed calls from writers who were being made to wait for their money. We could not afford to lose a single ad from either magazine; rather, we desperately needed to increase business. We had had a good start to the year with *Ms.*'s Women of the Year issue (a tradition that I thought should continue), published in January 1989, a very healthy 166 pages book size. The women we had chosen to honour included Oprah Winfrey; movie star Anne Archer, chosen for her pro-choice views; gun control activist Sarah Brady; and Marjory Stoneman Douglas, a 98-year-old journalist and novelist who'd saved The Everglades in Florida;[1] and they all attended a splashy breakfast at the Waldorf Astoria with movie star Alan Alda, our MC, conferring the awards. We'd achieved a lot of positive media coverage. You would never have known that morning the trouble we were in and the desperate measures we were taking to keep our little empire afloat.

In early February, I decided that our April issue should feature as our cover the harrowing story of Hedda Nussbaum, a former Random House children's book editor who had been charged, along with her partner, Joel Steinberg, a lawyer, with the murder of their six-year-old adopted daughter,

Lisa Steinberg. It was a horrifying story of the tiny neglected girl beaten to death in a filthy apartment in an elegant old brownstone in the heart of the Greenwich Village, in a house where Mark Twain had once lived (and where I had been tempted the previous year to rent an apartment). But in deciding to commission several articles to address this story, I had no inkling that it would lead to a mass advertiser exodus and a rupture with Gloria Steinem, together a perfect storm that had me concluding that *Ms.* was probably doomed.

It was a story that electrified New York: middle-class people in one of the city's most iconic neighbourhoods, revealed to have lived a hellish existence of drugs, degradation and extraordinary brutality. Constant complaints from neighbours to police about cries and crashing noises from the apartment had not ended the nightmare. Instead, in the early hours of a November morning in 1987, medics from a nearby hospital entered the squalid apartment—one of them said later it resembled a 'cave'—to find the unconscious six-year-old on a bathroom floor, another small child tethered to a playpen, sitting in his own excrement and drinking spoiled milk and the severely injured Hedda. The two went on trial in October 1988, but early on the charges against Hedda were dropped and she became the major prosecution witness against her former partner. The trial was the first ever to be televised 'gavel-to-gavel' live on a major network, and the entire city watched transfixed as the visibly still injured Hedda told the story of what had happened that night. She was a polarising witness. The judge told the jury they could not rely on her evidence except to corroborate other testimony, and it was later revealed that the jury had largely disregarded her evidence.[2] In late- January 1989, Joel Steinberg was convicted of second-degree manslaughter and given a lengthy prison sentence.

The question of how much culpability Nussbaum should have for Lisa's death divided the city, but it was tearing the women's movement apart. The opposing sides could be characterised, broadly, as the Brownmiller and the Steinem camps. Susan Brownmiller, whose early 1970s masterpiece *Against Our Will* had redefined the way we understood rape, had written an op-ed piece for the *New York Times* that argued Hedda Nussbaum bore at least some responsibility for the death of Lisa Steinberg. She had just published a novel *Waverly Place* that was based on the Nussbaum/Steinberg story. I asked Susan if she would cover the trial for *Ms.* I knew she would turn in a well-written, powerful account of the crime and the court case, but she would also take a position on Hedda's responsibility for Lisa's death (and she did not disappoint). I also commissioned Marilyn French, author of *The Women's Room*. Her essay, which we titled 'A Gothic Romance', argued Hedda's dependency on Joel fit an archetype of male power/female bondage that still had a powerful hold on women's imagination, even in this feminist era. The rest of the package would comprise my essay and several other pieces on various aspects of domestic violence, written by staff members. When Gloria learned that Susan was writing, she called me. Hedda Nussbaum was a total victim, Gloria argued, who in no way could be blamed for Lisa's death and she put to me most forcefully that it would be a betrayal of everything *Ms.* had ever stood for if the magazine were to publish the Brownmiller position. This view encapsulated for me so much of what I saw as being wrong with the 'old' *Ms.* The magazine tended to adopt purist positions as articles of faith, allowing for no discussion or contrary views. This alienated many women who had tried to read *Ms.*—they felt shut out or, worse, patronised, if their own views differed. 'With fewer real victories to report, and an acute fear of revealing divisions within the movement to the voraciously hostile outside world, *Ms.* fell into a pattern,' wrote Peggy Orenstein in *Mother Jones* in a scathing assessment of where the magazine had ended-up shortly before our acquisition. 'It continued to remind its readers that the same old inequities were still the same old inequities, and it found smaller, individual victories to exult in, victories that often seemed sugar-coated.'[3] I thought *Ms.* would be more relevant, and appeal to a wider audience, if we explored issues, including highly charged and difficult subjects such as this one, by bringing in different voices, including dissenting ones. Guide our readers, rather than preach at them. Many years later, in her memoir about the women's movement, Brownmiller praised me for giving her this commission: 'We agreed it was time to stop excusing the behaviour of all battered women by claiming each one was a helpless victim, a politically correct but, to our minds, a psychologically and morally untenable stance that damaged the movement's credibility'.[4]

In fact, although I had no hesitation about running articles representing a spectrum of views in our coverage of this excruciating case, I was actually very torn about Hedda. I knew from my experience at Elsie Women's Refuge in the early 1970s, and from constant dealings since with women victims of violence, that relentless abuse can lead to total loss of agency. I knew the complex answers to the question 'Why doesn't she leave?' Hedda *had* left— five times.[5] But she had always returned, despite warnings from colleagues that her own life could be in danger, and eventually she stopped working and became so socially isolated that there was no one to turn to. On the morning Lisa was discovered, Hedda's injuries were massive, a broken nose, blackened eyes, a split lip, big clumps of her hair were missing, she was limping and looked dazed and confused.[6] Her leg was so badly ulcerated that one observer described it as life threatening. Her nose was broken so severely it could never be repaired despite plastic surgery, and years later one eye wept permanently from a damaged tear duct, and she still walked with a limp. How could a woman so damaged herself possibly intervene to save a child? I was conscious, too, of the assumptions used by child protection agencies that women's interests, and safety, were always secondary to those of the child. As a feminist I could not subscribe to that, but I also knew it was rare even for women who themselves had been battered into stupefied submission, not to try to protect their children. Often the catalyst for finally being able to leave was when the abuse of a child began. Feminists needed to champion the interests of women but how did we reconcile these with a mother's failure to raise the alarm about her brutalised child? Hedda testified that after Lisa had sustained the injuries, Joel had laid her inert body on the bathroom floor and gone out to dinner. It is impossible to understand, and difficult to be sympathetic to why Hedda did not pick up the phone during the three hours he was gone. Was she so addicted to crack cocaine that she was unable to act? When Joel returned, he and Hedda free-based cocaine for most of the night. It was not until early the next morning that they rang 911. Lisa had been lying on that bathroom floor for ten hours. Medics said she could have been saved if she had received immediate medical attention. Instead, after three days, her life-support was turned off.[7] In the end, I concluded that while Hedda's failure to save Lisa was mitigated by her own horrendous abuse, it did not totally absolve her. She had a duty to Lisa that she was, or should have been, capable of exercising and she had failed to do so.

———⋅◆⋅———

The circulation department had been thrilled that I planned to run a newsy cover, featuring a close-up image of Hedda Nussbaum's bruised and swollen face. *Newsweek* had had great newsstand success with a similar cover shot and our people were predicting that this would be our biggest-selling issue of the year. This was exactly the kind of boost we needed, but our advertising sales director, Marsha Metrinko, had a very different reaction. Metrinko, as she liked to call herself—and she always addressed me as 'Summers'—was a hard-boiled character with statuesque good looks, tall with a helmet of short platinum hair that made her resemble Brigitte Nielsen. She mostly revelled in the challenge of selling advertising for *Ms.*, but she cried foul when she heard about our cover. 'Summers', she said, talking out of the side of her mouth as if she was telling me something secret, 'Summers, you're breaking my heart. We've just cracked the beauty category. You can't do this to me'.

She laid out the situation as she saw it. If we ran with the Hedda cover, we would lose seven pages of advertising. Not only that, Metrinko said, four advertisers would punish us by staying out for two issues while a new client, Bristol-Myers, which had four products it might place in *Ms.*, had said they would *never* come in. I was angry that these companies even knew about our cover. This kind of blackmail was horrifying, and I would have liked nothing more than to tell them we did not want their lousy business. But I also knew that our only chance of survival was to meet or, if possible, exceed our advertising budget of 40 pages per issue. There was no guarantee that those who had pulled their ads would come back if I capitulated and changed the cover, but we were absolutely certain to suffer financially if I didn't. Advertisers who did not like the editorial environment surrounding their ads simply refused to pay. *Ms.* had compromised in the past to avoid offending advertisers. They had not covered issues like the health impact of smoking on women, so as not to alienate cigarette advertisers and, Steinem told Peggy Orenstein, she had once changed a mention of Porsche in an article to 'expensive car', to keep Volkswagen happy.

We had worked hard to retain the automobile advertising. It was a lucrative category—they almost always wanted two-page spreads –and they did not demand supportive editorial. We did not have to run articles about cars, for instance, but it would have been foolhardy to criticise their product so I was stricken when Barbara Ehrenreich proposed her next column be a satire on fast cars. I explained to her how sensitive and demanding these advertisers were, how we could not afford to lose them. Would she be willing to change topics? 'If it was anyone but *Ms.*,' was her generous response.

These advertisers were influencing, even dictating, content. I could see no other way to look at it. We had to give them what they wanted—nice, non-controversial 'happy edit'—or they simply would not grace our pages. The automobile makers did not stipulate content directly but they dictated the way they wanted readers to feel when they glanced at their pages: happy, not challenged or confronted by the story of a battered woman or a murdered child. Without them, there would be no us, because they paid our production costs. We had to comply. Only the cigarette companies, who knew they were living on borrowed time, acknowledged they were in no position to dictate editorial. Our readers hated the cigarette ads, and so did I, but I did not see how we could survive without them. We also all hated the 'flying pad', as we called the large image of a sanitary napkin that ran across two pages. It was reasonable enough for us to advertise such products, but did the ads have to be so, so ugly? Proctor & Gamble, America's biggest advertiser of cosmetics and pharmaceuticals, would only advertise if they were guaranteed that their ads would not appear in an issue that mentioned any of a stipulated list of topics, which included abortion, gun control and the occult. They did not care what position the editorial adopted on these topics, they could not even be mentioned. It was often difficult to create credible editorial while conforming to such guidelines. Sometimes we found ourselves having to concoct bland copy to place near these ads. When added to the other advertiser demands, that their ads run close to the front and on a right-hand page, the task of putting together the magazine became very challenging. I sometimes envied the fashion magazines who could easily slot-in pages of beauty, jewellery and clothing between the ads at the front, and run their feature stories in the 'well', that section in the middle of the magazine where there were no ads and where controversy could reign free.

My background was newspapers where, as far as I was aware, advertisers did not have this kind of power. I had never been asked to change a story, or refrain from mentioning a topic, because of advertiser demands, so I was unprepared for these battles and the editorial challenges they created. We soon learned that the constraints *Sassy* and *Ms.* were experiencing were not unique. Throughout the magazine and broadcast industries, articles and on-air programs were being pulled, toned-down or simply not written, not because they might offend *readers* or *viewers* but because they could upset advertisers or religious groups. At the same time, special bland editorial was being manufactured to give advertisers the non-controversial 'happy-edit' they were increasingly demanding. We thought our situation was dire because we believed that our magazines had a special mission: we were not there just to create edit to place between the ads. We believed that the ads should pay for the edit *we* and *our readers* wanted. But increasingly, in an environment that was so competitive and so dependent on advertising, other media met the demands—at the cost of unfettered freedom of expression—and made it that much tougher for the rest of us.

The new April cover was an arty, grainy image of the chest and lower face of a naked woman, her arms crossed to cover her breasts. It was sensual and visually attractive but in no way did it represent the Hedda Nussbaum stories inside. We had quickly switched tack, making the cover story a report about the dangers of estrogen and relegating the Hedda and Joel package to just a cover line. I justified my caving to advertisers as a survival tactic, but I sometimes had to ask myself what I was doing in this mad magazine world. I was used to serious journalism. Now I was having to pander to advertisers whose only journalistic criteria, seemingly, was that an article be inoffensive. Three of those that pulled their ads in the April issue did not come back, including the cosmetics company, and Bristol-Myers did not come in with their pharmaceutical products, but Metrinko was able to save Chevrolet's two-page spread and got commitments from the others that they would be back for the May issue. She also managed to haul-in several totally new pages so, although we did not make budget, the issue was not a total disaster.

The passions aroused by the Hedda Nussbaum case were quite extraordinary. There had been petitions and rallies, as well as warring public op-eds and bitter private arguments. Susan Brownmiller later wrote that her opinions in the *NYT* and *Ms.* were seen by 'enraged battered-women's advocates ... as a stab in the back to the movement'[8] and reported that 'some of my movement friendships never recovered from the debate'. Gloria Steinem publicly associated herself with the pro-Hedda forces, speaking at a rally in Hedda's defence on the steps of the criminal court building (and in 2006 would write the introduction to Hedda's book and appear with her to promote it), and she wanted *Ms.* to back her. She seemed to assume she was still entitled to influence the editorial. I felt caught. While I frequently consulted Steinem, and often found her advice valuable, I also needed to put my own stamp on the magazine and that included abandoning the women-can-do-no-wrong mantra that seemed to underpin the editorial in the 'old' *Ms.* I wanted to take a more modern and nuanced approach that acknowledged women were not perfect and, in some cases, actually wrong. But in the end I compromised, or as Brownmiller put it, 'the new team at *Ms.* capitulated, adding their names to the Hedda petition and printing a few self-serving words from Nussbaum in a subsequent issue'.[9] (I ran a one page article by Hedda Nussbaum.)

This episode made brutally clear to me that while I was nominally editor-in-chief of *Ms.*, I was not fully in control of the editorial agenda. The advertisers would not allow it and neither, it seemed, would Gloria Steinem. She still loomed large over the magazine in most people's eyes—including, apparently, her own. She no longer owned the magazine but she could not let go. Maybe we should have opted for a clean break, and not retained Steinem, and Carbine, as consultants. It was often tricky for me to explain my vision for *Ms.* In April 1989 I was on an American Society of Magazine Editors panel 'Remaking a Magazine', along with Mort Zuckerman who talked about his makeover of *US News* and *World Report*. Tina Brown, who was editor-in-chief of *Vanity Fair*, chaired the session. 'That must have been tough,' she said to me sympathetically during the break, 'having to talk about what was wrong with *Ms.* with Gloria's boyfriend there'.

I had disregarded Steinem when she'd tried to dissuade me from running an interview with Betty Friedan to mark the 25th anniversary of the publication of *The Feminine Mystique*. There was tremendous enmity between Steinem and Friedan and, I was astonished to discover, Friedan's name had never once appeared in *Ms*. These two giants of the women's movement barely spoke to each other. They represented different strands of feminism. Steinem was more utopian and visionary, whereas Friedan was a pragmatist who wanted clear political victories now. Their political differences spilled over into the personal realm and they barely had a civil word to say to, or about, each other, but I did not see that as a reason for me not to acknowledge one of the most influential books of the twentieth century. I interviewed Friedan in her tiny apartment in a sprawling block across from Lincoln Centre on the Upper West Side of Manhattan and published the article, together with a photo of the two of us, in the December 1988 issue. Friedan's insights mirrored many of my own. I, too, was puzzled why, when women's lives had changed so dramatically in so many ways, they were still reluctant to seize political power and change the world. 'What is wrong that a new generation of women leaders has not arisen?' Friedan said to me. 'We can't leave until they come'. That, it seemed to me, should be a key question for *Ms*. to pursue. If I could only get some clear air.

———

In early May, Holmes à Court told us he would not proceed. He had been our last hope as, one after another, the major media companies had been deterred by *Sassy*'s deteriorating situation. Holmes à Court had signed a letter of intent, so we thought it was a done deal, but he had changed his mind. We were under-capitalised and could never succeed, he told us. Of course, without his injection of cash, that now seemed inevitable. After that, events were largely taken out of our hands, as the cash flow got worse and a controversial article in the June issue of *Sassy* sent the bankers into a total tailspin. The article was a very matter-of-fact account of a girl's experience of incest with her grandfather. It was written in such a way as to warn girls about such relationships. I could see nothing wrong with it and nor did we lose any further advertisers, but for the bankers it was the last straw. *They* were the ones who could no longer stand the heat, who wanted this mess behind them, and they took precipitous action, insisting that Sandra resign, that an external CEO be appointed and that I take charge of *Sassy*'s editorial. It was devastating for Sandra to have the media company she had created taken from her. The day it happened, she and I locked ourselves in her office with a bottle of Scotch. It was just 21 months since our lunch at Café Un Deux Trois. In that short time, Sandra had reinvented magazines for teenage girls. Our adventure was over, but her legacy would stretch far into the future. It did not seem that way at the time, of course, although Sandra put on a show of extraordinary grace as she addressed the hastily brought-together staff of the two magazines, and told them she was leaving.

At first, I had thought it would be cool to spend time with the groovy young team at *Sassy*. It would be a refreshing change from *Ms.* where it was a constant struggle to convince the editors that we had to change the sensibility of the magazine. Even when they agreed we needed to change, the long-term staffers often simply could not adjust their mindsets and, all too often, they seemed to want to make it their mission to make *me* adapt to theirs. It was exhausting, especially on top of the ongoing financial struggles. *Sassy* would be fun. While the advertising director was trying to convince jittery advertisers that it was safe to come back, I needed to ensure the magazine did nothing to jeopardise this. I insisted on seeing page proofs, so I could peruse every tiny detail, captions as well as headlines, in addition to having already being briefed on the overall contents. I found myself utterly ill-equipped to deal with the content. I knew nothing about teenage culture and worried that Jane Pratt and her staff were trying to hoodwink me. Was there really a band called the Butthole Surfers? Because I had not seen anything wrong with the incest piece, I now became ultra-cautious about anything that might backfire. I pulled an article on one-night stands, and another on animal testing of cosmetics, and soon found myself the object of sullen resentment by the *Sassy* staff. Jane was aware of our financial troubles, but she and her team did not act as if they understood just how vulnerable their magazine now was. In just a few months *Sassy* had gone from being the hottest thing in town to facing the real risk that if we could not find a buyer she—and *Ms.*—might have to close.

1989 still stands as both the best and the worst year of my life. It was the year I lost the magazines, lost my job and, I feared, the very foundations of my identity, but it was also the year that I met the man who would become the love of my life. My marriage had ended 30 years earlier, although John Summers and I had not got around to divorcing. I'd had romances in Sydney in the 1970s, a couple of which had lasted a year or more, but the 1980s had been a bleak time for me, in Canberra and in New York. It was so long that I could scarcely remember what it felt like to lie in someone's arms, to surrender to passion, to experience that kind of joy. I realised I had become something of a constant voyeur of other people's love lives, with no emotional life of my own. Even so, I was utterly confident that I was going to meet someone. I was undeterred by the *Newsweek* cover story a few years earlier that asserted a woman over 40 in New York had a better chance of being killed by a terrorist attack than of getting married. Not that I wanted to get married, but I did want a soul mate. I don't know what made me so sure, but I never doubted that it would happen. Eventually. I just never expected that when it did he would turn out to be an exceptionally good-looking, smart-as-a-tack Texan, who was nineteen years younger than me and who worked at our company.

Chip Rolley was employed in the marketing department of *Ms.* but I had had limited dealings with him until late one night I had found him in the photocopier room. I had asked that every member of Congress be sent *Ms.* each month and I had provided copy for a cover letter to accompany the issue. I was astonished to find Chip painstakingly inserting a small slip of paper with my signature onto each letter before copying it—535 times!

'There's no need for them all to be signed!' I said to him. 'You will be here all night.'

Chip seemed a little embarrassed that I had found him doing this, but he insisted that the letters should be signed. 'It won't take me that long,' he said.

After that, I began to notice him. Although he was one of the few men in our mostly female organisation, he was neither intimidated nor defensive. In fact, he had quite a mouth on him, always ready with a quick comeback or a witty retort. After our finances collapsed and we had to undertake a drastic reorganisation to save as many positions as possible, Chip had agreed to leave marketing and work—temporarily, he was assured—as Sandra's PA. That meant he was on a different floor from me, so I didn't see him often, but I did make a point of inviting him to a farewell party I was throwing at my apartment for Joanne Edgar, one of the founding staffers of *Ms.*, who was leaving to pursue philanthropic work. It was an all-staff party, everyone was relaxed, and I found myself flirting with Chip. At the end of the night, I asked if he would stay back and help me clean up. He readily agreed.

The next day I felt tremendously guilty. Although there was certainly no coercion involved, I wondered if I had abused my position. As a part-owner of the company that employed him, I was, technically, one of his bosses, even though he did not report to me. But we very quickly developed a strong attachment to each other, based on an attraction that was not just physical, and which seemed to transcend any technical workplace considerations. I told Sandra and, while she laughed wickedly and teased Chip mercilessly for the rest of that day, she could not see a problem. Within a very short time he had moved into my apartment and, although he kept his room in the apartment he shared with a friend in the Beacon Hotel just around the corner until the end of the year, we have been together ever since.

I soon learned that Chip was the name Americans use for a 'Junior', someone who shares their father's name. His actual name was Chester. His father was in the military and returned to Vietnam shortly after Chip's birth. The new baby was given his name, Chester Harrison Rolley—with Jr added. Many 'Juniors' are known as Chip: it signifies the person is a chip off the old block. We soon stopped being conscious, or even aware, of the difference in our ages. It was something other people noticed—and occasionally had a problem with—but for us it has always been immaterial except for an occasional disagreement about music—impossibly, he does not care for Bob Dylan—as our younger selves grew up to different sound tracks. We saw things in each other we liked and admired and that was what brought us together. He liked my fierceness and my willingness to speak my mind and not worry what people thought of me. I was knocked out by his wisdom and calmness, and what today we would call emotional intelligence, qualities that were unexpected in a man in his mid-twenties. He had acquired a strong feminist outlook from his mother, which meant that he and I had a common frame of reference through which we both viewed the world. More than that, he was not at all intimidated—or threatened—by me. Men of my age tended to be defensive around me, as if they were expecting me to direct my feminist wrath at them if they got out of line. I found this exhausting and it was refreshing to meet someone who was totally relaxed with me. Not only that, he would take me on. That was a change; few men I'd been involved with in the past felt able to do that.

Chip had endured some very tough times as an adolescent, so he had had to grow up fast. He had developed a protective armour that he used when he needed to navigate stressful situations of his own and it was this, I think, that enabled him to understand and comfort me during what was undoubtedly the most stressful time of my life. There were times when I did not think I would be able to keep going. When things were at their most grim, with me having to fire people or not pay them or front up for yet another futile meeting with a potential investor or cope with further resentment from editors at *Ms.* or *Sassy*, I would come home, pour myself a glass of Scotch—and burst into tears. All my life I have made sure *never* to cry in front of work colleagues and I never have, but for those few months in 1989, when I was wrung dry and was physically and emotionally a spent force, I would let it all out once I was safely inside my apartment. I was amazed Chip did not run a million miles from the wreck of a woman I was during that time. Instead he was soothing, or said nothing, just listened as I poured out my frustration and anger at the situation I had so unwittingly found myself in. His just being there helped me stay sane. It must have been very hard for him. He knew more than most employees about the company's precarious financial situation because of his job with Sandra, and he knew his own future could be in doubt, but he managed to set aside his own anxieties while I vented and raged and gathered the strength to face another day. I have never stopped being grateful because I wonder how I would ever have got through it without him.

By June we had reached the end of the line. There was just one offer remaining on the table, and it was totally unacceptable. I told Steve Sherrill this and he offered me *Ms.* for $10—provided I could raise the operating capital. Fat chance! But I went on one, final, last-ditch search for funds because unless I was able to find a new partner, I would be unable to deflect Citibank from selling *Ms.* and *Sassy* to Dale Lang, the owner of Lang Communications, publisher of *Working Woman*, *Working Mother* and until very recently the mass-circulation *McCall's*. 'Whatever you do, don't sell to Dale', Gloria Steinem had said to me several times during the long and difficult struggle to find new financing. She and Pat Carbine had been horrified when I'd told them of Lang's interest. During their ownership, his *Working Woman* ad sales staff had cruelly targeted *Ms.*, circulating to advertisers blown-up copies of classified advertisements that contained the word 'lesbian'. Back then, that was a lethal weapon. This was before Ellen Degeneres, before *The L Word*, before same-sex marriage, before the widespread acceptance of lesbian, gay, bisexual, transgender, queer and intersex individuals (as evidenced by mainstream politicians, even candidates for the US Presidency, now feeling required to reference LGBTQ communities). This tactic had cost *Ms.* advertising business and they were rightly bitter about it. They had staved off Lang once before—and sold to Fairfax. It was unconscionable that the man Steinem referred to as 'the Pilsbury Doughboy'—a strikingly accurate reference to his pudgy appearance—could now get his hands on *Ms.* We made a pact: ABD. Anyone but Dale. Which is how I came to be in some pretty strange places while I frantically tried to find other money.

Wilma Jordan arranged for me to meet with TorStar, the publishers of the *Toronto Star*. More talk, more balance sheets and deal points, and more inconclusive discussions. For one mad week, I had talks with Harlequin Enterprises, a subsidiary of TorStar, and publisher of the internationally best-selling Mills and Boon romance novels, who were seriously interested in both magazines. I could imagine the jokes: 'Feminist icon teams up with bodice-ripper.' It would be worth it, I thought, if it kept us afloat, but in the end this deal, too, collapsed. I was amused almost fifteen years later, when Rupert Murdoch's News Corporation bought the company and all the jokes were at his expense; even the *New York Times* speculated that the newly-single media mogul might be 'suddenly in the mood for love'.[10] Anita Roddick of the Body Shop was helpful although she had no funds of her own to invest. She introduced me to Josh Mailman, a wealthy young Manhattanite who two years earlier had co-founded Social Venture Capital Network, an organisation designed to connect good causes with socially aware investors. As I travelled down in the elevator after leaving Mailman's posh Upper East Side apartment, the doors had opened to admit Carl Bernstein, the celebrated Watergate journalist. He expertly undressed me, the only other occupant, with his eyes and clearly not attracted by what he saw, turned back to face the door. I flew to San Francisco to the Social Venture annual conference, but these well-heeled philanthropists were looking to invest hundreds of thousands. I needed millions. And their favoured causes tended to be cutting-edge New Age or counter-cultural, not tired old feminists and their faltering magazines.

Peter Blazey offered money. Blazey, as everyone called him, was a very old friend, an Australian, a journalist, political activist and all round good time boy, described by his publisher as a 'millionaire wastrel', who was now working his way through his Hortico inheritance, living in Los Angeles in a dilapidated mansion in the Hollywood Hills that had once belonged to Barbara Stanwyck. When Chip and I had swum in the pool during a visit to LA, Blazey had taken a series of great pictures of us in the cool blue water, documenting our early relationship with accompanying louche commentary about Chip's good looks and my even better good fortune. 'How much do you need?' Blazey had said to me over dinner in New York. I had no idea how much money Blazey had, or was willing to part with, so I hedged. 'Would $50,000 do it?' he asked. I almost burst into tears, at his generosity and his innocence. That was the trouble. None of my friends could comprehend the sums involved. How could they? Two years earlier I, who had never even heard of mezzanine debt, could not have imagined that I would become so blasé about the massive sums that were needed to rescue us. I gently turned down Blazey, who underneath his often coarse patois was the sweetest of men. He died of AIDS in 1997, and left behind *Screwloose*, a wonderfully wicked memoir, whose munificence was one of the few consolations during those bleak days.

I was grateful for another kind of consolation when I was a guest lecturer at the University of Wisconsin in Madison in June 1989. My host was Chancellor Donna Shalala, who would later become a Cabinet Secretary in the Clinton administration. It was a nice break from the fundraising ordeal although I could not help myself from telling my audience about the impending disaster for *Ms.* They were sympathetic, but uncomprehending. No one outside the small media world seemed to be able to get their head around the disaster that had befallen us. Who could blame them, especially those in the otherworld of academia? I got to spend time with two giants of women's studies: Gerda Lerner and Linda Gordon. They had both been intellectual heroes of mine in a previous life, back when the only work-related stress I suffered were sore eyes after a long day at the library trying to decipher hand-written manuscripts. Linda Gordon had been an examiner for my PhD who had praised the work unreservedly. I thought she lived in Boston, so was surprised to finally meet her, in Madison. 'Do you miss women's history now that you are doing something really important?' I was startled to hear her ask. 'You were so good at it. It's a pity you no longer do it.' For a moment, I almost regretted that I had abandoned that life—one where I had been content to analyse the wrongs of the past, for the one I had now, and the at times almost unendurable pressures of trying to make the future a better place for women.

In August 1989 with all other options exhausted, Citibank agreed that Dale Lang could buy both magazines. Despite being a board member of Matilda Publications, the entity that was being sold, I was increasingly side-lined as Steve Sherrill and Dale Lang negotiated one-on-one. On the advice of a friend, I had hired a big-time corporate lawyer, Irwin Jay Robinson, who I knew from work he had done for Fairfax. Robbie, as everyone called him, had a courteous demeanour that belied his Machiavellian assess-ment of situations and his tough negotiating tactics. He ultimately got me back to the table, preserved my contract and ensured that I had work, and recognition, at the new owner's company. Part of Robbie's strategy had been to boost my public profile and he frequently took me to New York's hottest restaurants for lunch. I have to admit I loved watching heads turn as I strutted behind the maître'd, turned out in the best outfit I could possibly manage, towards the prominent table where Robbie would already be waiting. Although it was part of a war game, it was still a welcome break from the corporate trenches and the wearing ego clashes and bitter betrayals that came to characterise this deal. When it was finally sealed, in mid-October 1989, Lang had acquired 70 per cent of Matilda Publications while Citibank retained 30 per cent.[11] What was not made public, but which Robbie and I knew from the deal sheet that he insisted on perusing on my behalf, was that Lang had paid no purchase price. Nor had he committed to invest in the two titles. Citibank had forgiven half its debt, agreed to freeze interest payments on the rest until 'break-even', and would invest a further

$3 million. In other words, Lang had been able to pick up *Ms.* and *Sassy* for nothing.

Lang had claimed he had little interest in *Sassy*, saying he really only wanted *Ms.*, and that turned out to be partly true. He wanted *Ms.* so he could kill her. To Madison Avenue it looked as if Lang was trying to undermine *Ms.*, reported Peggy Orenstein in her account of *Ms.*'s fight for survival.[12] He fired our advertising staff then engineered a collapse in ads for our December issue by excluding *Ms.* from a group discount deal being offered for *Sassy* and his two magazines. Even though the December issue was ready for pre-press, he ordered it not to be printed. He demanded we hand over our subscriber lists, then folded them into *Working Woman* to take it to over one million circulation for the first time ever. Our subscribers were unpleasantly surprised when *Working Woman* landed in their mailboxes instead of *Ms.* Lang then made us cancel the circulation deal with NOW, demanding we get them to do a similar deal to boost the circulation of *Working Woman*. All that was left of *Ms.* was a totally demoralised editorial staff and no apparent future. Our publication was cancelled, we had nothing to do but we hadn't been fired either, so we were in a weird kind of limbo. We occupied ourselves cleaning out our desks and playing endless games of Scrabble.

It was a welcome distraction from this state of uncertainty when on 6 November Marcia Gillespie and I went to lunch at the White House along with other top women's magazine editors from New York. I was pleased to see that no other Lang people had been invited. Our host was Barbara Bush, the First Lady, and she mightily impressed us all by having the lunch in the private quarters and treating us to a tour first. We got to see the Lincoln Bedroom, which contains the only signed copy of the Gettysburg Address, the Queen's Bedroom where Winston Churchill says he saw Lincoln's ghost, and the Bush's sitting room which had been Ronald Reagan's study. We had lunch in a large and pretty room that used to be Alice Roosevelt's bedroom. But first we lined up for our one-on-one photos with Mrs Bush. Just before I stepped forward to shake the First Lady's hand, I felt a voice whisper in my ear, 'Put your bag on your other shoulder so it doesn't show in the picture.'

It was Jill Krementz who passed on this sage advice. She was a top photographer in New York, and married to the novelist Kurt Vonnegut, and she was standing behind me. As a result, the photograph of me with Mrs Bush, which my mother displayed proudly in her sitting room for many years, was unsullied by an unsightly shoulder strap. I got to sit at Mrs Bush's table although she made no effort to talk to me, confining her efforts to the powerful editors, Anne Fuchs from *Woman's Day* and Myrna Blyth from *Ladies' Home Journal*, on either side of her. I had to settle for Marilyn Quayle, wife of the much-mocked Vice-President Dan Quayle, but I interpreted the seating as some kind of positive affirmation, a nod in the direction of feminism. Not that it would save me from what lay ahead. Also at my table was a woman whose husband used to be the governor of Oklahoma and who had become a strong supporter of women's industries in his home state. We were each presented with a Raggedy-Ann doll. It was Barbara Bush's ultimate joke on us all, having those sophisticated New York editors walk out of the White House with a doll under their arms.

When he first took over Lang had had me develop various new editorial proposals for *Ms.* I had complied reluctantly as I did not believe he was sincere, but I'd worked up the two options he requested: an eight-page 24-times-a-year newsletter, and a six-times-a-year publication printed on pulp stock. Lang then conducted a very public recruitment process for a new editor; several well-known and competent women turned him down but, astonishingly, Robin Morgan, the well-known feminist, agreed to take the job. She had just agreed to start on a project with the UN Development Program to write a big book on AIDS, and a staff researcher at *Ms.* had resigned to go work with her, so this turnaround was bewildering. So was the revelation that it was Gloria Steinem who had recruited her to the job. Once the deal with Lang was inevitable Steinem had—surprisingly—agreed to meet with him and soon was conferring regularly with him to plot the future of *Ms.* It seems that Dale Lang had come to the realisation that he could have his cake and eat it too. He could remove *Ms.* from the advertising and mainstream circulation market, and thereby protect *Working Woman*, while earning kudos, and the eternal gratitude of Gloria Steinem and all that that debt would entail, by enabling her to do a massive makeover of what she could once again claim as her magazine. Dale Lang 'saved' *Ms.*, he said in an interview in 2013, when he 'helped Gloria hatch the plan to ask readers, 'Does the world still need *Ms.*?' then came up with the campaign that 'convinced them to vote with their wallets by paying three times more for the product, enabling its publisher to break even and *Ms.* to go ad free'.[13]

I was fired as editor of *Ms.* on 19 December. A week earlier Dale Lang had called me over to his office and informed me he did not want me to continue. Lang's headquarters were in the Pan Am building where eighteen months earlier Sandra and I had signed the deal papers that had made us media mogulettes. Lang said he proposed to appoint me editor-at-large of *Ms.*, to honour my contract and provide me with an office and a secretary provided I wrote twelve articles a year for his various publications, including *Ms.* I had been expecting, and in many ways wanting, to be shown the door. Psychologically I did not see how I could work for this man who had been so untrustworthy, so manipulative and who had treated us all so badly. Financially, though, I was not sure that I could refuse. My contract had four years to run and I had a mortgage. Lang had said I could also write for any other magazine that was not in direct competition with his stable. That left practically every decent magazine in America; I could try to build a reputation as a magazine writer. I owed Robbie big time for my contract being honoured. A few weeks earlier, I had been dead meat. Of course, I should have known not to believe a word of it. I got no office, no secretary, and I had to battle to get assignments from Lang's editors, including from *Ms.* Lang had promised not to dissolve Matilda Publications but that also turned out to be a hollow undertaking. Soon, our brave little company would cease to exist. Sandra and I were media mogulettes no more, but we could be proud that both magazines were at the highest-ever circulations: *Ms.* with 550,000 and *Sassy* at 450,000.

My last day at *Ms.* was 20 December. I'd tried to maintain morale among the staff, but I was so battle-weary by then that I was barely functioning. I felt tremendous guilt that I had let down the magazine, its subscribers and everyone who had helped me during my 27 months as editor-in-chief so I was incredibly moved on that last day when the staff presented me with a quickly mocked-up fake *Ms.* cover. In those days before Photoshop they'd had to make do with crude cut and paste. *Our Woman of the Year* was the main cover line, my head replaced Pat Schroeder's on the image from my very first cover and each of the other cover lines had been reworked in tribute to me: 'Who's crying now! The Unsinkable Anne Summers', 'Editor's Essay: Enough is Enough' 'Exclusive! The Harrowing saga of a Mogul with a Mission' and finally, in what we referred to as the ear, that small slash in the top right-hand corner of the cover, 'We will Ms. you!'

It was two years and three months since the Fairfax Board had agreed to buy *Ms.*, two years since Young Warwick had decided to sell us and just seventeen months since Sandra and I had done our management buyout. We had started out with such joy and optimism about the wildly unexpected path we had carved for ourselves, but then we had crashed, and crashed hard. I did not know it was possible to absorb so much trauma. I was exhausted, emotionally and physically and probably more crazed than I realized, but I had not cracked up. I was still standing and although much of the fight had gone out of me, at least for now, I was not bitter. At least not yet. I went back to Adelaide and stayed with my mother, trying to get my body and soul back into some kind of equilibrium. At an absurdly early hour, the phone rang.

'It's for you,' my mother called from the room where the phone was. 'It's the ABC.'

I did not want to talk to the ABC or to anyone else. I would simply have slammed down the phone, but my mother was much too polite. I staggered sleepily towards the receiver she was holding out for me.

'Hello,' I said, somewhat blearily. 'What do you want?'

It was Pru Goward on the line. She was the host of an early morning national radio program and she was live on air. With absolutely no introduction (that presumably happened while I was walking towards the phone) she launched straight into it:

'Anne Summers, you are back from New York. What does it feel like to be a failure?'

'I don't feel like a failure,' I said feebly.

'Well,' she said briskly, 'you would say that wouldn't you.'

Welcome home, Anne, I thought to myself, to the country where if you succeed they tear you down, and if you fail they dance on your grave. I was glad I was returning to New York the following week. I might not have a real job, but I would be in a city where effort was encouraged and where everyone was trying. If someone succeeded, everyone applauded because that showed it could be done and, who knows, next time it might be you.

Back in New York, for the first time in more than two years I was now free from the constant pressure of meeting financial as well as editorial deadlines. I no longer had to rush from meetings to lunches and back to the office and could start to enjoy the city again, the way I had when I had first arrived. I needed time to think about what I would do next, but I could not stop myself from thinking about the brutal events of the recent past. Part of me felt I had failed. I had been unable to make *Ms.* work. It would have been so easy to scuttle *Ms.* as Sandra and I did our various deals, but we had refused. We had kept her alive for another two years after she faced almost certain closure in 1987. That was something, I supposed. And I'd been proud of the editorial. When I look now at the issues I edited, I am surprised how good they are, so much better than I remembered. Trying to get some perspective on those two years, I wonder: did we merely survive? or did we actually manage to do some good during that pitiless time? There was no doubt that Sandra had changed magazine publishing for teenage girls with *Sassy*, but did I have any lasting impact on how to frame feminist editorial for the mainstream magazine market of the late 1980s? Looking back on that tumultuous time I can see that our little venture probably did not have a chance. The outsider status and courage that enabled us to succeed initially also hampered our longer-term prospects. There were too many things we did not understand about America. We were as blind-sided by the reticence of liberal groups to support us in the face of the boycott as by the effectiveness of the evangelicals who had instigated it. We were confounded that advertisers could effectively censor our plans to shatter genres and take readers on exciting new editorial journeys. But, most of all, we were just too small. We had no ballast when the storm struck. It was probably amazing we lasted as long as we did.

I became quite depressed for a time, unable to sleep or to work. I knew I now had a second—or was it a third?—chance to make something of myself in New York but I was having trouble revving myself up. I wondered if I had the toughness to survive in this town. On my last day at *Ms.* several people had told me that I was 'just too nice'. It was not meant as a compliment. 'You are the nicest person I have ever worked for,' one of the editors had said, 'but to succeed in this business you have to be a barracuda.' I did not have what it takes, in other words. I had had my chance in the spotlight but, even with significant goodwill from most quarters, I had not been able to invent a new future for myself. Instead, I would find myself writing consumer reports on 'the best cities for childcare' for *Working Mother* and getting glummer about where I had ended up. 'You're only happy when you're important,' Elisabeth Wynhausen said to me one day. It was a cruel observation, but she was probably right. For the past fifteen years, since I started at the *National Times*, I had been in high-profile jobs, constantly in the spotlight, basking in the attention. It was who I was. Now I no longer had the armour of a job title, no one reported to me, my name was not in the newspapers, no one called. Had I lost my identity? I was starting again, on a new track, not knowing quite where I was going and just hoping that the best of my life was not already behind me.

⋯⋯

We were a party of about ten who flew from Newark to Jacksonville, Florida where we were picked up by vans and driven to Yulee, the site of the 7400 acres White Oak estate, which had been owned by the Gilman family since 1938. David Hay, Chip and I were being escorted by Charlie Milhaupt, who had worked in film in California for many years, but who was now in New York working for our host Howard Gilman who was already at White Oak. In my post-*Ms.* life, I was exploring possible projects in film and in theatre as well as journalism, and had become friendly with Charlie who promised to open doors for me. The rest of the party comprised Natalie Moody, Howard's long-term executive assistant, and a number of other guests, including Linda Fairstein, who was New York's sex crimes prosecutor who was currently dealing with an especially lurid high-profile sexual assault and homicide case known as 'the Preppy murder', and her husband Justin Feldman. White Oak was a timber plantation that supplied the extremely lucrative Gilman Paper Company. Gilman was the grandson of an immigrant from Belarus, who when he had stepped off the boat in America had seen a piece of paper fluttering on the wharf. He took it as a sign of the business he should pursue in his new homeland. Within a generation, the Gilman company would become immensely wealthy and would support Howard's enormously generous philanthropy in the arts, especially the ballet; his unparalleled collection of early photography, which he later endowed to the Metropolitan Museum of Art where there is a gallery named for him; and the nature conservancy, which he established at White Oak in 1982. Wealth sat lightly on Howard, a tall soft-spoken gentle man with white hair and a cool, observant eye. He was extraordinarily generous to friends as well as to individuals and organisations whose work he admired, and he surrounded himself with beautiful things and people, especially young men and prima ballerinas, but he spent nothing on himself. No holidays or luxuries of any kind. He appeared to own just one pair of shoes and his suits and weekend wear were years, if not decades, old. When he died suddenly, of a heart attack age 73 in early 1998, his estate had assets of more than $1 billion.

Because it was our first visit, Chip and I were put in the special suite in what was referred to as the Old Hunting Lodge, the main building where we had all our meals and where the walls were adorned with stag heads and other hunting trophies. Our wooden twin beds were said to have been owned by Ulysses S. Grant, the 18th President of the United States, and the man who led the Union to victory over the Confederacy states. It was where 'Mischa and Jessica' always stayed, we were told. When the dancer Mikhail Baryshnikov defected from Russia in 1974, Howard Gilman had taken him in, taken care of him and set him up financially. More than a decade later, Howard was still managing Mischa's financial affairs, hosting him and his partner Jessica Lange to regular weekends at White Oak and in 1990 would finance what became known as the White Oak Dance Project, a ballet studio where Baryshnikov and Mark Morris collaborated and created a program of touring works. This was the place where Annie Leibovitz shot her celebrated portrait of Baryshnikov, against a white roll in front of the pines of White Oak. Many eminent people were invited to White Oak. (There was no other way to get there, Charlie told us, as solicitations to visit were ignored; he recounted with sardonic pleasure how he and Howard had knocked back an overture from Madonna.) Nearly a decade later, it was the place where Bill and Hillary Clinton licked their wounds from the Lewinsky affair and plotted her Senate run. A few weeks later, we would be invited back. Isabella Rossellini, a good friend of Howard's who served on the board of his foundation, was there with her twin sister Ingrid and on Saturday night we celebrated their birthdays, and Chip's, whose was a week earlier.

But this weekend in May 1990 was all about the nature conservancy. Howard himself took us on the tour of several hours through this truly remarkable place that he had set up to breed endangered species. There were more than 300 animals, including rhinoceroses, giraffes, cheetahs, antelopes, buffalo, zebras and many other exotic and unfamiliar animals. They all had large enclosures and, unlike zoos, the animals could roam free. We were shown a video of the birth of seven cheetah cubs just the night before we had arrived, a further example of the continuing success of the breeding program at White Oak which boasted more than 100 births a year. It was strange to look from the window of our bedroom directly into the enclosure that contained three black rhinoceroses. In Florida!

Not all of the animals at White Oak were endangered. Howard bred horses, too, and had owned a quarter stake in the great racehorse Secretariat that had died just a few months before. Secretariat's last foal, named Plantation, had been born at White Oak a week earlier. And the Bengal tigers were there because they had been confiscated by Florida police from various drug dealers and other loonies, who were keeping them as pets without a permit. Not knowing what to do with them, the police asked Howard if he would take them. Now White Oak had a special park, including a large lake, because they liked to swim and a very, very high fence that not even a Bengal tiger could leap over.

There was also a bird sanctuary which included some black swans from Western Australia and, I was soon to discover, Howard worked closely with the Western Plains Zoo in Dubbo in outback New South Wales, donating a white rhino for their breeding program. Maybe Howard had a thing about Australians because he and I became very good friends, staying in touch by letter after I returned to Australia. He used to send me photographs of newborns at White Oak, especially the giraffes which he loved even more than the rare rhinos, writing engagingly about each one as if it were a new grandchild.

In July 1990, *Ms.* was relaunched as an 'advertiser-free' publication with Robin Morgan as editor-in-chief. The old logo was restored and the cover story, written by Gloria Steinem and titled 'Sex, Lies and Advertising', was an impassioned denunciation of advertising and the way it had constrained *Ms.* in the past. No longer a glossy magazine, its original mission of trying to create a mass-circulation commercial feminist publication abandoned, with fewer than 100,000 subscribers,[14] and production values and design that made *Ms.* resemble a movement publication, it looked as if it had given up the fight.

After my own experiences with advertisers, I could totally empathise with Steinem's desire to escape their yoke. I would have applauded this radical change in direction as a welcome and timely reimagining of the original goals of *Ms.*, except that the new *Ms.* included several attacks on 'my' *Ms.* The strained friendliness with Gloria and her gang of the past three years seemed to have evaporated faster than you could say sisterhood is powerful. Robin Morgan's editor's letter contained a list, apparently supplied by readers, of topics they did not want to see in *Ms.* The list included fashion, celebrities ('unless clearly feminist') and gardening. This was clearly a crack at 'Earthly Delights', the column I'd created, which Gloria had named and which Robin herself had written for. She had sent me a beautiful poem 'Upstairs in the Garden' which she described in her cover letter as 'my own rather unusual version of a gardening piece'. I had placed it in the December 1989 issue, the one that Dale Lang had refused to print. Now 'gardening' apparently was code for what was wrong with what I'd done at *Ms.* The 'new' *Ms.* also included a couple of very specific repudiations. It reprinted the 'We're Not the *Ms.* We used To Be' trade ad in their 'No Comment' section of sexist or demeaning advertisements. This was the ad showing a hippie-looking woman evolving into a 1980s glamour puss that had upset Gloria and her friends three years earlier. They claimed it was meant to represent—and repudiate—Gloria and no amount of disavowal on our part would convince them otherwise. The masthead of the new *Ms.* confirmed that I was not being overly sensitive. My agreement with Lang stipulated that in return for relinquishing the editorship-in-chief (to make way for Morgan), my new title was to be 'Editor at Large for *Ms.*', and that I was to be listed as such in the magazine. Instead, I was there as Editor at Large for Lang, in the corporate section of the masthead. Nothing to do with *Ms.*, in other words. Suzanne Braun Levine was there, however, with the Editor Emirata title that I had declined to give her. I wrote to Robin Morgan, pointing out the contractual obligation and 'to respectfully request'—my lawyer Robbie had guided the drafting of this letter—I be listed correctly in future issues. She replied saying the title no longer existed. And that was that.

From now on, I had to accustom myself to hearing, or reading, almost non-stop criticisms of my tenure at *Ms.* Much of it was hurtful because it was so inaccurate. I got no credit for anything, even the widely praised political coverage. Instead I was criticised for how I had supposedly corrupted the magazine with fashion, celebrities and, of course, gardening. Steinem told her biographer Carolyn Heilbrun that I never consulted her about *Ms.* editorial, forgetting apparently our regular meetings, her generous annual consultancy fee—and the entire Hedda Nussbaum episode. At the same time, the story of how Sandra and I had managed to buy *Ms.*, first via Fairfax and then through our MBO, was rewritten. In the retelling we were no longer 'real feminists with real money', we were 'the Australians' and, increasingly, this term came to refer not to us but to Fairfax. Steinem several times misrepresented how Sandra and I enabled *Ms.* to survive, by stating that the money we raised came from Australia rather than from Wall Street. As late as 2015, such inaccuracies appeared in interviews she did to promote her new book *My Life on the Road*. It was surprising, for instance, to read in the *New Yorker*, which used to pride itself on its fact-checking, about 'the Australian media group that took over the magazine during a slump in 1987' and that 'two years later, a group of American feminists was able to buy it back, and eventually Steinem helped form a foundation to keep the magazine in print, ad-free, as a monthly.'[15] Almost every single assertion in that sentence is inaccurate. The truth is that Dale Lang owned *Ms.* from 1989 to 1996 when he sold it to Jay MacDonald, an entrepreneur backed by a Florida-based media company. It was not until 1999—a full ten years after Matilda reluctantly relinquished control—that Steinem put together a consortium of wealthy women under the name Liberty Media for Women and, once again, got *Ms.* back.[16]

'You have to understand,' Pat Carbine had said to me over dinner one night in July 1989 when it was apparent that Dale Lang might end up as the new owner, 'that *Ms.* is the child Gloria never had. She can never walk away from it.' Perhaps this explained the attacks now being directed at me. It also now made sense of the time, over breakfast in the Pierre Hotel back in April 1989, just after the fiasco with advertisers over the Hedda Nussbaum cover, when Steinem had said to me with some bitterness, 'You will never get advertising. You are wasting your time.' I had been taken aback by the comment, and by the vehemence with which it had been delivered. I had thought—naively as it turned out—that if we worked harder, were more original, pitched better, etc., we would be able to crack advertiser resistance to *Ms.* Now here was Steinem not only saying it wasn't possible, but almost sounding as if she did not want us to. For the first time, it dawned on me that she would never be able to let go, and so long as we did not succeed there was a chance for her. And then Dale Lang had come along, she had been able to set aside her revulsion and grab the opportunity he presented. Now that she had *Ms.* back, she seemed to be trying to expunge those years when her baby had slipped out of her hands. If they never existed, perhaps the pain they caused would go away. At times she talked as if she had never left. She told the *Guardian* in 2015 that she had once sent [Susan] Brownmiller to cover a domestic violence case in which 'a man beat his wife and killed their baby and that Brownmiller had filed a piece for *Ms.* that blamed the mother'. 'Not even the legal system came to this conclusion!' said Steinem.[17] This was a very unreliable recollection of what had happened at *Ms.* over the Hedda Nussbaum case, when I had commissioned the Brownmiller article and Steinem had tried to stop it being published.

In August 1991 I received a warm handwritten letter from the journalist Susan Faludi thanking me for my letter in which I had congratulated her on winning a Pulitzer Prize and saying she'd call me in September when she was in New York so we could get together. This was part of an exchange of letters with Faludi that had begun when she had asked me to sign a release, agreeing she could quote from the interview she had done with me for her forthcoming book about the backlash against women's equality in America. So I was astonished when I received my copy of *Backlash: The Undeclared War Against American Women* to find more than three pages attacking 'my' *Ms.* Billed as the next great book of the women's movement and documenting the ways in which the achievements of the 1970s women's movement were being undermined or reversed, *Backlash* quickly became a must-read in feminist circles. Faludi worked for the *Wall Street Journal* so she knew how to get information, marshall facts and report accurately—she'd just won a Pulitzer for a series in the *Wall Street Journal*—but *Backlash* was not just factually wrong about so much of what I had done, there was a tone to the writing that made it sound almost malicious. Why? I was stunned because in my several interviews with Faludi she had given no clue she was going to attack me in this fashion.

Faludi's description of *Ms.* under my stewardship suggested I covered nothing but celebrities and that every issue was a celebration of fashion and makeup: 'The magazine that had once investigated sexual harassment, domestic violence, the prescription-drug industry and the treatment of women in third-world countries now dashed off gushing tributes to Hollywood stars, launched a fashion column, and delivered the real big news—pearls are back.'[18] She 'reported' that I had 'pulled' a photo of Hedda Nussbaum from a cover 'to pacify advertisers', and noted that now *Ms.* was not-for-profit again and could endorse candidates: 'Instead', Faludi wrote, 'the magazine wound up endorsing beauty products.'[19] She compared me with the editor of *Good Housekeeping*, more interested in upscaling the magazine than in covering issues. No mention of our Washington Bureau, our regular political coverage, our tough reporting on women's health, violence against women, abortion and countless other topics.

As a journalist with a financial newspaper you'd think Faludi might have had some appreciation of the business pain our little media group was suffering because of the *Sassy* boycott and its impact on *Ms.* but no. Her take on what happened? 'Finally, with the advertiser exodus threatening to push *Ms.* into financial collapse, Summers gave up', she wrote. 'She turned the female-run publication over to male publisher Dale Lang . . .'[20] I could not let this stand. It was inaccurate, it was cruel and it was going to be read by hundreds of thousands of people around the world. Once again, I called on Robbie. His initial tough letter of complaint to Random House landed a few days before the *Time* magazine cover promoting the book appeared. 'Fighting the backlash against feminism,' was the main cover line. 'Susan Faludi and Gloria Steinem sound the call to arms.' It made them sound like co-authors and the accompanying photograph suggested it really was the two of them against the world. In the weeks that followed, there was extensive correspondence between Random House and Robbie. Initially they merely offered an apology but then agreed to make substantial changes. Susan Faludi had not meant to attack me, her publisher said. She 'feels badly' about it. She would write a letter of apology. Ultimately, a very large number of changes were made to the section about *Ms.* and me in all subsequent US hardcover and paperback and all foreign editions. I was not satisfied because the new version still badly misrepresented what I had tried to do with *Ms.*, and the tone was still sneering, but Robbie's letters had already cost me several thousand dollars and I could not afford to take it to court. There was nothing more I could do but I was very unhappy. I still am. Faludi's letter of apology must have been lost in the mail, because I never received it.

On 5 April 1992 several hundred thousand people marched through the streets of Washington DC, the route taking them past the US Supreme Court which was about to consider the constitutionality of a Pennsylvania state law that would restrict rights to abortion. It was one of the largest marches ever seen in the national capital and it culminated in a rally at a park where a huge crowd gathered to hear speaker after speaker denounce the proposed threats to women's right to choose. Gloria Steinem was one of the speakers, but during her address she departed from the abortion script to talk about the magazine: 'We got *Ms.* back!' she yelled at the crowd—who roared back their appreciation.

It was almost two years now since the relaunch of *Ms.*, so Steinem had had her magazine 'back' now for almost as long as we had 'had' it. Except, I wondered, did she really have the magazine 'back' when Dale Lang was the owner and could ultimately call the shots? It was no longer my problem but still I could not rest in the face of yet another public denigration of me and what I had done. On 22 April I wrote her an angry letter, pointing out that if Fairfax had not come along in 1987 *Ms.*, with its more than $8 million in debt, was most unlikely to have survived. I also got a few other things off my chest. Why, I asked, were she and Robin Morgan continuing their attacks on me, in the magazine and around the traps in New York, accusing me of having removed all 'substance' from *Ms.* by introducing 'gardening', celebrity covers and beauty and fashion editorial? I reminded her that *Ms.* had run celebrity covers and articles on fashion and beauty long before I came along. She might want to pretend those two and a half years never existed, I wrote, but then so would I: 'Some parts of me, too, would like to be able to expunge the memory of what was in many ways a nightmare and which continues to have unpleasant consequences,' I wrote. 'It was bad enough having to deal with bankers who were inflexible, advertisers who were unyielding and fundamentalists who were determined to put us out of business. I did not expect, after that was all over, to be subjected to a campaign of denigration by mean-spirited feminists.' She never replied.

———◦◦◦———

In mid-2012, the City of New York hosted a morning tea function at City Hall to mark the 40th birthday of *Ms.* magazine. Presumably the City did this because *Ms.* had been founded in NYC, but it was now based in Los Angeles and had been for eleven years since its acquisition in 2001 by the Feminist Majority Foundation. This women's activist group was run by the admirable Ellie Smeal, who I knew from when I was at *Ms.* She had served three terms as president of the National Organisation for Women (NOW) and she and her successor, Molly Yard, visited me early on. I was impressed by their pragmatism, their clear focus on the need for tangible wins and to protect rights, such as abortion, that were under threat. We quickly concluded a membership deal with NOW that would have given us an additional 150,000 subscribers by January 1990. Smeal had established the Feminist Majority as a lobbying vehicle in 1987 with the aid of a $15 million gift from feminist philanthropist Peg Yorkin and, more than a decade later, had been savvy enough to see that *Ms.* could be an effective mouthpiece to serve the organisation's lobbying and activism.

Although Steinem and Morgan remained on the masthead of the new *Ms.*, they did not appear to have day-to-day influence, judging by the generous article the magazine's online news service published upon Betty Friedan's death in 2006. Nor was there any antipathy to me; even today, back copies of 'my' *Ms.* are offered for sale on their website. I was visiting New York at the time of the City Hall morning tea and Letty Pogrebin got me invited. She and I had stayed in touch over the more than three decades. The gathering was small and characteristically laden with symbolism, comprising a bunch of much older women, the founders, and a group of girls representing the future. A large square Wonder Woman cake formed the centerpiece around which everyone gathered. Gloria Steinem was there, of course, but she studiously avoided any eye or other contact with me while she posed for the cameras, signed autographs and talked to fawning fans. Should I confront her? I debated with myself but then I decided: what was the point? This magazine was nothing to do with me anymore. I felt no nostalgia, or regrets. I was unfettered. I walked away.

CHAPTER NINE

PAUL KEATING AND THE LAMINAR FLOW

In May 1992, I returned to Canberra to take up a short-term job as a political adviser to Paul Keating, who in December the year before had become Prime Minister. A few months earlier I had received a late-night phone call from Don Watson, the writer and former academic; he, along with Hilary McPhee, his wife at the time, were friends of mine and he had recently joined Keating's office as The Speechwriter. 'Paul's got a bit of a problem with women,' Don told me. 'We want you to come and help out.'

It had been Hilary's idea to ask me to come back and advise on how to improve the gender gap in Keating's support, he said, and while I was tantalised, I took a fair bit of persuading. Not that I did not think I could do it, despite having been away from Australia for seven years, but I just didn't see how Paul Keating would want me anywhere near his office. I was too closely identified with his mortal enemy, my previous Prime Ministerial boss, Bob Hawke, whom I'd publicly supported during the leadership stoush. I'd even written, in a cover story for Max Suich's the *Independent Monthly* a year earlier, that Keating was 'despised by about a third of the population' and had quoted trade union sources describing him as 'unfocused and undisciplined'. I'd described how Keating punished journalists who displeased him by denying them access. In my Press Gallery days, I had myself been on the receiving end of a couple of Keating telephone 'sprays', and he had once handwritten a vitriolic letter denouncing one of my articles, so I presumed he would be unforgiving for my criticisms the previous year.

'If he wants me to work for him, he is going to have to ask me himself,' I told Don.

Leaving New York could be risky for me. I was finally starting to find a niche for myself post *Ms.* magazine. I had a Green Card which meant I could stay in the US and I could work, and I had three Rolodexes full of great contacts, not all of whom had dropped me when I lost the editorship of *Ms.* I had a literary agent, Gloria Loomis, who was helping me develop a book proposal and I was getting newspaper op-eds published. I hadn't yet cracked the *New York Times*, my measure of 'making it', but I was getting encouraging notes from editors in response to my submissions, so I hoped it would not be long now. Leaving, even for just three months, might mean I'd never recover the momentum. I had a year left on my Matilda contract, which Dale Lang had picked up, so I could pay my mortgage and other expenses. My prospects were good, I liked to think. Would I be throwing it all away? But my strongest tie to New York was Chip. We had been together for almost three years now, and both of us felt that we'd found our life's partner. I was not willing to jeopardise that. But what if Chip agreed to come too?

Keating eventually called me and we agreed I would come for three months. Most of my New York friends were mightily impressed that I had received a phone call from my country's leader, and I was influenced by the American view that it was a public duty to agree if a political leader asks you to serve. Although it would temporarily throw me off my chosen course, I saw it as a chance to put into practice some of my ideas about how to integrate women's issues into the mainstream political agenda. 'To put my mouth where my money was,' as I said to friends. How could I not do it? Especially as Chip had agreed to accompany me.

Although I fully expected to return to New York, I took the opportunity of this break from my usual patterns to give up smoking. I had tried many times but could never break a habit I'd had since I was fourteen, and which

I associated so closely with writing. I feared I would never produce another sentence without a cigarette burning in the ashtray beside my computer. It was not just the physical addiction; it was who I was. I was a smoker. I lit up when I picked up the phone, or when I sat down to my desk, at parties where I knew no one, after a satisfying meal, whenever I had a drink, or after sex. But I knew that it would undermine my credibility in Canberra if I was one of those people who had to leave not just their desk, but the very building, to huddle outside in the frigid weather to drag on their cigarettes. If I expected to command respect in this job, I had to get rid of the awful habit. I was recommended a hypnotherapist who, I was told, had helped Linda Ronstadt quit. I took a train to Connecticut and spent an hour with a man who got me to tell him why I wanted to stop smoking. He then put me into some kind of hypnotic state, recited these reasons back to me, and sent me on my way. I never smoked again.

I'd known Paul Keating and got on well with him when I ran the Canberra bureau of the *Financial Review* and he was Labor's Minerals and Energy spokesman. He was a frequent visitor to the only bureau in the Press Gallery that properly covered mining and related issues. He was always elegantly dressed himself and he noticed what other people wore. One day, as I walked with him and Max Walsh over to the Lobby Restaurant for lunch, Paul had commented on my new Weiss suit:

'You always were a snappy dresser, Annie.'

He was the only parliamentarian—probably the only man—I knew who could say something like that without it sounding like a come-on.

It was apparent then that Paul Keating was an unusual Labor man. He was an independent thinker and even though he was from the notoriously muscular New South Wales Labor right faction, he maintained a close friendship with Tom Uren, the much older leader of the left. He was open to ideas, and to people, from outside his formative experiences. He was married to a beautiful Dutch woman, who had piercing brown eyes and a tangle of long, dark-blonde curly hair. She had been an air hostess (as they were called then) on KLM and they had met on one of her flights. His marriage to Annita was another thing that distinguished Paul Keating from his Labor colleagues, who mostly married girls they had grown up with. And, unlike many of his parliamentary colleagues, he did not have a wandering eye. It was an article of faith in Canberra when I worked in the Press Gallery that Paul Keating was a one-woman man, and that woman was his wife Annita. They had four children and, as I was to learn when I worked for him, Paul was intensely devoted to his kids.

On my first day in Parliament House, I was taken into the Prime Minister's office, through the front door, to meet him. The last time I'd seen Paul Keating had been in New York in 1988 at a function for the visiting Treasurer. We'd posed for a photograph, both of us grinning toothily, me holding the latest issue of *Ms.* with Oprah Winfrey on the cover. Four years later and he had changed. The weight of office and the hard years of getting there showed in the tired lines on his face. His tall, lean frame was encased in the trademark dark Zegna suit, the shirt was white and spotless. His hooded eyes gave him a look of great solemnity. Those eyes would appear expressionless or even cold as he surveyed the room while he talked. It was as if he was scoping for possible pitfalls but then he could, in a second, break into an impish grin that showed too much gum, but which gave him an irresistible and instant charisma. The man who had said he could, if necessary, 'throw the switch to vaudeville' once he became Prime Minister, was in fact something of a performer. He could ham it up for the office or crack a joke (which he often found funnier than his audience) or display a lighter side that would have astonished those who knew him only from his combative Question Time performances. My expected three-months in Canberra would turn into eleven months, and I would be part of the team that delivered Keating his unexpected election victory in March 1993. I got caught up in what became a thrilling and rewarding political journey, one where I developed a deeper appreciation for Paul Keating, and where I gained new insights into what is needed for women to achieve the supposedly simple goal of equality within a democracy. But there were some unanticipated high personal costs and my life would change far more radically than I'd expected when I agreed to do that short-term stint.

Perhaps unsurprisingly, not everyone welcomed me back as Keating and most of his team in the PMO, as the Prime Minister's Office was called, did. Some of my new colleagues were worried that I was too much in the limelight, committing the cardinal crime of a staffer taking attention away from her boss. I gave no interviews but that did not diminish the non-stop media interest, at times verging on obsession, in my presence on Keating's staff. There were constant stories, including a lengthy profile in *Good Weekend*, that described me as responding to 'a Prime Ministerial SOS'. It was accompanied by a lurid illustration that depicted Keating and me on a small boat using a fish hook to catch women.[1] None of this helped me, or the job I had been asked to do. The national ALP, which already had a poor relationship with the PMO, was affronted. The team at OSW was nervous about what it meant for them to have a former head of the Office at the centre of power. I soon learned that relations were severely fractured after OSW had made disparaging comments about a PMO-drafted, and very poorly received, speech Keating had delivered on International Women's Day in Brisbane. Peter Walsh, who had been Minister for Finance in the Hawke government, and an old foe from my days at OSW, later wrote that Keating had 'recycled Anne Summers . . . [who] quickly set about inflicting policy damage on the government.'[2]

As I understood it, my job was to help improve Paul Keating's standing with women, but I was given no specific brief or guidance about how to do that. That was fine with me as it meant I was not curbed by a rulebook or precedents, but first I needed to understand *why* women did not like the Prime Minister. Perhaps then we could set about persuading them to look at him differently, maybe even vote for him. ALP National Secretary Bob Hogg had briefed the advisers that there was a 3 to 4 per cent gender gap *against* the government. In the 1980 election, Labor had closed what had been big gender gaps in the previous two elections—setting them up for victory in 1983—he said, and in 1983 and 1984 more women than men had voted Labor. In the previous three elections—1984, 1987 and 1990—women had started out being anti-Labor but that gap had closed during the campaign. Now, Hogg told us, the polls were suggesting an entrenched resistance. The ALP's private polls were more encouraging than the published polls that had a gender gap of 7 per cent in women's approval, which was better than the 10 per cent it had been earlier in the year, but still not enough to put Keating in a winning position. I had come to the job thinking that it would not be any kind of gimmickry, but rather sound policy, that would be most likely to persuade women to rethink their views on Keating. But I was keen to know what my new colleagues thought.

The PMO was a large, busy set of offices located on the ground floor at the rear of what I could not stop myself calling the 'new' Parliament House. (It was four years now since the Parliament and the several thousand people who worked in it had decamped from the 'old', and supposedly temporary, building it had occupied further down the hill towards Lake Burley Griffin since 1927, and where I had worked ten years earlier in the Press Gallery.) The PMO was remarkably quiet for a place where 30 or more people worked, usually on deadlines, always with urgency and often with a fair amount of friction among us. And that was before you took into account the disputes and, at times, outright brawls, that walked through the door in the form of the Prime Minister's cabinet colleagues. The PMO was the centre of gravity of the government, where the power resided, the deals were done, and the future course of the nation decided. But being there did not feel as exciting as I'd imagined. Everyone was calm, and supercool. Unless, as sometimes happened, tempers broke through, shouts replaced the usual murmurs and, once or twice, someone even threw something. But there was laughter. Lots of it. That, more than tension, was our lubricant.

Each of the advisers had their own office. Even me, the latecomer for whom there was initially no space. In a surprisingly generous gesture, the drivers gave up their sitting room. They decamped to an area just outside, where there were couches and a television and where those staff who did not go into the House with Paul would gather on sitting days to watch Question Time. My room was large and windowless, but I found that I could rent paintings from Art Bank and soon my walls were covered with large dramatic works, all of them by women. Might as well advertise what I'm here for, I thought.

I already knew several of the advisers. Apart from Don Watson, whose office was close to mine so that we were constantly running in to each other; there was John Edwards, now an economics adviser but whom I'd known for many years through his several incarnations as a journalist in Sydney and Washington, ministerial adviser to Clyde Cameron in the

Whitlam government and author of a book on the MX missile; and Simon Balderstone, the amiable environmental adviser who had previously worked for Graham Richardson and my old friend Mary Ann O'Loughlin who, I was surprised and delighted to discover, was social policy adviser. I soon got to know the others. Anne de Salis, who had been the first woman to be appointed to the senior executive service in Treasury and was now in charge of administering the PMO as well as advising on immigration; Ric Simes, another economist; and political advisers Stephen Smith, a former ALP State Secretary from WA, and Mark Ryan, who'd moved from running media for Premier John Cain in Victoria initially to become Keating's press secretary. Smith would leave soon to become a candidate for a federal seat back in his home state. Ashton Calvert was the foreign policy adviser, a calm and quintessential bureaucrat on the surface, but when a few months later Keating decided to overturn the ban on allowing gays to serve in the military and he and I were the unlikely duo given carriage of the issue, I saw his steely core and his deft strategic mind. He left the PMO to become Ambassador to Japan and, later, served for seven years as Secretary of the Department of Foreign Affairs and Trade. I had less to do with the Press Office, where there were five or six people in a separate suite of rooms that were connected to the PMO, but not accessible to the journalists, although Greg Turnbull, the press secretary, was always around.

The secretaries and assistants were a tireless and talented lot, without exception all women, whose job was to answer non-stop ringing phones, take dictation and produce letters, speeches, memos or whatever other documents the Prime Minister or his advisers needed, and to generally ensure the place ran efficiently. Gina Bozinovski was assigned to me; she already had two other advisers to look after but she took on the extra burden without complaining, and was always cheerfully competent in the midst of the chaos that invariably accompanied the producing of a major speech or policy announcement. She later went to law school and is now a successful corporate counsel in Queensland. There were other staffers: the person in charge of the diary, and someone who tried to coordinate all movements, and Guy Nelligan who was officially called a butler and whose job was to ensure Paul had his constant cup of tea or whatever other sustenance he required. Deborah Hope, who I'd known from her days as a Fairfax journalist, was an adviser to Annita Keating. She and husband John Edwards used to arrive in the office each morning with hair still wet from their morning swim and were known—behind their backs—as 'John and Ilsa', after the champion teenage swimmers Jon and Ilsa Konrads, who during the 1950s and 60s had broken virtually every world swimming record. Presiding over all of us was Don Russell, the former Treasury official who had been with Paul since his days as Treasurer and was now Chief of Staff. His tall, sinewy frame, topped by a totally bald pate, was a calm and unifying presence seemingly able to absorb any amount of bad news without appearing ruffled.

Although I kept my head down while I surveyed the scene, assessing how I would do the job, I was soon receiving a never-ending stream of visitors, most of them women. They were lobbying, putting their case for or against measures the government was, or was rumoured to be, about to implement. And there was the massive volume of phone calls, letters and faxes. There was tremendous excitement about my presence in Canberra, and a lot of gratitude that there was now access in the PMO of a kind that had not existed since Elizabeth Reid had been women's adviser to Gough Whitlam in the early 1970s. I saw, or talked to, as many people as possible. I wanted to reconnect. I wanted to hear what was on women's minds. I felt humbled to receive a visit from Edna Ryan, the lifelong fighter for women's rights who was then aged 89 and who was upset about the government's proposed changes to superannuation that, she argued, would disadvantage women. My visitors also included backbenchers and even ministers, who calculated that mine was yet another voice that could get to the Prime Minister and help them with whatever their case was.

It was an article of faith in the PMO that women were antagonised by Keating's aggressive behaviour in Parliament, principally during Question Time, but I was not convinced that it was such a problem. I knew plenty of women who admired Keating for precisely this reason. They, along with the rest of the country, roared when Keating responded to Opposition Leader John Hewson asking during Question Time on 15 September 1992, why he would not call an early election: 'The answer is, mate, because I want to do you slowly.' There was a similar reaction on 2 November, when he referred to the Senate as 'unrepresentative swill'.

Keating was a superb parliamentary performer, able to home in on his opponents' weaknesses, always finding the right phrase, with perfectly timed delivery. It was essential to who he was and I thought people liked this about him. There was, I discovered, widespread admiration of Keating among some lesbians, mainly academics, for his style and wit. There were other women who'd despised Hawke and who felt Keating was a man who, despite his old-fashioned attitudes towards women, had passions and a vision that the country sorely needed. But my friends were hardly a representative sample; we needed to know what the wider population of women thought.

I was surprised to find that there was no qualitative research. Karen Luscombe, the ALP's Perth-based researcher, did only quantitative, telephone polling, intended to track voting intentions. I felt we needed research that probed what was influencing women's views on the government. We needed someone like Barbara Riley, the expert facilitator of focus groups whose report on what we needed to do to fix *Ms.* had been so devastatingly accurate. Barbara had since married and was now Riley-Smith; she did a lot of work for the NSW ALP, so her credentials were acceptable to the PMO. The only problem was we did not have any money and the ALP was not prepared to pay for it. In the end, Mike Keating, the head of PM&C, said that so long as the research was not party-political it could come from the OSW budget. This would not be a problem. I firmly believed we needed policy solutions, not political gimmicks, to address whatever the research revealed, so it was perfectly legitimate to use taxpayer funds. Even the Opposition, when it found out about the research, was not able to mount a credible case against it. The project had to go to tender and fortunately Barbara's proposal won. When she had completed the research, we had a report that contained the most thorough exploration of the views of Australian women that had ever been conducted for non-commercial purposes. And it was the first time an Australian government had ever asked women what they wanted.

The twenty focus groups were conducted in every capital city and two regional centres, Geelong and Mackay. In each place there were two groups that were, on Barbara's recommendation, divided according to age, either under or over 40. Participants were selected on the basis of income; they had to be eligible for some form of government assistance, which in those days was all income-tested, and which cut out at a combined family income of $55,000. There was a mixture of employed and stay-at-home mothers but there were no professionals, no so-called yuppies, and no one who was not struggling financially. Every woman who was in receipt of family allowances (the money for each child paid directly to mothers) knew down to the last cent exactly what her payment was, and most of them said they needed that money for food and other essentials.

The overarching question asked of these women was: what do you think about your own lives and about what the government is doing for women? We were attempting to probe their knowledge of, and satisfaction with, existing policies and services, but we also wanted to tap into how they felt about their lives. Maybe not the government's business, perhaps, but to me it was impossible to separate the two because, in Australia at least, government programs such as childcare (and, back then, the lack of a government-paid maternity leave scheme) were such big factors in determining whether women could participate in the economy after they had had children.

Mary Ann O'Loughlin and I observed each of the groups, sitting behind the two-way mirror (so that we could not be seen), and listened to these women speaking with remarkable frankness about their lives. In the smaller centres, where there were no professional research rooms, we listened on a loudspeaker strung under the door of an adjoining motel room. It meant we could not see them but their voices came through clearly enough. We listened as Barbara asked the women to describe their lives, to talk about the things that mattered and the things that worried them. They needed little encouragement. It was obvious that many of them rarely got to talk about themselves. The focus groups gave them a chance, especially as they could open up in front of people they knew they would never see again. It turned out to be a great lubricant for honesty and some startling findings.

Inevitably, although Barbara was scrupulous about not asking, many of the women volunteered opinions of the Prime Minister and his wife. We were surprised at how big an issue it was that he wore Italian suits. Some of the women blamed Annita, saying she must have insisted that he wear European, not Australian, clothes. One woman in Brisbane said,

'Remember when he was Treasurer, he told us to buy Australian but he doesn't himself.'

The women tended to think that Keating was 'arrogant' and 'cold' and 'not interested in ordinary people'. Several expressed distaste for the way he had come to power (by 'stabbing Bob Hawke in the back'—a sentiment that would also haunt Julia Gillard almost twenty years later). Others liked the way that Keating was so clearly devoted to his family, but they wanted him to engage them more.

'Smile!' was the advice many of them gratuitously offered. 'Lighten up.'

Some time later, I was travelling with the Prime Minister in suburban Perth. We pulled up at traffic lights, and people in the car beside us noticed him. They started pointing and gesticulating, and not in a friendly way. Paul ignored them.

'Smile!' I urged him. I was sitting directly behind Paul and had a clear view of the people in the next car.

'Why?' he said. He was impatient with such trite political gestures.

'Please,' I begged him. 'Just do it.'

He turned his face, gave them a wave, and one of his big, beautiful and infectious grins. The transformation was remarkable. The people in the car broke into huge smiles, and their hands, which a moment earlier had been giving him the finger, returned the wave. Then the lights changed. We zoomed off and Paul went back to muttering into his mobile. Persuading Paul that he needed to engage with the public was a frustrating and mostly futile job. It wasn't who he was. Which, of course, was what made him special. But there was an election to be won.

The focus group findings were utterly unambiguous and remarkably uniform across the entire country; there were no discernible state or regional differences. Australian women valued the independence and choices their lives provided, even when those choices were accompanied by the stress of the double load of housework and raising children with outside employment. They did, however, feel their work was undervalued and that men did not do enough to share the load. When asked what issues were important to the country, they nominated employment (including unemployment), and education and training. But when asked what was important to them *as women*, the answers were unanimous. They had three overwhelming concerns: childcare, women's health and violence against women. Stark and simple and, for a federal government, extremely challenging.

Childcare was of course a federal responsibility, but as I knew from my time in OSW a decade earlier, one that was contentious—and expensive. But clearly we had to do something. Barbara interpreted the 'women's health' response in two ways. It was women caring for their family's well-being—and thus wanting to preserve Medicare, which was under threat from the Coalition—but it was also a way of expressing their need for 'me' time, some respite from always having to be on duty as mothers or wives or employees. They wanted to be seen as individuals, as the women and girls they once were, before all these responsibilities enveloped their lives. Not a lot we could do about that except by having the Prime Minister respectfully acknowledge the contribution women were making to the country. To let them know they were appreciated. But we needed to look at health and see what we might do—apart from assuring Australians that Medicare would be safe under a Keating government.

But it was the response on violence that staggered us. Almost every woman mentioned it. In order to get rankings of what the women viewed as the most important issues, Barbara asked them to imagine they had a budget of $100 and to allocate the money according to their priorities. In Mackay, Queensland only one of the nine women in the group did not include violence on her list, and two of them allocated 40 per cent of their entire budget to dealing with violence. I found this outcome extremely confronting. I had no idea violence against women was so extensive, and I did not have a clue how to respond to it. Domestic and sexual violence were state responsibilities, covered by state laws. The federal government had no role—but perhaps it needed to find one. Mary Ann and I briefed the two Dons on the findings and said we would come back with recommendations on what we could do in response to these issues that so clearly troubled Australian women. We had uncovered some very serious problems, issues that had previously not been paid sufficient attention by government. That would have to change, and not just because there was an election looming. Campaign and policy material coming from the state and federal Liberal and National parties was highlighting the same three issues. The budget of the NSW Liberal Fahey government, delivered in early September 1993, emphasised women's health, childcare and violence against women. All the political parties were uncovering the same discontent and, I was pleasantly surprised to discover, they all felt the need to respond. Maybe, finally, women were about to get the political attention they deserved. What they wanted was clear enough. We just had to work out how to deliver.

Figuring that out, and then doing my best to get it delivered, would occupy most of the time I spent in the PMO. I spent a lot of time consulting widely with women's groups and key individuals, and I worked closely with Mary Ann on policy ideas. But while we worked on the big policy items—'kicking goals' as it was referred to in the office—we also had day-to-day decisions, crises and the occasional opportunity to deal with. For instance, in mid-1992 a vacancy loomed on the board of the Reserve Bank, Australia's central bank, and arguably the most important board in the country. It had never had a woman member, so I suggested to Keating that he could make history. He was amenable and asked his Treasurer, John Dawkins, to recommend someone. I remember a meeting with a Dawkins staffer who explained that he'd asked Treasury for the names of some suitable women but 'they couldn't find any'. They still 'couldn't find any' after several prompts, so Mary Ann and I realised we'd have to find someone ourselves. We consulted OSW's Register of Women. I was not optimistic, remembering from my days at OSW that this list of women who were nominally suitable for board appointments was not very comprehensive. But, I hoped, maybe it had been upgraded. In fact, almost the very first name the coordinates produced was ideal. We ran it past the Prime Minister and then went back to Dawkins' office. We've 'found one', we said, trying not to smirk. They couldn't argue with Janet Holmes à Court, who was one of Australia's leading businesswomen, head of the largest construction company as well as helming a number of other companies that had been part of the empire of her late husband, Robert. In fact, they should have been able to find her themselves. The government appointed her to the Reserve Bank Board in August 1992 and she served for five years. Sadly, when her term expired in 1997, Prime Minister John Howard defied usual practice and did not reappoint her, despite her meeting with him and saying she'd like to stay on.[3] Instead, a few months later, he appointed Jillian Broadbent, a banker. This helped cement the tradition we had created of appointing women. Fortunately, it has continued and expanded. In 2017, three of the nine Reserve Bank Board members are women. It seems they are no longer so hard to find.

I'd arrived in the office one morning to discover workmen crawling all over my desk.

'Someone must like you, love,' I was told when I asked what they were doing.

They were hooking me up to the PM's communications system, I learned. This meant that Keating could 'buzz' me as he could the other advisers. It meant I was no longer just a transient blow-in, but part of the team. Shortly afterwards, I was asked to stay on until the election—whenever that would be. Chip decided to return to New York. He'd spent the three months of our expected stay in Canberra and was bored out of his brain. I was in the office for long hours, he did not have a job, and there were only so many times he could run around Lake Burley Griffin to increase his already peak fitness. More than anything, though, he needed to return to deal with the financial catastrophe that was unfolding back in New York.

Dale Lang had peremptorily cancelled my employment contract, meaning we had no money to pay the mortgage on my apartment. There were no grounds for the cancellation; my contract allowed me to return to Australia for short-term work assignments, and I had done this in the past, but Lang apparently calculated that I would not have the resources to sue for restitution of the payments. And he was right. I learned from the Australian Consulate in New York that someone from the *Ms.* offices had called, wanting to know how long I would be in Canberra. They made no attempt to ask me. I presumed the $200,000 Lang saved went straight to the *Ms.* editorial budget. Great for them, if true, but a very nasty problem for me. We could rent out the apartment, although that income would not cover the mortgage and Chip would need to find somewhere cheap to live. My PMO salary was $86,882 per year, pro-rated to my tenure. Starting in July, when Chip returned to New York, I began to send him almost the entire amount each pay period to meet our mortgage payments. With an exchange rate hovering around 50 cents, it was a brutal experience. I moved out of our Yarralumla rental and began to rely on the hospitality of friends.

I was under no illusions that I was an office insider. I was not, and did not expect to be, party to the big political decisions. I could not contribute to discussions about economic settings or foreign policy—although I was gratified when Paul asked me to be the note-taker for his meeting with Irish

President Mary Robinson. He spent the first ten minutes or so trying to get her to comprehend the size and complexity of Indonesia. Unlike her tiny island homeland, which you could drive across in a day, Paul demonstrated—with lots of hand gestures—that it took seven hours to fly from one end of the Indonesian archipelago to the other.

I was thrilled that I could now be buzzed, but I also knew that it would never happen. If Paul wanted you, he'd come to you. I'd heard from a former staffer that Malcolm Fraser, when he was impatient, would angrily sweep his hand across the entire console, buzzing every single person in the PMO, to ensure he got the attention of whoever it was he needed to talk to. Paul was not at all like that. I'd be on the phone and look up and see the familiar figure in my doorway.

'When you've got a moment, love,' he'd say and sit himself down in front of my desk.

'I have to go,' I'd say into the phone. No hurry, the Prime Minister would gesture.

Those who saw only the brutality of Keating against his political enemies in Question Time would be amazed at how kind and considerate he could be with people. He knew all the personal stories of his staff and was always ready with advice or practical help. When a staff member had a miscarriage, Keating wanted her to try some of the Chinese remedies that he and Annita used to maintain their health. Whenever you went to The Lodge, the pungent smell of whatever concoction of roots and powders was boiling away on the stove would waft through the rooms. On election night, in March 1993, amid the euphoria and exultation of his unexpected win, and before he had made his victory speech, Keating had taken me aside and said, 'On Monday, get yourself a ticket to New York and see Chip for a couple of weeks, and then come back and we'll talk.'

Some in the office thought Keating was too much of a softie. He would take someone into his private office to give them the bad news that they had to be let go. The longer the meeting went, we'd learned from previous experience, the less likely it was to achieve its mission. Yes, there they were emerging from Paul's office, laughing and shaking hands. Not only not sacked, but now the best of buddies. Very few people ever left the office and almost everyone who has ever worked for Paul Keating is still in touch with him. No other Prime Minister has an annual get-together with his staff as Keating and his PMO still do, more than two decades after he left office. To celebrate the twentieth anniversary of his becoming Prime Minister, in December 2012, there was a really big party at the Bellevue Hotel in Sydney that brought together almost everyone who had ever worked for Paul Keating, including all the federal police and the drivers. The loyalty and affection former staffers have for him is a remarkable commentary on the man, although it is not easy to explain. Perhaps we want to be part of his aura because we all admire his continuing boldness and creativity. He is never short of a killer aphorism to capture the essence of a problem, or a person. ('All tip and no ice-berg', to describe former federal Treasurer Peter Costello, showed he has turned this aptitude into an art form.) But more than all that, I think we are dazzled by the breadth and depth of this boy from Bankstown. He had shaped himself into a person who understood in profound detail how the world worked, from economics to geopolitics to aesthetics and beyond, and he was constantly seeking to make it work better. And although he had made it to the very top of the political tree, first as Treasurer and then Prime Minister, he had never left anyone behind. If you were part of any of his story, you remained there. Unless you chose to leave or behaved in such a way that earned his enmity. Once that happened, it was hard to come back.

The first time I flew on the VIP aircraft with Keating was to Perth. As soon as we'd boarded, Paul delved into his battered leather attaché case and, grabbing a handful of CDs, handed them to the steward.

'He'll put them on as soon as we're up,' he told me, indicating I should sit next to him.

I assumed this was a privilege accorded to first-time flyers. As we taxied to takeoff, Paul retrieved a blue clothbound volume from the attaché case that, he soon revealed to me, was a set of maps of Georgian Sydney. As the music—I think it was Mahler—filled the cabin, he leafed through the book, jabbing with his forefinger to show me the few buildings that still remained. If your only knowledge of Keating's aesthetic was from the media you would know about his love for French clocks, but you would scarcely be aware of how broadly his taste ranged, and the extent of his expertise. I later learned about an official trip to the UK during which the Prime Minister took a late-night detour to a county somewhere, to the impressive Georgian residence of an Englishman who wanted Keating's advice on some of the finer points of the restoration he was undertaking.

We were running early for our event so Paul took us to the shop at the Art Gallery of Western Australia, which was near the venue where he was due to speak.

'Hi, Paul,' said the women behind the counter.

They were totally unfazed by the sight of the Prime Minister and his entourage filling-up their tiny space; it turned out he was a frequent visitor. While the rest of us pretended to browse, Paul went straight to the section containing books on architecture.

'Have you read this one?' he asked Mark Ryan, showing him a slim volume. 'I'll buy it for you.'

But when he put his hand in his pocket, there was no money so Ryan ended up paying for his gift. It was not the first time this had happened, Ryan told me as we trooped out, farewells from the shop women ringing in our ears.

'I've got quite a collection of art books Paul thinks I should read,' he said.

I remembered how in May 1980 I'd run into Keating, then an Opposition frontbencher, just outside the new High Court building which had been officially opened by the Queen the night before.

'What a shocking waste of public money that building is,' I'd said to him, echoing the cynicism that was popular among journalists and some Labor politicians.

'You can never invest too much in the public,' he'd said with an intensity I found surprising.

It was unexpected to have my complacent disparagement challenged. Exciting even. Who else in cosy, self-reinforcing Canberra ever did that? I realised then that there was a lot more to Paul Keating than politics and self-promotion. He proceeded to treat me to a passionate defence of public buildings, arguing that such investment was integral to civic pride. 'That place up there,' he said gesturing up the hill towards where construction of the new Parliament House had just begun, 'will ensure that local manufactures and crafts are maintained. Every element of that building will be a tribute to the Australian people, including the skills of the carpenters and stonemasons and all the craftsmen who will make that place.'

Back then I did not know about Keating's appreciation of music, architecture and the decorative arts, or that he was in the process of becoming a world-renowned collector of furniture and other objects from 1795 to 1799, the *Directoire* period, the final five years of the French Revolution that was succeeded by Napoleon's military rule. For those few years an executive of five men (the Directory) and a bi-cameral legislature governed France. Keating has been known to talk in almost reverential terms about this period, not just as the apogee of classicism, which he considers was reached in 1800, but as a time when many of the political values and freedoms we enjoy today were both established and confirmed. All I knew back in 1980 was that this young Labor politician from the western suburbs of Sydney knew enough to tell me, when he heard I was going to Paris for a holiday, not to worry too much about the Louvre, but to spend every moment I could at the Jeu de Paume.

There were many sides to Paul Keating, I learned during the eleven months I spent working for him. I thought I'd known him well enough, that I'd understood this man to be a unique combination of hard and soft, as well-versed in the finer points of Georgian architecture as in the robust requirements of politics and government. But I came to appreciate that these various strands were not just seemingly conflicting elements that he somehow managed to reconcile; each of them was essential to who he was. He is a complicated and arresting man, capable of moving in the one conversation from the complexities of the design of his beloved superannuation scheme to the unique elements of a pair of American girandoles and then returning to the subject in hand which, if it was me sitting patiently through this exposition, might be how we were going to design a new childcare scheme.

One afternoon as we advisers watched Question Time on the television set outside my office, we heard the Prime Minister refer in one of his answers to 'the laminar flow'. We looked at each other. Nope. No one had a clue. We knew better than to ask him when he returned from the chamber because we knew how draining Question Time was. He always needed some time to recover because, as he told the singer Tom Jones over dinner in Canberra one night in April 1993, it left him exhausted. I was lucky enough to be at that small dinner, and in fact had helped arrange it. The promoter of Jones' 1993 Australian tour, John Hanson, was a childhood friend of mine; he'd got front row tickets at the Royal Theatre in Canberra for Paul and Annita—and me—and then set up the dinner at Belluci's Trattoria in the Canberra suburb of Dickson. Annita and I were very much on the sidelines as the two great performers, who took to each other instantly, compared notes on what it was like to put on a show.[4] Paul admired Jones's voice but, he told him, he thought it was wasted on popular music.

'You should sing opera,' Keating urged the Welshman.

Jones laughed it off, but after this tremendous compliment from the Prime Minister, the two men could not stop talking.

After Question Time that day it took us some time, in those pre-Google days, to learn that the laminar flow is a scientific term that refers to the flow of viscous fluid, in which the various elements—or laminates—remain separate and unique as they move. Keating used the term again when talking with Laurie Oakes on the *Sunday* television program in March 1994. He referred to 'that laminar flow from various parts of the community into employment, one of those laminations has to be from the long term unemployed.'[5] It was a somewhat arcane form of political communication, as not many people would be familiar with the term, but when I thought about it, I realised that it was the perfect language with which to describe Paul Keating himself. He exemplified the laminar flow. Many laminates, or layers, made up his character, his skills and his panoply of expertise and interests. There was no one else like him in politics, and the only person I could think of who had come even close in complexity, erudition and range was Gough Whitlam. The difference between Whitlam and Keating was that Keating was self-taught. Whitlam could converse in Latin but Keating had something else. In delivering the eulogy for an old friend, Keating said: 'With his own eyes and his own taste, and without any specific education in the arts, he developed an acute sense of shape and form both of decoration and of architecture . . .'[6] He was referring to the antiques dealer Bill Bradshaw, but he could just as easily have been talking about himself.

There was also, of course, the Paul Keating who was the familiar tough political operator, who took no prisoners and who often used crude language to bludgeon opponents into shocked submission. This was another essential layer of the whole man. I'd witnessed that side of him plenty of times, but no more spectacularly than in late October 1992, when he summonsed the heads of the television networks to Canberra to demand they 'do something' about screening violent movies. A week earlier, his youngest daughter Alexandra, who was aged seven, had a nightmare after watching on television a movie based on a Stephen King horror story. Keating was outraged that such fare was on early enough in the evening for young children to be exposed—and he said so, very publicly. Some of us in the office felt that parents ought to be supervising their children's television-watching and did not think it was an issue for government, so we were totally unprepared for what followed. There were hundreds of phone calls, letters, and faxes from parents, overwhelmingly from women, and all of them with the same message: Please do something about violence on television. A large number of women wrote: 'I've always hated you, but if you get rid of violence from our television, I will vote for you.' That certainly got our attention. It was quickly decided that the Prime Minister should invite the TV network chiefs to an emergency meeting, to sort out what to do. Because it was judged to be a 'women's issue', I was put in charge—which is how, a few days later, I came to be sitting with the four network chiefs and the head of their industry association, while we waited for the Prime Minister to join us. Unlike today's confected confrontations between Prime Ministers and industry bosses, there were no cameras present and no press release afterwards.

Keating strode in and without handshakes or any other niceties, pointed out to the five men—in extremely crude and forceful terms—that the current licensing arrangements provided extraordinarily profitable protection from competition, and suggested they see it in their interest to do something about this issue of overwhelming public concern. The meeting lasted less than half-an-hour, and ended with the television stations proposing a new category of program rating, the MA, which would denote that a film contained violence and which could only be screened after 9 p.m. It was one of the fastest policy developments I had ever witnessed. Although it might have seemed liked a small change, it did Keating an enormous amount of good because he was seen to have responded to parents' worries—and to have done something about it. The MA rating and 9 p.m. screening time for violent programs is still in force today.

'She came back to Australia, to join my staff, and then set about feminising me, which she knew was basically a hopeless task,' Keating said in 1994, a year after I'd left his office.[7] In fact, he was not 'hopeless' at all. Mostly, he was willing to listen to what I put to him and to grapple with issues that had not previously been on his radar. But it was always easier when he could make a connection from someone or something he already knew. I organised a small roundtable in his office with Susan Ryan, Labor's first female cabinet minister and a former Minister assisting the Prime Minister on the Status of Women; Jennie George who was President of the ACTU; Mary Ann O'Loughlin, and me to talk about women and the economy. It was a good and easy meeting. Keating got on well with all of us. It was a background session, designed to introduce him to current issues in the area rather than ask for specific policy changes, and of course it was closely related to a subject he knew backwards: the economy. I was frustrated that Treasury and the other economic policy analysts never thought to include women's labour-market participation, and the policy tools such as childcare needed to support it, in their analyses or forecasts. It was as if they were oblivious to this major force that helped shape outcomes. Not only that, as I'd found at OSW, they often actively resisted even wanting to consider the impact of millions of women becoming economically active. Keating was not like that. He understood the points we were making and, as he'd tell me many years later, having three daughters in a world where women's fortunes were changing rapidly made him think about the opportunities he wanted them to enjoy—and what might be necessary for governments to do to facilitate that.

Several of the girls Keating had been to school with were now single mothers, struggling after their husbands had walked-out on them. He responded with both anger and sympathy, and understood the government had a role in supporting them. Similarly with carers. He met regularly with his mother, Mim, and a group of her elderly friends. Several of them had ill or disabled husbands to care for, and he could see at first-hand how debilitating and exhausting it was to have to care full-time for another adult human being.

'Let's give the old darlings something,' he'd said during preparation of the 1992/93 budget, one that all current polling suggested was going to be his last. There had been no departmental submission seeking extra money.

But domestic violence was utterly beyond his personal experience. He knew no one who had been a victim, or at least no one who had talked about it. I had to find a way for him to understand what it was like for women who had been subjected to such violence. I also needed to convey to him, and to his office, how big and how terrifying an issue this was for so many Australian women. Not all of them were convinced, despite the results of the research. In his biography of Keating, John Edwards recounts a staff meeting in August where we all argued about the best way for Paul to improve his sagging popularity. Don Watson, Mark Ryan and I—the so-called 'bleeding hearts' of the office—all argued that he needed to talk about subjects other than the economy. I reminded them of the research about violence. But Edwards, Don Russell and the other economists—who Watson had labelled 'the pointy heads'—would have none of it.

'As an economic adviser, I disagreed,' Edwards wrote. 'I said we had not talked nearly enough about the economy, that we had a good story to tell, and that Keating should go after Hewson day after day on economic issues.'[8]

I was exasperated that the economic advisers could not seem to understand that a Prime Minister had to talk about a whole lot of different things. Keating was no longer Treasurer. He could not just talk about the economy. I argued whenever I saw an opportunity that Keating should include references to women in his speeches, and I became quite creative at devising plausible excuses for him to do this. But I often found myself nagging, because without my interventions, it never happened. It was not something the speechwriters did without prompting. I got worried I would wear out my welcome, but I was also annoyed that it was so hard just to do what I thought was the job they had brought me in to do.

At the same time, I was worried about what to propose in response to the research. Childcare and health were relatively straightforward, although probably expensive, but Mary Ann and I were less certain how to achieve something immediate, tangible, credible and effective on violence. We decided to make it an agenda item for the Premiers' Conference in October. The premiers had never discussed violence against women, so this was at least a gesture of our intention to take it seriously. There was, I discovered, a Violence Against Women Strategy document that had been tortuously developed by a group of Commonwealth and state bureaucrats. OSW wanted the Prime Minister to launch it. Getting him to launch a dry bureaucratic 'strategy' seemed inadequate, insulting almost, given the passion with which the women in the focus groups had talked about violence. We had to do something big. This would do for now but it was not enough.

I thought the best way to introduce Keating to the issue would be for him to meet some ordinary women who could tell him their stories about suffering domestic abuse. That would be more effective than any amount of briefing I could give him. I decided we would arrange for him to visit a women's refuge. Something very low-key, no media, no publicity of any kind. The best place to do it, I figured, would be in his electorate.

I rang the area coordinating group (few individual refuges were in the phone book, for security reasons) and explained what I hoped to do. The woman who took my call was suspicious; she did not want to get caught up in any publicity stunt. I did my best to reassure her; just three or four people, I said, and no pressure at all on the residents of the refuge if they did not want to meet the Prime Minister. She said she'd have to take it to her committee.

'Fair enough,' I said. 'When does it next meet?'

'In three months' time.'

I explained we could not wait that long, but thanks anyway.

Next I tried a Catholic refuge, run by St Vincent de Paul in Sydney's Arncliffe. Again, I thought Paul might feel more comfortable if he could identify with the religion of the people who ran the place. But when I visited I found that not a single resident spoke English. There were Vietnamese women, Turkish women, Chinese women, dozens of them with their children, most of them recently arrived in the country. I was stunned by the appalling realisation that for so many women, their first experience of Australia was brutality at the hands of their husbands. These men were no doubt angry, bitter and frustrated at how they were being treated by their new country, but it was their wives and kids who were bearing the brunt. But this was not the right place for what I had in mind. There were just too many other issues involved and, besides, the women would need interpreters. This was not the way for Keating to hear women telling their own stories.

In the end, I found a place in suburban Perth. It was a modest dwelling and the residents were all young working-class women; Keating would be able to talk easily with them, I thought. I explained to the very accommodating woman who ran the place that they need not do anything special, that we would be there for an hour at the most. The federal police would come the day before to check the place out—that was a routine security requirement—but on the day it would just be Paul and me, with possibly one of the advisers and a federal policeman, who would stay in the car with the driver.

'Offer him a cup of tea, if you like,' I said. 'But don't go to any trouble.'

'There was just one thing,' the refuge manager said. 'We've got an application for funding in. Do you think you can help with that?'

I promised her I'd do what I could.

It turned out Keating was going to be in Perth in just a few weeks. We'd go to the refuge on 8 December 1992. The day before, I went there with federal police officer Peter Holder, a friendly relaxed guy with a wide smiling face, who immediately put the women at their ease.

'You see,' I said to them as we left, 'there's nothing to be nervous about.'

As it turned out, I was the one who should have been anxious.

As we drove into the street the next day I had trouble recognising the house. Then I saw a huddle of people and a couple of cameras.

'I'm really sorry,' I said to Paul. 'This was supposed to be a totally private visit.'

Instead, we had a reception committee. The mayor was there, and the local state member of Parliament and Stephen Smith, who had been on Paul's staff when I'd first arrived but was now a full-time candidate for the federal seat of Perth. (He would win the seat and go on to be Minister for Foreign Affairs and Defence Minister during the Rudd and Gillard governments.) And, being politicians, these people could not go anywhere without the media.

'It's just local stuff,' Smith assured me. 'You can't expect us to ignore that the Prime Minister is visiting our area.'

It got worse. The house had been freshly painted, inside and out, and did not even remotely resemble the run-down place I'd described to Paul.

The bedraggled backyard had been transformed into a gaily decorated party scene: umbrellas provided shade to brand-new wooden tables that were stacked with party pies and cupcakes and glasses of orange cordial. There were balloons everywhere. The children who a few days earlier had been sullen or aggressive, now tore around with the excitement that all kids bring to parties. As for their mothers, they were all in their best party frocks, most had had their hair done, they wore makeup. They looked nothing like the defeated women I'd met just the day before. Most of them had cameras.

'I told you there was no need to go to any trouble,' I said weakly.

'Do you think I wanted to meet him looking the way I did the other day?' one of them said to me. 'I've never met a Prime Minister before.'

She had a point. Paul was soon posing with them, cup of tea in hand. Later I was able to get him to one side with a couple of the women.

'Just tell him your stories,' I encouraged them. 'He wants to understand domestic violence.'

But these women did not want to sully their meeting with the country's leader by sharing their painful stories. The festive atmosphere was totally at odds with the private terrors they had experienced. How to convey on a sunny afternoon against the laughter of, at least momentarily, happy children the sickening sound of a fist to a face, the screams, the bruises and broken bones, the despair?

The whole exercise was a total failure, I thought. I had not enabled Paul to hear the stories that I thought would aid his understanding of what was happening with so many Australian women and why it was so urgent that we do something.

⊷⊶

Developing a childcare policy was almost simple, by comparison. Mary Ann and I began brainstorming. We asked OSW for policy options and informed PM&C and Treasury that we were looking for ideas to reduce the cost of care for families on moderate incomes, who did not qualify for fee relief. We were not attracted to the idea of tax deductibility of fees which was being pushed by the Women Lawyers' Association and other high-earning professional women. Heather Carmody, from the Business Council of Australia's Council for Equal Opportunity, told me that everyone she talked to in private industry wanted tax deductibility. I was sympathetic to their argument that childcare was an essential expense in earning an income, and to the double standard whereby men could claim professional expenses on their taxes. Nevertheless, Mary Ann and I felt equity principles took precedence. This issue had long been debated within the women's movement and the lines were clearly drawn. Full deductibility was hugely expensive and would divert too much of the childcare dollar into the purses of high-earning women. At the same time, we both thought that if we could somehow use the tax system to recompense at least part of the cost of childcare, that would be some acknowledgement that it was a work-related expense. We were determined that childcare should no longer be seen—by the government or the community—as a welfare issue. Childcare was an economic issue, a necessary cost to women's ability to earn an income, either through employment or preparing for work through study. We also wanted to take away from childcare the inevitable stigma that attached to welfare programs.

Early in September at a meeting with Don Russell, Mark Ryan and Ric Simes, Mary Ann and I put on the table the bones of a possible package. I loved working with Mary Ann. Not just because she had such an acute social policy brain and could always figure out a solution to what we wanted to do, but she was always so exuberant. With her, doing wonky policy was never boring. It was fun. Our proposed package would include a major expansion of supply—that is, more places, a rebate for childcare spending above the level of current fee relief, an accreditation package, and the possibility of a fee-relief credit card. We had figures that showed that of the 1.8 million families with children under twelve, only 230,000 were in the government childcare system, and there was an estimated unmet demand for 540,000 places. The Tax Office had provided an estimate that as many as 200,000 people would be likely to benefit from the tax rebate. At the same time, I raised the possibility of cashing out the Dependent Spouse Rebate (DSR), converting the tax rebate men received for their stay-at-home wives to a cash payment for the women. The DSR was loathed by feminists, because it was a deterrent to women working; it gave high-earning husbands a tax benefit (in addition to the benefits they received from having a full-time wife doing housework, childcare, shopping, etc.). We also included a proposal for a $1000 one-off payment to new mothers; 'the baby grand', Mary Ann called it. That one did not survive the cut, but the meeting did agree we would have departments look at the cost of providing total coverage: childcare for all who needed it by 2000. We were going to do something very big.

But it had to be kept secret. There was enormous opposition within the Labor Party to the notion of a tax rebate because it was seen, erroneously in my view, as the thin end of the wedge towards tax deductibility. In fact, it was the opposite. A rebate was a flat amount and thus of greater benefit to lower-income earners, whereas tax deductibility, especially for the total costs of childcare, could significantly reduce the overall tax burden of higher-earners. I hoped the rebate would come to be seen as a more equitable alternative that would take the heat out of the push for full deductibility. Some purists thought that the only policy solution was to simply directly fund more centres. I had lunch with Neal Blewett, an old friend and a former political scientist—he had taught me politics at the University of Adelaide in the 1960s—who had been given the big ministry of Social Security by Keating. He reminded me of how toxic childcare politics still were within the Labor Party: 'I suggested there is some hangover from ferocious Walshian attitudes,' Blewett wrote of our meeting in his political memoir, 'but pointed out also that childcare is an expensive program and in these tight budgetary times restrictive attitudes still predominate.'[9] I told him that, given the views of women across Australia that affordable childcare was needed, the government had to do something substantial. When I mentioned we were thinking of a rebate, Blewett responded that his 'worry' was that a rebate would benefit the better off and leave no funds to expand fee-relief. I explained this was not the case but Blewett's reaction was salutary. If someone of his progressive views, whose portfolio required him to support disadvantaged groups, had qualms about our proposal, how would we fare with the full cabinet? Contrary to the myth invented by some on the right of the ALP, that Labor governments were putty in the hands of feminists, when it came to childcare policy, almost the reverse was true. We were portrayed as 'special interests', on a par with lobbyists for business or mining, annoying intrusions into the political conversation. Anyone would have thought that the evil feminists wanted to put those childcare billions in their own pockets. In fact, we were trying to make women's lives easier as they contributed to the economy—*and* kept the population going and the home fires burning. Our only leverage was the need to attract votes from women, and we had to make that case to the PMO and, of course, the Prime Minister. If he was on board, everyone else would fall into line.

We had the support of the ACTU which, without knowing the details of what we were planning, argued strongly for more support for childcare. The ALP was another matter. There was no love lost between the National Secretariat and the PMO. Bob Hogg, the National Secretary, was concerned that no one in the PMO had any campaign experience. The PMO felt Hogg was too negative and not willing to cut Keating any slack. Nor did the ALP see any need to conduct a special campaign for women; there was not a single woman on the ALP Campaign Committee. My activities were dismissed with derision. But, the government was seeing some light. Wayne Swan, the Queensland State Secretary of the ALP, who would successfully contest the federal seat of Lilley in the next election, reported to the PMO that the Goods and Services Tax (GST) was turning out to be a major negative for the Liberals. Keating's image was seen as softening somewhat (I liked to take a little credit for that), and he was benefiting from a 'devil you know' feeling, as voters contemplated the unknown terrors of John Hewson's GST.

I consulted widely, while not being able to say exactly what we were considering. The word had got out, though, so while I would not confirm that a tax rebate was on the table, I was willing to canvass the views of key constituencies. In late September I met with Eva Cox and Helen Leonard from the Women's Electoral Lobby. Eva was very opposed to a rebate. Instead, she suggested, why not have a tax credit that could either be added to a woman's Family Allowances or deducted from her tax liability. I could not see a significant difference between a credit and a rebate, especially as we were hoping to be able to offer it as a fortnightly cash payment (perhaps able to be collected from Medicare offices) for women who did not want to wait until tax time to claim the benefit. But I was encouraged that there might be scope to reach an accommodation with the women's movement.

On 9 February, just two days after he'd called an election for 13 March, Keating launched his economic policy at the National Press Club in Canberra. It was a major set-piece speech of the campaign, as important in many ways as the formal campaign launch that would come a fortnight later. The central announcements were a total surprise, even to some of his cabinet colleagues. There was a dramatic cut in company tax, development assistance for business—and a major boost for childcare. The Prime Minister announced a tax rebate of 30 per cent of the costs of childcare, up to a maximum of $28 a week for one child in work-related childcare. Commenting in his diary, Neal Blewett described the policy as 'not a particularly egalitarian proposal' but 'electorally smart'.[10] I thought he was flat-out wrong in not seeing that it was an egalitarian response to how to reimburse women for their childcare costs. There were other elements to the package, including a cashing out of the dependent spouse rebate (which was never to happen; the DSR was one of those policies so beloved by senior bureaucrats, many of whom were beneficiaries, that no matter what governments promised, it never went away). Mary Ann and I were ecstatic. We had got what we thought was a fair and sensible policy *and* it had been announced as economic policy. This was in some ways as significant as the policy itself.

In his book about Keating, Don Watson writes that the Prime Minister complained that I 'forced' him to do things he did not want to do. I'm still deciding whether to be offended or complimented by the notion that I could 'force' Paul Keating to do anything, but perhaps what he had in mind when he said this was the speech to launch the National Agenda for Women on 10 February 1993. What had been intended as a routine speech had taken on a new significance once the election was called; it was now a major campaign event. I had written a speech that made several announcements we hoped would appeal to the women in the focus groups, including one that tangentially addressed the issue of violence. The night before, Mark Ryan, Don Watson and I had gone over the speech and decided what the 'grab' should be. This is the section of the speech that would be highlighted for the television cameras. There was no guarantee they would follow our advice or, if they did, whether their news directors would put it to air, but it was usually a safe bet that the television-watching population that night would see on the news the 'grab' we had selected.

Mark wanted us to go very hard on some remarks made in January 1993 by Judge Derek Bollen, of the South Australian Supreme Court, who when instructing the jury in a rape in marriage trial had said: 'There is, of course, nothing wrong with a husband faced with his wife's refusal to have inter-course, in attempting in an acceptable way, to persuade her to change her mind, and that might involve a measure of rougher than usual handling.'[11]

'I was shocked,' I had written into the speech, 'to hear . . .' and I'd quoted the latter few words and then put in our announcement about gender training for members of the judiciary.

When Paul read the speech at Kirribilli House, just a couple of hours before he was due to deliver it, he baulked at this section. He did not want to discuss it with me, but he told Mark in extremely colourful language that he would not say it. After some to-ing and fro-ing, Paul said to me:

'I don't want to say "shocked". That sounds too strong. Can't I say "surprised", or something like that?'

'Say what you like,' I said.

I was angry that he had not read the speech sooner, giving me no time to rewrite it. I was also angry that he was unwilling to strongly condemn the judge's atrocious comments. I did not tell him that the speech had already been distributed to the media. That would have meant another fight as we were supposed to have the PM's clearance before release, but when he was late reading them we often had no choice. All speeches were marked 'To Be Checked Against Delivery'. I just had to hope the media would not make a big deal out of the Prime Minister watering down his comments on the subject of rape.

We arrived at Bankstown where the place was absolutely packed, and the goodwill towards Paul was palpable. Quentin Bryce, the Sex Discrimination Commissioner and Elizabeth Evatt, who was President of the Australian Law Reform Commission, as well as a group of Labor women MPs and senators greeted him. I hung back at the rear of the hall as he was guided to the stage. I began to tense up as he got to the key part of the speech:

'I was shocked,' he said.

I relaxed. He'd said it. Thank goodness, I thought to myself, no chance the media can make anything of this now. But then I realised that the room had erupted and it was quickly apparent that Paul really was shocked: by the cheers and wild applause that greeted his comment. He went on to read the lines about gender-based training for judges and magistrates and the room went crazy again. He looked out at the sea of yelling, clapping women and said it again, only this time with the kind of pizzaz that only Paul Keating can produce:

'It's back to school for judges and magistrates.'

I wish I could have written a line like that. It got the crowd on its feet again. Paul smiled, repeated the line—and went on with the speech. The 'grab' was all over television that night, and women columnists and opinion makers responded positively to Paul's comments on the recalcitrant judge.

When Keating went on to say that while he could have made his major childcare announcement today, rather than in his economic statement, he had decided 'it is time childcare was included amongst our mainstream issues', there was further wild applause. Then a standing ovation at the words: 'The time is long past, as far as I am concerned, where childcare was tagged as "a women's issue" or a "welfare issue" and only attracted the crumbs from the table where the budget banquet was enjoyed.' I felt hugely vindicated. Not only had Keating agreed to the massive childcare announcement being included in the economic speech, but now he was getting almost hysterical applause from a crowd of 600 women. It was a big moment. We had succeeded in wrestling women's policy away from welfare and into the economic mainstream, where of course it belonged, and the significance of this was certainly not lost on the audience.

Today, when talk about childcare and paid parental leave is mostly couched within the debate about women's workforce participation, this does not sound like a big deal. In the early 1990s, there was still far from a consensus that mothers even be in the workforce, let alone that policy could boost economic activity by facilitating this. The *Australian* editorialised in response to Keating's announcement that encouraging women into employment, as this policy was designed to do, was 'a strange argument to make at a time of record unemployment'.[12] Nor was there support from the media for treating childcare as an economic policy lever. I'd travelled on the press bus a few days later and was challenged by the *Sydney Morning Herald*'s Tom Burton. He first berated me for including childcare in the economic statement, and then he got stuck into me for steering Keating towards 'middle-class welfare'. This would not be the last time I would have this argument with journalists, but that day while I tried to maintain a sunny exterior, inside I seethed with anger and frustration. What was behind this savage opposition to including women's work, and its necessary supports, in a mainstream economic policy? Why were these journalists so obtuse that they could not see the broad economic benefits of supporting mothers returning to work? How come they never denounced benefits such as tax-deductible conferences in places like Venice, or barristers being able to depreciate their libraries as 'middle-class welfare'? Why was it only policies that benefited women that were disparaged in this way? I could not answer these questions—and neither could they—because there were no rational answers. It was prejudice, pure and simple.

I'd also included a couple of other announcements in the women's speech. The most important, to my mind, was the establishment of a longitudinal study of women's health. I'd heard about a similar study in the United States and it seemed to me that gathering vital data about women's health and well-being, over time, would provide an invaluable tool for informing policy for decades to come. I worked closely with Jenny Macklin who was the senior adviser to Brian Howe, the Deputy Prime Minister and Minister for Health, to ensure the project had the backing of all the right people in the health field. Jenny, of course, went on to become a distinguished federal member of Parliament, a senior member of the Rudd and Gillard cabinets, and the first woman deputy leader of the ALP. This was not an announcement that would bring an audience to its feet, or even be reported in the press, but it was a solid and important initiative and a further response to women's expressed concerns about health issues. It is one of the things I accomplished during my time in the PMO of which I am still the most proud. The Australian Longitudinal Study of Women's Health (ALSWH) is now run as a collaboration between the federal Department of Health and the Universities of Newcastle and Queensland. Since 1996, it has tracked the physical and emotional health and important life-events (marriage, birth etc.) of 58,000 Australian women throughout their lives. A new, younger cohort was added in 2012.[13] The data is shared with 650 researchers and is linked to Medicare and Pharmaceutical Benefits Scheme usage, to test take-up of services and medications relating to health issues ranging from depression to weight gain. It is almost impossible to exaggerate the ongoing benefits for Australian women's health of this research. Fortunately it has won international acclaim for successive governments which have funded its continuance for more than two decades.[14]

This was just one example of relatively small, but carefully targeted, policy announcements on women's health in direct response to women in the focus groups. A few months earlier, Brian Howe had announced a $64 million program for the Early Detection of Breast Cancer and named Dr Mary Rickard to be the public face of a campaign that, within five years, would be able to screen 860,000 Australian women. This followed an earlier decision to allocate $23 million for a cervical cancer-screening program and to appoint Dr Edith Weisberg as the spokeswoman for that. I had arranged for Howe to make these two announcements to a group of women's magazine editors in Sydney—in the cabinet room in the federal government offices. There had never before been a media briefing there, so I was pretty sure the editors would all turn up—just so they could say they had been there—and they did. Once the official business was over, I had a quiet word with Nancy Pilcher who was the editor-in-chief of *Vogue*.

'Would you be interested in an interview with Annita Keating?'

'We've been trying for months,' she said, smiling widely.

It took several months as magazines have very long lead times, but the March issue of *Vogue* featured a spread of photographs of the Prime Minister's wife looking ultra-stylish and, sensationally, her usual tangle of curls replaced by long, straight hair. All the media picked-up the photographs. They were reproduced on the front pages of all the newspapers and featured on television news bulletins meaning that few Australians would not be aware that Annita Keating, mother of four, could hold her own in the country's top fashion magazine, wearing Australian apparel and looking absolutely stunning. I'd also been instrumental in talking to Kathy Bail, editor of *Rolling Stone* magazine, about featuring the Prime Minister on the cover. I'd gone with him to the photo shoot, at Lorrie Graham's Surry Hills loft studio, where Keating was surprisingly receptive to being treated like a rock star. Perhaps it reminded him of his early days in Sydney, when he'd managed a band called the Ramrods, before he'd opted for a career in politics. The cover showed him looking supercool, peeking out over the top of a pair of Ray-Bans. Inside was an interview conducted by the musician Reg Mombassa, and writers Linda Jaivin and Peter Corris. The Prime Minister stated that he did not think marijuana should be legalised and revealed that his favourite Beatle was Paul McCartney. No surprises there. The PMO was ecstatic. 'Annita in *Vogue* and Paul in *Rolling Stone* . . .' enthused one staff member to the *Sydney Morning Herald*, mocking the Opposition efforts with far less-groovy publications.[15]

My final media effort was with *Woman's Day*, which had been only too happy to accept my offer of unprecedented shots of the Keating family relaxing on the lawns at Kirribilli House. The children were young and, like their parents, arrestingly photogenic. They even had a good-looking dog. These media gigs were not a substitute for policy initiatives, and were never intended to be. They merely added a few more pieces to the mosaic of altering perceptions about Paul Keating, especially by women. They were not artificial; instead they revealed things about Keating and his wife and family that were apparent to anyone who was close to them, but which had never before been on public view. I thought it was totally appropriate for the people who would be deciding who should govern the country for the next three years to know more about the Prime Minister, to see his lighter side and to watch him interact with the family he adored. It was part of who he was, but it was a part that he had always been reluctant to share before.

———

Paul looked exhausted and dispirited when he arrived at the State Theatre in Market Street, Sydney at midday on Sunday 28 February 1993, for what was ostensibly the launch of Labor's arts policy, but in fact was a concert to honour him. I was waiting at the kerb with the movie actor Sam Neill, who would escort Paul and Annita to their seats. Garry McDonald was there too, in character as Norman Gunston, getting in the way with his camera crew, trying to engage with the Prime Minister. As he emerged from the car, Paul swatted at him as if he were a troublesome insect.

'I don't think I've got a twenty-minute speech in me today, Annie,' Paul said as I hurriedly briefed him on what to expect inside and handed him some notes Don Watson had prepared.

I followed them into the theatre; it was dark, except for the spotlight on a lone Circus Oz aerialist who, clinging to a rope, swung daringly across the void above the heads of the audience. He was a bit like Paul Keating the politician, who was also a high-wire act performer, putting on a dazzling show, taking risks, no net. You could see, as the Prime Minister watched the brave performer swing from side-to-side in that cavernous space, that he felt something of a connection. He seemed to perk-up a bit. Then the audience realised that Keating had arrived and there was a mighty roar. A tumultuous wave of sound swirled around the room that bore within it the affection, the admiration, the gratitude and, also, the fear of what was to come if this man were to be swept from office and replaced by John Hewson. That morning, when he had spied Sam Neill handing out pro-Labor pamphlets at the Double Bay shopping centre, the Liberal leader had threatened him with the words, 'You will never work in this town again.' The applause was raw and raucous, and it bore Keating down the aisle towards the front row seat from where he would watch the performance. You could see his shoulders lift as he surveyed the screaming adoring crowd, a huge grin breaking across his face. He sat down, and the show began.

The concert started with a short piece by Russell Page from Bangarra, the notable Aboriginal dance company. Then, following a scene-setting speech from leading actor Bryan Brown, there was a short, sizzling dance by Jan Pinkerton and Paul Mercurio, the star of the current Baz Luhrmann hit film *Strictly Ballroom*. Mercurio was wearing his trademark white singlet, the same one that—unwashed and still smelling of sweat—would be auctioned-off at the end of the week, along with many other significant items, including a Prime Ministerial tie, to raise money to pay for the costs of this extraordinary show.[16]

It had been made to happen by a high-powered group of people from various parts of the arts industry who decided that, whatever the election outcome, they wanted to thank Keating for the support he had given them throughout his public life. Arts for Labor, as they decided to call themselves, first met at the Birchgrove, Sydney home of publicist Rae Francis. I was invited and soon found myself the liaison person between the PMO and the group. Its core members included Anne Britton, the federal secretary of the Media Arts and Entertainment Alliance; film producers Erroll Sullivan, Michael Thornhill and Hal McElroy; literary agents Rosemary Creswell and Jane Cameron; the Writers' Guild's Jeanette Paramour; and Michael Lynch, who was general manager of the Sydney Theatre Company.

They had met regularly over a couple of months and conceived a show that would be part-performance, part-tribute, showcasing the best of Australian arts in an unprecedented act of gratitude. One Saturday I drove up to the northern beaches with Erroll Sullivan to Bryan Brown's home to persuade him to lend his support by emceeing the event. Once he was on board, the other big names quickly followed.

After the first performances, the actor Robyn Nevin read excerpts from scores of testimonials from grateful recipients of government financial support for the arts, including almost every single living person who had benefited from a 'Keating'. This was the unofficial name given to the generous two-year Australian Artists Creative Fellowships, instigated by Keating in 1989 when he was still Treasurer, to provide financial security for mature artists across all genres. Between 1989 and 1996, 65 artists received Keatings. They included writer Frank Moorhouse, who used his to produce two of the books of his impressive League of Nations trilogy; theatre director Neil Armfield, who created *Cloudstreet*, based on Tim Winton's novel and which became one of the most successful theatrical productions ever staged in Australia; poets Les Murray and John Tranter, who produced significant collections; writer Kate Grenville, who wrote *The Idea of Perfection* which won the UK Orange Prize for Women's fiction; and a host of other Australian greats, such as Emily Kame Kngwarreye, Dorothy Hewett, Thea Astley, Richard Meale, Geoffrey Tozer, John Bell, Reg Livermore and Garth Welch.

Paul Keating understood the concept, and the value, of 'soft power' long before it was touted as a tool of diplomacy. The 'Keatings' cost a total of $11.7 million over their lifetime (they were abolished by the Howard government). Compare the value of this investment in Australian creativity and its value to the nation (even if it cannot be measured with any precision) with, for instance, the embarrassing and unsuccessful tourist campaign on television in 2006, that featured a bikini-wearing blonde woman on a beach shouting 'Where the bloody hell are you?' and which cost $180 million.

That afternoon in the State Theatre the words were followed by more performance: the Hermannsburg Ladies Choir—a group of middle-aged Aboriginal women who had never before travelled from the former mission in Central Australia, and who were brought to Sydney by Roger Foley; Jane Rutter did a sexy flute performance; Reg Mombassa performed with his band Mental as Anything; and a vocal ensemble, The Song Company. All the while, Roger Foley, in his capacity as lighting-master Ellis D. Fogg, projected brightly coloured psychedelic images onto a screen at the rear of the stage. Mardi Gras, Sydney's boisterous annual gay pride march, had been on the night before and quite a few members of the audience had not yet been to bed. There was a lot of nervous energy in the room, and the kind of low hysteria brought about by exhaustion and anxiety. It was almost hypnotic in its allure.

I had been living in New York for almost seven years and, I realised, that despite my frequent visits home and the American tours to the Big Apple of everyone from Midnight Oil to the Sydney Symphony Orchestra, I was totally out-of-touch with Australian creativity. I watched spellbound. I had never seen anything like it. Not just the array of talent, although that was impressive and stirring; it was also the generosity and the gratitude. This was so different from the cynical and backbiting Sydney arts community I remembered from the late 1970s, it told me something was happening in this country. Something good, that perhaps I wanted to be part of.

The final performance, by several more men from Bangarra, was a moving reminder of the ancient culture on which everything else we do rests. When they had finished, Keating walked onto the stage. He was a radically different man from the one who had dragged himself out of his car an hour earlier. He stepped lightly, he was grinning. You could tell that he was profoundly moved—by the show itself, and that it had all been put on for him. He said later that it was the turning point in the campaign. He was suddenly energised—and motivated. He was not going to let-down these people, nor this country. As Don Watson describes the event in his book, '. . . the prime minister could not stop smiling and bowing.'[17]

He threw aside the notes Watson had prepared and launched into a passionate address. 'There's no way the Liberal Party would understand this,' he said of the performances he had just witnessed. 'They don't understand that the Arts resonate the opportunity and energy of Australia . . . they don't see its importance and they never have.'

He told his avid audience that 'even though we pulled the budgets back in the '80s we always kept the Arts budget growing, and we did because we know to let the Arts down is to let ourselves down'.

'How many countries have had the chance to put together a new society,' he said. 'Here we are on the oldest piece of crust on the earth's face, with one of the oldest nations of the earth, Aboriginal Australians, with ourselves as though we were towed on a raft into one of the most interesting parts of the world, next door to a civilisation 900 years old, 180 million people—what a phenomenal opportunity we have to develop a new country, a multicultural country, a new society, with new expression, new feelings, and new resonances.' He spoke for 40 minutes, and as he unfolded his theme, drawing on historian Manning Clark's language, of Labor as the enlargers 'out there feeling the resonances and pushing out the boundaries', something in me responded. I considered, for the first time, whether I might want to stay in Australia if Keating won.

When it was over, an exuberant throng of performers joined Keating on stage. The newspapers the next morning showed photographs of the Prime Minister in his slightly rumpled light grey Zegna suit, standing close between two Bangarra dancers who were wearing not much more than lap-laps and a bit of body paint. It was an arresting image: representatives of this ancient civilisation beside the modern man who, if he won, would follow through on his promises in his already famous Redfern speech[18] two months earlier, that Australia's first inhabitants deserved to be treated with dignity.

The Saturday after next he'd be on another stage, in the Bankstown Sports Club in the western suburbs, in the heart of his electorate, again unable to stop grinning as he stepped onto the stage and proclaimed:

'This is the sweetest victory of all.'

The night before his entire staff, including the cops and the drivers, had gathered at a Chinese restaurant in The Rocks. Most of us wore 'Keating is Right' badges. Don Russell had them made as a take on the 'Lang is Right' buttons worn in 1932 by supporters of the controversial NSW premier, who had been Paul's political mentor. Unlike the originals, our buttons did not bear an image of the Prime Minister; just simple white letters on a solid black background. We wore them with irony, and to distract from the tension we all felt. When Paul spoke, he said that Labor 'might be able to win'. Unlike at ALP headquarters, which had written us off and briefed a gullible national media accordingly, there were pockets of optimism in the PMO. Weeks earlier, on the Sunday that Keating had called the election, when along with all the advisers I had gone into the office, I was overcome with gut-churning apprehension. Elections can change everything and this one could very well alter the course of Australian history but now I was convinced, after being based in Sydney for the weeks before the election and talking to a lot of different people, that Keating could win. I had even accepted a $1000 bet from Barbara Riley-Smith's husband, who was an out-and-out Lib. If Labor lost, I did not know how I would be able to pay him. Perhaps that's why I was so fervent when I yelled out at the dinner, 'You're going to win, you're going to win!' 'Let's hope so, Annie,' Keating had replied. 'If we win, it will be the win of the century.'[19]

The early votes from Tasmania the next afternoon (they were an hour ahead of the mainland, due to daylight saving having ended early) were promising. We staffers mooched around in a room somewhere out the back of the Sports Club, trying to keep our hopes contained while the numbers guys crunched furiously with their computers. I found it hard to breathe, and not just because the ghastly carpet had absorbed decades of spilt beer and cigarette smoke. As the night wore on and certainty grew, we allowed ourselves a few self-congratulatory smirks, and then the key advisers were gathering around Paul while he went over his speech. Just before he walked onto the stage, I grabbed his arm.

'Don't forget to thank the sheilas,' I urged him.

The crowd eventually calmed and settled back to hear Paul Keating claim his win and to tell them: 'This is a victory for the true believers, the people who in difficult times have kept the faith . . .' His speech that night was subsequently criticised for being insufficiently humble, and for suggesting that he would govern only for those who had voted for him, but it did not sound that way on the night. At least, not to me or, it seemed, the rest of the team. We were exultant. He had won.

And then he said, 'an extra special vote of thanks for the women of Australia who voted for us believing in the policies of this government.'

Although I had asked him to, I could scarcely believe he was saying it. Putting us at the heart of who he was and how he would govern.

Later that night a group of us gathered at Zanzibar's in Kellett Street, Kings Cross which was one of the few restaurants in Sydney to stay open into the early hours. Paul and Annita, Laurie and Trish Brereton, Baz Luhrmann and Catherine Martin (who'd designed the backdrop curtain for Bankstown), Tara Morice (the star of *Strictly Ballroom*), Mark Ryan, Don Watson, maybe a few others—and me. It was late, well past 3 a.m., when the doors of the restaurant burst open and in came another bunch of revellers. We looked up at them when we heard a woman scream. It was Anna Cronin, Hewson's chief-of-staff. Of all the gin joints, the team we had literally just defeated in the 'unwinnable election' had chosen this one. They looked at us and fled.

On the way back from Bankstown I'd rung Chip who was in Washington DC, with ABC journalists Heather Ewart and Barrie Cassidy, at an Embassy party where the diplomats had clearly expected, and seemingly wanted, a different result. I had trouble telling Chip how I felt. To say I was happy would be trite and insufficient. I had turned 48 the day before the election, but I'd barely stopped to acknowledge this milestone. Nor did I now, as I was so overwhelmed by waves of relief, of gratitude, of pure joy that I actually did not feel a thing.

I offered to spend my final couple of weeks in the PMO organising a special celebration to mark the extraordinary election win. Paul agreed and no one else demurred, not at first anyway, but the immediate feedback from ALP headquarters was that my proposed True Believers Victory Dinner, to be held in the Great Hall at Parliament House on 23 March, was 'too American' and, at $100 a ticket, plus the cost of travel to Canberra, 'too expensive'. I argued that some American traditions were worth imitating, and celebrating an unexpected victory with grace and style was one of them. I suggested we allocate a certain number of freebies for party supporters, to be subsidised by the more affluent attendees. I promised that I could bring in a classy event that would pay for itself. I got grudging agreement and then I went to work.

I had a very grand plan and I knew exactly who could help me bring it off: the team who had delivered the Arts for Labor concert at the State Theatre in Sydney, less than a month earlier. Most of them were showbiz people, and not only did they know exactly what was needed, but they were very motivated: Keating's victory had invigorated the whole sector. They knew now that they had a future and they were more than happy to help pay tribute to the man who would deliver it. Roger Foley agreed to dress and light the room, and someone persuaded Yothu Yindi, the Indigenous band led by Mandawuy Yunupingu, that was the hottest group in Australia at the time, to perform for free.

With the physical arrangements in these capable hands, there was nothing for me to do on the day, which was just as well because Keating was finalising the new cabinet that afternoon and I was determined to have my say about what happened with the women's portfolio. It had to be in cabinet, I argued forcefully to Don Russell, to avoid the absurd and humiliating current situation where OSW staff members had access to cabinet documents—such as the budget—they could not show their minister because she was not in cabinet. There was currently just one woman in cabinet, Ros Kelly, and I was dead-set against her getting the job for the simple reason she had never shown any interest in women's issues. I could not see her as the kind of advocate who would ensure the extraordinary election promises became policy and were faithfully implemented. Keating agreed, according to Don Watson's account of what happened, that Kelly lacked the 'gravitas' for the job.[20] The solution was unusual but, to me, obvious. Keating was considering promoting the talented Bob McMullan, a former ALP National Secretary who was now a senator from the ACT. McMullan was unaligned which meant he missed out on promotion in a factional deal. The only way to do it would be to expand the cabinet to nineteen members, something which both Keating and Don Russell were reluctant to do, but nor were they willing to remove an existing cabinet minister, so they had to give way. McMullan was summonsed, and Don Watson and I had the job of telling him he was being promoted and would have the portfolios of Administrative Services, Arts and Women. To my absolutely astonishment, and then rage, he said he'd take Arts and Admin Services, but not Women.

'This is not a smorgasbord, mate,' I barely stopped myself from saying.

McMullan argued it would be 'a political mistake' to put a man in charge of women's policy. I countered by saying there were respected precedents: Bob Ellicott and Tom McVeigh had both held the portfolio, which was then located in Home Affairs, during the Fraser years. But while I was trying to make the political argument that the portfolio needed the status someone credible like McMullan would bring to it, I was called to the phone where disastrous news awaited me.

The unions in Parliament House were demanding they be paid for the evening's event. They would not actually be working because Roger Foley's team of volunteers was doing all the big electrical and other jobs involved in lighting the room, and the band's roadies would manage the instruments on stage. The in-house catering and wait staff were, of course, on the job and would be paid their usual rates, but I was being held hostage by union rules that insisted the electricians and some other technicians be paid for work being done on their site.

That evening Paul and Annita walked into the candle-lit room, packed with more than 600 people from all around the country, to the music of 'The Jupiter Suite' from Gustav Holst's *The Planets*. It was exactly what I'd hoped for: stirring and emotional, glamorous and celebratory. The Great Hall had never looked so magical, but I was in no mood to party. McMullan had held his ground. He was in cabinet, but women's policy was not. I had the Parliament House unions' bill to contend with and now, I was discovering, although the Yothu Yindi band members were 'free', their roadies and other crew were not. I'd spent an awful hour on the phone to the ALP that afternoon, begging for money. They had been against the dinner from the outset, and even though Bob Hogg was seated at the top table, next to the Prime Minister, he was far from happy. Some MPs present attacked the event, from the safety of several decades worth of hindsight, as 'too much self-glorification'.[21] Most of those present, however, laughed and revelled, drank and danced. Keating spoke of 'the great Australian democracy' his party would deliver, and especially thanked the Arts community 'who stood up and were counted'. He reached out to Hogg and to Bob Hawke, acknowledging the previous election victories that had allowed his own. Hawke stood and waved as he absorbed the adulation of the crowd. Later, a *Sunday Telegraph* gossip item commented that Paul Keating 'stole the show ... dancing to "Achy Breaky Heart"'.[22] While the True Believers partied into the night, I sat on the floor at the back of the room, sobbing with humiliation and rage. Every so often, someone would tap me on the shoulder and ask me to approve 'another bottle of Bundy for the band'. The final bill for the evening was $35,000, which the ALP had to pick up. Every account of that evening blames me for hubris and for overspending. Even 23 years later, in 2016, a new book about Keating felt it necessary to point to my 'misjudgement' for thinking the ALP was entitled to celebrate an astonishing and unexpected victory.[23]

In late April I finally left the office. I had been there for eleven months. Despite the awfulness of the victory dinner, I was in something like a state of euphoria. Keating had been re-elected and we had achieved the promise of some important and, I was sure, lasting policy changes for women. I was still angry about McMullan's cowardice, meaning women's policy was not in cabinet, but I was confident that Keating, with the support of Mary Ann O'Loughlin, would steer them through. Keating, the economic hardhead, the man who held the Press Gallery in the palm of his hand, who influenced, even dictated, the thinking of the major chroniclers of the age, had now signed-off on what he would later call 'a landmark change'.[24] Using childcare policy to encourage women into the workforce was 'something which we'd never had before, even though the Government extended childcare opportunities with childcare places' and it signalled that, finally, women's policy was at the big table.

My farewell dinner was at the National Gallery, in a private room with Jackson Pollock's *Blue Poles* looking over us. Or so I thought. It turned out to be a copy of the famous and controversial painting that had been acquired by the Whitlam government, and which was still a forceful reminder that it was Labor governments and Labor Prime Ministers who understood how essential the arts were to a society's soul and its confidence in itself. In my farewell speech I thanked Paul Keating for allowing us to 'kick a few goals' by 'taking policy to a new level', with the childcare rebate, and the cashing out of the DSR and I announced that although I was leaving the PMO, I was staying in the country. Three events had influenced my decision, I told my about-to-be-former colleagues: the Arts for Labor event at the State Theatre; the election-eve arts auction at the Bellevue Hotel, where the generosity and optimism of Sydney's arts world was once again on display; and the staff dinner later that night where I'd realised that, if Keating won, the country was in for an exhilarating time.

———※⊛≪———

With Keating returned to power, we had a leader who understood our country's past and present, and how we needed to fit into the region. He knew that in order to mature, Australia had to come to terms with its past, and he believed fervently that the artistic soul of a country was as much a part of who we were as our economy and our politics. It was going to be a dramatic time in Australian history, perhaps the most significant era since white settlement. We were going to become a Republic. It was going to be bigger than even the Whitlam era had been, and I wanted to be part of it. It had not been easy to sell Chip on the idea of Keating's Australia versus Bill Clinton's USA. After twelve years of Republican rule, the Democrats were finally back in the White House. Bill Clinton was a young modern President whose wife, Hillary, was his equal, and whose administration was going to restore fairness to the country. As a student, Chip had campaigned for Walter Mondale and Geraldine Ferraro; in 1988 he had hoped for a Dukakis victory to wipe away the memory of the Reagan years; now, in 1993, he most definitely did not want to miss out on the Clinton era. But, in an act of tremendous love and generosity, he eventually allowed himself to be persuaded and began the far-from-easy process of demonstrating that he met the various requirements to become an Australian resident. Another benefit of the Sex Discrimination Act, I realised gratefully. No discrimination on the basis of marital status meant that the fact we were not married did not prevent Chip from getting a visa. In future years, several of our same-sex couple friends would also be able to become residents and, eventually, citizens because of this far-sighted provision of Australia's national anti-discrimination laws.

'An even greater achievement than winning the election is not just the promise of the sort of country that could lure me back,' I said to Paul Keating that night. 'Your greatest achievement, as far as I'm concerned, is that you've been able to get Chip to come back!'

My farewell present was a framed front cover of the *Sydney Morning Herald*, signed by the Prime Minister, where a story by Jenna Price

reported the pollster AGB McNair as saying 1993 was the first election
where the overall female vote for the ALP equalled the male vote.[25] Much
of the analysis after the election had attributed the victory, at least in part,
to Labor's pitch to women—particularly the childcare policy, the cashing
out of the DSR into a home carers' payment, the extension of Medicare
and other health initiatives—and it felt good to have this acknowledged by
my colleagues.

Eight months later, Keating launched a new edition of my book *Damned
Whores and God's Police*. A lot had changed since 1975 when it was first
published, and my publishers agreed it was time for a fresh appraisal. I had
written a very long new introduction that tried to chronicle and make sense
of the changed landscape for women, drawing especially on the differences
between Australia and the United States, which I judged to be far less progressive than the country I was once again calling home. I also included
what was to become quite a controversial 'Letter to the Next Generation', in
which I urged young women to pick up the feminist torch. In his speech,
Keating praised me for deciding I was now 'a fervent pragmatist'.

'Pragmatism is not cynicism,' he said. 'It is about learning the lessons of
things and seeing how one can advance visions and objectives.'

His entire speech was a master class from the man who had done so
much to transform Australia, but his final words totally blew me away, and
convinced me that, thanks to him, Australia was set to become a different,
better place:

'We have had a lot of talk in this country in the last year or so about reconciliation between Aboriginals and non-Aboriginal Australians,' Keating
said. 'The word reconciliation has been used a lot and used with all the
meaning that it deserves to be used with. But one of the great reconcilia-
tions which is underway now is a reconciliation between men and women
and the lives they now lead, with the changed role of women, the changed
opportunities of women . . . and I think men understand that and they
are adjusting their view of life and society and opportunity, in terms of
the changes which have taken place, and the new reconciliation which is
required of it.'

I left the launch for a literary lunch where I was to talk about the book and where, with faltering voice, I told the audience that the Prime Minister of Australia had just made the profound observation that what was now needed in this country was reconciliation between women and men.

It was 1994 and it felt to me as if, finally, we were on our way.

CHAPTER TEN

THE GETTING OF ANGER

In May 1993 I was back at Fairfax. This time as editor of *Good Weekend*, the magazine inserted in the *Sydney Morning Herald* and the *Age* each Saturday and reaching around one million readers. The call had come from David Hickie, my partner in crime-writing from the *National Times*, who had just been appointed editor of the *Herald*. Conrad Black, the Canadian newspaper publisher, had acquired a controlling stake in Fairfax after it went into receivership following Young Warwick's disastrous takeover bid back in the late 1980s. The new editorial director was Michael Hoy, who'd been brought in from News Ltd, and he had agreed to a reporting structure where I would answer directly to him rather than, as previous editors had, to the editor of the *Herald*. Both Hickie and Alan Kohler, editor of the *Age*, signed-off on my appointment. But I started the job to something less than the widespread approval of my peers. Newspaper journalists still looked down on magazines as being lightweight, serving up entertainment, not news, and therefore not to be taken seriously. It was an argument that was fast losing validity as newspapers began using more colour in their news pages and magazines such as *Good Weekend* published articles and, especially, well-observed profiles of a depth and quality of writing that harried daily journalists seldom had time to deliver. I was determined to draw on my New York magazine experience to further improve the range and quality of our journalism, accompanied by great art direction. But few people cared about my lofty ambitions. Most did not take *Good Weekend* seriously. It wasn't news, it wasn't 'real' journalism; it was derisively described as a 'supplement'. Our offices, a few blocks away from the Jones Street headquarters of Fairfax, were mockingly referred to as Palm Beach. This was a reference to the leisurely hours supposedly worked by the six staff writers, whose deadlines admittedly were less stressful than those of daily journalists. Hardly anyone took my appointment at face value. People searched for ploys or hidden agendas. There was speculation that I was being 'warehoused' to take over the *Herald* or some other 'real' job. Although I suppose these were meant to be compliments of a kind, I found them pretty insulting. But it was true *Good Weekend* had not been my first choice. As I was finishing up at the PMO, Paul Keating had offered me the job of Australian Consul-General in New York.

'Go back to New York and be with Chip,' he'd said to me.

When I told Chip about Keating's offer, he was emphatic that I should take it.

'Imagine,' he said, only half-joking, 'living in that Beekman Place apartment.'

The job came with a splendid piece of real estate. We had been there many times, to dinners and receptions hosted both by Chris Hurford, who had been a minister in the Hawke government before his appointment to New York which had just recently ended, and his urbane predecessor John Taylor, who had previously been Secretary of the Department of Aboriginal Affairs in Canberra. The Australian government had two apartments in a classic 1930s building in ritzy Beekman Place in New York's midtown, off 57th Street. Australia's Ambassador to the United Nations occupied the other, somewhat larger, one. I had never thought of myself as a diplomat but I was very alive to the possibilities of being able to promote Australia in a new and more interesting way. I admired the way Annie Cohen-Solal did the job for France. She had written an acclaimed biography of Jean-Paul Sartre and was now Cultural attaché at the French Consul-General's office. She was constantly written-up in the New York media for her chic events. Why couldn't Australia have a similarly alluring presence in New York? Did our representation have to be confined to investment and trade? What if

Australia's rich cultural and artistic offerings were integrated into our story, into the way we sold ourselves? Australian companies such as the Sydney Dance Theatre, Sydney Symphony Orchestra, Circus Oz, and Midnight Oil had all performed while I was living in New York. There was usually a reception afterwards, with a few 'Aussie-friendly' local media people invited, but there did not seem to be an aggressive attempt to showcase our art, music and dance. The astounding and enduring success of Australian actors and directors in Hollywood was a tantalising clue that there was more to the country than the lazy stereotypes we used to promote ourselves. I was under no illusion that Australia could hope to match France when it came to cultural offerings, but there was a lot more to us than Paul Hogan's 'I'll slip an extra shrimp on the barbie . . .' tourism television advertisement implied. This, like *The Thornbirds* a decade earlier, projected a country that bore no relation to the lives of most Australians. In fact, it was quite misleading. Americans had no idea of the country that had shown itself off to the Prime Minister in March 1993 at the State Theatre. I was excited at the prospect of being able to introduce *that* Australia, to show that creativity and a thriving economy were not in conflict, in fact could feed off each other. I am sure this was part of Keating's thinking in suggesting I take on the job.

But it did not happen. I was worried about what would happen at the end of the four years. There was no chance I would be able to stay in the diplomatic world, and it was unlikely that I could go back to journalism after such a political appointment. I look back today sadly, and with amazement, at my decision. Why did I turn down an opportunity that would have been so interesting, and such fun? I know how I rationalised it: at the end of the four years I would be 53, with no job and no prospects. In reality, I think I was fearful that I would be seen as not up to the job, as a token appointment, as not being worthy or capable. It was a stupid and self-loathing way to look at it. Instead, I took the other job on offer, and determined to turn *Good Weekend* into a must-read powerhouse of Australian journalism. It was a great opportunity, I told myself.

Chip and I eventually found a house we wanted to buy, in Victoria Street in Sydney's Kings Cross. It was a smallish terrace but with three storeys, and it faced out over the Domain towards the city, giving us what we liked to call our 'mini-Manhattan' view. Both of us loved the informality of the house and the spaces it gave us for work, relaxation and sleep. The two rooms plus tiny galley kitchen on the ground floor were, we'd say, for dining and relaxation. Once we'd got some furniture we started to have friends for dinner, making up for all those years of being away. The second floor was for personal maintenance, with its bathroom and two bedrooms while the top floor, with the two attic rooms converted to offices for each of us, was the factory. In June 1994, after we had a large party to celebrate Chip's 30th birthday, we began to feel that we were putting down roots in Sydney. Chip was doing freelance journalism, getting assignments for the *Wall Street Journal*, *Rolling Stone* and similar publications, and he joined the Sydney Philharmonia Choir, where for almost a decade he sang some of the great choral works, including 'Mahler 8' at the Royal Albert Hall as part of the proms concerts—and I waited in line for hours to get a standing room ticket to be part of this absolutely thrilling experience. During the same trip the choir also performed at King's College, Cambridge, and that afternoon we'd gone out on the river, both of us in summer whites, Chip punting and me savouring being propelled along, an unfamiliar treat. But the biggest gig was undoubtedly the Sydney Olympics, where he was part of the massed choir that performed in the Opening Ceremony.

It would take almost a year before *Good Weekend* began to reflect my sensibility and many months before I could even signal what I wanted to do. The three-week long production lead times and the weeks, sometimes months, it took a writer to produce a profile or feature article meant that I had to plan a long way ahead. I eventually overhauled, removed or improved every single one of the many elements that go to make up a magazine, but meanwhile we still needed to produce an issue each week. I drew on already-commissioned pieces while I made my plans, and got to know the lay of the land at *Good Weekend*, I concentrated on the one element that was readily available to me: the cover. I was very fortunate to have in Jeff Allan an art director who was a creative risk-taker and extremely talented; there was nothing he would not try and over the four years we worked together we created some memorable work, most often advertised by a striking cover.

We first showed what we could do in late July 1993 when we published a cover that appeared to show a naked Jeff Kennett, then premier of Victoria, addressing a public meeting. The cover line, 'Unreal, Jeff', provided a clue that perhaps what you saw was not entirely believable. And of course, it was not. The story, titled 'The Lying Eye', was a serious and pioneering piece of journalism dissecting 'the new world of the digital image,'[1] the recently available technology that enabled photographs to be manipulated. 'From now on,' our piece reported, 'the camera can never be relied on to tell the whole truth.' The article looked at the technology itself, the ethics of such manipulation and the fact that there were no guidelines, let alone laws, to curb the use of this technology for mischievous or even sinister purposes. We reproduced a couple of digitally-altered photographs that had recently appeared in newspapers to illustrate this, but I felt we needed to create our own arresting image to really make the point. Photoshop and other programs for digitally-altering photographs are now within the reach of anyone with a smart phone or a computer, but in 1993 few people understood the potential—and the risks—involved. We devoted a full page to showing how in the *Good Weekend* studio we had photographed a model, standing in a similar pose, to a stock news photo of Kennett addressing a public gathering in Geelong in 1991. An artist using a Qantel Graphics Paintbox XL positioned the model's naked body over the suited-image of Kennett, substituted Kennett's head, and created another head in the crowd 'in front of the groin area to spare the Premier's blushes', as we put it in our caption.

I thought the final result was wonderful. Using such a well-known person clearly showed how a photo could be manipulated. The cover attracted a lot of attention, including from the Victorian premier himself. We had given him a heads-up, as a matter of courtesy, and I had expected him to enjoy the joke. But Kennett's sense of humour did not apply to himself. He made a formal complaint. I think it even went to the board. I got my knuckles rapped.

Five months later, we published a full-page Christmas greeting to our readers. All of the staff, wearing dark green T-shirts and holding candles and decorations, arranged themselves in the shape of a Christmas tree. We called it the Good Weekend Family Tree. I was at the top, the angel or the boss, whichever way you wanted to look at it. We also had the image printed as a Christmas card; some people received the version where the photograph had been digitally-altered so that I was sitting atop that tree naked. I hoped Jeff Kennett would get the joke.

While our primary editorial task was to produce big feature stories on subjects—be they people or issues—that were of current relevance, I also relished the opportunity to have some fun, to be quirky and to generally try to reward readers with a few surprises at least every few weeks. I had already renovated the cooking page, upgrading what had been a small column into a lavish three-page spread, which I called Appetites. Each week we featured a leading Australian chef, such as Stephanie Alexander, Maggie Beer, Tony Bilson, Jill Dupleix or Gay Bilson, writing about food. (I also tried to bring on new talent by encouraging previously unknown food writers, such as Siu Ling Hui.) Huon Hooke and Mark Shield contributed shorter columns on wine and beer and spirits respectively. The chef's words were accompanied by a gorgeous image created by the top photographer, George Seper, and styled by Tom Rutherfood, who was a caterer who went on to create his own restaurants. It was the era of so-called gastro-porn. Australians were into food, shopping for it, cooking it, eating it, looking at it. Cookbook sales were in the stratosphere. Celebrity chefs had entered our lives and long before television, shows such as *Masterchef* had a profound impact on everyday Australians enthusiasm for food, it seemed we could not be too extravagant or excessive when it came to food. It turned out that you could, and it was a June 1994 column by Gay Bilson where she wrote about trying to make sausages from her own blood that provoked reader outrage and disgust.[2] I had been enthusiastic about the article, encouraging Gay to be as frank and explicit as she wished. I'd had some fun positioning the piece, giving it the title 'The Blood of Others', in what I thought was a witty allusion to Simone de Beauvoir's 1945 novel of the same name. While de Beauvoir certainly wasn't a cook, as a Frenchwoman she would have eaten her share of *boudin noir* and I had written, 'Only the most sanguine of cooks would contemplate using themselves as a principal ingredient', to guide readers into the article.

It was a wonderful piece of writing in which Gay described how a year earlier she had decided to make sausages 'from my own blood for a dinner centred around the body, our bodies'. She would, she wrote, 'prove my blood to be safe, freeze it over the period needed to obtain about three litres, then personally make the sausages. Our blood has similar properties to pig's blood, so as "food" I knew they would be palatable.' No one could ever accuse Gay Bilson of being frivolous, and this article was certainly not meant to be anything other than a serious rumination on blood and its value as food. It included a reference to the famous pig-killing scene in Thomas Hardy's *Jude the Obscure*. But Bilson was unable to persuade any of her coterie of cooks and servers to take part in such a dinner. Was it the time of AIDS that made it so unacceptable? Or was it that a woman proposed to use her own blood? In 1993 the London artist Marc Quinn had carved a bust of his head from his frozen blood. Was that acceptable because 'his blood became sculpted material, not food'? Bilson asked.[3] *Good Weekend*'s readers made clear they would prefer more conventional food columns in the future. One described it as 'stomach-churning', another suggested she donate her blood to the Red Cross. But I relished the unconventional, and counted this article as one of those I was most proud to publish.

I had been similarly unrepentant about another unusual editorial choice earlier in 1994, when I had devoted a total of eight pages to reprinting a New York *Village Voice* article they had titled 'A rape in cyberspace', but which I chose to call 'Data rape'.[4] It was unheard of for us to run an article of this length—it was almost 10,000 words—let alone on such an esoteric topic. The article explored what were fast becoming increasing interactions between our actual lives and those that existed virtually in cyberspace. In this case, a man who went by the online name of Mr Bungle committed several acts of sexual violence, including rapes, on other virtual characters in a fictional world that went by the name of LambdaMOO. The question as to how someone who does not exist could be violated by another fictional character was quickly overtaken by an urgent online debate, about how real people, using their fictional persona, could perpetrate such acts. The article was an early foreshadowing of the issues of online violence, trolling and similar uses of the internet to intimidate—and even kill people—that we are grappling with today. Back then, scarcely anyone knew what we were even talking about and I did not win any friends in the upper echelons of Fairfax, let alone from the advertising department, for publishing something most people thought was, frankly, weird. I did, however, receive a congratulatory phone call from Bruce Gyngell, the Nine Network's television guru (and the man who was known as Mr Television for having been the first person to appear on Australia's television screens some 40 years earlier). 'It was the most interesting thing I have read in a long time,' Gyngell told me. That was good enough for me.

⎯⎯►◄⎯⎯

In early March 1995, Fairfax relocated from its long-term headquarters in Jones Street, Broadway to a glass tower perched on the edge of Darling Harbour, on the western side of the central business district of Sydney. Whatever the original rationale was for locating *Good Weekend* away from the mothership was forgotten, and we too found ourselves in a spanking-new set of offices on the 24th floor. After the move, everything changed. We were now part of the Fairfax 'family', sharing spaces, running into colleagues from other parts of the company in the lifts or the coffee shop downstairs. People actually came to see us (something that never happened while we were at Palm Beach). There was also a perceptible change in my status. Our masthead was on the wall of the company reception area. That rankled with some people who thought it incongruous, if not downright impertinent, for a magazine, a mere supplement, to have a separate billing from its host the *Sydney Morning Herald*, and equal status with the *Sun-Herald* and the *Australian Financial Review*. Michael Hoy included me in all editors' gatherings, so I often found myself at dinners or meetings with the men who ran the major mastheads. While I appreciated being treated as an equal, even I could not make a plausible case that my responsibilities, let alone staff numbers and budget, even came close to those of the editors of the newspapers. I also differed from these editors in having more of a public profile than any of them. I received constant invitations to give speeches, attend conferences and other public events. At the same time, being *Good Weekend* editor automatically conferred A list guest status. I'd been astonished when I started the job to find my inbox brimming with invitations to opening nights at the opera and the theatre, movie premieres and all sorts of fancy social events. Not to mention the gifts. Endless cosmetics and other beauty products, liquor, homewares and all kinds of other usually very stylish and rather expensive goods arrived so regularly, my office started to resemble a gift shop. It was very different from just being a journalist; I was sneered at as a 'celebrity editor' by former colleagues, who questioned whether I would be capable of applying journalistic impartiality if any of the pals I socialised with found themselves in trouble. The name Carmen Lawrence was mentioned as an example. I was occupying a strange place in the journalistic pantheon. *Good Weekend* was publishing good and important stories but there were plenty of traditionalists who, as well as questioning my credentials, viewed anything published in a magazine as inferior to the 'real thing' in newspapers. And, it would turn out, there were also some for whom my newfound status was intolerable.

On 14 June 1995, after I had been at *Good Weekend* for just over two years, I received a phone call from my good friend Elisabeth Wynhausen, who was now working at the *Australian*. Did I know, she asked me, that rumours were circulating that I had sexually harassed a member of my staff? No. I most certainly did not. I asked her for details. It seemed, she said, that I had been, or was about to be, formally accused of harassment by a *Good Weekend* male photographer. The story was apparently being spread with especially malevolent glee, spreading like wildfire, especially in media circles, up and down the east coast of Australia for almost a week before I knew anything about it. Suddenly, a number of things made sense: people looking at me sideways in the lift at Fairfax; people who normally greeted me avoiding my gaze and I'd had some strange phone calls from friends who, I later learned, when I said nothing had simply assumed I did not want to talk about it. The story had assumed the force of fact before I was even aware of it.

'Have you heard the rumour about Anne Summers?' I later heard one colleague was asked.

'It's not a rumour,' she was informed by another Fairfax journalist. 'It's a fact.'

The story was especially insidious because of its veneer of apparent verisimilitude. The so-called harassment had taken place at a Christmas party. I was soon to learn that this was a key word in the lexicon of sexual harassment complaints. (So much so that Chris Ronalds, a barrister friend of mine who handles a number of harassment complaints, told me she thought

Christmas parties should go the way of Guy Fawkes Night and be outlawed altogether.) People who would not normally believe that I would harass an employee might concede that anything was possible at a Christmas party. Worse, there were supposedly photographs. Proof, in other words. It had taken an especially Machiavellian mind to construct this scenario, but the people who were putting the story around (and I learned later that the story was, most likely, deliberately concocted and circulated) found that it fell on fertile ground. It was a damn good story: one of Australia's leading feminists hoist with the petard of the very laws she'd had a hand in developing. (While I worked in Paul Keating's office in 1992, I had helped with amendments to the Sex Discrimination Act that implemented recommendations of a review of the legislation by Michael Lavarch that, among other things, extended the sexual harassment provisions of the 1984 Act from employment to education and the provision of goods and services.) Not long before, she'd defended Helen Garner's book *The First Stone*, a sympathetic account of a man accused of sexual harassment at a university college in Melbourne. It was a story that people simply could not resist repeating and, before long, reporting.

Miranda Devine, the well-known right-wing and anti-feminist columnist, then employed by Sydney's *Daily Telegraph-Mirror*, who in more than two decades has rarely bypassed an opportunity to comment unfavourably about me, wrote a colourful column about the 'fabulous characters' who 'peopled' the rumour:

'There's Summers herself, 50, blonde, leggy and sharp. Her toothy young American-born boyfriend Chip. Her serious short-haired deputy Deborah Tarrant fighting for her job with two small children at home to support. Then of course there is the mysterious anti-hero, *Good Weekend* photographer Brendan Read, who takes beautiful pictures and looks beautiful himself, in a long-haired beefcake way,' she wrote. 'There were great props, too, like the *Good Weekend* staff's festive season poster with Summers as a nude angel on top of a human Christmas tree. And, of course, there's The Tape, recording an acrimonious meeting on July 7 between Summers and Tarrant, complete with intimate exchanges.'[5]

As this florid account suggests, this workplace drama was so bizarre that it resembled a soap opera. Even more than twenty years later and recounting only an outline of what happened, the story is scarcely believable. But at the time I had to believe it, because it was happening—and it was happening to me. I tried frantically to find out if a complaint *was* going to be made, and what conduct on my part could possibly have prompted it. Ultimately, there was no complaint—nor any reason for one—but that did not stop the rumours from escalating and accumulating more salacious detail on every retelling. Nor did it prevent the journalists' union from escalating the matter into a full-blown industrial dispute and, in the three months before it was finally over, several people losing their jobs.

Essentially what happened was this: the *Good Weekend* photographer involved told Fairfax management he did not propose to lodge a complaint *and* that there was no behaviour of mine that he wished to complain about, but it took him two weeks to sign a letter to this effect; I fired my deputy editor for disloyalty for behaviour associated with the matter; the Media Entertainment and Arts Alliance (MEAA), the journalists' union, instigated industrial action, first directing a work-to-rule at *Good Weekend*, then a Fairfax-wide stoppage, to protest my management style. Ultimately the photographer resigned, the MEAA ended its campaign, several of my staff left and I continued in the job. But this bland summary scarcely does justice to a situation where other agendas were being brought into play, old scores against the company being settled, and individual grievances that had nothing to do with me became part of the mix. And I was the one in the spotlight, I was the one who, in defending herself and her reputation against insidious rumours of poor behaviour, became the target. As well, intimidatory tactics were used to pressure those of my staff who were loyal into lining up against me. All the time this was happening, I was trying to control my emotions. I could not afford to crack-up but I came very close. How do you retain composure, and continue to try to put out a magazine, when you are the subject of such lurid speculation?

In late July, a full six weeks after I first learned about the rumours, I wrote an op-ed piece for the *Sydney Morning Herald*. I decided to tell the whole story, make it absolutely clear that I had been fully exonerated of whatever the rumours had me doing, and thereby warn off the rest of the media. But instead of killing the story, the sensational treatment of my piece by the *Herald*, with its front-page banner headline 'My sexual harassment nightmare', complete with a photograph of me, gave it oxygen. Now every single media outlet in the country could pick it up, *and* they could name names. The media circus that followed was quite extraordinary. Every radio host wanted an interview and the newspapers, especially the Murdoch-owned tabloids, had a field day. The *Daily Telegraph-Mirror* ran a two-page spread, entitled 'The dismissal. Office politics gone wrong at Fairfax'[6] that included the *Good Weekend* Christmas card with me, ostensibly, naked on the top of the tree, and a transcript of the conversation in which I had advised my deputy that she no longer had a job because of her disloyalty. Another article the previous day had been accompanied by a photograph of me at *Good Weekend*'s tenth anniversary party a few months earlier. I'm clearly in a party mood, holding a glass of wine and leaning in towards my partner Chip Rolley. Just to keep the innuendo going, reminding readers of my predilection for younger men. Chip gave me unwavering support, without which I wonder if I could have got through those three months, but it was very hard on him. He had to put up with sneering and innuendo, as well as the insinuation that I had a roving eye. Not only that, but the allegation that I had harassed a staff member at a Christmas party that had occurred at our house—our small house in Victoria Street—and where Chip was present, implied that the behaviour had taken place in front of him. He hid it from me but I later learned it had taken an emotional toll. And, like me, he found the sheer ferocity of the assault inexplicable and very hard to take.

My op-ed article had precipitated a round of commentary, including from right-wing journalists, who used my situation to argue that the Sex Discrimination Act unfairly laid men open also to being subjected to fabricated accusations of sexual harassment. I was attacked by journalists and the union who claimed I had taken advantage of privileged access to the opinion pages of the *Herald*, that other people simply did not have. Maybe that was true—although I would expect that any public figure who had been shredded in the media unremittingly for weeks the way I had been would be welcome to write an article in response. But there was also a lot of sympathy for me. 'I was in tears as I read what happened to Anne,' Quentin Bryce told the *Australian*, 'she is the best boss I have ever had.'[7] Letters, faxes, telephone messages and lots and lots of flowers started to arrive at the office. For many people, what was happening to me was starting to look like a pile-on. I was astonished to read the names on the messages. Many came from influential and powerful people, whom I had never met, all exhorting me to ride it out. A few came from high-profile women. Several, I knew, had been subjected to similar campaigns of vilification in the media, and their handwritten notes were especially heartfelt. They recognised a witch-hunt when they saw one. A number of people sent the same message: *Nolite te bastardes carborundorum* (Don't let the bastards get you down). There was even an especially extravagant arrangement of flowers bearing the tag, 'From your friends at *The Australian*'. At least not everyone in the media was trying to bring me down.

I had read in the press that my staff had problems with me. I was 'imprecise', 'disorganised' and 'frequently absent at luncheons and speaking engagements'. I did receive many invitations to speak, but I tried to achieve a workable balance between doing my job and continuing my role as an advocate and commentator. Maybe I was imprecise. I liked to try new things and to keep changing layouts and headlines until they were as good as they could be. I don't think being organised is itself a virtue, especially not in a creative job, but if I was really as disorganised as was made out I doubt that I could have done that job, let alone those I have done before and since. But this, it turned out, was a minor complaint compared with what some staff *really* thought. Sandra Coates, my dedicated and utterly loyal assistant, became an undeserving and unwilling go-between with several staff members telling her what they thought was *really* wrong with my editorship. That I had a problem with male staff, I could not get on with men, I had no empathy and that it was because I did not have children.

That was when I knew that this was not just about me. It was not just a few staff members with grievances real or exaggerated; it was not just the usual resentment of my decisions as editor to reject and thus disappoint people. It was true that some inside Fairfax were resentful, perhaps jealous, at how I'd come back from outside to a top editorial job. Others within the company were manoeuvring to force me out. There were plenty of people motivated to lend a hand in trying to tear me down. But the way it was done revealed deep and disturbing undercurrents of resistance to women in positions of power and authority. Even Miranda Devine as good as acknowledged this when she commented: 'Even if the unflattering stories about her management style . . . were just familiar attempts to undermine a senior woman, Angry White Males gleefully counted her scalp as a trophy.'[8]

I was not attacked for being incompetent or lazy or tyrannical or any of the charges that might be laid against a boss, male or female. I was characterised, instead, as a sexual predator and attacked for not being a mother. Just about the two worst things you could say about a woman, even in 1995, just a few years away from the end of the century that had seen women win the vote, obtain the means to control their fertility, enter education and the workforce in massive numbers, move into politics and management and, supposedly, be able to do 'anything'. Yet we were still either madonnas or whores. I was not a mother, so I must be a whore. It seemed unbelievable, yet it was happening—to me. And so many people, including in the media, even the journalists' union itself, were all buying it. It began to dawn on me that what was happening to me was part of a pattern of hounding prominent women. Carmen Lawrence, who in 1990 had become Australia's first female premier, of Western Australia, was one of the first to be the target of malicious and mendacious slurs designed to unsettle and unseat her, and Joan Kirner in Victoria, Australia's second woman premier later that same year, became another.

———❖———

Carmen Lawrence was now in Canberra where she was Minister for Human Services and Health in the Keating government. She had been wooed to Canberra by Keating himself, who wanted someone high-profile and clearly competent to boost the numbers of women in his government. Despite the defeat of her government in the 1993 WA state elections, she was seen as a political star. She was immensely popular. We had run a profile of Lawrence in *Good Weekend* in March[9] in which our reporter Jane Cadzow had remarked on the adoring crowds, especially women, she attracted wherever she went. The media monitored her every move. Her high visibility would, Lawrence correctly predicted in a speech in Sydney in August 1995, become a 'two-edged sword'. More precisely, it made her a target. Even among her colleagues in cabinet who, Cadzow reported, gave her an

exceptionally tough time in her first appearance before the Expenditure
Review Committee prior to the budget. Earlier, back in Perth, Lawrence
had endured, and apparently survived, intense parliamentary scrutiny over
a scandal about an immensely complicated story that became known as
the 'Easton affair' because one of the principals, Penny Easton, had committed suicide. However, in May 1995, Richard Court, who as Leader of
the Opposition was involved in the original parliamentary brouhaha, and
who had become premier in Western Australia after defeating Lawrence's
government, announced a Royal Commission into the Easton affair. Paul
Keating denounced this as a 'political stunt', which it undoubtedly was—and
it had deadly effect. The Royal Commission found Lawrence had misled
Parliament. Charges of perjury were brought against her; she stood down
from her position as a front bench member of Labor, which was by now in
Opposition. For the next two years, until she was acquitted of all charges
in July 1999, Lawrence fought ferociously and with immense dignity to
preserve her reputation, but she never recovered the political lustre that had
propelled her to Canberra. Mission accomplished, you might say, if you had
been one of those trying to derail the brilliant career of one of Australia's
most talented political leaders.

Joan Kirner was attacked for her political management, as any incumbent of the premiership at that particularly difficult time undoubtedly
would have been. But no male premier would have been subjected to a
cruel public campaign that mocked his body size and clothing choices.
Kirner was caricatured as fat and frumpy, a housewife who'd mistakenly
found herself in the corridors of power. She was even ridiculed for wearing
a polka-dot dress, a fashion crime she had not committed but, as I had
found, the truth has nothing to do with what finds its way into the armoury
of those who want to bring down women. Jennie George would become
the first woman President of the ACTU in 1996, and be subjected to media
scrutiny about her sex life and other intimate details that male unionists
were not probed about. Even before the attacks on me, I had noticed the
emergence of this trend of trying to wound women in public life, and it
had troubled me. It was a sobering rejoinder to the elation many of us had
felt when women had, at long last, finally breached these previously male-
only bastions. But it never occurred to me that I would become a target.

I was not in elected office; I was not in a high-profile public job; nor was I a pioneer in a previously all-male field. All but one of my predecessors at *Good Weekend* had been women, so I had not robbed a man of his job. It was true that I had more power than previous editors, reporting to the more senior editorial director rather than the top editor of the *Sydney Morning Herald*. But was that reason enough to go after me? It turned out that it might have been. Although in standing or influence I did not even remotely resemble the position of premiers or trade union leaders, I had, seemingly and unwittingly, found myself occupying a position more powerful than a lot of people liked.

I had been hearing whispers about women in senior jobs who were doing it tough. These were women who ran institutions, or headed cultural organisations, or otherwise were prominent and whose views were often sought by the media about being pathfinders for women. I met several of these women, for lunch, or by chance encounter at functions and I probed, asking them how things were. I heard fragments of stories, or muttered asides, and lots of shrugged shoulders, but no one wanted to come out and talk about the price they were paying for their ostensible success. I found it sickening, even if it was not surprising. We had seen it before. It had happened to the courageous women who had taken what used to be called 'non-traditional' jobs in the police, the fire department, the steel works, the water board— all those complacently all-male essential services that were shaken-up by the anti-discrimination laws of the 1970s. These pioneers had endured such shocking pushback in the form of verbal and physical abuse, often with some pretty gruesome pornography thrown in, that many of them had gone to court and won. They blazed the blue-collar trails with little fanfare and precious little appreciation. But, I had always supposed, their court victories had opened pathways for other women to follow. Things would be better for those who came after. Now I wondered whether these women had, in fact, been the canaries in the coalmines.

A generation later, the white-collar citadels were being stormed and the reaction seemed to be the same. The women in these jobs were educated, articulate and forceful women—they had to be, to be there in the first place—and they, like me, were utterly astounded at the hostility they faced. More than ten years after the passage of the Sex Discrimination Act, and the employment affirmative action laws passed by the Hawke government, women were finding not just glass ceilings that prevented their getting to the very top, but impenetrable walls of hostility, and colleagues ready to go to almost any length to demonstrate just how unwelcome they were.

Fifteen years later, in 2010, when Julia Gillard became Australia's first female Prime Minister, the initial jubilation at finally reaching this historic milestone soon was replaced in many sections of society by expressions of hostility that were shocking for their brazen crudity. When I grappled with how best to describe this situation, I could only agree with Gillard's own characterisation in her famous 'sexism and misogyny' speech on 9 October 2012,[10] and conclude that what we were seeing was misogyny. It was not a word that had been used much in recent decades. It had not been needed, we thought. In the mid-1990s we had but the dimmest understanding of how profound the assault on us was going to be. In the second decade of the 21st century, we found the word needed to be revived to describe the surprising and distressing rise in public hostility to women, especially women in public roles. Somehow 'sexism' was not sufficient to describe what was going on. These women, and perhaps even most women, were being treated differently and unequally just because they were women. But there was more to it than that. There was a naked hostility evident in the way women were being scrutinised and judged. This hostility was being directed especially at women who had entered areas of public life that were once the exclusive domain of men. Women were now newsreaders, company directors, commentators, surgeons, professors, cabinet ministers, prime ministers. Hostility had become a new weapon. It was being deployed in ways that we had scarcely seen before, both offensively—and defensively. The savage appraisals of women's appearance, both their body shapes and their apparel, and often entailing demeaning sexual evaluations, were full-frontal assaults. But just as insidious, and in some ways more hostile, were the defensive plays. As more and more women began to take seats around boardroom tables, in corporations, not-for-profits, sporting organisations, many were subjected to pushback that was almost laughably pathetic. I heard of women being criticised for bringing shopping to board meetings (men didn't have to do that as their food shopping was generally done by other people), for their handbags being 'too big', or for talking too much. Perhaps for talking at all, was what the critics meant. Stay away, lady, was the message. We don't want you here; if you force your way in, we will make it so hard and horrible you will regret the day you ever walked through that door.

In April 1997 I was at a board meeting of the Balmain Tigers, the Sydney Rugby League team later renamed the Wests Tigers, when a board member noticed a mistake, a wrong date, in a report being presented by a fellow director:

'I'll have to take that up with my wife—she typed it,' said the man who was making the presentation.

'Don't hit her too hard,' interjected another board member.

'Don't worry; you can still see the marks from last time,' the man replied.

I looked in disbelief at these two, and the rest of the men around the table. Sure, they were joking—they must be!—but no one seemed embarrassed or uncomfortable about the subject of the joke.

I had—very reluctantly—become the first woman to join a Rugby League Club board when Murray Sime had talked me into becoming a Tigers director the year before. I had known Murray for years, from around the Push and from when I had lived in Balmain in the early 1970s. Murray was a Balmain fixture. He was a flamboyant character, a big bloke whose rumpled appearance might lead you to suppose he was as down-and-out as the poets and gamblers and grifters who also made up the Balmain Push. But then you noticed the sharp green eyes he fixed on you through his gold-rimmed glasses, and you heard the astute comments he had for any situation, and you would then not be surprised to learn he was a very successful banker. As well as being very radical in his politics. Years before he had got into trouble for using his position at the NSW Attorney-General's office to organise people to take part in an anti-Vietnam Moratorium march; the AG's phone number had appeared on brochures that were distributed all around Sydney. Every Boxing Day, he held what became a legendary party for all-comers at his Balmain waterside house, to mark Chairman Mao's birthday. It was at one of these parties that I'd first met Germaine Greer. I had had too many glasses of Jim Beam, a drink I had never tried before (or since) and, embarrassingly, had thrown up in front of her. She had looked at me with a mixture of disdain and compassion. Despite our both being champions of feminism, we have never really connected; it was probably our first meeting that saw to that.

Murray worked for years for Citibank, presumably making lots of money for them as a Vice-President before, in 1998, establishing his own merchant bank. Murray was a constant source of advice and money for the writers and artists of Balmain. He, along with his good friend the writer Frank Moorhouse, whose patron he also was, helped establish the Copyright Agency that ensured writers got remunerated when their works were photo-copied. Murray also loved his football and he had persuaded the Balmain Tigers Board, of which he was a long-time member, that they needed to recruit a woman member to help them change their brutish male image (there had recently been a rape charge against a prominent former player). Murray argued that they needed to boost the attendance of families at their games and he said he'd speak to me about coming on board. I was absolutely the wrong person for this job. I had no children, I had no interest in football, let along rugby league which I considered to be a violent and boorish game; there would be better women, I said, women who actually liked the game and would kill for the opportunity to be the first woman member of a rugby league board. But Murray would not take no for an answer. He wanted a prominent feminist, he said, to send a signal that the club was serious, and so I allowed myself to be persuaded. I knew from the first time I sat at that boardroom table that it was a mistake.

My very being there was wrong. They did not want me and I did not want to be there. I had nothing to contribute. Even my supposed reason for being there was undermined within a few weeks when Rupert Murdoch's News Corporation launched the rebel Super League to take on the existing competition. Suddenly, the Tigers were fighting for their very existence. All thought of women and families was forgotten. It was now a matter of survival in a new and unexpected world. I had absolutely nothing to offer here, but Murray was adamant that I should not resign.

'Hang in,' he said. 'It will get better.'

It got worse. At another board meeting, the coach reported that a new sponsor had come to the club on Monday morning and given 'the boys' several thousand in cash for winning the game over the weekend. The Tigers did not win very often and this victory was a big deal.

'What did they do with the money,' asked one of the directors.

'I can't say,' said the coach. 'Not with Anne here.'

'Don't worry,' said Murray, 'Anne's broadminded.'

And so we learned that 'the boys' had used the money to treat themselves at a local brothel that afternoon.

I wondered whether such conversations took place around the board-room table of BHP. Probably not, but nor were there any women at that table—or at most blue-chip company board tables in those days—so any similar 'jokes' about hitting women or reports of rewarding employees with sexual treats would not need to be held back, and would probably not attract any criticism. Just as that evening I did not say anything to my fellow Tigers directors. Where would I begin? It merely added to my growing unease that things were starting to unravel for women. Just as rugby league's efforts to become 'family friendly' had been swept aside by the brutal power of Rupert Murdoch's desire to dominate the sport, I could not help but see a similar thing starting to happen in Canberra where John Howard had begun to reverse many of the policy reforms for women of the Keating, Hawke and even Whitlam governments. Something sinister was happening here; why on earth would the Prime Minister want to turn back the clock for women? I watched, first with disbelief, then with growing unease and, finally, with anger.

There had been a 5 per cent swing against Paul Keating's government in March 1996, giving John Howard a gain of 26 seats. The new members of the House of Representatives included the surprisingly large number of thirteen women, mostly from marginal seats that the Liberals had not expected to win. Howard posed on a bridge outside Parliament House with the new women MPs, all of them wearing brightly coloured suits, facing into their political futures with an optimism that, if they had any solidarity at all with their sex, would quickly turn out to be utterly misplaced. The new Prime Minister began, systematically and ruthlessly, to dismantle almost all of the reforms and protections for women that had been so painstakingly put together over previous decades. Howard tore into the Sex Discrimination Act, the Human Rights and Equal Opportunity Commission that administered the

Act, the Office of the Status of Women, and the Affirmative Action Agency. He diluted the childcare rebate I'd been so proud to have helped bring to life in 1993 and he slashed other forms of childcare assistance, turning an essential prop for women's employment into a welfare program, only able to be accessed by those with very low incomes. He changed the family payments benefits arrangements so they penalised families where women worked and he began to put in place what would ultimately become the 'baby bonus', generous payments for having babies which—unlike childcare support—was not income tested.[11] He had soon closed down or totally emasculated (I chose the word advisedly) all of the offices and agencies that were there to facilitate or monitor women's progress towards equality, especially in employment. It was nothing less than an all-out assault on the employment of women, especially of women with children.

But I did not think for a moment that Howard would get rid of the Women's Bureau. This had been established in 1963 by his political godfather, Sir Robert Menzies—admittedly after a lot of pressure from Liberal Party women, led by the redoubtable Victorian Senator Ivy Wedgwood, who was a strong advocate for women's rights—with the pragmatic purpose of ensuring women got a fair deal in employment. It was the only government agency that monitored maternity leave entitlements and other working conditions, and kept track of Australia's dismal progress in implementing equal pay. But Howard brutally demolished the Bureau and with it the women's unit in the Australian Bureau of Statistics, so that reliable and up-to-date data about women's workforce participation became almost impossible to obtain. 'What gets measured gets done' is a mantra of business. John Howard made sure that nothing got done on his watch to ensure women had equal opportunities in employment. In fact, he did exactly the reverse. By 2002, only 54.4 per cent of employed women worked full-time; in 1982 the figure had been 63.8 per cent.[12] John Howard's 'white picket fence' view of women, and the role they should play in society was now firmly entrenched in policy, and the country was falling into line. It was an appalling reversal of fortune for the women of Australia.

It took some time to see it for what it was: a war against women. It was an onslaught on a scale we had never previously experienced, because we had never before accumulated the rights and the legal protections that we now enjoyed in 1996. I was beside myself with fury and rage, but I was also grappling with an even more profound response. For the first time in my adult life, I no longer felt optimistic. It had been an article of faith for me—indeed, you could probably call it my secular religion—that our societies were inexorably headed towards equality and fairness; that politics was about righting wrongs, ending injustices and creating the conditions whereby all citizens could thrive. I had absorbed this view of the world, and of politics, in the 1960s when I had first become aware of the writings of John Stuart Mill on liberty, R.H. Tawney on equality and Beatrice and Sidney Webb on socialism. My later, and brief, foray into Marxism had merely reinforced the idea that progress and justice were inevitable. Martin Luther King Jr had said 'the arc of the moral universe is long, but it bends towards justice', and every social reformer I could think of had argued similarly. I knew that conservatives resisted change and sought to conserve what they regarded as sacred institutions or policies. I disliked and disagreed with them for their trying to hold back progress, for their championing of institutions and policies whose foundations all too often were discriminatory or even oppressive. I saw them as standing in the way of progress, but they were not wreckers. Now I had to confront a phenomenon I had not known possible: the actual destruction of so much that we had fought for. I knew that I had to document what was happening. I had to bear witness so that this destruction did not go unnoticed or be forgotten. I was stunned, because I never thought that we would have to do this. I really believed that the changes won by the battles of the past five or six decades were permanent. I could not understand why any political leader would want to turn back the clock for women.

Why was John Howard doing this? As a former Treasurer, surely he understood the economic value of women participating in the workforce. Apparently not; in a contest between ideology and economics, with Howard it was ideology that won. At least when it came to women. Howard had famously told me a decade earlier 'the times will suit me' when he became Prime Minister. He had thought that in 1987, when the next federal election was due, Australians would have tired of Bob's Hawke's more interventionist role for government and be ready for the free-market economics adopted by Ronald Reagan in the US and Margaret Thatcher in the UK. Instead, Hawke had been re-elected, three times, and then Paul Keating succeeded him and remained in power until March 1996. While Howard had won decisively, there was nothing to suggest that Australians wanted him to take them back to the 1980s. Nevertheless, he hopped into his time machine and took us even further back, to the 1950s, an era when women were supposed to be content to be what used to be called 'home makers'. Howard appeared to be incapable of dealing with the times he now found himself in. Instead, he imposed his atavistic view of women and their role in society onto a country that neither saw it coming, nor appreciated until far too late, just how much damage he had done to the social fabric of Australia. Many of his policies were dire for women themselves. For instance, he seriously tried to implement a fundamental revision to the Sex Discrimination Act in order to prevent single women and lesbians having access to IVF. He wanted such access restricted to 'married or de facto heterosexual couples'.[13] In November 1996, Howard's office struck me and several other prominent women associated with Labor off the invitation list to a small gathering to meet Hillary Clinton who was visiting Sydney with her husband, US President Bill Clinton.[14] Mrs Clinton had requested to meet with senior Australian women who shared her interests. Instead she got Janette Howard, the wife of the Prime Minister, and her handpicked guests, most of whom could not be accused of sharing Clinton's interest in women's equality and children's rights. It was a petty gesture on Howard's part, but it was typical of his small-mindedness. As was his reaction of surprise and disdain when he and I brushed past each other in the makeup trailer set up at Mrs Macquarie's Chair by NBC's *Today Show*, at the time the highest-rating program on US television, which was doing a series of outdoor broadcasts from the Sydney Harbour foreshore during the Olympic Games in September 2000.[15] Howard looked at me with astonishment. What is *she* doing here? he seemed to be thinking. He must have known, as I did, that there were only four guests. I bet he did not have the same reaction to the other two: Paul Hogan and John Williamson.

⎯⎯⎯◆⎯⎯⎯

In August 1998 I spoke at a women's fundraiser in Byron Bay and, in a speech entitled 'A Dangerous Liaison: Women and the Howard Government', reported on the contraction of choices for women, especially when it came to their reproductive freedom, being orchestrated by John Howard, in partnership with Senator Brian Harradine, the rabidly religious zealot from Tasmania who held the balance of power in the Senate. What, I asked rhetorically, would such men do if they wanted to force women out of employment into full-time motherhood:

'They'd probably start by taking the razor to the family planning agencies—even the Catholic ones (forcing Catholic women back to "Vatican roulette"?); then they'd ban non-surgical alternatives to abortion like the drug RU–486 and after that they'd get officials working on a new model criminal code to replace existing state abortion laws with a new national code that was significantly more restrictive than the current situation in New South Wales and Victoria. They'd amend the Sex Discrimination Act to ensure that only married women had access to fertility programs.'[16]

That was just for starters. I went on to describe the deregulation of casual and part-time work, where women were concentrated, and the resultant pushing down of wages; the cuts to childcare, including afterschool care, further restricting women's workforce options. We were, I said in another speech, going back to the future.[17]

I literally shuddered to think that we might be returning to the days so brilliantly expounded by Betty Friedan in her classic 1963 book *The Feminine Mystique*. According to *Future Shock* author Alvin Toffler, this was the book that 'pulled the trigger on history'. It was the book that lifted the veil on the misery of the legions of educated middle-class housewives in affluent mid–twentieth century America, whose failure to find fulfilment from shopping, cooking, chauffeuring, running a perfect house and trying to be a faultless wife made them feel guilty and depressed. It was, Friedan wrote, 'the problem that has no name', so she set out to identify, document and label it. She called it 'the feminine mystique'. Her book sent shock waves around America and then much of the Western world. Yet here we were a mere 35 years later, seemingly forcing women to return to a world that had made their grandmothers so miserable. It was not just the government trying to restrict women's options when it came to combining motherhood and employment, it was the government seemingly saying that motherhood was women's destiny. If you were not a mother, you did not matter.

If that was the case, where did it leave women like me? I am nobody's mother and I am not the least bit unhappy about it. While I was still in my twenties I decided my life would be freer and fuller if I did not have children. Would my life have been different if I'd had them? Of course it would. Would it have been better? I do not think so. I am very happy with the choice I made. Back in the 1970s, childless people were criticised for being 'selfish'. This was an almost explicit admission by parents that having children was such a burden that they needed everyone else to be similarly encumbered. It was another way of expressing the envy many parents felt for the freedom enjoyed by their childless friends. In the 1980s, when I was in my late-thirties and early-forties, it became fashionable to talk about 'the ticking' of our supposed biological clocks. Women my age were made to feel that we might 'miss out' if we did not 'hurry up'. And quite a few women felt this way, or were made to. There was a blip of baby-having among my single friends in the late 1980s, a trend that was happening with educated and economically self-sufficient women across the developed (or at least English-speaking) world. It was exemplified, even glorified, in *Murphy Brown*, the US TV sitcom starring Candice Bergen as a single mother, that ran for ten years from 1988. And I thought about it. Despite my firm resolve in my twenties to never allow myself to be encumbered by children, of course I did.

In the early 1980s, I was heading for 40, which was seen then as the absolute age-limit for having a first baby, I had no partner and there seemed no prospect of one while I lived in Canberra. But there was probably no better town in which to raise a child as a single mother. I had a good job, I owned a house (well, almost), and I lived and worked in an environment that would support my making such a choice. The services were there and in Canberra you had none of the stresses like traffic and overcrowded childcare centres that made Sydney such a nightmare. But when I looked at friends who had done it, I saw them struggling. Some of them, if they were honest with themselves, were regretting their choice, but of course there was no going back on a decision like this. The child was there, with all its needs and the mother had to deal with them. I saw domestic tragedies: a child who was difficult, a mother unable to cope, physically or emotionally, with what she'd taken on. For me, this was a needed dose of reality. You would have to *really* want to do this. And, when I thought about it, deep down, honest to God, I didn't. Maybe I was different from other women, but I did not have the maternal hankerings so many women talked about. I simply did not feel that same desperate need I'd heard some women describe. Nor did I understand how a modern woman in the 1980s or 1990s, able to earn an income and with freedoms her grandmother could not even have dreamed of, could claim that her very identity was dependent on having a child. I had absorbed earlier in life that many of the women I admired did not have children. Simone de Beauvoir for example. I was astonished to discover that Doris Lessing actually had three kids. I could not recall her mentioning children in those life-changing novels of hers that I devoured as a young woman. I guess I did not notice. I absorbed literature that matched my needs and interests, and families and children were just not on my horizon, so I remained oblivious to the maternal status of many of the women whose books I read. Later, when I made a study of these things, I would discover that having children was almost impossible for artists, but that many women were able to combine motherhood and writing. But I was not to be one of them. I guess I was lucky because it meant that I did not suffer the psychological pain that was clearly the lot of some women. I felt some sympathy for them, although I could not understand their feelings, but I also felt relief that I was not that way. Plenty of women, including a number of my close friends, chose to have children. Others already had them when the women's movement came along and they had no option but to figure out how to make the new ideas work with their existing obligations. But I was able to get on with my life, with no pangs and absolutely no regrets. It meant, as well, that I had no constraints when opportunities presented themselves. I could take a job with the government that would involve a lot of travel. I could move to New York. And I could move back to Sydney, not fettered by considerations of schools and children's friendships and all the other complications of parenting.

❧

In late 1993, Betty Friedan visited Sydney as a guest of the NSW government. Chip and I, along with Chip's mother Beverly Rogers who was visiting us from Boston, took her and her companion to dinner at The Pier, a restaurant that juts out into Rose Bay. Betty was a short, fierce woman who exuded energy, but whose argumentative style could make her exhausting company. Yet here she was, the mother of modern feminism, in Sydney, being charming and relaxing herself into a good time. You got the feeling that this was not something she often allowed herself to do. During our conversation over martinis and a meal of some of the city's finest seafood, I asked her how she would describe herself. Her answer initially floored me.

'First I am an American,' she said. 'Secondly I am Jew, and third, I am a woman.'

The woman who had coined the term 'the feminine mystique', who had revolutionised the lives of millions of women around the world, now ranked being female as behind her national and ethnic identities. And, although she had three children, she did not mention being a mother. I looked at her and wondered if she was simply tired of the struggle. She was 72 and she was now concentrating on the issue of ageing (she was in Sydney to take part in Seniors Week). Perhaps she was now ready to leave the women's fight to others. Yet just the year before I had joined her in Dublin where she and I and Irene Natividad were running a Global Summit of Women,[18] a gathering hosted by the Irish President Mary Robinson. The Summit, which is still in existence and now run solely by Natividad, had brought together women from around the world, aiming to internationalise the women's movement. I could not see Betty Friedan retreating from that ambition. And yet she had paid a heavy price for her activism. I recalled the awful story I'd read about Friedan not showing up to a major protest she was due to lead at the Plaza Hotel in New York in February 1969. A group of women planned to invade the Oak Room, that genteel bastion of Yankee privilege that would not permit women to be present between the hours of 12 and 3 p.m., when the power lunches were held. Friedan herself had been humiliated there five years earlier; she'd turned up to meet the publisher Clay Felker for lunch, and been denied entry. Felker had invited her, apparently blissfully unaware that in the past he was surrounded only by men when he dined there at lunch times. Now, at precisely noon, a bunch of fur-coat wearing women (they were not going to allow dress codes to be an excuse for denying them entry) was about to storm this hallowed sanctum. The media was there in droves but Betty Friedan was not.[19] She could not come, Betty told the woman who'd rung to see where she was, because she had a black eye and a big bruise on her cheek. The previous night Betty's husband, Carl, had hit her. He did this often before she had a big public engagement, Betty told her friend. The friend was resourceful: a theatrical-makeup artist was hastily dispatched to Betty's apartment and, her bruises artfully concealed, America's most famous feminist made it to the Oak Room in time for the protest.

Friedan had eventually divorced Carl, but her life was a series of fights of one kind or another. She was a difficult person, argumentative and almost impossible to mollify once she was exercised about something. I admired Betty greatly for her writing and thinking but I knew how hard she could be to work with. I agreed with her pragmatism and her realism and I had managed to work fruitfully with her a number of times, but I'd been horrified by the patronising cruelty she dispensed to women she regarded as unimportant. She was a polarising figure in the women's movement, and the hatred she and Gloria Steinem had for each other was legendary. I had had an earful of it from Gloria the first time I'd mentioned Betty's name to her. And Betty had of course earned the undying enmity of huge numbers of women when she had warned that what she called 'the lavender menace'— the large presence of lesbians in the women's movement—might deter mainstream women from joining.

Yet, I thought, perhaps I understand what Betty meant when she downplayed her sex in her description of herself. Perhaps she was just tired of the struggle, worn-out by constantly having to be the one to point out where women were missing out; always the spoiler, never able to relax and just 'be'. I sometimes felt the same way. It was often a lonely place to be. There was camaraderie in the women's movement, of course, but the sisterhood was less enveloping and intense than it had been in the early days. Now it was the occasional meeting, a march on International Women's Day, and a bit of informal contact. We all had other lives now. But I could never look away and ignore something I thought was unjust or unfair. I could not stop myself from naming it and condemning it but I, too, was weary of a struggle that seemed never to end. I longed to be able to be 'just' another person, enjoying my life and work, and not needing to always be the one

who was alert to the putdowns, the humiliations and the outright discrimi-
nation that women still had to endure so much of the time. But nor did
I have a choice because women often approached me, wanting to talk.
Sometimes the stories were ugly, even brutal, other times just sad. But they
were almost always stories that women had kept sequestered, hidden away
in secret compartments of their hearts, often unable to be talked about.
Sometimes it was just they had no one to tell. There was usually not much
I could do except listen but back then, before a movement like #MeToo
emerged in 2017 that encourages women to share these stories and to have
such bad behaviour banished from the workplace, mostly that was enough.
It happened a lot. It might be a knock on my front door in Canberra back
in the early 1980s, with a well-known journalist and her husband on my
doorstep, there to tell me the story of her harassment by a famous editor.
It might be the woman from the *Herald* switchboard telling me about the
abortion she had always kept a secret. It might be a 'typist', the demeaning
title once used for the women, always women, who provided stenographic
and administrative assistance to bosses who were invariably men, who had
been brought down from one of our Scandinavian embassies to Paris to
help out with a prime ministerial visit. Very late at night, after the correspondence was done, this woman rang my hotel room and asked if she
could meet me for a drink. She had a story of assault in a foreign country
that the Ambassador and his senior staff chose to not treat seriously. Or it
might be a long-time friend, finally finding the words to talk about her rape.
When you wove together all these stories you saw that so many Australian
women had so little power over their lives, if not always at least during
these episodes when they were vulnerable, and when there was no one to
turn to for consolation or redress.

Friedan had famously warned of a backlash against women's equality
and, as with so many of her pronouncements, she proved to be distressingly
prescient. In 2005, the *New York Times* columnist Maureen Dowd asked:
'If we flash forward to 2030, will we see all those young women who thought
trying to Have It All was a pointless slog, now middle-aged and stranded in
suburbia, popping Ativan, struggling with rebellious teenagers, deserted by
husbands for younger babes, unable to get back into a workforce they never
tried to be part of?'

If this happens, Dowd wrote, these domestic robots will be 'desperately seeking a new Betty Friedan'.[20]

After *Good Weekend*, I intended to establish myself as a full-time writer. I had already done my 'big book' on women with *Damned Whores* back in 1975 and, it seemed to me that I had said all that I wanted or needed to say. I had other topics I wanted to write about. I intended the first book of my new writing life to be an autobiography. This would inevitably explore what it was like to be a woman in Australia in the 1960s and 70s, and the consequent founding of the women's movement, the setting up of Elsie Women's Refuge, and the fight for legal abortion—but it was also a broader story of family and country and I intended it to set me on a path to writing books on a wide range of subjects. But I found that I simply could not look the other way to what was happening to Australian women under John Howard so in 2003 I wrote a book I called *The End of Equality*.[21] It would be a tough book, tough on Howard but also tough on the women in Canberra who I considered were mere bystanders, saying nothing while our rights were being stripped from us. Joan Kirner read the chapter I'd initially called 'Political kewpie dolls' and told me that it was unfair. I thought she was being unduly protective of her politician sisters, but I respected her enough to tone it down somewhat; I changed the title to 'Political eunuchs'.

I was disappointed, and surprised, that there was not more of a backlash against John Howard by women. So were my publishers. Random House had put a lot of effort, and money, into promoting *The End of Equality*. Based on a poll of young women in their office who had read the book and responded with outrage at learning what was being taken away from them, they expected the book to run off the shelves. It didn't. The world was turning-in on itself. It was the era of privatisation against collective ownership, of individualism versus social actions, of DIY feminism rather than a women's movement, of private solutions to 'problems' such as childcare or workplace opportunities. People endured alone and suffered in silence. John Howard had helped engineer this climate and he was very very lucky that, at the time, so few people saw through what he was doing.

So I thought that would be my last word—or at least my last book—on the subject of women but again I was wrong. In 1994, after Keating had launched the new edition of *Damned Whores*, I would have been startled to know that over the next 20 years, I would continually return to the subject of the unequal and, at times, brutal treatment of women in Australian society. I was an unwilling witness and an even more reluctant chronicler of our country's seemingly ingrained disparagement of women, but the turn of events kept sending me back to the keyboard. I was astounded at the hostility directed at our first female Prime Minister, Julia Gillard, during her three years in office and at first unable to fathom the rationale for the pornographic images that were part of the artillery directed against her. I tried to make sense of it in 2013 in a short book, *The Misogyny Factor*. The Gillard factor was, I believed, responsible for the amazing resurgence in feminism, especially among young women, that began around that time and which led to a period of intense self-scrutiny that continues today. Yet at the same time as we were pondering why women were finding it so hard to make headway in the world outside the home, motherhood and the domestic arts were getting a 21st century makeover.

Women were having more babies than they'd had in years. In 2006 the birthrate rose to 1.90 for the first time in fifteen years and continued to hover around that level for the next six years. It seemed that women had responded with enthusiasm to the 2004 exhortation of the federal Treasurer Peter Costello in 2004 that they 'have one for mum, one for dad and one for the country'. The federal government's baby bonus, a non-means tested payment of $5000 per baby, introduced in 2004, helped too. Evidence showed that women timed their pregnancies to be able to take advantage of this payment.[22] Surprisingly, to me at least, this rise in the birthrate also led to a revival of domesticity. Young women began baking and doing craftwork and other home-based activities that my generation had dispensed with, as emblematic of women's domestic subjugation. Plus we simply did not have time; especially those who had jobs and kids. Now, young women were deciding not to return to work after they had children. We saw the rise of the 'yummy mummy'. Motherhood was cool in a way it had not been since the baby boom of the 1940s and '50s. Yummy mummies, with their extravagant baby showers and massive baby buggies, were right up there competing with their be-suited employed sisters in the status stakes. In fact, sometimes the balance seemed to tilt towards the mummies, and working mothers were made to feel guilty about having their kids in childcare, not doing tuck-shop duty or having freshly baked snacks ready when the children came home from school. I watched this development with amazement and sadness. Why did these young women not want to combine having children with having an economic life outside the home? What we in the women's movement always wanted was for women to be able to choose when and whether to have children, and to be able to combine that choice with continued engagement with the economy. We wanted to relieve women of what an early suffragette had called 'the unconscionable choice' women had had to make in the early twentieth century between love and work; in those early days of unreliable contraception, choosing love invariably meant motherhood. The option that many women, including myself, enjoy today—of love without children—simply did not exist. Were we now surrendering that option? It seemed that full-time motherhood was once again becoming the preferred option for young women, especially young women with tertiary education whose workforce participation rates dropped precipitously during the early years of the 21st century. Today, women without children are no longer called 'selfish'. Now we are more likely to be objects of pity. This is another form of social control, of course, a quite insidious one that has the effect of making childless women feel inadequate, or unfulfilled, especially now motherhood is back in vogue. Women themselves mostly seem to welcome this, but it seemed in so many ways that we were back to where we were when I'd first written about women. The God's Police stereotype that I had described in 1975 had not disappeared, but had merely been updated.

Once again, I felt compelled to write about this. Forty-one years after its original publication, in 2016, in a new edition of *Damned Whores and God's Police*[23] I argued that the two stereotypes still had a powerful grip on modern Australia, even if they had been modernised to adjust to the times. Moreover, I argued that it was women themselves who were reluctant to surrender the role of running their families, physically and emotionally. It was their one area of undisputed power and authority, and they were not going to give that up lightly. 'We have not disavowed that motherhood is still the central, preferable and most admired option for women,' I wrote in the new introduction. 'We might not overtly punish women who are not mothers but we have our ways of letting them know they have fallen short of the ideal. By calling them "deliberately barren", for instance.'[24] Or, in my case, certain people at Fairfax trying to undermine me by saying I had no empathy, and was a bad boss, because I had no children.

———⸙———

I stayed another two years at *Good Weekend*. A number of my staff members who had most disliked me left, while a couple of those who'd been at the forefront of trying to get rid of me apologised and decided to stay. Those who had kept their heads down throughout the entire gruesome episode were just glad it was over. So was I, of course, but I was never going to forget the effort that had been made to try to destroy me. And who knew how much of the dirt had stuck? Years later, I still kept being asked about it. People wanted to know: what *really* happened? What was behind all that? I wasn't bitter but I was incredulous. If it had been intended to force me to leave, the gambit had failed. There was no way I was going to leave with that hanging over me. I recruited new staffers, including the wonderfully droll Tom Dusevic, who came over from the *Australian* to be deputy editor. The new mix of personality and talent revived the kind of energy that had driven our reinvention in 1994, and it felt as if we were back to where we had been trying to get to all along. We received a swag of nominations in the 1995 Australian Society of Magazine Editors awards, and took out the Best Reporting and Best Columns categories, the only magazine to win more than one award. Nikki Barrowclough won Best Reporting for her harrowing account of the Australian men who were serial importers of Filipina 'mail order brides', many of whom were summarily divorced, or simply disappeared after marriage, meaning the husband was able to bring in another wife.[25] It was just horrible to know that women were being treated this way, in Australia, in 1995.

In November 1996 we ran David Leser's astonishing profile of the newly elected Queensland federal MP Pauline Hanson. She had made headlines for her maiden speech, attacking Asian immigration and multiculturalism, and for stating that she would not represent any Aboriginal people who lived in her electorate of Oxley.[26] Our cover, shot by the brilliant Tim Bauer, was a very tight closeup of Hanson's face; her green eyes and pinched scarlet lips looked out at the reader with what seemed like obdurate indifference. 'Inside the mind of Pauline Hanson', was the cover line—and David Leser certainly delivered that. After his many requests for an interview had been ignored or refused, he simply got on a plane, put himself in Hanson's path, and managed to secure himself a dinner invitation to her property outside town. His discursive interview with her was revelatory. He showed the conflicts within her family, the previously unmentioned several prior husbands—and the former mother-in-law, who was a Holocaust survivor who trembled in fear at the thought her erstwhile relative might have her deported.

'There are a couple of risks in doing this story,' Leser had written. 'First, there will be those who will argue that it further boosts the profile of a woman who should never have been given a forum in the first place; that, now when the dust is perhaps settling, we are continuing to turn, in the words of one commentator, a "misfit into a megastar".'

'The second risk is that in trying to examine Pauline Hanson's life, we end up on an excursion through the ugly, primal landscape of the Australian character where bigotry and racism have always played their part, but which a noble bipartisanship in recent decades has attempted to obviate. By re-visiting such tribal prejudices we're in danger of causing further offence at home and abroad.'

As editor, I felt the risk was worth taking. I was strongly of the view that we needed to shine a light on this woman and her ideas that were starting to roll like a tsunami across the Australian political landscape. We were not to know then that Pauline Hanson would remain a political phenomenon for the next two decades at least, would have her party win seats in state parliaments and that, after just one term as the member for Oxley and a subsequent brief term in prison for electoral fraud (her conviction was later overturned)[27] she, along with three One Nation colleagues, would be elected to the Australian Senate in 2016. The supposed misfit has had a very long political life.

Leser concluded his piece with the following observation: 'For a brief moment I actually feel sorry for her. I look at Pauline Hanson and see a woman hopelessly out of her depth. I see a media circus and a political neophyte who has lost virtually all privacy. I see, in part, a scapegoat for all the ugly sentiments that gnaw away at the human heart, including those of our more slippery politicians.'

But then he looked once more 'and what I see again are the cold, sharp features of bigotry and racism'. He feels he is justified in writing about her. And so did I.

Twelve days after Pauline Hanson's maiden speech, Prime Minister John Howard travelled to Queensland where he addressed the Liberal Party. In his remarks he noted that in the six months since his—and, let's not forget, Hanson's—election, 'people do feel able to speak a little more freely and a little more openly about how they feel. In a sense the pall of censorship on certain issues has been lifted . . .'[28] He went on to welcome the fact that people could speak freely 'without living in fear of being branded a racist or a bigot'.

Remember that date: 22 September 1996. Australian politics changed forever that day. Here was the Prime Minister abrogating his responsibility to lead, his duty to curb the baser instincts of many in the population and to ensure the country moved forward together. Instead the Prime Minister encouraged people to express 'how they feel'. He literally opened the floodgates to aggrieved or angry people setting aside civic restraint and pouring out whatever vitriol or bile was bubbling away inside them. I remember walking through the streets of Bankstown one afternoon in early 1993 with Paul Keating when one of his constituents fell into step beside him and offered a complaint about the number of shops that now had Chinese names, and Chinese characters written across their windows. Keating quickly deflected the racist sentiment the man was trying to express. I can't remember now exactly what he said, but I do recall how easily he was able to mollify the man, treating him seriously but at the same time giving him a quick lesson on how times were changing and we had to change with them. By contrast, John Howard opened a different door: say what you feel, he said. Let it rip. And people have been doing exactly that ever since. Astonishingly hateful racist abuse is now commonplace in our streets and on social media. And the more people engage in it, the worse it gets. The tenor and content of abuse against our fellow citizens because of their race, their sex, their religion or whatever characteristic disturbs the abuser has become frightening, because it points to a barely concealed violence simmering away beneath the surface of our society. At the same time, Howard was also fostering a total revision of how we as Australians saw ourselves. A whole

new rewriting of our national story was underway, which denied the deci-
mation of the Indigenous inhabitants at the hands of the British. Howard
dismissed what he called 'the black armband view of history', and was ably
assisted by craven collaborators only too willing to provide the 'evidence' for
this shameful revisionism.

As a result of these two moves, whole sections of our population have
become fair game. Sexist abuse is now also part of our daily discourse. So
much so that on 12 March 2013, a woman felt able to yell down from the
public gallery of the nation's Parliament to the Prime Minister: 'Moll!' This
was beyond anything we had experienced in Australia before, and I feel justified in blaming John Howard for putting the prime ministerial imprimatur
on hate speech. He encouraged it and look where it has led us. And that is
why I am so angry with him.

In early 1997, I took stock. Chip and I with a bunch of friends had just
enjoyed a two-week visit to Vietnam, my first trip to that part of Asia.
We'd travelled from north to south on the Reunification Express, seen the
remnants of the war that had ended just 22 years earlier, and observed with
wonder the grit and resilience of a people who were remaking their country
after more than a century of occupation and combat. I realised I was ready
for a remaking myself. I was proud of what we were doing at *Good Weekend*,
but editing the magazine had stopped being fun. The battles were never-
ending. As the economy slowed, advertisers became more demanding,
expecting editorial favours we had never had to accede to in the past. There
were neverending turf battles and other attacks on me and my tenure in the
job. This constant corporate slugfest was exhausting and, as I'd experienced
in the bureaucracy when I was at OSW, enervating. My enemies were there
for the long game, whereas I was totally disenchanted with its pettiness.
It was all about power, I recognised that, but the stakes did not interest me
enough to devote my life to the fight. So one Monday morning in March,
after an act of treachery from a supposed colleague that was designed to
undermine and demoralise me, I stormed into the CEO's office and resigned.
I had no qualms about accepting the package they offered. It gave me a bit of
a cushion as I sailed off towards my next adventure.

CHAPTER ELEVEN

PEACE AND WAR

In September 2000 I was elected chair of the board of Greenpeace International. It was so different from anything I had ever done before that many people had trouble grasping it. 'Greenpeace?' they'd say. 'We didn't know you were a greenie.' Or, 'Don't you mean Greenpeace Australia?' No one seemed able to accept that I could have got myself a position on the international board of the world's most famous environmental organisation—and that I had actually been headhunted for the position. The media was equally sceptical, even sneering, in its coverage: 'The appointment of Dr Summers . . . has surprised some Australian observers who do not recall the former head of the Office of the Status of Women taking any particular interest in environmental issues', said a page one article in the *Sydney Morning Herald*.[1]

This job did not fit most people's preconceptions of me; it wasn't 'women', or journalism. Why on earth had I stepped off my familiar path to do something so out of character? Why not? I retorted. Hadn't I left a safe job in the public service in Canberra to go to New York in 1986? And risked my newly created post-*Ms.* identity in 1992 to go to Canberra for what was meant to be just a three-month job with Prime Minister Paul Keating? Wasn't such risk-taking and adventure-seeking what I did? I was no longer the girl who'd been too frightened to stay in New York in the 1970s. Now I was up for practically anything. Most people could not fathom themselves doing anything unpredictable or risky. Nor could they see past their assumptions about the person they thought I was. And being a board chair, for an *international* organisation, an environmental one at that, did not fit that picture. And I resented this; I was tired of being pigeonholed. I wanted to go wherever life was going to take me.

Yet this step was a huge one—and not just because it defied people's expectations. It was an abrupt departure from the course I had set for myself. There was no doubt that this serious and important job would disrupt the life that I was feeling contented with because, at last, I was where I wanted to be. It was two years since I had left *Good Weekend* and I was finally living the writing life. I had just finished a book, an autobiography to be called *Ducks on the Pond*, which would be published later in 1999. It was my first book in more than fifteen years. I'd been scared that perhaps I did not have another book in me, so I was as relieved as I was proud to have accomplished something large and, I hoped, worthy. (Although I had written a lengthy new introduction for a revised edition of *Damned Whores and God's Police* in 1994, I had not completed a new book since *Gamble for Power* in 1983.) My regular column with the *Sydney Morning Herald* was my only published writing (and income) at the time. In April, Chip and I had got the job of editing the *Australian Author*, a three-times a year magazine for writers published by the Australian Society for Authors. We had brought our magazine experience to the task: hiring an art director, insisting on articles being edited, introducing photography and illustrations. We hoped we were turning it into a livelier, well-written and better-looking publication. It was a job we would hold for six years and while it wasn't *Les Temps Modernes*, our editing partnership was yet one more rewarding element in the life we continued to enjoy together. We sparked off each other, liked each other's ideas and got considerable satisfaction from crafting these into interesting magazine pieces. When people asked me what I did, I could point to the magazine, to writing books, journalism, giving speeches and some political activism. It was the life I had yearned for, but always found a rationale for not doing. Now I had finally broken the old patterns. I would soon start my next book. So what was I doing in the Netherlands in July 1999, putting myself forward for a job that, despite being part-time, would involve lots of work and a great deal of international travel? Was I, yet again, trying to sabotage myself? Or was I simply unable to refuse yet another great adventure?

Eindhoven is a small thirteenth-century city in the south of Holland, where Greenpeace International was holding its annual general meeting. As we'd driven in from Amsterdam, we saw that virtually nothing remained of the medieval city; it had been almost completely destroyed by Allied bombs during the liberation in September 1944. The new city, like the conference centre, was squat and ugly, steel and glass, with none of the charm of the canals and centuries-old houses that I'd glimpsed in Amsterdam during my transit. I was in Eindhoven because of a quite unexpected and intriguing opportunity to seek election to the Greenpeace Board. If I was chosen, I would become involved in the leadership of the world's most famous environmental organisation. While I waited to make my presentation, I stayed in my room, checking the proofs of *Ducks*; once they were corrected, I would send copies to my mother and to my four surviving brothers, to whom I planned to dedicate the book. It was a story that they were mostly familiar with. Indeed, much of my story was also theirs. I had taped several lengthy conversations with my mother about her life, so she knew what I was proposing to write. I was not expecting my family to have problems with what I had written. I could not have been more wrong.

Meeting the Greenpeace people was a revelation. I suppose I was expecting earnest individuals wearing dreadlocks and sandals. Instead I was confronted with, among others, a surgeon from Brazil, an Israeli sociologist, scientists from England and Germany, a Greek shipping magnate, a Chinese barrister from Hong Kong, and a member of the British House of Lords, all of whom were either Trustees or Executive Directors (EDs) of their national Greenpeace offices. There were 27 of these national and regional offices, mostly in Europe, but also in the Americas, Russia, China (Hong Kong), Japan and Southeast Asia. These people had flown in just for the weekend; some of them, like the Latin Americans and those from Asia, had had to endure flights almost as long as we Australians routinely put up with. I should have realised from the way in which I had been head-hunted that Greenpeace was a totally professional organisation. The head of its international board search committee was Ann de Wachter, a long-time member of Greenpeace's Australian board, who lived in Sydney and had her own public relations firm. When she first approached me, I was sceptical. I had no experience and, frankly, not a huge amount of interest in environmental issues. I was undoubtedly an instinctive greenie, but my previous activism had been mostly around women's equality issues or, two decades earlier in Sydney, prisons or resident action activities. Ann assured me that Greenpeace had plenty of environmental expertise. They were looking to bring onto the seven-person board someone with a good strategic mind and with media and communications experience.

After I made my presentation, the Trustees (who would elect the new board members) questioned me intently. In introducing myself, I had described my work at OSW, doing the management buyout in New York, and my work in Paul Keating's office in helping him win an unexpected electoral victory. None of these examples had any direct bearing on the work of Greenpeace, I conceded, but I made the argument that my skills were adaptable and could easily be transferred to the service of this organisation as it headed towards the new millennium. I had not expected either the quality of the discussion, nor the range of subjects put to me. Had I been anticipating talk of zodiacs and whales? Swapping stories on banner drops and other daring exploits? Instead, among other subjects, we talked about population and pacifism. Peter Melchett, the long-term British ED who had previously been a minister in the Callaghan Labor government and who was also an hereditary peer, acknowledged that population growth was one of the biggest threats to the world's ecology. But it was not a discussion the organisation was prepared to have, he told me. Perhaps a quarter of Greenpeace's offices were located in countries that were nominally Catholic, and the organisation did not want to embroil itself in the perilous politics of abortion. I absorbed this and resolved to think further about its implications. Then George Vernicos, the gruff-seeming Greek guy who owned ships and who, I later learned, had been imprisoned and tortured during the *junta* of 1967–74, asked me if I was a pacifist.

'No, I am not a pacifist, and nor do I think that Greenpeace is a pacifist organisation,' I responded, 'its flagship is, after all, called the *Rainbow Warrior*.'

They seemed to like that answer, but the question had thrown me. I knew non-violence was one of the core principles of Greenpeace, but did that mean it was anti-war? But how could a non-violent organisation support war? I was starting to see that this was a very different Greenpeace from the one I'd imagined. This Greenpeace agonised over the politics, the philosophy and the ethics of what it was trying to do; this was before they even got to the daring campaign strategies that had made Greenpeace a globally known organisation. I had initially been taken aback when I walked into the meeting room and had seen that the Trustees were seated around a three-sided table in alphabetical order according to country, with the country names on white cards in front of them, just like the United Nations. They might as well have had little flags as well. I had assumed a radical body like Greenpeace would have been less formal, less country-focused. I would later learn that the national basis of the organisation's structure was one of its biggest problems. But after my two days with them, I decided I liked these people. And I liked what they were trying to do. I wanted to be part of it—if they'd have me.

I was elected, but because of a quirk in the meetings calendar, my life with Greenpeace would not start until seven months later, at the board meeting of February 2000 which was held in Italy, at the Castello di Gargonza, a former monastery in Tuscany, not far from Florence. It was not luxurious but it was very classy, because it was so old and was situated on top of a mountain surrounded by forests of fir trees. Again, it was not what I had expected of Greenpeace. (Neither did most of those attending, it turned out, and Italy was reprimanded for choosing such an unsuitable venue. In future, we were to opt for more Spartan accommodation.) But it was in Tuscany that I was exposed to the true complexity of the organisation that was trying to globalise its structure and adapt to the challenges created by the newer offices from the developing world, wanting issues like food and energy security added to the traditional Greenpeace campaigns on whales, nukes, forests, GMOs, toxics and oceans. The organisation's growth had seemingly stalled, and although it still had more than two million members worldwide, newly energised groups like WWF were becoming competitive. As a body that shunned corporate and government donations, relying solely on individuals and philanthropy, Greenpeace needed to protect and grow its fundraising base while maintaining its campaign integrity. I would discover that funds were more easily raised to save animals or for scary campaigns like toxics

launch my book about the vicissitudes of being a woman in Australia in the mid-twentieth century, but I was not expecting the frank outpouring contained in her speech. She had received great sustenance from reading *Damned Whores and God's Police* back in the 1970s, she said: 'At a difficult time in my life, and my relationship with Bob, this sort of understanding [my explanation of the damned whores and God's police roles] that put my own troubles in a wider (and yet a very Australian) context, was a valuable gift.'

But although Hazel Hawke had liked the book, and the beloved Australian novelist Ruth Park had written a generous preface, my mother had taken a very different view. She was beside herself with anger, humiliation and grief at what I had revealed about our family. She especially could not bear, she told me in several letters, that I had told the story of my father's drinking and of his ill-treatment of me. She conceded it was all true but, she wrote, there was no need to tell the world. And she was horrified at my 'startlingly sordid' description of an early and humiliating sexual relationship. 'Is it necessary to give such salacious detail?' she'd asked. 'This is written by Anne Summers, PhD AO, not Barbara Cartland or someone of that ilk.' I found the letters very hard to read, especially when she told me about the physical and emotional toll it was taking. She had woken one morning after just a few hours sleep: '. . . I felt there was a band of lead across my head, and I immediately remembered that was how I felt when I woke up the morning after Jamie died'. (In 1976 her youngest child, and my little brother, Jamie, had died of cancer at the age of seventeen.) At the same time, I could not understand her anger and her misery. I could not believe she had not understood that I was going to write about these things. I had *interviewed* her about it! And while I was upset that she was upset, I also was sick of her trying to control and manipulate me, to portray me as someone I was not. She could not accept me as I was. She took the bits she liked, the public acclaim, the Order of Australia, the doctorate, the working for Prime Ministers and knowing famous people (especially when she had photographs of me with them she could display to her friends), but she did not want the rest: the unconventional elements of which she disapproved, the not-staying married, not having children, the essential person I was. She could never understand, or acknowledge, that what made it possible for me to do the things that she could brag about was that I had become a very different person—from her and from the woman she had wanted me to be. I had rejected that person, and the constraints she had had to endure, and I had made my own way. Now I was supposed to suppress my story so she could preserve appearances in front of her snobbish friends. They would be saying that I should have waited till she was dead, she told me. But I was not prepared to pretend that none of these things happened. My father *had* treated me appallingly, I *had* been used and abused by a lover, and I *had* had a botched illegal backyard abortion in 1965 that I was lucky did not kill me. She had spent her life trying to survive by putting on a good front, and while I understood the strategy, it was not the way I was, or wanted to be. I had become a different kind of woman, and the book I had written was my attempt to start telling the story of how I managed it.

For me, the family story was only part of what *Ducks on the Pond* was about. I'd tried to paint a bigger picture, to capture what life was like for girls like me who grew up in Catholic families in the 1950s, and who were given no encouragement to do anything with their lives except become wives and mothers. My family, and my school, had mirrored the wider society that offered women few opportunities in those grim days. The book's title had come from a warning phrase called out when a woman was approaching the shearing sheds. It was to alert the men to watch their language, but it had seemed to me the perfect metaphor for the ways women were excluded from most areas of life outside the home. I was part of the generation that decided to challenge and to change that, and my book told my part of the story of how we'd gone about it. I chronicled the early days of the women's liberation movement, the setting up of Elsie Women's Refuge, my taking on the huge task of retelling the story of Australian history and society through feminist eyes. But I also had to tell my personal story: having to leave home at seventeen—at a time when that was highly unusual—because of my father's hostility towards me, getting married at age 22 then separating three years later. I had been frank, perhaps brutal, in the way I told my story, but I felt that I needed the truth as my shield. I had grown up in conservative Adelaide, a city built on secrets and denial, where appearances were what counted and the truth about people's lives was more often than not concealed. This had damaged me and, I decided, I needed to confront my past in order to give myself a future. It had become almost the mantra of the women's movement to speak with utter honesty about one's life, whether it was to reveal a long-sublimated rape, to admit to never having had an orgasm, to confess to fear of speaking out. We called it consciousness-raising, and we believed that the truth gave us both strength and courage. It was high-risk and often disastrous, as not everyone could handle the consequences of having their past lives unfurled to public view, but to me it was logical and self-evident. I had to deal with my past, to try to understand who I now was, and how I had become that person. I could not do that without dealing with my terrible relationship with my father.

I had been looking forward to our family story being read and recognised as the common Australian story that it was. I had naively thought that it might even join the well-known and loved books that sit on so many people's shelves, because they resonate with who we are. None of this happened. I had some wonderful letters from people who enjoyed my story, including one from a Sydney businesswoman I knew who, astonishingly, revealed to me a life that was almost identical to my own, right down to her father being in the Air Force in the very same town as mine had been, who had also liked to wear women's clothes and who, also like my father, over time became a spectacular drunk. But my mother was not interested in learning that our life-story had been very common, post World War One. In her view, I had betrayed a trust, I had broadcast our secrets and I had shamed her. She travelled to Sydney to tell me face-to-face how angry and upset she was. I expected an all-out war, as we'd had so many times in the past, such as when I told her I was getting married in a registry office rather than in the Catholic Church, but this time she surprised me. She told me that I had placed a terrible burden on her, but that she would nevertheless return to Sydney for the book launch. She wanted to put on a public display of support for her daughter. On the night you would never have guessed she was anything other than a proud mother of the writer, whose book was being launched in the company of a large crowd of friends at a cocktail party at a fancy restaurant, just across from the Art Gallery of NSW.

In the weeks and months that followed, she wrote to many people, especially to priests and nuns, seeking confirmation for her views. Without exception, they gently disagreed. Friends counselled her to understand the need for writers to tell the truth. Within a year she had reconciled herself to the book, even harassing bookshops to move it to a more prominent position, and proudly noting in her diary when it sold out. She loved and admired Chip—finally there was something or rather someone in my life she could be unreservedly pleased about—and to her immense credit, she had no problem with the difference in our ages. Now she also immersed herself in my Greenpeace life, demanding I send her my detailed itineraries so she could follow my travels, and while she really had no idea what my job involved, she was proud of me. And she was no doubt relieved that her daughter had provided her with another story, something else she could genuinely brag about, which pushed back into the recesses of her pride the book that had caused her such pain.

Bill Darnell, a young Canadian social worker, dreamed up the name Greenpeace in 1971. It was, says an official history of the organisation, a 'dynamic combination of words that bound together concern for the planet and opposition to nuclear arms in a forceful new vision that would inspire some of the most effective environmental protests of all time'.[2] Darnell was one of twelve activists, all of them men and most with either a Quaker or environmentalist background, who in September that year sailed from Vancouver to Amchitka in the Aleutian chain of islands in an old dilapidated 24-metre boat, *Phyllis Cormack* that was hastily renamed *Greenpeace*. They were intending to bear witness to a proposed US test of a nuclear bomb in this remote, earthquake-prone part of the world. Their action did not stop that test, which took place on 6 November, but they did unleash a tidal wave of enduring political protests that led to an end to nuclear testing on Amchitka and the beginning of a new, radical and global movement. As the name implied, the movement saw nuclear annihilation as the greatest threat to the environment, and in the early years Greenpeace focused only on that one issue. There were some who believed that opposition to nukes, as they became known in the Greenpeace world, should be the sole campaign. But by 1975 this view was being contested by a group who argued the International Whaling Commission was not doing its job of protecting endangered species of whales. In 1975 the first Greenpeace boats set out to confront the Soviet whaling fleet. Using zodiacs, crewmembers got close to the harpooned and bleeding animals, filmed their death agonies and so initiated what would become a signature form of campaigning for Greenpeace.

Twenty-eight years later, when I joined the Greenpeace Board, the methods were essentially the same—creative and daring actions to dramatise the issues—but the issues themselves had been broadened. Greenpeace now described its mission as being to protect the global commons (its oceans, its climate/ozone, its very existence against the threat of nukes) by campaigning on issues such as ancient forests, toxic substances, nuclear disarmament and genetically modified organisms (GMOs). The organisation was also expanding into trade issues, opposing globalisation and many of the actions of international organisations such as the World Bank, the International Monetary Fund and the World Trade Organization. Greenpeace was now global, having opened its first office in a developing country, in Argentina in 1987, and with a growing presence in Asia, the Middle East and Latin America. Africa would soon be the next horizon. It was grappling with the challenges of operating globally while preserving local ties and loyalties. Greenpeace was also an organisation that had been severely traumatised in July 1985, when agents of the French government had blown up the *Rainbow Warrior*, which was docked in Auckland Harbour, destroying the boat and killing a photographer who was on board. The stakes had suddenly escalated. Greenpeace was, as they liked to say, making waves. If a government had engaged in murderous actions to stop a Greenpeace boat from observing its nuclear tests then clearly the organisation was having an impact. But it was paying a heavy, perhaps unacceptable, price. Greenpeace was accustomed to run-ins, often violent ones, with governments, and to imprisonment, injunctions, fines and other penalties for taking on powerful interests, but it had never before been the target of a state-sponsored act of terrorism.

During my seven years at Greenpeace, I learned to see the world differently. I developed an informed understanding of the fragility of the planet and I acquired an unexpected and fervent admiration for the people who went to such lengths to protect our earth—and us—from those who, from ignorance or greed, were bringing us closer to extinction. Simply to acquit myself in the job, I needed to acquire a great deal of specialist knowledge in addition to being across our campaign issues and methods, and all the complexities involved in supervising a global organisation in a volatile world. As a board we needed a policy in case a staff member was kidnapped and we had to determine whether it would be a breach of our non-violence policy to have armed guards protect staff in our Amazon office, who had received extremely specific death threats. We pondered having our very right to exist being revoked by governments trying to curb our effectiveness, and we assessed the financial impact of losing tax-deductible status in a major fundraising market. The only boats I'd been on before were ferries but now I had to get my head around a fleet plan, understand the costs of refuelling at sea (and therefore the ongoing viability of the whaling campaign in the Great Southern Ocean) and deal with staffing and pay issues for crews that were totally different from those for the rest of our employees. Probably my proudest moment on the board was in 2006 when I led the decision to commission a new ship. The 58-metre *Rainbow Warrior III* would be Greenpeace's first-ever purpose-built boat. It was going to cost 20.8 million euro, but we had guaranteed contributions from the NROs and were confident our supporters would kick-in to ensure Greenpeace could continue to sail this eco-warrior of the waters. I was long gone by the time the ship was launched in July 2011, but the world's first-ever custom built environmental campaigning vessel was, on all accounts, a masterpiece.

I met some extremely smart people at Greenpeace. It is one thing to be dedicated and courageous and be willing to hang your arse from a fast-moving inflatable to stop illegal fishing or logging, and Greenpeace had dozens of such people, and admirable as they were, the world is not changed by bravery alone. It took big thinking to outwit the world's governments and corporations, and Greenpeace was fortunate to have plenty of people also able to do that. The challenge was to keep doing it, to adapt to growth, to changing geopolitics and evolving technologies, to learn to age as an organisation without growing sclerotic or failing to plan succession. Like the women's movement, which was about the same age but whose agenda and tactics were very different, the environmental and anti-war movements that were brought together in Greenpeace helped define my generation. I felt extraordinarily privileged to gain insights into how the organisation survived and endured that those years on the inside gave me.

At the end of 2000, after just a year on the Greenpeace Board, I was per-suaded to accept the position of Board Chair. It was an extraordinary honour, and a singular vote of confidence in me, a newbie. I had never chaired a board; indeed, my board experience was quite limited, but I did not let that discourage me. I had leapt in the deep-end before and shown I could learn quickly and adapt to a new culture, and although this was far bigger than anything I'd taken on in the past, I saw no reason why I could not do so again. I was now the titular leader of a global entity with an annual income of around 150 million euro, some 1100 staff, plus the crews of the various Greenpeace ships, and members, defined as anyone who made a donation, numbering 2.4 million. Board Chair was not a high-profile position, because the head of the organisation and the main spokesperson was the International Executive Director (IED) but, as my predecessor set out for me in a handover letter, 'it requires real leadership ability: vision, strategic thinking, commitment, stamina and the ability to listen to, persuade and inspire people from many different backgrounds and countries.' The Board Chair, she told me, is 'the person ultimately responsible for ensuring the core values of the organisation are upheld, namely: non-violence, non-party political, bearing witness, peaceful confrontation and respect for all life'. In practical terms, this meant I was required to lead the board's supervision of the performance of the IED, including oversight of his management of the global campaigns, and to approve and monitor the 27 million euro annual budget of Greenpeace International (GPI). Those two simple-sounding tasks entailed being across every aspect of the operations of this large and complex organisation, and since I was so new I had a lot of learning to do. I had to learn the history, the culture, the politics and the people, and fast. When I'd started new jobs in the past, I'd always immersed myself in the history of the place, reading as much as I could, and I'd talk to people from inside and outside, people who knew what was what, people I knew would not mislead me. I'd done this at PM&C and at *Ms.* magazine, and I would do the same at Greenpeace but while I could learn a lot in Amsterdam, where GPI was headquartered, I would also need to travel. I decided to try to visit every one of our offices, adding a side trip to at least one new country each time I travelled. It turned out to be too ambitious a plan, but I did manage to visit all our offices in Latin America, East Asia, North America and most of Europe. I did not make it to Turkey or Israel or Lebanon or India, and my trip to Russia was cut short so that, sadly, I did not get to experience the eleven time zones and vast differences of that remarkable country, including a planned visit to Lake Baikal.

I made around six international trips a year, to Amsterdam and to whichever country was hosting that year's AGM, had weekly phone meetings with the IED, as well as wrangling a never-ending email feed. It was not a full-time job, although it often felt as if it was. I was the first Board Chair from the Southern Hemisphere in the organisation's almost 30-year history which meant my (economy class) travel was long and exhausting, and the weekly phone meetings with the IED were always at a difficult time of the day or—more often—night. Despite Greenpeace being nominally a global organisation, in reality it was utterly Eurocentric. Fourteen of the 27 national offices were in Europe, which distorted global governance, as each office had an equal vote. It meant that, for instance, Switzerland, or tiny Luxembourg, had on paper at least the same influence as the United States or the soon-to-be established offices in India and China. I spent a great deal of my tenure arguing for a more representative structure, but while there was some agreement that we *should* change, no office wanted to surrender its power.

The beginning of my tenure at Greenpeace coincided with Chip spending a year in Beijing where he undertook advanced studies in Mandarin at Tsinghua University. The time apart meant co-editing the *Australian Author* remotely and celebrating the beginning of the new millennium at separate iconic global locations—he on the Great Wall, me at the Sydney Opera House. But when I visited we travelled widely, to a number of cities and to more remote places such as the sacred island of Putuoshan, giving us both experiences and insights into China. These were invaluable for me when Greenpeace opened an office in Beijing in 2002, and helped Chip develop a fascination with China that saw him return to live there for a further year in 2004, this time in Shanghai, teaching English. Our lives also developed parallel paths, when in the early 2000s, Chip became a member of the international board of the writers' organisation, PEN International, which required him to travel, mostly to Europe, almost as often as I did. We found there were many similarities with these two global bodies, each trying to reconcile their international focus with their European origins.

For the seven years I served on the board, six of them as chair, in addition to whatever specific topics or emergencies might present themselves, we also engaged in a never-ending discussion about the future direction of Greenpeace. Very early in my tenure, we were presented with an impressive argument for why we should abandon all other campaigns and concentrate just on climate. Elaine Lawrence, the international campaigns director, a phlegmatic Englishwoman with long straight dark hair that was starting to fleck with grey, made the presentation. She had been with Greenpeace for many years, initially in the UK before she moved to Amsterdam, and she had an outstanding strategic brain. She also had the ability to reach rapid and wryly delivered assessments of people. Elaine had observed to me one day that because every one of the young Dutch women who had recently applied for jobs at Greenpeace had been more than 182 centimetres tall, she expected the organisation would soon be transformed into an Amazonian army.

Elaine laid out for the board with cool precision the evidence of the changes that were occurring to the climate that would impact on the earth's temperature and, in time, its very viability. Climate change was, she argued, as big a threat to the actual existence of the planet as nukes had once been. On that logic, the organisation ought to set aside all its other work and devote itself entirely to campaigning against climate change. It was hard to disagree. But I was still very new. I had yet to understand the silo mentality of campaigners for the other issues, and the tenacity with which they resisted any suggestion 'their' issue ought not to be Greenpeace's top priority. These arguments around climate would dominate my time at Greenpeace and they were, I was given to understand, every bit as impassioned as the first big policy division over nukes and whales in the mid-1970s. It was never resolved. There were other factors apart from the resistance from other campaigns. Climate change was a complex issue. It did not have the emotional appeal of Saving the Whales, or the immediacy of the threat of a hole in the ozone layer. Climate change was abstract. The dangers it posed could not be summed-up in a simple slogan. We had banners that said Save the

Climate, but what did that mean? In places like Russia, global warming was seen as welcome relief from their frigid winters, so we learned to stick to the language of 'climate change'. And there was now further competition from new issues like food security being put on the Greenpeace agenda by our new offices in the developing world. These were impossible to ignore, or to relegate to reduced importance.

———◆———

Greenpeace's head office in Amsterdam was in a grand 1905 building, designated a national monument, on the corner of Keizersgracht, one of the three major canals that circle the city, and Leliegracht, a smaller feeder canal. The grey-stone building with its clock tower, steep slate roofs and a mural painted high-up on the front wall, was an architectural curiosity. Now it housed a group of people dedicated to peace and to saving the world's environment. The building sprawled over six floors, around a magnificent central wooden staircase, with leaded-glass windows and dozens of tiny rooms that cascaded off passageways in all directions. It was a beautiful place, but totally impractical for modern office arrangements. I was sad, but could not make a plausible counter-argument, when the board had to agree to the organisation's relocation to a soulless office block in the suburbs. It made sense to have everyone on just two floors, with open planning, everyone in sight of each other, constantly in contact and everyone aware of what was happening.

One of my first tasks as Board Chair had been to lead the search for a new IED. The organisation could have been severely disrupted by an unexpected turn of events, that resulted in the unprecedented situation of its two top leadership positions becoming vacant at the same time. With me being essentially an outside recruitment, it seemed important to try to fill the IED job from within Greenpeace, and fortunately in Gerd Leipold we had the ideal candidate. Although he was currently working outside the organisation, he had been the ED of the German office in the 1980s and had run the international disarmament campaign from 1987 to 1992. He had a deep knowledge of and was widely known and respected within Greenpeace, and thus could jump right in without a lengthy induction. During his six years in the job, among many other achievements, Leipold presided over the global expansion of Greenpeace, opening offices in India, China and the Amazon and began the first steps for a presence in Africa, a new frontier for Greenpeace.

Despite our very different backgrounds, Leipold and I got on immensely well. He was a scientist, a meteorologist and oceanographer, and a multi-lingual European. Both of us tried to shuck-off the stereotypes of our nationalities; I made sure to be extremely punctual and efficient, while Gerd allowed himself to relax and joke in ways that were in contrast to the usual seriousness of many of our German colleagues. In Crete in 2004, we had all been amazed at the extraordinary number of corpulent middle-aged German tourists sharing the hotel where we were having our AGM. 'Which was worse,' Gerd asked our bemused waiter. 'The German invasion of 1941, or this one?'

In August 1983, Gerd and an Englishman John Sprange had flown a hot-air balloon over the Berlin Wall into East Germany, in an action for peace and disarmament. It was a very dangerous operation; they risked being shot out of the sky by the trigger-happy East German military. Fortunately, they were allowed to land, arrested and, after a five-hour detainment, expelled back to the West.[3] Gerd told me later that during the 40-minute flight he had not had time to be frightened, because he and Sprange had been arguing about a girl they both liked.

I'd been surprised to discover that Greenpeace's largest office was not Canada, where the organisation was founded, nor the United States, the world's richest country. It was Germany that was the financial and political backbone of Greenpeace. The German office was the largest, the richest, the best organised, and it underwrote the rest of Greenpeace for the time I was there. There was tremendous support for Greenpeace among the German population, enabling them to be immensely innovative. They branched into service provision, opening an alternative power company and developing Greenfreeze, an ozone-friendly refrigerant that is in widespread use today. Germany was very into 'green'—the world's first Green Party had been started there—but it was also obsessed with peace. The anti-nuke sentiments were stronger in Germany than perhaps anywhere else. I found myself wondering what drove these German people, how much their activism and optimism was driven by an element of atonement. Most Germans I encountered were of an age to have parents who would have been involved in the war, but we never talked about it. Nor, it seems, did they. I began to understand why, when I came across the writings of W.G. Sebald, a German writer who had lived in England for most of his life until his premature death in a road accident in December 2001. I had read Sebald's essay, 'A Natural History of Destruction', in the *New Yorker*[4] in 2002, an excerpt from his book of the same name, about the carpet-bombing of Hamburg by the British. Sebald argued that the utter destruction of most German cities at the end of the war, causing more than 600,000 deaths, had brought about a kind of collective amnesia in the post-war population. The subject was simply not discussed, nor written about—even by writers like Heinrich Böll, who explored every other area of Germany's wartime conduct.

'There was a tacit agreement, equally binding on everyone, that the true state of material and moral ruin in which the country found itself was not to be described,' Sebald wrote. 'The darkest aspects of the final act of destruction, as experienced by the great majority of the German population, remained under a kind of taboo like a shameful family secret, a secret that perhaps could not even be privately acknowledged.'

I gave a copy of the essay to Gerd. I think we were in Hamburg at the time. We talked about the horrors of the firebombing where hundreds of people simply melted, and the rebuilding of the city from the rubble, but we did not talk about Sebald's central proposition which, if I read him correctly, was that many Germans felt they deserved this retaliatory bombing, but it was not something that could be acknowledged publicly and, thus, it was 'forgotten', and never discussed. But the Germans in Greenpeace were addressing the subject by remaking their society, doing what they could to ensure history was not repeated.

I started my Greenpeace education in Hamburg. If Amsterdam was the head of global Greenpeace, the warehouse in Hamburg was, in many ways, its operational headquarters. Harald Zindler guided me around. He was a solid man with a big head of grey hair, who was even more legendary than the warehouse itself. He had been an original member of the German office in 1981 and his aphorism, 'The optimism of the action is better than the pessimism of the thought', adorned the title page of the official history of Greenpeace. He'd previously been an anti-nukes campaigner. Now he was custodian of the warehouse. It was located on an island in the middle of Hamburg harbour and was spread over several storeys with various rooms designated for particular activities. It was able to support and equip any Greenpeace action anywhere in the world. An enormous internal space at water level contained dozens of inflatable boats of every conceivable size; these were the workhorses of the organisation. We needed protective clothing just to go into the state-of-the-art hazmat facility. Greenpeace had the capability to assess the toxicity of any waste dump, any toxic spill, any nuclear mishap. Standing in that room in Hamburg, looking up at shelf-upon-shelf of the most toxic substances known to humankind, I shuddered. Greenpeace's hazmat stockpile was easily the most comprehensive in the country, if not the whole of Europe. Zindler told me that the German police and fire department experts regularly came over to the warehouse to top up their knowledge.

My favourite part of the warehouse was the banner-making department. It occupied a huge space with natural light pouring in through large square windows. There were massive tables, able to take metres-long rolls of canvas, where banners were made using the same techniques as for sail-making. It was hardly surprising that a nautical organisation such as Greenpeace would have expertise in sail-making, but what fascinated me was the way they had adapted that process to serve a political end. Most of the smaller Greenpeace offices could not afford such facilities, so the Germans had designed a system to fulfill orders for banners from around the world. The designs and the required dimensions were emailed to the German warehouse. It was, of course, critical that there be no errors in the wording that was most often in a language other than German (or English, which most of the German office staff spoke fluently). They were now also having to accommodate themselves to different scripts as our offices in Thailand and China started doing actions. I was shown the steps whereby the little design on the email would be blown up onto a large screen from which the banner would be printed. Some of these banners were many metres wide, or long. They would be shipped-off to their destination and, weeks later, their German creators, if they happened to be watching the television news, might see their handiwork draped over a building in Brazil, or hanging from a ship in the Indian Ocean. It was an impressive display of international cooperation and smart use of resources. I could see why the German warehouse was spoken of in awe almost everywhere in the Greenpeace world I visited.

I learned to appreciate that behind the romantic images of Greenpeace ships on the high seas, or the daring exploits of activists abseiling down high buildings, was a highly skilled and developed organisation. I came to respect the meticulous planning and the risk assessments that went into every activity. Of course, it would have been irresponsible, even murderous, to allow activists to engage in some of the dangerous actions that were the organisation's signature, without taking every care to protect their lives. In 30 years, despite the extraordinary feats many of them undertook, for example, dangling a sign from the top of London's Big Ben or Rio's Christ the Redeemer, or playing chicken from a rubber inflatable with a US nuclear warship, no campaigner had been killed or disabled during an action. A couple of people had suffered serious injuries, however, and we had a duty of care towards helping with their recovery. And as a non-violent organisation, Greenpeace was committed to ensuring that no one else was harmed as a result of our actions. I was told about a staff member who had been disciplined for cutting the anchor chain of a boat moored in a European port harbour, potentially endangering the crew onboard. And during my time there was a fierce debate in the UK office about whether invading fields and ripping out GM crops was a violent act and therefore unjustifiable, or whether it was a legitimate destruction of plants that had the capacity to contaminate the food chain.

There were just two ships in the Greenpeace fleet when I started: the MV *Arctic Sunrise* as well as the flagship, the MV *Rainbow Warrior*. There were also a couple of smaller, European-based boats that did not count as part of the fleet, and some planes, including our helicopter, *Tweety*. The ships were easily identifiable, their hulls painted a deep green with the rainbow across their bows. They were a familiar and inspiring sight. The first time I saw the *Rainbow Warrior* was when it sailed into Sydney Harbour for the 2000 Olympics. I found myself feeling quite emotional as I watched the totemic boat passing the iconic Sydney Opera House. The *Rainbow Warrior* was as famous and, in its own way, as significant a force for peace as any human world figure.

The fleet expanded when the MV *Esperanza*, its refit completed, was launched in February 2002. It was a former Russian firefighting boat, previously named the *Echo Fighter*; the organisation had spent several million euro refitting it for Greenpeace purposes, installing cranes to lift the inflatables, and a helicopter landing-pad. There had been an internal competition to name this newest boat with the Spanish and Latin American offices waging a fierce fight to ensure the Spanish word for 'hope', would beat *Gaia*, the other contender. The *Esperanza* also had the advantage of being ice-class, which meant it could be deployed in Arctic or Antarctic waters. It was the largest ship in the Greenpeace fleet, with 33 berths, a speed of 16 knots and able to accommodate two large and four small inflatables.

The inflatables, often referred to disparagingly as Greenpeace's 'rubber boats', but whose technical name is RHIBs, or rigid-hulled inflatable boats, were a critical element in any marine operation. The larger ships of the fleet would get the activists as close as possible to the whaling ship or the logging boat, the inflatables would then be lowered, and the actions crew would clamber down and roar off to undertake the planned action. The inflatables came in many sizes, able to accommodate from four to more than twenty people. What made them indispensable was their ability to travel at high speeds through rough seas. The only time I was on one, ferried from the *Rainbow Warrior* to the shore in New Zealand, I found the ride terrifying as we bumped hard across the waves, at what seemed like a dangerously fast speed.

I had worked hard and was now feeling relatively comfortable in my role as Chair of GPI. I had mastered the lingo, including a mind-numbing array of acronyms that people in Greenpeace used to talk to each other, I knew all the key people and was across most of the policy issues. I was now someone who could confidently chair a rambunctious meeting of Trustees and EDs. As with the board, I ran tight meetings that always got through the agenda and finished on time. I'd got rid of the three-sided table and the country nametags. Everyone now sat comfortably at round tables at what conference organisers call 'cabaret-style', and were free to move around during proceedings. I'd also started an internal newsletter to keep the organisation informed about what the board was up to, and created a 'buddy system' between board members and Trustees, as an induction and knowledge-sharing tool. Notionally, we liked to describe ourselves as 'One Greenpeace' but we needed to reduce geographic, cultural and language barriers. In 2001 we welcomed India's new ED to his first international meeting. Ananthapadmanabhan Guruswamy, who insisted we simply called him Ananth, had been selected from 1000 applicants. He was a brilliant choice who would soon make an impact on the entire organisation. Our Beijing office opened the next year. Greenpeace was going to places it needed to be, and I felt proud to be there while it was happening. Sometimes, I had to ask myself, Am I really here? Doing this? I felt lucky, but I also knew that I would not be where I was without the lift I'd been given early in my life.

———

In December 1999, I had received an extraordinary handwritten letter from Wales, from a man called Roger Ellis. He had been sent *Ducks on the Pond*, he told me, by a former nun at Cabra Convent in Adelaide, where I had gone to school. He wanted me to know that for the past 30 years he had been happily married to the nun who had been my primary school teacher at Cabra, the woman who had changed my life. I'd recounted in the book how Sr Mary Vianney had pulled me aside after I'd been in trouble for some larrikinish behaviour, and spoken to me sharply. She'd told me to stop hanging-out with girls who were idiots, to stop behaving like an idiot myself, and to start using the brain that I so obviously had.

'You do not have to accept the given,' she had said to me. 'You have the ability to be different, to shape the world to your liking.'

No one had ever spoken to me like that. Without her words, I doubt I would be the person I am today, so I was quite overwhelmed to get this letter. Two months later, during a Greenpeace trip to London, I took an extra day and in February 2000 I travelled to Wales by train to meet Kate Vianney. She had been Lillian Horgan before she entered the convent, and I wondered why she had retained her religious name. It was too much part of her to relinquish, I surmised, but I had no idea where Kate had come from. Roger had warned me that Kate had Alzheimer's and probably would not remember me. It had been more than forty years. Her face was scarcely recognisable but those eyes that I remembered still flickered with the fierce intelligence she'd used to rescue this lost girl. She did not need to know I was there. I was the one who needed to honour and thank her. Just as I needed to make another pilgrimage, this time to Paris in the winter of 2001, in order to acknowledge another debt.

I was there to meet the French office and attend a local board meeting, but instead of the hotel recommended by Greenpeace, I'd booked myself into the Hotel la Louisiane at 60 rue du Seine, a few paces off Boulevard Saint Germaine on the Left Bank. It was a ratty little place, with maybe three stars, but it had a history. The Rolling Stones used to stay in the 1960s as did a number of black jazz musicians fleeing racism in 1950s America whose lives were depicted in the 1986 Bertrand Tavernier movie *Round Midnight*. But I was there because during World War II, Simone de Beauvoir had lived there and it was in Room 50, 'a large round room with a kitchenette', according to her biographer Deirdre Bair, that she had written at least part of *The Second Sex*.[5] I had booked myself into one of the hotel's three 'round rooms', rooms that because they were at the apex of the v-shaped building were much larger than the hotel's other mean-sized chambers. Although the room numbers were different now, I believed from a photograph in Hazel Rowley's book[6] that I was in the room in which de Beauvoir had begun the book that was the other major influence in starting me on the road to who I am today.

Despite all my travelling to Greenpeace offices, I had never managed to take part in an action until September 2002 when I travelled to Manaus, the city in the heart of the Amazon. Manaus is famous for its opulent Teatro Amazones Opera House, opened in 1897 and built from the rubber fortunes that had transformed this tiny hamlet into the thriving town it now was. Although we already had a longstanding office in Brazil, located in Sao Paulo, GPI decided we also needed a presence in the heart of the Amazon. It would serve as a base for campaigning against the destruction of the Amazon basin by deforestation through illegal logging and, an increasing threat, mass clearance of lands for agriculture, especially soya and cattle. Anne Dingwall, another Greenpeace veteran, was appointed Amazon

Campaign Coordinator and it was her job to open the office, find the staff
and get the operation underway. She was experienced at this, having already
set up the Russian and Hong Kong offices. Anne was Canadian, rail thin,
a bundle of nervous energy who seldom had a cigarette out of her hand,
and who radiated a compelling aura of warmth and competence. I liked
her immediately and she was an excellent guide as she took me around the
multiple terrains of Greenpeace. She was almost as indispensable as Jenny
Stannard was during my six years as Board Chair. Jenny was board assistant, responsible for all logistics around our meetings including producing,
assembling, then dispatching our voluminous board papers—Greenpeace
liked its paper—as well as keeping me on top of everything I needed to
be doing. She was a vivacious and perpetually cheerful person, originally
from England, but who had lived in the Netherlands for decades now. She
had been McTaggart's right-hand woman for years, which meant there was
nothing about Greenpeace she did not know, and she had become a kind of
unofficial guardian of the organisation's history. She was always there, my
beacon and my support. My enduring image of Jenny is her listening to *Kind
of Blue* while she transcribed the minutes of an especially rambunctious
session of an AGM meeting in Mexico. She could always find tranquillity in
the heart of any turmoil. A truly excellent person to work with.

I inspected the new office in Manaus with its already-impressive amount
of equipment, including of course a good supply of inflatables, then Anne
and I flew in the *Fat Duck*, Greenpeace's small aquaplane, to Porto de Moz,
a region in northern Brazil where anti-logging action was happening on a
tributary of the Amazon. Greenpeace was there to support the local community who wanted to protect their lands from illegal logging. For the
several hours it took us to travel the almost 900 kilometres, we skimmed
above the dense vegetation. As someone who was an extremely nervous
flyer then, I was amazingly relaxed, enjoying it even. We were more connected to earth than in a jetliner, I told myself, and that made it feel safer. As
we came into land on the river we could see MV *Veloz*, the bright blue river-
boat Greenpeace had chartered. The rest of the team was already on board.
The local community had formed a barricade across the river, comprising
approximately 50 boats, with some 400 people on board, that was intended
to block the expected barge of illegal logs. We settled in to wait. I was only

able to stay a couple of days, and I wasn't even sure if I wanted to still be there if a confrontation happened. I admit to being nervous, scared even. We were well aware of the loggers' reputation for violence. Many people had been murdered for trying to resist them. We were in a very isolated part of the Amazon basin. There were less than a handful of police in Porto de Moz, and we didn't know if they would intervene if the loggers became violent. Everyone was tense, but we all knew better than to show it. Shipboard routine had to be adhered to and that mostly meant cooking, serving and cleaning up after the three meals each day. I did my best to be useful. Anne and I were by far the oldest people on board and we found we had lots to talk about, including (we were surprised to discover, since we were from different countries) that we were both taking the same brand of HRT.

That night we settled into the deep darkness of the river. It was still and, at first, quiet. Then we began to hear a noise that sounded like someone slapping themselves and, it turned out, that is exactly what it was. The people on the boats making up the barricade were slapping their skin each time a mosquito landed. We on the big blue boat, with our tropical-strength repellant, were protected but the locals had no such luxury. All night, until I eventually fell asleep, I could hear the gentle slaps. As soon as it was light, I noticed a number of small boats were heading towards us.

'What is going on?' I asked one of the crew.

'They know we have a doctor on board.'

For the rest of the day, after patiently waiting their turn, the occupants of the next boat would come alongside and a child, or an old man, or anyone who needed medical assistance would be helped on board. Our doctor, a young woman, worked all day, bandaging, medicating, soothing. One old man had a machete gash so deep I wondered that his arm did not fall off. A number of children were feverish. I felt humbled and proud watching this. I had known of Greenpeace's rescue efforts during Hurricane Mitch in 1998, when we'd sent the *Rainbow Warrior* to Nicaragua with clothes, food and medical supplies. I was to learn that although Greenpeace is not an aid organisation, it frequently helped out if needed. Our ships turned out to have many uses apart from chasing Japanese whalers. It was not a role we had sought and certainly not one that we had advertised, but we could not turn these people away, even though by the end of the day our own medical supplies were running low. We needed to be prepared in case of a violent reaction from the loggers. Then, as the light was fading, a new boat approached. On board was a young woman who was moaning. She was helped on board, but soon it was apparent that there was a problem. The doctor conferred with the action team. The RHIB jet boat was deployed, the engine revved up, the woman was lowered onto the boat and, with the doctor and two young Greenpeace men beside her, they sped off into the gathering darkness.

The woman was miscarrying. The doctor said she needed urgent medical help, beyond what she could offer. There was no hospital anywhere near us but Porto de Moz, the small town about an hour's fast ride up the river, had a clinic. The fit young men did not hesitate and I found myself strangely moved by the way they quickly readied the inflatable and prepared to take off in near darkness. When they got there the clinic was closed. The Greenpeace team did their best, waking up the town trying to find help, but there was none to be had. The young woman lost her baby. I have seldom seen young men more dejected and defeated than these two actions guys when they returned. To me, they were heroes, but they were more than that. They were the kind of men who could tend a miscarrying young woman one evening and, a few days later, engage in an extraordinary act of bravery that saved as many as 80 lives when the confrontation finally came.

It happened a few hours after I left. After three days the *Fat Duck* had picked me up and sped me back to Manaus, so I missed the arrival of the barge of logs being pushed by a tugboat. I am indebted to Anne Dingwall for this account of what happened next. The tugboat was captained by Andre Campos, whose brother was the mayor of nearby Porto de Moz, and since it was unable to proceed due to the barricade, Campos secured the tug to trees on the riverbank with cables, leaving the barge drifting perilously close to the boats forming the barricade. There followed a tense discussion between Campos and community leaders, who wanted it moved further upstream. Campos agreed to secure the cables more tightly, but would not move the barge. It was agreed they would negotiate further the next morning. However, just after midnight, when almost everyone was asleep, Campos released the cables and began trying to crash through the barricade. David Logie and Todd Southgate, the Greenpeace action guys, were having a few drinks on the deck of the *Veloz* when they heard the sound of the tug starting. Yelling a warning to the small boats to get out of the way, the two young men deployed the jet boat, and at full throttle rammed the barge, forcing it into the riverbank. The *Veloz* then started up and used its weight to keep the tug pinned to the bank. There was some fighting, several people were injured, but the tugboat's keys were seized and the blockade was ended.

Subsequently Andre Campos was arrested, the barge with its illegal cargo of over 100 logs was seized, and its owners fined a substantial sum. Two years later, the Federal Verde para Sempre (Green Forever) Extractive Reserve for sustainable use of Amazon rainforest resources was established. The local population of approximately 2250 families had won the right to their land. It was a low-key action by Greenpeace standards, conducted far away from the media spotlight, but it succeeded in assisting a local community and it marked another milestone in the battle for the Amazon. I was sorry I was not there to witness it.

In October 2001, I had gone to Prague to attend Forum 2000, an exclusive invitation-only five-day event hosted by President Vaclev Havel, the formerly imprisoned political dissident, poet and playwright, who was now the President of the Czech Republic. It was rare for me to represent the organisation in a gathering such as this, but the ED in Greenpeace's Czech office was insistent that it would help their standing if the international Board Chair attended. Forum 2000 had been founded five years earlier as a joint initiative of Havel, Japanese philanthropist Yohei Sasakawa, and Nobel Peace Prize Laureate Elie Wiesel. It was designed to address human rights, civil society, and other issues relevant to the globalising 21st century, and the guest list each year included famous political, cultural and religious figures. Hillary Clinton, Madeleine Albright, Henry Kissinger and the Chinese dissident Wei Jingsheng had attended in previous years. I was both excited and slightly in awe of what awaited me.

I'd flown in from Amsterdam on 14 October and discovered that another invitee, Francis Fukuyama the famous political scientist, was on the same flight. We'd been given VIP treatment upon arrival at Prague Airport, escorted from the plane before the other passengers and, bypassing immigration, taken straight to the tarmac, where a line of cars waited. Following what I thought were my directions, I started to climb into the first car, a silver Mercedes. There was some shouting, which I could not understand, from the men who had met us, and I was roughly pulled from the Merc and pushed towards the car behind it, a small battered Skoda. The Mercedes was for Dr Fukuyama. A little over a month earlier, the terrorist attacks on the United States seemed to disprove Fukuyama's celebrated thesis that we had arrived at 'the end of history'. He had posited in his best-selling book of the same name that the end of the Soviet era, dramatised by the fall of the Berlin Wall in 1989, showed ideology no longer mattered. We had reached 'the end point of mankind's ideological evolution and the universalization of Western liberal democracy as the final form of human government'. The West had won, in other words. His thesis was now looking a little shaky. Nevertheless, he got the good ride. He was a man, and this was indisputably a man's world. Only nine of the 50 invited guests were women. There might have been notional equality of the sexes prior to the Velvet Revolution that had brought Havel to power in Czechoslovakia, but as I discovered during the Forum, it was no longer in evidence, seemingly discarded as just one more superfluous communist value. These Eastern European flunkeys made no effort to disguise their hostility towards me, even when a couple of them came to get me for my audience with the President.

Havel had asked to see me. He was very interested in Australia and had visited several times. I'd joined the throng in an old pub in The Rocks a year or so earlier when the visiting President had expressed a wish to meet writers and journalists in a relaxed environment. It had been too crowded to get close to him that evening, but now it was just the two of us. He looked just like his photographs, but he seemed slightly harried, which was not surprising given the big crowd of important guests, and that he was having to deal with the last-minute cancellation by some of the American participants, a few short weeks after the 11 September attacks. We were in a small anteroom in the lavish castle that could not have been further away, in style and comfort, from the prison cells where he had spent more than five years as a political prisoner. Havel was polite and tried to engage me but our meeting was perfunctory and awkward. He wanted to talk about Australia's Aboriginal people but his English was poor, my Czech non-existent, and no one had thought to provide an interpreter. We gave up after a few stilted moments, and I was escorted away by the same grim-looking men who had forced me to ride in from the airport in the crappy little car while the male guest travelled in style.

The Forum took place in the magnificent Prague Castle, supposedly the largest castle in the world, dating from the ninth century, and displaying a wide array of architectural styles. We met in lavish chambers where the walls were gold, the furniture baroque and the chandeliers crystal. It reminded me of Versailles. My fellow guests included Shimon Peres, F.W. de Klerk, HRH Prince El Hassan bin Talal of the Jordanian royal family, José Ramos-Horta, and several dozen other current or up-and-coming world leaders, whose names I was not yet familiar with.[7] In mid-October all of us were still trying to digest the shocking events of the terrorist attacks on the United States on 11 September that was the reason for many of the American guests cancelling. Jeffrey Sachs, the once conservative economist who'd become an activist against poverty in developing countries, was beamed in via videolink. Bianca Jagger who was supposed to be on a panel with me did not show and Jeane Kirkpatrick, who had been Ronald Reagan's (and the first woman) US Ambassador to the United Nations, was another who was afraid to fly. I was asked to deliver a keynote in her stead. But to everyone's amazement, Bill Clinton came.

I'd been in Toronto, intending to fly to New York later that day, when the planes struck. Greenpeace had been founded in September 1971 and we were planning to celebrate 30 years of activism and innumerable victories in defence of the planet with a series of events, including some very high-level fundraising activities, in New York. The *Rainbow Warrior* was sailing up the east cost of the US, headed for the Chelsea Piers where we were going to hold a fancy cocktail party on 12 September. I tried without success that crazy, scary day to reach Gerd Leipold, who was somewhere on the west coast; we had planned to meet up in New York that evening. Once we connected, the next day, we had to try to digest the implications for Greenpeace of this unprecedented act of terrorism. We would need to find the right words to console and reassure our American colleagues, to set the tone to guide the rest of the organisation as it began to grapple with this new kind of war, and its yet-unknown consequences. Before long, the Americans would dictate new maritime rules that would restrict our free movement on and off our ships wherever they docked around the world, political surveillance would increase, as would the aggressive prosecution of our activists, especially around our opposition to nuclear issues such the 'Star Wars' missile defence system.

The day before the attack, on 10 September, I'd found myself surrounded by the Canberra Press Gallery as I flew from Sydney to Los Angeles, en route to Toronto. John Howard was flying commercial for some reason, so the travelling party was all aboard that Qantas jet. I was chatting with Michelle Grattan when they were all summonsed to the front of the plane; the Prime Minister wanted to talk to them. When they returned some 30 minutes later, Grattan told me that Howard had briefed them that he was excising Christmas Island from Australia. They would file the story when we landed at Los Angeles in about ten hours time. In future, no people arriving by boat at this remote Indian Ocean Island that, until now, had been part of Australia, would be able to claim asylum. As we flew across the Pacific, we pondered the politics of this extraordinary move, this pitiless declaration of war on some of the most vulnerable people on earth, none of us knowing how much worse it was going to get for them when the world changed so profoundly the very next day.

Bill Clinton had been in Australia, holidaying in Port Douglas in Far North Queensland, at the time of the attacks. The Australian military had helped get him back to the US while commercial flights remained restricted, but he was not grounding himself in the aftermath. His presence in Prague that day was an exemplary act of courage. There are several things for which I cannot forgive Bill Clinton: the pardoning of financial fugitive Marc Rich, nor the abuse of his power with the exploitation of a young woman's emotions in the Monica Lewinsky episode, but he was absolutely a hero for making this trip to the Forum. Until January that year he had been President of the United States, and while he was now technically just a private citizen, albeit one who would forever be able to use the title President, his very presence was a powerful act of moral leadership. He sat at the head of a simple table in that extravagantly baroque gilt and mirrored room as dozens of us delegates crammed around. He spoke in those low, slow tones of his so that we had to lean forward to catch his words. He consoled us, he empathised with the shock most of us were still feeling and, most important of all, he encouraged us not to lose sight of the issues that had brought us all to Prague.

Bill Clinton has a remarkable way with words, and that day those of us who were privileged to be present experienced the kind of healing that made him such a potent politician.

At my session, there were just two others at the table: Vandana Shiva the Indian environmentalist and F.W. de Klerk, the former President of South Africa. He was the man who on 11 February 1990 had released Nelson Mandela after 27 years of imprisonment. In 1993, he and Mandela had jointly received the Nobel Peace Prize. De Klerk was that rare kind of man in politics: both brave and creative. He had shocked his colleagues, and the world, on 2 February 1990 by announcing the end of apartheid and the introduction of democracy to South Africa. He was already preparing the ground for Mandela's release nine days later.

I had read Allister Sparks's long and illuminating article in the *New Yorker*, in April 1994, that described the lengthy talks and processes that preceded Mandela's release. Most of them were conducted outside the prison, in government buildings, including an initial meeting between de Klerk and Mandela in the Prime Minister's office, even in ministers' private homes. (Mandela recalled later being offered his first alcoholic drink in 22 years at one of these gatherings; it was a creamed sherry, and he said it tasted like nectar.) De Klerk understood that South Africa's—indeed the world's—most famous prisoner would need time to adjust to the outside world after his long incarceration. He arranged for Mandela, who by now had been transferred to a prison in Paarl, not far from Cape Town, to be driven around, to towns and to the countryside, to see the way the world had changed. He was taken, in what must have been an unconscious act of ironic cruelty, to Stellenbosch. It was the nearest town, but it was still the ideological centre of apartheid. The whole thing was a very risky operation. Mandela's release might have been thwarted if word had got out that it was about to happen. Once, at a petrol station, Mandela spoke to the attendant who appeared to recognise him.[8]

De Klerk was kind and courteous towards me but I found myself tongue-tied; I so wanted to tell him how much I admired what he had done, but I did not want to appear gauche. This was a serious political gathering, not a fan club. I envied the facility with which the natives of this world of international politics so easily made their way through these social trenches.

I did not have their easy ice-breaking phrases with which to engage people I'd never before met. At the first reception for delegates, where I'd found the luxury of the chamber dazzling and distracting, I knew no one. I didn't have the moxie to stride-up boldly to a world leader with outstretched hand, so I cast my eyes around hoping they might land on someone who was as stranded as I. Soon an attractive and expensively dressed couple engaged me as if I were a lifelong friend. They turned out to be minor European royalty, and they knew how to do this. Not for the first time, I regretted that I had not forced myself to acquire the art of small talk. It would have helped me glide more gracefully around New York society, and it certainly would have made it easier for me in Prague. There were so many luminaries there and I had easy access to all of them. But none of them had ever heard of me and, despite my star billing, I had not given the attention-grabbing performance that might have put me on their radar. Had I had more experience in performing in public for Greenpeace, I might have been able to do better at Forum 2000. Instead I was disappointed in myself, and that unnerved me. It is not easy to be assured when you are the object of the kind of open contempt exhibited by the men who had escorted me from the airport. In my head, I was a second-class attendee, riding around the Forum in that battered little Skoda, and it affected the way I conducted myself. I did not exude the authority or the bearing that said, I am the Board Chair of Greenpeace International, and so no one of any importance approached me or showed any interest in the organisation I represented. Shimon Peres, Israel's Minister for Foreign Affairs (and, of course, sometime Prime Minister and future President), swept past me several times, surrounded by a clutch of bodyguards. His room was in the same corridor as mine in the grim concrete bunker that was our hotel. He always nodded and gave a slight smile; he certainly did not emanate the incipient hostility I felt from other men at the Forum, but I could not find the words to greet him.

The Forum provided my first encounter with political leaders as peers—all invitees were supposedly of equal status. I had met plenty of political leaders before, of course, but this was not the same as sitting across from Caspar Weinberger, my reporter's notebook at the ready, or interviewing the President of Argentina. I had nothing these men wanted—I wasn't a

reporter; or an influential thought-leader; not even, given my age, a potential roll in the hay—so mostly they simply ignored me. In this setting
women were mostly inconsequential, unless they happened to be very
famous or very powerful, and I found this invisibility difficult. Although
Greenpeace was often portrayed as male-dominated, a perception fed by
our action teams being mainly men, the culture of the organisation was
far from hostile. We knew we needed more women in senior management roles, but a woman invariably led the board, which itself managed
to achieve gender and geographical diversity. And, interestingly enough,
it was women who had done the work to open each of our non-European
offices. Apart from Anne Dingwall's efforts in Russia, Hong Kong and
Manaus, Lyn Goldsworthy had opened India and Southeast Asia while,
earlier, Tani Adams had opened the three Latin American offices. I was
treated with courtesy and respect wherever I went in the organisation, even
in countries that traditionally were unaccustomed to women in leadership
roles. This sheer rudeness in Prague was a shock and I found myself inter-
nalising the contempt.

Maybe it would have been easier if I'd been there as a journalist. The
reporter's notebook would have given me cover—and access. I knew I could
have written a powerful article about this extraordinary gathering. Here
were world leaders and other influential people who were among the first
to try to articulate what the September 11 attacks meant for democracy and
human rights. The sessions were all open to local media, and transcripts of
all the proceedings were on the Forum 2000 website for many years (sadly,
those for 2001 were taken down in October 2016), but as far as I could tell,
there was no international media coverage. The press tends to cover only
people who are currently in power, not those who might be influencing,
or even determining, events from other positions and perspectives. Havel
apparently no longer attracted US or even European media attention. I don't
know if I could have persuaded an editor to run my report on Forum 2000,
but I would have liked to have been able to try.

I had finally achieved reconciliation with my father in 1988, the year of
his death, and while this pleased my mother immensely, and brought me

an unanticipated sense of peace, it turned out there was other unfinished business in our family that would not be resolved for another quarter century. During those years we had to deal with the shock of the deaths of my mother and my oldest brother David. Both deaths were sudden, and while my mother was 81, an age where death is not unexpected, she was healthy and fit so we were unprepared. She had died in her sleep, at home, in her own bed, in exactly the way she wanted to go. Once we got over the shock, my brothers and I were relieved that she had not suffered, she had not lost her faculties, nor had to endure the indignity of losing her drivers' licence or having to go into a nursing home. We were sad of course, but our grief was tempered by the knowledge that she was finally at peace. One of my Greenpeace Board colleagues informed the Trustees of my bereavement, and I was immensely moved to receive letters of condolence, many of them intensely personal, from every one of the 27 Trustees, including some with whom I was in constant and not always amicable battle over governance matters. That they could set aside these squabbles to write such words of consolation demonstrated that while Greenpeace could be a tough and even ruthless organisation, it was also a family, and one with plenty of heart.

David's death, in 2010, was different. He'd fallen from a ladder on his farm, struck his head on soft soil yet died instantly, in front of his wife Annie and second son Patrick. He was 63. Just a year earlier they had sold their house in Adelaide and, fulfilling a lifelong dream, moved to a property on Kangaroo Island, where he intended to build a house with his own hands. He and Annie were managing their first flock of sheep, and preparing to start on the house, when the terrible accident occurred. Less than three weeks earlier, my brothers and I had all gathered for something of a family reunion at David and Annie's holiday house at Penneshaw, on the other side of Kangaroo Island. It was my first visit to this unique part of Australia, reached by a ferry that was an hour's drive away from Adelaide. Our reunion was the result of a determined effort on the part of a family that rarely got together. We'd wanted to remember our mother and to acknowledge ourselves as a family of adult orphans who for all the little we had in common, were bound inextricably and permanently as siblings. We'd vowed to do it again, perhaps in a year's time. Then came the phone call and we headed back to Kangaroo Island, our numbers augmented by our mother's two surviving brothers and their wives, all in their eighties, a few of our cousins and Annie's family. The service was in a tiny multi-faith picture-perfect church facing the water and later we stood by David's grave, on a hillside overlooking his favourite fishing spot. There had been too many deaths in our family, I thought, as I watched David being lowered into the ground. We'd been six kids. Now we were four.

The year my father died was the same year that I became a business owner in New York, raised what seemed (then anyway) a huge amount of money on Wall Street; got a Green Card which gave me permanent residence in the United States; and become a well-known and, for a short time, sought-after person in the place where, according to the song, if you can make it there . . . I was unrecognisable as the sullen teenager who had stirred up so much anger in him. Nor was I any longer the 'ratbag' radical of the 1970s who enraged him. I'd met my parents once in Sydney, after I'd been to a political demonstration, and as I stomped across the grass in Hyde Park to our meeting point, I could see the disappointment—or was it disgust?—on their faces. Their only daughter—and look at her. Both he and my mother had had such conventional hopes for me, about the sort of person I might marry. They'd hoped for a doctor or a lawyer, someone whose status I would automatically assume. They had never expressed any ambition for *me*. My father had actually told me, while I was a teenager, that sending me to university would be a waste of money. Not that it cost him anything when I finally made it there, thanks to a Commonwealth Scholarship and the fact that I had totally supported myself since the age of fourteen. Now, both my parents were proud of me—of what I was doing and how I looked. I had my share of designer clothes, although many of them had been bought cheaply from Loehmann's, their labels snipped off. My photograph was in the *New York Times*, in *New York* and *Time* magazines, and similar arbiters of achievement. I was under orders to send home copies of all such mentions, and my mother meticulously documented my life. After his death, I discovered that my father had fixed to the wall beside his bed a framed glam photo of me, taken in 1983 by Australian *Vogue*. This was the daughter of his dreams. Finally, he was pleased with the way I was. In July 1988, after Sandra and I had done the deal in New York, he'd written a letter telling me how proud he was of me. I flew to Adelaide for my brother Paul's wedding on 20 August. My father looked wretched; he was gaunt and slow to move. Again, we did not talk. I did not even acknowledge that he had written to me. But back in Sydney, just before I returned to New York, from a friend's house in Rozelle, sitting on the floor to be close to the telephone, I rang. Finally, we had the conversation that had been building up inside both of us for almost three decades. It was still hard. Neither of us was accustomed to expressing towards each other any feelings, except hostility. But we both knew this might be the last time we talked and perhaps it was easier that we could not see each other. He raised it first. He said he knew that we'd had 'difficult periods' in the past, and he got upset as he tried to say how sorry he was for the way he'd treated me. I listened with astonishment, and was so overcome with unfamiliar emotions that I barely knew how to respond. I kept saying, 'It's all right. I forgive you. I forgive you.' And, in the end, sobbing, just before I hung up: 'I love you.'

Back in New York I wrote to him. I told him how much I'd appreciated *his* letter and, especially the business advice he had given me. 'It is pretty ironic, as I'm sure you appreciate' I'd written, 'that of all your kids I am the one to end up a capitalist.' I assured him that the 'difficulties' we had had were 'long forgotten' and that he should not 'harbour any feelings of remorse about that time'. Then, not knowing if I even believed what I was saying, I set out for him why I thought he should be proud of his life, of his family, of his accomplishments. I told him that he and I were more alike than we had ever wanted to acknowledge. I told him that as I wrote, I was listening to Kiri Te Kanawa singing Verdi: 'My love of opera is something else I learned from you.' I told him that I admired how he had finally been able to stop drinking, acknowledging how hard that must have been for him, and how glad I was that I'd been able to play a small part in helping it happen. 'I would like to be able to help you now,' I wrote, 'as you deal with a difficult and painful illness.' I told him he needed to accept that he was sick: 'As you have shown in the past, you have the strength and character to deal with it'. I folded the four sheets of heavy cream paper and placed them in the matching envelope, with its maroon-coloured tissue lining. I addressed the envelope, using the same Montblanc fountain pen with my signature brown ink that I'd used for the letter and stamping it Air Mail, sent it on its way. It arrived the day after he died.

He was alone, in the Repat Hospital in Adelaide on 20 September 1988, when he succumbed. My mother had left just an hour or so before. She'd recounted in her diary later that day, 'because of his drowsiness I probably wouldn't get to say all the things to him that I wanted to.' She'd been on the phone to her sister Gwen and when she hung up, it rang again immediately. It was the hospital 'telling me my darling had died just fifteen minutes before'. When my letter arrived, my mother was overcome with happiness that her husband and her daughter had finally reconciled. She determined the moment should survive so she scrawled in capital letters on the envelope: 'VIP. NEVER TO BE DESTROYED.' Seventeen years later, after her own death, I found it among her papers.

In New York the night my father died, I'd been touched by the immense practical kindness shown by Joanne Edgar, one of the senior editors and a member of the original *Ms.* team. She immediately got on the phone to Qantas and organised a ticket for the next day. The problem was that I had submitted a Green Card application. If you left the country during the application process, you were deemed to no longer want to proceed. With my immigration lawyer, I headed for the offices of the Immigration and Naturalization Services (INS) early the next morning and, after the inevitable wait, told the officer that I was seeking a temporary parole so I could return to Australia.

'Not possible.'

'My father just died. I want to go to his funeral.'

'Everyone says that,' he told me.

Thank goodness for new technology. My brother Greg faxed me a copy of the death certificate, the only proof INS would accept. I made it back to Adelaide with just hours to spare, arriving at St Ignatius Church in Norwood where I'd been to Mass as a teenager, where in 1976 seven Jesuit priests presided at Jamie's Requiem Mass and where, in 2005, we would celebrate the life of my mother, with the consoling sound of Gounod's *Ave Maria* soaring towards the vaulted ceilings of this suburban church. My father's was a far more modest service, with nothing like the 600 who'd attended Jamie's funeral, just a few people he'd worked with, a couple of AA mates and other friends, together with members of both his and my mother's families, but my father would have been tickled pink to know that among the small number of floral tributes laid beside his coffin was one from Gloria Steinem.

In July 2005, just a few weeks after we'd buried my mother, I joined the *Rainbow Warrior* in Auckland to set sail for Mataui Bay, an idyllic spot with clear turquoise waters near the tip of the north island of New Zealand. It was the resting place of the first *Rainbow Warrior*, which had been scuttled there in December 1987, two years after she had been sunk in Auckland Harbour in an act of terrorism by the French government. Although I had now been with Greenpeace for six years and had been on board most of our ships, I had never actually sailed with one. Finally, although it was just for one night, I was on our iconic flagship. We were not sailing into any kind of confrontation; the only risk on this voyage was seasickness. I had followed the onboard doctor's advice, and was very glad I'd taken the pills when I saw the Japanese students who were travelling with us green faced and retching, because they had decided to tough it out. I felt honoured to be on board this boat because of what we were about to do, and because I finally felt joined to the history of this remarkable organisation.

The next morning we dropped anchor above the scuttled ship. It was 10 July, twenty years to the day since the bombing. Several of our divers went down to inspect the hull while we on board made preparations for the formal commemorative ceremony. We would be honouring both the ship and its decades of service to the cause of world peace and environmental integrity, but also the memory of Fernando Pereira, the young photographer who had been killed in the explosion. His daughter was with us as we threw flowers into the water. She had been eight-years-old when the French government murdered her father. It was still hard to believe a government had done such a thing, that it had attacked a non-government organisation whose mission had merely been to try to secure a more peaceful planet. I would still not call myself a pacifist because there are times when force is needed but I recoiled from any kind of violence. Whether it was dispensed by soldiers on behalf of governments, by individuals pursuing their demented fantasies, or men against members of their own families, I felt sickened with apprehension and fear whenever I contemplated the scale and intensity of the wanton violence that seems endemic in our world and which engulfs so many of us. Even my own family.

On an overcast day in October 2014, in a far corner of the Catholic section of Adelaide's West Terrace Cemetery, my family gathered in front of the unmarked grave that for 79 years had held the remains of our grandfather, John Patrick Cooper. We were there for a final act of reconciliation.

When my father's father died suddenly aged 51 in 1935, his wife and sons bought him a hole in the ground, but that was all. No headstone, no marker of any kind. Not even his name was recorded. He had lain unlamented in the ground ever since. Nor, until my brother Greg Cooper decided in 1988 to search for his grave, had anyone visited him. Greg had been shocked to discover the plot was full of weeds, and that a tree was growing up through it. Now, all these years later, his five surviving grandchildren—my three brothers, Tony, Greg and Paul, my cousin Pam Kelly, and I—had decided to give him a headstone.

My father never spoke about his father. As we were growing up we knew practically nothing about him, apart from a few fragments of family legend. He'd been a stretcher-bearer on the Western Front during World War I, my mother had told us. He was the only survivor when the four men carrying a loaded stretcher across No Man's Land had stepped on a land mine. We were given to understand he was a violent man, but we were told no details. And we never asked. It was only as they approached their own deaths—my father in 1988 and his brother Arthur in 1997— that they started to open up to their children about the brutality of their upbringing. My father visited Greg at his home one night early in 1988, when his wife and kids were out, and spoke for hours about the horrors of his childhood.

There were stories of smashed toys and holes in walls.

My cousin Pam Kelly also had a conversation with her father Arthur as he lay close to death, and learnt that in 1928 our grandfather had put him, then aged seven, in hospital with a broken arm and jaw, injuries so severe the medical staff refused to believe that a father could have inflicted them.

There are no records of any of this beyond our fathers' late-in-life disclosures. We have tried to find more, but while official records have yielded details of his work as a clerk for the tramways, and that he played the banjo in a small band that entertained prison inmates and performed at weddings, there is nothing that tells us what kind of man he was. We will never know how much the brutal experience of the trenches contributed to the way our grandfather was. We know war has a brutalising effect, and that his generation of returned soldiers often made their families bear the brunt of how the war had changed them. That was what had happened to our fathers. We grew up living with what World War II did to them with their 'surly moods and intermittent brutalities', as George Johnston put it in *My Brother Jack*, his brilliant novel about young men of our fathers' generation. We had not, until now, really confronted what World War I had done to *their* fathers, and how that had shaped them as well.

Richard Flanagan begins *The Narrow Road to the Deep North*, his powerful novel that won the 2014 Man Booker Prize, with a scene about the impact of those who returned from the First War on the men who went to the Second. Flanagan's central character is Dorrigo Evans, who endures the murderous conditions of the Japanese forced-labour camps. As a young boy Dorrigo had watched, astonished, when his older brother Tom returned from France: 'He had swung his kitbag onto the hot dust of the siding and abruptly burst into tears.' In 1918, men did not cry. It was so rare that it was frightening: 'It was a sound like something breaking.'

Thousands of Australian families have lived for almost a century with the consequences of that breaking. John Cooper was 32 when he enlisted and his wife, our beloved Nana, tried to leave him then but was forced back to the marriage by her own father. This suggests he may already have been a violent man. We know he hit his wife so hard, she fell backwards against a door and knocked it off its hinges. We can speculate that his elder son's relationships with his own children may have been affected by the cruelty of his childhood. We do know that he, his mother and brother wanted nothing to do with his memory once he was gone. Over the years, both sons accumulated enough money to buy their father a headstone. They chose not to.

They buried their mother in another cemetery altogether, many kilometres away from her husband, with a handsome headstone that, inexplicably to us grandkids, mentioned her 'loving husband'.

I'd written some of this in *The Lost Mother* in 2009 and it had prompted Patricia Smith, a woman in her 80s, the daughter of a World War I soldier, to contact me. She had visited France, she told me, and 'wept in countless graveyards and read the inscriptions on headstones, and the thousands of those whose names were not known and read down the lists of those who have no known burial place'.

'You do know where your grandfather is buried,' she wrote, 'It is too late for forgiveness, but bring him "home", give him a name and a defined resting place and hope that his story shows the young in the family the utter futility of war.'

I showed the letter to my brothers and my cousin. Greg and Tony reminded me that they had initially talked about placing some kind of marker on the grave when Greg had first found it, back in 1988. Smith's email gave that idea a new impetus. We were also influenced by Rosie Batty. After her son Luke was murdered at cricket practice in a small Victorian town by his father earlier that year, she had spoken of the need for families to talk about the violence so many of us harbour. We decided we would give our grandfather a headstone.

We talked a lot about what it would mean to do this. Were we forgiving him his violence? One brother was sentimental in that he just wanted to complete our family. Another felt we should respect the inaction of Nana and her two sons: the violence must have been pretty bad for them to have done this, was his thinking. I was insistent that our action not be seen as condoning this man's behaviour. Then there was the question of what should be written on the headstone. We concluded that it was not for us to countermand the decision of Nana and her sons by now including their names. We did eventually agree that his war service should be acknowledged. He was the only member of our family to serve in World War I (Mum's father, a good Melbourne Irish Catholic, had obeyed Archbishop Mannix's stricture about not getting involved in what he saw as primarily a British war). Greg obtained permission from the War Graves Commission to use the AIF emblem. The headstone we erected on the dismal patch of ground that had been his resting place for so long listed his name, and gave his dates of birth and death. 'Served in WWI on the Western Front,' it read. 'Remembered by his grandchildren Anne, Pam, David, Tony, Greg & Paul.' Greg had checked with David's widow, Annie, about including his name as we were sure that David would have wanted to be part of this.

Joining Pam, my cousin, and her husband Steve, and my brothers and me at the graveside that day was Greg's older son Matthew, Tony's son Jake and Paul's older son Richard, as well as David's daughter-in-law Linda and her three children, Jasmine, Josh and Chelsea. Three generations of Coopers confronting our grandfather's violence, the younger ones listening as we, the grandchildren, made clear that while we were bringing him 'home', we condemned the way he had treated his wife and children. We understand more these days about the ongoing trauma inflicted on those who go to war—how it damages people, often permanently (especially if left unacknowledged)— but we have talked less about the lethal impact on their families and the cycle of violence it perpetuates across generations. My family hoped that by acknowledging the person while repudiating his behaviour, we might help start to break these cycles, so men can learn to deal differently with buried pain and raging emotions. I was grateful that my brothers were the kind of men who could talk about these things. I hoped the cycle of violence in our family was now spent. As it needs to be in so many other families. Looking around that unkempt corner of the cemetery, at the plots up and down the rows where our grandfather now lay acknowledged, it was chilling to see just how many unmarked graves there were.

CHAPTER TWELVE

UNFETTERED AND ALIVE

——⟫⟡⟨——

I've had what I wanted, and, when all is said and done, what one wanted was always something else. There is an emptiness in man, and even his achievements have this emptiness. That's all. I don't mean that I haven't achieved what I wanted to achieve but rather that the achievement is never what people think it is.

Simone de Beauvoir *The Paris Review*, 1965

In 2011, I was named one of the world's wisest women by *Vogue*; one of the world's most influential women by *Good Weekend*; and my face appeared on a postage stamp, along with three other well-known feminists, as an Australian Legend. I was not as thrilled by these accolades as I should have been. I might have felt better if they were gratifying little peaks in the roiling ocean of my everyday activities. But they were, essentially, all that was happening in my life. Greenpeace was long behind me and my nine-year tenure at Sydney's Powerhouse Museum, first as Trustee and then Deputy President, had ended in 2009. I had very little work and what I did have was mostly making me unhappy. I had a very well paid part-time corporate consultancy, but I hated it. My job had been to produce a newsletter on gender equity issues for the company and its clients but the innate conservatism of that company (my copy was vetted by around nine different people, each of whom usually had 'a few suggestions'), and its fear of offending any of their many clients meant what I was permitted to produce was bland and boring. Then an act of sabotage by a female careerist inside the company had me floundering. I was unsure of how or even whether to save myself. The newsletter was abruptly cancelled. Now no one knew what to do with me, and I was not sure what I could offer. My patron inside the company said she wanted me to stay on 'forever', but she was undecided about what I might do to justify my big monthly fee. 'Would I like to advise some of their clients on how to increase the number of women in their employment?' No, I would not. I was a thinker and a writer, not a gender equity practitioner. That called for an expertise that I simply did not have. I supposed I could have studied up and forced myself to do it, but my heart just wasn't in it. I saw my job as being to research and identify the wrongs, and leave it to other more practical souls to make them right. Perhaps I could write a history of the company, it was suggested. Nothing came of that, and nor could anyone think of anything for me to do. Before long, I followed the advice I used to give to the mostly female audiences who asked me to talk about 'women's leadership'. I would say: 'If you are not happy in your job, leave. Life is too short.' Easy to say, of course. I was very glad to leave the constant humiliation of so patently being just a ticked box. I had no other income, but we would not be broke. Chip was in his second year as Artistic Director of the Sydney Writers' Festival, where he was having great success broadening the program and its audience. I was happy to be the supportive partner at home, helping however I could with his wonderful job, as he had so many times in the past supported me, while I looked for something to do.

A year earlier I'd ended my involvement with a businesswomen's conference I had curated and emceed for almost a decade. 'Serious Women's Business' was an annual event created by Taren Hocking, a talented and energetic young events organiser from Adelaide, who realised there was an opening for an intelligently designed, beautifully presented, high-level private conference for women aspiring to succeed in the corporate world. SWB brought together some of the biggest female names in business and politics who, because the conference was Chatham House rules and they could speak freely and frankly, shared their experiences of trying to work the non-fiction of my previous works. I wanted my next book to be similarly testing. I considered a biography, a big book about an important Australian whose story deserved re-telling or even being told for the first time. I'd enjoyed researching the Australian art scene of the early to mid-twentieth century; maybe I could stay in that world. I wondered about a biography of Sam Atyeo, the avant-garde artist whose 1933 work *Organised Line to Yellow* is credited with being the first abstract work exhibited in Melbourne, if not Australia. He left Australia in 1936 and later became a diplomat but he, and the few works he left behind, had enormous influence on the next generation of artists, including Sidney Nolan, who saw *Yellow* hanging at Heide, the home of art collectors John and Sunday Reed. But would anyone be interested in reading about Atyeo in the 2010s? I could not afford to write a book no one would read. I needed a subject people still cared about. Maybe Nolan himself? I could not believe there was not a major biography. I thought hard about whether I was the right person to do it. Did I know enough? Was it too late, given that so many people close to him were now dead? It would take three or four years. I was tempted, but I also wondered how I would fare immersing myself in the life of a man who, by reputation, was pretty obnoxious. What if I came to hate him? Could I write about someone I despised as a person, even if I admired his work? This was a question that had preoccupied feminism for decades now and has been subjected to an even sharper scrutiny in the wake of the #MeToo movement that emerged in late 2017. Should a male artist's personal conduct, particularly misogynous behaviour, be held against him when evaluating his work? How do we reconcile the demands of art with the conduct of everyday life? The question had been asked about such artists as Philip Roth, Philip Glass, Norman Mailer and, of course, Picasso. Drusilla Modjeska had addressed it in *Stravinsky's Lunch*,[1] a book whose opening scene had the composer demanding that his family eat lunch in total silence so as not to interrupt his creative processes. If I was to tackle Nolan, I would have to address this, and that would mean taking on the art world, where such issues tended to be mostly ignored. Then I heard that a big biography of Nolan was in the works; it would eventually be published in 2015. I turned my attention elsewhere.

I wondered about H.V. Evatt, the idiosyncratic Labor leader from the 1950s. Maybe it was time to introduce to a new generation of Australians this brilliant and erratic man, whose extraordinary career has never been matched. He had been one of the founders of the United Nations, was the youngest person ever to be appointed a High Court judge, had been a state MP, then federal Attorney-General, Minister for External Affairs and, eventually, leader of federal Labor, before leaving politics for his final destination: Chief Justice of New South Wales. Evatt had been central to some of the biggest political contretemps of the era: the Egon Kisch affair, the attempt to ban the Communist Party of Australia, and The Split of the ALP. There had scarcely been a political life like his. He and his wife, Mary Anne, were also avid art collectors, supporting local artists by buying their works, and they owned a number of European modernist paintings. Evatt's story had been told many times, of course, but I felt I could bring a new perspective, and cast a feminist eye over a man who had always been more accommodating of women's participation in public life than was usual at that time. It was Evatt who had ensured that Jessie Street attended the meeting in San Francisco in 1945 that established the United Nations. Street was one of the handful of women there; they banded together to ensure that sex discrimination was outlawed in the inaugural UN Charter and that women could be employed at this new global body. I could perhaps add another chapter to the feminist history of Australia through the story of H.V. Evatt. And perhaps a reassessed 'Doc' (as he was known, something we shared) might fare better than he had while he was still alive? I spoke to a few people but received nothing but discouragement. No one, it seemed, wanted to restore Evatt's somewhat tarnished reputation. I could not afford to spend years on a book that no one wanted to read. I reluctantly abandoned that idea.

For a while I tinkered with the idea of telling the story of Australia's most famous colonial criminal, Ned Kelly, from the point of view of his mother. The tough and formidable Ellen Kelly outlived most of her nine children, and was reputed to have said to Ned as he faced the gallows: 'Die like a Kelly, son.' I soon realised, though, that the Kelly literature was immense, dense and constantly growing. I feared there might not be an inexhaustible appetite for the Kellys. Again, it was too risky. I toyed with a biography of a house. The dwelling I had in mind was a terrace house in Challis Avenue in Sydney's Potts Point. I thought I could tell a sliver of the story of Sydney through the lives of some of the beguiling inhabitants of this particular house.

because of a 2009 column entitled 'White is the new Black'. (The Court ultimately found against Bolt.) Naparstek readily agreed, and my 6800-word
profile ran over ten pages in the October 2011 issue.[2] It attracted a lot of
attention, in part because I had a scoop about a past personal relationship
of Bolt's but also because of the proposition I advanced in the piece. Based
on the very large number of interviews I had conducted with people who'd
known Bolt over decades, including when he had very different politics
years earlier, I argued that he was a political opportunist. He had seen
an opening in the newly expanding and increasingly polarised world of
opinion and commentary for a strong right-wing voice, especially one that
was not afraid to be contentious. He had stepped into that role and rapidly
made it seem as if this was who he had always been. He quickly assumed
a huge media profile with his regular nationally syndicated columns that
attracted a massive online commentary, plus his daily radio and weekly
television shows. Bolt had not cooperated with me; he'd even refused to
confirm details of his biography, arguing that to do so would give credence
to anything else I wrote about him. But he was enraged after publication,
angry about what I'd said about his family, his former fiancée and, I suspect
most of all, how I'd positioned him as entrepreneurial rather than principled
in his politics.

The response was astonishing. I was suddenly getting work again, lots of
it: more commissions from the *Monthly*, and I returned to regular appearances in the *Sydney Morning Herald* with the *Age*, too, now interested in my
views. There were invitations to give speeches including, early in 2012, one
from the University of Newcastle asking me to deliver its annual Human
Rights and Social Justice lecture on 31 August that year. And Andrew Leigh,
the ALP federal member for Fraser in the ACT, had asked me to deliver the
bi-annual Fraser oration, in July. This was a perfect opportunity to set out
my thoughts on why what I was now calling 'the equality project' was still
not even close to being realised.[3] Why, I asked in the oration, was Australia
so successful with huge nation-building projects such as the Snowy River
Project or the Overland Telegraph, but so hopeless at what should have been
the much simpler social project of achieving equality of the sexes: 'Why
have we Australians denied ourselves the benefits of equality? Why have
we been so irrational as to forego the economic and other advantages that

would stem from the equality project?' In addressing this question, I drew
on what I regarded as an extraordinarily perceptive speech delivered in 2011
by US Secretary of State, Hillary Clinton. Speaking at an APEC Women and
the Economy Summit in San Francisco, Clinton asked a similar question
to the one I was posing. 'Why, when we have already achieved so much,
do we need to keep pushing further?' The answer: 'because evidence of
progress is not evidence of success.'[4] It was a light-bulb moment for me. We
had spent the past 40 years measuring our progress, counting and tallying
up what we had achieved, but we had not asked what success looked like.
Perhaps, I speculated, we had assumed the two things were synonymous.
They weren't, but our preoccupation with progress had had the unintended
consequence of blinding us to where we were headed—and whether we
were even close to getting there.

The speech got some attention, including from Kathy Bail, an old friend
who was now publisher at NewSouth Books, the publishing arm of the
University of New South Wales. Would I be interested in turning the speech
into a short ebook? It could feed into the growing discussion around re-
actions to Julia Gillard's prime ministership? Sure, I told Kathy, but you might
want to also include the speech I'll be giving next month in Newcastle which
will directly address that topic. I called the Newcastle speech 'Her Rights at
Work: the political persecution of Australia's first female Prime Minister'[5]
and I used it to take a hard look at the extent to which our Prime Minister,
Julia Gillard, had been subjected to unfair attack because of her sex. The
speech needed a lot of research because I had decided to frame the lecture
through a 'rights at work' perspective and explore whether, if she were an
ordinary employee, the way she had been treated would be in breach of discrimination and industrial relations laws. I sought the advice of lawyers and
various practitioners in industrial relations and discrimination law. I had
also begun seeing some of the sexualised material about Gillard that was
circulating via email and on websites, so I sent out a call to friends and to
the world, via Facebook, asking people to send me more examples. Soon I
was seeing an avalanche of material, some of it breathtakingly crude in itself,
but when 'enhanced' with photoshopped images of the Prime Minister, or
'jokes' about her, were the most sickening things I had ever seen about a
public figure. It was then I discovered, too, the images the cartoonist Larry

Pickering was emailing to every member of federal Parliament. Pickering had once been a mainstream artist employed by major newspapers including, just before my time, the *National Times*, but he had now retreated to the hate cave where he produced a daily dose of vitriol, most of it sexually based, and a great deal of it directed at Gillard. He drew her carrying a massive dildo. In a former life, Pickering had produced a famous annual calendar of male politicians with enormous penises; this 'joke' now seemed to have transformed itself into a view that to be a political leader, you had to have a dick. If you were a woman, you'd have to make do with a fake one. I spoke to several serving federal MPs, who confirmed they received these disgusting cartoons virtually every day. Several sent me copies. None had thought to complain about it. 'I just delete them,' one MP told me. I started to compile a PowerPoint presentation to accompany my speech. I realised I would have to warn the audience before I showed it.

On the way up to Newcastle, I heard on the radio a report that the shock jock broadcaster Alan Jones had that morning attacked a number of prominent women, including Gillard, accusing them of wanting to 'destroy the joint'. The attacks on the Prime Minister were already in the news, in part because she herself had made some remarks about 'misogynist nutjobs on the internet' who had been attacking her. My speech became an instant hit. Australia, it seemed, was ready to confront why it was engaging in the cruel and inexplicable demolition of the woman who just two years earlier we had celebrated with such pride and exuberance. I received a huge number of emails and posts on social media responding to what I had said. Many people thanked me for standing-up against the vilification of Gillard, and for giving them some means of fighting back—by sharing my speech. I also received a number of letters of apology, mostly from men, who told me they had shared some of these hateful emails and now they felt ashamed. I had dozens of requests: for interviews, to reprint excerpts or even the full speech. It became part of the conversation, the zeitgeist. Articles commented on it; there was furious dispute about the culpability of the Canberra Press Gallery for not reporting the Pickering onslaught against Gillard. Almost 8000 people read the speech on my website in the first few days after I delivered it. Because of the obscene nature of some of the content, I posted two versions: Vanilla and R-rated, and gave people the choice as to which one they wanted to read. I also included an X-rated appendix of material that was just too pornographic to present on the day. Large numbers also watched the video on the University of Newcastle's website that showed me delivering it. Then some five weeks later, Gillard gave her famous 'sexism and misogyny' speech to Parliament[6] that instantly went viral and everything went totally crazy. In turn, my speech went international, picked-up and praised—and, all importantly, linked to—by the *New Yorker*. That night I got another 10,000 visits to my website as a direct result of that endorsement. The traffic continued to grow, with many people coming back to the site time and again, to re-read the lecture or to share it with colleagues. By the end of the year, a phenomenal 200,000 visitors had been to my little website. The talk around what I'd said kept growing; I became a bit of a 'go to' person for any media wanting a view on Gillard. A year earlier, I'd been miserable because I had no work. Now, I could scarcely keep up with all the assignments.

I was working on a big profile for the *Monthly* of the businessman David Gonski, who had recently completed a review of education for the federal government, that recommended a radical needs-based school-funding model. This was a popular finding with the public education sector and soon the union had everyone wearing buttons that said 'I give a Gonski'. Yet, it seemed to me, that unless they were regular readers of the business pages of newspapers, no one really knew anything about this man. I had followed Gonski around, observing him give several big speeches, I'd spoken to dozens of people who knew or had worked with him, and I sat down twice with the man himself for formal on-the-record interviews. A full-on profile, in other words. I took particular care in crafting this piece. I wanted to get it right: the tone, the man himself, the significance of this South African immigrant teaming up with a Prime Minister who was herself an immigrant, from Wales, to deliver unprecedented and much-needed reforms to the way Australian schools were funded. Most of all, I wanted the piece to dispel any preconceptions readers might have that it was impossible to write an interesting piece about a businessman. I was pleased with what I submitted, but I soon became anxious and then angry when I saw how the article had been edited. John van Tiggelen had recently replaced Ben Naparstek as editor and he took astonishing liberties, not just rewriting key paragraphs but actually inserting new material of a political nature that I not only had not written, but totally disagreed with. I told him that I would not tolerate such interference. He agreed to restore my original text, but a few days later when I received the copy-edit I saw that a new set of changes had been made. Just one of them, replacing my description of Gonski's 'soft South African' accent with the word 'Afrikaans', was enough to have me yelling down the phone and resisting all pleas and promises from the editor. I withdrew the article from publication. Trust was broken, they were totally unprofessional, I would never work with the *Monthly* again. But what was I going to do with the piece? I'd done a lot work, it was a good article and—I could not forget—I had been expecting to be well-paid for it.

I offered the piece around, but no one wanted it. Although it had a lot to say about a man whose name had now become synonymous with education funding reform, it seemed that magazine editors were only interested in articles they themselves commissioned. I understood this. A magazine must embody its editor's ideas, interests, obsessions and quirks; otherwise it has no shape or, as we used to say about women's magazines back in New York, no personality. (One of the favourite ploys of the marketing people was to have the editor try to describe the kind of person the magazine was; they would then construct their sales pitches around this persona.) I suddenly understood something else. If my Gonski profile was to be published, I would have to publish it myself. My new career as a magazine editor and publisher was born in that moment. It was a totally impetuous act. I had no money, I had no business plan, I had no plan at all, really, but I did have an idea, a very strong one that had been bubbling away in the back of my brain for a long time now. I had my own website where I posted some of my writing, but I still hankered for a publication where I could also bring together the work of others. And not just writing, either. I wanted art and photography, design and architecture, and my take on fashion. In fact, the more I excitedly thought about it, what I wanted was my own magazine. I wanted to edit, to commission and create something unique, something I considered absent from the current Australian publishing scene. Even though it would be a digital publication—there was no way I could even consider print, given the cost of paper, printing and postage—I saw it as a magazine. It was not going to be a blog or a website. It would *look* like a magazine, with pages that could be flipped, like an ebook, and so each page would be designed as if it were for print. It would report, not opine. The opinion industry in Australia was already large and growing. Earlier in the year, Chip had left the Sydney Writers' Festival for the ABC, and he was now in charge of the national broadcaster's opinion and analysis website, *The Drum*. His work epitomised this trend; it was his job to oversee the commissioning and publication of up to ten pieces a day that analysed or commented upon current political, economic and social issues. We were both now back in the media, although in very different places. Soon we would be jokingly comparing with each other how our respective publications represented the two major strands in contemporary journalism.

My publication would report and reflect on the world not just as it was but as we wanted it to be. Its reporting, and choice of subject matter, would reflect the diversity and complexity of our society—and the world. But it would not confine its editorial agenda to the daily or even weekly news cycle. We would try to fill gaps left by other publications. And we would be rigorously edited. I had learned in New York that rigorous fact checking, tough editing and, where needed, numerous rewrites were essential to producing a credible and interesting publication. We would read well but, just as important, we would look great which meant we needed to have the very best art director. It would be, I explained excitedly to the people I wanted to help me realise this crazy ambition, 'a mixture of the *New Yorker*, *Rolling Stone* and the old *Esquire*.' I hoped that description conveyed my lofty ideals: big ideas, great writing, startling photography. My first call was to Ricky Onsman, the amazingly-creative digital producer who had created and maintained my website for years now: 'I have this great idea, Ricky!' I heard him groan, but he came on board immediately. In short order, I found the rest of the team: Foong Ling Kong, the brilliant editor who had done such a great job with *The Lost Mother* and who was now freelancing; Ashley Hogan, who'd worked as a researcher and speechwriter for Senator John Faulkner and now volunteered herself as a writer, researcher and general helper; and Stephen Clark, who had a full-time design job with Fairfax but who gamely offered to give up nights and weekends to create a stunningly designed magazine. My longstanding friends David Hay in New York and Paula Weideger in

London agreed to write regularly, giving me a small core of top-notch writers. Coming up with the name for the magazine was surprisingly easy. I worried that it would sound too self-promotional, but everyone I consulted advised that I was trusted as a reporter so by using my own name readers would know exactly what to expect.

The first issue of *Anne Summers Reports*, which we quickly shortened to *ASR*, was published at the end of November 2012, just six weeks after the *Monthly* had rejected my Gonski profile which was now our cover story. 'Get Gonski. Meet the man behind the schools report' was our main cover line. Everyone donated their talent, which meant we were able to produce that first issue for just the $70 it cost to register the business name. But I'd need money for subsequent issues. The production team would in future be paid market rates for their work, and so would the writers, artists and photographers. I despised the growing trend of internet publications not paying contributors; if we could not be professional, we did not deserve to exist. I had decided that *ASR* should be free to subscribers, although I'd ask for donations. I hoped this way we would grow quickly, creating a large audience that would be attractive to advertisers. Digital advertising was taking off; I was confident we could make it work. But it seemed necessary, both for readers and for potential advertisers, to position the magazine more precisely. I think it was me who came up with the tag line 'Sane. Factual. Relevant'. People loved its directness, and they appreciated a pledge that few other media at that time could credibly make. We got around 750 subscriptions and almost $4000 in donations in the first fortnight. I had hoped for more, but I had to admit that for a crazy idea that was less than two months old, we were doing pretty well. Out of nothing, something special had happened. I could not wait to see where it would go.

While I was producing the second issue, to be published in March 2013, I was rushing to complete the book Kathy Bail had commissioned a year earlier. She had agreed that it should now be a print book, and a somewhat bigger project that tried to make sense of the widespread hostility towards women that had so publicly manifested itself with Julia Gillard. *The Misogyny Factor* was published on 1 June 2013 and immediately caused a stir. Its bright yellow cover with the arresting image of a traffic stop sign conveyed a simple, direct and uncompromising message. It provided an immediate talking-point, especially now that Gillard was being publicly and pitilessly stalked by Kevin Rudd, the man she had deposed three years earlier. He succeeded in returning the favour on 26 June. That evening Julia Gillard made a dignified exit speech, in which she said she was certain it would be easier for the next woman, and even more so for the one after that. Reflecting on the role gender had played in the difficulties she had faced as Prime Minister, she said, 'It doesn't explain everything, it does not explain nothing, it explains some things. And it is for the nation to think in a sophisticated way about those shades of grey'. She had been in the job three years and three days, longer than Gough Whitlam, and longer than Kevin Rudd would be, even after he shouldered her aside to grab his second term.

Now as I went from bookshops to libraries to writers' festivals, talking to enormous crowds about my book, everywhere I went men and women, but especially women, were upset; they were really upset. It was quite extraordinary the way people were grieving. These literary events seemed to take on the aura of funerals. People kept asking me, 'Is she all right?' Everyone seemed to assume that because I had written so much about Gillard, not just in the book and in the Newcastle speech, but also in my newspaper columns over the past year, that I knew her, that we were friends. In reality, I had met her only once or twice and only in a professional capacity. I did not have her email or her phone number. But these questions got me thinking.

The last time I had spoken with Gillard was on 10 June, the Monday of the Queen's Birthday holiday, when I had interviewed her for the cover story of just the third issue of *ASR*.[7] She had also agreed to a photoshoot with Peter Brew-Bevan, a top Sydney photographer, who had worked with me at *Good Weekend* and who had shot Qantas CEO Alan Joyce for the cover of our second issue. It was a tremendous coup for a tiny start-up like mine to secure a prime ministerial interview, especially while she was under such duress. I knew it was her way of thanking me for my support and I was determined to produce a memorable issue. None us knew that day that Gillard had less than three weeks left in the job but she seemed to sense that the clock was running out. Apart from arriving in the hefty, bullet-proof white car with the necessary complement of Australian Federal Police, she brought none of the trappings of her office: no press secretary or advisers. She was accompanied just by a young woman who helped her with her clothes. She did not even bring a phone or a handbag. Peter Brew-Bevan had put a lot of thought into the images, and what he produced that day encapsulated the dignity and warmth of this woman who had served us so well. Our cover shot showed a close-up portrait of Gillard in a plain white shirt, looking straight to camera, a light bulb just above her head. It was simple and arresting; here she is, it said, the real person you never got to know. Inside we used a shot of her in a bright pink jacket, smiling warmly, sitting on a stool in front of a blackboard on which was scrawled, in schoolkid chalk, a list of the amazing number of reforms she had achieved as Prime Minister: National Disability Insurance Scheme, Gonski, paid parental leave, a computer for every student, plain packaging of tobacco, $3 billion in tax cuts, $7 billion in jobs creation, the Murray–Darling water agreement, apology for forced adoptions, removing combat restrictions on women serving in the military, the Asian Century White Paper. I am now sorry that we neglected to include what I believe will be the reform that changed this country most profoundly, and which would never have happened if she had not ordered it: the Royal Commission into Institutional Responses to Child Sexual Abuse.

In early July, I had accepted an invitation to meet the entrepreneur and philanthropist Catriona Wallace in her North Sydney office. Wallace cuts a striking figure; she is tall and skinny with long red hair, and she likes to wear flamboyant outfits with very high heels. She does not fit the template for a business woman, yet she had been extraordinarily successful running several businesses specialising in customer engagement; she also had a hand in programs to help women newly released from prison, disadvantaged kids, and others needing a leg-up. She employed a number of refugees waiting for their asylum status to be assessed. She'd asked to meet me, she said, because she admired my work and wondered if she could help me: her expertise in digital publishing was perhaps something we could explore? Her publisher, Julie Trajkovski, a super-friendly dark-haired young woman who exuded competence, joined us. The trend in digital, Catriona explained, was to create ways to bring the publication to life so that readers could engage more fully with what they had absorbed from the screen. One way to do this was with events. Catriona and Julie were impressed that I had snagged an interview with Julia Gillard. They suggested I put on an event with Gillard as a way for *ASR* readers to engage with the publication; we could start to build an emotional connection with what currently only existed in cyberspace. It was an intriguing idea. We talked about a lunch at a big city hotel. You could attract a couple of hundred people to something like that, they said. You also need to make money from this, Catriona reminded me. Her focus was all about business. What she was in effect offering me was a business mentorship, something I sorely needed. I was full of ideas for the magazine but I did not have a clue about how to leverage these ideas into the income I needed if I was to keep going.

After I'd been on the road for my book tour, I reported back to Catriona and Julie that I thought if we could get Gillard our event needed to be bigger, open to a wider audience than businesswomen, and needed to be in more places than Sydney. We started checking out venues. I drafted a two-page letter addressed to 'Ms. Gillard', in which I described the emotional responses I had been witnessing. 'These outpourings have made me think that it would be great to be able to provide a means whereby people could come and hear you—and see you—to express their feelings, to hear that you are all right and to perhaps get from you a takeaway on how to view the extraordinary story of Australia's first female Prime Minister', I wrote. 'Perhaps you could even lead the "mature discussion" you urged us all to have on the evening of 26 June about the relevance of gender to your Prime Ministership.' I proposed events in Sydney and Melbourne, in 'a controlled and classy environment' that would also serve as fundraisers for *ASR*. I emailed the letter to her chief of staff Bruce Wolpe. I got my reply the next day. It was a Yes.

On the night, 30 September 2013, Gillard was allocated the conductor's suite at the Sydney Opera House, a group of rooms that looked out across the water to the Bridge and which included a grand piano. I was next door, in a much smaller room. After we'd formally greeted each other, we both retreated to have our hair and makeup done. I had had my first conversation with her about the event just the morning before. She had flown back in from an overseas trip and I was worried she would be tired, but she sounded fresh, looking forward to a birthday celebration that Tim Mathieson her partner was planning for later that day. I asked if she wanted to go through the subjects I was thinking of for our conversation, and whether there was anything she wanted me to avoid. She had no restrictions, just two requests. She wanted an opportunity to rebut reports in the *Australian Financial Review* that she and Tim had split up, and she wanted to be able to announce that she had just secured a position with the Brookings Institution in Washington.

My whole body was thumping as I waited in that little room. My hair was done, my face was as good as it was ever going to look. I tugged at my flimsy little black jacket with its pattern of appliqued sequined flowers. It was not the sort of thing I usually wore, but this was my first time on the stage of the Sydney Opera House. I wanted to look a little bit show-bizzy. Gillard obviously felt the same way; she wore a grey lurex jacket she'd picked up in Washington the week before. The Opera House had asked me if we'd like a call. Why not, I thought, but when I heard it, my heart beat even harder.

'Miss Gillard, Miss Summers. Ten minutes to stage'. The words reverberated around the corridors of this building where so many legends had performed. I had seen a fair share of them—Pavarotti, Sutherland, Bryn Terfel, Renee Fleming, the Berlin Philharmonic—sitting out the front, enjoying myself. Now I was getting a tiny taste of what it was like to be the performer, to walk out onto that stage and face the thousands of eager upturned faces. The five-minute call came. Gillard and I followed our escort through a maze of corridors until we reached the stairs that led to the small room where the stage manager worked. I don't know how some of the larger performers managed those stairs. I had to take off my stilettos. Gillard and I, both outwardly calm, said nothing to each other as we waited. Catriona Wallace, who was emceeing the event, walked on stage from the other side. People were still finding their seats while she explained how the evening would work. The crowd began to quieten, but nothing could quell the undercurrent of excitement that crackled like electricity in the air. The concert hall was packed to its 2600 capacity, with even the choir stalls behind the stage full. A large orange banner, announcing *Anne Summers Conversations*, hung in front of them. I had not known Catriona and Julie had done this. Was this really happening! Catriona announced me and I walked onto the stage. We'd rehearsed it several times that afternoon so I knew where I had to go, but I felt dazed and disoriented as I heard the crowd roar. It wasn't me they should be cheering. Just wait, I tried to gesture, she'll be here in a minute. Then the music started.

I think I spent more time worrying about what music to play for Gillard's entrance than the questions I'd ask her. We needed the right sound, but what would that be? Classical? Funky? Female? I asked friends. It was Sandra Yates who came up with the perfect solution. But could we afford it? It turned out that the Opera House had rights to every piece of music in existence, and it was covered by the rent we'd paid. I don't think there was a person in the place who did not recognise the first chords of 'Respect', and as they reverberated throughout the concert hall, the audience went absolutely crazy. Aretha Franklin began belting out that she just wanted 'a little respect', Julia Gillard walked on stage, and the roar that went through the room was like nothing I had ever heard before. Afterwards, Donna Ingram, the Waradjuri woman who a few moments earlier had welcomed us to country and now was standing beside Gillard just offstage, said that as the music started and the crowd began to roar, Gillard had lifted her shoulders and exhaled deeply. A shiver made its way through her frame, Donna said, as she stepped through the door into the light. It was as if all the hatred and the vitriol and the pain that she had had to absorb during those years was finally leaving her body. She walked out of the darkness towards the love and admiration and the sheer joy at her presence that awaited her that night. She glowed as she sat down, and we began our conversation.

The excitement around the event had been unprecedented. As was the learning curve Catriona, Julie and I embarked upon as we organised our very first major events. We'd quickly upgraded to the Sydney Opera House and Melbourne's Town Hall, in part because smaller venues were not available but also because I felt if we were going to do this, we should aim for the stars. We confirmed both venues on back-to-back nights. Catriona put the $25,000 deposit for the Opera House on her credit card; fortunately, her company also had a $20 million public liability insurance policy, a requirement to make the booking. Bruce Wolpe emailed me to say Gillard was worried the venues, with a combined capacity of more than 4000, were too big. She 'hope[s] you have a fantastic marketing plan to fill all those seats'. He wanted to talk about our media plan. But for now there would be no publicity. None. The deal was that no one but our small circle was to know about this. Gillard did not want any announcement to overshadow Kevin Rudd's electioneering. If it leaked, the deal was off. We managed these two momentous events with fewer than ten people knowing. The Opera House did not know who they were reserving the Concert Hall for. On Gillard's advice we waited until Tuesday—three days after Saturday's election—to announce, so that Monday would be free for any post-election media wash up. She was right; once we announced, no other news registered. At 6.45 a.m. on Tuesday 10 September, three days after Tony Abbott, Gillard's nemesis and the object of her 'Sexism and Misogyny' speech, was elected Prime Minister, I emailed the name to the Opera House Box Office. They began printing the tickets ready for a 9 a.m. onsale. We sent out a press release and an email to our subscribers. Ten minutes later my website crashed, as people piled-on trying to link to the Opera House box office. Someone put it on Facebook and I think it was Catherine Devaney in Melbourne who first tweeted it. That was it. Tickets started being gobbled up in both Melbourne and Sydney at a startling rate. We had not yet issued our offer, based on another Gillard suggestion, to give schoolgirls tickets at a discount price. We never did. By lunchtime, Melbourne's 2000 tickets had gone and by early afternoon, the Opera House was asking if we wanted to open up the choir stalls behind the stage, another 400 seats which, in our wildest dreams we'd never thought we would need, which we now agreed could be sold for $20 each. By 4 p.m. the Opera House, too, was sold out. Its website had crashed a few times, but it managed to get through what they later told me was one of the fastest-selling events in the organisation's history. Had my father still been alive, it would have been his 100th birthday. I could imagine him looking down at my latest business venture, which was starting to look as if it would be a lot more successful than the New York one he'd been so worried about. It was an unexpected and joyous turn of events.

It was Gillard's first public appearance since she left the Prime Minister-ship fourteen weeks earlier, so there was extraordinary interest in just seeing both of us. I also hired Helen Johnstone, who had worked at the Sydney Writers' Festival as a marketing and partnership manager. Christine had the only other desk in my attic, so Helen had to work from home. We turned remote into an art form as she ran down every corporation and potential sponsor in town, to try to get them on board. She was very pregnant at the time.

There was an incredible allure to the conversations, to being live onstage talking with a well-known person in front of a rapt audience. At times I was almost delirious with disbelief. Was I really on stage at Sydney Theatre, talking with Cate Blanchett? Did I actually just ask the head of the Australian Army, Lieutenant General David Morrison, about rape in war? I'd been bold enough to approach Blanchett because I'd seen her on British television, mentioning my name and *The Misogyny Factor*, while she was promoting her new movie *Blue Jasmine*. She agreed to the event which of course was a massive sell-out as well, and she allowed us an interview and a photoshoot for the June 2014 issue of *ASR* where, once again, Peter Brew-Bevan showed his singular talent. Blanchett rarely allowed herself to be photographed in Australia, so this was a very special gift.[8] After Blanchett, it was easy to approach people and no one refused; we even had publicists chasing us, suggesting clients they argued would be good talent. I found myself constantly amazed at how quickly we had created legitimacy and respect.

I was becoming increasingly proud of what our little team was able to achieve with both the magazine and the events. It was nerve-wracking constantly stepping into the unknown, but I loved this living dangerously. What would we do next? We talked of inviting Hillary Clinton. We had had a Yes from Christine Lagarde, head of the IMF, who was going to be in Australia for the G20 meeting in November 2014. I ran into Robyn Archer, the extraordinarily talented singer and international festival director at the University of Adelaide. We were both getting honorary degrees at our old alma mater, and she greeted me with a huge enthusiastic grin: 'It's amazing the way you have reinvented yourself.' I loved getting such comments. I took it as validation that what I'd become was worthwhile. There seemed to be no limit to where our imagination and energy might take us, and I was revelling in it. It was just two years since I'd been marooned in lassitude and

misery, because nobody wanted me. Now I was so much in demand that I
worked frenetically. And now I could appreciate the awards: being named
by *Daily Life* as one of 2012's 'most influential female voices' and, in 2013,
Julia Gillard and I being ranked equal No. 7 on the Cultural Power list of the
Financial Review's Power List for that year. It was satisfying that these accolades were in recognition not of past glories, but for what I doing now. The
Financial Review citation read: 'Gillard made the speech. Summers prosecuted the case. And their live talk shows sold out within hours.'[9]

I look back in amazement at just how much I did during those three
years and yet the more I did, the more energised I became, and the more
I felt I could do. Far from winding down, as we used to believe was both
inevitable and desirable as one passed what used to be the official retirement
age, my life has had more challenges, become more demanding and offered
greater rewards than almost any other time in my life. I was the busiest I had
ever been, producing the magazine, curating and presenting the conversation events, giving large numbers of speeches, writing what had become
a more regular opinion column for Fairfax media, and trying to find the
time to work on this book. I was annoyed, but not deterred, when LaGarde
cancelled at the last moment. I set about trying to secure another big-name
international guest. Sometimes I thought I was pushing myself a little too
much but slowing down was not in my nature. I was not going to stop until
I was forced to.

On 11 March 2015, the day before I turned 70, I went to see Dr Ben
Jonker the man I now had to call 'my neurologist'. The news he had was
not good. In August 2014 he had detected a tumour at the front of my
brain. It was a meningioma. 'Nothing to worry about,' he'd said, 'but let's
check again in a year.' Now the MRI showed it had grown slightly, from
18.5×13 millimetres to 20×15 millimetres. 'Not too big', he said, but
neither was it 'small'. It was on the edge of my brain rather than inside it,
which was good, but it was 'sitting very close to the nerve that controls the
eye'; there was a small risk to my vision. We had three options: do nothing
and see if it keeps growing; try to blast it away with radiation or take it
out. Because the tumour was accessible he recommended the latter. Brain

surgery. It was not urgent, he said, just whenever I—and he—could fit it in. I took out my diary. My next conversation event, with Sex Discrimination Commissioner Elizabeth Broderick, was locked in for 7 May. What about the following week? That worked for Dr Jonker. He explained in excruciating detail where and how he was going to cut open my skull. The surgery was set for 14 May.

Whatever fear I had about what was to happen I buried so deeply that I could not feel it. I was utterly calm and totally methodical as I worked out what needed to be done over the coming nine weeks. I had initially thought I would tell everyone, even put out a press release that would announce I'd be out of action for a few months, but the reaction of the first couple of people was so extreme that I thought better of it. One friend literally screamed. I learned that you simply couldn't say the words 'brain tumour' without people really freaking out. I decided I would tell my family, a few close friends and only those others who absolutely had to know.

The next nine weeks were as hectic as any over the past year. I presided over the editing and production of the April/May 2015 issue of *ASR*—our twelfth—and wrote the cover story, an intensely researched and lengthy profile of Elizabeth Broderick. I ran two Conversation events, the one with Broderick and, a few weeks earlier, another with the football legend Adam Goodes. In an effort to sell tickets and build up our revenue, I'd put enormous effort into marketing both these events, including hiring Luisa Low, a smart young woman who'd run social media for the Greens during the recent NSW state election. She was to work all-out for a month to sell the Broderick event, especially to schools. And on 17 April, with my brother Tony, I'd driven the nine hours from Sydney to Deniliquin in the Riverina district of New South Wales for a two-day family reunion. Ten days earlier I'd found myself unaccountably nervous before the Goodes event. I supposed it was because I knew so little about football and while the conversation was supposed to deal with Goodes's personal story of how he found his way as a young Indigenous Australian, and his championing of issues such as ending violence against women, I worried that my total ignorance of the game might somehow make the whole event seem unauthentic. I wanted to hide in my dressing room and try to calm myself with peppermint tea but Adam, perhaps sensing my stage fright, engaged me. Everyone else had left the backstage area, so it was just the two of us, standing awkwardly in a doorway. I'd met him just once before, at the Sydney Swans headquarters a few weeks earlier, when I had run through the topics for tonight's discussion. It had taken more than a year of chasing to get Goodes. In 2014 he was Australian of the Year, which meant multiple speaking engagements as well as his football commitments, but he had promised to make time early in 2015. By April when we finally scheduled it, Goodes was having a very rough time on the field, being routinely booed. The hostility was widely seen as payback for his strong stance on Indigenous issues; he'd copped a lot of flak the year before when he'd singled out from the yelling crowd at a Melbourne game a young girl—she turned out to be just thirteen-years-old—for calling him an 'ape'. She was escorted off. Later she apologised, she and Goodes had a conversation and he'd dismissed what happened as due to her youth and ignorance, but many football fans still booed whenever he came on the field. He became so demoralised that he did not play several games and in September 2015, refused to undertake the lap of honour accorded to all retiring champions in his final game. It was a shameful episode in Australian sport but that April night at the City Recital Hall in Sydney's Angel Place you would never have guessed this young man was undergoing such a crisis as he tried to calm me. He told me he often got nervous before big games, especially those being played at iconic locations such as the MCG. 'How did he deal with those nerves?' I asked him. He'd run up to the top of the stand a few times, he said. That usually settled him down. I laughed. 'There's no way I'm doing that,' I said, pointing to my high heels. He used language to settle me. I don't remember what he said but the effect of him—a man, a *footballer*, half my age—talking, working to calm me, to give me the confidence to go on, was something that moved me profoundly. On stage, he revealed himself to be as smart and self-deprecating a man as everyone who knew him had assured me he was. There were a lot of little boys in the audience that night, brought along by their mothers to experience a different kind of role model. He lifted them up, along with the rest of the audience in a way that I have seldom seen. As for me, I felt comfortable enough to ask him a few questions about football.[10]

Just four weeks later I was back at the City Recital Hall to converse with Elizabeth Broderick. I felt more relaxed this time. I was familiar with the subject matter, I got on well with Liz, I was pleased that we'd varied the usual format of the event to enable Qantas CEO Alan Joyce and Macquarie Bank chairman Kevin McCann, two leading businessmen who were members of her Male Champions of Change group, to join us on stage for part of the event. Most of all I was thrilled and relieved that we'd sold a huge number of tickets . . . Kevin McCann could not believe the crowd: 'You must have 700 people here', he said. Close enough, and everyone was buzzing with excitement. It was nearly two years since Julia Gillard had been deposed and the ripple effect was continuing; everyone was here to learn how women could overcome the obstacles that still stood in the way of full equality. How could it get better? Several questioners challenged the CEOs, but it was the line of schoolgirls in uniform waiting to ask questions that was a gratifying confirmation that the next generation was stepping up.

<hr>

The day before the surgery was busy. I had to be at St Vincent's Hospital in Darlinghurst early for another MRI; this would provide Dr Jonker with the latest possible image of the tumour. I then rushed down to the lawyer's office in East Sydney to sign a will and documents to give Chip power to make decisions on my behalf. Just in case. Then back to St Vincent's, for pre-admission form-filling. I am looking forward to being in hospital, I told myself, I could do with the rest. The next morning, carrying my small overnight bag, I walked the four blocks along Victoria Street back to the hospital. I passed Bar Coluzzo where I often had an almond croissant and a bitter espresso. I passed the snazzy new cancer centre which Elisabeth Wynhausen visited several times even though she, like the rest of us, knew her pancreatic cancer was unstoppable. She had died on 5 September two years earlier. Soon I was in pre-surgery wearing a blue and white striped robe, lying on a bed in front of a window looking over the street. I took a selfie and sent it to Chip. Just in case. The photo is still in my phone; you can see the plane trees of Victoria Street, and cars driving past. Just a normal day for everyone else. Before my last big surgery, more than 30 years earlier, I'd stared at myself in the mirror, at the Textacolour lines the surgeon had drawn on my chest, and knew that if nothing went wrong I would wake up a different, more confident person. Now I was about to have my skull cut open, and I had a letter from Dr Jonker outlining everything that could go wrong, 'including death'. In the photograph I do not make eye contact. I am looking downwards, but I am smiling. I do not look worried. Or even resigned. I am simply there. Waiting.

After surgery of some three and half hours, I was transferred to the ICU for a night that was incredibly stressful and made worse by Chip not being allowed to stay for more than a few minuites. It was not the whisper-quiet attentive place one sees on television. There was a hierarchy of ministration; the hearts got one-on-one constant care, while we brains had to wait for a passing nurse to notice our parched mouths and lips. I was relieved the next morning to escape to the greater democracy and comparative quiet of the ward. Dr Jonker looked with approval at his handiwork as he photographed it on my iPhone. That strip of shaved scalp and the black cross-hatching of the stitches, was that still me? I had had something cut out of my brain, my head hurt a lot, and my skull resembled a baseball. Now that it was over, I allowed myself to feel a little bit scared.

I stayed in hospital for six days, until the pain subsided. I read Keith Richards' highly entertaining autobiography, *Life*, on my phone. Dr Jonker told me about his neurosurgeon friend in New Zealand who had cared for Richards after he'd injured his head falling from a palm tree in Fiji. Neurologists from all over America kept calling, he said, but Richards decided to stay where he was. Later, the doctor accompanied the Rolling Stones on their European tour. Just to keep an eye on the patient, he said, but his rather envious colleagues felt that maybe he had rather too good a time with his newfound friend. Like Keith Richards, I fully recovered. Dr Jonker had been able to remove the entire tumour. It was benign. 'No further treatment required', his follow-up letter said. As I lay in my hospital bed, I thought of my many friends who had died in this hospital or across the road at the hospice: Peter Wilenski, Mick Young, Peter Blazey, Peter Field, Sasha Soldatow, Elisabeth Wynhausen. Once again, I was the lucky one. If you had to get something, and most of us will, I was fortunate that while what I got sounded terrifying, it had been easily treatable. I had no side-effects or ongoing problems. Two years later, my fingers could barely find the scar, my hair grew back the same as it had been and, unless I mentioned it, no one was any the wiser. Unlike so many of my friends, I did not need chemo, or radiation; I did not lose a limb, a faculty or

Richard Mahony in 2009, I took a totally different view of these two characters. Now I saw Mary as long-suffering, put-upon, even abused by her
erratic and irresponsible spouse.) The fictional character who most influenced me in my twenties was Martha Quest, the woman whose life from
girlhood to middle-age was chronicled in five novels by Doris Lessing, in
what was known as the 'Children of Violence' series. I empathised with
Martha's emotional turmoil, her striving for individual freedom and her
struggle to know who, underneath everything, she really was. But the books
were set in what was then known as Southern Rhodesia (Zimbabwe today),
and Martha's colonial life and communist politics had scarce resemblance to
my own. I had thought I would be better imitating the lives of real women,
even if they were French, like Simone de Beauvoir, and much older than me.
I thought the way she lived was ideal: a free relationship with her lifelong
lover, no marriage, no kids, a life of writing and reading and political
activity conducted in cafés, and travelling to exotic places like Algiers. Her
life was, I used to think, a template for the one I wanted. More than any of
the American or British feminists, most of whom were closer to my age and
still figuring life out for themselves, this strange French woman was a model
for this young Australian woman. It wasn't just the feminism—a word we
did not use then—it was the freedom, the escape from suburban dreariness,
the life of the mind, conducted with elegance and sophistication. Decades
later, de Beauvoir's life was revealed to have flaws that would have horrified
me when I was younger. She had been sexually rejected by Sartre while she
was still in her twenties; the free and open relationship he had proposed
turned out to be very one-sided but she stayed loyal to him, working side by
side with him almost every day and editing his work until the end of his life.
She agreed to find girlfriends for him, often by first seducing them herself. It
was not until she began her affair with the American writer Nelson Algren
in Chicago in 1947 that, at the age of 39, she experienced her first orgasm.
Nor, until she began work on *The Second Sex* in 1946, she claimed later in
her life, did she have any understanding that women were systematically
subordinated.[12] Despite her very considerable literary achievements, her
decades-long fame and her being practically worshipped by younger generations of feminists, de Beauvoir was a doormat when it came to men. These
revelations, laid out in Deirdre Bair's important biography,[13] in de Beauvoir's

own letters and Hazel Rowley's marvellous book about the relationship of these two important existentialists,[14] forced us to see our heroine's flaws and shortcomings. I did not feel a sense of betrayal on learning these things. Once, I might have judged her more harshly, but now I understood that we still are prisoners of our early formation, even when we think we have repudiated it. Doris Lessing, a decade younger, says she started writing around the same time as de Beauvoir but maintains, 'She didn't like being a woman, you see. She talks with real dislike and disgust about her body'.[15] Perhaps she just did not like what being a woman meant more than seven decades ago. French women had only recently won the right to vote (in 1944) and while she proved that women could rebel against the bourgeois strictures they had been raised to conform to, could get an education, practise free love, refuse to be a mother or a wife, it turned out she could not completely escape the tyranny of her sex. She documented her journey of freedom, with all its contradictions and heartbreaks, so that we too can retrace the troubled road to emancipation. But none of that mattered in the 1970s, when I was learning about a life that women like her made possible for women like me.

I received another shock, in 2015, when I discovered that the first line of *The Second Sex*, the words that had guided my life, had been mistranslated. De Beauvoir had actually written 'One is not born but rather one becomes woman . . .' Not 'a' woman, as the battered copy of my 1970 book had it. It might seem innocuous but there is a world of difference between 'a woman'—the individual—and 'woman'—the category. Not only that, the quote which had changed my life is on page 283 of the newly translated book. Not the opening line, not even in the first chapter; rather it appears in volume two of a book that is considerably larger and more complex than the one that had been my bible. *The Second Sex* was first translated into English in 1953 at the instigation of Blanche Knopf, the wife of Alfred Knopf, de Beauvoir's American publisher. She apparently thought the book, which she knew was a literary sensation in France, was a highbrow sex manual so she sought out H.M. Parshley, a retired professor of zoology at Smith College in the US, to do the translation. Pashley knew nothing about philosophy, French literature or feminism, and he was under instructions to condense the text because Alfred Knopf considered that de Beauvoir 'suffers from verbal diarrhea'.[16] De Beauvoir protested that 'so much of what seems important to me' had been omitted, but she signed-off on the edition and that was the version that sustained my generation of feminists. Amazingly, it was not until 2011 that de Beauvoir's work received a meticulous, accurate and complete English translation, by Constance Borde and Sheila Malovany-Chevallier. They 'translated *Le deuxieme sexe* as it was written, unabridged and unsimplified, maintaining de Beauvoir's philosophical language,'[17] and the key sentence was revised. De Beauvoir's intended formulation was stronger than the one served up to us, but in the end it probably does not matter. We got the message. And, finally, her epic and ground-breaking book has been restored.

⋯⋯⋯

By mid-July I was back at work. I was not just alive, I felt and looked fine. My hair covered the scar, which was already fading fast, and my energy levels were back to where they used to be. Just as well, because the next few months would be among the most hectic of my new entrepreneurial career. In August we published the thirteenth issue of *ASR*. The cover was the brilliant young British Somalian woman Nimco Ali, who is a flamboyant activist against female genital mutilation, using her own story of having been cut as a young girl as she campaigns to end FGM in Britain as well as in Africa. Nimco is an arrestingly beautiful young woman, and this means people pay her attention; they are drawn to her and they listen to her. She is blunt and forceful, talking about 'fannies' and 'cunts' in polite society and having no compunction about walking the streets of London dressed as a vagina. One of her proudest achievements, she says, was to get former British Prime Minister David Cameron to use the words 'clitoris' and 'vagina' in a speech. Nimco and I had got on famously when we'd been on a panel together in London at the Women of the World festival the year before, and I was so pleased that she had agreed to make the long trip to Australia. Destroy the Joint, now a fully fledged online activist group created by Sydney journalist and academic Jenna Price and others, spurred into existence by Alan Jones's disparaging remark two years earlier, had agreed to pay her fare so she could take part in a conference to mark the 40th anniversary of the publication of *Damned Whores and God's Police*.

Nimco was one of a lineup of speakers and panelists that included luminaries such as Quentin Bryce, David Morrison, Larissa Behrendt, Senator
Penny Wong as well as other terrific writers, historians and activists. The
super-energetic Jenna Price had used her powers of persuasion to get UTS,
the university where she works as a journalism lecturer, to donate the
rooms and services for the conference, while Christine Howard, her temporary side-kick Justine Merrony and I made up the rest of the organising
team. We amazed even ourselves at what we managed to pull off: three days
of talking, arguing, getting ourselves fired-up, celebrating and managing to
remind ourselves that feminism can, and should, be intellectually engaging
as well as a lot of fun.

Once the conference was over, I escorted Nimco around Sydney and
Melbourne. She was not only our very first international conversation
guest, but she was also the first to not be a household name. That did not
matter, because what I had in mind this time were not big money-raising
events but more targeted, community-focused gatherings designed to
raise awareness of an issue that has not had much attention in Australia.
This meant we were reaching out to entirely different audiences, and I was
thrilled to know we had at least partly succeeded when a group of Somalian
women, many of them in traditional dress, walked into the lecture theatre
at the University of Sydney for our event. Nimco generated huge interest
because of her eloquence and her single-minded insistence that FGM be
treated not as a cultural practice but as a criminal act of violence against
women and children. She and I went to Parramatta and Auburn in Sydney,
and to Footscray and the Royal Women's Hospital in Melbourne, to talk
to a number of different groups of women who were dealing with FGM
and the myriad of issues it threw up. We learned how Australian maternity wards were dealing with women who had had stage 3 FGM (the most
invasive form, involving removal of external genitalia and the sewing up of
the remaining wound). The biggest issue, it turned out, was dealing with
husbands who insisted their wives be sewn up again after the birth. This
practice, known as re-infibulation, is outlawed in Australia, as are all forms
of FGM. We met field workers who had threatened to inform the police of
parents who planned to take their young daughters out of the country to get
'cut', as it was called. Nimco reacted to all this with the professionalism of the

expert she was, while I was having trouble keeping my emotions in check. I was horrified to learn what was happening in Australia, of the courageous battles being fought by African, Egyptian, Middle Eastern and Indonesian women to protect the next generation of girls, all the while dealing with the trauma experienced by the women who had already been subjected to it. All of this pretty much under the radar. Few people wanted to know about it, but in any event forcing FGM into the public arena risked stirring up ugly anti-immigrant and refugee sentiments in a society where these were already dangerously ever-present. I learned more about the experiences of some immigrant women in Australian society in those few days with Nimco than I could possibly have imagined. I was especially glad that we had devoted so much space to Nimco Ali and FGM, because it turned out that issue of *ASR* would be the last.

Despite a loyal group of monthly donors, and the responsiveness of others when I appealed for funds, we were simply not bringing in enough revenue to cover our costs. Digital advertising turned out to be elusive. We had cut as much as we could. Christine now worked part-time, Helen Johnstone had not been replaced when she went on maternity leave. I did not pay myself for writing or editing, or any of the other work I did, but I was adamant that if we could not afford to pay everyone else then we could not afford to be in business. I held two more events in 2015, a small Masterclass with the business and bureaucratic whizz Kerry Schott, and a final Conversation at the City Recital Hall in Angel Place in Sydney with the wonderful Annabel Crabb. Both made money, but not enough to make much of a dent in the line of credit that was keeping us afloat. I tried to find a business partner or investor, but it soon became clear that I could not afford to keep going. It was stressful and it was sad, but it was not as horrible as it had been at *Ms.* where people's livelihoods were at stake. Fortunately, everyone at *ASR* had other sources of income. On Tuesday 21 June 2016, just before 4 p.m., we sent out our last email. It was headed 'Nothing lasts for long', words I had taken from a Joni Mitchell song. 'I am sad,' I told our 16,500 subscribers, 'but my overwhelming feeling is one of pride at what we managed to achieve over the past three and a half years: thirteen issues of *ASR*, four *Digests*, eight *Conversation* events and one Masterclass. That is a lot, especially considering the size of our team and how little money we had. I want us to be judged not by how long we lasted but by how good we were.'

Christine and I sat at the computer and had the spooky experience, via the Google maps facility on our direct mail program, of watching people opening the email. Little flags popped up, with the email address of the person opening the message. First it was dozens of flags in Sydney and Melbourne and elsewhere in Australia, then we saw them pop up in Japan, in the UK, the US, in Germany and even—given the time of night it must have been there—Brazil. About half our subscribers lived outside Australia. Many of these were probably expats, but we never knew for sure as most people had Gmail addresses. But whatever their country of origin, I was immensely proud of the fact that we were a global publication. Soon, it got too sad tracing our demise and we stopped watching.

For the next few weeks messages of shock, disappointment and regret came flooding in. The sentiments were heartfelt and they reinforced my conviction that my overwhelming feeling should be one of pride rather than sadness. As did the flow of money. More than $40,000 was donated after I'd closed the business, a most practical way of expressing appreciation and it could not have been more welcome. Even more surprising was that people continued to subscribe, even months later. I still get an occasional new sub even now, two years later. But what pleased me most of all was the number of people who said they could not wait to see what I did next. I was now 71, but no one was writing me off.

I'd been born into a world that expected very little of women like me. We were not expected to have jobs or not to stay in them once we'd had the children we were meant to have. We were meant to tread lightly on the earth, influencing events through our husbands and childen, if at all. We were meant to fade into invisibility as we aged, to be docile and accepting as we waited to depart this earth. I defied all of these expectations and so have hundreds of thousands, if not millions, of women like me. Forty years ago, Jill Neville and I rued that there were not yet many of us. Now we are everywhere, in all countries, all ages, all races and ethnicities and colours and sexualities, and our numbers are exploding as the next generations rightfully take for granted their entitlement to be unfettered and in charge of their lives. Women like me changed the world so we could have a place in it, and we had to change ourselves to make that happen. We are still discovering, and inventing, what it means to be a woman. No longer occupying that space between man and eunuch, women have become a new kind of person, one that scarcely existed before, and we are still evolving. We do not know where we will end up. All I can say about myself is that I know that am not yet finished and I never will be.

ACKNOWLEDGEMENTS

This book simply would not have happened without Foong Ling Kong. Not only did she nag me (ever so gently, as is her style) that I needed to write it, but she found a publisher and hovered until a contract was signed. That was five years ago but finally I can, with a lot of pride and even more amazement, formally thank her for her persistence.

Even though this book is principally about my life, I needed plenty of help to research and recollect events and people. I am indebted to the staff at the Australian National Library, especially Catriona Anderson, Sarah Cowan, Emma Jolley, Nicola Mackay-Sim and Bronwyn Ryan, as well as to Michael Duffy, Peter Duncan, the Fairfax Library, the Media Library at Greenpeace International, Susan Grusovin, David Hay, Rowena Johns, Tom Kelly, Mary Murnane, Barbara Riley-Smith, Chris Ronalds, Tegan Sadlier at Fairfax Magazines, Michael Stutchbury, Max Suich, Sue Wills and Sandra Yates who all helped me in various ways. I very much appreciated the assistance of my brothers Tony Cooper, Greg Cooper and Paul Cooper and my cousin Pam Kelly in helping me with details of the story of our grandfather.

I am grateful to the following people who provided a quiet place for me to write when I was unable to work at home: Sally Irwin and Roger Simpson, Mary Murnane, Nell Wheeler and The Writers Room in New York where executive director Donna Brodie and Liz Sherman, assistant director, came to my rescue at very short notice when a flooded apartment left me with nowhere to work as the final deadline loomed.

And I am especailly indebted to Quentin Bryce, Anne de Salis, Anne Dingwall, Roger Foley, Phillip Frazer, Bruce Haigh, Foong Ling Kong, Wendy McCarthy, Mary Murnane, Mary Ann O'Loughlin, Chris Ronalds,

Max Suich, Carol Treloar and Sandra Yates who read all or parts of the manuscript and provided valuable coments and feedback. If, despite their assistance, I have got anything wrong, the fault is entirely mine.

I have been blessed to have a great publisher in Patrick Gallagher and I thank him for his forebearance over the years it took for me deliver the final words, and I am very fortunate to have been able to work with his excellent team: publisher Elizabeth Weiss, editorial director Rebecca Kaiser and publicity manager Christine Farmer. And it was such a pleasure to work again with Clare O'Brien on the final edit of the manuscript.

I am very lucky to have Chip Rolley as my partner and I can't thank him enough for the way he sustained me during the writing of this book. He read every draft, helped with ideas and recollections and always had the right words whenever my enthusiasm flagged. Chip is my soul-mate, phrase-maker and my intellectual sparring partner. My life, and work, are enriched by being with him.

NOTES

Introduction

1 Madeleine Gobeil, 'Simone de Beauvoir, The Art of Fiction No. 35', *Paris Review*, No. 34, Spring–Summer, 1965, https://www.theparisreview.org/interviews/4444/simone-de-beauvoir-the-art-of-fiction-no-35-simone-de-beauvoir

Chapter 1 'What's the Story, Morning Glory?'

1 Tom Wolfe, 'The Birth of "The New Journalism": Eyewitness Report by Tom Wolfe', *New York Magazine*, 14 February 1972, http://nymag.com/news/media/47353/

2 Its full title was: 'Radical chic: that party at Lenny's', *New York Magazine*, 8 June 1970, http://nymag.com/news/features/46170/

3 Evan Whitton, 'VJ Carroll and the essence of journalism', 22 April 2013, http://netk.net.au/Whitton/Whitton1.pdf

4 Gavin Souter, *Company of Heralds. A Century and a half of Australian Publishing*, Melbourne University Press, Melbourne, 1981, p. 473

5 Anne Summers, 'The day the screws were turned loose', *The National Times*, 19–24 April 1976, pp. 4–5, 17; Anne Summers, 'If prison is purgatory, then Grafton is hell', *The National Times*, 26 April–1 May 1976, pp. 8–9; Anne Summers, 'Life at Supermac's. Is the new Grafton just one more prison problem', *The National Times*, 3–8 May 1976, pp. 12–13; Anne Summers, 'For women. Prison is enforced "femininity"', *The National Times*, 10–15 May 1976, pp. 12–13; Anne Summers, 'NSW prison officers declare: "we won't be the scapegoats"', *The National Times*, 31 May–5 June 1976, pp. 8–9; Anne Summers, 'How prisoners were bashed', *The National Times*, 12–17 July 1976, pp. 8–9 There were also several subsequent follow-up articles published in 1977

6 Report of the Commission (Royal Commission into New South Wales Prisons), 1978, p. 108, https://www.records.nsw.gov.au/series/1604

7 Anne Summers, 'Rumbles from the concrete blockhouse', *The National Times*, 31 October–5 November 1977, pp. 14–15

8 Bernie Matthews, *Intractable*, Pan Macmillan, Sydney, 2006

9 David Brown, 'The Nagle Royal Commission 25 years on: Gaining perspective on two and a half decades of NSW prison reform', *Alternative Law Journal*, 37 (2004), http://www.austlii.edu.au/au/journals/AltLawJl/2004/37.html

10 For an account of Jamie's final days, death and the aftermath see Anne Summers, *Ducks on the Pond*, Penguin, Ringwood, Vic., 1999, pp. 392–411

11 David Marr and Anne Summers, 'How women are used: the animal act of the year', *The National Times*, 21–26 November 1977, pp. 8–9, 11–12, 14

12 Kelsey Munro, 'St Paul's College boycotting Elizabeth Broderick review into college culture', *Sydney Morning Herald*, 18 November 2016, http://www.smh.com.au/nsw/st-pauls-college-boycotting-elizabeth-broderick-review-into-college-culture-20161117-gsrfq7.html

13 Naaman Zhou, 'St. Paul's College joins University of Sydney's review of "culture of sexism"', *The Guardian*, 2 June 2017, https://www.theguardian.com/australia-news/2017/jun/02/st-pauls-college-joins-university-of-sydneys-review-of-culture-of-sexism

14 For a fuller account of the end of Brifman's relationship with Krahe and her subsequent escape to Brisbane and her death, see: Michael Duffy and Nick Hordern, *Sydney Noir, The Golden Years*, NewSouth Publishing, Sydney, 2017, pp. 186, 189–90, 204–05, 216–19, 254–55

15 no byline [Anne Summers], 'Police corruption allegations', *The National Times*, 13–18 March 1978, pp. 8–9

16 Telephone interview with Peter Duncan, 22 May 2017

Chapter 2   Home of the Brave

1 Hazel Rowley, *Tete-a-Tete. The Lives and Loves of Simone de Beauvoir and Jean-Paul Sartre*, Chatto & Windus, London, 2006, p. 71

2 Editorial, 'On Wounded Knee', *New York Times*, 23 October 2012

3 Marlon Brando, 'That Unfinished Oscar Speech', *New York Times*, 30 March 1973

4 Brando, 'That Unfinished Oscar Speech'

5 A.A. Phillips, 'The Cultural Cringe', *Meanjin*, vol. 9 no. 4, Summer 1950, pp. 299–302

6 Simone de Beauvoir, excerpt from Preface of *Crimes Against Women. Proceedings of the International Tribunal*, Compiled and edited by Diana E.H. Russell and Nicole Van de Ven, Les Femmes, Millbrae, California, 1976

7 For a detailed account of Jane Alpert's time on the run, see Lucinda Franks, 'The Four Year Odyssey of Jane Alpert, from revolutionary bomber to feminist', *New York Times*, 14 January 1975. And for an account of how Alpert's essay, and her cooperation with the FBI, split the women's movement, see: Alice Echols, *Daring to be Bad. Radical Feminism in America, 1967–1975*, University of Minnesota Press, Minneapolis, 1989, pp. 247–62

Chapter 3   The Press Gallery

1 Andrew Clark, 'Max Walsh', Biography for Australian Media Hall of Fame induction n.d.[2017], http://halloffame.melbournepressclub.com/article/max-walsh

2 *For the record. Gough Whitlam's mission to China, 1971*, https://www.whitlam.org/gough_whitlam/china/fortherecord. The full transcript, which was described as 'extraordinary' and 'powerful' by Eric Sidoti, Director of the Whitlam Institute, can be found in this document: https://www.whitlam.org/__data/assets/pdf_file/0007/493279/For_the_Record_-_Gough_Whitlams_mission_to_China,_1971.pdf

3 An account of this can be found in Anne Summers, *Ducks on the Pond*, p. 335

4 Anne Summers, 'Number C/57/61: What ASIO knew' in Meredith Burgmann (ed.), *Dirty Secrets. Our ASIO Files*, NewSouth Books, Sydney, 2014

Chapter 4   Foreign Correspondence

1 Samora Machel was killed in a plane crash in 1986 that the Soviet Union alleged had been caused by a technology provided by the South African government. His widow, Gracha Machel, married Nelson Mandela in 1998 and became the First Lady of South Africa

2 I discovered only while I was writing this, from Bruce Haigh, that Zwelakhe Sisulu had been arrested and charged, and subsequently imprisoned, under the Terrorism Act for activities that had no connection with me. But I did not know this at the time and could only blame myself for his being detained

3 Pakistan left the Commonwealth between 1972 and 1989 in protest at Bangladesh being given membership; during that period other Commonwealth nations such as Australia were represented by Ambassadors—not the usual High Commissioners

4 Anne Summers, *Gamble for Power. How Bob Hawke beat Malcolm Fraser. The 1983 federal election*, Thomas Nelson, Melbourne, 1983

Chapter 5   Mandarins versus Missionaries

1 Anne Summers, 'Mandarins or Missionaries: Women in the Federal Bureaucracy' in Norma Grieve and Ailsa Burns (eds). *Australian Women New Feminist Perspectives*, Oxford University Press, Melbourne, 1986, p. 64

2 R.J.L. Hawke, Foreword to Susan Ryan and Gareth Evans, *Affirmative Action for Women. A Policy Discussion paper*, Volume 1, Australian Government Publishing Service, Canberra, 1984

3 Organisation for Economic Cooperation and Development, *The Integration of Women into the Economy*, Paris, 1985, p. 76

4 ABC News, 'Women earn 23 per cent less than men', 15 November 2016, http://www.abc. net.au/news/2016-11-16/australian-women-earn-23-per-cent-less-than-men/8028802

5 Subsequently other Prime Ministers have introduced legislation that was especially important to them. In November 2012 Julia Gillard introduced the National Disability Insurance Scheme legislation, for instance

6 Peter Walsh, *Confessions of a Failed Finance Minister*, Random House, Sydney, 1995, p. 224

7 Australian Government. Department of Education, Employment and Workplace Relations, *Child Care in Australia*, August 2013, p. 15

8 Marian Sawer, *Sisters in Suits: Women and Public Policy in Australia*, Allen & Unwin, Sydney, 1990, p. 80

9 Senator Don Grimes, Child Care Amendment Bill 1985, Second Reading Speech *Australian Senate*, 14 November 1985

10 Sawer, *Sisters in Suits*, p. 81

11 Angelique Chrisafis, 'Just call me Nell', *The Guardian*, 22 November 2004, http://www. theguardian.com/books/2004/nov/22/biography.gayrights (accessed 30 October 2014)

12 Anne Summers, *Ducks on the Pond*, Penguin, Ringwood, Vic., 1999

Chapter 6   'The Times Will Suit Me'

1 F. Scott Fitzgerald, *My Lost City*, typescript, 1935–36, http://fitzgerald.narod.ru/ crackup/068e-city.html

2 Bruno Bertuccioli, *The Level Club. A New York City story of the twenties splendor, decadence and resurgence of a monument to human ambition*, Watermark Press, Maryland, 1991

3 Anne Summers, 'The times will suit me, says John Howard', *Australian Financial Review*, 7 July 1986, p. 1

4 Anne Summers, 'Smut reigns in new TV network of "Dirty Digger"', *Australian Financial Review*, 7 April 1987

5　Anne Summers, 'Murdoch's News group pays $428m for Harper & Row', *Australian Financial Review*, 1 April 1987

6　Anne Summers, 'Hollywood mogul gazumps the President', *Australian Financial Review*, 18 August 1986, p. 1

7　Anne Summers, 'Malcolm Fraser's Memphis Blues', *Australian Financial Review*, 31 October 1986, p. 1

Chapter 7　'Real Feminists With Real Money'

1　Anne Summers, 'Packer in personal talks on Ms. deal', *Australian Financial Review*, 23 March 1987, p. 1

2　Carolyn G. Heilbrun, *The Education of a Woman: The Life of Gloria Steinem*, Dial Press, New York, 1995, p. 23

3　Heilbrun, *The Education of a Woman*, p. 381

4　Heilbrun, *The Education of a Woman*, p. 389

5　Kurt Anderson, 'Felkerisim', *New York*, 1 July 2008, http://nymag.com/news/features/48013/

6　Peggy Orenstein, 'Ms. fights for its life', *Mother Jones*, November/December 1990, http://www.maryellenmark.com/text/magazines/mother%20jones/904Y-000-005.html

7　Michael Kelly, 'Ted Kennedy on the Rocks', *GQ*, 14 April 2016 (Originally published in *GQ* in 1990), https://www.gq.com/story/kennedy-ted-senator-profile

8　The first was Linda Wachner who in 1986 had raised $550 million to buy the lingerie company Warnaco; when she took over she was, at the time, the only female CEO of a Fortune 500 company

9　The Magazinist 'Stolley's Laws' http://themagazinist.com/Stolley_s_Laws.html

Chapter 8　Media Mogulettes in New York City

1　After Marjory Stoneman Douglas died, in 1998 at the age of 108, a local high school was named for her. The school became famous after a mass shooting there in 2018, resulting in seventeen deaths. This led a number of its students to become nationally known and celebrated activists for gun control and against the National Rifle Association

2　Ronald Sullivan, 'Steinberg is Guilty of First-Degree Manslaughter', *The New York Times*, 31 January 1989, http://www.nytimes.com/1989/01/31/nyregion/steinberg-is-guilty-of-first-degree-manslaughter.html

3　Orenstein, 'Ms. fights for its life'

4　Susan Brownmiller, *In our Time. Memoir of a Revolution*, The Dial Press, New York, 1999, p. 278

5　Interview with Hedda Nussbaum, *Larry King Live*, 16 June 2003, http://transcripts.cnn.com/TRANSCRIPTS/0306/16/lkl.00.html

6　Ronald Sullivan, 'Jurors see Graphic Tape of Nussbaum', *New York Times*, 4 November 1988, http://www.nytimes.com/1988/11/04/nyregion/jurors-see-graphic-tape-of-nussbaum.html

7　Ronald Sullivan, 'Steinberg is Guilty of First-Degree Manslaughter', *New York Times*, 31 January 1989, http://www.nytimes.com/1989/01/31/nyregion/steinberg-is-guilty-of-first-degree-manslaughter.html?pagewanted=all

8　Brownmiller, *In Our Time*, p. 278

9　Brownmiller, *In Our Time*, p. 278

10 Jonathan Mahler, 'Bodice-ripper in New Hands', *New York Times*, 2 May 2014, http://newsdiffs.org/article-history/www.nytimes.com/2014/05/03/business/media/news-corp-to-acquire-harlequin-enterprises.html

11 The Associated Press, 'Stakes sold in magazines', *The New York Times*, 17 October 1989

12 Orenstein, 'Ms. fights for its life'

13 Brennan Nardi, 'Tracing Our Roots. How our founder became a nationally known magazine maverick', *Madison Magazine*, 15 January 2013, https://www.channel3000.com/madison-magazine/opinion/tracing-our-roots/158720523

14 Orenstein, 'Ms. fights for its life'

15 Jane Kramer, 'After Fifty Years, Gloria Steinem is Still at the Forefront of the Feminist Cause', *The New Yorker*, 19 October 2015

16 Lang continued to publish *Sassy* until 1994, when he sold it to the Pedersen Publishing Company which in 1996 folded it into its *Teen* magazine and *Sassy* was no more, although it continues to have an almost cult-like following in some media, fashion and cultural circles. http://www.nytimes.com/1994/12/08/business/the-media-business-petersen-will-restart-sassy-with-push-for-older-readers.html

17 Emma Brockes, 'Gloria Steinem, If Men Could Get Pregnant Abortion Would be a Sacrament', *The Guardian*, 17 October 2015

18 Susan Faludi, *Backlash. The Undeclared War Against American Women*, Random House, New York, 1991, p. 108

19 Faludi, *Backlash*, p. 109

20 Faludi, *Backlash*, p. 110

Chapter 9   Paul Keating and the Laminar Flow

1 Nikki Barrowclough, 'Keating goes a-wooing', *Good Weekend*, 6 June 1992, pp. 12–17

2 Walsh, *Confessions of a Failed Finance Minister*, 1995, p. 248

3 Patricia Edgar, *Bloodbath. A Memoir of Australian Television*, Melbourne University Publishing, Melbourne, 2006, p. 364

4 'PM finds words of praise for the pop singer', *The Canberra Times*, 24 April 1993, p. 7

5 Laurie Oakes, 'Interview with the Prime Minister one year after the election', *Sunday*, 13 March 1994. http://pmtranscripts.pmc.gov.au/sites/default/files/original/00009157.pdf

6 Paul Keating, *Eulogy on the death of Bill Bradshaw*, Woollahra, Sydney, 25 November 2009, http://www.keating.org.au/shop/item/funeral-of-bill-bradshaw---25-november-2009

7 Hon P.J. Keating, *Launch of Anne Summers' book 'Damned Whores and God's Police'*, Sydney, 24 January 1994, typescript copy held by author

8 John Edwards, *Keating. The Inside Story*, Penguin, Ringwood, Vic., 1996, p. 494

9 Neal Blewett, *A Cabinet Diary. A personal record of the first Keating government*, Wakefield Press, Kent Town, SA 1999, p. 220

10 Blewett, *A Cabinet Diary*, p. 301

11 Cited in Anne Summers, *The End of Equality. Work, Babies and Women's Choices in 21st century Australia*, Random House, Sydney, 2003, p. 111

12 'Keating's uneven childcare', *The Australian*, 11 February 1993, p. 12

13 http://www.alswh.org.au/about/about-the-study

14 http://www.ands.org.au/working-with-data/publishing-and-reusing-data/data-reuse/benefiting-womens-health

15 John O'Neill, 'PM throws the switch to rock 'n' roll', *Sydney Morning Herald*, 22 February 1993

16 The following Facebook post by folklorist Warren Fahey contains reports and interviews with people involved in making this event happen, together with a detailed account by Roger Foley of how he got the Hermannsburg Ladies Choir to come to Sydney, and other important details of how it all happened. It is a very good summary of how the event was organised. https://www.facebook.com/warren.fahey.10/posts/10151871054926495

17 Don Watson, *Recollections of a Bleeding heart. A Portrait of Paul Keating PM*, Knopf, Sydney, 2002 p. 337

18 Hon Paul Keating, 'Redfern Speech—Year of the world's Indigenous people', 10 December 1992, http://www.keating.org.au/shop/item/redfern-speech-year-for-the-worlds-indigenous-people---10-december-1992

19 Hon. P.J. Keating, 'Address to staff', Imperial Peking Restaurant, Sydney, 12 March 1993, typescript copy held by author

20 Watson, *Recollections of a Bleeding Heart*, p. 362

21 Troy Branston, *Paul Keating. The Big-Picture Leader*, Scribe, 2016, p. 476

22 Melissa Hoyer, 'True-believing heavyweights', *Sunday Telegraph*, 28 March 1993, p. 165

23 Branston, Paul Keating, p. 476

24 Paul Keating, Launch of Anne Summers' book

25 Jenna Price, 'Women gave ALP equal share', *Sydney Morning Herald*, 15 March 1993, p. 1

Chapter 10   The Getting of Anger

1   Lindsay Simpson, 'The Lying Eye', *Good Weekend*, 31 July 1993, pp. 18–22

2   Gay Bilson, 'The blood of others', *Good Weekend*, 14 May 1994, pp. 67–8

3   Bilson, 'The blood of others', p. 68

4   Julian Dibbell, 'Data rape. A tale of torture and terrorism on-line', *Good Weekend*, 19 February 1994, pp. 30–8

5   Miranda Devine, 'Angry White Males rejoice', *Daily Telegraph-Mirror*, 3 August 1995, p. 10

6   Peter Lalor and Kate de Brito, 'The dismissal. Office politics gone wrong at Fairfax', *The Daily Telegraph-Mirror*, 29 July 1995, pp. 26–7

7   Amanda Meade, 'Women support distressed Summers', *The Australian*, 28 July 1995, p. 3

8   Devine, 'Angry white males rejoice'

9   Jane Cadzow, 'Carmen Lawrence's year of living dangerously', *Good Weekend*, 11 March 1995, pp. 23–33

10 Julia Gillard, The Hansard transcript of the speech: http://bit.ly/2uuc82t/
    Watch the speech: https://www.youtube.com/watch?v=SOPsxpMzYw4
    Read the transcript: http://www.smh.com.au/federal-politics/political-news/transcript-of-julia-gillards-speech-20121009-27c36.html

11 For a full description of how John Howard reversed every policy and other form of government support designed to facilitate women in employment see Anne Summers, *The End of Equality*, pp. 142–71

12 Summers, *The End of Equality*, p. 163

13 Summers, *The End of Equality*, p. 252

14 Jodie Brough and Leonie Lamont, 'Struck off list; the women Hillary won't meet', *Sydney Morning Herald*, 21 November 1996, p. 1

15 Anthony Dennis, 'US breakfast show still has a cuddly kangaroo on the menu', *Sydney Morning Herald*, 12 September 2000, p. 4

16 Anne Summers, A Dangerous Liaison: Women and the Howard Government, Address to Australian Women's party fundraiser, Byron Bay, 1 August 1998, http://www.annesummers. com.au/speeches/a-dangerous-liaison-women-and-the-howard-government/

17 Anne Summers, Back to the Future. Urgent issues for the men and women of Australia, ACTU Whitlam Lecture Series, 25 June 1997, http://www.annesummers.com.au/ speeches/back-to-the-future-urgent-issues-for-the-men-and-women-of-australia/

18 This conference was captured in a wonderful documentary made by Anne Deveson and Eve Mahlab, *Not a bedroom war*, 1993, See: http://trove.nla.gov.au/work/10408122? selectedversion=NBD11070822

19 This incident was reported in Marcia Cohen, *The Sisterhood. The Inside Story of the Women's Movement and the Leaders Who Made it Happen*, Fawcett Colunbine, New York, 1989, pp. 13–22

20 Maureen Dowd, 'What's a modern girl to do?', *New York Times*, 30 October 2005, http:// www.nytimes.com/2005/10/30/magazine/whats-a-modern-girl-to-do.html?_r=0

21 Summers, *The End of Equality*

22 Michael Klapdor, *Abolishing the baby bonus*, Parliament of Australia, nd, 2013, http://www. aph.gov.au/About_Parliament/Parliamentary_Departments/Parliamentary_Library/ pubs/rp/BudgetReview201314/BabyBonus

23 Anne Summers, *Damned Whores and God's Police*, NewSouth Books, Sydney, 2016

24 Summers, *Damned Whores and God's Police*, 2016, p. 10. Liberal Party Senator Bill Heffernan accused the childless Julia Gillard of being 'deliberately barren' in 2007, just as she was about to become Australia's Deputy Prime Minister

25 Nikki Barrowclough, 'The shameful story of Australia's serial husbands', *Good Weekend*, 6 May 1995, http://www.smh.com.au/good-weekend/gw-classics/the-shameful-story-of-australias-serial-husbands-20140827-109b5i.html

26 David Leser, 'Pauline Hanson's bitter harvest', *Good Weekend*, 30 November 1996, pp. 18–28

27 'Hanson and Ettridge convictions overturned, ABC PM, 6 November 2003, http://www. abc.net.au/pm/content/2003/s983982.htm

28 John Howard, Address to the Queensland Division of the Liberal Party State Council, 22 September 1996, http://pmtranscripts.pmc.gov.au/release/transcript-10114

Chapter 11   Peace and War

1 Laura Tingle, 'Summers to head Greenpeace board', *Sydney Morning Herald*, 23–24 September 2000, p. 1. Interestingly—and for me, gratifyingly—all of the people from whom the *Herald* sought quotes about the appointment, including Paul Keating, had nothing but positive comments to make about my appointment and the contribution I would make

2 Michael Brown and John May, *The Greenpeace Story*, Dorling Kindersley, London, 1989 p. 9

3 Brown and May, *The Greenpeace Story*, p. 98

4 W.G. Sebald, 'A Natural History of Destruction', *The New Yorker*, 4 November 2002, http://www.newyorker.com/magazine/2002/11/04/a-natural-history-of-destruction

5 Deirdre Bair, *Simone de Beauvoir A Biography*, Vintage, London, 1991, p. 285

6 Rowley, *Tete-a-Tete*, photograph between pp. 206–07

7 http://www.forum2000.cz/en/projects/human-rights-search-for-global-responsibility
Note: the conference program included in the Documents PDF on this website is the

scheduled program, and does not reflect who ultimately participated as a number of the American guests listed did not attend in the wake of the 9/11 attacks on the US

8 Allister Sparks, 'The Secret Revolution', *The New Yorker*, 11 April 1994, p. 65

Chapter 12   Unfettered and Alive

1 Drusilla Modjeska, *Stravinsky's Lunch*, Picador, Sydney, 1999

2 Anne Summers, 'The Bolt Factor. The making of an opportunist', *The Monthly*, October 2011, pp. 18–27

3 Anne Summers, 'The Equality Project: progress v. success', The Fraser Oration 2012, Canberra, 25 July 2012, http://www.annesummers.com.au/speeches/the-equality-project-progress-v-success/

4 Sadly, this speech is no longer available on the US State Department's archive. There is a fact sheet that summarises Clinton's remarks to this Summit but which fails to include the key insight that so impressed me

5 Anne Summers, 'Her rights at work. The political persecution of Australia's first female prime minister', Human rights and social justice lecture, University of Newcastle, 31 August 2012, http://www.annesummers.com.au/speeches/her-rights-at-work-the-political-persecution-of-australias-first-female-prime-minister/

6 http://www.youtube.com/watch?feature=player_embedded&v=ihd7ofrwQX0

7 Anne Summers, 'The prime ministership according to Julia Gillard', *Anne Summers Reports*, No. 3, July 2013, http://annesummerspull.issimoholdingspt.netdna-cdn.com/wp-content/uploads/2014/11/pmjuliagillard1.pdf

8 Anne Summers, 'Incomparable Cate', *Anne Summers Reports*, No. 8, June 2014, pp 24–37

9 Sarah Oakes, 'The 20 Most Influential Female Voices of 2012', *Daily Life*, 11 December 2012, http://www.dailylife.com.au/news-and-views/dl-opinion/the-20-most-influential-female-voices-of-2012-20121210-2b55h.html; Matthew Drummond, 'Cultural power', *Australian Financial Review*, 25 October, 2013, http://www.afr.com/it-pro/australias-top-power-brokers-revealed-20131024-jjzb6

10 A video of Adam Goodes in conversation with Anne Summers can be watched at http://www.annesummers.com.au/conversations/adam-goodes/

11 Frank Moorhouse, *Grand Days*, Picador, London, 1993; Frank Moorhouse, *Dark Palace*, Vintage Books, Sydney, 2000; Frank Moorhouse, *Cold Light*, Vintage Books, Sydney, 2012

12 Joan Acocella, 'The Frog and the Crocodile', *The New Yorker*, 24 and 31 August 1998, p. 144

13 Bair, *Simone de Beauvoir*

14 Rowley, *Tete-a-Tete*

15 Natasha Walter, 'Interview: The Golden Journey. After a lifetime of novels, Doris Lessing has written her autobiography', *Independent*, 14 October 1994

16 Judith Thurman, 'Introduction' to Constance Borde and Sheila Malovany-Chevallier, *The Second Sex*, Vintage Books, New York, 2011, p. xiii

17 Borde and Malovany-Chevallier, *The Second Sex*, p. xvii

INDEX

Abbott, Prime Minister Tony 149, 429
ABC (Australian Broadcasting
    Corporation) 12, 31, 77, 91, 95, 97,
    274, 325, 422, 430, 437
Abeles, Sir Peter 156
Aboriginal Australians 117, 151, 323, 326,
    330, 367, 416, 433–4
    and Andrew Bolt 416–7
Aboriginal land rights 41, 117
Aboriginal Women's Task Force 151
abortion 7, 9, 44, 60, 66, 67, 96, 97, 154,
    170, 188–9, 260, 282, 284, 355, 360,
    361, 371, 375
    Control abortion clinic 60, 96
    rackets 11, 60
    rally, Washington DC 1992 283
Abraham, F. Murray 195–6
ABS (Australian Bureau of Statistics) 352
Abzug, Congresswoman Bella 69–71, 220,
    234
*A Cabinet Diary. A Personal Record of the First
    Keating Government see* Blewett, Neal
Academy Awards 51
ACLU (American Council for Civil
    Liberties) 251–2
ACTU (Australian Council of Trade
    Unions) 134, 151, 156, 313, 346
Adams, Glenda 42
Adams, Tani 400
Adams, Trudie 34
Adelaide xii, xiii, 22, 24, 31, 36, 39, 41,
    100, 157, 162, 274, 312, 375, 389, 401,
    403, 404, 406, 411, 431
Adelaide Festival of Arts 41

Adelaide Writers Week 36
Affirmative Action Agency 156, 175, 352
affirmative action legislation 153, 155–6,
    158, 169, 347
    pilot program 156
    Quotas 156
Affirmative Action Research Unit (AARU)
    156
    see also OSW
Afghanistan 99, 125, 127, 128
Africa xvi, 167
    see also Mozambique, Namibia, South
        Africa, Zambia, Zimbabwe
Against Our Will 65, 256
    see Brownmiller, Susan
Agora Ballroom 63
AIDS 152, 201–2, 269, 272, 358
AIDS Advisory Council 152
AIM (American Indian Movement) 49, 50
Albright, Madeleine 394
Alda, Alan 255
Alfonsin, President Raúl 202
Algonquin hotel 67
Algren, Nelson 438
Ali, Muhammad 57
Ali, Nimco 440–1, 442
Allan, Jeff 335
Allen, Peter 187
Allen, Woody 185
Alexander, Stephanie 337
Allis, Janine 412
Altman, Dennis 44
ALP (Australian Labor Party) 290, 294,
    313, 323, 327, 328, 415

Alpert, Jane 68–9
ALSWH (Australian Longitudinal Study of Women's Health) 317
Alther, Lisa 9
Ambassador for Global Women's Issues 251
American Family Association 250
Amsterdam 370, 380, 381, 382, 383, 385, 394
Ananth 389
Anderson, Don 64
Andrews Sisters 187
Angelou, Maya 36
Anglo-American Corporation 108
Angola 102
'Animal Act of the Year' 27–9
Anne Summers Conversations 427–8, 431–2, 433–5
Anne Summers Reports 423, 430, 433, 442
Ansett Airlines 156
Ansonia Building 185, 186–7
Anthony, Susie 2
ANZUS 191
apartheid 101, 102, 103, 104–5; 106–7, 114, 116, 119
    see also Africa, South; Biko, Steve; Haigh, Bruce; Koornhof, Piet; Soweto
APEC Women and the Economy Summit 418
Appleby, Sir Humphrey 168
Archer, Anne 255
Archer, Robyn 431
Arctic Sunrise 387
Argentina 202–3
Argyle Mines 156
Armani, Georgio 236
Armfield, Neil 321
Arnhem Land 54
Arts for Labor 319–23, 325–6, 328
ASIO 98, 100, 122
    and Summers' lost luggage 122
ASIS 100
ASME (American Society of Magazine Editors) 262
Associated Communications 254
Associated Newspapers 236, 237
Astley, Thea 36, 321
Atkinson, Ti-Grace 43

Atlanta 63, 248
Atlantic Monthly 206
Attenborough, Richard 103
Atwood, Margaret 36, 39
Atyeo, Sam 414
Auden, W.H. 187–8
Australian Artists Creative Fellowships ('the Keatings') 321
Australian Author 369, 381,
Australian Consolidated Press 206, 253
Australian Consul-General, New York 189, 299, 333
Australian Democrats 158
Australian Financial Review 5, 8, 9, 10, 11, 36, 46, 65, 72–99, 122, 129, 140, 144, 174, 178, 179, 180, 181, 198, 206, 212, 214, 254, 288, 333, 427
    Power List 2013 honours Gillard and Summers 432
Australian Law Reform Commission 315
Australian Media Hall of Fame 74
Australia Post Australian Legend 410
Australian Society of Magazine Editors 364
Australian War Memorial 90
Avon Products 208
A Woman to Blame 170
    see McCafferty, Nell
Aza Khel 127

Baader, Andreas 10
'baby bonus' 352, 362
Bacall, Lauren 247
Bacon, Wendy 7
Backlash: the Undeclared War against American Women 282–3
    see Faludi, Susan
Bail, Kathy 318, 423
Bain & Co 181
Bair, Deirdre 390, 438
Baker, Suzanne 13
Baldeagle, Curtis 49
Balderstone, Simon 292
Balmain Push 12, 350
Balmain Tigers 349, 350–1
Bangarra Dance Theatre 320, 323
Baran, Paul 194–5
Barnes, Alan 73

Barnett, David 77, 87, 91, 93, 94, 95, 97–99
  relations with Malcolm Fraser 77–8,
  transcribed historic China meeting 78
Barron, Peter 141
Barrowclough, Nikki 364
Barton, Gordon 3
Baryshnikov, Mikhail 277
Bastion, General Gert 171
Bates, Kathy 195–6
Bathurst Jail 16, 17, 18, 19
Batty, Rosie 408
Batty, Luke 408
Bauer, Tim 364
Beaurepaire, Dame Beryl 154
Beazley, Kim 191–2
Beecher, Eric 430
Beer, Maggie 337
Begg, Ken 91
Beijing 15, 381, 389
Beineix, Jean-Jacques 195
Bell, Glennys 11, 14
Bellecourt, Curtis 49
Bellevue Hotel 301, 328
Bergen, Candice 356
Berkman, Alexander 187
Berlin Philharmonic 427
Bernstein, Carl 268
Bernstein, Leonard 2, 247
Berry, Edith Campbell 437
  see Moorhouse, Frank
'best dressed bag ladies in New York' 236
Betty Blue 195
BHP 254, 255, 351
Bhutto, Prime Minister Zulfikar Ali 124
Bhutto, Benazir 129, 133, 134
Biko, Steve 103
Bilson, Gay 337–8
Bilson, Tony 337
bin Laden, Osama 125
Bjelke-Petersen, Premier Joh 153, 154
Black, Conrad 332
Black Panthers 3
Blade Runner 40
Blanchett, Cate 431
Blazey, Peter 269, 436
Blewett, Neal 152, 312, 314
Blue Note 200
Blue Jasmine 431

Blue Poles 328
Blyth, Myrna 272
Bollen, Judge Derek 314
Bolt, Andrew 416–7
Bophuthatswana 104
Border, Constance 439
BOSS (South African Bureau of State
  Security) 122
Boston 191, 200, 249, 270, 357
Botha P.W. 105
Bowers, Peter 72
Bowie, David 220
Boyd, Martin 59
Bozinovski, Gina 292
Bradshaw, Bill 304
Brady, Sarah 255
Brando, Marlon 50–1
Brenchley, Fred 9, 36, 73, 212
Brereton, Laurie 325
Brereton, Trish 325
Brew-Bevan, Peter 424–5, 431
Brifman, Shirley 30–3
Brisbane 24, 31, 87, 135, 154, 290, 295, 446
Bristol-Myers 259
Brittain, Vera 36
Britton, Anne 320
Broadbent, Jillian 298
Broadway 4, 12, 177, 184, 196, 2325, 240,
  339
Broderick, Elizabeth 29, 432, 433, 434
Broederbond 105, 118
Brookings Institution 427
Brown, Bryan 320, 321
Brown, David 15, 21
Brown, Tina 230, 262
Brown, Wally 90, 137
Brownmiller, Susan 65, 66, 219, 281
  and Hedda Nussbaum 256–7, 262
Bruce, Lenny 187
Bryce, Michael 154
Bryce, Quentin 154–5, 315, 343, 440
  Governor-General 412
Buckley, Brian 90
Bugg, Dennis 18–19
Bukharin, Nikolai 187
Burke, Brian 157
Burn This 196
Burns, Tim 42

Burroughs, William 187
Burton, Robert 143
Burton, Tom 316
Bush, Barbara 271–2
Bush, George H.W. 14, 190, 248
Bush, George W. 248
Business Council of Australia 156, 310, 412
Butkus, Nancy 216, 218
Butthole Surfers 264

Cabra Convent 389
Cadillac Bar 214
Cadzow, Jane 345
Café Un, Deux, Trois 204, 211, 239, 264
Cail, Barbara 174
Cain, John 292
Callil, Carmen 36
Calloway, Cab 186
Calvert, Ashton 292
Cameron, Clyde 5, 291,
Cameron, David 440
Cameron, Jane 320
Canada 38, 384
Canberra 5, 8, 9, 17, 34, 46, 48, 64, 65,
	72–5, 77, 80–1, 83–4, 87, 89–93, 95,
	99, 101, 111, 114, 118, 123–4, 128,
	131, 132, 135, 139, 141, 143–4, 149,
	159, 160, 161, 162, 168, 170, 174–5,
	184, 188, 191, 196, 203, 212, 254, 265,
	286–330, 333, 345–6, 351, 356, 360,
	361, 368, 397, 419, 437, 447
	See also Charlies; Keating PMO; National
		Press Club; OSW; press gallery
'Canberra Observed' 72, 75, 80, 95
Canberra Press Gallery, see press gallery
Cantor, Pat 237
Carbine, Pat 205, 206, 207, 209, 213,, 216,
	218, 225, 232, 262, 268, 281
Carey, Gabrielle 35
Carmody, Heather 3 10
Carnegie Hall 195
Carrington, Lord Peter 116
Carroll, Vic 8, 9, 11, 74
Carter, Betsy 221, 228
Carter, President Jimmy 38, 46, 69–70,
	96, 97
Cartland, Barbara 374
Caruso, Enrico 186

Cassidy, Barrie 325
Catholic Church 170, 183, 376
Central Park 64, 184, 200, 230
Cervical cancer screening program 318
CEW (Chief Executive Women) 174
chador 124, 129
Chairman Mao 349
Chalmers, Gill 211, 228
Chalmers, Rob 137
Chappaquiddick Island 233
Charlies 83, 84, 144
Chassler, Sey 239
Cher 242
Chess Studios 62
Chicago 46, 60, 61, 62, 63, 191, 224, 438,
Chicago Sun-Times 60
Chicago Tribune 46
Chief Big Foot 50
Chief Chingachgook 52
Chief Elijah Whirlwind Horse 49
Child, Joan 158
Childcare 66, 154, 161, 169, 174, 276,
	295–7, 303, 306, 307, 310–14, 316, 328,
	330, 352, 355, 356, 361, 362
	accreditation scheme 154
	opposition to 160–2, 312
	childcare rebate 311–14, 328, 352
	see also Blewett, Neal; O'Loughlin, Mary
		Ann; Roche, Michael; Walsh, Peter
China 14, 15, 46, 381, 384, 386
Chios 171, 172
Chisholm, Congresswoman Shirley 229
Choice 14
Chrysler Building 244
Circus Oz 199, 319, 334
Citibank (Australia) 350
Citibank Venture Capital Fund 241, 244,
	253, 267, 270
City Lights Bookstore 39, 192
Claridge's Hotel 96
Clark, Andrew 11, 34, 74
Clark, Stephen 422
Cleo 206
climate change 382–3
Clinton, President Bill 232, 248, 249, 278,
	329, 354, 396, 397–8
Clinton, Hillary 278, 329, 354, 394, 431
	Secretary of state speech 418

Cloudstreet 321
Club 33 30
Club L 173, 174
Coates, Sandra 344
Codd, Mike 203
Cohen-Solal, Annie 333
Collins, Cheryl 211
Commonwealth Heads of Government
    (CHOGM) 101, 102, 110, 111,
    115–16, 123
  Lusaka Declaration on Racism and
      Racial Prejudice 115
Commonwealth Style Manual 152
Conde Nast 237, 239, 240, 242, 253
Confessions of a Failed Finance Minister
    160
  see also Walsh, Senator Peter
Constance, Meryl 11, 14
Continental Baths 186–7
Control abortion clinic 60, 96
Cook, Patrick 11, 12
Cooper, Annie 401, 409
Cooper, Annie Beatrice (Nana) 407–8
Cooper Arthur 406–7
Cooper, Austin 164, 196–8, 253, 402–3,
    404, 406–7
Cooper Chelsea 409
Cooper, David 401–2, 408, 409
Cooper, Eileen (Tun) xii, 374–77, 401
  see also The Lost Mother
Cooper, Greg 404, 406
Cooper, Jake 409
Cooper, James Fenimore 1 87
Cooper, Jamie 22, 197, 374
Cooper, Jasmine 409
Cooper, John Patrick 406–9
Cooper, Josh 409
Cooper, Linda 409
Cooper, Matthew 409
Cooper, Patrick 401
Cooper, Paul 402, 406
Cooper, Richard 409
Cooper, Tony 406, 433
Coopes, Jenny 11, 14
Copyright Agency 350
Corris, Peter 318
Costello, Peter 301, 362
Costigan, Peter 137

Court, Sir Charles 23
Court, Richard 346
Cox, Eva 313
Crabb, Annabel 437, 442
Creswell, Rosemary 24, 320
Crikey 430
'Crocodile' Dundee 199, 217, 222
Cronin, Anna 325
Crowley, Peter 144
Cry Freedom 103
'cultural cringe' 59
Cuomo, Mario 248

Daily Dispatch 103
Daily Life 432
Daily Mirror 10, 74
Daily News 206
Daily Telegraph-Mirror 341, 343
Dakota Building 247
Dale, David 2
Dalla-Camina, Megan 412
D'Alpuget, Blanche 373
Damned Whores and God's Police 1, 8, 23,
    35, 36, 44, 48, 361, 374
  American responses 65, 71
  1994 edition launched by Paul Keating
      330–1
  2016 new edition 363
  40th anniversary conference 440–1
Darnell, Bill 377
Davidson, Gay 73
Dawkins, John 145, 298
Daylight, Phyllis 151
de Beaumont, Gustave 20
de Beauvoir, Simone xiii, xv, 8, 47, 66, 158,
    188, 337, 357, 390, 438–40
  death 188
  see also Algren, Nelson; Sartre, Jean-Paul;
      The Second Sex
de Castella, Robert 200
Deere and Company 53–5
Degeneres, Ellen 268
de Klerk, F.W. 396, 398
Della Femina McNamee 223
Democratic Party 46, 69, 228, 229, 248–9
Dempsey, Jack 186
Deniliquin 164, 433
de Salis, Anne 292

d'Estaing, Giscard 97, 173
Destroy the Joint 419, 440
De Tocqueville, Alexis 20
Devaney, Catherine 429
Deveson, Anne 451 n.18
Devine, Miranda 341, 345
de Wachter, Ann 370–1
Diana, Princess 242
Didion, Joan 234, 249
Dingwall, Anne 390–3, 400
Dirty Harry 62
Discipline and Punish 21
    see Foucault, Michel
Diva 195
Dodd, Senator Christopher 233
Dolly 204, 211, 250
domestic violence 5, 258–9, 307–10, 405,
    406–7
Doughty, Maureen 2
Douglas, Marjory Stoneman 255, 448 n. 1
Dowd, Maureen 360
Downhearted Blues 65
Dreiser, Theodore 186
DSR (Dependent spouse rebate) 311, 314,
    328, 330
Ducks on the Pond 370, 373, 374, 375, 389
    see also Summers, Anne
Duffy, Michael 30
Dugan, Darcy 19, 34
Dukakis, Michael 248, 329
Duke, David 47
Duncan, Peter 31–2
'Dunera boys' 44
Dunn, Irina 220
Dunstan, Don 17, 41, 141
Dupleix, Jill 337
Dusevic, Tom 364
Dworkin, Andrea 234
Dylan, Bob 266

Earhart, Amelia 175
Early Detection of Breast Cancer 318
'Earthly Delights' 219, 221, 279, 284
Earthworks Collective 7
East Village 187
Easton, Penny 346
Eastwood, Clint 62
Edgar, Joanne 209, 266, 404

Edwards, John 5, 11, 12, 291, 293, 307
Eggerton, Sir Jack 89
Eggleton, Tony 78
Ehrenreich, Barbara 260
Eisenhower, President Dwight 51
Eisenstein, Hester 194
Electric Circus 187
El Hassan bin Talal, HRH Prince 396
Elizabeth Bay 28, 29
Elle 235, 250
Ellicott, Bob 326
Elliott, Chuck 71
Ellis, Roger 389
Elsie Women's Refuge 5, 6, 35, 80, 258,
    361, 375
Eminent Persons Group 116, 202
Empire State Building 40, 178
England xiii, 37, 96, 370, 385, 391
equal pay see women, earnings and equal
    pay
ERA (Equal Rights Amendment) 56, 70
Esperanza 388
Esquire 229, 235, 422
Essence 227
Evans, Ted 84
Evatt, Elizabeth 315
Evatt, H.V. 414–5
Evatt, Mary Anne 415
Ewart, Heather 325

Fahey government (NSW) 297
Fahey, Warren 450 n.16
Fairfax 8, 9, 29, 32, 75, 88, 174, 204, 205,
    280, 422
    Fairfax Building, Ultimo 12–13,
    buys *Ms.* magazine 205–214
    privatization bid by 'Young Warwick'
        209–10, 211–12
    relocated to Darling Harbour 339
    see also John Fairfax (US) Ltd
Fairfax, James 210
Fairfax, Sir Warwick 17–18, 209, 210
Fairfax, Warwick ('Young Warwick')
    209–10; 211, 212, 332
    decides to sell *Ms.* and *Sassy* 234–5
    visits Summers and Yates in New York
        238–9
Fairstein, Linda 276

Fairway 184–5
Fallaci, Oriana 111, 132
Faludi, Susan 281–3
Falwell, Jerry 250–1
Fat Duck 391, 393
Faulkner, Senator John 422
FBI 50, 68
Fear of Flying 39
  see Jong, Erica
federal election 1980 134
federal election 1983 135
federal election 1984 160–1
federal election 1993 313–4, 323–4
federal election 1996 351
Feldman, Justin 277
Felker, Clay 221, 228, 358
female genital mutilation (FMG) 440,
feminism 43, 141, 172, 206, 208, 224, 229,
    233, 263, 272, 283, 350, 358, 361, 362,
    376, 414, 438, 439, 440–1
  American feminists 43, 65–71
  radical feminism 43, 68–9
  and fashion 142, 221
  and US electoral politics 229
  and domestic violence 256–9
  feminist history 415
  see also femocrats; lesbians; *Ms.*
    magazine; OSW
Feminist Majority Foundation 284
femocrats 143, 150, 151, 152, 169
Fergusson, Don 30
Ferlinghetti, Lawrence 39, 192
Ferraro, Geraldine 329, 441–2
Field, Peter 436
Financial Mail 108
financial deregulation 179
Firestone, Shulamith 187
Fitchett, Ian 137
Fitzgerald, F. Scott 47, 178
Five Spot jazz club 187
Flanagan, Richard 407
Focus on the Family 250
Fogg, Ellis D. 322
Foley, Roger 321, 322, 326, 327
Fonda, Bridget 185
Fonda, Jane 86
Forbes Club 30
Foreman, Milos 195

Forrestal, James V. 182
Forum 2000 394–400
Foucault, Michel 21
Fox, Margot 200
Fox Network 201
Francis, Rae 320
Frankie and Johnny in the Claire de Lune
  195
Franklin, Aretha 428
Fraser, Malcolm 5, 76, 78, 89, 92, 93, 95,
    99, 102, 300
  St Patrick's Day breakfast 87
  VIP plane travel with 87, 97, 99, 136
  media management 91
  Lusaka CHOGM 110, 111
  clash with Margaret Thatcher 111, 116
  anti-racism 115, 116–17
  Eminent Persons Group 116, 202
  federal election 1980 134
  federal election 1983 135
  Fraser government and women 152,
    154
  loses trousers in Memphis 202
Fraser, Tamie 202
Frazer, Phillip 39, 41, 42, 200
French, Marilyn 39,
Freud 197
Friedan, Betty 238, 262–3, 285, 355,
    357–60, 361
  enmity with Gloria Steinem 262–3, 359
  beaten by husband 359
  'the lavender menace' 359
Fuchs, Anne 272
Fukuyama, Francis 394–5

Galbraith, J.K. 195
Gamble for Power 136, 369
  see Summers, Anne
Gandhi, Indira 111
Gardiner, Greg 212, 238
Garner, Helen 35, 341
Gates, Bill 180
Gaudron, Mary 158
gay baths 186, 187
Gellhorn, Martha 48
Gem Spa 187
George, Jennie 306, 346
Germany 169, 370, 384–7, 443

Geyer, Renee 412

Giles, Senator Pat 165

Gillard, Prime Minister Julia 296, 362, 367, 412, 416, 418, 419, 423, 424–5, 426, 435
  farewell speech xv, 424
  'sexism and misogyny' speech 348, 420
  sexualised attacks 417–8
  achievements as PM 425
  Sydney Opera House talk with Anne Summers 426–30

Gillespie, Dizzy 200

Gillespie, Marcia Ann 227, 271

Gillette 251

Gilligan, Carol 69

Gilman, Howard 276–9

Ginsberg, Allen 39, 187, 192

Glass, Philip 414

Global Summit of Women 358

'God's Police' stereotype 363

Goldman, Emma 187

Goldstein, Vida 35

Goldsworthy, Lyn 400

Gonski, David 420–1, 423

Good Housekeeping 282

Good Weekend 290, 332–3, 334–445, 361, 364–5, 367, 369, 410, 424

Goodes, Adam 433–4

Gorbachev, Secretary-General 182

Gordon, Linda 270

Gore, Lesley 187

Gorton, Prime Minister John 135

Go Set 39

Goss, Wayne 154

Gottliebsen, Robert 8

Goward, Pru 274

Grade, Sir Lew 254

Grady, Diane 412

Grafton Gaol 16, 19–21

Graham, Lorrie 318

Grahame, Jack 15

Gramm-Rudman amendment 182

Grange Hermitage 88, 89

Grant, President Ulysses S. 277

Grattan, Michelle 72, 73, 82, 87, 88, 90, 117–18, 397

Greece 169, 171, 172

Greenhouse, Linda 7

Greenpeace 138, 368–73, 377–81, 382–9, 390–7, 400, 405–6
  see also climate change; Dingwall, Anne; Leipold, Gerd; McTaggert, David; Manaus; Rainbow Warrior; Stannard, Jenny

Greenwich Village 40, 64, 177, 193

Greer, Germaine 349

Gribble, Di 35

Guilfoyle, Senator Margaret 131

Gunston, Norman 319

Gyngell, Bruce 338–9

Haigh, Bruce 103–4; 105–8

Haines, Janine 158

Hancock, Lang 179

Hanford, Bruce 25

Hannah and her Sisters 185

Hanson, John 304

Hanson, Pauline 364–5, 366

Harper & Row 201

Harradine, Senator Brian 355

Harriman, Pamela 232

Harvard Business School 247

Harvey, Peter 82, 91

Haupt, Robert 203

Havel, Vaclev 394–5

'having it all' 216, 224

Hay, David 188, 200, 201, 276, 422

Hayden, Bill 79–80, 135, 145, 167–8

Hayes, Terry 10

Hawke, Bob 134, 146, 151, 152, 156, 158, 286, 296, 327, 373
  leads ALP to victory 135–6
  and Simone de Beauvoir 158
  introductions to US leaders 180–1

Hawke, Hazel 152, 373–4

Hearst Corporation 235, 237, 253

Heide 414

Heilbrun, Carolyn 213, 220, 280

Henry Ansbacher Inc. 205, 211

Hepburn, Katharine 201

Hermannsburg Ladies Choir 321

Hershey, Lenore 239, 242

Hewett, Dorothy 321

Hewett, Jenni 212

Hewitt, William 54

Hewson, John 293, 313, 320

Heydon, Dyson 27
Hickie, David 11, 33, 34, 332
Higgins, Chris 84
High Court of Australia 158
'Hill Arches' 53
Hinch, Derryn 10
Hoare, Judith 81
Hobart Women's Actin Group 11
Hocking, Taren 411
Hodgman, Michael 85
Hoffey, Frank 12, 32–3, 121
Hoffman, Abbie 187
Hogan, Ashley 422
Hogan, Gwen (SM Mercedes) xii, 404
Hogan, Nance xii
Hogan, Paul 217, 334, 354
Hogan, Sheila xii
Hogg, Bob 161, 290, 313, 327
Hogue, Cavan 166
Holder, Peter 309
Holiday Cocktail Lounge 188
Holmes à Court, Janet 298
Holmes à Court, Robert 212, 244, 298
  interest in Ms. and Sassy 254–5, 263
Homer 171
homosexuality 17, 41
  gays in the military 292
Hooke, Huon 337
Hooker, John 71
Hope, Deborah 292
Hordern, Nick 30
Horin, Adele 11, 14
Houston Conference 70
Hove, Richard 117
'How women are trained' 25–7
  see also Ingham; rape; The National
    Times
Howard, Christine 430, 440, 442
Howard, Janette 354
Howard, John 90, 189–91, 298, 365–7, 397
  reference for Summers RBT charge 145
  'the times will suit me' 190–1, 353
  reverses women's gains 351–5, 361
  'black armband view of history' 366
Howe, Brian 317, 318
Hoy, Michael 332, 339
Hughes, Robert 71
Hui, Siu Ling 337

Human Rights and Equal Opportunity
    Commission 351
Humphrey, Hubert 46
Hunter, Alberta 65
Hunter, Bob 373
Hurford, Chris 333
Hywood, Greg 81

Ilfracombe 154
Illiad 171
Iman 220
Indian Relocation Act, 1956 51
Ingham 24–7
Ingleton, Sue 159
Ingram, Donna 428
'Insider Baseball' 249
International Press Association 33
International Whaling Commission 377
Interview with History 111
  see Fallaci, Oriana
Iran 134
  Shah of 53, 111,
Iraq 134
Ireland xiii, 169–70, 196
Isherwood, Christopher 188
Islamabad 124, 125, 129, 132

Jackson, Jesse 46, 61
Jackson, Margaret 4 12
Jacobs, Gloria 230–1
Jagger, Bianca 396
Jagger, Mick 62, 186
Jaivin, Linda 318
Japan 9, 35, 179, 183, 292, 370, 392, 394,
    443
Jennings, Kate 121
Jingsheng, Wei 394
Jinnah, Muhammad Ali 124
Jockel, Gordon 134
Johannesburg 103, 114, 118, 119
John Fairfax (US) Ltd 211, 233
John Fairfax & Sons see Fairfax
Johnson, Lady Bird 219
Johnson, Mary 151
Johnston, George 407
Johnstone, Helen 431, 442
Jolie, Angelina 186
Jones, Alan 88–9, 419, 440

Jones, Carlos 60–3
Jones, Margaret 14–15
Jones, Tom 304
Jong, Erica 39, 234
Jonker, Dr Ben 432, 433, 435–6
Jordan, Congresswoman Barbara 57, 251
Jordan, Hamilton 70
Jordan, Wilma 235–7, 244, 248, 253, 254, 268
Joseph, Helen 120
Jost, John 11
journalism 4, 45, 130, 131–2, 136–8, 203–4
    drinking culture 12–13, 84
    women in 13–15
    investigative reporting 18
    foreign correspondence 198, 203
    newspapers versus magazines 332
    starting Anne Summers Reports 421–3
    digital journalism 423
    see also Australian Financial Review;
        The National Times; Press Gallery;
        World Press Institute
Joyce, Alan 424, 434
Juilliard School 195
junk bonds 179

Kahlo, Frida 67
Kane-Berman, John 108, 121
Kangaroo Island 401, 402
Karachi 129, 133
Katingal Supermax Jail 16, 20, 21
Keating, Annita 288–9, 293, 295, 300, 304, 318, 319, 325, 327,
Keating, Mike 294
Keating, Paul 73, 92, 94, 254, 286–331, 366, 416
    Keating PMO 289–90, 291–3, 294, 298, 301
    gender gap in support 290, 330
    Question Time 293, 300, 303–4
    focus group research on women 294–7
    kindness towards staff 300–1
    appreciation of art, architecture, decorative arts 301–3
    violence on television 303–4
    childcare policy 314, 316
    domestic violence policy 307–10

cover of Rolling Stone 318–9
    Arts for Labor event 319–23
    'the sweetest victory of all' 323
Kelly, Ellen 415
Kelly, Gail 412
Kelly, Ned 415
Kelly, Pam 406, 409
Kelly, Paul 11, 34, 72, 86, 91
Kelly, Petra 170–1
Kelly, Ros 326
Kelly, Steve 409
Kelly, Tom 15
Kelty, Bill 151
Kennedy, Senator Edward 233
Kennedy, President John 233
Kennedy, Robert 233
Kennedy, Trevor 2, 8, 206, 253
Kennett, Jeff 335–7
Kerouac, Jack 39, 187, 192
'Kerry babies' 170
Keyes, Alan 166
KGB 100
Khyber Pass 125, 127
Killen, Jim 90–1
Kinflicks 39
    see Alther, Lisa
King, Billie Jean 234
King, Martin Luther Jr 60, 353
King, Peter 44
King, Peter (Fairfax) 238
King, Stephen 196
Kings College, Cambridge 335
Kings Cross 29, 32, 324, 334
Kirkpatrick, Jeane 234, 396
Kirner, Joan 345, 346
Kirribilli House 152, 315, 319
Kissinger, Henry 111, 394
Klein, Anne 236, 243
Klu Klux Klan 47
Kngwarreye, Emily Kame 321
Knopf 71
Knopf, Alfred 439
Knopf, Blanche 439
Kohler, Alan 332
Kong, Foong Ling 422
Koornhof, Dr Piet 104–5, 106, 107
Kopechne, Mary Joe 233
Krahe, Fred 30, 31, 32, 34

Krementz, Jill 272
Kyburz, Rosemary 26

LaBelle, Patti 187
Ladies Home Journal 239, 272
Lagarde, Chrstine 431, 432
Lahey, Katie 412
Lakota Sioux Nation 50
La Louisiane, Hotel 390
Lang Communications *see* Lang, Dale
Lang, Dale 267–8, 272–3, 279–81, 283, 287
   acquires *Ms.* and *Sassy* 270–1
   cancels Summers' contract 299
Lange, George 230–1
Lange, Jessica 277
Lavarch, Michael 341
Lawrence, Carmen 340, 345–6, 412
Lawrence, D.H. 47
Lawrence, Elaine 382
Lawson, Valerie 10, 203
Lear, Norman 251
Lecter, Hannibal 52
Leibowitz, Annie 277
Leigh, Andrew 417
Leigh, Jennifer Jason 185
Leipold, Gerd 383–5, 396
Lennon, John 242
Lent 90
Leonard, Helen 313
Lerner, Gerda 270
lesbians 43, 67, 224–5, 268,
   negative view of by *Ms.* focus groups
      224
   and Paul Keating 294
   access to IVF 354
   see also Atkinson, Ti-Grace; feminism;
      Friedan, Betty; *Working Woman*
Leser, Bernard 253
Leser, David 365
Lessing, Doris 357
Lessore, Henry 199
leveraged buyouts (LBOs) 179–80
Levine, Suzanne Braun 217, 218, 225, 280
Lewinsky, Monica 278, 397
Lewis, Ann 232
Lewis, Daniel-Day 52
Lewis, Michael 180
Ley, Sussan 412

LGBTQ 268
Liar's Poker 180
Liberaction 11
Liberal Party 26, 78, 134, 191, 202, 322,
   352, 366
Lies and Stories 42
Life 62, 436
Light, Deborah 10
Lincoln Centre 185, 263
Literary Women 66
   see Moers, Ellen
Littlefeather, Sasheen 51
Livermore, Reg 321
Loehman's 247, 402
Logie, David 3 93
London 36, 44, 66, 95, 96, 99, 100, 115,
   196, 200, 254, 338, 387, 389
Long Bay Prison 16
Longendyke, Paula 39, 40
'Look!' 13
Loomis, Gloria 287
Los Angeles 191, 121, 217, 224, 269, 284,
   397
Low, Luisa 433
Lowy, Frank 253
Luhrmann, Baz 320, 325
Lusaka 101–2, 110, 111, 112,
Luscombe, Karen 294
Lynch, Michael 320
Lynch, Philip 90

McCafferty, Nell 169–70
McCall's 268
McCann, Kevin 434–5
McCarthy, Wendy 154, 174, 209
McCulloch, Deborah 140–1, 142
McCullough, Colleen 59
McDonald, Garry 3 19
McElroy, Hal 320
McGuinness, P.P. (Paddy) 9, 11, 77
McMahon, Prime Minister William 74
McMullan, Bob 236–7, 238
McNally, Terence 195
McPhee, Hilary 35, 286
McPhee Gribble Publishers 35
McTaggert, David 373
McVeigh, Tom 326
Ma, Yo-Yo 195

Macalester College 45, 47, 49, 56
MacCallum, Mungo 81, 82, 83
Machel, Gracie 446 n. 1
Machel, Samora 109
Mackellar, Michael 95
Mackenzie, Midge 66
Mackinolty, Chips 7
Macklin, Jenny 317
Macquarie Network 212
Macquarie University 8
Madame Butterfly 197
Madigan, Russell 179
Madison Avenue 208, 223, 271
Madonna 278
Madgwick, Rod 15
Magli, Bruno 189, 200
Mahlab, Eve 451 n.18
Maiden, Malcolm 197
Mailer, Norman 47, 414
Mailman, Josh 268
Makoni, Simba 117
Male Champions of Change 435
Malkovich, John 196
Malone, Paul 81
Malovany-Chevallier, Sheila 439
Man Booker Prize 407
management buyout (MBO) 235, 244, 280
Manaus (The Amazon) 390, 391, 393, 400
Mandela, Nelson 105, 107, 108, 115, 120, 398
Mandela, Winnie 106
Manfield, Chris 412
Manhattan Inc. 221, 229
Manhattan Theatre Club 195
Manilow, Barry 187
Mapplethorpe, Robert 187
Maputo 109, 112
Markson, Elaine 71
Marr, David 11, 27–9, 203
'marriage bar' 158
Married with Children 201
Marsh, Jan 154
Martin, Catherine 325
Mathieson, Tim 427
Matilda Publications Inc. 240, 245, 248,
    270, 281, 287
  dissolved by Dale Lang 273
  financial collapse as result of boycott
    252–3

Matthews, Bernie 20
Max's Bar 240–1
Mayer, Professor Henry 44
Meale, Richard 321
Means, Russell 50–2
Media Arts and Entertainment Alliance
    (MEAA) 342–3
'media mogulettes' 247–8, 273
Meinhof, Ulrike 10
Meir, Golda 111
Melbourne 10, 11, 35, 36, 39, 88, 89, 143,
    162, 174, 192, 254, 351, 408, 414, 416,
    426, 428, 429, 430, 434, 441, 443
Melbourne Herald 137
Melbourne Sun-Pictorial 73
Melchett, Peter 371
Menstruation and Menopause 67
  see Weideger, Paula
Mental as Anything 322
Menzies, Prime Minister Sir Robert 147,
    352
Mercurio, Paul 320
Merrony, Justine 440
#MeToo 414
Metrinko, Marsha 259, 261
Metropolitan Museum of Art 277
Metropolitan Opera 186, 197
Microsoft Corp. 180
'middle-class welfare' 316–17
Midler, Bette 187
Midnight Oil 199, 322, 334
Mikulski, Senator Barbara 232
Milhaupt, Charlie 276
Mill, John Stuart 353
Miller, Henry 47
Millett, Kate 47, 219
Milliken, Robert 11
Mills and Boon 268
Minelli, Liza 186
Mingus, Charlie 187
Minneapolis 45, 46, 47, 53
Minneapolis Star and Tribune 53
Minnesota 45–9, 53, 58, 59, 171
Misery 196
misogyny xvi, 47, 348, 362, 420, 423, 429,
    431
Mitchell, Joni 189, 442
Mitchell, Dame Roma 157

Modjeska, Drusilla 414
Moers, Ellen 66
Mombassa, Reg 318, 321
Mondale, Walter 46, 329
monetary policy 84, 179, 180
Monk, Thelonius 187
Monopoly Capital 194
Moody, Natalie 276
Moore, Henry 54
Moorhouse, Frank 321, 350, 437
Moral Majority 250
Morgan, Robin 219, 220, 272, 279–80, 284
Morgan Stanley 1 90
Moriarty, Eileen 215–16
Morice, Tara 325
Morris, Mark 277
Morrison, Lt Gen. David 431, 440
Mother Jones 257
'Mother Right' 68
Motlana, Dr Nthato 107, 120
Mozambique 101, 109–12, 120
Mozart 196
Ms. magazine 68, 69, 205–244, 247
    acquired by Fairfax 205–214
    and Kerry Packer 206
    financial problems 207,
    difficulties with advertising 207–8,
        222–3, 259–61
    history of 208–9
    Ms. Reporter 221, 231–2
    circulation problems 222
    focus group research 223–5
    repositioning to advertisers 225
    moves in with *Sassy* 224–5
    first African-American woman
        appointed to senior position 227
    targeted by *Working Woman* over lesbian
        ads 268
    acquired by Dale Lang 270–1
    relaunched advertiser-free 279–80
    bought by Jay MacDonald 280
    bought by Liberty Media 281
    40th birthday 284–5
    see also Carbine, Pat; Edgar, Joanne;
        Gillespie, Marcia Ann; Levine,
        Suzanne Braun; Orenstein, Peggy;
        Pogrebin, Letty Cottin; Smeal, Ellie;
        Steinem, Gloria; Summers, Anne

Ms. Foundation 209, 211, 213
    see also Carbine, Pat; Steinem, Gloria,
Ms. Women of the Year 1988 255
    see Archer, Anne; Brady, Sarah, Douglas,
        Marjory Stoneman; Winfrey, Oprah
Mugabe, Robert 106, 110, 111, 112
Mulawa Women's Prison 17
Murdoch, Rupert 74, 96, 199, 201, 217,
        237, 253
    starts Fox Network 201
    gazumps Ronald Reagan 201
    and Clay Felker 221
    buys *Seventeen* 237
    buys Mills and Boon publisher 268
    launches Rugby Super League 350, 351
Murphy, Tony 31
Murphy Brown 356
Murray, Les 321
Museum of Australian Democracy 76
Muzorewa, Bishop Abel 102
My Brother Jack 407
    see Johnston, George
My Life on the Road 280
    see Steinem, Gloria

9/11 terrorist attacks on the United States
        395, 396, 397, 400
Nagle, Justice John 16, 19
    see also Royal Commission into New
        South Wales Prisons
Namibia 101, 120
Naparstek, Ben 416–7, 420
Nation Review 3
National Advisory Committee for Women
        69, 70
National Agenda for Women 314
National Crime Authority 416
National Economic Summit 135
National Gallery of Art, Washington 182
National Organisation for Women (NOW)
        238, 271, 284
National Press Club, Canberra 84, 152, 313
National Press Club, Washington 14–15,
        104
National Women's Advisory Council
        (NWAC) 154
National Women's Consultative Council
        (NWCC) 151, 162

Native Americans 49–52, 57
Natividad, Irene 358
Nausea 48
 see Sartre, jean-Paul
Navratilova, Martina 234
NBC's *Today Show* 354
Neary, Jenni 147
Neill, Sam 319, 320
Nelligan, Guy 292
Nell's 220
Neville, Jill 37, 443
Nevin, Robyn 321
New Delhi 123, 124, 125, 134
New Journalism 2, 3, 25
New York 38, 39, 40–42, 43, 50, 60, 64, 65,
 66–71, 118, 119, 120, 121, 123, 165,
 175, 176–8, 181, 184–204, 206–9, 211,
 213, 214, 215, 217, 219, 220–2, 226,
 229–30, 236–8, 241, 244, 246–51, 253,
 255–7, 259, 261, 263, 265, 267–77,
 280–1, 283–5, 287, 289, 299–300, 322,
 332–4, 338, 357–8, 360, 368–9, 371,
 399, 402, 404, 421, 422, 429
New York 2, 64–5, 183–8, 221, 402
 Ms. insert 208–9
New York Financial Writers 181
New York Marathon 200
New York Newsday 211, 217
New York Post 237
New York Review of Books 200, 249
New York Woman 221
New Zealand 32, 41, 191, 199, 234, 388,
 405, 436
Newhouse, Si 239, 253
Newsweek 259, 265
Newton, Max 74
Nicholls, Linda 412
Nielsen, Juanita 32
Nissman, Barbara 5
Nixon, Peter 90
Nixon, President Richard 69, 70, 182
Nkomo, Joseph 116
Nobel Peace Prize 398
Nolan, Sidney 414
Nonon, Jacqueline 173
Not a Bedroom War 451 n.18
Novy Mir 187
Noxelle 251

NSW police 6–7
 corruption 30–4
Nussbaum, Hedda 255–9, 261–2, 280–1,
 282
 and Susan Brownmiller 256–7, 262
 and Gloria Steinem 256–7, 262
Nyoka, Justin 110, 115

Oakes, Laurie 72, 73, 86, 91, 92, 304
Obama, President Barack 61, 249, 251
OECD Working Party on the Role of
 Women in the Economy 150, 165
Office of the Parliamentary Counsel 155
Office of the Status of Women (OSW) 136,
 139–175, 290, 306, 310, 352
 see also affirmative action; childcare;
 O'Loughlin, Mary Ann; Roche,
 Michael; Register of Women; Sex
 Discrimination Act; Women's
 Budget Program
Office of Women's Affairs 136, 152
O'Loughlin, Mary Ann 145, 161, 166, 292,
 295, 297, 306, 307, 328
 childcare package 310–14,
Olsen, Tillie 66
Onassis, Jacqueline 215
One Nation Party 365
O'Neill, Gary 83, 137, 163
O'Neill, John 241
O'Neill, Kevin 241
O'Neill, Maureen 166
O'Neill, Mez 83, 84, 144, 163–4
Ono, Yoko 247
Onsman, Ricky 422
On the Road 39
 see Kerouac, Jack
Operation PUSH 46, 61
O'Reilly, Jane 229–231
O'Reilly, Neil 90
Orenstein, Peggy 257, 259, 271
Organised Line to Yellow 414
Osmond, Warren 44
Overground Telegraph 417

Packer, Clyde 206
Packer, Kerry 206, 212, 244, 253
 rights deal with *Ms.* magazine 206–7
Page, Russell 320

Pakistan xvi, 101, 123–33
Palmer, Ros 416
Pan Am 95, 118, 121–2
Pan Am Building 243, 273
Pankhurst, Emmeline 35
Papandreou, Prime Minister Andreas 171
Papandreou, Margaret 171, 172
Papp, Joe 249
Paramour, Jeanette 320
Paris 95, 97, 99, 100, 173, 174, 177, 303,
    360
Park, Ruth 374
Parker, Charlie 187
Parker, Dorothy 34
Parliament House, Canberra 76–9
Parramatta Jail 18
Parshley, H.M. 439
Patriotic Front 115, 116, 117
Pavarotti 427
Peacock, Andrew 90, 110, 115, 161, 191
Pearl, Daniel 125
Pearl Harbour 97
Peck, Abe 60
Peking 15
    see also Beijing
Penberthy, Jeff 203
Penguin Books 36, 48, 71
Pentagon 182, 183
People 242
People for the American Way 251
Pereira, Fernando 405
Peres, Shimon 396, 399
Perkins, Charles 151
Perrett, Janine 181
Perth 23, 157, 254, 294, 296, 301, 309,
    346
Peshawar 126, 127
Phelan, Michael 30
Phillips, A.A. 59
Phyllis Cormack 377
Piano Red 63
Picasso 414
Pickering, Larry 418–9
Piercy, Marge 219
Pierre Hotel 223, 281
Pilcher, Nancy 318
Pine Ridge Indian Reservation 49, 51
Ping, Deng Xiao 46

Pinkerton, Jan 320
Plaza Hotel 220, 358
Pogrebin, Letty Cottin 227–8, 285
Pollock, Jackson
Pol Pot 133–4
Portfolio 206
Powerhouse Museum 410
Prague 394, 396, 397, 399, 400
Prague Castle 396
Pratt, Jane 211, 255, 264
Press Gallery 46, 72–100, 111, 136–7, 138,
    178, 397, 419
    journalists nick-names 81–2, 93, 95
    lack of coverage of women's policy 142
Preston, Yvonne 5, 11, 14
Price, Jenna 329, 440
Prime Minister and Cabinet, Department
    of (PMC) 100, 136, 137, 139–42,
    146–57, 166, 310
    Mike Codd 203
    Mike Keating 294
    see also Yeend, Sir Geoffrey
Printing and Kindred Industries Union
    (PKIU) 13
prisons 6, 15–22, 51–3
    see also Bathurst; Foucault, Michel;
        Grafton Gaol; Katingal Supermax
        Prison; Long Bay Prison; Means,
        Russell; Mulawa Women's Prison;
        Nagle, Justice John; Parramatta,
        Royal Commission into New
        South Wales Prisons; South Dakota
        Penitentiary; Women Behind Bars
Procter & Gamble 260
Puberty Blues 35
    see Carey, Gabrielle and Lette, Kathy
Public Theatre 249
Pulitzer Prize 281, 282

Qantas 121, 404, 424, 434
Quayle, Vice-President Dan 272
Quayle, Marilyn 272
Queensland 24, 25–6, 31, 71, 87, 89, 149,
    153–4, 155, 292, 297, 313, 317, 364,
    366, 397
Queensland Irish Club 87
Queensland Women's Information Service
    (QWIS) 153

Quest, Martha 437–8
Quinn, John 166
Quinn, Marc 338

'radical chic' 2
Rainbow Warrior 371, 378–9, 387, 388,
    392, 396, 405
Ramjan, Barbara 28
Ramos-Horta, Jose 396
Ramsey, Alan 80
Random House 255, 283, 361
rape 24–7, 65, 79, 256, 315, 350, 376
    rape in marriage 41, 314–5
    rape in war 431
    see also Brownmiller, Susan; Ingham;
        St Paul's College
Rashidi, Ken 120
Read, Brendan 341
Reagan, Maureen 166
Reagan, President Ronald 46, 171, 190,
    191, 201, 271, 353
    and AIDS 201
Recollections of a Bleeding Heart
    see Watson, Don
Redbook 239
Reebok 251
Reed, John and Sunday 414
Reeves, Tony 31
Refractory Girl 6
Regan, Donald 181
Register of Women (ROW) 153, 298
Reid, Alan 90, 137
Reid, Elizabeth 11, 293
Republican Party 69, 229, 248
Reserve Bank of Australia 298
'Respect' 428
Reuters 133
Revolution from Within 213
    see Steinem, Gloria
Revolutionary Front for the Independence
    of East Timor (FRETILIN) 109
Rich, Adrienne 66, 68
Rich, Marc 397
Richards, Ann 248
Richards, Keith 62, 436
Richardson, Graham 292
Richardson, Henry Handel 59
Rickard, Dr Mary 318

Riley, Barbara
    see Riley-Smith, Barbara
Riley-Smith, Barbara 224, 294–7
Rhodesia 101–2, 109, 117, 120
    see also Fraser, Malcolm; Mugabe,
        Robert; Patriotic Front; Tekere,
        Edgar; Thatcher, Margaret;
        Zimbabwe
Robben Island 120
Robinson, Eric 89
Robinson, Irwin Jay ('Robbie') 270, 273,
    280, 283
Robinson, President Mary 300, 358
Robinson, Peter 8, 9
Roche, Imelda 174
Roche, Michael 145, 161, 166
Roddick, Anita 268
Rogers, Beverly 357
Rolley, Chip 265–7, 269, 276, 277, 278, 286,
    325, 333, 334–5, 343, 367, 377, 435–6
    returns to New York after Canberra 299
    moves to Australia 329, 334–5
    Sydney Philharmonia Choir 335
    year in Beijing 381
    joins board of PEN International 381–2
    Sydney Writers Festival artistic director
        411
    joins the ABC 422
Rolling Stone 229, 318–9, 335, 422
Rolling Stones 390, 436
Ronalds, Chris 155, 340
Roosevelt, President Franklin Delano 179,
    190
Rose, Alan 140, 146
Rosenthal, Marshall 60
Ross, Heather 24
Rossellini, Ingrid 278
Rossellini, Isabella 278
Roth, Philip 414
Rothermere, Lord 236
Round Midnight 390
Rowley, Hazel 390, 438
Roxon, Nicola 412
Royal Albert Hall 336
Royal Commission of Inquiry into Drug
    Trafficking 416
Royal Commission into New South Wales
    Prisons 6, 16, 20–1,

Rubin, Jerry 187
Rudd, Kevin 424, 429
Rudd, Mark 68
Rugby League 349
   Super League 350
Rush, Paula 146
Russell, Diana 66
Russell, Don 293, 307, 311, 323, 326
Russia 96, 98–99, 102, 126, 127, 128, 277, 370, 381, 383
Russian anarchists 187
Russian Tea Room 215
Ruth, Babe 186
Rutherford, Tom 337
Rutter, Jane 321
Ryan, Chris 22
Ryan, Edna 293
Ryan, Mark 292, 302, 307, 311, 314, 325
Ryan, Senator Susan 87, 136, 141, 145, 149, 154, 155, 158, 162, 306

Sachs, Jeffrey 396
Sadat, Anwar 57
Saffron, Abe 31–2
Saint Therese 22
Salami Sisters 35
same-sex marriage 268
San Francisco 39, 66, 191–2, 269, 415, 418
Sartre, Jean-Paul 8, 47, 333, 438
   see also de Beauvoir, Simone
Saskawa, Yohei 394
Sassy 204, 211
   launch party 214
   and Ms. move in together 226–7
   massive success of debut issue 235
   boycott by religious right 246, 249–252, 282
   folded into Teen 449 n.16
   see also Pratt, Jane; Yates, Sandra
Sawer, Marian 161
Schering-Plough 251
Schilling, William 52–3
Schmidt, Helmut 97
Schott, Kerry 442
Schroeder, Pat 228–9, 231, 234, 274
Schultz, George 181
Scorsese, Martin 251
Scott, Evelyn 154

Scott, Mary 83
Screwloose 269
   see Blazey, Peter
Seamen's Union 35
Sebald, W.G. 385
Secret Service 192, 198
Secretariat 278
Seeds 60
Seidler, Harry 195
Seper, George 337
Serious Women's Business (SWB) 411–13
Seven Days 41
Seven Little Australians 437
Seventeen 237
sex and the single feminist 67
sex discrimination 41, 95, 174
   anti-discrimination laws 153–4, 158, 347
Sex Discrimination Act (SDA) 148, 155, 172, 329, 341, 343, 347, 351
   exemptions for Defence 148
   resistance to 153
   and fertility programs 354, 355
   see also Ronalds, Chris
Sex Discrimination Commissioner 154, 315, 432
   see also Broderick, Elizabeth; Bryce, Quentin
sexism xvi, 80, 85–6, 87, 229, 348, 420, 429, 446
sexual abuse 27–9
sexual harassment 86,
Sexual Politics 47
   see Millett, Kate
Shahi, Aga 129–30
Shalala, Donna 269
Sheehan, Paul 202
Shelley, Jeanne 213
Sherrill, Steve 241, 242, 244, 245, 267, 270
Sherry, Ann 412
Shield, Mark 337
Shiva, Vandana 398
Short, John 93, 95
Shoulder to Shoulder 66
Silences 66
   see Olsen, Tillie
Silha, Otto 53, 54, 171
Sime, Murray 349–51

Simes, Ric 292, 311

Simonet, Puck 173

Simpson, Peggy 231, 232, 248

Single White Female 185

Sisterhood is Powerful 219
  see Morgan, Robin

Sisters Inc. 36

Sisulu, Walter 120

Sisulu, Zwelakhe 120, 122

Skinner, Michael 240

slut-shaming 29

Smark, Peter 73

Smeal, Ellie 284

Smith, Bessie 65

Smith, Ian 102, 115

Smith, Senator Margaret Chase 229

Smith, Patti 41–2, 187

Smith, Patricia 408

Smith, Stephen 292, 309

Snowy River Project 417

Social Venture Capital Network 268, 269

Soldatow, Sasha 436

Solem, Herman S. 50, 52

Solzhenitsyn, Aleksandr 21

Sontag, Susan 249

Souter, Gavin 13

South Africa 55, 101, 102–8; 112, 113–14,
    116, 117, 118–123, 398

South Australia 17, 31–3, 41, 141, 314

South Dakota 49–52
    State Penitentiary 50–2

Southgate, Todd 393

Soviet Union 111, 182

Soviet women 171

Soweto 105–8, 114
    children's uprising 103

Sparks, Allister 398

Special Broadcasting Service (SBS) 117

Spender, Stephen 188

Sprange, John 384

Stage Deli 197

Stannard, Bruce 11, 24–5

Stannard, Jenny 391

Stanwyck, Barbara 269

Staples, Jim 15

'Star Wars' 171, 183, 397

Starrett, Cam 208

State Bank of NSW 241, 244, 253

Steinberg, Joel 256–8,

Steinberg, Lisa 256–9

Steinem, Gloria 69, 70, 219, 220–1, 224–5,
    232, 247, 256, 259, 262, 268, 272, 273,
    279, 280, 281, 283–5, 405
  selling *Ms.* magazine to Fairfax 205–14
  retained as consultant 218
  and fashion 221
  and Hedda Nussbaum 257–62
  enmity with Betty Friedan 262–3, 359
  'Sex, Lies and Advertising' 279
  see also Carbine, Pat; Heilbrun, Carolyn;
      Lang, Dale; Morgan, Robin;
      Revolution from Within; Zuckerman,
      Mort

Stella, Frank 40

Stellenbosch 119, 121, 398

Stern, Isaac 195

Stewart, Donald 416

St Marks Place 187

St Paul 45, 47, 49, 50, 57

St Paul's College 27–9

Stimpson, Catherine 239

stock market crash 1987 214

Stolley, Richard 242

Stone, John 77, 84 , 149

Stott-Despoja, Senator Natasha 412

Stratas, Teresa 185–6

Stravinsky, Igor 186

Stravinsky's Lunch 414
  see Modjeska, Drusilla

Street, Jessie 415

Strictly Ballroom 320, 325

Strydom, Hans 118

Studio 54 187

suffragettes 66

Surfacing 39

Suich, Jennie 94

Suich, Max 1–7, 9–10, 12–14, 16–17, 23,
    25, 32, 34–5, 174, 175
  appointed editor *National Times* 9
  and economic reporting 179–80
  casualty of 'Young Warwick' takeover
      212
  The Independent Monthly 286
  Sullivan, Erroll 320, 321

Summers, Anne
  early dreams of being a writer xi–xiii

early days as a journalist 1–15
learning to swim 23–4
series on NSW prisons 15–22
wins Walkley Award 23
first trip to the US 38–71
awarded Ph.D for *Damned Whores &
  God's Police* 44–5, 270
awakening to misogyny 47
typewriters xii, 48, 112
encountering New York feminists 65–71
in Canberra Press Gallery 72–100
refused loan to buy a house 84–5
clash with Malcolm Fraser 93–99
abortions 96–7, 170, 188–9
reporting on southern Africa 101–23
interview with Edgar Tekere 111
South African government spying on
  118–23
ASIO files 100
elected President of the Parliamentary
  Press Gallery 130
running the Office of the Status of
  Women 139–175
breast surgery 143
RBT charge 144–5
developing affirmative action policy
  155–6
appoints Quentin Bryce 154
40th birthday 162
appointed to Fairfax in New York 175–7
foreign correspondent in the US 178–83;
  198–9; 202–3
interviews Caspar Weinberger 181–3
'the times will suit me' interview with
  John Howard 189–91
getting mugged 194
Café Un, Deux, Trois lunch with Sandra
  Yates 203
passed over as editor of the *National
  Times* 203–4
getting Fairfax to buy *Ms.* magazine
  205–214
dealings with *Ms.* editorial staff 214–19
induction by Gloria Steinem 219–21
producing first issue of *Ms.* 226–31, 234,
  238
introduces political coverage to *Ms.*
  231–2, 234

Ms. Washington launch party 232
buying *Ms.* and *Sassy* from Fairfax
  234–245
rupture with Gloria Steinem over Hedda
  Nussbaum 256–7, 262
appointed editorial director of *Sassy* 264
involvement with Chip Rolley 264–7
fired as editor of *Ms.* 273
advising Paul Keating 286–331
gives up smoking 287–8
editing *Good Weekend* 332–3, 335–45,
  364–5, 367
sexual harassment furore 340–45
not having children 356–7
tenure at Greenpeace International
  368–73, 378–81, 382–9, 390–6, 401,
  405–6
Forum 2000 Prague 394–400
letter to Daddy 403
giving our grandfather a headstone
  406–9
appears on a postage stamp 410
'Her rights at work' Gillard speech 418,
  419–20
Sydney Opera House interview with
  Gillard 426–430
brain surgery 432–3, 435–6
*see also Damned Whores and God's
  Police*; feminism; *Gamble for* Power;
  misogyny; Rolley, Chip; Suich, Max;
  The End of Equality; *The Misogyny
  Factor*; *The Lost Mother*; *The
  National Times*; Walsh, Max; Yates,
  Sandra
Summers, John 141, 200, 265
Sunday 137, 304
Sun-Herald 35, 74, 90
Sutherland, Joan 191, 427
Suzman, Helen 108, 120
Swan, Wayne 313
Sweezy, Paul 194
'swingeing' 75
Sydney 1–3, 5–10, 12–16, 18–19, 21, 22,
  24–5, 27–31, 33–4, 37, 42, 43, 44, 50,
  59, 60, 64, 66, 72, 74, 75, 77, 79, 80, 81,
  84, 88, 94, 95, 97, 121, 122, 133, 134,
  154, 159, 162, 168, 174, 175, 179, 191,
  194, 195, 199, 201, 202, 203, 204, 209,

210, 211. 212, 224, 235, 237, 241, 248,
265, 291, 301, 303, 308, 316, 318–9,
320–5, 328, 329, 332, 334, 335, 339–49,
354–6, 357, 358, 368, 369, 371, 376,
381, 387, 402, 403, 410–11, 4`3, 4`5,
417, 422, 424, 425–31, 433–7, 440–1,
442, 443
Sydney casino 195
see also Trump, Donald
Sydney Dance Theatre 334
Sydney Morning Herald 7, 9, 13, 80, 202,
203–4, 316, 342, 347, 360, 368, 413,
417, 430
Sydney Opera House 381, 387, 426,
427–30
Sydney Push 5, 7, 11, 79
Sydney Symphony Orchestra 199, 237,
322, 334
Sydney Writers Festival 411, 422, 431, 437

Taliban 125
Tambrands 250, 251
Taperell, Kath 152
Tarrant, Deborah 341
Tavernier, Bertrand 390
Tawney, R.H. 353
Tax Summit 166
Taylor, John 189, 333
Teen Vogue 252
Te Kanawa, Kiri 403
Tekere, Edgar 110, 111, 115, 117–18
Ten Network 253
Tereshkova, Valentina 171–2
Terfel, Bryn 427
Terkel, Studs 60
Thatcher, Margaret 97, 102, 111, 190, 353
  clash with Malcolm Fraser 111, 116
The Advertiser xii
The Age 73, 332, 417
The Argonauts xii
The Armagh Women 169
  see McCafferty, Nell
The Australian 74, 181, 316, 344, 364
The Body Shop 268
The Bulletin 12, 90, 137, 142
The Canberra Times 73, 144, 212
The Courier Mail 90
The Daily Mirror 10

The Daily Telegraph 11
The Dialectic of Sex 187
  see Firestone, Shulamith
The Digger 39
The Drum 422
The End of Equality 361
  see Summers, Anne
The Feminine Mystique 263, 355
  see Friedan, Betty
The First Stone 341
  see Garner, Helen
The Fortunes of Richard Mahony 437
  see Richardson, Henry Handel
The Godfather 51
The Gulag Archipelago 21
  see Solzhenitsyn, Aleksandr
The Hollywood Reporter 201
The Independent Monthly 286
The Last of the Mohicans 52
The Last Temptation of Christ 251
The Level Club 183, 185, 186, 192–3, 243
The Lost Mother 408, 413–4, 422
  see Summers, Anne
The L Word 268
The Misogyny Factor 362, 423, 431
  see Summers, Anne
The Monthly 416–7, 420, 421, 423
The Muslim 129
The Narrow Road to the Deep North 407
  see Flanagan, Richard
The National Times 1–35, 41, 42, 74, 83,
100, 121, 203, 276, 419
  see also Carroll, Vic; Cook, Patrick;
    Coopes, Jenny; Hoffey, Frank;
    journalism; Kelly, Paul; Suich, Max;
    Times on Sunday; Whitton, Evan;
    Wynhausen, Elisabeth
The New York Times 7, 50, 178, 195, 256,
268, 287, 360, 402, 422
  Longacre Square 226
The New York Times Company 253
The New Yorker 67, 385, 398, 420
  fact-checking 224, 280
The Paris Review xiii
The Ramrods 318
The Second Sex xiii, 158, 390, 438
  mistakes in translation of 1949 edition
    438, 439

new English translation 438–9
The Silence of the Lambs 52
The Song Company 322
The Southern Cross xii
The Spectator 210, 234
The Strategic Basis of Australian Defence Policy 91
The Sun 10
   The Super-Afrikaners. Inside the Afrikaner Broederbond 118
   see Wilkins, Ivor and Strydom, Hans
The Thornbirds 59, 199 , 334
   see McCullough, Colleen
The Times on Sunday 178, 203, 212
The Weekend Australian 11
The Women's Room 39
   see French, Marilyn
Theresa's Tavern 60–3
Thiess, Sir Leslie 89
This Side of Paradise 47
   see Fitzgerald, F. Scott
Thompson, Hunter S. 5, 83
Thornhill, Michael 320
Tilsen, Ken 49
Time 71, 283, 402
Time Inc. 237, 253
Times Square 176, 177, 227, 239, 247
Tin Sheds 7
Tindall Air Force base 147
Titian 182, 183
Toffler, Alvin 355
Toohey, Brian 203
Toronto Star 268
Torsh, Dany 22
Tosca's 191
Towards Equality 148
Tozer, Geoffrey 321
Trajkovski, Julie 425–6, 428
Tranter, John 321
Troeth, Senator Judith 412
Trotsky, Leon 187, 188
'True Believers' victory dinner 325–6, 327–8
Trump, Donald 195
Truth 11, 25, 145
Tsinhua University 381
Turandot 186
Turnbull, Greg 292
Twain, Mark 193, 256

Udall, Rochelle 240
Ullman, Tracey 208
United Fruit 55
United Nations 165, 415, 437
   founding meeting 1945 415
   UN Conference on Women, Copenhagen 154, 167
   UN Conference on Women, Nairobi 165, 166, 167–8
   United Nations Convention on the Elimination of All Forms of Discrimination Against Women (CEDAW) 165
United States of America 39
   Americans' view of Australia 199
University of Adelaide 31, 157, 431
University of New South Wales 15
University of Newcastle 317, 417, 420
University of New South Wales 417
University of Queensland 317
University of Sydney 2, 7, 27–9, 44, 74, 441
University of Technology, Sydney 12, 440
University of Wisconsin 269
Uren, Tom 288
US News and World Report 206, 262

Valentino 236
Vanity Fair 207, 230, 262
Vaughan, Sarah 186
Verdi 403
Veronis, John 239
Vernicos, George 371
Verveer Melanne 251
Vianney, Kate 389
Victoria Street 32, 334, 343, 435
Vietnam War 39, 367
Village Voice 338
Virago Press 36
Visbord, Ed 140, 145, 146
Vogue 142, 143, 318, 319, 402, 410
Voice of Free Africa 117
Volcker, Paul 180–1, 199
von Adlerstein, Marion 142
Vonnegut, Kurt 272
Vorwoerd, Hendrik 105

Wachner, Linda 448 n.8
Waldorf Astoria 181, 209, 255

Walkley Awards 15, 23, 40
Walkley, Sir William 23
Walker, Alice 220
Wall Street 39, 179–81, 190, 198, 239, 240,
  247, 280, 335, 402
Wall Street Journal 125, 282
Wallace, Catriona 425–6, 427–8
Wallace, Lois 71
Walmart 251
Walsh, Adela Pankhurst 35
Walsh, Max 8, 9, 46, 64, 72–6, 80–1, 93–7,
  99, 133, 137, 288
 'swingeing' 75
 fight with Malcolm Fraser 94–7
 70th birthday party 94
 influence on Paul Keating 94
 sending journalists on overseas
  assignments 101, 123–4
 See also Australian Financial Review;
  journalism; Keating, Paul
Walsh, Senator Peter 160, 175, 290
Walsh, Tom 35
War Graves Commission 408
Waradjuri woman 428
Ward, Barry 31
Ware, Helen 165, 166, 167
Warhol, Andy 187
Warner Communications 209
Washington DC 17, 14, 48, 60, 78, 95,
  97, 104, 182–3, 189, 190, 198–9, 224,
  230–3, 247, 248, 282, 283, 291, 325,
  427
Watergate 69, 70, 268
Waters, Muddy 62, 63–4
Waterston, Sam 185
Watkins, Alison 412
Watson, Don 286, 307, 314, 319, 322, 325
Watson, Lex 44
Waverly Place 257
 see Brownmiller, Susan
Weather Underground 68–9
Webb, Beatrice and Sidney 353
Wedgwood, Senator Ivy 352
Weideger, Paula 67–8, 199, 422
Weinberger, Caspar 181–3, 192, 199
Weisberg, Dr Edith 318
Weiss 143
Welch, Garth 321

Wells, Junior 62–3
Western Plains Zoo Dubbo 278
White House, The 198, 201, 229, 236,
  271–2
White Oak 276–9
 nature conservancy 277–9
White Oak Dance Project 277
Whitlam, Gough 5, 6, 11, 17, 76, 80, 304,
  424
 government 122, 135, 157
 staffers 141, 193
Whitton, Evan 10–11, 16, 23, 25–6, 34, 203
Wiesel, Elie 394
Wilenski, Peter 141, 175, 436
Wilkins, Ivor 118
Wilkinson, Graham 33
Wilkinson, Lisa 206
Williams, Helen 149, 157
Williams, Max 19–20, 21
Williamson, John 354
Wills, Sue 44
Willson, Sandra 21–2
Wilson, Laurie 91
Winfrey, Oprah 255, 289
Winton, Tim 321
Wolfe, Tom 2–3, 245
Wolfensohn, James 195, 206
Wolpe, Bruce 426, 429
Woman's Day 129, 142, 211, 228, 319
Woman's Day (US) 272
women 69–71,
 in prison 17, 21–2
 writers 36–7, 39
 getting the vote 41
 violence against 66, 282, 296–7
 the economy as a women's issue 70, 146
 employment 147, 159, 304, 352
 on boards 153, 348–9
 earnings and equal pay 157
 health 296–7,
 reversal of fortunes under John Howard
  351–5
 revival of domesticity ('yummy
  mummies') 362–3
 see also domestic violence; FGM;
  journalism
Women Against Pornography 66
Women Aglow 250

Women Behind Bars 21
Women of the World Festival 440
Women's Budget Program 149–50, 169, 174
Women's Bureau 147, 352
Women's Business 151
Women's College 27–8, 154
Women's Electoral Lobby 87
Women Lawyers Association 310
Women's Legal Defense Fund 233
women's movement 379
Women's Peace Army 35
women's units in federal departments 149
Wong, Senator Penny 440
Wood, Police Commissioner Mervyn 33
Woods, Donald 103
Woolford, Melissa 241, 242,
Working Mother 267, 276
Working Woman 267–8, 272
World Bank 195
World Economic Forum 174
World Press Institute (WPI) 45–63
World Trade Centre 40, 197
Wounded Knee 50–1
Wran, Neville 17, 33, 80
Wynhausen, Elisabeth 11–12, 14, 64, 94, 200, 276, 340
  death 435, 436

Yard, Molly 284
Yates, Sandra 204, 280, 428
  getting Fairfax to buy *Ms.* magazine 205–214
  negotiates option to buy *Ms.* and *Sassy* from Fairfax 235–7

buying *Ms.* and *Sassy* from Fairfax 234–245
  response to *Sassy* boycott 251–2, 253
  resigns 263
  legacy 275
  see also Matilda Publications Inc.; *Ms.* magazine; *Sassy*; Summers, Anne
Yeend, Sir Geoffrey 100, 140, 141, 145,
  Task Force on the Status of Women 148–9
  Women's Budget Program 149–50, 169
Yes Minister 168
Yippies 187
Yorkin, Peg 284
Yothu Yindi 336, 337
Young, Ambassador Andrew 63
Young, Mick 436
Yousafzai, Malala xvi
Yunupingu, Mandawuy 236

Zabars 184
Zambia 101, 116
Zampatti, Carla 174
Zanzibar's 324
Zemiro, Julia 412
Zia ul-Haq, President 124, 130, 133
Zimbabwe 102, 106, 111, 115, 116, 123, 438
Zimbabwean African National Union (ZANU) 106, 110, 111, 116
Zimbabwean African People's Union (ZAPU) 106, 116
Zindler, Harald 385–6
Zuckerman, Mort 206, 207, 262
Zwicky, Fay 36